Introduction to SOCIOLOGY

THIRD EDITION

ANTHONY GIDDEN

london school of economics

Introduction to

SOCIOLOGY

THIRD EDITION

MITCHELL DUNEIER

university of wisconsin–madison
and university of california, santa barbara

W. W. NORTON & COMPANY, INC.
New York · London

Editor: Stephen Dunn
Project Editor: Margaret Farley
Manufacturing Director: Roy Tedoff
Photograph Editor: Scott McCord
Editorial Assistant: Scott McCord
Book and Cover Designer: Antonina Krass
Layout Artist: Roberta Flechner
Compositor: UG / GGS Information Services, Inc.
Manufacturer: R.R. Donnelley

The text of this book is composed in Sabon
with the display set in Tekton, Mona Lisa, and Rockwell.

Library of Congress Cataloging-in-Publication Data
Giddens, Anthony.
    Introduction to sociology / Anthony Giddens, Mitchell Duneier.—
3rd ed.
        p.   cm.
    Includes bibliographical references and index.
    ISBN 0-393-97186-4 (pbk.)
    1. Sociology.   I. Duneier, Mitchell.   II. Title.
HM585.G53 1999
301—dc21   99-30545

W. W. Norton & Company, Inc., 500 Fifth Avenue, New York, N.Y. 10110
www.wwnorton.com

W. W. Norton & Company Ltd., 10 Coptic Street, London WC1A 1PU

1 2 3 4 5 6 7 8 9 0

CONTENTS

6 CONFORMITY, DEVIANCE, AND CRIME

PART THREE
Structures of Power

7 STRATIFICATION, CLASS, AND INEQUALITY

8 GENDER INEQUALITY

9 ETHNICITY AND RACE

11 GOVERNMENT, POLITICAL POWER, AND WAR

PART FOUR
Social Institutions

12 WORK AND ECONOMIC LIFE

13 MARRIAGE AND THE FAMILY

14 EDUCATION AND THE MASS MEDIA

15 RELIGION IN MODERN SOCIETY

PART FIVE
Social Change in the Modern World

16 THE SOCIOLOGY OF THE BODY: HEALTH AND ILLNESS, SEXUALITY, AND AGING

17 URBANIZATION, POPULATION, AND THE ENVIRONMENT

PREFACE

This book was written in the belief that sociology has a key role to play in modern intellectual culture and a central place within the social sciences. Our aim has been to write a book that combines some originality with an analysis of all the basic issues of interest to sociologists today. In many places, we attempt to bring the reader into a subject through the use of ethnographies written for this book. The book does not try to introduce overly sophisticated notions; nevertheless, ideas and findings drawn from the cutting edge of the discipline are incorporated throughout. We hope it is not a partisan treatment; we endeavored to cover the major perspectives in sociology and the major findings of contemporary American research in an even-handed, although not indiscriminate, way.

MAJOR THEMES

The book is constructed around a number of basic themes, each of which helps to give the work a distinctive character. One main theme is that of the *world in change*. Sociology was born of the transformations that wrenched the industrializing social order of the West away from the ways of life characteristic of preceding societies. The world that was created by these changes is the primary object of concern of sociological analysis. The pace of social change has continued to accelerate, and it is possible that we stand on the threshold of transitions as significant as those that occurred in the late eighteenth and nineteenth centuries. Sociology has prime responsibility for charting the transformations that have taken place in the past and for grasping the major lines of development taking place today.

A second fundamental theme of the book is the *globalizing of social life*. For far too long, sociology has been dominated by the view that societies can be studied as independent unities. But even in the past, societies have never really existed in isolation. In current times, we can see a clear acceleration in processes of global integration. This is obvious, for example, in the expansion of international trade across the world. The emphasis on globalization also connects closely with the weight given to the interdependence of First and Third Worlds today.

Third, the book takes a strongly *comparative* stance. The study of sociology cannot be taught solely by understanding the institutions of any one particular society. While we have slanted the discussion toward the United States, such discussion is always balanced by a rich variety of materials drawn from other cultures. These include researches carried out in other Western countries, but we also refer often to Russia and the Eastern European societies, which are currently undergoing substantial changes. The book also includes much more material on Third World countries than has been usual hitherto in introductions of sociology. In addition, we strongly emphasize the relationship between sociology and anthropology, whose concerns overlap comprehensively. Given the close connections that now mesh societies across the world with one another, and the virtual disappearance of traditional social systems, sociology and anthropology increasingly become indistinguishable.

A fourth theme is the necessity of taking a *historical approach* to sociology. This involves more than just filling in the historical context within which events occur. One of the most important developments in sociology over the past few years has been an increasing emphasis on historical analysis. This should be understood not solely as applying a sociological outlook to the past, but as a way of contributing to our understanding of institutions in the present. Recent work in historical sociology is discussed throughout, and provides a framework for the interpretations offered within most of the chapters.

Fifth, particular attention is given throughout the text to *issues of gender*. The study of gender is ordinarily regarded as a specific field within sociology as a whole—and this volume contains a chapter that specifically explores thinking and research on the subject (Chapter 8). However, questions about gender relations are so fundamental to sociological analysis that they cannot simply be considered a subdivision. Thus, many chapters contain sections concerned with issues of gender.

A sixth theme is the *micro and macro link*. In many places in the book, we show that interaction in micro-level contexts affects larger social processes and that such macro-level processes influence our day-to-day lives. We emphasize to readers that one can better understand a social situation by analyzing it at both the micro- and macro-level.

A seventh theme is the relation between the *social* and the *personal*. Sociological thinking is a vital help to self-understanding, which in turn can be focused back on an improved understanding of the social world. Studying sociology should be a liberating experience: the field enlarges our sympathies and imagination, opens up new perspectives on the sources of our own behavior, and creates an awareness of cultural settings different from our own. Insofar as sociological ideas challenge dogma, teach appreciation of cultural variety, and allow us insight into the working of social institutions, the practice of sociology enhances the possibilities of human freedom.

ORGANIZATION

There is very little abstract discussion of basic sociological concepts at the beginning of this book. Instead, concepts are explained when they are introduced in the relevant chapters, and we have sought throughout to illustrate them by means of concrete examples. While these are usually taken from sociological research, we have often used material from other sources (such as newspaper reports). We have tried to keep the writing style as simple and direct as possible, while endeavoring to make the book lively and full of surprises.

The chapters follow a sequence designed to help achieve a progressive mastery of the different fields of sociology, but we have taken care to ensure that the book can be used flexibly and is easy to adapt to the needs of individual courses. Chapters can be deleted, or studied in a different order, without much loss. Each has been written as a fairly autonomous unit, with cross-referencing to other chapters at relevant points.

STUDY AIDS

The chapters in this book have been carefully structured to make the learning process as entertaining yet systematic as possible. Each begins with a chapter organizer, which highlights the learning objectives of each section and allows students to preview that chapter's discussion. Throughout the chapter appear several "Key Concepts in Review" boxes. These boxes enable students to review the important terms and concepts discussed in the preceding section, ensuring that they know the basic concepts the following discussion builds upon. In addition, whenever a new term is first mentioned in the text itself, it is printed in boldface. All major concepts and terms are included in the glossary at the end of the text.

Another helpful aid is the use of a global icon to indicate examples of the changing world or the globalization process, or comparisons of U.S. society with other societies. Social change, the globalization of social life, and comparative analysis are all important themes of this text. The icon will help alert readers to discussions of these themes.

FURTHER RESEARCH: READING AND LIBRARIES

Libraries contain abundant sources of information that can be used to follow up or expand on issues discussed here. References are given throughout the text and listed fully in the Bibliography at the end. Also, we have included a short appendix that provides a guide to library resources and how to use them.

Acknowledgments

During the writing of both editions of this book, many individuals offered comments and advice on particular chapters and, in some cases, large parts of the text. They helped us see issues in a different light, clarified some difficult points, and allowed us to take advantage of their specialist knowledge in their respective fields. We are deeply indebted to them.

Anthony Troy Adams, Eastern Michigan University
Angelo A. Alonzo, Ohio State University
Deirdre Boden, Washington University, St. Louis
Richard J. Bord, Pennsylvania State University
Gerard A. Brandmeyer, University of South Florida
Phil Brown, Brown University
Annette Burfoot, Queen's University
Lee Clarke, Rutgers University, New Brunswick
Stephen E. Cornell, University of California, San Diego
Steven P. Dandaneau, University of Dayton
Lynn Davidman, University of Pittsburgh
Judith F. Dunn, Pennsylvania State University
Mark Eckel, McHenry County College
John V.A. Ehle, Jr., Northern Virginia Community College
Eliot Freidson, New York University
J. William Gibson, California State University, Long Beach
Richard H. Hall, University of Albany, SUNY
John Hartman, University at Buffalo, SUNY
Rick Helmes-Hayes, University of Waterloo
Wanda Kaluza, Camden County College
Paul Kingston, University of Virginia
Janet Koenigsamen, West Virginia University
Cora B. Marrett, University of Wisconsin
Garth Massey, University of Wyoming
Greg Matoesian, Fontbonne College
William H. McBroom, University of Montana

Katherine McClelland, Franklin and Marshall College

Greg McLauchlan, University of Oregon

Angela O'Rand, Duke University

Celia J. Orona, San Jose State University

Thomas Petee, Auburn University

Jennifer L. Pierce, University of Minnesota

Brian Powell, Indiana University

Allan Pred, University of California, Berkeley

Tomi-Ann Roberts, Colorado College

Roland Robertson, University of Pittsburgh

Craig St. John, University of Oklahoma

Martin Sanchez-Jankowski, University of California, Berkeley

Jack Sattel, Normandale Community College

Andrew Scull, University of California, San Diego

David R. Segal, University of Maryland, College Park

Peter Singelmann, University of Missouri, Kansas City

Judith Stepan-Norris, University of California, Irvine

Joel C. Tate, Germanna Community College

Christopher K. Vanderpool, Michigan State University

Henry A. Walker, Cornell University

Chaim I. Waxman, Rutgers University, New Brunswick

Timothy P. Wickham-Crowley, Georgetown University

Paul Root Wolpe, University of Pennsylvania

Dennis H. Wrong, New York University

Irving M. Zeitlin, University of Toronto

We would like to thank the numerous readers of the text who have written with comments, criticisms, and suggestions for improvements. We have often adopted their recommendations in this new edition.

We have many others to thank as well. We are especially grateful to Margaret Farley at Norton, who did a marvelous job of copyediting the book. To her we owe numerous suggestions for alterations and improvements that have contributed in important ways to the final form of the volume.

Our greatest debt is to Steve Dunn. He has poured an enormous amount of work into the book and has given the text much of whatever is worthwhile in it. He has helped to creatively restructure the text as a whole, has made many direct contributions to the various chapters, and has ensured that we have made reference to the very latest research. We are immensely grateful to him.

Particular thanks are due also to Deborah Carr of the University of Michigan and Neil Gross of the University of Wisconsin–Madison, two of the most outstanding young sociologists in the United States. Both had a tremendous influence on almost every chapter in the book. We would also like to register our thanks to a number of other University of Wisconsin graduate students whose contributions have proved invaluable: Katherin Zippel, Paul LePore, Wendy Carter, Josh Rossol, and David Yamane. Finally, Scott McCord, photo editor at Norton, has shown unusual flair and originality in the selections he has made for illustrating the book.

Introduction to SOCIOLOGY

THIRD EDITION

PART ONE

the study of sociology

We live in a world today that is increasingly more complex. Why are the conditions of our lives so different from those of earlier times? How will our lives change in the future? These are the types of questions that lead us to the study of sociology. Throughout your reading of this text, you will encounter examples from different people's lives that will help us to answer these important questions.

In Chapter 1, we begin to explore the scope of sociology and learn what sort of insights the field can bring to our lives. Among these insights are the development of a global perspective and an understanding of social change. Sociology is not a subject with a body of theories everyone agrees on. As in any complex field, the questions we raise allow for different answers. In this chapter, we compare and contrast differing theoretical traditions.

Chapter 2 is an exploration of the tools of the trade, how sociologists set about doing

research. A number of basic methods of investigation are available to help us find out what is going on in the social world. We must be sure that the information upon which sociological reasoning is based is as reliable and accurate as possible. The chapter examines the problems with gathering such information and indicates how they are best dealt with.

Chapter One

Learn what sociology covers as a field and how everyday topics like love and romance are shaped by social and historical forces.

Developing a Sociological Perspective

Recognize that sociology is more than just acquiring knowledge; it also involves developing a sociological imagination. Learn that studying sociology leads us to see that we construct society through our actions and are constructed by it. See that our actions have both intended and unintended consequences. Understand that two of the most important components of the sociological imagination are developing a global perspective and understanding social change.

The Development of Sociological Thinking

Learn how sociology originated and how it developed. Think about the theoretical issues that frame the study of sociology. Be able to name some of the leading social theorists and the concepts they contributed to the study of sociology. Learn the different theoretical approaches modern sociologists bring to the field.

Is Sociology a Science?

Learn how sociology is similar to and different from natural sciences.

How Can Sociology Help Us in Our Lives?

See the practical implications that sociology has for our lives.

WHAT IS SOCIOLOGY?

from the tragic mass murder at Columbine High School in Littleton, Colorado, to the "ethnic cleansing" and war in Kosovo, Yugoslavia, we live today in a world that is intensely worrying, yet full of the most extraordinary promise for the future. It is a world awash with change, marked by deep conflicts, tensions, and social divisions, as well as by the destructive onslaught of modern technology on the natural environment. Yet we have possibilities of controlling our destiny and shaping our lives for the better that would have been unimaginable to earlier generations.

How did this world come about? Why are our conditions of life so different from those of our parents and grandparents? What directions will change take in the future? These questions are the prime concern of sociology, a field of study that consequently has a fundamental role to play in modern intellectual life.

Sociology is the scientific study of human social life, groups, and societies. It is a dazzling and compelling enterprise, as its subject matter is our own behavior as social beings. The scope of sociological study is extremely wide, ranging from the analysis of passing en-

In the past, the relationship between a man and a woman had more to do with financial prosperity than romantic love. The painting above, Van Eyck's Arnolfini Marriage, *is filled with symbols of fertility and prosperity. In the movie* Titanic, *romantic love prevails over class differences and family traditions.*

counters between individuals on the street to the investigation of global social processes. A brief example will provide an initial taste of the nature and objectives of sociology.

Have you ever been in love? Almost certainly you have. Most people who are in their teens or older know what being in love is like. Love and romance provide, for many of us, some of the most intense feelings we ever experience. Why do people fall in love? The answer at first sight seems obvious. Love expresses a mutual physical and personal attachment two individuals feel for one another. These days, we might be skeptical of the idea that love is "forever," but falling in love, we tend to think, is an experience arising from universal human emotions. It seems natural for a couple who fall in love to want personal and sexual fulfillment in their relationship, perhaps in the form of marriage.

Yet this situation, which seems so self-evident to us today, is in fact very unusual. Falling in love is *not* an experience most people across the world have—and where it does happen, it is rarely thought of as having any connection to marriage. The idea of romantic love did not become widespread until fairly recently in our society and has never even existed in most other cultures.

Only in modern times have love and sexuality become seen as closely connected. In the Middle Ages and for centuries afterward, men and women married mainly in order to keep property in the hands of family or to raise children to work the family farm. Once married, they may have become close companions; this happened after marriage, however, rather than before. People sometimes had sexual affairs outside marriage, but these inspired few of the emotions we associate with love. Romantic love was regarded as at best a weakness and at worst a kind of sickness.

Romantic love first made its appearance in courtly circles as a characteristic of extramarital sexual adventures indulged in by members of the aristocracy. Until about two centuries ago, it was wholly confined to such circles, and kept specifically separate from marriage. Relations between husband and wife among aristocratic groups were often cool and distant—certainly compared to our expectations of marriage today. The wealthy lived in large houses, each spouse having his or her own bedroom and servants; they may rarely have seen each other in private. Sexual compatibility was a matter of chance and was not considered relevant to marriage. Among both rich and poor, the decision of whom to marry was made by family and kin, not by the individuals concerned, who had little or no say in the matter.

This remains true in many non-Western countries today. In India, for example, the vast majority of marriages are arranged by parents or other relatives. The opinions of prospective marriage partners are quite often taken into account, but by no means always. A study of marriage in Kerala, a state in India, showed that just over half the young people thought that meeting the prospective spouse before marriage was relevant to marital happiness. Among parents, only one percent were willing to let their children choose their own marriage partners. Romantic love is recognized to exist, but it is equated with temporary infatuation, or actually seen as a barrier to a happy marriage.

Neither romantic love, then, nor its association with marriage, can be understood as "given" features of human life. Rather, it has been shaped by broad social and historical influences. These are the influences sociologists study.

Most of us see the world in terms of the familiar features of our own lives. Sociology demonstrates the need to take a much broader view of why we are as we are, and why we act as we do. It teaches us that what we regard as natural, inevitable, good, or true may not be such, and that the "givens" of our life are strongly influenced by historical and social forces. Understanding the subtle yet complex and profound ways in which our individual lives reflect the contexts of our social experience is basic to the sociological outlook.

DEVELOPING A SOCIOLOGICAL PERSPECTIVE

In the aftermath of the mass murder at Columbine High School in Littleton, Colorado, in 1999, many Americans asked themselves how and why two high school students could murder thirteen of their classmates and teachers and then take their own lives. You undoubtedly encountered many explanations for this massacre in the mass media. One such explanation focused on the social cliques at Columbine High, which divided into "jocks," "preps," "geeks," "goths," and other groups. It was well known that the two murderers, part of a group called the "Trenchcoat Mafia," were teased and embarrassed by their classmates, especially the "jocks." It was also reported that the two teens were obsessed with the video game "Doom," in which each player tries to make the most kills. Many saw this as the embodiment of American culture's glorification of violence. The police also investigated how the two killers procured the guns and bombs used in the massacre. Many commentators denounced the easy availability of these weapons in American society. Others saw the tragedy as a symbol of the emptiness of suburban life, where people have few public places to go and socialize with others.

While explanations like these focus on the social causes of violence in the United States, sociology can bring an even deeper understanding of events like this mass murder. Sociology shows us the need to look beyond the surface of people's actions and study the social context in order to understand what happened. Sociology can also teach us to try to identify general patterns of behavior in particular individuals and to be systematic in explaining the social influences on these behavioral patterns (Berger, 1963). A sociologist must look at a wide array of evidence before accepting any single explanation. Thus a sociologist studying the Columbine High killings might study other mass murders and look to see if there was a pattern in the group characteristics—such as social class, race, gender, age, or cultural background—of the murderers and victims. This might lead a sociologist to ask why mass murders like the one at Columbine High seem to be mostly the doing of young, middle-class, white men and then explain why this is the case (Patterson, 1999). In other words, a sociologist would not simply ask "What led these two students at Columbine High to commit mass murder?" but also "What social factors explain why mass murders have occurred in the United States?"

Learning to think sociologically—looking, in other words, at the broader view—means cultivating the imagination. As sociologists, we need to imagine, for example, what the experience of sex and marriage is

globalization and everyday life

THE SOCIOLOGY OF COFFEE

"The world drinks about 2.25 billions cups [of coffee] per day—the United States alone drinks one fifth of this. Coffee drinking is a cultural fixture that says as much about us as it does about the bean itself. Basically a habit forming stimulant, coffee is nonetheless associated with relaxation and sociability. In a society that combines buzzing overstimulation with soul-aching meaninglessness, coffee and its associated rituals are, for may of us, the lubricants that make it possible to go on.

"Perhaps for this reason coffee occupies a distinctive niche in our cultural landscape. Along with alcohol, it is the only beverage to engender public houses devoted to its consumption. . . . Uniquely, though, coffee is welcome in almost any situation, from the car to the boardroom, from the breakfast table to the public park, alone or in company of any kind. Since its adoption as a beverage, coffee has been offered as an antipode to alcohol—more so even than abstinence, perhaps in recognition of a human need for joyfully mood-altering substances and the convivial social interactions that go along with them.

"Only a handful of consumer goods has fueled the passions of the public as much as coffee. . . . [C]offee has inspired impassioned struggles on the battlefields of

like for people—the majority of humankind until recently—to whom ideals of romantic love appear alien or even absurd. Or we need to image what life was like for the victims and the murderers at Columbine High. Studying sociology *cannot* be just a routine process of acquiring knowledge. A sociologist is someone who is able to break free from the immediacy of personal circumstances and put things in a wider context. Her work depends on what the American sociologist C. Wright Mills, in a famous phrase, called the **sociological imagination** (Mills, 1959).

The sociological imagination requires us, above all, to *"think ourselves away" from the familiar routines of our daily lives in order to look at them anew.* Consider the simple act of drinking a cup of coffee. What could we find to say, from a sociological point of view, about such an apparently uninteresting piece of behavior? An enormous amount. We could point out economics, human rights, politics, and religion, since its use first spread. Coffee may be a drink for sharing, but as a commodity it invites protectionism, oppression, and destruction. Its steamy past implicates the otherwise noble bean in early colonialism, various revolutions, the emergence of the bourgeoisie, international development, technological hubris, crushing global debt, and more. These forces, in turn, have shaped the way coffee has been incorporated into our culture and economy. Colonialism, for example, served as the primary reason for and vehicle of coffee's expansion throughout the globe; colonial powers dictated where coffee went and where it did not and established trading relationships that continue to this day.

"The story of coffee also reveals how (and why) we interact with a plethora of other commodities, legal or not. Surprising similarities exist, for example, between coffee's early history and the current controversy over marijuana. Today's national debate over the merits of marijuana, although young by comparison, is the modern version of the strife surrounding coffee in other ages. The social acceptability of each has been affected by religious and political opinion, conflicting health claims, institutionalized cultural norms, and the monied interests of government and private industry. The evolution of coffee's social acceptability highlights the delicate dance of interests and "truths" that governs the ways in which we structure our societies.

"Coffee is consumed with great fervor in rich countries such as the United States yet is grown with few exceptions in the poorest parts of the globe. In fact, it is the second most valuable item of legal international trade (after petroleum), and the largest food import of the United States by value. It is the principal source of foreign exchange for

dozens of countries around the world. The coffee in your cup is an immediate, tangible connection with the rural poor in some of the most destitute parts of the planet. It is a physical link across space and cultures from one end of the human experience to the other.

"The coffee trading system that has evolved to bring all this about is an intricate knot of economics, politics, and sheer power—a bizarre arena trod . . . by some of the world's largest transnational corporations, by enormous governments, and by vast trading cartels. The trip coffee takes from the crop to your cup turns out not to be so straightforward after all, but rather a turbulent and unpredictable ride through the waves and eddies of international commodity dynamics, where the product itself becomes secondary to the wash of money and power."

SOURCE: Gregory Dicum and Nina Luttinger, *The Coffee Book: Anatomy of an Industry from Crop to the Last Drop* (New York: The New Press, 1999), pp. ix–xi. Used with permission.

first of all that coffee is not just a refreshment. It possesses *symbolic value* as part of our day-to-day social activities (see "Globalization and Everyday Life"). Often the ritual associated with coffee drinking is much more important than the act of consuming the drink itself. Two people who arrange to meet for coffee are probably more interested in getting together and chatting than in what they actually drink. Drinking and eating in all societies, in fact, provide occa-

sions for social interaction and the enactment of rituals—and these offer a rich subject matter for sociological study.

Second, coffee is a *drug,* containing caffeine, which has a stimulating effect on the brain. Coffee addicts are not regarded by most people in Western culture as drug users. Like alcohol, coffee is a socially acceptable drug, whereas marijuana, for instance, is not. Yet there are societies that tolerate the consumption of marijuana or even cocaine, but frown on both coffee and alcohol. Sociologists are interested in why these contrasts exist.

Third, an individual who drinks a cup of coffee is caught up in a complicated set of *social and economic relationships* stretching across the world. The produc- tion, transport, and distribution of coffee require continuous transactions between people thousands of miles away from the coffee drinker. Studying such global trans- actions is an important task of sociology, since many aspects of our lives are now affected by worldwide social influences and communications.

Finally, the act of sipping a cup of coffee presumes a whole process of *past social and economic development*. Along with other now-familiar items of Western diets—like tea, bananas, potatoes, and white sugar—coffee only became widely consumed from the late 1800s. Although the drink originated in the Middle East, its mass consumption dates from the period of Western colonial expansion about a century and a half ago. Virtually all the coffee we drink in the Western countries today comes from areas (South America and Africa) that were colonized by Europeans; it is in no sense a "natural" part of the Western diet.

Studying Sociology

As individuals, we all know a great deal about ourselves and about the societies in which we live. We tend to think we have a good understanding of why we act as we do, without needing sociologists to tell us! And to some degree this is true. Many of the things we do in our day-to-day lives we do because we understand the social requirements involved. Yet there are definite boundaries to such self-knowledge, and it is one of the main tasks of sociology to show us what these are.

The sociological imagination allows us to see that many events that seem to concern only the individual actually reflect larger issues. Divorce, for instance, may be a very difficult process for someone who goes through it—what Mills calls a personal trouble. But divorce, he points out, is also a public issue in a society like the present-day United States, where over half of all marriages break up within ten years. Unemployment, to take another example, may be a personal tragedy for someone thrown out of a job and unable to find another. Yet it is much more than only a matter for private despair when millions of people in a society are in the same situation: it is a public issue expressing large social trends.

Try applying this sort of outlook to your own life. It isn't necessary to think only of troubling events. Consider, for instance, why you are turning the pages of this book at all—why you have decided to study sociology. You might be a reluctant sociology student, taking the course only to fulfill a requirement. Or you might be enthusiastic to find out more about the subject. Whatever your motivations, you are likely to have a good deal in common, without necessarily knowing it, with others studying sociology. Your private decision reflects your position in the wider society.

Do the following characteristics apply to you? Are you young? white? from a professional or white-collar background? Have you done, or do you still do, some part-time work to boost your income? Do you want to find a good job when you leave school, but are you not especially dedicated to studying? Do you not really know what sociology is but think it has something to do with how people behave in groups? More than three-quarters of you will answer yes to all these questions. College students are not typical of the population as a whole but tend to be drawn from more privileged backgrounds. And their attitudes usually reflect those held by friends and acquaintances. The social backgrounds from which we come have a great deal to do with what kinds of decisions we think appropriate.

But suppose you answer no to one or more of these questions. You might come from a minority-group background or one of poverty. You may be someone in midlife or older. If so, however, further conclusions probably follow. You will likely have had to struggle to get where you are; you might have had to overcome hostile reactions from friends and others when you told them you were intending to go to college; or you might be combining school with full-time parenthood.

Although we are all influenced by the social contexts in which we find ourselves, none of us are simply *determined* in our behavior by those contexts. We possess, and create, our own individuality. It is the business of sociology to investigate the connections between *what society makes of us and what we make of ourselves*. Our activities both structure—give shape to—the social world around us and at the same time are structured *by* that social world.

The concept of **social structure** is an important one in sociology. It refers to the fact that the social contexts of our lives do not just consist of random assortments of events or actions; they are structured, or *patterned*, in distinct ways. There are regularities in the ways we behave and in the relationships we have with one another. But social structure is not like a physical structure, such as a building, which exists independently of human actions. Human societies are always in the process of **structuration**. They are reconstructed at every moment by the very "building blocks" that compose them—human beings like you and me.

Intended and Unintended Consequences

This permanent process of the construction and reconstruction of social life is based on the meanings people attach to their actions. But our actions may bring about different results from those we desired. Sociologists therefore draw an important distinction between the purposes of our behavior—what we intend to bring about—and the unintended consequences of that behavior. For instance, two parents might want to make their children conform to socially accepted ways of acting. To achieve their goal, the parents act in a strict and authoritarian way. The unintended consequences of their authoritarianism, however, might be to drive the children to rebel and break loose from orthodox standards of behavior.

Sometimes actions undertaken with a particular aim in view have consequences that actually *prevent* the achievement of that aim. Some years ago, laws were introduced in New York City compelling the owners of deteriorating buildings in low-income areas to renovate them up to a minimum standard. The intention was to improve the basic level of housing available to poorer sections of the community. The result was that owners of run-down buildings abandoned them altogether or put them to other uses, so that there was a greater shortage of satisfactory accommodation than before (Sieber, 1981).

What we do in our lives and the ways in which our actions affect others must be understood in terms of a mix of intended and unintended consequences. It is sociology's task to study the resulting balance between **social reproduction** and **social transformation**. Social reproduction refers to how societies "keep going" over time; social transformation, to the

---

KEY CONCEPTS IN REVIEW

Sociology is the study of human social life, groups, and societies, focusing on the modern world.

The **sociological imagination** refers to our ability to break ourselves free from our particular circumstances and see our social world in a new light.

Social structure refers to the patterns in our social behavior. **Structuration** is the two-way process by which we shape our social world through our individual actions and by which we are shaped by society.

Social reproduction is the way societies keep going over time. **Social transformation** refers to processes of change in a society. Perhaps the most important process of change is **globalization**, the development of social and economic relationships that stretch across the world.

changes they undergo. Social reproduction occurs because there is continuity in what people do from day to day and year to year and in the social practices they follow. Changes occur partly because people intend them to occur, and partly because of consequences that no one either foresees or intends.

Developing a Global Perspective

As we just saw in our discussion of the sociological dimensions of drinking a cup of coffee, all our local actions—the ways in which we relate to one another in face-to-face contexts—form part of larger social settings that extend around the globe. And they also reflect large-scale processes of social change—processes that have drawn different parts of the world into interrelation with one another. The world in which we live today makes us much more *interdependent* with others, even thousands of miles away, than people have ever been previously.

These connections between the *local* and the *global* are quite new in human history. They have accelerated over the past thirty or forty years, as a result of the dramatic advances in communication, information technology, and transportation. The development of jet planes, large, speedy container ships, and other means of fast travel has meant that people and goods can be continuously transported across the world. And our worldwide system of satellite communication, established only some thirty years ago, has made it possible for people to be in touch with one another instantaneously.

American society, and the individual lives of Americans, is influenced every moment of the day by **globalization**, the growth of world interdependence, a social phenomenon that will be discussed throughout this book. Globalization should not be thought of simply as the development of worldwide networks—social and economic systems that are remote from our individual concerns. It is a local phenomenon, too. For example, only a few years ago, when they dined out, most Americans were faced with a limited choice. In many U.S. towns and cities today, a single street might feature Italian, Chinese, Japanese, Thai, French, and other types of restaurants next door to one an-

other. In turn, the dietary decisions we make are consequential for food producers who might live on the other side of the world. Another everyday aspect of globalization can be found in your closet and drawers. If you take a look at the labels of your clothing and see the many various countries in which they are manufactured, then you are experiencing globalization firsthand. In fact, many college students are now keenly aware of their ties to the many people around the world who work in low-wage factories. At dozens of college campuses in recent years, rallies have been held protesting the use of low-paid sweatshop workers to produce sweatshirts, t-shirts, baseball caps, and other clothing items with university logos. As University of California, Berkeley student Joanna Evelan said at one rally, "We want to raise awareness among students that they wear Cal clothes from manufacturers that are socially responsible."

Developing a global perspective has great importance for sociology. A global perspective not only allows us to become more aware of the ways that we are connected to people in other societies, it also makes us more aware of the many problems the world faces as it enters the twenty-first century. The global perspective opens our eyes to the fact that our interdependence with other societies means that our actions have consequences for others and that the world's problems have consequences for us.

Understanding Social Change

The changes in human ways of life in the last two hundred years, such as globalization, have been far-reaching. We have become accustomed, for example, to the fact that most of the population do not work on the land, and live in towns and cities rather than in small rural communities. But this was *never* the case until the middle of the nineteenth century. For virtually all of human history, the vast majority of people had to produce their own food and shelter and lived in tiny groups or in small village communities. Even at the height of the most developed traditional civilizations—like ancient Rome or traditional China—less than 10 percent of the population lived in urban areas; everyone else was engaged in food production in a rural setting. Today, in most of the industrialized societies, these proportions have become almost completely reversed. Quite often, more than 90 percent of the people live in urban areas, and only 2 to 3 percent of the population work in agricultural production.

It is not only the environment surrounding our lives that has changed; these transformations have radically altered, and continue to alter, the most personal and intimate side of our daily existence. To extend a previous example, the spread of ideals of romantic love was strongly conditioned by the transition from a rural to an urban, industrialized society. As people moved into urban areas and began to work in industrial production, marriage was no longer prompted mainly by economic motives—by the need to control the inheritance of land and to work the land as a family unit. "Arranged" marriages—fixed through the negotiations of parents and relatives—became less and less common. Individuals increasingly began to initiate marriage relationships on the basis of emotional attraction, and in order to seek personal fulfillment. The idea of "falling in love" as a basis for contracting a marriage tie was formed in this context.

Sociology as a discipline was born in an attempt to explain the social changes resulting from the Industrial Revolution during the nineteenth century. One such change was the employment of young children as factory workers.

Sociology had its beginnings in the attempts of thinkers to understand the initial impact of these transformations that accompanied industrialization in the West. It remains the basic discipline concerned with analyzing their nature. Our world today is radically different from that of former ages; it is the task of sociology to help us understand this world and what future it is likely to hold for us.

THE DEVELOPMENT OF SOCIOLOGICAL THINKING

When they first start studying sociology, many students are puzzled by the diversity of approaches they encounter. Sociology has never been a discipline in which there is a body of ideas that everyone accepts as valid. Sociologists often quarrel among themselves about how to go about studying human behavior and how research results might best be interpreted. Why should this be so? Why can't sociologists agree with one another more consistently, as natural scientists seem able to do? The answer is bound up with the very nature of the field itself. Sociology is about our own lives and our own behavior, and studying ourselves is the most complex and difficult endeavor we can undertake.

Theories and Theoretical Approaches

Trying to understand something as complex as the impact of industrialization on society raises the importance of theory to sociology. Factual research shows *how* things occur. Yet sociology does not just consist of collecting facts, however important and interesting they may be. We also want to know *why* things happen, and in order to do so we have to learn to construct theories. For instance we know that industrialization has had a major influence upon the emergence of modern societies. But what are the origins and preconditions of industrialization? Why do we find differences between societies in their industrialization processes? Why is industrialization associated with changes in ways of criminal punishment, or in family and marriage systems? To respond to such questions, we have to develop theoretical thinking.

Theories involve constructing abstract interpretations that can be used to explain a wide variety of empirical situations. A theory about industrialization, for example, would be concerned with identifying the main features that processes of industrial development share in common, and would try to show which of these are most important in explaining such development. Of course, factual research and theories can never completely be separated. We can only develop valid theoretical approaches if we are able to test them out by means of factual research.

We need theories to help us make sense of facts. Contrary to popular assertion, facts do not speak for themselves. Many sociologists work primarily on factual research, but unless they are guided by some knowledge of theory, their work is unlikely to explain the complexity of modern societies. This is true even of research carried out with strictly practical objectives.

"Practical people" tend to be suspicious of theorists, and may like to see themselves as too "down-to-earth" to need to pay attention to more abstract ideas, yet all practical decisions have some theoretical assumptions lying behind them. A manager of a business, for example, might have scant regard for "theory." Nonetheless, every approach to business activity involves theoretical assumptions, even if these often remain unstated. Thus the manager might assume that employees are motivated to work hard mainly by money—the level of wages they receive. This is not only a theoretical interpretation of human behavior, it is also a mistaken one, as research in industrial sociology tends to demonstrate.

Without a theoretical approach, we would not know what to look for in beginning a study or in interpreting the results of research. However, the illumination of factual evidence is not the only reason for the prime position of theory in sociology. Theoretical thinking must respond to general problems posed by the study of human social life, including issues that are philosophical in nature. Deciding to what extent sociology should be modeled upon the natural sciences, how we should best conceptualize human consciousness, action, and institutions—these are questions that do not admit of easy solutions. They

have been handled in different ways in the various **theoretical approaches** that have sprung up in the discipline.

Early Theorists

We human beings have always been curious about the sources of our own behavior, but for thousands of years our attempts to understand ourselves relied on ways of thinking passed down from generation to generation, often expressed in religious terms. (For example, before the rise of modern science, many people believed that natural events such as earthquakes were caused by gods or spirits.) Although writers from earlier periods provided insights into human behavior and society, the systematic study of society is a relatively recent development, whose beginnings date back to the late 1700s and early 1800s. The background to the origins of sociology was the series of sweeping changes ushered in by the French Revolution of 1789 and the emergence of the Industrial Revolution in Europe. The shattering of traditional ways of life wrought by these changes resulted in the attempts of thinkers to develop a new understanding of both the social and natural worlds.

A key development was the use of science instead of religion to understand the world. The types of questions these nineteenth-century thinkers sought to answer—what is human nature? why is society structured like it is? how and why do societies change?—are the same questions sociologists try to answer today. Our modern world is radically different from that of the past; it is sociology's task to help us understand this world and what the future is likely to hold.

AUGUSTE COMTE

No single individual, of course, can found a whole field of study, and there were many contributors to early sociological thinking. Particular prominence, however, is usually given to the French author Auguste Comte (1798–1857), if only because he invented the word "sociology." Comte originally used the term "social physics," but some of his intellectual rivals at the time were also making use of that term. Comte wanted to distinguish his own views from theirs, so he

Auguste Comte (1798–1857).

introduced "sociology" to describe the subject he wished to establish.

Comte believed that this new field could produce a knowledge of society based on scientific evidence. He regarded sociology as the last science to develop—following on from physics, chemistry, and biology—but as the most significant and complex of all the sciences. Sociology, he believed, should contribute to the welfare of humanity by using science to understand and therefore predict and control human behavior. In the later part of his career, Comte drew up ambitious plans for the reconstruction of French society in particular and for human societies in general, based on scientific knowledge.

ÉMILE DURKHEIM

The works of another French writer, Émile Durkheim (1858–1917), have had a much more lasting impact on modern sociology than those of Comte. Although he drew on aspects of Comte's work, Durkheim thought that many of his predecessor's ideas were too speculative and vague and that Comte had not successfully carried out his program—to establish sociology on a scientific basis. To become scientific, according to Durkheim, sociology must study **social facts,** aspects of social life that shape our actions as individuals, such as the state of the economy or the influence of religion. Durkheim believed that we must study social life with the same objectivity as scientists study the natural world. His famous first principle of sociology was "Study social facts as *things*!" By this

he meant that social life can be analyzed as rigorously as objects or events in nature.

Like a biologist studying the human body, Durkheim saw society as a set of independent parts, each of which could be studied separately. A body consists of various specialized parts (such as the brain, heart, lungs, liver, and so forth), each of which contributes to sustaining the continuing life of the organism. These necessarily work in harmony with one another; if they do not, the life of the organism is under threat. So it is, according to Durkheim, with society. For a society to have a continuing existence over time, its specialized institutions (such as the political system, religion, the family, and the educational system) must work in harmony with one another and function as an integrated whole. Durkheim referred to this social cohesion as **"organic solidarity."** He argued that the continuation of a society thus depends on cooperation, which in turn presumes a general consensus, or agreement, among its members over basic values and customs.

Another major theme pursued by Durkheim, and by many others since, is that the societies of which we are members exert **social constraint** over our actions. Durkheim argued that society has primacy over the individual person. Society is far more than the sum of individual acts; when we analyze social structures, we are studying characteristics that have a "firmness" or "solidity" comparable to those of structures in the physical world. Think of a person standing in a room with several doors. The structure of the room constrains the range of her or his possible activities. The

Émile Durkheim (1858–1917).

position of the walls and the doors, for example, defines the routes of exit and entry. Social structure, according to Durkheim, constrains our activities in a parallel way, setting limits to what we can do as individuals. It is "external" to us, just as the walls of the room are.

Like the other major founders of sociology, Durkheim was preoccupied with the changes transforming society in his own lifetime. His analysis of social change was based upon the development of the **division of labor** (the growth of complex distinctions between different occupations). Durkheim argued that the division of labor gradually replaced religion as the basis of social cohesion and provided organic solidarity to modern societies. He argued that as the division of labor expands, people become more and more dependent on one another, because each person needs goods and services that those in other occupations supply. Another of Durkheim's most famous studies was concerned with the analysis of suicide (Durkheim, 1966/1897). Suicide seems to be a purely personal act, the outcome of extreme personal unhappiness. Durkheim showed, however, that social factors exert a fundamental influence on suicidal behavior—**anomie,** a feeling of aimlessness or despair provoked by modern social life being one of these influences. Suicide rates show regular patterns from year to year, he argued, and these patterns must be explained sociologically. Many objections can be raised against Durkheim's study, but it remains a classic work whose relevance to sociology today is by no means exhausted. According to Durkheim, processes of change in the modern world are so rapid and intense that they give rise to major social difficulties, which he linked to anomie. Traditional moral controls and standards, which used to be supplied by religion, are largely broken down by modern social development, and this leaves many individuals in modern societies feeling that their daily lives lack meaning. Later in his life, Durkheim came to be especially concerned with the role of religion in social life. In his study of religious beliefs, practices, and rituals—*The Elementary Forms of Religion* (1912)—he focused particularly on the importance of religion in maintaining moral order in society.

KARL MARX

The ideas of Karl Marx (1818–1883) contrasted sharply with those of Comte and Durkheim, but like

Karl Marx (1818–1883).

them, he sought to explain the changes in society that took place over the time of the Industrial Revolution. When he was a young man, Marx's political activities brought him into conflict with the German authorities; after a brief stay in France, he settled permanently in exile in Britain. His writings covered a diversity of areas. Even his sternest critics regard his work as important for the development of sociology. Much of his writing concentrated on economic issues, but since he was always concerned to connect economic problems to social institutions, his work was, and is, rich in sociological insights.

Marx's viewpoint was founded on what he called the **materialist conception of history.** According to this view, it is not the ideas or values human beings hold that are the main sources of social change, as Durkheim claimed. Rather, social change is prompted primarily by economic influences. The conflicts between classes—the rich versus the poor—provide the motivation for historical development. In Marx's words, "All human history thus far is the history of class struggles."

Though he wrote about various phases of history, Marx concentrated on change in modern times. For him, the most important changes were bound up with the development of **capitalism.** Capitalism is a system of production that contrasts radically with previous economic systems in history, involving as it does the production of goods and services sold to a wide range of consumers. Those who own capital, or factories, machines, and large sums of money, form a ruling class. The mass of the population make up a class of wage workers, or a working class, who do not own the means of their livelihood but must find employment provided by the owners of capital. Capitalism is thus a class system, in which conflict between classes is a commonplace occurrence because it is in the interests of the ruling class to exploit the working class and the interests of the workers to seek to overcome that exploitation.

According to Marx, in the future capitalism will be supplanted by a society in which there are no classes—no divisions between rich and poor. He didn't mean by this that all inequalities between individuals will disappear. Rather, societies will no longer be split into a small class that monopolizes economic and political power and the large mass of people who benefit little from the wealth their work creates. The economic system will come under communal ownership, and a more equal society than we know at present will be established.

Marx's work has had a far-reaching effect on the twentieth-century world. Until recently, before the fall of Soviet Communism, more than a third of the earth's population lived in societies whose governments claimed to derive their inspiration from Marx's ideas. In addition, many sociologists have been influenced by Marx's ideas about class divisions.

MAX WEBER

Like Marx, Max Weber (pronounced "Vaber," 1864–1920) cannot simply be labeled a sociologist;

Max Weber (1864–1920).

his interests and concerns ranged across many areas. Born in Germany, where he spent most of his academic career, Weber was an individual of wide learning. His writings covered the fields of economics, law, philosophy, and comparative history as well as sociology, and much of his work was also concerned with the development of modern capitalism. Like other thinkers of his time, Weber sought to understand social change. He was influenced by Marx but was also strongly critical of some of Marx's major views. He rejected the materialist conception of history and saw class conflict as less significant than did Marx. In Weber's view, economic factors are important, but ideas and values have just as much impact on social change.

Some of Weber's most influential writings were concerned with analyzing the distinctiveness of Western society as compared with other major civilizations. He studied the religions of China, India, and the Near East, and in the course of these researches made major contributions to the sociology of religion. Comparing the leading religious systems in China and India with those of the West, Weber concluded that certain aspects of Christian beliefs strongly influenced the rise of capitalism. This outlook did not emerge, as Marx supposed, only from economic changes. In Weber's view, cultural ideas and values help shape society and affect our individual actions.

One of the most persistent concerns of Weber's work was the study of bureaucracy. A bureaucracy is a large organization that is divided into jobs based on specific functions and staffed by officials ranked according to a hierarchy. Industrial firms, government organizations, hospitals, and schools are all examples of bureaucracies. Weber believed the advance of bureaucracy to be an inevitable feature of our era. Bureaucracy makes it possible for these large organizations to run efficiently, but poses problems for effective democratic participation in modern societies. Bureaucracy involves the rule of experts, whose decisions are made without much consultation with those whose lives are affected by them.

Weber's contributions range over many other areas, including the study of the development of cities, systems of law, types of economy, and the nature of classes. He also produced a range of writings concerned with the overall character of sociology itself. Weber was more cautious than either Durkheim or

KEY CONCEPTS IN REVIEW

INTERPRETING MODERN DEVELOPMENT

DURKHEIM

1. The main dynamic of modern development is the **division of labor** as a basis for social cohesion and "**organic solidarity.**"
2. Durkheim believed that sociology must study **social facts** as things, just as science would analyze the natural world. His study of suicide led him to stress the important influence of social factors, qualities of a society external to the individual, on a person's actions. Durkheim argued that society exerts **social constraint** over our actions.

MARX

1. The main dynamic of modern development is the expansion of **capitalism.** Rather than being cohesive, society is divided by class differences.
2. Marx believed that we must study the divisions within a society that are derived from the economic inequalities of capitalism.

WEBER

1. The main dynamic of modern development is the **rationalization** of social and economic life.
2. Weber focused on why Western societies developed so differently from other societies. He also emphasized the importance of cultural ideas and values on social change.

Marx in proclaiming sociology to be a science. According to Weber, it is misleading to imagine that we can study people using the same procedures that are applied to investigate the physical world. Humans are thinking, reasoning beings; we attach meaning and significance to most of what we do, and any discipline that deals with human behavior must acknowledge this.

Modern Theoretical Approaches

While the origins of sociology were mainly European, in this century the subject has become firmly established worldwide, and some of the most important de-

velopments have taken place in the United States. The following sections explore these developments.

SYMBOLIC INTERACTIONISM

The work of George Herbert Mead (1863–1931), a philosopher teaching at the University of Chicago, had an important influence on the development of sociological thought, in particular through a perspective called **symbolic interactionism.** Mead placed particular importance upon the study of *language* in analyzing the social world. According to him, language allows us to become self-conscious beings—aware of our own individuality. The key element in this process is the **symbol**, something that *stands for* something else. For example, the word "tree" is a symbol by

THE SOCIOLOGICAL DEBATE

UNDERSTANDING THE MODERN WORLD

From Marx's time to the present day many sociological debates have centered upon the ideas that Marx set out about the influence of economics on the development of modern societies. According to Marx, as was mentioned earlier, modern societies are *capitalistic*—the driving impulse behind social change in the modern era is to be found in the pressure toward constant economic transformation produced by the spread of capitalist production. Capitalism is a vastly more dynamic economic system than any other that preceded it in history. Capitalists compete with one another to sell their goods to consumers, and to survive in a competitive market, firms have to produce their wares as cheaply and efficiently as possible. This leads to constant technological innovation, because increasing the effectiveness of the technology used in a particular production process is one way in which companies can secure an edge over their rivals.

There are also strong incentives to seek out new markets in which to sell goods, acquire cheap raw materials, and make use of cheap labor power. Capitalism, therefore, according to Marx, is a restlessly expanding system, pushing outward across the world. This is how Marx explains the spread of Western industry globally.

Marx's interpretation of the influence of capitalism has found many supporters. Subsequent Marxist authors have considerably refined Marx's own portrayal. On the other hand, numerous critics have set out to rebut Marx's view, offering alternative analyses of the influences shaping the modern world. Virtually everyone accepts that capitalism *has* played a major part in creating the world in which we live today. But other sociologists have argued both that Marx exaggerated the impact of purely *economic* factors in producing change, and that capitalism is *less central* to modern social development than he claimed. Most of these writers have also been skeptical of Marx's belief that a socialist system would eventually replace capitalism.

One of Marx's earliest, and most acute, critics was Max Weber. Weber's writings, in fact, have been described as involving a lifelong struggle with "the ghost of Marx"—with the intellectual legacy that Marx left. The alternative position that Weber worked out remains important today. According to Weber, noneconomic factors have played the key role in modern social development. Weber's celebrated and much discussed work, *The Protestant Ethic and the Spirit of Capitalism*, proposes that religious values—especially those associated with Puritanism—were of fundamental importance in creating a capitalistic outlook. This outlook did not emerge, as Marx supposed, only from economic changes.

Weber's understanding of the nature of modern societies, and the reasons for the spread of Western ways of life across the world, also contrasts substantially with that of Marx. According to Weber, capitalism—a distinct way of organizing economic enterprise—is one among other major factors shaping social development in the modern period. Underlying capitalistic mechanisms, and in some ways more fundamental than them, is the impact of *science* and *bureaucracy*. Science has shaped modern technology and will presumably continue to do so in any future socialist society. Bureaucracy is the only way of organizing large numbers of people effectively, and therefore inevitably expands with economic and political growth. The development of science, modern technology, and bureaucracy are examples of a general social process that Weber refers to collectively as **rationalization**. Rationalization means the organization of social, economic, and cultural life according to principles of efficiency, on the basis of technical knowledge.

Which interpretation of modern societies, that deriving from Marx, or that coming from Weber, is correct? Again, scholars are divided on the issue. It must be remembered that within each camp there are variations, so not every theorist will agree with all the points. The contrasts between these two standpoints inform many areas of sociology.

Neglected Founders

Although Comte, Durkheim, Marx, and Weber are, without doubt, foundational figures in sociology, there were other important thinkers from the same period whose contributions must also be taken into account. Sociology, like many academic fields, has not always lived up to its ideal of acknowledging the importance of every thinker whose work has intrinsic merit. Very few women or members of racial minorities were given the opportunity to become professional sociologists during the "classical" period of the late nineteenth and early twentieth centuries. In addition, the few that were given the opportunity to do sociological research of lasting importance have frequently been neglected by the field. These individuals deserve the attention of sociologists today.

Harriet Martineau

Harriet Martineau (1802–1876) was born and educated in England. She has been called the "first woman sociologist," but, like Marx and Weber, cannot be simply thought of as a sociologist. She was the author of over fifty books, as well as numerous essays. Martineau is now credited with introducing sociology to England through her translation of Comte's founding treatise of the field, *Positive Philosophy* (Rossi, 1973). In addition, Martineau conducted a firsthand systematic study of American society during her extensive travels throughout the United States in the 1830s, which is the subject of her book *Society in America*. Martineau is significant to sociologists today for several reasons. First, she argued that when one studies a society, one must focus on all its aspects, including key political, religious, and social institutions. Second, she insisted that an analysis of a society must include an understanding of women's lives. Third, she was the first to turn a sociological eye on previously ignored issues, including marriage, children, domestic and religious life, and race relations. As she once wrote, "The nursery, the boudoir, and the kitchen are all excellent schools in which to learn the morals and manners of a people" (Martineau, 1962, p. 53). Finally, she argued that sociologists should do more than just observe, they should also act in ways to benefit a society. As a result, Martineau was an active proponent of both women's rights and the emancipation of slaves.

Harriet Martineau (1802–1876)

W. E. B. Du Bois

W. E. B. Du Bois (1868–1963) was the first African American to earn a doctorate at Harvard University. Du Bois's contributions to sociology were many. Perhaps most important is the concept of "double consciousness," which is a way of talking about identity through the lens of the particular experiences of African Americans. He argued that American society only let African Americans see themselves through the eyes of others: "It is a particular sensation, this double consciousness, this sense of always looking at one's soul by the tape of a world that looks on in amused contempt and pity. One ever feels his two-ness—an American, a

W. E. B. Du Bois (1868–1963)

Negro, two souls, two thoughts, two unreconciled strivings, two warring ideals in one dark body, whose dogged strength alone keeps it from being torn asunder" (Du Bois, 1903, p. 2). Du Bois made a persuasive claim that one's sense of self and one's identity are greatly influenced by historical experiences and social circumstances, in the case of African Americans, the impact of slavery, and following emancipation, segregation and prejudice. Throughout his career, Du Bois was focused on race relations in the United States; as he said in an often repeated quote, "the problem of the twentieth century is the problem of the color line." His influence on sociology today is evidenced by continued interest in the questions that he raised, particularly his concern that sociology must explain "the contact of diverse races of men." Du Bois was also the first social researcher to trace the problems faced by African Americans to their social and economic underpinnings, an issue that most sociologists now widely agree with. Finally, Du Bois became known for connecting social analysis to social reform. He was one of the founding members of the National Association for the Advancement of Colored People (NAACP) and a long-time advocate for the collective struggle of African Americans. Later in his life, Du Bois became disenchanted by the lack of progress in American race relations and moved to the African nation of Ghana, where he died in 1963.

means of which we represent the object tree. Once we have mastered such a concept, Mead argued, we can think of a tree even if none is visible; we have learned to think of the object symbolically. Symbolic thought frees us from being limited in our experience to what we actually see, hear, or feel.

Unlike the animals, according to Mead, human beings live in a richly symbolic universe. This applies even to our very sense of self. Each of us is a self-conscious being because we learn to look at ourselves as if from the outside—we see ourselves as others see us. When a child begins to use "I" to refer to that object (herself) whom others call "you," she is exhibiting the beginnings of self-consciousness.

Virtually all interactions between individuals, symbolic interactionists say, involve an exchange of symbols. When we interact with others, we constantly look for clues to what type of behavior is appropriate in the context and how to interpret what others are

A symbolic interactionist studying romantic love in a society might observe two people on a date and focus on the symbolic meaning of gestures, such as touching one's hair or the other person's arm, as well as the broader meanings associated with love, intimacy, commitment, and relationships.

up to. Symbolic interactionism directs our attention to the detail of interpersonal interaction and how that detail is used to make sense of what others say and do. For instance, suppose two people are out on a date for the first time. Each is likely to spend a good part of the evening sizing the other up and assessing how the relationship is likely to develop, if at all. Neither wishes to be seen doing this too openly, although each recognizes that it is going on. Both individuals are careful about their own behavior, being anxious to present themselves in a favorable light; but, knowing this, both are likely to be looking for aspects of the other's behavior that would reveal their true opinions. A complex and subtle process of symbolic interpretation shapes the interaction between the two.

FUNCTIONALISM

Symbolic interactionism is open to the criticism that it concentrates too much on the small scale. Symbolic interactionists have found difficulty in dealing with more large-scale structures and processes—the very thing that a rival tradition of thought, **functionalism,** tends to emphasize. Functionalist thinking in sociology was originally pioneered by Comte, who saw it as closely bound up with his overall view of the field.

To study the *function* of a social activity is to analyze the contribution that that activity makes to the continuation of the society as a whole. The best way to understand this idea is by analogy to the human body, a comparison Comte, Durkheim, and other functionalist authors made. To study an organ like the heart, we need to show how it relates to other parts of the body. When we learn how the heart pumps blood around the body, we then understand that the heart plays a vital role in the continuation of the life of the organism. Similarly, analyzing the function of a social item, such as religion, means showing the part it plays in the continued existence of a society. According to Durkheim, for instance, religion reaffirms people's adherence to core social values, thereby contributing to the maintenance of social cohesion.

Functionalism became prominent in sociology through the writings of Talcott Parsons and Robert K. Merton, each of whom saw functionalist analysis as providing the key to the development of sociological theory and research. Merton's version of functionalism has been particularly influential.

Merton distinguished between manifest and latent functions. **Manifest functions** are those known to, and intended by, the participants in a specific type of social activity. **Latent functions** are consequences of that activity of which participants are unaware. To illustrate this distinction, Merton used the example of a rain dance performed by the Hopi Tribe of Arizona and New Mexico. The Hopi believe that the ceremony will bring the rain they need for their crops (manifest function). This is why they organize and participate in it. But the rain dance, Merton argued, using Durkheim's theory of religion, also has the effect of promoting the cohesion of the Hopi society (latent function). A major part of sociological explanation, according to Merton, consists in uncovering the latent functions of social activities and institutions.

Merton also distinguished between functions and dysfunctions. To look for the dysfunctional aspects of social behavior means focusing on features of social life that challenge the existing order of things. For example, it is mistaken to suppose that religion is always functional—that it contributes only to social cohesion. When two groups support different religions or even different versions of the same religion, the result can be major social conflicts, causing widespread so-

A functionalist approach to studying marriage in a society would emphasize the contribution that marriage makes to the society as a whole. Thus, functionalists might argue that one of the functions of marriage is to combine the economic resources of two families, as is suggested by this Indian bridegroom's traditional offering of food to his spouse's family.

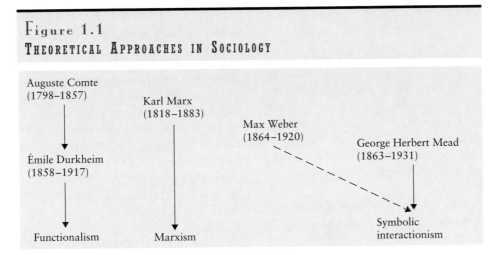

Figure 1.1
THEORETICAL APPROACHES IN SOCIOLOGY

Auguste Comte
(1798–1857)

Karl Marx
(1818–1883)

Max Weber
(1864–1920)

George Herbert Mead
(1863–1931)

Émile Durkheim
(1858–1917)

Functionalism   Marxism   Symbolic
                                                  interactionism

The unbroken lines indicate direct influence, the dotted line an indirect connection. Mead is not indebted to Weber, but Weber's views—stressing the meaningful, purposive nature of human action—have affinities with the themes of symbolic interactionism.

cial disruption. Thus, wars have often been fought between religious communities—as can be seen in the struggles between Protestants and Catholics in European history.

For a long while, functionalist thought was probably the leading theoretical tradition in sociology, particularly in the United States. In recent years, its popularity has declined as its limitations have become apparent. While this was not true of Merton, many functionalist thinkers (Talcott Parsons was an example) unduly stressed factors leading to social cohesion at the expense of those producing division and conflict. In addition, it has seemed to many critics that functional analysis attributes to societies qualities they do not have. Functionalists often wrote as though societies have "needs" and "purposes," even though these concepts make sense only when applied to individual human beings.

MARXISM AND CLASS CONFLICT

Functionalism and symbolic interactionism are not the only theoretical traditions of any importance in sociology. A further influential approach is **Marxism.** Marxists, of course, all trace their views back in some way to the writings of Karl Marx. But numerous interpretations of Marx's major ideas are possible, and there are today schools of Marxist thought that take very different theoretical positions.

In all of its versions, Marxism differs from non-Marxist traditions of sociology in that its authors see it as a combination of sociological analysis and political reform. Marxism is supposed to generate a program of radical political change. Moreover, Marxists lay more emphasis on conflict, class divisions, power, and ideology than many non-Marxist sociologists, especially most of those influenced by functionalism. The concept of **power**—and a closely associated notion, that of **ideology**—are of great importance to Marxist sociologists and to sociology in general. By power is meant the capability of individuals or groups to make their own concerns or interests count, even where others resist. Power sometimes involves the direct use of force, but is almost always accompanied by the development of ideas (ideologies), which are used to *justify* the actions of the powerful. Power, ideology, and conflict are always closely connected. Many conflicts are *about* power, because of the rewards it can bring. Those who hold most power may depend mainly on the influence of ideology to retain their dominance, but are usually able also to use force if necessary.

FEMINISM AND FEMINIST THEORY

Feminist theory is one of the most prominent areas of contemporary sociology. This is a notable development, since issues of gender are scarcely central in the work of the major figures who established the discipline. Sociologists did not add the study of women and gender inequality to their concerns without a pitched battle. The success of feminism's entry into sociology required a fundamental shift in the discipline's approach.

Many feminist theorists brought their experiences in the women's movement of the 1960s and 1970s to their work as sociologists. Like Marxism, feminism makes a link between sociological theory and political reform. Many feminist sociologists have been advocates for political and social action to remedy the inequalities between women and men in both the public and private spheres.

Feminist sociologists focus on the inequalities between women and men in a society and the ways that social action, such as forming political groups like the National Organization for Women, can remedy these inequalities.

Feminist sociologists argue that women's lives and experiences are central to the study of society. Sociology, like most academic disciplines, has presumed a male point of view. Driven by a concern with women's subordination in American society, feminist sociologists highlight gender relations and gender inequality as an important determinant of social life in terms of both social interaction and social institutions such as the family, the workplace, and the educational system. Feminist theory emphasizes that gendered patterns and gendered inequalities are not natural, but socially constructed. (We will cover this point in more detail in Chapter 8).

Today, feminist sociology is characterized by a focus on the intersection of gender, race, and class. A feminist approach to the study of inequality has influenced new fields of study, like men's studies, sexuality studies, and gay and lesbian studies.

Theoretical Thinking in Sociology

So far in this chapter we have been concerned with theoretical approaches, which refer to broad, overall orientations to the subject matter of sociology. However, we can draw a distinction between theoretical approaches and theories. Theories are more narrowly focused and represent attempts to explain particular social conditions or types of event. They are usually formed as part of the process of research, and in turn suggest problems to which research investigations should be devoted. An example would be Durkheim's theory of suicide, referred to earlier in this chapter.

Innumerable theories have been developed in the many different areas of research in which sociologists work. Sometimes theories are very precisely set out, and are even occasionally expressed in mathematical form—although this is more common in other social sciences (especially economics) than in sociology.

Some theories are also much more encompassing than others. Opinions vary about whether it is desirable or useful for sociologists to concern themselves with very wide-ranging theoretical endeavors. Robert K. Merton (1957), for example, argues forcefully that sociologists should concentrate their attention upon what he calls *theories of the middle range*. Rather

KEY CONCEPTS IN REVIEW

MODERN THEORETICAL APPROACHES

Symbolic interactionism stresses the exchange of symbols between individuals in social interaction. Unlike other theories, symbolic interactionism emphasizes the small-scale interactions of an individual, not society as a whole.

Functionalism looks at society as a whole, emphasizing the contribution a social activity makes to society. Merton, whose version of functionalism has been particularly influential, stressed that **manifest functions,** those intended by the participants in a social activity, are sometimes less important than **latent functions,** the unintentional consequences of a social act. Merton believed that a major part of sociological explanation is to uncover the latent functions of social acts and institutions.

Many contemporary social theorists are still influenced by Marx and his emphasis upon **power, ideology,** and social conflict. For instance, the study of inequality using the concepts of gender, class, and race is at the heart of feminist sociology, which has changed the field by directing its attention to women's lives and the subordination they have experienced. One way to think about sociology's theoretical approaches is to think in terms of level of analysis. **Microsociology** is the study of everyday behavior in situations of face-to-face interaction. **Macrosociology** is the analysis of large-scale social systems. The two are closely connected.

---

than attempting to create grand theoretical schemes (in the manner of Marx, for instance), we should be concerned with developing more modest theories.

Middle-range theories are specific enough to be directly tested by empirical research, yet sufficiently general to cover a range of different phenomena. A case in point is the theory of *relative deprivation*. This theory holds that how people evaluate their circumstances depends upon who they compare themselves to. Thus, feelings of deprivation do not conform directly to the level of material poverty individuals experience. A family living in a small home in a poor area, where everyone is in more or less similar circumstances, is likely to feel less deprived that one living in a similar house in a neighborhood where the majority of homes are much larger and the people more affluent.

It is indeed true that the more wide-ranging and ambitious a theory is, the more difficult it is to test empirically. Yet there seems no obvious reason why theoretical thinking in sociology should be confined to the "middle range."

Assessing theories, and especially theoretical approaches, in sociology is a challenging and formidable task. Theoretical debates are by definition more abstract than controversies of a more empirical kind. The fact that there is not a single theoretical approach that dominates the whole of sociology might seem to be a sign of weakness in the subject. But this is not the case at all: the jostling of rival theoretical approaches and theories is an expression of the vitality of the sociological enterprise. In studying human beings—ourselves—theoretical variety rescues us from dogma. Human behavior is complicated and many-sided, and it is very unlikely that a single theoretical perspective could cover all of its aspects. Diversity in theoretical thinking provides a rich source of ideas that can be drawn upon in research, and stimulates the imaginative capacities so essential to progress in sociological work.

Levels of Analysis: Microsociology and Macrosociology

One important distinction between the different theoretical perspectives we have discussed in this chapter involves the level of analysis each is directed at. The study of everyday behavior in situations of face-to-face interaction is usually called **microsociology**. **Macrosociology** is the analysis of large-scale social systems, like the political system or the economic order. It also includes the analysis of long-term processes of change, such as the development of industrialism. At first glance, it might seem as though micro and macro analysis are distinct from one another. In fact, the two are closely connected (Knorr-Cetina and Cicourel 1981; Giddens 1984).

Macro analysis is essential if we are to understand the institutional background of daily life. The ways in which people live their everyday lives are greatly affected by the broader institutional framework, as is obvious when the daily cycle of activities of a culture like that of the medieval period is compared with life in an industrialized urban environment. In modern societies, as has been pointed out, we are constantly in contact with strangers. This contact may be indirect and impersonal. However, no matter how many indirect or electronic relations we enter into today, even in the most complex societies, the presence of other people remains crucial. While we may choose to send an acquaintance an e-mail message on the Internet, we can also choose to fly thousands of miles to spend the weekend with a friend.

Micro studies are in their turn necessary for illuminating broad institutional patterns. Face-to-face interaction is clearly the main basis of all forms of social organization, no matter how large-scale. Suppose we are studying a business corporation. We could understand much about its activities simply by looking at face-to-face behavior. We could analyze, for example, the interaction of directors in the boardroom, people working in the various offices, or the workers on the factory floor. We would not build up a picture of the whole corporation in this way, since some of its business is transacted through printed materials, letters, the telephone, and computers. Yet we could certainly contribute significantly to understanding how the organization works.

In later chapters, we will see further examples of how interaction in micro contexts affects larger social processes, and how macro systems in turn influence more confined settings of social life.

IS SOCIOLOGY A SCIENCE?

Durkheim, Marx, and the other founders of sociology thought of it as a **science**. But can we really study human social life in a scientific way? To answer this question, we must first understand what the word means. What is science?

Science is the use of *systematic methods of empirical investigation, the analysis of data, theoretical thinking, and the logical assessment of arguments* to develop a body of knowledge about a particular subject matter. Sociology is a scientific endeavor, according to this definition. It involves systematic methods of empirical investigation, the analysis of data, and the assessment of theories in the light of evidence and logical argument.

Studying human beings, however, is different from observing events in the physical world, and sociology shouldn't be seen as directly like a natural science. Unlike objects in nature, humans are self-aware beings who confer sense and purpose on what they do. We can't even describe social life accurately unless we first grasp the concepts that people apply in their behavior. For instance, to describe a death as a suicide means knowing what the person in question was intending when he died. Suicide can only occur when an individual actively has self-destruction in mind. If he accidentally steps in front of a car and is killed, he cannot be said to have committed suicide.

The fact that we cannot study human beings in exactly the same way as objects in nature is in some ways an advantage to sociology. Sociological researchers profit from being able to pose questions directly to those they study—other human beings. In other respects, sociology creates difficulties not encountered by natural scientists. People who are aware that their activities are being scrutinized frequently will not behave in the same way as they do normally. They may consciously or unconsciously portray themselves in a way that differs from their usual attitudes. They may even try to "assist" the researcher by giving the responses they believe she wants.

HOW CAN SOCIOLOGY HELP US IN OUR LIVES?

Sociology has several practical implications for our lives, as C. Wright Mills emphasized when developing his idea of the sociological imagination.

Like an integrated classroom, sociology hopes to encourage awareness of cultural differences.

Awareness of Cultural Differences

First, sociology allows us to see the social world from many perspectives. Quite often, if we properly understand how others live, we also acquire a better understanding of what their problems are. Practical policies that are not based on an informed awareness of the ways of life of people they affect have little chance of success. Thus, a white social worker operating in an African-American community won't gain the confidence of its members without developing a sensitivity to the differences in social experience that often separate white and black in the United States.

Assessing the Effects of Policies

Second, sociological research provides practical help in assessing the results of policy initiatives. A program of practical reform may simply fail to achieve what its designers sought or may produce unintended consequences of an unfortunate kind. For instance, in the years following World War II, large public housing blocks were built in city centers in many countries.

These were planned to provide high standards of accommodation for low-income groups from slum areas, and offered shopping amenities and other civic services close at hand. However, research showed that many people who had moved from their previous dwellings to large apartment blocks felt isolated and unhappy. High-rise apartment blocks and shopping malls in poorer areas often became dilapidated and provided breeding grounds for mugging and other violent crimes.

Self-Enlightenment

Third, and in some ways most important, sociology can provide us with self-enlightenment—increased self-understanding. The more we know about why we act as we do, and about the overall workings of our society, the more likely we are to be able to influence our own futures. We should not see sociology as assisting only policy makers—that is, powerful groups—to make informed decisions. Those in power cannot be assumed always to consider the interests of the less powerful or underprivileged in the policies they pursue. Self-enlightened groups can often benefit from sociological research and respond in an effective way to government policies or form policy initiatives of their own. Self-help groups like Alcoholics Anonymous and social movements like the environmental movement are examples of social groups that have directly sought to bring about practical reforms, with some degree of success.

The Sociologist's Role in Society

Finally, it should be mentioned that many sociologists concern themselves directly with practical matters as professionals. People trained in sociology are to be found as industrial consultants, urban planners, social workers, and personnel managers, as well as in many other jobs. An understanding of society can also help one in careers in law, journalism, business, and medicine.

Those who study sociology also frequently develop a social conscience. Should sociologists themselves actively advocate, and agitate for, programs of reform or social change? Some argue that sociology can preserve its intellectual independence only if sociologists

are studiously neutral in moral and political controversies. Yet are scholars who remain aloof from current debates necessarily more impartial in their assessment of sociological issues than others? There is often a connection between studying sociology and the prompting of social conscience. No sociologically sophisticated person can be unaware of the inequalities that exist in the world today, the lack of social justice in many social situations, and the deprivations suffered by millions of people. It would be strange if sociologists did not take sides on practical issues, and it would be illogical to try to ban them from drawing on their expertise in so doing.

In this chapter, we have seen that sociology is a discipline in which we set aside our personal view of the world to look more carefully at the influences that shape our lives and those of others. Sociology emerged as a distinct intellectual endeavor with the development of modern societies, and the study of such societies remains its principal concern. But sociologists are also preoccupied with a broad range of issues about the nature of social interaction and human societies in general.

Sociology isn't just an abstract intellectual field but has major practical implications for people's lives. Learning to become a sociologist shouldn't be a dull academic endeavor! The best way to make sure it doesn't become so is to approach the subject in an imaginative way and to relate sociological ideas and findings to situations in your own life.

SUMMARY

1. *Sociology* can be identified as the systematic study of human societies giving special emphasis to modern, industrialized systems. The subject came into being as an attempt to understand the far-reaching changes that have occurred in human societies over the past two to three centuries.

2. Major social changes have also occurred in the most intimate and personal characteristics of people's lives. The development of romantic love as a basis for marriage is an example of this.

3. The practice of sociology involves the ability to think imaginatively and to detach oneself as far as possible from preconceived ideas about social relationships.

4. A diversity of theoretical approaches is found in sociology. The reason for this is not particularly puzzling. Theoretical disputes are difficult to resolve even in the natural sciences, and in sociology we face special difficulties because of the complex problems involved in subjecting our own behavior to study.

5. Important figures in the early development of sociological theory include Auguste Comte (1798–1857), Émile Durkheim (1858–1917), Karl Marx (1818–1883), and Max Weber (1864–1920). Many of their ideas remain important in sociology today.

6. The main theoretical approaches in sociology are *symbolic interactionism, functionalism, Marxism,* and *feminism.* To some extent, these approaches are complementary to one another. However, there are also major contrasts between them, which influence the ways in which theoretical issues are handled by authors following different approaches.

7. The study of face-to-face interaction is usually called *microsociology*—as contrasted to *macrosociology*, which studies larger groups, institutions, and social systems. Micro and macro analyses are in fact very closely related and each complements the other.

8. Sociology is a science in that it involves systematic methods of investigation and the evaluation of theories in the light of evidence and logical argument. But it cannot be modeled directly upon the natural sciences, because studying human behavior is in fundamental ways different from studying the world of nature.

9. Sociology is a subject with important practical implications. Sociology can contribute to social criticism and practical social reform in several ways. First, the improved understanding of a given set of social circumstances often gives us a better chance of controlling them. Second, sociology provides the means of increasing our cultural sensitivities, allowing policies to be based upon an awareness of divergent cultural values. Third, we can investigate the consequences (intended and unintended) of the adoption of particular policy programs. Finally, and perhaps most important, sociology provides self-enlightenment, offering groups and individuals an increased opportunity to alter the conditions of their own lives.

Chapter Two

Sociological Questions

Be able to name the different types of questions sociologists try to answer in their research—factual, theoretical, comparative, and developmental.

The Research Process

Learn the steps of the research process, and be able to complete the process yourself.

Understanding Cause and Effect

Be able to differentiate between causation and correlation.

Research Methods

Familiarize yourself with all the different methods available to sociological research, and know the advantages and disadvantages of each.

Research in the Real World: Methods, Problems, Pitfalls

See how research methods were combined in a real study, and recognize the problems the researcher faced.

Asking and Answering Sociological Questions

In the auditorium of the Delta Airlines Stewardess Training Center in Atlanta, 123 flight attendant trainees sat and listened to a pilot explain that the smile is the flight attendant's main asset. Arlie Hochschild, a sociology professor at the University of California, Berkeley, went to Atlanta to sit in on these classes and wrote about them in her book, *The Managed Heart*.

"Now girls, I want you to go out there and really *smile*," the pilot instructed the trainees. "Your smile is your biggest asset. I want you to go out there and use it. Smile. *Really* smile. Really *lay it on*."

On the basis of her research with the flight attendants, Hochschild was able to add a new dimension to the way sociologists think about the world of work. As the American economy has become increasingly based on the delivery of services, the emotional style of the work we do needs to be understood.

The job of flight attendant is like many jobs that you and your friends work in today. Whether you are serving espresso or parking cars, many of today's jobs require that you do more than physical labor. It is necessary that you do what Hochschild calls "emotional labor"—labor that requires that you manage your feelings in order to create a publicly observable (and acceptable) facial and bodily display. According to Hochschild, the companies you work for lay claim not only to your physical motions, but to your emotions. They own your smile when you are on the job (Hochschild, 1983).

WHY HANG OUT AT DELTA'S TRAINING SESSIONS?

Hochschild spent an extended period of time in the training classes because an excellent way to understand social processes is to participate in and observe them. She also conducted interviews that enabled her to gather more information than she would have obtained by simply observing the classes. Hochschild's research opened a window upon an aspect of life that most people think they understand, but which needed to be understood at a deeper level. Her work is based upon systematic research, but it also carries a note of passion.

In the nineteenth century, most work required physical labor. Although there is a difference between physical labor and emotional labor, Hochschild found that the flight attendants had one thing in common with physical laborers. Both kinds of workers feel a sense of distance from the particular aspect of themselves that is given up in work. The physical laborer's arm, for example, might come to feel like a piece of machinery, and only incidentally a part of the person moving it. Likewise, service workers often told Hochschild that their smiles were *on* them but not *of* them. In other words, these workers felt a sense of distance from their own emotions. This is quite interesting when one considers the fact that emotions are usually thought of as a deep and personal part of ourselves.

SOCIOLOGICAL QUESTIONS

It is the business of sociological research in general to go beyond surface-level understandings of ordinary

The Columbine school shootings inspired sociologists to pose questions aimed at discovering the motives and effects of the disaster: What caused two young men to conceive their plan to shoot certain types of students? Why do these students grieve using these specific rituals? Will the high-school community become more interested in reconciling different social circles?

life as Hochschild did. Good research should help us understand our social lives in a new way. It should take us by surprise, in the questions it asks and the findings it comes up with. The issues that concern sociologists, in both their theorizing and their research, are often similar to those that worry other people. But the results of such research frequently run counter to our commonsense beliefs.

What are the circumstances in which minority groups live? How can mass starvation exist in a world that is far wealthier than it has ever been before? What effects will the increasing use of information technology have on our lives? Is the family beginning to disintegrate as an institution? Sociologists try to provide answers to these and many other problems. Their findings are by no means conclusive. Nevertheless, it is always the aim of sociological theorizing and research to break away from the speculative manner in which the ordinary person usually considers such questions. Good sociological work tries to make the questions as precise as possible and seeks to gather factual evidence before coming to conclusions. To achieve these aims, we must know the most useful **research methods** to apply in a given study and how to best analyze the results.

Some of the questions sociologists ask in their research studies are largely **factual,** or empirical. For example, many aspects of crime and justice need direct and systematic sociological investigation. Thus, we might ask: What forms of crime are most common? What proportion of people who engage in criminal behavior are caught by the police? How many of these are in the end found guilty and imprisoned? Factual questions such as these are often difficult to answer; official statistics on crime are of dubious value in indicating the real level of criminal activity. Researchers who have studied crime levels have found that only about one-half of all serious crimes are reported to the police.

Factual information about one society, of course, will not always tell us whether we are dealing with an unusual case or a very general set of influences. Sociologists often want to ask **comparative questions,** relating one social context within a society to another, or contrasting examples drawn from different soci-

eties. There are significant differences, for example, between the social and legal systems of the United States and Canada. A typical comparative question might be: How much do patterns of criminal behavior and law enforcement vary between the two countries? (Some important differences are in fact found between them.)

In sociology, we need not only to look at existing societies in relation to one another, but also to compare their present and past. The questions sociologists ask here are **developmental.** To understand the nature of the modern world, we have to look at previous forms of society and also study the main direction that processes of change have taken. Thus we can investigate, for example, how the first prisons originated and what they are like today—an issue already touched upon earlier.

Factual—or what sociologists usually prefer to call empirical—investigations concern *how* things occur. Yet sociology does not consist of just collecting facts, however important and interesting they may be. We always need to interpret what facts mean, and to do so we must learn to pose **theoretical questions.** Many sociologists work primarily on empirical questions, but unless they are guided in research by some knowledge of theory, their work is unlikely to be illuminating (see Table 2.1).

In this chapter, we shall begin by looking at the stages involved in sociological research. We shall then

Table 2.1 A Sociologist's Line of Questioning

Factual question	What happened?	During the 1980s, there was an increase in the proportion of women in their thirties bearing children for the first time.
Comparative question	Did this happen everywhere?	Was this a global phenomenon, or did it occur just in the United States, or only in a certain region of the United States?
Developmental question	Has this happened over time?	What have been the patterns of childbearing over time?
Theoretical question	What underlies this phenomenon?	Why are more women now waiting until their thirties to bear children? What factors would we look at to explain this change?

In looking at this painting by Brueghel, we can observe the number of people, what each is doing, the style of the buildings, or the colors the painter chose. But without the title, Netherlandish Proverbs, *these facts tell us nothing about the picture's meaning. In the same way, sociologists need theory as a context for their observations.*

compare the most widely used research methods as we consider some actual investigations. There are often large differences between the way research should ideally be carried out and real-life studies!

THE RESEARCH PROCESS

Let us first look at the stages normally involved in research work. The research process takes in a number of distinct steps, leading from when the investigation is begun to the time its findings are published or made available in written form.

Defining the Research Problem

All research starts from a research problem. This is sometimes an area of factual ignorance: we may simply wish to improve our knowledge about certain institutions, social processes, or cultures. A researcher might set out to answer questions like, What proportion of the population holds strong religious beliefs? Are people today really disaffected with "big govern-

ment"? How far does the economic position of women lag behind that of men?

The best sociological research, however, begins with problems that are also puzzles. A puzzle is not just a lack of information, but a *gap in our understanding.* Much of the skill in producing worthwhile sociological research consists in correctly identifying puzzles.

Rather than simply answering the question "What is going on here?" puzzle-solving research tries to contribute to our understanding of *why* events happen as they do. Thus, we might ask: Why are patterns of religious belief changing? What accounts for the decline in the proportions of the population voting in presidential elections in recent years? Why are women poorly represented in high-status jobs?

No piece of research stands alone. Research problems come up as part of ongoing work; one research project may easily lead to another because it raises issues the researcher had not previously considered. A sociologist may discover puzzles by reading the work of other researchers in books and professional journals or by being aware of specific trends in society. For example, over recent years, there has been an increasing number of programs that seek to treat the mentally ill in the community rather than confining them in asylums. Sociologists might be prompted to ask: What has given rise to this shift in attitude toward the mentally ill? What are the likely consequences both for the patients themselves and for the rest of the community?

Reviewing the Evidence

Once the problem is identified, the next step taken in the research process is usually to review the available evidence in the field; it might be that previous research has already satisfactorily clarified the problem. If not, the sociologist will need to sift through whatever related research does exist to see how useful it is for his purpose. Have previous researchers spotted the same puzzle? How have they tried to resolve it? What aspects of the problem has their research left unanalyzed? Drawing upon others' ideas helps the sociologist to clarify the issues that might be raised and the methods that might be used in the research.

Making the Problem Precise

A third stage involves working out a clear formulation of the research problem. If relevant literature already exists, the researcher might return from the library with a good notion of how the problem should be approached. Hunches about the nature of the problem can sometimes be turned into definite **hypotheses**—educated guesses about what is going on—at this stage. If the research is to be effective, a hypothesis must be formulated in such a way that the factual material gathered will provide evidence either supporting or disproving it.

Working Out a Design

The researcher must then decide just *how* the research materials are to be collected. A range of different research methods exists, and which one is chosen depends on the overall objectives of the study as well as the aspects of behavior to be analyzed. For some purposes, a survey (in which questionnaires are normally used) might be suitable. In other circumstances, interviews or an observational study such as that carried out at Delta Airlines by Arlie Hochschild might be appropriate. We shall learn more about various research methods later.

Carrying Out the Research

At the point of actually proceeding with the research, unforeseen practical difficulties can easily crop up. It might prove impossible to contact some of those to whom questionnaires are to be sent or whom the researcher wishes to interview. A business firm or government agency may be unwilling to let the researcher carry out the work planned. Difficulties such as these could potentially bias the result of the study and give her a false interpretation. For example, if the researcher is studying how business corporations have complied with affirmative action programs for women, then companies that have not complied might not want to be studied. The findings could be biased as a result.

Interpreting the Results

Once the material has been gathered to be analyzed, the researcher's troubles are not over—they may be just beginning! Working out the implications of the data collected and relating these back to the research problem are rarely easy. While it may be possible to reach a clear answer to the initial questions, many investigations are in the end less than fully conclusive.

Reporting the Findings

The research report, usually published as a journal article or book, provides an account of the nature of the research and seeks to justify whatever conclusions are drawn. In Hochschild's case, this report was the book *The Managed Heart*. This is a final stage only in terms of the individual research project. Most reports indicate questions that remain unanswered and suggest further research that might profitably be done in the future. All individual research investigations are part of the continuing process of research taking place within the sociological community. Many other scholars have built upon Hochschild's research findings.

Reality Intrudes!

The preceding sequence of steps is a simplified version of what happens in actual research projects (see Figure 2.1). In real sociological research, these stages rarely succeed each other so neatly, and there is almost always a certain amount of sheer "muddling through." The difference is a bit like that between the recipes outlined in a cookbook and the actual process of preparing a meal. People who are experienced cooks often don't work from recipes at all, yet they might cook better than those who do. Following fixed schemes can be unduly restricting; most outstanding sociological research could not in fact be fitted rigidly into this sequence, although most of the steps would be there.

UNDERSTANDING CAUSE AND EFFECT

One of the main problems to be tackled in research methodology is the analysis of cause and effect. A **causal relationship** between two events or situations is an association in which one event or situation produces another. If the parking brake is released in an automobile pointing down a hill, it will roll down the incline, gathering speed progressively as it does so. Taking the brake off *caused* this to happen; the reasons for this can readily be understood by reference to the physical principles involved. Like natural science, sociology depends upon the assumption that all events have causes. Social life is not a random array of occurrences, happening without rhyme or reason. One of the main tasks of sociological research—in combination with theoretical thinking—is to identify causes and effects.

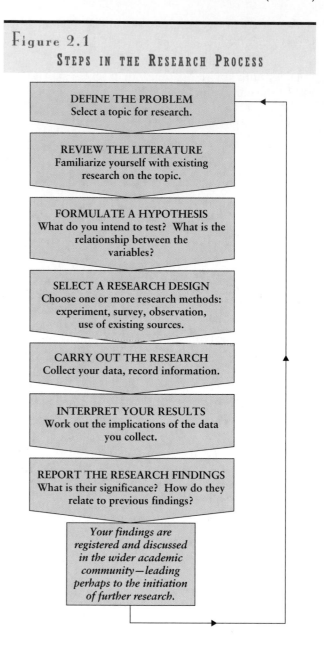

Figure 2.1

STEPS IN THE RESEARCH PROCESS

DEFINE THE PROBLEM
Select a topic for research.

REVIEW THE LITERATURE
Familiarize yourself with existing research on the topic.

FORMULATE A HYPOTHESIS
What do you intend to test? What is the relationship between the variables?

SELECT A RESEARCH DESIGN
Choose one or more research methods: experiment, survey, observation, use of existing sources.

CARRY OUT THE RESEARCH
Collect your data, record information.

INTERPRET YOUR RESULTS
Work out the implications of the data you collect.

REPORT THE RESEARCH FINDINGS
What is their significance? How do they relate to previous findings?

Your findings are registered and discussed in the wider academic community—leading perhaps to the initiation of further research.

Causation and Correlation

Causation cannot be directly inferred from **correlation**. Correlation means the existence of a regular relationship between two sets of occurrences or **variables**. A variable is any dimension along which individuals or groups vary. Age, differences in income, crime rates, and social-class differences are among the many variables sociologists study. It might seem as though when two variables are found to be closely correlated, one must be the cause of another; such is often not the case. There are many correlations without any causal relationship between the variables. For example, over the period since World War II, a strong correlation can be found between a decline in pipe-smoking and a decrease in numbers of people who regularly go to the movies. Clearly one change does not cause the other, and we would find it difficult to discover even a remote causal connection between them.

There are many instances, however, in which it is not so obvious that an observed correlation does not imply a causal relationship. Such correlations are traps for the unwary and easily lead to questionable or false conclusions. In his classical work *Suicide*, Émile Durkheim (1966/1897) found a correlation between rates of suicide and the seasons of the year. In the societies Durkheim studied, levels of suicide increased progressively from January up to around June or July. From that time onward they declined toward the end of the year. It might be supposed that this demonstrates that temperature or climatic change is causally related to the propensity of individuals to kill themselves. Perhaps as temperatures increase, people become more impulsive and hot-headed? However, the causal relation here has nothing directly to do with temperature or climate at all. In spring and summer most people engage in a more intensive social life than they do in winter. Individuals who are isolated or unhappy tend to experience an intensification of these feelings as the activity level of other people rises. Hence they are likely to experience acute suicidal tendencies more in spring and summer than in autumn and winter, when the pace of social activity slackens. We always have to be on our guard both in assessing whether correlation involves causation, and in deciding in which direction causal relations run.

CAUSAL MECHANISM

Working out causal connections involved in correlations is often a difficult process. There is a strong correlation, for instance, between level of educational achievement and occupational success in modern societies. The better the grades an individual gets in school, the better paying the job he is likely to get. What explains this correlation? Research tends to show that it is not mainly school experience itself; levels of school attainment are influenced much more by the type of home from which the person comes. Children from better-off homes, whose parents take a strong interest in their learning skills and where books are abundant, are more likely to do well than those coming from homes where these qualities are lacking. The causal mechanisms here are the attitudes of parents toward their children, together with the facilities for learning that a home provides.

Causal connections in sociology should not be understood in too mechanical a way. The attitudes people have, and their subjective reasons for acting as they do, are causal factors in relationships between variables in social life.

CONTROLS

In assessing the cause or causes that explain a correlation, we need to distinguish **independent variables** from **dependent variables.** An independent variable is one that produces an effect upon another variable. The variable affected is the dependent one. In the example just mentioned, academic achievement is the independent variable and occupational income the dependent variable. The distinction refers to the direction of the causal relation we are investigating. The same factor may be an independent variable in one study, and a dependent variable in another. It all depends on what causal processes are being analyzed. If we were looking at the effects of differences in occupational income upon lifestyles, occupational income would then be the independent variable rather than the dependent one.

To find out whether a correlation between variables is a causal connection we use **controls,** which means we hold some variables constant in order to look at the effects of others. By doing this, we are able to judge between explanations of observed correlations, separating causal from noncausal relationships. For example, researchers studying child development have claimed that there is a causal connection between maternal deprivation in infancy and serious personality problems in adulthood. ("Maternal deprivation" means that an infant is separated from its mother for a long period—several months or more—during the early years of its life.) How might we test whether there really is a causal relationship between maternal deprivation and later personality disorders? We would do so by trying to control, or "screen out," other possible influences that might explain the correlation.

One source of maternal deprivation is the admission of a child to a hospital for a lengthy period, during which it is separated from its parents. Is it attachment to the mother, however, that really matters? Perhaps if a child receives love and attention from *other* people during infancy, she might subsequently be a stable person? To investigate these possible causal connections, we would have to compare cases where children were deprived of regular care from anyone, with other instances in which children were separated from their mothers, but received love and care from someone else. If the first group developed severe personality difficulties, but the second group did not, we would suspect that regular care from *someone* in infancy is what matters, regardless of whether or not it is the mother. (In fact, children do seem to prosper normally as long as they have a loving, stable relationship with someone looking after them—this does not have to be the mother herself.)

IDENTIFYING CAUSES

There are a large number of possible causes that could be invoked to explain any given correlation. How can we ever be sure that we have covered them all? The answer is that we cannot be sure. We would never be able to carry out, and interpret the results of, a piece of sociological research satisfactorily if we were compelled to test for the possible influence of every causal factor we could imagine as potentially relevant. Identifying causal relationships is normally guided by previous research into the area in question. If we do not have some reasonable idea beforehand of the causal mechanisms involved in a correlation we would probably find it very difficult to discover what the real causal connections are. We would not know what to test *for*.

A good example of how difficult it is to be sure of the causal relations involved in a correlation is given by the long history of studies of smoking and lung cancer. Research has consistently demonstrated a strong correlation between the two. Smokers are more likely to contract lung cancer than nonsmokers, and very heavy smokers are more likely to do so than light smokers. The correlation can also be expressed the other way around. A high proportion of those who have lung cancer are smokers, or have smoked for long periods in their past. There have been so many studies confirming these correlations that it is generally accepted that a causal link is involved; but the exact causal mechanisms are thus far largely unknown.

However much correlational work is done on any issue, there always remains some doubt about possible causal relationships. Other interpretations of the correlation are possible. It has been proposed, for instance, that people who are predisposed to get lung cancer are also predisposed to smoke. In this view it is not smoking which causes lung cancer, but rather, some built-in biological disposition to smoking and cancer.

KEY CONCEPTS IN REVIEW

A **causal relationship** between two events or situations is one in which one event or situation brings about the other. **Causation** must be distinguished from **correlation**, which refers to the existence of a regular relationship between two **variables**. A variable can be differences in age, income, crime rates, etc.

We need also to distinguish **independent variables** from **dependent variables**. The former is a variable that produces an effect upon another. Sociologists often use **controls** to ascertain a causal relationship.

RESEARCH METHODS

Let's now look at the various research methods sociologists commonly employ in their work.

Ethnography

Hochschild used **ethnography** (or studies of people at firsthand using **participant observation** or interviewing) as her main research method. Here, the investigator hangs out or works or lives with a group, organization, or community and perhaps takes a direct part in their activities. An ethnographer cannot just be present in the place she studies, but must explain and justify her presence to its members. She must gain the cooperation of the community and sustain it over a period of time, if any worthwhile results are to be achieved. Gaining the confidence of the trainers and flight attendants of Delta wasn't something Hochschild could take for granted. She had to work very hard for that acceptance.

For a long while, it was usual for research based on participant observation to exclude any account of the hazards or problems that had to be overcome, but more recently the published reminiscences and diaries of fieldworkers have been more open about them. Frequently, feelings of loneliness must be coped with—it isn't easy to fit into a social context or community where you don't really belong. The researcher may be constantly frustrated because the members of the group refuse to talk frankly about themselves; direct queries may be welcomed in some contexts, but meet with a chilly silence in others. Some types of fieldwork may even be physically dangerous; for instance, a researcher studying a delinquent gang might be seen as a police informer or might become unwittingly embroiled in conflicts with rival gangs.

In the traditional works of ethnography, accounts were presented without very much information about the observer. This was because it was believed that an ethnographer could present objective pictures of the things they studied. Even Hochschild's research, written during the early 1980s, presents little information about herself or the nature of her connection to the people she studied. More recently, ethnographers

A sociologist studying members of a group must gain their acceptance if the study is to have any value.

have increasingly tended to talk about themselves and the nature of their connection to the people under study. Sometimes, for example, it might be a matter of trying to consider how one's race, class, or gender affected the work, or how the power differences between observer and observed distort the dialogue between them.

ADVANTAGES AND LIMITATIONS OF FIELDWORK

Where it is successful, ethnography provides information on the behavior of people in groups, organizations, and communities, and also how those people understand their own behavior. Once we see how things look from inside a given group, we are likely to develop a better understanding not only of that group, but of social processes that transcend the situation under study. Hochschild's study helps sociologists understand far more than just the lives of flight attendants or even service workers. Her book also contributes to an understanding of the nature of emotion itself.

But fieldwork also has major limitations. Only

fairly small groups or communities can be studied. And much depends on the skill of the researcher in gaining the confidence of the individuals involved; without this skill, the research is unlikely to get off the ground at all. The reverse is also possible. A researcher could begin to identify so closely with the group that she becomes too much of an "insider" and loses the perspective of an outside observer. Or, a researcher may interpret the situation she is studying and reach conclusions that are more about her own effects than she or her readers ever realize. These did not seem to be problems in Hochschild's study of emotional labor.

Surveys

Interpreting field studies usually involves problems of generalization. Since only a small number of people are under study, we cannot be sure that what is found in one context will apply in other situations as well, or even that two different researchers would come to the same conclusions when studying the same group. This is usually less of a problem in survey research. In a survey, questionnaires are either sent or given directly in interviews to a selected group of people—sometimes as many as several thousand. This group of people is referred to by sociologists as a **population.** Fieldwork is best suited for in-depth studies of small slices of social life; survey research tends to produce information that is less detailed, but that can usually be applied over a broad area.

STANDARDIZED AND OPEN-ENDED QUESTIONNAIRES

Two sorts of questionnaires are used in surveys. Some contain a standardized, or fixed-choice, set of questions, to which only a fixed range of responses is possible—for instance, "*Yes/No/Don't know*" or "*Very likely/Likely/Unlikely/Very unlikely.*" Such surveys have the advantage that responses are easy to compare and count up, since only a small number of categories are involved. On the other hand, because they do not allow for subtleties of opinion or verbal expression, the information they yield is likely to be restricted in scope, if not misleading.

Other questionnaires are open-ended: respondents

have more opportunity to express their views in their own words; they are not limited to making fixed-choice responses. Open-ended questionnaires typically provide more detailed information than standardized ones. The researcher can follow up answers to probe more deeply into what the respondent thinks. On the other hand, the lack of standardization means that responses may be more difficult to compare statistically.

Questionnaire items are normally listed so that a team of interviewers can ask the questions and record responses in the same predetermined order. All the items must be readily understandable to interviewer and interviewees alike. In the large national surveys undertaken regularly by government agencies and research organizations, interviews are carried out more or less simultaneously across the whole country. Those who conduct the interviews and those who analyze the results could not do their work effectively if they constantly had to be checking with each other about ambiguities in the questions or answers.

Questionnaires should also take into consideration the characteristics of respondents. Will they see the point the researcher has in mind in asking a particular question? Have they enough information to answer usefully? Will they answer at all? The terms of a questionnaire might be unfamiliar to the respondents. For instance, the question "What is your marital status?" might baffle some people. It would be more appropriate to ask, "Are you single, married, separated, or divorced?" Most surveys are preceded by **pilot studies** in order to pick up problems not anticipated by the investigator. A pilot study is a trial run in which a questionnaire is completed by just a few people. Any difficulties can then be ironed out before the main survey is done.

SAMPLING

Often sociologists are interested in the characteristics of large numbers of individuals—for example, the political attitudes of the American population as a whole. It would be impossible to study all these people directly, so in such situations research studies concentrate on a **sample,** or small proportion of the overall group. One can usually be confident that results from a population sample, as long as it was properly chosen, can be generalized to the total population. Studies of only two to three thousand voters, for instance, can give a very accurate indication of the attitudes and voting intentions of the entire population. But to achieve such accuracy, a sample must be **representative:** the group of individuals studied must be typical of the population as a whole. Sampling is more complex than it might seem, and statisticians have developed rules for working out the correct size and nature of samples.

A particularly important procedure used to ensure that a sample is representative is **random sampling,** in which a sample is chosen so that every member of the population has the same probability of being included. The most sophisticated way of obtaining a random sample is to give each member of the population a number and then use a computer to generate a random list, from which the sample is derived—for instance, by picking every tenth number.

"The People's Choice?"

One of the most famous early examples of survey research was "The People's Choice?," a study carried out by Paul Lazarsfeld and a number of colleagues about half a century ago (Lazarsfeld, Berelson, and Gaudet, 1948). This study, which investigated the voting intentions of residents of Erie County, Ohio, during the 1940 campaign for the U.S. presidency, pioneered several of the main techniques of survey research in use to this day. In order to probe a little more deeply than a single questionnaire would do, the investigators interviewed each member of a sample of voters on seven separate occasions. The aim was to trace, and understand the reasons for, changes in voting attitudes.

The research was set up with a number of definite hypotheses in view. One was that relationships and events close to voters in a community influence voting intentions more than distant world affairs, and the findings on the whole confirmed this. The researchers developed sophisticated measurement techniques for analyzing political attitudes; yet their work also made significant contributions to theoretical thinking. Among the concepts they helped to introduce were those of "opinion leaders" and the "two-step flow of communication." The study showed that some individuals—opinion leaders—tend to shape the political opinions of those around them. People's views are not formed in a direct fashion, but in a two-step process.

In the first step, opinion leaders react to political events; in the second step, those leaders influence people around them—relatives, friends, and colleagues. The views expressed by opinion leaders, thus filtered through personal relationships, influence the responses of other individuals toward political issues of the day.

Advantages and Disadvantages of Surveys

Surveys are widely used in sociological research, for several reasons. Questionnaire responses can be more easily quantified and analyzed than material generated by most other research methods; large numbers of people can be studied; and given sufficient funds, researchers can employ an agency specializing in survey work to collect the responses. The scientific method is the model for this kind of research, as surveys give researchers a statistical measure of what they are studying.

Many sociologists are critical, however, of the survey method. They argue that an appearance of preci-

One hazard of surveys.

A "prisoner" being arrested (left), frisked (middle), and in his cell (right).

sion can be given to findings whose accuracy may be dubious, given the relatively shallow nature of most survey responses. Levels of nonresponse are sometimes high, especially when questionnaires are sent and returned through the mail. It is not uncommon for studies to be published based on results derived from little over half of those in a sample, although normally an effort is made to recontact nonrespondents or to substitute other people. Little is known about those who choose not to respond to surveys or refuse to be interviewed, but survey research is often experienced as intrusive and time-consuming.

Experiments

An **experiment** can be defined as an attempt to test a hypothesis under highly controlled conditions established by an investigator. Experiments are often used in the natural sciences, as they offer major advantages over other research procedures. In an experimental situation, the researcher directly controls the circumstances being studied. As compared with the natural sciences, the scope for experimentation in sociology is quite restricted. We can bring only small groups of individuals into a laboratory setting, and in such experiments, people know that they are being studied and may behave unnaturally.

Nevertheless, experimental methods can occasionally be applied in a helpful way in sociology. An example is the ingenious experiment carried out by Philip Zimbardo, who set up a make-believe jail, assigning some student volunteers to the role of guards and other volunteers to the role of prisoners (Zim-

bardo, 1972). His aim was to see how far playing these different parts led to changes in attitude and behavior. The results shocked the investigators. Students who played at being guards quickly assumed an authoritarian manner; they displayed real hostility toward the prisoners, ordering them around and verbally abusing and bullying them. The prisoners, by contrast, showed a mixture of apathy and rebelliousness often noted among inmates in real prisons. These effects were so marked and the level of tension so high that the experiment had to be called off at an early stage. The results, however, were important. Zimbardo concluded that behavior in prisons is more influenced by the nature of the prison situation itself than by the individual characteristics of those involved.

Life Histories

In contrast to experiments, **life histories** belong purely to sociology and the other social sciences; they have no place in natural science. Life histories consist of biographical material assembled about particular individuals—usually as recalled by the individuals themselves. Other procedures of research don't usually yield as much information as the life-history method about the development of beliefs and attitudes over time. Life-historical studies rarely rely wholly on people's memories, however. Normally sources such as letters, contemporary reports, and newspaper descriptions are used to expand on and check the validity of the information individuals provide. Sociologists' views differ on the value of life histories: some feel they are too unreliable to provide useful information, but others believe they offer sources of insight that few other research methods can match.

Life histories have been successfully employed in studies of major importance. A celebrated early study was *The Polish Peasant in Europe and America*, by W. I. Thomas and Florian Znaniecki, the five volumes of which were first published between 1918 and 1920 (Thomas and Znaniecki, 1966). Thomas and Znaniecki were able to provide a more sensitive and subtle account of the experience of migration than would have been possible without the interviews, letters, and newspaper articles they collected.

Comparative Research

Each of the research methods described above is often applied in a comparative context. **Comparative research** is of central importance in sociology, because making comparisons allows us to clarify what is going on in a particular area of research. Let's take the American rate of divorce—the number of divorces granted each year—as an example. Divorce rates rose rapidly in the United States after World War II, reaching a peak in the early 1980s. Current trends suggest that as many as 60 percent of couples marrying today will divorce before their tenth wedding anniversary—a statistic that expresses profound changes taking place in the area of sexual relations and family life. Do these changes reflect specific features of American society? We can find out by comparing divorce rates in the United States with those of other countries. Such a comparison reveals that although the U.S. rate is higher than in most other Western societies, the overall trends are similar. Virtually all Western countries have experienced steadily climbing divorce rates over the past half century.

Historical Analysis

As was mentioned in Chapter 1, a historical perspective is often essential in sociological research. For we frequently need a *time perspective* to make sense of the material we collect about a particular problem.

Sociologists commonly want to investigate past events directly. Some periods of history can be studied

in a direct way, when there are still survivors around—such as in the case of the Holocaust in Europe during World War II. Research in **oral history** means interviewing people about events they witnessed at some point earlier in their lives. This kind of research work, obviously, can only stretch at the most some sixty or seventy years back in time. For historical research on an earlier period, sociologists are dependent upon the use of documents and written records, often contained in the special collections of libraries or the National Archives.

An interesting example of the use of historical documents is sociologist Anthony Ashworth's study of trench warfare during World War I (Ashworth, 1980). Ashworth was concerned with analyzing what life was like for men who had to endure being under constant fire, crammed in close proximity for weeks on end. He drew on a diversity of documentary sources: official histories of the war, including those written about different military divisions and battalions, official publications of the time, the notes and records kept informally by individual soldiers, and personal accounts of war experiences. By drawing on such a variety of sources, Ashworth was able to develop a rich and detailed description of life in the trenches. He discovered that most soldiers formed their own ideas about how often they intended to engage in combat with the enemy, and often effectively ignored the commands of their officers. For example, on Christmas Day, German and Allied soldiers suspended hostilities, and in one place the two sides even staged an informal soccer match. (See Table 2.2.)

Combining Comparative and Historical Research

Ashworth's research concentrated on a relatively short time period. As an example of a study that investigated a much longer one, and that also applied comparative research in a historical context, we can take Theda Skocpol's *States and Social Revolutions* (1979), one of the best-known studies of social change. Skocpol set herself an ambitious task: to produce a theory of the origins and nature of revolution grounded in detailed empirical study. She looked at

Table 2.2 Four of the Main Methods
Used in Sociological Research

RESEARCH METHOD	STRENGTHS	LIMITATIONS
Fieldwork	Usually generates richer and more in-depth information than other methods.	Can only be used to study relatively small groups or communities.
	Ethnography can provide a broader understanding of social processes.	Findings might only apply to the groups or communities studied; it is not easy to generalize on the basis of a single fieldwork study.
Surveys	Make possible the efficient collection of data on large numbers of individuals.	The material gathered may be superficial; where a questionnaire is highly standardized, important differences between respondents' viewpoints may be glossed over.
	Allow for precise comparisons to be made between the answers of respondents.	Responses may be what people profess to believe rather than what they actually believe.
Experiments	The influence of specific variables can be controlled by the investigator.	Many aspects of social life cannot be brought into the laboratory.
	Are usually easier for subsequent researchers to repeat.	The responses of those studied may be affected by their experimental situation.
Documentary research	Can provide sources of in-depth materials as well as data on large numbers, according to the type of documents studied.	The researcher is dependent on the sources that exist, which may be partial.
	Is often essential when a study is either wholly historical or has a defined historical dimension.	The sources may be difficult to interpret in terms of how far they represent real tendencies—as in the case of some official statistics.

processes of revolution in three different historical contexts: the 1789 revolution in France, the 1917 revolution in Russia (which brought the Communists to power and established the Soviet Union, in 1989 again dissolved), and the revolution of 1949 in China (creating Communist China).

By analyzing a variety of documentary sources, Skocpol was able to develop a powerful explanation of revolutionary change, one that emphasized the underlying social structural conditions. She showed that social revolutions are largely the result of unintended consequences. Before the Russian Revolution, for instance, various political groups were trying to overthrow the preexisting regime, but none of these—including the Bolsheviks, who eventually came

to power—anticipated the revolution that occurred. A series of clashes and confrontations gave rise to a process of social transformation much more radical than anyone had foreseen.

RESEARCH IN THE REAL WORLD: METHODS, PROBLEMS, PITFALLS

All research methods, as was stressed earlier, have their advantages and limitations. Hence, it is common to combine several methods in a single piece of research, using each to supplement and check on the others in a process known as **triangulation.** We can see the value of combining methods—and, more generally, the problems and pitfalls of real sociological research—by looking at an influential study in the sociology of religion: Roy Wallis' investigation of the movement known as Scientology.

Roy Wallis and Scientology

The founder of Scientology, L. Ron Hubbard, developed religious doctrines that came to form the basis of a church. According to Scientology, we are all spiritual beings—Thetans—but we have neglected our spiritual nature. We can recover forgotten supernatural powers through training that makes us aware of our real spiritual capacities. Wallis was first drawn to the research because of the "exotic" nature of Scientology. The movement was very controversial but had attracted a large following. Why had this movement in particular become so prominent?

Initiating the research presented problems. Wallis knew that the leaders of the movement were likely to be unwilling to cooperate in sociological research because they had already been investigated by various government agencies. Then, while reading about the movement's history, he came across a book by one of its former members. He contacted the author, and was eventually put in touch with a number of his acquaintances who had also mostly severed their ties with Scientology. Many of these people agreed to be interviewed, and some still maintained contact with believers. These early interviewees provided Wallis with a range of documents and literature, including the mailing list of a Scientology organization. Wallis drew up and sent off a questionnaire to a sample of the names on the list. But the list proved so out of date that many among the sample had moved from the addresses given; others had been placed on the list merely because they had bought a single book on Scientology and had no real connections with the movement.

The survey thus proved of limited value as a sample of Scientologists in general. Yet it provided Wallis with further contacts. Some respondents to the questionnaire indicated that they would be willing to be interviewed. Wallis therefore traveled around the United States and Britain conducting interviews and collecting more documentary information at the same time. He began with a fixed set of questions, but found it more profitable to adopt a more flexible style, allowing respondents to talk at length on matters they regarded as important. Some people were willing to be tape-recorded; others were not.

Wallis soon came to believe that he needed to understand more about the particular doctrines of Scientology, so he signed up for an introductory "communications" course taught by a Scientology group. He thus began participant observation, but he did not reveal his identity as a researcher. Staying at the Scientology house during the course, Wallis found the role of covert participant observer difficult to sustain. Conversation with other members required a display of commitment to ideas he did not share. Expressing disagreement with these views led to such difficulties that it became clear he couldn't continue without publicly assenting to some of the main principles of Scientology, which he wasn't willing to do. He therefore slipped away quietly without finishing the course.

Later Wallis wrote to the leaders of the movement, explaining that he was a sociologist engaged in research into Scientology. Pointing out that the movement had been under much attack, he suggested that his own research would provide a more balanced view. He subsequently visited the headquarters of the sect in Britain and spoke to one of the officials there. This person was concerned about his having dropped out of the communications course; he also knew about the questionnaires sent to those on the list of Scientologists. Nonetheless, he gave Wallis permission to interview some staff members and students and supplied addresses of people to be contacted in the United States. Eventually Wallis managed to gather enough material to complete his work (Wallis, 1977). He concluded that Scientology drew its appeal less from the ideas it advocated than from its energetic attempts to attract new members—and from the pressures toward conformity placed upon them once they had become involved.

Ethical Problems: Strategy and Publication

All research concerned with human beings can pose ethical dilemmas. Wallis was less than truthful to those whose behavior he studied because he didn't reveal his identity as a sociologist when registering for the Scientology course. He tried to avoid any direct lies, but he did not give the real reason for his participation. Was this behavior ethical? The answer is that on balance, it probably was. Had Wallis been completely frank at every stage, the research might not have gotten as far as it did, and it could be argued that it is in society's interest to know what goes on inside secretive organizations. On these grounds, we might consider his strategy justified.

Ethical issues are also often posed in sociology by the potential consequences of the publication of research findings. Before publishing his book, Wallis sent his manuscript to the Scientology headquarters. Although he made alterations to meet some of their objections, the Scientologists sent the manuscript to a lawyer experienced in libel cases. On his advice, further deletions were made. A commentary on the book, highly critical of Wallis' research methods and conclusions, was prepared by a sociologist who was also a practicing Scientologist, and it was eventually incorporated into the published work as an appendix. The Scientologists also published an article analyzing Wallis' research in one of their own periodicals. In their discussion, they quoted the Panel on Privacy and Behavioral Research set up by the Office of Science and Technology in Washington, which had stressed that "informed consent should be obtained by researchers engaged in work on human subjects." Informed consent, the Scientologists emphasized, had not been secured, and they added that Wallis' published work was based on information gained from only a small circle of people, mostly hostile to the Church of Scientology.

Wallis was dealing with a powerful and articulate group, who were able to persuade him to modify early versions of his research reports. Other individuals or groups studied by sociologists do not have similar influence. In studying people who are vulnerable or relatively powerless, such as mental patients or prisoners, the researcher has a particular obligation to weigh the ethical implications of her research. For the ability of such people to answer back in a direct way is likely to be limited.

The subjects of a study may find its published results offensive, either because they are portrayed in a light they find unappealing—the reaction of the Scientologists—or because attitudes and behavior they would prefer to keep private are made public. In most settings of social life, people engage in practices they wouldn't want to become public knowledge. Some people working in factories and offices regularly pilfer materials; hospital nurses sometimes wrap terminally ill patients in morgue sheets before they die and give them little care; prison guards may accept bribes from inmates and recognize certain prisoners as "trusties," allowing them to perform tasks they should take care of themselves.

THE INFLUENCE OF SOCIOLOGY

Sociological research is rarely of interest only to the intellectual community of sociologists. Its results are often disseminated throughout society. This was the case with Wallis' work, which so concerned the Scientologists. It was also true of *The Managed Heart*, which has been read by a generation of sociology students, as well as a general audience including many service workers who themselves do emotional labor.

Sociology, it must be emphasized, is not just the *study* of modern societies; it is a significant element *in the continuing life* of those societies. Take the example mentioned in Chapter 1: the transformations taking place in the United States in marriage, sexuality, and the family. Few people living in a modern society do not have some knowledge of these changes, as a result of the filtering down of sociological research. Our thinking and behavior are affected by sociological knowledge in complex and often subtle ways, thus reshaping the very field of sociological investigation. A way of describing this phenomenon, using the technical concepts of sociology, is to say that sociology stands in a **reflexive** relation to the human beings whose behavior is studied. "Reflexive" describes the interchange between sociological research and human behavior. We should not be surprised that sociological findings often correlate closely with common sense. The reason is not simply that sociology comes up with findings we knew already; it is rather that sociological research continually influences what our commonsense knowledge of society actually *is*.

Statistical Terms

Research in sociology often makes use of statistical techniques in the analysis of findings. Some are highly sophisticated and complex, but those used most often are easy to understand. The most common are **measures of central tendency** (ways of calculating averages) and **correlation coefficients** (measures of the degree to which one variable relates consistently to another).

There are three methods of calculating averages, each of which has certain advantages and shortcomings. Take as an example the amount of personal wealth (including all assets such as houses, cars, bank accounts, and investments) owned by thirteen individuals. Suppose the thirteen own the following amounts:

1 $	000 (zero)	8 $	80,000
2 $	5,000	9 $	100,000
3 $	10,000	10 $	150,000
4 $	20,000	11 $	200,000
5 $	40,000	12 $	400,000
6 $	40,000	13 $	10,000,000
7 $	40,000		

The **mean** corresponds to the average, arrived at by adding together the personal wealth of all thirteen people and dividing the result by 13. The total is $11,085,000; dividing this by 13, we reach a mean of $852,692.31. This mean is often a useful calculation because it is based on the whole range of data provided. However, it can be misleading where one or a small number of cases are very different from the majority. In the above example, the mean is not in fact an appropriate measure of central tendency, because the presence of one very large figure, $10,000,000, skews all the rest. One might get the impression that most of the people own far more than they actually do.

In such instances, one of two other measures may be used. The **mode** is the figure that occurs most frequently in a given set of data. In our exam-ple, it is $40,000. The problem with the mode is that it doesn't take into account the *overall distribution* of the data, i.e., the range of figures covered. The most frequently occurring case in a set of figures is not necessarily representative of their distribution as a whole, and thus may not be a useful average. In this case, $40,000 is too close to the lower end of the figures.

The third measure is the **median**, which is the middle of any set of figures; here, this would be the 7th figure, again $40,000. Our example gives an odd number of figures, 13. If there had been an even number—for instance, 12—the median would be calculated by taking the mean of the two middle cases, figures 6 and 7. Like the mode, the median gives no idea of the actual *range* of the data measured.

Sometimes a researcher will use more than one measure of central tendency to avoid giving a deceptive picture of the average. More often, he will calculate the **standard deviation** for the data in question. This is a way of calculating the **degree of dispersal**, or the range, of a set of figures—which in this case goes from zero to $10,000,000.

Correlation coefficients offer a useful way of expressing how closely connected two (or more) variables are. Where two variables correlate completely, we can speak of a perfect positive correlation, expressed as 1.0. Where no relation is found between two variables—they have no consistent connection at all—the coefficient is zero. A perfect negative correlation, expressed as −1.0, exists when two variables are in a completely inverse relation to one another. Perfect correlations are never found in the social sciences. Correlations of the order of 0.6 or more, whether positive or negative, are usually regarded as indicating a strong degree of connection between whatever variables are being analyzed. Positive correlations on this level might be found between, say, social class background and voting behavior.

Reading a Table

You will often come across tables in reading sociological literature. They sometimes look complex, but are easy to decipher if you follow a few basic steps, listed below; with practice, these will become automatic. (See Table 2.3 as an example.) Do not succumb to the temptation to skip over tables; they contain information in concentrated form, which can be read more quickly than would be possible if the same material were expressed in words. By becoming skilled in the interpretation of tables, you will also be able to check how far the conclusions a writer draws actually seem justified.

1. Read the title in full. Tables frequently have longish titles, which represent an attempt by the researcher to state accurately the nature of the information conveyed. The title of Table 2.3 gives first the *subject* of the data, second the fact that the table provides material for comparison, and third the fact that data are given only for a limited number of countries.
2. Look for explanatory comments, or *notes*, about the data. A note at the foot of Table 2.3 linked to the main column heading indicates that the data cover only licensed cars. This is

Table 2.3 Automobile Ownership: Comparisons of Several Selected Countries

	NUMBER OF CARS PER 1,000 OF THE ADULT POPULATION[a]				
	1971	1981	1984	1989	1993
Brazil	12	78	84	98	NA
Chile	19	45	56	67	NA
Eire	141	202	226	228	NA
France	261	348	360	475	420
Greece	30	94	116	150	NA
Italy	210	322	359	424	500
Japan	100	209	207	286	300
Sweden	291	348	445	445	410
U.K.	224	317	343	366	360
USA	448	536	540	607	570
West Germany	247	385	312	479	470[b]

[a]Includes all licensed cars.
[b]Germany as a whole in 1993.

SOURCE: International Road Federation, *United Nations Annual Bulletin of Transport Statistics*, reported in *Social Trends* (London: HMSO, 1987), p. 68; Statistical Office of the European Community, *Basic Statistics of the Community* (Luxembourg: European Union, 1991). Data for 1993 from *The Economist, Pocket World in Figures*, 1996.

Several interesting trends can be seen in the figures in our table. First, the level of car ownership varies considerably between different countries: the number of cars per 1,000 people is nearly ten times greater in the USA than in Chile. Second, there is a clear connection between car ownership and the level of affluence of a country. In fact, we could probably use car ownership ratios as a rough indicator of differential prosperity. Third, in nearly all countries represented, the level of car ownership has increased between 1971 and 1993, but in some the rate of increase is higher than in others—probably indicating differences in the degree to which countries have successfully generated economic growth or are catching up.

important, because in some countries the proportion of vehicles properly licensed may be less than in others. Notes may say how the material was collected, or why it is displayed in a particular way. If the data have not been gathered by the researcher but are based on findings originally reported elsewhere, a **source** will be included. The source sometimes gives you some insight into how reliable the information is likely to be, as well as showing where to find the original data. In our table, the source note makes clear that the data have been taken from more than one source.

3. Read the *headings* along the top and left-hand side of the table. (Sometimes tables are arranged with "headings" at the foot rather than the top.) These tell you what type of information is contained in each row and column. In reading the table, keep in mind each set of headings as you scan the figures. In our example, the headings on the left give the countries involved, while those at the top refer to the levels of car ownership and the years for which they are given.

4. Identify the units used; the figures in the body of the table may represent cases, percentages, averages, or other measures. Sometimes it may be helpful to convert the figures to a form more useful to you: if percentages are not provided, for example, it may be worth calculating them.

5. Consider the conclusions that might be reached from the information in the table. Most tables are discussed by the author, and what he or she has to say should of course be borne in mind. But you should also ask what further issues or questions could be suggested by the data.

SUMMARY

1. Sociologists investigate social life by posing distinct questions and trying to find the answers to these by systematic research. These questions may be *factual, comparative, developmental*, or *theoretical*.

2. All research begins from a *research problem*, which interests or puzzles the investigator. Research problems may be suggested by gaps in the existing literature, theoretical debates, or practical issues in the social world. There are a number of clear steps in the development of research strategies—although these are rarely followed exactly in actual research.

3. A *causal relationship* between two events or situations is one in which one event or situation brings about the other. This is more problematic than it seems at first. *Causation* must be distinguished from *correlation*, which refers to the existence of a regular relationship between two *variables*. A variable can be differences in age, income, crime rates, etc. We need to also distinguish *independent variables* from *dependent variables*. The former is a variable that produces an effect upon another. Sociologists often use *controls* to ascertain a causal relationship.

4. In fieldwork, or *participant observation*, the researcher spends lengthy periods of time with a group or community being studied. A second method, *survey research*, involves sending or administering questionnaires to samples of a larger *population*. Documentary research uses printed materials, from archives or other resources, as a source for information. Other research methods include *experiments*, the use of *life histories*, historical analysis, and *comparative research*.

5. Each of these various methods of research has its limitations. For this reason, researchers will often combine two or more methods in their work, each being used to check or supplement the material obtained from the others. This process is called *triangulation*.

6. Sociological research often poses ethical dilemmas. These may arise either where deception is practiced against those who are the subjects of the research, or where the publication of research findings might adversely affect the feelings or lives of those studied. There is no entirely satisfactory way to deal with these issues, but all researchers have to be sensitive to the dilemmas they pose.

the individual and society

In this part of the book, we start our exploration of the diverse field of sociology by looking at the connections between individual development and culture and by analyzing the major types of society in which human beings live today, or have lived in the past. Our personalities and outlooks are strongly influenced by the culture and society in which each of us happens to exist. At the same time, in our day-to-day behavior we actively recreate and reshape the cultural and social contexts in which our activities occur.

In the first chapter of this part (Chapter 3), we examine the unity and the diversity of human culture. We consider how far human beings resemble animals and how far they differ from them; and we analyze the range of variations found between different human cultures. The extent of human cultural variability has only come to be studied as a result of changes that have in fact altered or destroyed many cultures in which people lived prior to modern times. These changes are outlined, and the main types of society that dominate the world today are contrasted to those that preceded them in history. We con-

clude by returning to one of the most important themes guiding sociology today, the increasing interdependence of different societies around the world.

Next, Chapter 4 discusses socialization, concentrating upon the process by which the human infant develops into a social being. To some degree, socialization continues through the life span, so studying socialization thus also means analyzing the "cycle of the generations"—the relationships between young, middle-aged, and older people.

In Chapter 5, we discuss how people interact with each other in everyday life. We look at the delicate, yet profoundly important, mechanisms whereby individuals interpret what others say and do in their face-to-face encounters. The study of social interaction can in fact tell us a great deal about the larger social environments in which we live. Chapter 6 moves on to look at wider social processes, beginning with the study of deviance and crime. We can learn much about the way the majority of a population behaves by studying people whose behavior deviates from generally accepted patterns.

Learn how both biological and social/cultural factors affect the development of human beings. Learn how societies have changed throughout history, most recently through the impact of globalization.

The Concept of Culture

Know what culture consists of, and recognize how it differs from society. Begin to understand how both biological and cultural factors influence our behavior. Learn the ideas of sociobiology and how others have tried to refute them by emphasizing cultural differences.

Disappearing World: Premodern Societies and Their Fate

Learn how societies have changed over time.

Societies in the Modern World

Recognize the factors that changed premodern societies, particularly how industrialization and colonialism influenced global development. Know the differences between the First, Second, and Third Worlds and how they developed.

The Impact of Globalization

Recognize the impact of globalization on your life and the lives of people around the world.

CULTURE AND SOCIETY

Until two centuries ago, no one held the "overall" view of the world that we now take for granted. The Europeans who traveled to the Americas in the 1500s went looking for giants, amazons, pygmies, and the Fountain of Eternal Youth—women whose bodies never aged and men who lived for several hundred years. The voyagers carried with them familiar images of traditional European myths. Native Americans, for example, were initially regarded as wild creatures, having more affinity with animals than with human beings. Paracelsus, the sixteenth-century medical writer, pictured North America as a continent peopled with creatures that were half human, half beast.

At the same time, the Europeans who established contact with the Chinese Empire during the seventeenth and eighteenth centuries were themselves treated with disdain by its rulers. In 1793, King George III of England sent a trade mission to China to foster commercial exchange. The "barbarian" visitors were allowed to set up some trading outposts in

China and to benefit from the luxuries that country could provide. The Chinese themselves, the visitors were told, were uninterested in anything the Europeans had to offer: "Our Celestial Empire possesses all things in prolific abundance and lacks no products within its borders. There is therefore no need to import the manufactures of outside barbarians in exchange for our own produce." A request for permission to send Western missionaries to China met with this answer: "The distinction between Chinese and barbarians is most strict, and your Ambassador's request that barbarians shall be given full liberty to disseminate their religion is utterly unreasonable" (Worsley, 1968). The gulf between East and West was so great that each held the most bizarre beliefs about the other. For example, even as late as the end of the nineteenth century, it was widely believed in China that foreigners, particularly the English, would die of constipation if deprived of rhubarb.

One of the most dramatic first contacts between Westerners and other cultures occurred as late as 1818. An English naval expedition looking for a passage to Russia between Baffin Island and Greenland, within the Arctic Circle, by chance encountered some polar Inuit. Until that day, the Inuit had thought they were the only people in the world!

Women in the Louvre: an illustration of both the everyday and sociological meanings of "culture." We might think only of the paintings on the walls as culture, while a sociologist would focus on everything else in this picture as well.

THE CONCEPT OF CULTURE

In this chapter, we shall look at the unity and diversity of human life and culture, and at how individuals become a part of different cultures. The concept of culture is one of the most widely used in sociology. **Culture** consists of the values the members of a given group hold, the norms they follow, and the material goods they create. **Values** are abstract ideals. Thus, monogamy—being faithful to a single marriage partner—is a prominent value in most Western societies. In other cultures, on the other hand, a person may be permitted to have several wives or husbands simultaneously. **Norms** are definite principles or rules people are expected to observe; they represent the dos and don'ts of social life. Norms of behavior in marriage include, for example, how husbands and wives are supposed to behave toward their in-laws. In some societies, they are expected to develop a close relationship with parents-in-law; in others, they keep a clear distance from one another. Finally, **material goods** refer to the physical objects that a society creates, which influence the ways in which people live. A central aspect of a society's material culture is technology.

When we use the term in ordinary daily conversation, we often think of culture as equivalent to the higher things of the mind—art, literature, music, dance. As sociologists employ it, the concept includes these activities, but also far more. Culture refers to the ways of life of the individual members or groups within a society: how they dress, their marriage customs and family life, their patterns of work, religious ceremonies, and leisure pursuits. The concept also covers the goods they create and goods that become meaningful for them—bows and arrows, plows, factories and machines, computers, books, dwellings. We should think of culture as a "design for living" or "tool kit" of practices, knowledge, and symbols acquired—as we shall see later—through learning rather than by instinct (Kluckhohn, 1949; Swidler, 1986).

How might we describe American culture? It involves, first, a particular range of values shared by many, if not all, Americans—such as the belief in the merits of individual achievement, or in equality of opportunity. Second, these values are connected to specific norms: for example, it is usually expected that people will work hard in order to achieve occupational success (Parsons, 1964; Bellah et al., 1985). Third, it involves the use of material artifacts created mostly through modern industrial technology, such as cars, mass-produced food, clothing, and so forth.

"Culture" can be distinguished from "society," but there is a close connection between these notions. A **society** is a *system of interrelationships* that connects individuals together. No culture could exist without a society; and equally, no society could exist without culture. Without culture, we would not be human at all, in the sense in which we usually understand that term. We would have no language in which to express ourselves, no sense of self-consciousness, and our ability to think or reason would be severely limited.

The chief theme of this chapter is the biological versus cultural inheritance of humankind. What distinguishes human beings from the animals? Where do our distinctively human characteristics come from? What is the nature of human nature? These questions are crucial to sociology because they set the foundation for the whole field of study. To answer them, we shall analyze what human beings share in common and how cultures differ.

Cultural variations among human beings are linked to differing types of society, and we will compare and contrast the main forms of society found in history. The point of doing this is to tie together closely the two aspects of human social existence—the different cultural values and products that human beings have developed, and the contrasting types of society in which such cultural development has occurred. Too often, culture is discussed separately from society as though the two were quite disconnected; whereas in fact, as has already been emphasized, they are closely meshed. Throughout the chapter, attention will be concentrated upon how social change has affected human cultural development—particularly since the time when Europeans began to spread their ways of life across the world.

The Human Species: Nature and Nurture

As human beings, we all have physical characteristics that are part of our genetic makeup. We are all also members of a society and adopt some of its cultural characteristics. In other words, nature and nurture intermingle in our actions. But what is the relationship between them? Is our behavior directly influenced by our biological constitution (nature)? The fundamental importance of culture (nurture) in human life is not denied by anyone. But disagreements exist about whether or not some forms of human activity are genetic rather than cultural in derivation. To begin our exploration of these controversies, we turn to Charles Darwin, the founder of evolutionary theory in biology.

THE EVOLUTIONARY BACKGROUND

In 1859, after two journeys around the world on the ship HMS *Beagle*, Charles Darwin, an ordained minister of the Church of England, published *On the Origin of Species*. During his travels, Darwin had carefully observed different animal species on the Galapagos Islands off the western coast of South America. From these observations and drawing on his extensive knowledge of paleontology (the study of fossils), anatomy, embryology, and breeding, Darwin concluded that animal species can and do change over time. In other words, animals evolve.

What accounts for a species' evolution? Darwin proposed that evolution is a result of **natural selection**. The idea of natural selection is simple. All

Charles Darwin (1809–1882).

beings need food and other resources, such as protection from climatic extremes, in order to survive. But not enough resources exist to support all members of a species because each generation produces more offspring than the environment can provide for. Those best adapted to their environment survive, while those less able to cope with its demands perish. In the struggle for survival, members of the former group live longer, are able to reproduce, and pass their characteristics on to subsequent generations. They are "selected" to survive and reproduce.

The implications of Darwin's theory were tremendous. He showed that there exists an evolutionary relationship between all species, including the human. Our characteristics as humans have emerged from a process of biological change that can be traced back to the origins of life on earth, more than 3 billion years ago. Many religions, including Christianity, teach that animals and human beings resulted from divine creation. Evolutionary theory, by contrast, regards the development of animal and human species as entirely random.

Although the theory of evolution has been refined since Darwin's day, the essentials are still widely accepted. As a result, evolutionary theory allows us to understand the emergence of different species and their relation to one another.

The evolution of life, it is now generally agreed, began in the oceans. About 400 million years ago, the first land-based creatures emerged. Some of these gradually evolved into large reptiles, who were later displaced by mammals, warm-blooded creatures who reproduce through sexual intercourse. Although the mammals were much smaller in bodily size than the giant reptiles, they were more intelligent and maneuverable. Mammals have a greater capacity to learn from experience than other animals, and this capacity has reached its highest development in the human species. Human beings make up part of a group of higher mammals, the primates, which originated some 70 million years ago.

Our closest relatives among animal species are the chimpanzee, gorilla, and orangutan. On learning about Darwin's theory of evolution, the wife of the Bishop of Worchester, England, is said to have remarked: "Descended from monkeys? My dear, let us hope that it is not true. But if it is true, let us hope that it does not become widely known." Like many

others since, she misunderstood what evolution involves. Human beings are not descended from the apes; humans and apes all trace their evolution from more primitive species living millions of years ago.

SOCIOBIOLOGY

Although biologists recognized the evolutionary connections between animals and human beings, until twenty or thirty years ago most tended to emphasize the distinctive qualities of the human species. This position has been challenged by the work of sociobiologists, who see close parallels between human behavior and that of animals. The term **sociobiology** derives from the writings of Edward Wilson (1975, 1978) and refers to the application of biological principles to explain the social activities of animals, including human beings. According to Wilson, many aspects of social life are grounded in our genetic makeup. For instance, some species of animals engage in elaborate courtship rituals, whereby sexual union and reproduction are achieved. Human courtship and sexual behavior, according to sociobiologists, generally involve similar rituals, based also on inborn characteristics. In most species, to take a second example, males are larger and more aggressive than females and tend to dominate the "weaker sex." Some suggest that genetic factors explain why, in all human societies that we know of, men tend to hold positions of greater authority than women.

One way in which sociobiologists have tried to illuminate the relations between the sexes is by means of the idea of "reproductive strategy." A reproductive strategy is a pattern of behavior, arrived at through evolutionary selection, that favors the chances of survival of offspring. The female body has a larger investment in its reproductive cells than the male—a fertilized egg takes nine months to develop. Thus, according to sociobiologists, women will not squander that investment, and are not driven to have sexual relations with many partners; their overriding aim is the care and protection of children. Men, on the other hand, tend toward promiscuity. Their wish to have sex with many partners is sound strategy from the point of view of the species; to carry out their mission, which is to maximize the possibility of impregnation, they move on. In this way, it has been suggested, we can explain differences in sexual behavior and atti-

"Because my genetic programming prevents me from stopping to ask questions—that's why!" © *The New Yorker Collection 1991 D. Reilly from Cartoonbank.com. All rights reserved.*

tudes of men and women and even perhaps account for phenomena such as rape.

Critics of sociobiology reject this interpretation. There is no way, they say, that it could be proven. Moreover, not all men are promiscuous, and if we look at sexual behavior in modern societies, where women are much freer to choose their sexual involvement than they used to be, they now have as many affairs as men do. And even if the sociobiologists' generalization were correct, there are social and cultural factors that could account for it. For example, men hold the most power in society; in seeking many partners, they could be driven by the desire to exert that power and keep women under their overall control.

These issues remain highly controversial. Scholars tend to fall into two camps, depending to some degree on their educational background. Authors sympathetic to the sociobiological viewpoint are mostly trained in biology rather than the social sciences, while the majority of sociologists tend to be skeptical of sociobiology's claims. Probably sociologists know rather little about the genetic foundations of human life, and biologists have similarly limited knowledge of sociological research. Each side finds it difficult to

understand fully the force of the arguments advanced by the other.

Some of the passions generated early on by Wilson's work have now abated, and it seems possible to produce a reasonably clear assessment of the field. Sociobiology is important—but more for what it has shown about the life of animals than for what it has demonstrated about human behavior. Drawing on the studies of ethologists (biologists who carry out fieldwork among animal groups, rather than studying animals in artificial circumstances such as zoos or laboratories), sociobiologists have shown that many animal species are more social than was previously thought. Animal groups have considerable influence over the behavior of individual members of their species. On the other hand, little evidence has been found to demonstrate that genetic inheritance controls complex forms of human activity. The ideas of sociobiologists about human social life are thus at best speculative.

INSTINCTS

Most biologists and sociologists agree that human beings do not possess instincts. Such a statement runs contrary not only to the hypotheses of sociobiology, but also to what most people believe. Aren't there some things we do "instinctively"? If someone throws a punch, don't we instinctively blink or shy away? In fact, this is not an example of an instinct. As understood in biology and sociology, an **instinct** is a complex pattern of behavior that is genetically determined. The courtship rituals of many of the lower animals are instinctive. For example, the stickleback (a small fresh-water fish) performs an extremely complicated set of rituals that must be followed by both male and female if mating is to occur (Tinbergen, 1974). Each fish produces an array of movements, to which the other responds, resulting in an elaborate mating dance. This is genetically patterned for the whole species.

A spontaneous blinking of the eye or movement away of the head in the face of an anticipated blow is a reflex act rather than an instinct. It is a single, simple response, not an elaborate behavior pattern, and is not regarded as instinctive in the technical sense. Human beings are born with a number of basic reflexes similar to the eye-blink reaction, most of which seem to have some evolutionary survival value. Very young infants, for example, will suck when presented with a nipple or a nipple-like object. A young child will throw up her arms to catch at support when suddenly losing her balance, and will pull her hand back sharply if she touches a very hot surface. Each of these reactions is obviously useful in coping with the unpredictable occurrences of the environment. Humans also have a number of given biological needs. There is an organic basis to our needs for food, drink, sex, and the maintenance of certain levels of body temperature.

Cultural Learning

Although biology obviously influences our development, the ways in which these human needs are satisfied vary widely between, and within, different cultures. For example, all cultures tend to follow some kind of standardized courtship behavior. While this is related to the universal nature of sexual needs, the expression of these needs—even including the sexual act itself—varies enormously in different cultures. A common position for the sexual act in Western culture consists of the woman lying on her back and the man on top of her. This position is seen as absurd by people in some other societies, who are more likely to have intercourse lying side by side, with the woman on top of the man, with the man facing the woman's back, or in other positions. The ways in which people

In the West, puppies are adorable companions. In China and other parts of Asia, they are a prized meal.

seek to satisfy their sexual needs thus seem to be culturally learned, not genetically implanted.

Moreover, humans can override their biological needs in ways that appear to have no parallel among the animals. Religious mystics may fast for long periods. Individuals may choose to remain celibate for part or all of their adult lives. All animals, including human beings, possess a drive toward self-preservation, but humans are unlike other animals in being able deliberately to act against that drive, risking their lives climbing mountains or walking tightropes, or even committing suicide. Biological needs, therefore, condition but rarely determine what we do. Cultural learning exerts the greatest influence upon why we are as we are and why we act as we do.

CULTURAL DIVERSITY

The study of cultural differences highlights the importance of cultural learning on our behavior. Values and norms of behavior vary widely from culture to cul- ture, and often contrast radically with what people from Western societies consider "normal." For example, in the modern West, we regard the deliberate killing of infants or young children as one of the worst of all crimes. Yet in traditional Chinese culture, female children were frequently strangled at birth because they were regarded as a liability rather than an asset to the family. In the West, we eat oysters but we do not eat kittens or puppies, both of which are regarded as delicacies in some parts of the world. Jews don't eat pork, while Hindus eat pork but avoid beef. Westerners regard kissing as a normal part of sexual behavior, but in other cultures the practice is either unknown or regarded as disgusting. All these different kinds of behavior are aspects of broad cultural differences that distinguish societies from one another.

Small societies (like the "hunting and gathering" societies, discussed in the last chapter) tend to be culturally uniform, but industrialized societies are themselves culturally diverse, involving numerous different **subcultures**. In modern cities, for example, there are many subcultural communities living side by side. Gerald Suttles (1968) carried out a now classic fieldwork study of a slum area on Chicago's West Side. In just this one neighborhood, he found these different subcultural groupings: Puerto Ricans, blacks, Greeks,

Jews, gypsies, Italians, Mexicans, and Southern whites. All of these groups had their own "territories" and ways of life.

The number of subcultures in the United States reflects that Americans live in a multicultural society of multiple ethnic and racial groups, many of which have maintained their cultural identities. Multiculturalism holds that cultural diversity is good for a society, but multiculturalism has not been free of controversy in the United States. For instance, the debate over whether public schools should offer bilingual or multilingual education reflects that cultural diversity is not without critics.

CULTURAL IDENTITY AND ETHNOCENTRISM

Every culture displays its own unique patterns of behavior, which seem alien to people from other cultural backgrounds. As an example, we can take the Nacirema, a group described by Horace Miner. Miner concentrated his attention on the strange and exotic body rituals in which the Nacirema engage. His discussion is worth quoting at length:

> The fundamental belief underlying the whole system appears to be that the human body is ugly and that its natural tendency is to debility and disease. Incarcerated in such a body, man's only hope is to avert these characteristics through the use of the powerful influences of ritual and ceremony. Every household has one or more shrines devoted to this purpose.... The focal point of the shrine is a box or chest which is built into the wall. In the chest are kept the many charms and magical potions without which no native believes he could live. These preparations are secured from a variety of specialized practitioners. The most powerful of these are the medicine men, whose assistance must be rewarded with substantial gifts. However, the medicine men do not provide the curative potions for their clients, but decide what the ingredients should be and then write them down in an ancient and secret language. This writing is understood only by the medicine man and by the herbalists who, for another gift, provide the required charm....

> The Nacirema have an almost pathological horror of and fascination with the mouth, the condition of which is believed to have a supernatural influence on all social relationships. Were it not for the rituals of the mouth, they believe that their teeth would fall out, their gums bleed, their jaws shrink, their friends desert them, and their lovers reject them. They also believe that a strong relationship exists between oral and moral characteristics. For example, there is a ritual ablution of the mouth for children which is supposed to improve their moral fibre.

> The daily body ritual performed by everyone includes a mouth-rite. Despite the fact that these people are so punctilious about care of the mouth, this rite involves a practice which strikes the uninitiated stranger as revolting ... the ritual consists of inserting a small bundle of hog hairs into the mouth, along with certain magical powders, and then moving the bundle in a highly formalized series of gestures. (1956)

Who are the Nacirema, and in which part of the world do they live? You can answer these questions for yourself, as well as identify the body ritual described, simply by spelling "Nacirema" backward. The Nacirema, in other words, are Americans (and other Westerners), and the ritual is the brushing of teeth. Almost any familiar activity will seem strange if described out of context. Western cleanliness rituals are no more or less bizarre than the customs of some Pacific groups who knock out their front teeth to beautify themselves, or of certain South American tribal groups who place discs inside their lips to make them protrude, believing that this enhances their attractiveness.

We cannot understand these practices and beliefs separately from the wider cultures of which they are part. A culture must be studied in terms of its own meanings and values—a key presupposition of sociology. Sociologists endeavor as far as possible to avoid **ethnocentrism**, which is judging other cultures in terms of the standards of one's own. Since human cultures vary so widely, it is not surprising that people belonging to one culture frequently find it difficult to sympathize with the ideas or behavior of those from a different culture. In sociology, we must remove our own cultural blinkers in order to see the ways of life of different peoples in an unbiased light. The practice of judging a society by its own standards is called **cultural relativism**.

Cultural Universals

Amid the diversity of human behavior, there are some common features. Where these are found in virtually all societies, they are called **cultural universals**. For example, there is no known culture without a grammatically complex **language**. All cultures possess some recognizable form of family system, in which there are values and norms associated with the care of the children. The institution of **marriage** is a cultural universal, as are religious rituals and property rights. All cultures, also, practice some form of incest prohibition—the banning of sexual relations between close relatives, such as father and daughter, mother and son, or brother and sister. A variety of other cultural universals have been identified by anthropologists, including art, dancing, bodily adornment, games, gift giving, joking, and rules of hygiene.

Yet there are variations within each category. Consider, for example, the prohibition against incest. Most often, incest is regarded as sexual relations be-tween members of the immediate family; but among some peoples, it includes cousins, even in some instances all people bearing the same family name. There have also been societies in which a small proportion of the population have been permitted to engage in incestuous practices. This was the case, for instance, within the ruling class of ancient Egypt, when brothers and sisters were permitted to have sex with one another.

Among the cultural characteristics shared by all

KEY CONCEPTS IN REVIEW

Culture consists of the values held by a given group, the norms they follow, and the material goods they create. **Values** are abstract ideals, while **norms**, representing the dos and don'ts of social life, are definite rules people are expected to observe.

Culture and society are closely related. **Society** refers to the system of relationships that connects individuals who share the same culture.

"Nature," the biological characteristics that make up our genetic inheritance, and "nurture," social and cultural influences, both affect our actions. However, **sociobiology** argues that our genetic makeup accounts for most aspects of social life.

Most sociologists argue that human beings do not possess **instincts**, complex patterns of behavior that are genetically determined. We do have reflexes (such as the eye blink) and biological needs (such as eating) that are conditioned by social influences and are culturally learned.

Modern societies are composed of **subcultures**, smaller segments of society distinguished by unique patterns of behavior.

Sociologists seek to avoid **ethnocentrism**, the judging of other cultures by our own standards. The practice of judging a society by its own standards is known as **cultural relativism**.

Cultural universals are forms of human behavior found in all societies. They include language, family systems, religious rituals, and prohibitions against incest.

societies, two stand out particularly. All cultures incorporate ways of expressing meaning and communication, and all depend on material means of production. In all cultures, *language* is the primary vehicle of meaning and communication. It is not the only such vehicle, however. Material culture itself carries meanings, as we shall show in what follows.

LANGUAGE

Possession of a language is perhaps the most distinctive human cultural attribute, shared by all cultures (although thousands of different languages are spoken in the world). Animals can communicate with one another, yet no animal species possesses a developed language. Some of the apes can be taught linguistic skills, but only in a rudimentary way. One of the most famous chimpanzees known to sociology, called Washoe, was taught a vocabulary of over a hundred words using American Sign Language (Gardner and Gardner, 1969, 1975). Washoe was also able to put together a few simple sentences. For example, she could communicate "Come hug-love, sorry sorry," meaning that she wanted to apologize after acting in a way she knew was disapproved of.

The experiments with Washoe were much more successful than similar ones with other chimpanzees; hence her fame in the sociological literature. But Washoe was not able to master any rules of grammar and could not teach other chimps what she knew. Even after having been trained for several years, her linguistic capacity was far below that of the average child of two. Every competent adult human language speaker employs a vocabulary of thousands of words, and is able to combine them according to rules so complex that linguists spend their entire careers trying to find out what they are.

Language is one of the best examples for demonstrating both the unity and diversity of human culture. For there are no cultures without language, yet there are thousands of different languages spoken in the world. Anyone who has visited a foreign country armed with only a dictionary knows how difficult it is to either understand anything or to be understood. Although languages that have similar origins have words in common with one another—as for example, German with English—most of the world's languages have no words in common at all.

The use of language, and the ability to pass it on from one generation to the next, is a distinctly human attribute.

Language is involved in virtually all of our activities. In the form of ordinary talk or speech, it is the means by which we organize most of what we do. We will discuss the importance of talk and conversation in social life at some length in a subsequent chapter (Chapter 5: "Social Interaction and Everyday Life"). However, language is involved not just in mundane, everyday activities, but also in ceremony, religion, poetry, and many other spheres. One of the most distinctive features of human language is that it allows us to vastly extend the scope of our thought and experience. Using language, we can convey information about events remote in time or space, and can discuss things we have never seen. We can develop abstract concepts, tell stories, make jokes, and construct imaginative flights of fancy.

SPEECH AND WRITING

All societies use speech as a vehicle of language. However, there are other ways of "carrying" or expressing language—most notably, writing. The invention of writing marked a major transition in human history. Writing first began as the drawing up of lists. Marks would be made on wood, clay, or stone to keep records about significant events, objects, or people. For example, a mark, or sometimes a picture, might be drawn to represent each field possessed by a particular family or set of families (Gelb, 1952). Writing began as a means of storing information, and as such

globalization and everyday life

REGGAE MUSIC

When those knowledgeable about popular music listen to a song, they can often pick out the stylistic influences that helped shape it. Each musical style, after all, represents a unique way of combining rhythm, melody, harmony, and lyrics. And while it doesn't take a genuis to notice the differences between grunge, hard rock, techno, and hip-hop, musicians often combine a number of styles in composing songs. Identifying the components of these combinations can be difficult. But for sociologists of culture, the effort is often rewarding. Different musical styles tend to emerge from different social groups, and studying how styles combine and fuse is a good way to chart the cultural contacts between groups.

Some sociologists of culture have turned their attention to reggae music because it exemplifies the process whereby contacts between social groups result in the creation of new musical forms. Reggae's roots can be traced to West Africa. In the seventeenth century, large numbers of West Africans were enslaved by the British and brought by ship to work in the sugar cane fields of the West Indies. Although the

British attempted to prevent slaves from playing traditional African music for fear it would serve as a rallying cry to revolt, the slaves managed to keep alive the tradition of African drumming, sometimes by integrating it with the European musical styles imposed by the slave owners. In Jamaica, the drumming of one group of slaves, the Burru, was

was closely linked to the administrative needs of the early civilizations. A society that possesses writing can "locate itself" in time and space. Documents can be accumulated that record the past, and information can be gathered about present-day events and activities.

Writing is not just the transfer of speech to paper or some other durable material. It is a phenomenon of interest in its own right. Written documents or *texts* have qualities in some ways quite distinct from the spoken word. The impact of speech is always by definition limited to the particular contexts in which words are uttered. Ideas and experiences can be passed down through generations in cultures without writing, but only if they are regularly repeated and passed on by word of mouth. Texts, on the other hand, can endure for thousands of years, and through them those from past ages can in a certain sense "address" us directly. This is, of course, why documentary research is so important to historians. Through interpreting the texts that are left behind by dead generations, historians can reconstruct what their lives were like. The Biblical texts, for example, have formed an enduring part of the history of the West for openly tolerated by slaveholders because it helped meter the pace of work. Slavery was finally abolished in Jamaica in 1834, but the tradition of Burru drumming continued, even as many Burru men migrated from rural areas to the slums of Kingston.

It was in these slums that a new religious cult began to emerge—one that would prove crucial for the development of reggae. In 1930, a man named Haile Selassie was crowned emperor of the African country of Ethiopia. While opponents of European colonialism throughout the world cheered Selassie's ascension to the throne, a number of people in the West Indies came to believe that Selassie was a god, sent to earth to lead the oppressed of Africa to freedom. One of Selassie's names was "Prince Ras Tafari," and the West Indians who worshipped him called themselves "Rastafarians." The Rastafarian cult soon merged with the Burru, and Rastafarian music came to combine Burru styles of drumming with Biblical themes of oppression and liberation. In the 1950s, West Indian musicians began mixing Rastafarian rhythms and lyrics with elements of American jazz and black r & b. These combinations eventually developed into "ska" music, and then, in the late 1960s, into reggae, with its relatively slow beat, its emphasis on bass, and its stories of urban deprivation and of the power of collective social consciousness. Many reggae artists, such as Bob Marley, became commercial successes, and by the 1970s people the world over were listening to reggae music. In the 1980s and 1990s, reggae was fused with hip-hop (or rap) to produce new sounds, as can be heard in the work of the groups Wu-Tang Clan and the Fugees (Hebdige, 1987).

The history of reggae is thus the history of contact between different social groups, and of the meanings—political, spiritual, and personal—that those groups expressed through their music. Globalization has increased the intensity of these contacts. It is now possible for a young musician in Scandinavia, for example, to grow up listening to music produced by men and women in the ghettos of Los Angeles, and to be deeply influenced as well by, say, a mariachi performance broadcast live via satellite from Mexico City. If the number of contacts between groups is an important determinant of the pace of musical evolution, it can be predicted that there will be a veritable profusion of new styles in the coming years as the process of globalization continues to unfold.

the past two thousand years. We can still read, and admire, the plays of the great dramatists of ancient Greece.

SEMIOTICS AND MATERIAL CULTURE

The symbols expressed in speech and writing are the chief ways in which cultural meanings are formed and expressed. But they are not the only ways. Both material objects and aspects of behavior can be used to generate meanings. A **signifier** is any vehicle of meaning—any set of elements used to convey communication. The sounds made in speech are signifiers, as are the marks made on paper or other materials in writing. Other signifiers, however, include dress, pictures or visual signs, modes of eating, forms of building or architecture, and many other material features of culture (Hawkes, 1977). Styles of dress, for example, normally help signify differences between the sexes. In our culture, at least until relatively recently, women used to wear skirts and men pants. In other cultures, this is reversed: women wear pants and men skirts (Leach, 1976).

Semiotics—the analysis of nonverbal cultural meanings—opens up a fascinating field for both sociology and anthropology. Semiotic analysis can be very useful in comparing one culture with another. Given that cultural meanings are symbolic, it allows us to contrast the ways in which different cultures are structured. For example, the buildings in cities are not simply places in which people live and work. They often have a symbolic character. In traditional cities, the main temple or church was usually placed on high ground in or near the city center. It symbolized the all-powerful influence that religion was supposed to have over the lives of the people. In modern societies, by contrast, the skyscrapers of big business often occupy that symbolic position.

Of course, material culture is not simply symbolic, but is vital to catering for physical needs—in the shape of the tools or technology used to acquire food, make weaponry, construct dwellings, and so forth. We have to study both the practical and the symbolic aspects of material culture in order to understand it completely.

Culture and Social Development

Cultural traits are closely related to overall patterns in the development of society. The level of material culture reached in a given society influences, although by no means completely determines, other aspects of cultural development. This is easy to see, for example, on the level of technology. Much of the cultural paraphernalia characteristic of our lives today—cars, telephones, computers, running water, electric light—depend upon technological innovations that have been made only very recently in human history.

The same is true at earlier phases of social development. Prior to the invention of the smelting of metal, for example, goods had to be made of organic or naturally occurring materials like wood or stone—a basic limitation upon the artifacts that could be constructed. Variations in material culture provide the main means of distinguishing different forms of human society, but other factors are also influential. Writing is an example. As has been mentioned, not all human cultures have possessed writing—in fact, for most of human history, writing was unknown. The development of writing altered the scope of human cultural potentialities, making different forms of social organization possible than those that had previously existed.

We now turn to analyzing the main types of society that existed in the past and that are still found in the world today. In the present day, we are accustomed to societies that contain many millions of people, many of them living crowded together in urban areas. But for most of human history, the earth was much less densely populated than it is now, and it is only over the past hundred years or so that any societies have existed in which the majority of the population were city dwellers. To understand the forms of society that existed prior to modern industrialism, we have to call upon the historical dimension of the sociological imagination.

DISAPPEARING WORLD: PREMODERN SOCIETIES AND THEIR FATE

The explorers, traders, and missionaries sent out during Europe's great age of discovery met with many different peoples. As the anthropologist Marvin Harris has written in his work *Cannibals and Kings:*

> In some regions—Australia, the Arctic, the southern tips of South America and Africa—they found groups still living much like Europe's own long-forgotten stone age ancestors: bands of twenty or thirty people, sprinkled across vast territories, constantly on the move, living entirely by hunting animals and collecting wild plants. These hunter-collectors appeared to be members of a rare and endangered species. In other regions—the forests of eastern North America, the jungles of South America, and East Asia—they found denser populations, inhabiting more or less permanent villages, based on farming and consisting of perhaps one or two large communal structures, but here too the weapons and tools were relics of prehistory. . . .
>
> Elsewhere, of course, the explorers encountered fully developed states and empires, headed by despots and ruling classes, and defended by standing armies. It was these great empires, with

their cities, monuments, palaces, temples and treasures, that had lured all the Marco Polos and Columbuses across the oceans and deserts in the first place. There was China—the greatest empire in the world, a vast, sophisticated realm whose leaders scorned the "red-faced barbarians," suppliants from puny kingdoms beyond the pale of the civilised world. And there was India—a land where cows were venerated and the unequal burdens of life were apportioned according to what each soul had merited in its previous incarnation. And then there were the native American states and empires, worlds unto themselves, each with its distinctive arts and religions: the Incas, with their great stone fortresses, suspension bridges, over-worked granaries, and state-controlled economy; and the Aztecs, with their bloodthirsty gods fed from human hearts and their incessant search for fresh sacrifices. (Harris, 1978)

This seemingly unlimited variety of premodern societies can actually be grouped into three main categories, each of which is referred to in Harris's description: hunters and gatherers (Harris's "hunters and collectors"); larger agrarian or pastoral societies (involving agriculture or the tending of domesticated animals); and nonindustrial civilizations or traditional states. We shall look at the main characteristics of these in turn (see Table 3.1).

Table 3.1 Types of Human Society

TYPE	PERIOD OF EXISTENCE	CHARACTERISTICS
Hunting and gathering societies	50,000 B.C.E. to the present (now on the verge of complete disappearance).	Consist of small numbers of people gaining their livelihood from hunting, fishing, and the gathering of edible plants. Few inequalities. Differences of rank limited by age and sex.
Agrarian societies	12,000 B.C.E. to the present. Most are now part of larger political entities, and are losing their distinct identity.	Based on small rural communities, without towns or cities. Livelihood gained through agriculture, often supplemented by hunting and gathering. Stronger inequalities than among hunters and gatherers. Ruled by chiefs.
Pastoral societies	12,000 B.C.E. to the present. Today mostly part of larger states; their traditional ways of life are becoming undermined.	Dependent on the tending of domesticated animals for their material subsistence. Size ranges from a few hundred people to many thousands. Marked by distinct inequalities. Ruled by chiefs or warrior kings.
Traditional states or civilizations	6000 B.C.E. to the nineteenth century. All traditional states have disappeared.	Based largely on agriculture. Some cities exist, in which trade and manufacture are concentrated. Very large in size, some numbering millions of people (though small compared with larger industrialized societies). Distinct apparatus of government headed by a king or emperor. Major inequalities exist among different classes.

Members of a hunter-gatherer society in the Kalahari Desert.

The Earliest Societies: Hunters and Gatherers

For all but a tiny part of our existence on this planet, human beings have lived in **hunting and gathering societies**, small groups or tribes often numbering no more than thirty or forty people. Hunters and gatherers gain their livelihood from hunting, fishing, and gathering edible plants growing in the wild. Hunting and gathering cultures continue to exist in some parts of the world, such as in a few arid parts of Africa and the jungles of Brazil and New Guinea. Most such cultures, however, have been destroyed or absorbed by the spread of Western culture, and those that remain are unlikely to stay intact for much longer. Currently, less than a quarter of a million people in the world support themselves through hunting and gathering—only 0.001 percent of the world's population (see Global Map 3.1).

Compared with larger societies—particularly modern societies, such as the United States—little inequality was found in most hunting and gathering groups. The material goods they needed were limited to weapons for hunting, tools for digging and building, traps, and cooking utensils. Thus, there was little difference among members of the society in the number or kinds of material possessions—there were no divisions of rich and poor. Differences of position or rank tended to be limited to age and sex; men were almost always the hunters, while women gathered wild crops, cooked, and brought up the children.

The "elders"—the oldest and most experienced men in the community—usually had an important say in major decisions affecting the group. But just as there was little variation in wealth among members, differences of power were much less than in larger types of society. Hunting and gathering societies were usually "participatory" rather than competitive: all adult male members tended to assemble together when important decisions were to be made or crises faced.

Hunters and gatherers moved about a good deal, but not in a completely erratic way. They had fixed territories, around which they migrated regularly from year to year. Since they were without animal or mechanical means of transport, they could take few goods or possessions with them. Many hunting and gathering communities did not have a stable membership; people often moved between different camps, or groups split up and joined others within the same overall territory.

Hunters and gatherers had little interest in developing material wealth beyond what was needed for their basic wants. Their main concerns were with religious values and ritual activities. Members participated regularly in elaborate ceremonials, and often spent a great deal of time preparing the dress, masks, paintings, or other sacred objects used in such rituals.

Hunters and gatherers were not merely primitive peoples whose ways of life no longer hold any interest for us. Studying their cultures allows us to see more clearly that some of our institutions are far from being natural features of human life. We shouldn't idealize the circumstances in which hunters and gatherers lived; but the lack of major inequalities of wealth and power and the emphasis on cooperation rather than competition are instructive reminders that the world created by modern industrial civilization is not necessarily to be equated with progress.

Pastoral and Agrarian Societies

About twenty thousand years ago, some hunting and gathering groups turned to the raising of domesticated animals and the cultivation of fixed plots of land as

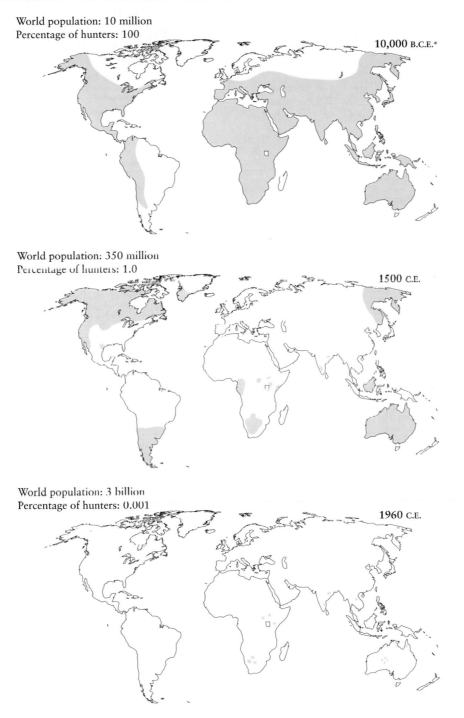

World population: 10 million
Percentage of hunters: 100

10,000 B.C.E.*

World population: 350 million
Percentage of hunters: 1.0

1500 C.E.

World population: 3 billion
Percentage of hunters: 0.001

1960 C.E.

*Historians now use B.C.E. (Before Common Era) and C.E. (Common Era) rather than B.C. and A.D.

SOURCE: Richard B. Lee and Irven De Vore, eds., *Man the Hunter* (Chicago: Aldine Press, 1968).

their means of livelihood. **Pastoral societies** relied mainly on domesticated livestock, while **agrarian societies** grew crops (practiced agriculture). Some societies had mixed pastoral and agrarian economies.

Depending on the environment in which they lived, pastoralists reared animals such as cattle, sheep, goats, camels, and horses. Some pastoral societies still exist in the modern world, concentrated especially in areas of Africa, the Middle East, and Central Asia. They are usually found in regions of dense grasslands or in deserts or mountains. Such regions are not amenable to fruitful agriculture but may support livestock.

At some point, hunting and gathering groups began to sow their own crops rather than simply collect those growing in the wild. This practice first developed as what is usually called "horticulture," in which small gardens were cultivated by the use of simple hoes or digging instruments. Like pastoralism, horticulture provided for a more assured supply of food than was possible by hunting and gathering, and therefore could support larger communities. Since they were not on the move, people gaining a livelihood from horticulture could develop larger stocks of material possessions than either hunting and gathering or pastoral communities. Some peoples in the world still rely primarily on horticulture for their livelihood (see Table 3.2).

Table 3.2 Some Agrarian Societies Still Remain

COUNTRY	PERCENTAGE OF WORKFORCE IN AGRICULTURE
Nepal	91.1
Rwanda	90.1
Ethiopia	88.3
Uganda	82.1
Bangladesh	64.2
Industrialized Societies Differ	
Japan	6.2
Australia	5.0
Germany	3.8
Canada	3.4
United States	2.8
United Kingdom	2.0

Nonindustrial Civilizations

From about 6000 B.C.E. onward, we find evidence of larger societies than ever existed before, which contrast in distinct ways with earlier types. These societies were based on the development of cities, showed pronounced inequalities of wealth and power, and were ruled by kings or emperors. Because writing was used and science and art flourished, they are often called civilizations.

The earliest civilizations developed in the Middle East, usually in fertile river areas (see Global Map 3.2). The Chinese Empire originated in about 2000 B.C.E., at which time powerful states were also founded in what are now India and Pakistan. A number of large civilizations existed in Mexico and Latin America, such as the Aztecs of the Mexican peninsula and the Incas of Peru.

Most traditional (premodern) civilizations were also empires: they achieved their size through the conquest and incorporation of other peoples (Kautsky, 1982). This was true, for instance, of traditional Rome and China. At its height, in the first century C.E., the Roman Empire stretched from Britain in northwest Europe to beyond the Middle East. The Chinese Empire, which lasted for more than two thousand years, up to the threshold of the twentieth century, covered most of the massive region of eastern Asia now occupied by modern China.

Global Map 3.2
TRADITIONAL SOCIETIES IN THE ANCIENT WORLD

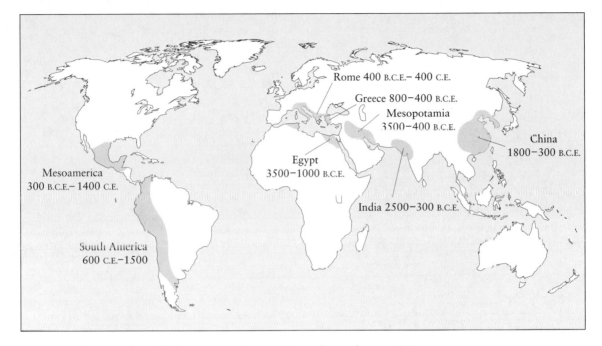

Rome 400 B.C.E.– 400 C.E.

Greece 800–400 B.C.E.

Mesopotamia
3500–400 B.C.E.

China
1800–300 B.C.E.

Egypt
3500–1000 B.C.E.

Mesoamerica
300 B.C.E.– 1400 C.E.

India 2500–300 B.C.E.

South America
600 C.E.–1500

The color areas on the map show the locations and approximate dates of some of the major traditional civilizations of the past.

Though some agrarian societies survive today, such as this one in Nepal, most of the world is industrialized.

SOCIETIES IN THE MODERN WORLD

What happened to destroy the forms of society that dominated the whole of history up to two centuries ago? The answer, in a word, is **industrialization**—the emergence of machine production, based on the use of inanimate power resources (like steam or electricity). The industrialized, or modern, societies differ in several key respects from any previous type of social order, and their development has had consequences stretching far beyond their European origins (see Table 3.3).

Table 3.3 Societies in the Modern World

First World societies	Eighteenth century to the present.	Based on industrial production and generally free enterprise. Majority of people live in towns and cities, few in rural agricultural pursuits. Major class inequalities, though less pronounced than in traditional states. Distinct political communities or nation-states, including the nations of the West, Japan, Australia, and New Zealand.
Second World societies	Early twentieth century (following the Russian Revolution of 1917) to the early 1990s.	Based on industry, but the economic system is centrally planned. Small proportion of the population work in agriculture; most live in towns and cities. Major class inequalities persist. Distinct political communities or nation-states. Until 1989, included the Soviet Union and Eastern Europe, but social and political changes began to transform them into free-enterprise economic systems, making them First World societies.
Third World societies	Eighteenth century (mostly as colonized areas) to the present.	Majority of the population work in agriculture, using traditional methods of production. Some agriculture produce sold on world markets. Some have free enterprise systems, others are centrally planned. Distinct political communities or nation-states, including China, India, and most African and South American nations.
Newly industrializing countries	1970s to the present.	Former Third World societies now based on industrial production and generally free enterprise. Majority of people live in towns and cities, a few in agricultural pursuits. Major class inequalities, more pronounced than First World societies. Average per capita income considerably less than First World societies. Include Hong Kong, South Korea, Singapore, Taiwan, Brazil, and Mexico.

The Industrialized Societies

Industrialization originated in eighteenth-century England as a result of the Industrial Revolution, a shorthand name for a complex set of technological changes affecting the means by which people gained their livelihood. These changes included the invention of new machines (like the spinning jenny for weaving yarn), the harnessing of power resources (especially water and steam) to production, and the use of science to improve production methods. Since discoveries and inventions in one field provoke more in others, the pace of technological innovation in industrialized societies is extremely rapid compared with traditional social systems.

In even the most advanced of traditional civilizations, most people were engaged in working on the land. The relatively low level of technological development did not permit more than a small minority to be freed from the chores of agricultural production. By contrast, a prime feature of industrialized societies today is that the large majority of the employed population work in factories, offices, or shops rather than in agriculture. And over 90 percent of people live in towns and cities, where most jobs are to be found and new job opportunities created. The largest cities are vastly greater in size than the urban settlements found in traditional civilizations. In the cities, social life becomes more impersonal and anonymous than before, and many of our day-to-day encounters are with strangers rather than with individuals known to us. Large-scale organizations, such as business corporations or government agencies, come to influence the lives of virtually everyone.

A further feature of modern societies concerns their political systems, which are more developed and intensive than forms of government in traditional states. In traditional civilizations, the political authorities (monarchs and emperors) had little direct influence on the customs and habits of most of their subjects, who lived in fairly self-contained local villages. With industrialization, transportation and communications became much more rapid, making for a more integrated "national" community.

The industrialized societies were the first nation-states to come into existence. **Nation-states** are political communities with clearly delimited borders dividing them from each other, rather than the vague frontier areas that used to separate traditional states. Nation-state governments have extensive powers over many aspects of citizens' lives, framing laws that apply to all those living within their borders. The United States is a nation-state, as are virtually all other societies in the world today.

The application of industrial technology has been by no means limited to peaceful processes of economic development. From the earliest phases of industrialization, modern production processes have been put to military use, and this has radically altered ways of waging war, creating weaponry and modes of military organization much more advanced than those of nonindustrial cultures. Together, superior economic strength, political cohesion, and military superiority account for the seemingly irresistible spread of Western ways of life across the world over the past two centuries.

Global Development

From the seventeenth to the early twentieth century, the Western countries established colonies in numerous areas previously occupied by traditional societies, using their superior military strength where necessary. Although virtually all these colonies have now attained their independence, the process of **colonialism** was central to shaping the social map of the globe as we know it today. In some regions, like North America, Australia, and New Zealand, which were only thinly populated by hunting and gathering communities, Europeans became the majority population. In other areas, including much of Asia, Africa, and South America, the local populations remained in the majority.

Societies of the first of these types, including the United States, have become industrialized. Those in the second category are mostly at a much lower level of industrial development and are often referred to as **Third World** societies. Such societies include China, India, most of the African countries (such as Nigeria, Ghana, and Algeria), and those in South America (for example, Brazil, Peru, and Venezuela). Since many of these societies are situated south of the United States and Europe, they are sometimes referred to collectively as the South, and contrasted to the wealthier, industrialized North.

The term "Third World" was originally part of a contrast drawn between three main types of society found in the early twentieth century (see Global Map 3.3). **First World** countries were (and are) the industrialized states of Europe, the United States, Australasia (Australia, New Zealand, Tasmania, and Melanesia), and Japan. Nearly all First World societies have multiparty, parliamentary systems of government. **Second World** societies meant the Communist countries of what was then the Soviet Union (USSR) and Eastern Europe, including Czechoslovakia, Poland, East Germany, and Hungary. Second World societies were centrally planned economies, which allowed little role for private property or competitive economic enterprise. They were also one-party states: the Communist party dominated both the political and economic systems. For some seventy-five years, world history was affected by

Labeling nations as part of one of the "Three Worlds" can be problematic for several reasons. First, as noted in the text, with the collapse of Communism in the former

Soviet Union, the Second World has effectively disappeared. The countries highlighted as Second World are these former Communist states in the process of transfor-

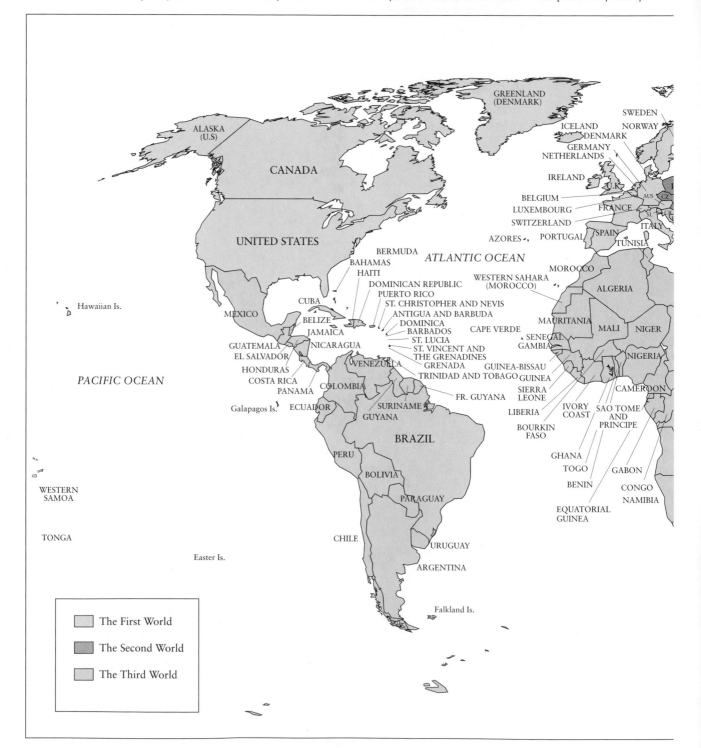

GREENLAND (DENMARK)

SWEDEN
ICELAND   NORWAY
DENMARK
GERMANY
NETHERLANDS
IRELAND
U.K
BELGIUM
LUXEMBOURG   FRANCE
SWITZERLAND
AZORES   PORTUGAL   SPAIN   ITALY
TUNISIA
AUS   CZ
SL

ALASKA (U.S)

CANADA

UNITED STATES

BERMUDA   *ATLANTIC OCEAN*
BAHAMAS
HAITI
DOMINICAN REPUBLIC
PUERTO RICO
ST. CHRISTOPHER AND NEVIS
ANTIGUA AND BARBUDA
DOMINICA
BARBADOS
ST. LUCIA
ST. VINCENT AND
THE GRENADINES
GRENADA
TRINIDAD AND TOBAGO
FR. GUYANA

CUBA
MEXICO
BELIZE
JAMAICA
GUATEMALA
EL SALVADOR
HONDURAS
COSTA RICA
PANAMA
NICARAGUA
VENEZUELA
COLOMBIA

Hawaiian Is.

WESTERN SAHARA (MOROCCO)
MOROCCO
ALGERIA
MAURITANIA   MALI   NIGER
CAPE VERDE
SENEGAL
GAMBIA
GUINEA-BISSAU
GUINEA
SIERRA
LEONE
LIBERIA
IVORY
COAST
BOURKIN
FASO
GHANA
TOGO
BENIN
EQUATORIAL
GUINEA
NIGERIA
CAMEROON
SAO TOME
AND
PRINCIPE
GABON
CONGO
NAMIBIA

PACIFIC OCEAN

Galapagos Is.   ECUADOR
SURINAME
GUYANA

BRAZIL

PERU
BOLIVIA

WESTERN
SAMOA

PARAGUAY

TONGA

CHILE

Easter Is.

URUGUAY
ARGENTINA

Falkland Is.

The First World

The Second World

The Third World

mation to capitalist societies. Second, as you will see later in this chapter, several Third World nations are experiencing rapid economic growth and may soon join the ranks of the First World. Third, ranking the world's nations reflects a value judgment that can be insulting to many. As noted in the text, the Three Worlds concept was developed earlier this century, and as the world undergoes dramatic changes, the concept may outlive its usefulness.

ABBREVIATIONS

ALB.	ALBANIA
AUS.	AUSTRIA
B.H.	BOSNIA AND HERZEGOVINA
BULG.	BULGARIA
CR.	CROATIA
CZ.	CZECH REPUBLIC
HUN.	HUNGARY
SL.	SLOVENIA
ROM.	ROMANIA
U.K	UNITED KINGDOM
YU.	YUGOSLAVIA

a global rivalry between the Soviet Union and Eastern European countries on the one hand and the capitalistic societies of the West and Japan on the other. Today that rivalry is over. With the ending of the Cold War and the disintegration of Communism in the former USSR and Eastern Europe, the Second World has effectively disappeared.

The End of the Second World: The Collapse of Communism

What was the Cold War? It was a situation of permanent armed confrontation between the First World societies of the West—with the United States most prominent—and the Communist societies, led by the Soviet Union. It was a "cold" war because no direct military battles ensued between the two sides; it was a sort of military standoff, with each side constantly prepared to go to war with the other but not actually doing so.

With the end of the Cold War, Russia and the other former Second World societies are in the process of moving toward a competitive market system like that of the Western countries. They are also trying to form democratic political institutions based on Western models. These changes, however, are creating major new social situations for other parts of the world, including the United States.

During the Cold War, important aspects of U.S. society and culture were affected by the existence of an "enemy"—the Soviet Union. For example, some major American industries, like the arms industry, electronics, and aviation, prospered from U.S. involvement in the Cold War. High rates of unemployment and economic recession followed the end of the war in states where those industries were strongly represented, such as California. In Russia and the other countries that made up the Soviet Union, the consequences of the ending of the Cold War have been much more marked. Alongside the move toward a market economy and a democratic political system, we find in these countries today the rise of aggressive nationalist movements, plus a great upsurge of tensions between different ethnic groups.

What's going on in Russia and the other ex-Communist countries might seem to have little to do with

The fall of the Berlin Wall changed the lives of Germans first, but by removing the structure the Cold War had imposed on the world, it soon produced effects felt far from Germany.

the lives of people in the United States. But this isn't so at all. In common with all the other industrial societies, the United States is increasingly locked into a global economy, such that events in other parts of the world have immediate effects upon the activities of Americans. What happens in the former Soviet Union, for instance, might actually determine whether you are able to get a good job, or even a job at all, when you leave college. For continuing U.S. economic prosperity depends on stable economic conditions worldwide. If Russia is able to achieve economic and political development, fruitful trade with the United States could be of benefit to both countries. Should there be an economic collapse in the societies of the former Soviet Union, however, damaging consequences might ensue for American social and economic stability too—affecting the prospects of most Americans.

Third World Societies

The large majority of Third World societies are in areas that underwent colonial rule in Asia, Africa, and South America. A few colonized areas gained independence early, like Haiti, which became the first autonomous black republic in January 1804. The Spanish colonies in South America acquired their freedom in 1810, while Brazil broke away from Portuguese rule in 1822.

Some countries that were never ruled from Europe were nonetheless strongly influenced by colonial relationships, the most notable example being China. By force of arms, China was compelled from the seventeenth century on to enter into trading agreements with European powers, by which the Europeans were allocated the government of certain areas, including major seaports. Hong Kong was the last remnant of these. Most Third World nations have become independent states only since World War II—often following bloody anticolonial struggles. Examples include India, which shortly after achieving self-rule split into India and Pakistan, a range of other Asian countries (like Myanmar, Malaysia, and Singapore), and countries in Africa (including, for example, Kenya, Nigeria, Zaire, Tanzania, and Algeria).

While they may include peoples living in traditional fashion, Third World countries are very different from earlier forms of traditional society. Their political systems are modeled on systems first established in the societies of the West—that is to say, they are nation-states. While most of the population still live in rural areas, many of these societies are experiencing a rapid process of city development. Although agriculture remains the main economic activity, crops are now often produced for sale in world markets rather than for local consumption. Third World countries are not merely societies that have "lagged behind" the more industrialized areas. They have been in large part created by contact with Western industrialism, which has undermined earlier, more traditional systems.

Immigration from global South to North as seen on a highway sign in southern California.

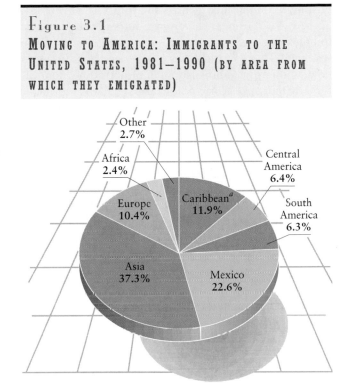

SOURCE: Center for Immigration Studies, *1990 Immigration and Naturalization Service Yearbook*, as reported in the *New York Times*, May 6, 1992.
[a]Antigua-Barbuda, the Bahamas, Barbados, Cuba, Dominica, Dominican Republic, Grenada, Haiti, Jamaica, St. Kitts and Nevis, St. Lucia, St. Vincent and the Grenadines, and Trinidad and Tobago.

Conditions in the more impoverished of these societies have deteriorated rather than improved over the past few years. It has been estimated that in 1993 there were 1.2 billion people living in poverty in the developing countries, nearly a quarter of the population of the world. Some half of the world's poor live in South Asia, in countries such as India, Myanmar, and Cambodia. About a third are concentrated in Africa. A substantial proportion, however, live on the doorstep of the United States—in Central and South America.

Once more, the existence of global poverty shouldn't be seen as remote from the concerns of Americans. Whereas in previous generations the bulk of immi- grants into the United States came from the European countries, most now come from poor Third World societies (see Figure 3.1). Recent years have seen waves of

Hispanic immigrants, nearly all from Latin America. Some U.S. cities near the entry points of much of this immigration, such as Los Angeles and Miami, have become "Third World cities." They are bursting with new immigrants and also maintain trading connections with Third World countries.

In most Third World societies, poverty tends to be at its worst in rural areas. Malnutrition, lack of education, low life expectancy, and substandard housing are generally most severe in the countryside. Many of the poor are to be found in areas where arable land is scarce, agricultural productivity low, and drought or floods common. Women are usually more disadvantaged than men. They encounter cultural, social, and economic problems that even the most underprivileged men do not. For instance, they often work longer hours and, where they are paid at all, earn lower wages (see also Chapter 8 for a lengthier discussion of gender inequality).

The poor in Third World countries live in conditions almost unimaginable to Americans. Many have no permanent dwellings apart from shelters made of cartons or loose pieces of wood. Most have no running water, sewage, or electricity. Nonetheless, there are millions of poor people in the United States, and there are connections between poverty in America and global poverty. Almost half of the people living in poverty in the United States originate from the global South. This is true of the descendants of the black slaves brought over by force centuries ago; and it is true of more recent, and willing, immigrants who have arrived from Latin America, Asia, and elsewhere.

The Newly Industrializing Countries

The Third World is not a unity. While the majority of Third World countries lag well behind societies of the West, some have now successfully embarked on a process of industrialization. These are sometimes referred to as **newly industrializing countries** (NICs), and they include Brazil, Mexico, Hong Kong (although not a country, it is customarily grouped with NICs), South Korea, Singapore, and Taiwan. The rates of economic growth of the most successful NICs, such as Taiwan, are several times those of the Western industrial economies. No Third World country figured among the top thirty exporters in the world in 1968, but twenty-five years later Hong Kong and South Korea were in the top fifteen.

The Asian NICs, as of the early 1990s, have shown the most sustained levels of economic prosperity.

KEY CONCEPTS IN REVIEW

The development and expansion of the West led to the conquest of many parts of the world, and the process of **colonialism** radically changed long-established social systems and cultures.

World society has become increasingly interdependent—a process known as **globalization**. The development of world social relations involves large-scale inequalities between the **First World**, or industrialized, and **Third World** societies. The largest disparities of wealth and living standards are those separating the rich industrialized countries from the poorer Third World states.

Most Third World societies are in areas of the world that underwent Western colonial rule. Many have only become independent states since World War II. Although most Third World societies are impoverished compared with the industrialized nations, a minority (the NICs, or **newly industrializing countries**) have experienced rapid economic development.

THE SOCIOLOGICAL DEBATE

EXPLAINING POVERTY: CULTURE OR SOCIAL STRUCTURE?

The concept of culture is one of the most widely used in sociology. Culture consists of the values the members of a given group hold, the norms they follow, and the material goods they create. Sociologists are also interested in the competing roles that culture and social structure play in guiding human behavior. An exemplar of this question is the "culture of poverty debate" of the 1960s and 1970s. Anthropologist Oscar Lewis proposed a "culture of poverty" theory, which argued that the "ghetto" poor have developed a unique subculture of behavior and attitudes, and this subculture is transmitted from generation to generation. Sociologist Elliot Liebow, among others, countered that the transmission of behavior and attitudes from poor parents to poor children is not "cultural," rather it is due to the fact that both generations face similar social and economic obstacles.

In his "culture of poverty" essay, Lewis elaborated that the social structural conditions to which the poor are exposed, such as "chronic unemployment, low income, lack of property ownership, and . . . chronic shortage of food, money, medical care, and other necessities of life" give rise to unique patterns of family and community disorganization. This disorganization, in turn, leads to the development of a distinct set of beliefs, attitudes, and values held by the poor such as helplessness and dependence.

Lewis emphasized that familial and community patterns of child rearing were the key to understanding the persistence of poverty. He wrote that "the culture of poverty . . . is not only an adaptation to a set of objective conditions of the larger society. Once it comes into existence, it tends to perpetuate itself from generation to generation because of its effect on the children. By the time slum children are age six or seven they have usually absorbed the basic values and attitudes of their subculture and are not psychologically geared to take full advantage of the changing conditions or increased opportunities that may occur in their lifetime" (Lewis, 1968, pp. 5–6).

Sociologist Liebow counters that new generations may resemble their parents and grandparents because they confront the same social-structural conditions and hardships. Children may very well share the values, beliefs, and attitudes of the larger society, but as they grow up and experience the same lack of socioeconomic opportunities as their parents, they may adopt the unique responses and attitudes that characterize the "subculture" of poverty.

In his classic 1967 book *Tally's Corner: A Study of Negro Streetcorner Men*, Liebow challenges the conclusions of Lewis: "the streetcorner man does not appear as a carrier of an independent cultural tradition. His behavior appears not so much as a way of realizing the distinctive goals and values of his own subculture, or of conforming to its models, but rather is his way of trying to achieve many of the goals and values of the larger society . . . Many similarities between the lower class Negro father and son (or mother and daughter) do not result from 'cultural transmission' but from the fact that the son goes out and independently experiences the same failures, in the same areas, and for much the same reasons as his father. What appears as a dynamic, self-sustaining cultural process is, in part at least, a relatively simple piece of social machine which turns out in rather mechanical fashion, independently produced look-alikes" (Liebow, 1967).

Whether policy makers believe that intergenerational transmission of poverty is cultural or social structural has important ramifications. Early adherents to the "culture of poverty" argument believed that the urban poor would have to be "rehabilitated culturally" before they would be able to advance in society (Banfield, 1970). If the urban poor are ingrained with unique cultural characteristics such as norms, values, and attitudes, then the implication is that *they*—not the economic structure—must change. Policy makers who believe structural obstacles account for the "inheritance" of poverty among generations would advocate efforts to change the opportunity structure, which would in turn change the values of the poor. We will return to the issue of poverty later in Chapter 7. Poverty was discussed here to illuminate a debate that has been central to sociology for many decades, the varying influence of culture and social structure on people's lives.

They are investing abroad as well as promoting growth at home. South Korea's production of steel has doubled in the last decade, and its shipbuilding and electronics industries are among the world's leaders. Singapore is becoming the major financial and commercial center of Southeast Asia. Taiwan is an important presence in the manufacturing and electronics industries. All these changes in the NICs have directly affected the United States, whose share of global steel production, for example, has dropped significantly over the past thirty years.

THE IMPACT OF GLOBALIZATION

In Chapter 1 it was pointed out that the chief focus of sociology has historically been the study of the industrialized societies. As sociologists, can we thus safely ignore the Third World, leaving this as the domain of anthropology? We certainly cannot. The industrialized and the Third World societies have developed in *interconnection* with one another and are today more closely related than ever before. Those of us living in the industrialized societies depend upon many raw materials and manufactured products coming from Third World countries to sustain our lives. Conversely, the economies of most Third World states depend upon trading networks that bind them to the industrialized countries. We can only fully understand the industrialized order against the backdrop of the Third World societies—in which, in fact, by far the greater proportion of the world's population lives.

Take a close look at the array of products on display the next time you walk into a local shop or supermarket. The diversity of goods we in the West have come to take for granted as available for anyone with the money to buy them depends on amazingly complex economic connections stretching across the world. The store products have been made in, or use ingredients or parts from, a hundred different countries. These parts must be regularly transported across the globe, and constant flows of information are necessary to coordinate the millions of daily transactions.

"Until our day," the anthropologist Peter Worsley has written, "human society has never existed" (1984), meaning that it is only in recent times that we can speak of social associations that span the earth. The world has become a single *social system*, as a result of growing ties of interdependence, both social and economic, that now affect virtually everyone. But it would be a mistake to think of this increasing interdependence, or **globalization**, of the world's societies simply as the growth of world unity. The globalizing of social relations should be understood primarily as the reordering of *time and distance* in social life. Our lives, in other words, are increasingly and quickly influenced by events happening well away from our everyday activities.

No society on earth any longer lives in isolation from others, and even in the wealthiest countries everyone is dependent on imported goods. In the United States, for example, nearly all TV sets sold are made and assembled abroad, mainly in the Far East. Another case in point is the automobile industry. Forty years ago, U.S. car production was greater than that of the whole rest of the world put together. Today the United States stands only third; more cars are made in both Europe and Japan. In 1955, imported cars accounted for less than 1 percent of American auto sales; this proportion had risen to 32 percent by 1993. Globalizing processes have brought many benefits to Americans: a much greater variety of goods and foodstuffs is available than ever before. At the same time, the fact that we are all now caught up in a much wider world has helped create some of the most serious problems American society faces.

Industrialized and Third World societies are radically different from the traditional types of social order that dominated world history for thousands of years up to some two centuries ago. The explorations that Western travelers undertook across the globe set off processes of change that have destroyed many premodern cultures. There remains enormous cultural diversity, however, both within and between societies. As human beings, we all share major traits in common—but we are also strongly influenced by the cultural values and habits of the societies in which we exist.

SUMMARY

1. *Culture* consists of the *values* held by a given group, the *norms* they follow, and the *material goods* they create.

2. The human species emerged as a result of a long process of biological evolution. Human beings are part of a group of higher mammals, the *primates*. There seems to be strong evidence that cultural development preceded, and probably shaped, the evolution of the human species.

3. *Sociobiology* is important primarily for its insights concerning animal behavior. The ideas of the sociobiologists about human social life are highly speculative. Our behavior is genetically influenced, but our genetic endowment probably conditions only the potentialities of our behavior, not the actual content of our activities.

4. Human beings have no *instincts* in the sense of complex patterns of unlearned behavior. A certain set of simple *reflexes*, plus a range of organic needs, are innate characteristics of the human being.

5. Forms of behavior found in all, or virtually all, cultures are called *cultural universals*. *Language*, the prohibition against incest, institutions of *marriage*, the *family*, *religion*, and *property* are the main types of cultural universals—but within these general categories there are many variations in values and modes of behavior between different societies.

6. Several types of premodern society can be distinguished. In *hunting and gathering societies*, people do not grow crops or keep livestock, but gain their livelihood from gathering plants and hunting animals. *Pastoral societies* are those that raise domesticated animals as their major source of subsistence. *Agrarian societies* depend upon the cultivation of fixed plots of land. Larger, more developed, urban societies form traditional states or civilizations.

7. The development of *industralized societies* and expansion of the West led to the conquest of many parts of the world, and the process of *colonialism* radically changed long-established social systems and cultures.

8. In industrialized societies, industrial production (whose techniques are also used in the production of food) is the main basis of the economy. *First World* industrialized countries include the nations of the West, plus Japan, Australia, and New Zealand. *Second World* countries are industrialized societies ruled by communist governments. *Third World* countries, in which most of the world's population live, are almost all formerly colonized areas. The majority of the population works in agricultural production, some of which is geared to world markets.

9. The increase in global communications and economic interdependence represents more than simply the growth of world unity. Time and distance are being reorganized in ways that bring us all closer together, but the new patterns of social relations that result are still subject to the same injustices and inequalities we have always struggled to understand and change.

Chapter Four

Culture, Society, and Child Socialization

Learn about socialization (including gender socialization), and know the most important agencies of socialization.

Socialization through the Life Course

Learn the various stages of the life course, and see the similarities and differences among different cultures.

Socialization and the Life Cycle

animals low down on the evolutionary scale, such as most species of insects, are capable of fending for themselves very soon after they are born, with little or no help from adults. There are no generations among the lower animals, because the behavior of the "young" is more or less identical to that of the "adults." As we go up the scale, however, these observations apply less and less; the higher animals have to *learn* appropriate ways of behavior. Among most of the more developed mammal species, the young are quite often completely helpless at birth and have to be cared for by their elders. The human infant is most dependent of all. A human child cannot survive unaided for at least the first four or five years of life.

Socialization is the process whereby the helpless infant gradually becomes a self-aware, knowledgeable person, skilled in the ways of the culture into which he or she is born. Socialization among the young allows for the more general phenomenon of social reproduction—the process whereby societies have structural continuity over time (a concept introduced in Chapter 1, "What Is Sociology?"). During the course of socialization, especially in the early years of life, children learn the ways of their elders, thereby perpetuating their values, norms, and social practices. All societies have characteristics that endure over long stretches of time, even though their members change as individuals are born and die. American society, for example, has many distinctive social and cultural characteristics that have persisted for generations—such as the fact that English is the main language spoken.

Socialization connects the different generations to one another (Turnbull, 1983). The birth of a child alters the lives of those who are responsible for its upbringing—who themselves therefore undergo new learning experiences. Parenting usually ties the activities of adults to children for the remainder of their lives. Older people still remain parents when they become grandparents, of course, thus forging another set of relationships connecting the different generations with each other. Although the process of cultural learning is much more intense in infancy and early childhood than later, learning and adjustment go on through the whole life cycle.

In the sections to follow, we shall continue the theme of "nature versus nurture" introduced in the previous chapter. We shall first analyze the development of the human individual from infancy to early childhood, identifying the main stages of change involved. A number of theoretical interpretations have been put forward by different writers about how and why children develop as they do, and we will describe and compare these, including theories that explain how we develop gender identities. Finally, we shall move on to discuss the main groups and social contexts that influence socialization during the various phases of individuals' lives.

CULTURE, SOCIETY, AND CHILD SOCIALIZATION

"Unsocialized" Children

What would children be like if, in some way or another, they were raised without the influence of human adults? Obviously no humane person could bring up a child away from social influence. There are, however, a number of much-discussed cases of children who have spent their early years away from normal human contact.

THE "WILD BOY OF AVEYRON"

On January 9, 1800, a strange creature emerged from the woods near the village of Saint-Serin in southern France. In spite of walking erect, he looked more animal than human, although he was soon identified as a boy of about eleven or twelve. He spoke only in shrill, strange-sounding cries. The boy apparently had no sense of personal hygiene, and relieved himself where and when he chose. He was brought to the attention of the local police and taken to a nearby orphanage. In the beginning he tried constantly to escape, and was only recaptured with some difficulty. He refused to tolerate wearing clothes, tearing them off as soon as they were put on him. No parents ever came forward to claim him.

The child was subjected to a thorough medical examination, which turned up no major physical abnormalities. On being shown a mirror, he seemingly saw an image, but did not recognize himself. On one occasion, he tried to reach through the mirror to seize a potato he saw in it. (The potato in fact was being held behind his head.) After several attempts, without turning his head, he took the potato by reaching back over his shoulder. A priest who was observing the boy from day to day, and who described this incident, wrote: "All these little details, and many others we could add prove that this child is not totally without intelligence, reflection, and reasoning power. However, we are obliged to say that, in every case not concerned with his natural needs or satisfying his appetite, one can perceive in him only animal behavior. If he has sensations, they give birth to no idea. He cannot even compare them with one another. One would think that there is no connection between his soul or mind and his body" (Shattuck, 1980; see also Lane, 1976).

Later the boy was moved to Paris and a systematic attempt was made to change him "from beast to human." The endeavor was only partly successful. He was toilet-trained, accepted wearing clothes, and learned to dress himself. Yet he was uninterested in toys or games, and was never able to learn or speak more than a few words. So far as anyone could tell, on the basis of detailed descriptions of his behavior and reactions, this was not because he was mentally retarded. He seemed either unwilling or unable to fully master human speech. He made little further progress, and died in 1828.

GENIE

It cannot be proved how long the wild boy of Aveyron lived on his own in the woods, or whether or not he suffered from some congenital defect that made it impossible for him to develop like a normal human being. However, there are more recent examples that reinforce some of the observations made about his behavior. One case is provided by the life of Genie, a California girl who was locked in a room from the age of about one-and-a-half until she was over thirteen (Curtiss, 1977). Genie's father kept his wife, who was going blind, more or less completely confined to the house. The main connection between the family and the outside world was through a teenage son, who attended school and did the shopping.

Genie had a hip defect from birth that prevented her from walking properly. Her father frequently beat her. When Genie was twenty months old, her father apparently decided she was retarded and put her away in a closed room with the curtains drawn and the door shut. She stayed there for the next eleven years, seeing the other members of the family only when they came to feed her. Genie had not been toilet-trained, and spent part of her time harnessed, naked, to an infant's potty seat. Sometimes at night she was removed, only to be put into another restraining garment, a sleeping bag within which her arms were imprisoned. Tied up in this way, she was also enclosed in an infant's crib with wire-mesh sides and a mesh cover overhead. Somehow, in these appalling circumstances she endured the hours, days, and years of her life. She had almost no opportunity to overhear any conversation between others in the house. If she attempted to make a noise, or to attract attention, her father would beat her. Her father never spoke to her, but instead made barking, animal-like sounds if she did anything to annoy him. She had no proper toys, or other objects with which to occupy her time.

In 1970 the mother escaped from the house, taking Genie with her. The condition of the girl came to the notice of a social worker, and she was placed in the rehabilitation ward of a children's hospital. When she was first admitted to the hospital, she could not stand erect, could not run, jump, or climb, and was only able to walk in a shuffling, clumsy fashion. She was described by a psychiatrist as "unsocialized, primitive, hardly human." Once in a rehabilitation ward, however, Genie made fairly rapid progress. She learned to eat quite normally, was toilet-trained, and tolerated being dressed like other children. Yet she was silent almost all of the time, except when she laughed, her laugh being high-pitched and unreal. She masturbated constantly in public situations, refusing to abandon the habit. Later she lived as a foster child in the home of one of the doctors from the hospital. She gradually came to develop a fairly wide vocabulary and could make a limited number of basic utterances. Yet her mastery of language never progressed beyond that of a three or four year old.

Genie's behavior was studied intensively and she was given a variety of tests over a period of some seven years. These seemed to indicate that she was neither retarded nor suffered from any other congenital defects. What seems to have happened to Genie, as to the wild boy of Aveyron, is that by the time she came into close human contact, she had grown beyond the age at which the learning of language and other human skills is readily accomplished by children. There is probably a "critical period" for the learning of language and other complex accomplishments, after which it is too late to master them fully. The wild boy and Genie provide some sense of what an "unsocialized" child would be like. Each retained many "nonhuman" responses. Yet, in spite of the deprivations they suffered, neither displayed any lasting viciousness. They responded quickly to others who treated them sympathetically, and were able to acquire a certain minimum level of ordinary human capabilities.

Of course, we have to be cautious about interpreting cases of this sort. In each of these examples it is possible that there was a mental abnormality that remained undiagnosed. Alternatively, the experiences to which the children were subjected may have inflicted psychological damage that prevented them from gaining the skills most children acquire at a much earlier age. Yet there is sufficient similarity between these two case histories, and others that have been recorded, to suggest how limited our faculties would be in the absence of an extended period of early socialization.

Theories of Child Development

One of the most distinctive features of human beings, compared to other animals, is that humans are *self-aware*. How should we understand the emergence of a sense of self—the awareness that the individual has a distinct identity, separate from others? During the first months of his life, the infant possesses little or no understanding of differences between human beings and material objects in his environment, and has no awareness of self. Children do not begin to use concepts like "I," "me," and "you" until the age of two or after. Only gradually do they then come to understand that others have distinct identities, consciousness, and needs separate from their own.

The problem of the emergence of self is a much-debated one, and is viewed rather differently in contrasting theoretical perspectives. To some extent, this is because the most prominent theories about child development emphasize different aspects of socialization. The American philosopher and sociologist George Herbert Mead gives attention mainly to how children learn to use the concepts of "I" and "me." The Swiss student of child behavior, Jean Piaget, worked on many aspects of child development, but his most well-known writings concern **cognition**—the ways in which children learn to *think* about themselves and their environment.

G. H. MEAD AND THE DEVELOPMENT OF SELF

Since Mead's ideas form the main basis of a general tradition of theoretical thinking, **symbolic interactionism,** they have had a very broad impact in sociology. Symbolic interactionism emphasizes that interaction between human beings takes place through symbols and the interpretation of meanings (see Chapter 1). But in addition, Mead's work provides an account of the main phases of child development, giving particular attention to the emergence of a sense of self.

According to Mead, infants and young children first of all develop as social beings by imitating the actions of those around them. Play is one way in which this takes place, and in their play small children often imitate what adults do. A small child will make mud pies, having seen an adult cooking, or dig with a spoon, having observed someone gardening. Children's play evolves from simple imitation to more complicated games in which a child of four or five years old will act out an adult role. Mead called this "taking the role of the other"—learning what it is like to be in the shoes of another person. It is only at this stage that children acquire a developed sense of self. Children achieve an understanding of themselves as separate agents—as a "me"—by seeing themselves through the eyes of others.

We achieve self-awareness, according to Mead, when we learn to distinguish the "me" from the "I." The "I" is the unsocialized infant, a bundle of spontaneous wants and desires. The "me," as Mead used the term, is the **social self.** Individuals develop **self-consciousness,** Mead argued, by coming to see themselves as others see them. A further stage of child development, according to Mead, occurs when the child is about eight or nine years old. This is the age at which children tend to take part in organized games, rather than unsystematic play. It is at this period that children begin to understand the overall *values* and *morality* according to which social life is conducted. To learn organized games, children must understand the rules of play, and notions of fairness and equal participation. Children at this stage learn to grasp what Mead termed the **generalized other**—the general values and moral rules involved in the culture in which they are developing.

JEAN PIAGET AND THE STAGES OF COGNITIVE DEVELOPMENT

Piaget placed great emphasis upon the child's active capability to make sense of the world. Children do not passively soak up information, but select and interpret what they see, hear, and feel in the world around them. Piaget described several distinct stages of cognitive development during which children learn to think about themselves and their environment. Each stage involves the acquisition of new skills and depends upon the successful completion of the preceding one.

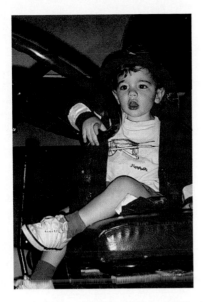

According to Mead, the early stages in a child's develop-ment are to imitate the actions of others and to act out the adult role such as "fireman."

Piaget called the first stage, which lasts from birth up to about age two, the **sensorimotor stage,** because infants learn mainly by touching objects, manipulating them, and physically exploring their environment. Until about age four months or so, infants cannot differentiate themselves from their environment. For example, a child will not realize that her own movements cause the sides of her crib to rattle. Objects are not differentiated from persons, and the infant is unaware that anything exists outside her range of vision. Infants gradually learn to distinguish people from objects, coming to see that both have an existence independent of their immediate perceptions. The main accomplishment of this stage is that by its close children understand their environment to have distinct and stable properties.

The next phase, called the **preoperational stage,** is the one to which Piaget devoted the bulk of his researches. This stage lasts from ages two to seven. During the course of it, children acquire a mastery of language and become able to use words to represent objects and images in a symbolic fashion. A four-year-old might use a sweeping hand, for example, to represent the concept "airplane." Piaget termed the stage "preoperational" because children are not yet able to

use their developing mental capabilities systematically. Children in this stage are **egocentric.** As Piaget used it, this concept does not refer to selfishness, but to the tendency of the child to interpret the world exclusively in terms of his own position. A child during this period does not understand, for instance, that others see objects from a different perspective to his own. Holding a book upright, the child may ask about a picture in it, not realizing that the other person sitting opposite can only see the back of the book.

Children at the preoperational stage are not able to hold connected conversations with another. In egocentric speech, what each child says is more or less unrelated to what the other speaker said. Children talk together, but not *to* one another in the same sense as adults. During this phase of development, children have no general understanding of categories of thought that adults tend to take for granted: concepts such as causality, speed, weight, or number. Even if the child sees water poured from a tall, thin container into a shorter, wider one, she will not understand that the volume of water remains the same—and conclude rather that there is less water because the water level is lower.

A third period, the **concrete operational stage,** lasts from age seven to eleven. During this phase, children master abstract, logical notions. They are able to handle ideas such as causality without much difficulty. A child at this stage of development will recognize the false reasoning involved in the idea that the wide container holds less water than the thin, narrow one, even though the water levels are different. She becomes capable of carrying out the mathematical operations of multiplying, dividing, and subtracting. Children by this stage are much less egocentric. In the preoperational stage, if a girl is asked, "How many sisters do you have?" she may correctly answer "one." But if asked, "How many sisters does your sister have?" she will probably answer "none," because she cannot see herself from the point of view of her sister. The concrete operational child is able to answer such a question with ease.

The years from eleven to fifteen cover what Piaget called the **formal operational stage.** During adolescence, the developing child becomes able to grasp highly abstract and hypothetical ideas. When faced with a problem, children at this stage are able to review all the possible ways of solving it and go through

KEY CONCEPTS IN REVIEW

Symbolic interactionism analyzes human interactions in terms of symbols and the interpretation of meanings. The crucial developmental stage for Mead is when children distinguish the "I" from the "me." The "I" is unsocialized, while the "me" is the **social self. Self-consciousness** is achieved by individuals when they see themselves as others view them. The next crucial stage occurs when children learn the **generalized other**, the values and norms of the culture in which they live.

Piaget stresses cognition, or the child's active capacity to make sense of the world. The first stage is the **sensorimotor stage**, where learning occurs through direct contacts with the outside world. In the **preoperational stage**, the child learns language and symbolic representation. At this stage, children are **egocentric** (*not* selfish) since they see the world only from their own point of view. The **concrete operational stage** is when the child learns to master abstractions and logical notions. The final, **formal operational stage** is not achieved by every adult since it depends partly on schooling. According to Piaget, each stage entails completing the previous one and acquiring new cognitive skills.

them theoretically in order to reach a solution. The young person at the formal operational stage is able to understand why some questions are trick ones. To the question, "What creatures are both poodles and dogs?" the individual might not be able to give the correct reply, but will understand why the answer "poodles" is right and appreciate the humor in it.

According to Piaget, the first three stages of development are universal; but not all adults reach the formal operational stage. The development of formal operational thought depends in part upon processes of schooling. Adults of limited educational attainment tend to continue to think in more concrete terms and retain large traces of egocentricism.

Agencies of Socialization

We can refer to the groups or social contexts within which significant processes of socialization occur as **agencies of socialization.** In all cultures, the **family** is the main socializing agency of the child during infancy. But at later stages of an individual's life, many other socializing agencies come into play.

The Family

Since family systems vary widely, the range of contacts that the infant experiences is by no means standard across cultures. The mother everywhere is normally the most important individual in the child's early life but the nature of the relationships established between mothers and their children is influenced by the form and regularity of their contact. This is, in turn, conditioned by the character of family institutions and their relation to other groups in society.

In modern societies, most early socialization occurs within a small-scale family context. The majority of American children spend their early years within a domestic unit containing mother, father, and perhaps one or two other children. In many other cultures, by contrast, aunts, uncles, and grandchildren are often part of a single household and serve as caretakers even for very young infants. Yet within American society there are many variations in the nature of family contexts. Some children are brought up in single-parent households; some are cared for by two mothering and fathering agents (divorced parents and stepparents). A high proportion of women with families are now employed outside the home and return to their paid work relatively soon after the births of their children. In spite of these variations, the family normally remains the major agency of socialization from infancy to adolescence and beyond—in a sequence of development connecting the generations.

Families have varying "locations" within the overall institutions of a society. In most traditional societies, the family into which a person was born largely determined the individual's social position for the rest of his or her life. In modern societies, social position is not inherited at birth in this way, yet the region and social class of the family into which an individual is born affects patterns of socialization quite distinctly. Children pick up ways of behavior characteristic of their parents or others in their neighborhood or community.

Varying patterns of child rearing and discipline, together with contrasting values and expectations, are found in different sectors of large-scale societies. It is easy to understand the influence of different types of family background if we think of what life is like, say, for a child growing up in a poor black family living in a run-down city neighborhood, compared to one born into an affluent white family living in an all-white suburb (Kohn, 1977).

Peer relationships are important agencies of socialization, and they can long outlast childhood.

Of course, few if any children simply take over unquestioningly the outlook of their parents. This is especially true in the modern world, in which change is so pervasive. Moreover, the very existence of a range of socializing agencies in modern societies leads to many divergences between the outlooks of children, adolescents, and the parental generation.

SCHOOLS

Another important socializing agency is the school. Schooling is a formal process: students pursue a definite curriculum of subjects. Yet schools are agencies of socialization in more subtle respects. Children are expected to be quiet in class, be punctual at lessons, and observe rules of school discipline. They are required to accept and respond to the authority of the teaching staff. Reactions of teachers also affect the expectations children have of themselves. These expectations in turn become linked to their job experience when they leave school. Peer groups are often formed at school, and the system of keeping children in classes according to age reinforces their impact.

PEER RELATIONSHIPS

Another socializing agency is the **peer group**. Peer groups consist of children of a similar age. In some cultures, particularly small traditional societies, peer groups are formalized as **age-grades** (normally confined to males). There are often specific ceremonies or rites that mark the transition of men from one age-grade to another. Those within a particular age-grade generally maintain close and friendly connections throughout their lives. A typical set of age-grades consists of childhood, junior warriorhood, senior warriorhood, junior elderhood, and senior elderhood. Men move through these grades not as individuals, but as whole groups.

The family's importance in socialization is obvious, since the experience of the infant and young child is shaped more or less exclusively within it. It is less apparent, especially to those of us living in Western societies, how significant peer groups are. Yet even without formal age-grades, children over four or five usually spend a great deal of time in the company of friends the same age. Given the high proportion of women now in the workforce, whose young children play together in day-care centers, peer relations are even more important today than before (Corsaro, 1997; Harris, 1998).

In her book *Gender Play,* Barrie Thorne, a sociologist now at the University of California, Berkeley, looked at socialization in this way. As others had before her, she wanted to understand how children come to know what it means to be male and female (you will learn three classic theories of gender socialization later in this chapter in "The Sociological Debate"). Rather than seeing children as passively learning the meaning of gender from their parents and teachers, she looked at the way in which children actively create and recreate the meaning of gender in their interactions with each other. The social activities that schoolchildren do together can be as important as other agents for their socialization.

Thorne spent two years observing fourth and fifth graders at two schools in Michigan and California, sitting in the classroom with them and observing their activities outside the classroom. She watched games such as "chase and kiss," "cooties," and "goin' with" and teasing to learn how children construct and experience gender meanings in the classroom and on the playground.

Thorne found that peer groups have a great influence on gender socialization, particularly as children talk about their changing bodies, a subject of great fascination. The social context created by these children determined whether a child's bodily change was couched with embarrassment or worn with pride. As Thorne observed, "If the most popular women started menstruating or wearing bras (even if they didn't need to), then other girls wanted these changes too. But if the popular didn't wear bras and hadn't . . . gotten their periods, then these developments were viewed as less desirable."

Thorne's research is a powerful reminder that children are social actors who help create their social world and influence their own socialization (Thorne, 1993). Still, the impact of societal and cultural influences is tremendous, since the activities that children pursue and the values they hold are determined by influences such as their families and the media.

Peer relations are likely to have a significant impact beyond childhood and adolescence. Informal groups of people of similar ages, at work and in other situations, are usually of enduring importance in shaping individuals' attitudes and behavior.

THE MASS MEDIA

Newspapers, periodicals, and journals flourished in the West from the early 1800s onward, but they were confined to a fairly small readership. It was not until a century later that such printed materials became part

KEY CONCEPTS IN REVIEW

Socialization is the process by which, through contact with other human beings, one becomes a self-aware, knowledgeable human being, skilled in the ways of a given culture and environment.

Agencies of socialization are structured groups or contexts within which significant processes of socialization occur. In all cultures, the family is the principal socializing agency of the child during infancy. Other influences include peer groups, schools, the mass media, and the work environment.

These agencies and groups also influence **gender socialization,** the learning of male versus female roles.

Peer groups are social groups with similar age and social background. When they are formalized, they are called **age-grades.**

of the daily experience of millions of people, influencing their attitudes and opinions. The spread of **mass media** involving printed documents was soon accompanied by electronic communication—radio, television, records, and videos. American children spend the equivalent of almost a hundred schooldays per year watching television.

Much research has been done to assess the effects of television programs on the audiences they reach, particularly children. Perhaps the most commonly researched topic is the impact of television on propensities to crime and violence.

The most extensive studies are those carried out by George Gerbner and his collaborators, who have analyzed samples of prime-time and weekend daytime TV for all the major American networks each year since 1967. The number and frequency of violent acts and episodes are charted for a range of programs. Violence is defined as physical force directed against the self or others, in which physical harm or death occurs. Television drama emerges as highly violent in character. On average, 80 percent of programs contain violence, with a rate of 7.5 violent episodes per hour. Children's programs show even higher levels of violence, although killing is less commonly portrayed. Cartoons depict the highest number of violent acts and episodes of any type of television program (Gerbner, 1985).

In general, research on the effects of television upon audiences has tended to treat children as passive and undiscriminating in their reactions to what they see. Robert Hodge and David Tripp (1986) emphasized that children's responses to TV involve interpreting, or "reading," what they see, not just registering the content of programs. They suggested that most research has not taken account of the complexity of children's mental processes. TV watching, even of trivial programs, is not an inherently low-level intellectual activity; children read programs by relating them to other systems of meaning in their everyday lives. According to Hodge and Tripp, it is not the violence alone that has effects upon behavior, but rather the general framework of attitudes within which it is both presented and read.

In recent years home video games have come into widespread use. In his book *Video Kids* (1991), Eugene Provenzo analyzes the impact of Nintendo. There are currently some 19 million Nintendo and

Most of you likely have played video games as children (or still do!). How would you assess the impact of video games on your socialization?

Sega games in the United States and many more in other countries. Nearly all are owned and operated by children. Social codes and traditions have developed based on the games and their characters. Of the thirty best-selling toys in the United States in 1990, twenty five were either video games or video equipment. The games are often directly linked to the characters or stories in films and TV programs; in turn, television programming has been based on Nintendo games. Video games, Provenzo concludes, have become a key part of the culture and experience of childhood today.

But is this impact a negative one? It is doubtful that a child's involvement with Nintendo harms her achievement at school. The effects of video games are likely to be governed by other influences on school performance. In other words, where there are strong pressures deflecting students from an interest in their schoolwork, absorption with TV or video pursuits will tend to reinforce these attitudes. Video games and TV then can become a refuge from a disliked school environment.

But it is also possible that video games can act to develop skills that might be relevant both to formal education and also to wider participation in a society that depends increasingly on electronic communication. According to Marsha Kinder, her son Victor's adeptness at Nintendo transferred fruitfully to other spheres. For example, the better he became at video games, the more interested and skillful he was at drawing cartoons. Patricia Greenfield has argued that "video games are the first example of a computer technology that is having a socializing effect on the next generation on a mass scale, and even on a worldwide basis" (Greenfield, 1993).

The mass media are an important influence upon socialization, in all forms of society. There are few societies in current times, even among the more traditional cultures, that remain completely untouched by the media. Electronic communication is accessible even to those who are unable to read and write, and in the most impoverished parts of the world it is common to find people owning radios and television sets.

WORK

Work is in all cultures an important setting within which socialization processes operate, although it is only in industrial societies that large numbers of people go "out to work"—that is, go each day to places of work separate from the home. In traditional communities many people farmed the land close to where they lived, or had workshops in their dwellings. "Work" in such communities was not so clearly dis-

How would you describe this child—as sweet and delicate (Beth) or sturdy and tough (Adam)? (The child's sex is revealed on page 89.)

tinct from other activities as it is for most members of the work force in the modern West. In the industrialized countries, going "out to work" for the first time ordinarily marks a much greater transition in an individual's life than entering work in traditional societies. The work environment often poses unfamiliar demands, perhaps calling for major adjustments in the person's outlook or behavior.

Gender Socialization

These agencies of socialization also play an important role in how children learn **gender roles.** Let's now turn to the study of **gender socialization,** the learning of gender roles through social factors such as the family and the media.

REACTIONS OF PARENTS AND ADULTS

Many studies have been carried out on the degree to which gender differences are the result of social influences. Studies of mother-infant interaction show differences in the treatment of boys and girls even when parents believe their reactions to both are the same. Adults asked to assess the personality of a baby give different answers according to whether or not they believe the child to be a girl or a boy. In one experiment, five young mothers were observed in interaction with a six-month-old called Beth. They tended to smile at her often and offer her dolls to play with. She was seen as "sweet," having a "soft cry." The reaction of a second group of mothers to a child the same age, named Adam, was noticeably different. The baby was likely to be offered a train or other "male toys" to play with. Beth and Adam were actually the same child, dressed in different clothes (Will, Self, and Datan, 1976).

GENDER LEARNING

Gender learning by infants is almost certainly unconscious. Before children can accurately label themselves as either a boy or a girl, they receive a range of preverbal cues. For instance, male and female adults usu-

Even for parents determined to raise children free of gender socialization, the prevailing culture of cooking for girls and Little League for boys is hard to combat.

ally handle infants differently. The cosmetics women use contain different scents from those the baby might learn to associate with males. Systematic differences in dress, hair style, and so on provide visual cues for the infant in the learning process. By age two, children have a partial understanding of what gender is. They know whether they are boys or girls, and they can usually categorize others accurately. Not until five or six, however, does a child know that a person's gender does not change, that everyone has gender, and that sex differences between girls and boys are anatomically based.

The toys, picture books, and television programs with which young children come into contact all tend to emphasize differences between male and female attributes. Toy stores and mail-order catalogs usually categorize their products by gender. Even some toys that seem neutral in terms of gender are not so in practice. For example, toy kittens and rabbits are recommended for girls, while lions and tigers are seen as more appropriate for boys.

Vanda Lucia Zammuner studied the toy preferences of children aged between seven and ten in Italy and Holland (Zammuner, 1986). Children's attitudes toward a variety of toys were analyzed; stereotypically masculine and feminine toys as well as toys presumed not to be sex-typed were included. Both the children and their parents were asked to assess which toys were suitable for boys and which for girls. There was close agreement between the adults and children. On average, the Italian children chose sex-differentiated toys to play with more often than the Dutch children—a finding that conformed to expectations, since Italian culture tends to hold a more traditional view of gender divisions than Dutch society. As in other studies, girls from both societies chose gender-neutral or boys' toys to play with far more than boys wanted to play with girls' toys.

STORYBOOKS AND TELEVISION

Over twenty years ago, Lenore Weitzman and her colleagues carried out an analysis of gender roles in some of the most widely used preschool children's books and found several clear differences in gender roles (Weitzman et al., 1972). Males played a much larger part in the stories and pictures than females, outnumbering females by a ratio of 11 to 1. Including animals with gender identities, the ratio was 95 to 1. The activities of males and females also differed. The males engaged in adventurous pursuits and outdoor activities demanding independence and strength. Where girls did appear, they were portrayed as passive and

THE SOCIOLOGICAL DEBATE

GENDER SOCIALIZATION

FREUD'S THEORY

Perhaps the most influential—and controversial—theory of the emergence of gender identity is that of Sigmund Freud. According to Freud, the learning of gender differences in infants and young children is centered on the possession or absence of the penis. "I have a penis" is equivalent to "I am a boy," while "I am a girl" is equivalent to "I lack a penis." Freud is careful to say that it is not just the anatomical distinctions that matter here; the possession or absence of the penis is symbolic of masculinity and femininity.

At around age four or five, the theory goes, a boy feels threatened by the discipline and autonomy his father demands of him, fantasizing that the father wishes to remove his penis. Partly consciously, but mostly on an unconscious level, the boy recognizes the father as a rival for the affections of his mother. In repressing erotic feelings toward the mother and accepting the father as a superior being, the boy identifies with the father and becomes aware of his male identity. The boy gives up his love for his mother out of an unconscious fear of castration by his father. Girls, on the other hand, supposedly suffer from "penis envy" because they do not possess the visible organ that distinguishes boys. The mother becomes devalued in the little girl's eyes, because she is also seen to lack a penis and to be unable to provide one. When the girl identifies with the mother, she takes over the submissive attitude involved in the recognition of being "second best."

Once this phase is over, the child has learned to repress his erotic feelings. The period from about five years old to puberty, according to Freud, is one of latency—sexual activities tend to be suspended until the biological changes involved in puberty reactivate erotic desires in a direct way. The latency period, covering the early and middle years of school, is the time at which same-sex peer groups are most important in the child's life.

Major objections have been raised against Freud's views, particularly by feminists, but also by many other authors (Mitchell, 1975; Coward, 1984). First, Freud seems to identify gender identity too closely with genital awareness; other, more subtle factors are surely involved. Second, the theory seems to depend on the notion that the penis is superior to the vagina, which is thought of as just a lack of the male organ. Yet why shouldn't the female genitals be considered superior to those of the male? Third, Freud treats the father as the primary disciplining agent, whereas in many cultures the mother plays the more significant part in the imposition of discipline. Fourth, Freud believes that gender learning is concentrated at age four or five. Most later authors have emphasized the importance of earlier learning, beginning in infancy.

CHODOROW'S THEORY

While many writers have made use of Freud's approach in studying gender development, they have usually modified it in major respects. An important example is the sociologist Nancy Chodorow (1978, 1988). Chodorow argues that learning to feel male or female derives from the infant's attachment to his parents from an early age. She places much more emphasis than Freud does on the importance of the mother rather than the father. Children tend to become emotionally involved with the mother, since she is easily the most dominant influence in their early lives. This attachment has at some point to be broken in order to achieve a separate sense of self—the child is required to become less closely dependent.

Chodorow argues that the breaking process occurs in a different way for boys and girls. Girls remain closer to the mother—able, for example, to go on hugging and kissing her and imitating what she does. Because there is no sharp break from the mother, the girl, and later the adult woman, develops a sense of self that is more continuous with other people. Her identity is more likely to be merged with or dependent on another's: first her mother, later a man. In Chodorow's view, this tends to produce characteristics of sensitivity and emotional compassion in women.

Boys gain a sense of self via a more radical rejection of their original closeness to the mother, forging their understanding of masculinity from what is not feminine. They learn not to be "sissies" or "mama's boys." As a result, boys are relatively unskilled in relating closely to others; they develop more analytical ways of looking at the world. They take a more active view of their lives, emphasizing achievement, but they have repressed their ability to understand their own feelings and those of others.

To some extent, Chodorow reverses Freud's emphasis. Masculinity, rather than femininity, is defined by a loss, the forfeiting of continuing close attachment to the mother. Male identity is formed through separation; thus, men later in life unconsciously feel that their identity is endangered if they become involved in close emotional relationships with others. Women, on the other hand, feel that the absence of a close relation to another person threatens their self-esteem. These patterns are passed on from generation to generation, because of the primary role women play in the early socialization of children. Women express and define themselves mainly in terms of relationships. Men have repressed these needs, and adopt a more manipulative stance toward the world.

Chodorow's work has met with various criticisms. Janet Sayers, for example, has suggested that Chodorow does not explain the struggle of women, particularly in current times, to become autonomous, independent beings (Sayers, 1986). Women (and men), she points out, are more contradictory in their psychological makeup than Chodorow's theory suggests. Femininity may conceal feelings of aggressiveness or assertiveness, which are revealed only obliquely or in certain contexts (Brennan, 1988). Chodorow has also been criticized for her narrow conception of the family, one based on a white, middle-class model. What happens, for example, in one-parent households or, as in many Chicano communities, families where children are cared for by more than one adult (Segura and Pierce, 1993)?

These criticisms don't undermine Chodorow's ideas, which remain important. They teach us a good deal about the nature of femininity, and they help us to understand the origins of what has been called male inexpressiveness—the difficulty men have in revealing their feelings to others (Balswick, 1983).

GILLIGAN'S THEORY

Carol Gilligan (1982) has further developed Chodorow's analysis. Her work concentrates on the images adult women and men have of themselves and their attainments. Women, she agrees with Chodorow, define themselves in terms of personal relationships, and judge their achievements by reference to the ability to care for others. Women's place in the lives of men is traditionally that of caretaker and helpmate. But the qualities developed in these tasks are frequently devalued by men, who see their own emphasis upon individual achievement as the only form of "success." Concern with relationships on the part of women appears to them as a weakness rather than as the strength that in fact it is.

Gilligan carried out intensive interviews with about two hundred American women and men of varying ages and social backgrounds. She asked all of the interviewees a range of questions concerning their moral outlook and conceptions of self. Consistent differences emerged between the views of the women and the men. For instance, the interviewees were asked, "What does it mean to say something is morally right or wrong?" Whereas the men tended to respond to this question by mentioning abstract ideals of duty, justice, and individual freedom, the women persistently raised the theme of helping others. Thus a female college student answered the question in the following way:

"It [morality] has to do with responsibilities and obligations and values, mainly values. . . . In my life situation I relate morality with interpersonal relationships that have to do with respect for the other person and myself." The interviewer then asked: "Why respect other people?" receiving the answer, "Because they have a consciousness or feelings that can be hurt, an awareness that can be hurt." (Gilligan, 1982)

The women were more tentative in their moral judgments than the men, seeing possible contradictions between following a strict moral code and avoiding harming others. Gilligan suggests that this outlook reflects the traditional situation of women, anchored in caring relationships, rather than in the "outward-looking" attitudes of men. Women have in the past deferred to the judgments of men, while being aware that they have qualities that most men lack. Their views of themselves are based upon successfully fulfilling the needs of others, rather than pride in individual achievement (Gilligan, 1982).

confined mostly to indoor activities. Girls cooked and cleaned for the males, or awaited their return. Much the same was true of the adult men and women represented in the storybooks. Women who were not wives and mothers were imaginary creatures like witches or fairy godmothers. There was not a single woman in all the books analyzed who held an occupation outside the home. By contrast, the men were depicted as fighters, policemen, judges, kings, and so forth.

More recent research suggests that things have changed somewhat, but that the large bulk of children's literature remains much the same (Davies, 1991). Fairy tales, for example, embody traditional attitudes toward gender and toward the sorts of aims and ambitions girls and boys are expected to have. "Some day my prince will come"—in versions of fairy tales from several centuries ago, this usually implied that a girl from a poor family might dream of wealth and fortune. Today, its meaning has become more closely tied to the ideals of romantic love. Some feminists have tried to rewrite some of the most celebrated fairy tales, reversing their usual emphases: "I really didn't notice that he had a funny nose. And he certainly looked better all dressed up in fancy clothes. He's not nearly as attractive as he seemed the other night. So I think I'll just pretend that this glass slipper feels too tight" (Viorst, 1986). Like this version of "Cinderella," however, these rewrites are found mainly in books directed to adult audiences and have hardly affected the tales told in innumerable children's books.

Although there are some notable exceptions, analyses of television programs designed for children conform to the findings about children's books. Studies of the most frequently watched cartoons show that most of the leading figures are male, and that males dominate the active pursuits. Similar images are found in the commercials that appear throughout the programs.

The Difficulty of Nonsexist Child Rearing

June Statham studied the experiences of a group of parents committed to nonsexist child rearing. Thirty adults in eighteen families were involved in the research, which included children aged six months to twelve years. The parents were of middle-class back-ground, mostly involved in academic work as teachers or professors. Statham found that most of the parents did not simply try to modify traditional sex roles by seeking to make girls more like boys, but wanted to foster new combinations of the feminine and masculine. They wished boys to be more sensitive to others' feelings and capable of expressing warmth, while girls were encouraged to seek opportunities for learning and self-advancement. All the parents found existing patterns of gender learning difficult to combat. They were reasonably successful at persuading the children to play with nongender-typed toys, but even this proved more difficult than many of them had expected. One mother commented to the researcher:

> If you walk into a toy shop, it's full of war toys for boys and domestic toys for girls, and it sums up society the way it is. This is the way children are being socialized: it's all right for boys to be taught to kill and hurt, and I think it's terrible, it makes me feel sick. I try not to go into toy shops, I feel so angry.

Practically all the children in fact possessed, and played with, gender-typed toys, given to them by relatives.

There are now some storybooks available with strong, independent girls as the main characters, but few depict boys in nontraditional roles. A mother of a five-year-old boy told of her son's reaction when she reversed the sexes of the characters in a story she read to him:

> In fact he was a bit upset when I went through a book which has a boy and a girl in very traditional roles, and changed all the he's to she's and she's to he's. When I first started doing that, he was inclined to say "you don't like boys, you only like girls." I had to explain that that wasn't true at all, it's just that there's not enough written about girls. (Statham, 1986)

Clearly, gender socialization is very powerful, and challenges to it can be upsetting. Once a gender is "assigned," society expects individuals to act like "females" and "males." It is in the practices of everyday life that these expectations are fulfilled and reproduced (Bourdieu, 1990; Lorber, 1994).

SOCIALIZATION THROUGH THE LIFE COURSE

The various transitions through which individuals pass during their lives seem at first sight to be biologically fixed—from childhood to adulthood and eventually to death. But the stages of the human **life course** are social as well as biological in nature. They are influenced by cultural differences and also by the material circumstances of people's lives in given types of society. For example, in the modern West, death is usually thought of in relation to old age, because most people enjoy a life span of seventy years or more. In traditional societies of the past, however, more people died in younger age-groups than survived to old age.

Childhood

To people living in modern societies, childhood is a clear and distinct stage of life. Children are distinct from babies or toddlers; childhood intervenes between infancy and the teen years. Yet the concept of childhood, like so many other aspects of social life today, has only come into being over the past two or three centuries. In earlier societies, the young moved directly from a lengthy infancy into working roles within the community. The French historian Philippe Ariès has argued that "childhood," as a separate phase of development, did not exist in medieval times (Ariès, 1965). In the paintings of medieval Europe, children were portrayed as little adults, with mature faces and the same style of dress as their elders. Children took part in the same work and play activities as adults, rather than the childhood games we now take for granted.

Right up to the twentieth century, in the United States and most other Western countries, children were put to work at what now seems a very early age. There are countries in the world today, in fact, in which young children are engaged in full-time work, sometimes in physically demanding circumstances (coal mines, for example). The ideas that children have distinctive rights and that the use of child labor is morally repugnant are quite recent developments.

Because of the long period of childhood that we recognize today, societies now are in some respects more child centered than traditional ones. But a child-centered society, it must be emphasized, is not one where all children experience love and care from parents or other adults. The physical and sexual abuse of children is a commonplace feature of family life in present-day society, although the full extent of such abuse has only recently come to light. Child abuse has clear connections with what seems to us today like the frequent mistreatment of children in premodern Europe.

It seems possible that as a result of changes currently occurring in modern societies, the separate character of childhood is diminishing once more. Some observers have suggested that children now grow up so fast that this is in fact the case. They point out that even small children may watch the same television programs as adults, thereby becoming much more familiar early on with the adult world than did preceding generations.

The Teenager

The idea of the "teenager," so familiar to us today, also didn't exist until recently. The biological changes involved in puberty (the point at which a person becomes capable of adult sexual activity and reproduction) are universal. Yet in many cultures, these do not produce the degree of turmoil and uncertainty often

The movie Sixteen Candles *depicts a teenager in the midst of adapting to the new demands of young adulthood.*

The child pictured on page 84 is a girl.

JAPANESE AND AMERICAN TEENAGERS

Studies comparing socialization in varying cultural settings show some interesting contrasts. For example, the idea of the teen years as an extended period of transition between childhood and adulthood emerged in America before it did in Japan. In fact, the Japanese term, *cheenayja*, is an adaptation of the American one. In premodern Japan, the movement from childhood to adulthood occurred in an instant, because it happened as part of an age-grade system (one that included girls). A child would become as an adult when he participated in a special rite. Japanese boys became adults at some point between ages eleven and sixteen, depending on their social rank. The parallel ceremony at which girls were recognized as women was the *kami* age, the age at which their hair was worn up rather than down.

Just as in most other nonmodern societies, including those of medieval Europe, young people in Japan knew who they would be and what they would be doing when they became adults. The teenage years weren't a time to experiment. Japanese children were schooled to follow closely the ways of their parents, to whom they owed strict obedience; family norms emphasizing the duties of children toward their parents were very strong.

Such norms have endured to the present day, but they

have also come under strain with the high pace of industrial development in contemporary Japan. So are Japanese teenagers now just like American ones? Mary White, a sociologist at Boston University, attempted to answer this question. White interviewed one hundred teens in each culture over a period of three years, trying to gain an in-depth view of their attitudes toward sexuality, school, friendship, and parents (White, 1993). She found big differences between the Japanese and American teenagers, but also came up with unexpected conclusions about both. In neither culture are most teenagers the rebels she expected to find. Instead,

found among young people in modern societies. In cultures that foster age-grades, for example, with distinct ceremonials that signal a person's transition to adulthood, the process of psychosexual development generally seems easier to negotiate. Adolescents in such societies have less to "unlearn" since the pace of change is slower. There is a time when children in Western societies are required to be children no longer: to put away their toys and break with childish pursuits. In traditional cultures, where children are already working alongside adults, this process of unlearning is normally much less severe.

In Western societies, teenagers are "betwixt and between": they often try to follow adult ways, but they are treated in law as children. They may wish to go to work, but they are constrained to stay in school. Teenagers live in between childhood and adulthood, growing up in a society subject to continuous change.

she found a fairly high degree of conformity to wider cultural ideas and an expressed respect for parents in both countries.

What the adults say of their teenage offspring in Japan and the United States is much the same: "Why don't you listen more to what I say?" "When I was your age . . . ." The Japanese and American teens also echo each other in some ways: "Do you like me?" "What should I aim for in my life?" "We're cool, but they aren't." Pop music, films, and videos figure large in the experience of both—as does at least a surface sexual knowledgeability, since from an early age in both cultures sexual information, including warnings about sexual disease, is widespread.

The Japanese teenagers, however, come out well ahead of the Americans in terms of school achievements: 95 percent of Japanese teenagers reach a level in academic tests met by only the top 5 percent of young Americans. And while both express respect for parents, the Japanese teenagers remain much closer to theirs than do most of the American teenagers.

The Japanese teenagers are certainly interested in sex but placed it at the bottom of a list of priorities White presented them with; the Americans put it at the top. Teenagers in Japan are nonetheless sexually very active, probably even more so than their American counterparts. Two-thirds of Japanese girls by age fifteen are sexually active. White reports that they are, by Western standards, amazingly forthcoming about their sexual fantasies and practices; nearly 90 percent of the Japanese girls reported that they masturbate twice or more a week.

The Japanese separate clearly three areas of sexuality that are more mixed up for the American teenagers: physical passion, socially approved pairing or marriage, and roman-

tic fantasies. "Love marriages," in which two people establish a relationship on the basis of emotional and sexual attraction, are now common in Japan. However, they are often the result of an initial introduction of suitable partners arranged by parents, followed by falling in love prior to marriage. Even the most sexually experienced young person may continue to prefer to have a mature adult arrange an appropriate marriage.

Japanese teenagers often stress that love should grow in marriage, rather than being the basis of choosing a partner in the first place. The sexual activity of young girls tends to involve several older boys and not be bound up with dating. White quotes as typical of young, unmarried Japanese women a respondent who was in her early twenties when interviewed. She first had sexual intercourse at fifteen—like three-quarters of her friends—and since had accumulated many "sex friends." These were not *boifurends* (boyfriends), a relationship that implies emotional attachment. She said, "I do it [have sex] because it is fun. However, marriage is a totally different story, you know. Marriage should be more realistic and practical" (White, 1993).

Young Adulthood

Young adulthood seems increasingly to be a specific stage in personal and sexual development in modern societies (Goldschneider and Waite, 1991). Particularly among more affluent groups, people in their early twenties are taking the time to travel and explore sexual, political, and religious affiliations. The importance of this postponement is likely to grow, given the extended period of education many people now undergo.

Mature Adulthood

Most young adults in the West today can look forward to a life stretching right through to old age. In premodern times, few could anticipate such a future

KEY CONCEPTS IN REVIEW

Socialization occurs throughout the **life course**, the various transitions individuals experience during their lives. The variation across cultures of childhood, adolescence, and old age indicates that no stage of the life course is fixed and is instead influenced by social and cultural factors.

with much confidence. Death through sickness or injury was much more frequent among all age groups than it is today, and women in particular were at great risk because of the high rate of mortality in childbirth.

On the other hand, some of the strains we experience now were less pronounced in previous times. People usually maintained a closer connection with their parents and other kin than in today's more mobile populations, and the routines of work they followed were the same as those of their forebears. In current times, major uncertainties must be resolved in marriage, family life, and other social contexts. We have to "make" our own lives more than people did in the past. The creation of sexual and marital ties, for instance, now depends on individual initiative and selection, rather than being fixed by parents. This represents greater freedom for the individual, but the responsibility can also impose difficulties.

Keeping a forward-looking outlook in middle age has taken on a particular importance in modern societies. Most people do not expect to be doing the same thing all their lives, as was the case for the majority in traditional cultures. Individuals who have spent their lives in one career may find the level they have reached in middle age unsatisfying and further opportunities blocked. Women who have spent their early adulthood raising a family and whose children have left their home may feel themselves to be without any social value. The phenomenon of a "midlife crisis" is very real for many middle-aged people. A person may feel she has thrown away the opportunities that life had to offer, or she will never attain goals cherished since childhood. Yet growing older need not lead to

resignation or bleak despair; a release from childhood dreams can be liberating.

Old Age

In traditional societies, older people were normally accorded a great deal of respect. Among cultures that included age-grades, the elders usually had a major—often the final—say over matters of importance to the community. Within families, the authority of both men and women mostly increased with age. In industrialized societies, by contrast, older people tend to lack authority within both the family and the wider social community. Having retired from the labor force, they may be poorer than ever before in their lives. At the same time, there has been a great increase in the proportion of the population aged over sixty-five. In 1900, only one in thirty people in the United States was over sixty-five; the proportion today is one in eight and will likely rise to one in five by the year 2030 (U.S. Bureau of the Census, 1999). The same trend is found in all the industrially advanced countries.

Transition to the age-grade of elder in a traditional culture often marked the pinnacle of the status an individual could achieve. In modern societies, retirement tends to bring the opposite consequences. No longer living with their children and often having retired from paid work, older people may find it difficult to make the final period of their life rewarding. It used to be thought that those who successfully cope with old age do so by turning to their inner resources, becoming less interested in the material rewards that social life has to offer. While this may often be true, it seems likely that in a society in which many are physically healthy in old age, an outward-looking view will become more and more prevalent. Those in retirement might find renewal in what has been called the "third age," in which a new phase of education begins (see also Chapter 16 on the sociology of the body).

Socialization, Culture, and Individual Freedom

Since the cultural settings in which we are born and come to maturity so influence our behavior, it might appear that we are robbed of any individuality or free will. We might seem to be merely stamped into preset molds that society has prepared for us. Some sociologists do tend to write about socialization, and even about sociology more generally, as though this were

the case. Yet such a view is fundamentally mistaken. The fact that from birth to death we interact with others certainly conditions our personalities, the values we hold, and the behavior in which we engage. Yet socialization is also at the origin of our very individuality and freedom. In the course of socialization, each of us develops a sense of self-identity and the capacity for independent thought and action.

This point is easily illustrated by the example of learning language. None of us invent the language we learn as a child, and we are all constrained by fixed rules of linguistic usage. At the same time, however, understanding a language is one of the basic factors making possible our self-awareness and creativity. Without language, we would not be self-conscious beings, and we would live more or less wholly in the here and now. Mastery of language is necessary for the symbolic richness of human life, for awareness of our distinctive individual characteristics, and for the practical control of our lives.

SUMMARY

1. *Socialization* is the process whereby, through contact with other human beings, the helpless infant gradually becomes a self-aware, knowledgeable human being, skilled in the ways of the given culture and environment.

2. According to G. H. Mead, the child achieves an understanding of being a separate agent by seeing how others behave toward him or her in social contexts. At a later stage, entering into organized games, learning the rules of play, the child comes to understand "the *generalized other*"—general values and cultural rules.

3. Jean Piaget distinguishes several main stages in the development of the child's capability to make sense of the world. Each stage involves the acquisition of new cognitive skills and depends upon the successful completion of the preceding one. According to Piaget these stages of cognitive development are universal features of socialization.

4. *Agencies of socialization* are structured groups or

contexts within which significant processes of socialization occur. In all cultures, the *family* is the principal socializing agency of the child during infancy. Other influences include *peer groups, schools,* and the *mass media.*

5. The development of mass communications has enlarged the range of socializing agencies. The spread of mass printed media was later accompanied by the use of electronic communication. TV exerts a particularly powerful influence, reaching people of all ages at regular intervals every day.

6. *Gender socialization* begins virtually as soon as an infant is born. Even parents who believe they treat children equally tend to produce different responses to boys than girls. These differences are reinforced by many other cultural influences.

7. Socialization continues throughout the life cycle. At each distinct phase of life there are transitions to be made or crises to be overcome. This includes facing death as the termination of physical existence.

Chapter Five

Familiarize yourself with the study of everyday life.

Nonverbal Communication

Know the various forms of nonverbal communication.

Social Rules and Talk

Learn the research process of ethnomethodology, the study of our conversations and how we make sense of each other.

Face, Body, and Speech in Interaction

Recognize the different contexts of our social life and how they are used to convey or hide meaning. Also learn how our social actions are organized in time and space.

Interaction in Time and Space

Understand that interaction is situated, that it occurs in a particular place and for a particular length of time. See that the way we organize our social actions is not unique by learning how other cultures organize their social lives.

Linking Microsociology and Macrosociology

See how face-to-face interactions and broader features of society are closely related.

SOCIAL INTERACTION AND EVERYDAY LIFE

eric Schmitz, 34, is a personal trainer and fitness director at the Santa Barbara Athletic Club, an upscale health club. He has been employed at the gym since he graduated from the University of Wisconsin–Madison with a degree in Exercise Physiology in 1987.

Schmitz knows hundreds of people who work out at the gym. Some of them he has worked with as fitness director as they were getting to know the machines in their early months there. He has met many others while teaching classes in spinning—a group cycling class. Others he came to know through casual contact, since many of the same people work out at the same time every week.

The personal space is limited within a gym environment, due to the proximity of the exercise equipment. For example, in the weight training circuit at SBAC, one section contains a number of Cybex machines near to one another. Members must work out in close proximity to one another, and their bodies constantly criss-cross as they move through their workouts.

It is almost impossible for Schmitz to walk any-where in this physical space without potentially mak-ing eye contact with someone he has at least met. He will greet certain of these patrons the first time he sees them in the day, but afterward it is usually under-stood that they will go about their own business with-out acknowledging one another in the way they did earlier.

When passersby quickly glance at one another and then look away again, they demonstrate what Erving Goffman (1967, 1971) calls the **civil inattention** we require of one another in many situations. Civil inat-tention is not the same as merely ignoring another person. Each individual indicates recognition of the other person's presence, but avoids any gesture that might be taken as too intrusive. Can you think of ex-amples of civil inattention in your own life? Perhaps when you are walking down the hall of a dormitory, or trying to decide where to sit in the cafeteria, or sim-ply walking across campus? Civil inattention to others is something we engage in more or less unconsciously, but it is of fundamental importance to the existence of social life, which must proceed efficiently and, some-times among total strangers, without fear. When civil inattention occurs among passing strangers, an indi-vidual implies to another person that she has no rea-son to suspect his intentions, be hostile to him, or in any other way specifically avoid him.

The best way to see the importance of this is by thinking of examples where it doesn't apply. When a person stares fixedly at another, allowing her face openly to express a particular emotion, it is normally with a lover, family member, or close friend. Strangers or chance acquaintances, whether encountered on the street, at work, or at a party, virtually never hold the gaze of another in this way. To do so may be taken as an indication of hostile intent. It is only where two groups are strongly antagonistic to one another that strangers might indulge in such a practice. Thus, whites in the United States have been known in the past to give a "hate stare" to blacks walking past.

Even friends in close conversation need to be care-ful about how they look at one another. Each individ-ual demonstrates attention and involvement in the conversation by regularly looking at the eyes of the other, but not staring into them. To look too intently might be taken as a sign of mistrust about, or at least failure to understand, what the other is saying. Yet if each party does not engage the eyes of the other at all, he is likely to be thought evasive, shifty, or otherwise odd.

The Study of Daily Life

Why should we concern ourselves with such seem-ingly trivial aspects of social behavior? Passing some-one on the street or exchanging a few words with a friend seem minor and uninteresting activities, things we do countless times a day without giving them any thought. In fact, the study of such apparently insignifi-cant forms of **social interaction** is of major impor-tance in sociology—and, far from being uninteresting, is one of the most absorbing of all areas of sociologi-cal investigation. There are two reasons for this.

First, our day-to-day routines, with their almost constant interactions with others, give structure and form to what we do; we can learn a great deal about ourselves as social beings, and about social life itself, from studying them. Our lives are organized around the repetition of similar patterns of behavior from day to day, week to week, month to month, and year to year. Think of what you did yesterday, for example, and the day before that. If they were both weekdays, in all probability you got up at about the same time each day (an important routine in itself). You may have gone off to class fairly early in the morning, making a journey from home to school or college that you make virtually every weekday. You perhaps met some friends for lunch, returning to classes or private study in the afternoon. Later, you retraced your steps back home, possibly going out later in the evening with other friends.

Of course, the routines we follow from day to day are not identical, and our patterns of activity at week-ends usually contrast with those on weekdays. And if we make a major change in our life, like leaving col-lege to take up a job, alterations in our daily routines are usually necessary; but then we establish a new and fairly regular set of habits again.

Second, studying social interaction in everyday life sheds light on larger social systems and institutions. All large-scale social systems, in fact, depend on the patterns of social interaction we engage in daily. This is easy to demonstrate. Consider again the case of two strangers passing on the street. Such an event may

Civil inattention, New York City.

seem to have little direct relevance to large-scale, more permanent forms of social organization. But when we take into account many such interactions, this is no longer so. In modern societies, most people live in towns and cities and constantly interact with others whom they do not know personally. Civil inattention is one among other mechanisms that give city life, with its bustling crowds and fleeting, impersonal contacts, the character it has.

In this chapter, we shall first learn about the nonverbal cues (facial expressions and bodily gestures) all of us use when interacting with each other. We will then move on to analyze everyday speech—how we use language to communicate to others the meanings we wish to get across. Finally, we will focus on the ways in which our lives are structured by daily routines, paying particular attention to how we coordinate our actions across space and time.

NONVERBAL COMMUNICATION

Social interaction requires numerous forms of **nonverbal communication**—the exchange of information and meaning through facial expressions, gestures, and movements of the body. Nonverbal communication is sometimes referred to as "body language," but this is misleading, because we characteristically use such nonverbal cues to eliminate or expand on what is said in words.

The Face, Gestures, and Emotion

One major aspect of nonverbal communication is the facial expression of emotion. Paul Ekman and his colleagues have developed what they call the Facial Action Coding System (FACS) for describing movements of the facial muscles that give rise to particular expressions (Ekman and Friesen, 1978). By this means, they have tried to inject some precision into an area notoriously open to inconsistent or contradictory interpretations—for there is little agreement about how emotions are to be identified and classified. Charles Darwin, the originator of evolutionary theory, claimed that basic modes of emotional expression are the same in all human beings. Although some have disputed the claim, Ekman's researches among people from widely different cultural backgrounds seem to confirm this. Ekman and W. V. Friesen carried out a study of an isolated community in New Guinea, whose members had previously had virtually no contact with outsiders. When they were shown pictures of facial expressions conveying six emotions (happiness, sadness, anger, disgust, fear, surprise), the New Guineans were able to identify these emotions.

According to Ekman, the results of his own and similar studies of different peoples support the view that the facial expression of emotion and its interpretation are innate in human beings. He acknowledges that his evidence does not conclusively demonstrate this, and it may be that widely shared cultural learning experiences are involved; however, his conclusions are supported by other types of research. I. Eibl-Eibesfeldt studied six children born deaf and blind to see how far their facial expressions were the same as those of normal individuals in particular emotional situations (1972). He found that the children smiled when engaged in obviously pleasurable activities, raised their eyebrows in surprise when sniffing at an object with an unaccustomed smell, and frowned when repeatedly offered a disliked object. Since they could not have seen other people behaving in these ways, it seems that these responses must have been innately determined.

Using the FACS, Ekman and Friesen identified a

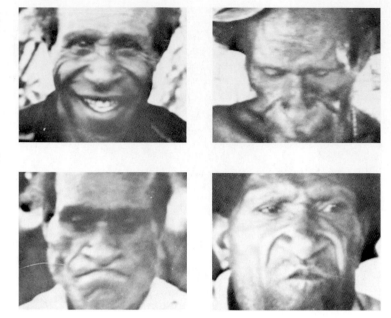

When New Guinea tribesmen were asked to show expressions of happiness, sadness, disgust, or anger, they displayed facial expressions similar to those of other cultures.

number of the discrete facial muscle actions in newborn infants that are also found in adult expressions of emotion. Infants seem, for example, to produce facial expressions similar to the adult expression of disgust (pursing the lips and frowning) in response to sour tastes. But although the facial expression of emotion seems to be partly innate, individual and cultural factors influence what exact form facial movements take and the contexts in which they are deemed appropriate. How people smile, for example, the precise movement of the lips and other facial muscles, and how fleeting the smile is all vary between cultures.

There are no gestures or bodily postures that have been shown to characterize all, or even most, cultures. In some societies, for instance, people nod when they mean no, the opposite of Anglo-American practice. Gestures Americans tend to use a great deal, such as pointing, seem not to exist among certain peoples (Bull, 1983). Similarly, a straightened forefinger placed in the center of the cheek and rotated is used in parts of Italy as a gesture of praise, but appears to be unknown elsewhere.

Like facial expressions, gestures and bodily posture are continually used to fill out utterances, as well as conveying meanings when nothing is actually said. All three can be used to joke, show irony, or show skepticism. The nonverbal impressions that we convey inadvertently often indicate that what we say is not quite what we really mean. Blushing is perhaps the most obvious example, but there are innumerable more subtle indicators that can be picked up by other people. Genuine facial expressions tend to evaporate after four or five seconds. A smile that lasts longer could indicate deceit. An expression of surprise that lasts too long may deliberately be used as a parody—to show that the individual is not in fact surprised after all.

"Face" and Culture

The word "face" can also refer to the *esteem* in which an individual is held by others. In daily social life, we normally pay a good deal of attention to "saving face." Much of what we call politeness or etiquette in social gatherings consists of disregarding behavior that might otherwise lead to a loss of face. We don't refer to episodes in an individual's past or personal characteristics that might produce embarrassment if mentioned. We refrain from making jokes about baldness if we realize that someone is wearing a hairpiece—unless we are among close friends. Tact is a sort of protective device that each person employs in the expectation that, in return, her own weaknesses will not be deliberately exposed to general view. Our day-to-day lives, therefore, do not just happen. Without realizing it most of the time, we skillfully maintain a close and continuous control over facial expression, body posture, and gesture in our interactions with others.

Some people are specialists in the control of facial expressions and tactful commerce with other people. A good diplomat, for example, must be able—giving every appearance of ease and comfort—to interact with others whose views he might disagree with or even find repellent. The degree to which this is managed successfully can affect the fate of whole nations. Skillful diplomacy might defuse tensions between countries and prevent a war.

SOCIAL RULES AND TALK

Although we routinely use nonverbal cues in our own behavior and in making sense of the behavior of others, much of our interaction is done through talk—casual verbal exchange—carried on in informal conversations with others. It has always been accepted by sociologists that language is fundamental to social life. Recently, however, an approach has been developed that is specifically concerned with how people use language in the ordinary contexts of everyday life. The study of conversations has been strongly influ-

enced by the work of Erving Goffman. But the most important influence in this type of research is Harold Garfinkel, the founder of ethnomethodology (Garfinkel, 1985).

Ethnomethodology is the study of the "ethnomethods"—the folk, or lay, methods—people use to *make sense* of what others do, and particularly what they say. We all apply these methods, normally without having to give any conscious attention to them. Often we can only make sense of what is said in conversation if we know the social context, which does not appear in the words themselves. Take the following conversation (Heritage, 1985):

A: I have a fourteen-year-old son.

B: Well, that's all right.

A: I also have a dog.

B: Oh, I'm sorry.

What do you think is happening here? What is the relation between the speakers? What if you were told that this is a conversation between a prospective tenant and landlord? The conversation then becomes sensible: some landlords accept children but don't permit their tenants to keep pets. Yet if we don't know the social context, the responses of individual B seem to bear no relation to the statements of A. *Part* of the sense is in the words, and *part* is in the way in which the social context emerges from the talk.

KEY CONCEPTS IN REVIEW

Social interaction is the process by which we act and react to those around us.

Civil inattention refers to the nonintrusive recognition of others, which is done more or less unconsciously.

Nonverbal communication is a form of social interaction that includes facial expressions, gestures, and body movements.

Shared Understandings

The most inconsequential forms of daily talk presume complicated, shared knowledge brought into play by those speaking. In fact, our small talk is so complex that it has so far proved impossible to program even the most sophisticated computers to converse with human beings. The words used in ordinary talk do not always have precise meanings, and we "fix" what we want to say through the unstated assumptions that back it up. If Maria asks Tom: "What did you do yesterday?" there is no obvious answer suggested by the words in the question themselves. A day is a long time, and it would be logical for Tom to answer: "Well, at seven-sixteen, I woke up. At seven-eighteen, I got out of bed, went to the bathroom and started to brush my teeth. At seven-nineteen, I turned on the shower. . . ." We understand the type of response the question calls for by knowing Maria, what sort of activities she and Tom normally carry on together, and what Tom usually does on a particular day of the week, among other things.

Many of the "rules" of everyday conversation become obvious only when someone breaks them.

Garfinkel's Experiments

The "background expectancies" with which we organize ordinary conversations were highlighted by some experiments Garfinkel undertook with student volunteers. The students were asked to engage a friend or relative in conversation, and to insist that casual remarks or general comments be actively pursued to make their meaning precise. If someone said, "Have a nice day," the student was to respond, "Nice in what sense, exactly?" "Which part of the day do you mean?" and so forth. One of the exchanges that resulted ran as follows (S is the friend, E the student volunteer):

S: How are you?

E: How am I in regard to what? My health, my finance, my school work, my peace of mind, my . . .

S (red in the face and suddenly out of control): Look! I was just trying to be polite. Frankly, I don't give a damn how you are.

(Garfinkel, 1963)

Why do people get so upset when apparently minor conventions of talk are not followed? The answer is that the stability and meaningfulness of our daily social lives depend on the sharing of unstated cultural assumptions about what is said and why. If we weren't able to take these for granted, meaningful communication would be impossible. Any question or contribution to a conversation would have to be followed by a massive "search procedure" of the sort Garfinkel's subjects were told to initiate, and interaction would simply break down. What seem at first sight to be unimportant conventions of talk, therefore, turn out to be fundamental to the very fabric of social life, which is why their breach is so serious.

Note that in everyday life, people on occasion deliberately feign ignorance of unstated knowledge. This may be done to rebuff the others, poke fun at them, cause embarrassment, or call attention to a double meaning in what was said. Consider, for example, this classic exchange between parent and teenager:

P: Where are you going?

T: Out.

P: What are you going to do?

T: Nothing.

The responses of the teenager are effectively the opposite of those of the volunteers in Garfinkel's experiments. Rather than pursuing inquiries where this is not normally done, the teenager declines to provide appropriate answers at all—essentially saying, "Mind your own business!"

The first question might elicit a different response from another person in another context:

A: Where are you going?

B: I'm going quietly round the bend.

B deliberately misreads A's question in order ironically to convey worry or frustration. Comedy and joking thrive on such deliberate misunderstandings of the unstated assumptions involved in talk. There is nothing threatening about this so long as the parties concerned recognize the intent to provoke laughter.

Forms of Talk

It is a sobering experience to hear a tape recording or read a transcript of a conversation to which one has contributed. Conversations are much more fractured, hesitant, and ungrammatical than most people realize. When we take part in everyday talk, we tend to think that what we say is fairly polished, because we unconsciously fill in the background to the actual words; but real conversations are quite different from conversations in novels, where characters speak in well-formed and grammatical sentences.

As with Goffman's work on civil inattention, it might be presumed that the analysis of ordinary conversations is rather marginal to the main concerns of sociology; indeed, many sociologists have been critical of ethnomethodological research for just this reason. Yet some of the arguments used to show why Goffman's work is so important to sociology also apply to ethnomethodology. Studying everyday talk has shown how complicated is the mastery of language that ordinary people command. The immense difficulties involved in programming computers to do what human speakers are able to carry out without effort is evidence of this complexity. In addition, talk is an essen-tial element of every realm of social life. The Watergate tapes of President Nixon and his advisers were nothing more than a transcript of conversation, but they provided a glimpse of the exercise of political power at the highest levels (Molotch and Boden, 1985).

Response Cries

Some kinds of utterances are not talk but consist of muttered exclamations, or what Goffman has called **response cries** (Goffman, 1981). Consider Lucy, who exclaims, "Oops!" after knocking over a glass of water. "Oops!" seems to be merely an uninteresting reflex response to a mishap, rather like blinking the eye when a person moves a hand sharply toward your face. It is not, however, as shown by the fact that people do not usually make the exclamation when alone. "Oops!" is normally directed toward others present. The exclamation demonstrates to witnesses that the lapse is only minor and momentary, not something that should cast doubt on Lucy's command of her actions.

"Oops!" is used only in situations of minor failure, rather than in major accidents or calamities—which also demonstrates that the exclamation is part of our controlled management of the details of social life. Moreover, the word may be used by someone observing Lucy, rather than Lucy herself; or it may be used to sound a warning to another. "Oops!" is normally a curt sound, but the "oo" may be prolonged in some situations. Thus, someone might extend the sound to cover a critical moment in performing a task. For instance, a parent may utter an extended "Oops!" or "Oopsadaisy!" when playfully tossing a child in the air. The sound covers the brief phase when the child may feel a loss of control, reassuring him and probably at the same time developing his understanding of response cries.

This may all sound very contrived and exaggerated. Why bother to analyze such an inconsequential utterance in this detail? Surely we don't pay as much attention to what we say as this example suggests? Of course we don't—on a conscious level. The crucial point, however, is that we take for granted an immensely complicated, continuous control of our appearance and actions. In situations of interaction, we are never expected just to be present on the scene.

Others expect, as we expect of them, that we display what Goffman calls "controlled alertness." A fundamental part of being human is continually demonstrating to others our competence in the routines of daily life.

Slips of the Tongue

"Oops!" is a response to a minor mishap. We also make mistakes in speech and pronunciation in the course of conversations, lectures, and other situations of talk. In his investigations into the "psychopathology of everyday life," Sigmund Freud, the founder of psychoanalysis, analyzed numerous examples of such **slips of the tongue** (Freud, 1971). According to Freud, mistakes in speaking, including mispronounced or misplaced words and stammering, are never in fact accidental. They are unconsciously motivated by feelings that are repressed from our conscious minds, or that we try consciously but unsuccessfully to suppress. These feelings often, but not always, involve sexual associations. Thus, one may mean to say "organism" but instead say "orgasm." In an example Freud gave, when a woman was asked, "What regiment is your son with?" she answered, "With the Forty-Second Murderers" (*Mörder* in German, rather than the word she intended to say, *Mörser*, or "Mortars").

Slips of the tongue are often humorous and could pass as jokes. The difference lies simply in whether or not the speaker consciously intended the words to come out as they did. Slips of the tongue shade over into other types of "inappropriate" speech, which Freud also believed are often unconsciously motivated—as when a person fails to see that something she says has a clear double meaning. These again can be taken as jokes if deliberately intended, but are otherwise lapses in the controlled production of talk that we expect people to sustain.

One of the best ways of illustrating these points is to look at lapses in the speech of radio and television announcers. Announcers' speech is not like ordinary talk, because it is not spontaneous but scripted. It is also expected to be more nearly perfect than ordinary talk, delivered with fewer hesitations and more clearly articulated. Hence, when news readers fluff what they have to say, it is much more obvious than in casual conversations. Yet announcers do, of course, make slips of the tongue, and many are funny or have the "only too true" nature to which Freud called attention. Here are two examples (Goffman, 1981):

> This is the Dominion Network of the Canadian Broadcorping Castration.

> Beat the egg yolk and then add the milk, then slowly blend in the sifted flour. As you do, you can see how the mixture is sickening.

Other examples come into the category of inappropriate speech, where a double meaning that should have been spotted comes through:

> Ladies who care to drive by and drop off their clothes will receive prompt attention.

> Folks, try our comfortable beds. I personally stand behind every bed we sell.

> The loot and the car were listed as stolen by the Los Angeles Police Department.

> And here in Hollywood, it is rumored that the former movie starlet is expecting her fifth child in a month.

We tend to laugh more at verbal mistakes when announcers (or teachers in lectures) make them than when they occur in ordinary conversation. The humor resides not only in what is missaid, but also in the discomfiture the broadcaster or teacher might show at delivering a less than perfect performance. We temporarily see behind the mask of cool professionalism to the ordinary individual.

FACE, BODY, AND SPEECH IN INTERACTION

Let us summarize at this point what we have learned so far. Everyday interaction depends on subtle relationships between what we convey with our faces and bodies and what we express in words. We use the facial expressions and bodily gestures of other people to fill in what they communicate verbally, and to check how far they are sincere in what they say. Mostly without realizing it, each of us keeps a tight and continuous control over facial expression, bodily posture, and movement in the course of our daily interaction with others.

Sometimes, however, we make verbal slips that, as Freud's example of the "murderers" indicates, briefly reveal what we wish to keep concealed, consciously or unconsciously. Many verbal slips inadvertently display our true feelings—like the one in the example of the cake mix, which the announcer probably thinks is really "sickening."

Face, bodily management, and speech, then, are used to convey certain meanings and to hide others. We also organize our activities in the *contexts* of social life to achieve the same ends, as we shall now see.

Encounters

In many social situations, we engage in what Goffman calls **unfocused interaction** with others. Unfocused interaction takes place whenever individuals exhibit mutual awareness of one another's presence. This is usually the case anywhere large numbers of people are assembled together, as on a busy street, in a theater crowd, or at a party. When people are in the presence of others, even if they do not directly talk to them, they continually communicate nonverbally through their posture and facial and physical gestures.

Focused interaction occurs when individuals directly attend to what others say or do. Except when someone is standing alone, say at a party, all interaction involves both focused and unfocused exchanges. Goffman calls an instance of focused interaction an **encounter**, and much of our day-to-day life consists of encounters with other people—family, friends, workmates—frequently occurring against the background of unfocused interaction with others present on the scene. Small talk, seminar discussions, games, and routine face-to-face contacts (with ticket clerks, waiters, shop assistants, and so forth) are all examples of encounters.

Encounters always need "openings," which indicate that civil inattention is being discarded. When strangers meet and begin to talk at a party, the moment of ceasing civil inattention is always risky, since

Unfocused interactions take place between everyone in a public place, such as a restaurant.

misunderstandings can easily occur about the nature of the encounter being established (Goffman, 1971). Hence, the making of eye contact may first be ambiguous and tentative. A person can then act as though he had made no direct move if the overture is not accepted. In focused interaction, each person communicates as much by facial expression and gesture as by the words actually exchanged. Goffman distinguishes between the expressions individuals "give" and those they "give off." The first are the words and facial expressions people use to produce certain impressions on others. The second are the clues that others may spot to check their sincerity or truthfulness. For instance, a restaurant owner listens with a polite smile to the statements of customers about how much they enjoyed their meals. At the same time, he is noting how pleased they seemed to be while eating the food, whether a lot was left over, and the tone of voice they use to express their satisfaction.

Markers

Most of us meet and talk to a variety of people in the course of an average day. Catherine, for example, gets up, breakfasts with her family, and perhaps accompanies her children to school, stopping briefly to exchange pleasantries with a friend at the school gates. She drives to work, probably listening to the radio. During the course of the day, she enters into interchanges with colleagues and visitors, ranging from transitory conversations to formal meetings. Each of these encounters is likely to be separated by **markers**, or what Goffman calls **brackets**, which distinguish each episode of focused interaction from the one before and from unfocused interaction taking place in the background (Goffman, 1974).

At a party, for example, people talking together will tend to position themselves and control their voice levels so as to create a "huddle," separate from others. They may stand facing one another, effectively making it difficult for others to intrude until they decide to break up, or until they soften the edges of their focused interaction by moving to different positions in the room. On more formal occasions, recognized devices are often used to signal the opening and ending of a particular encounter. To signal the opening of a play, for instance, the lights go down and the curtain is raised. At the end of the performance, the auditorium lights are turned on again and the curtain falls.

Markers are particularly important either when an encounter is especially out of the ordinary or when there might be ambiguity about what is going on. For example, when a model poses naked in front of an art class, he does not usually undress or dress in the presence of the group. Undressing and dressing in private allows the body to be suddenly exposed and hidden. This both marks the boundaries of the episode and conveys that it is devoid of the sexual meanings that otherwise might be conveyed.

In very confined spaces, such as elevators, it is difficult to mark off an area of focused interaction. Nor is it easy for other people present to indicate, as they will do in other situations, that they are not listening to whatever conversation is carried on. It is also difficult for strangers not to be seen looking at others more directly than the norms of civil inattention allow. Thus, in elevators, people often adopt an exag-

In Japan, businessmen mix traditional and Western markers for the opening of a focused interaction.

gerated "not listening" and "not looking" pose, staring into space or at the panel of buttons—anywhere but at their fellow passengers. Conversation is usually suspended or confined to brief exchanges. Similarly, if several people are talking to one another in an office and one is interrupted to take a phone call, the others cannot readily show complete inattention, and they may carry on a sort of hesitant, limp conversation on their own.

Impression Management

Goffman and other writers on social interaction often use notions from the theater in analyzing social interaction. The concept of **social role**, for example, originated in a theatrical setting. Roles are socially defined expectations that a person in a given **status** (or **social position**) follows. To be a teacher is to hold a specific position; the teacher's role consists of acting in specified ways toward her pupils. Goffman sees social life as though played out by actors on a stage—or on many stages, because how we act depends on the roles we are playing at a particular time. People are sensitive to how they are seen by others, and use many forms of **impression management** to compel others to react to them in the ways they wish. Although we may sometimes do this in a calculated way, usually it is among the things we do without conscious attention.

When Philip attends a business meeting, he wears a suit and tie and is on his best behavior; that evening, when relaxing with friends at a football game, he wears jeans and sweatshirt and tells a lot of jokes. This is impression management.

As we just noted above, the social roles that we adopt are highly dependent on our social status. A person's social status can be different depending on social context. For instance, as a "student" you have a certain status and are expected to act a certain way when you are around your professors. As a "son" or "daughter" you have a different status from a student, and society (especially your parents) has different expectations for you. Likewise, as a "friend" you have an entirely different position in the social order and the roles you adopt would change accordingly. Obviously, a person has many statuses at the same time. Sociologists refer to the group of statuses that you occupy as a **status set**.

Sociologists also like to distinguish between ascribed status and achieved status. An **ascribed status** is one that you are "assigned" based on biological factors such as race, sex, or age. Thus your ascribed statuses could be "white," "female," and "teenager." An **achieved status** is one that is earned through an individual's own effort. Your achieved statuses could be "high-school graduate," "athlete," or "employee." While we may like to believe that it is our achieved statuses that are most important, society may not agree. In any society, some statuses have priority over all other statuses and generally determine a person's overall position in society. Sociologists refer to this as a **master status** (Hughes, 1944; Becker, 1963). The most common master statuses are those based on gender and race. Sociologists have shown that in an encounter, one of the first things that people notice about one another is gender and race (Omi and Winant, 1994). As we shall see shortly, both race and gender strongly shape our social interactions.

FRONT AND BACK REGIONS

Much of social life, Goffman suggested, can be divided into front regions and back regions. **Front regions** are social occasions or encounters in which individuals act out formal roles; they are "onstage performances." Teamwork is often involved in creating front-region performances. Two prominent politi-

cians in the same party may put on an elaborate show of unity and friendship before the television cameras, even though each cordially detests the other. A wife and husband may take care to conceal their quarrels from their children, preserving a front of harmony, only to fight bitterly once the children are safely tucked up in bed.

The **back regions** are where people assemble the props and prepare themselves for interaction in the more formal settings. Back regions resemble the backstage of a theater or the off-camera activities of filming. When they are safely behind the scenes, people can relax and give vent to feelings and styles of behavior they keep in check when on front stage. Back regions permit

> profanity, open sexual remarks, elaborate griping . . . rough informal dress, "sloppy" sitting and standing posture, use of dialect or substandard speech, mumbling and shouting, playful aggressiveness and "kidding," inconsiderateness for the other in minor but potentially symbolic acts, minor self-involvement such as humming, whistling, chewing, nibbling, belching and flatulence. (Goffman, 1973)

Thus, a waitress may be the soul of quiet courtesy when serving a customer but become loud and aggressive once behind the swing doors of the kitchen. There are probably few restaurants customers would patronize if they could see all that goes on in the kitchens.

ADOPTING ROLES: INTIMATE EXAMINATIONS

For an example of collaboration in impression management that also borrows from the theater, let's look at one particular study in some detail. James Henslin and Mae Biggs studied a specific, highly delicate type of encounter: a woman's visit to a gynecologist (Henslin and Biggs, 1971, 1997). At the time of the study, most pelvic examinations were carried out by male doctors, and hence the experience was (and sometimes is) fraught with potential ambiguities and embarrassment for both parties. Men and women in the West are socialized to think of the genitals as the most private part of the body, and seeing, and particularly feeling, the genitals of another person is ordinarily associated with intimate sexual encounters. Some women feel so worried by the prospect of a pelvic examination that they refuse to visit the doctor, male or female, even when they suspect there is a strong medical reason to do so.

Henslin and Biggs analyzed material collected by Biggs, a trained nurse, from a large number of gynecological examinations. They interpreted what they found as having several typical stages. Adopting a dramaturgical metaphor, they suggested that each phase can be treated as a distinct scene, in which the parts the actors play alter as the episode unfolds. In the prologue, the woman enters the waiting room preparing to assume the role of patient, temporarily discarding her outside identity. Called into the consulting room, she adopts the "patient" role, and the first scene opens. The doctor assumes a businesslike, professional manner and treats the patient as a proper and competent person, maintaining eye contact and listening politely to what she has to say. If he decides an examination is called for, he tells her so and leaves the room; scene one is over.

As he leaves, the nurse comes in. She is an important stagehand in the main scene shortly to begin. She soothes any worries that the patient might have, acting as both a confidante—knowing some of the "things women have to put up with"—and a collaborator in what is to follow. Crucially, the nurse helps alter the patient from a person to a "nonperson" for the vital scene—which features a body, part of which is to be scrutinized, rather than a complete human being. In Henslin and Biggs's study, the nurse not only supervises the patient's undressing, but takes over aspects that normally the patient would control. Thus, she takes the patient's clothes and folds them. Most women wish their underwear to be out of sight when the doctor returns, and the nurse makes sure that this is so. She guides the patient to the examining table and covers most of her body with a sheet before the physician returns.

The central scene now opens, with nurse as well as doctor taking part. The presence of the nurse helps ensure that the interaction between doctor and patient is free of sexual overtones, and also provides a legal witness should the physician be charged with unprofessional conduct. The examination proceeds as though the personality of the patient were absent; the sheet across her separates the genital area from the rest of her body, and her position does not allow her to watch the examination itself. Save for any specific medical queries, the doctor ignores her, sitting on a low stool, out of her line of vision. The patient collaborates in becoming a temporary nonperson, not initiating conversation and keeping any movements to a minimum.

In the interval between this and the final scene, the nurse again plays the role of stagehand, helping the patient to become a full person once more. At this juncture, the two may again engage in conversation, the patient expressing relief that the examination is over. Having dressed and regroomed herself, the patient is ready to face the concluding scene. The doctor reenters and, in discussing the results of the examination, again treats the patient as a complete and responsible person. Resuming his polite, professional manner, he conveys that his reactions to her are in no way altered by the intimate contact with her body. The epilogue is played out when she leaves the physician's office, taking up again her identity in the outside world. Patient and doctor have thus collaborated in such a way as to manage the interaction and the impression each participant forms of the other.

Personal Space

There are cultural differences in the definition of **personal space**. In Western culture, people usually maintain a distance of at least three feet when engaged in focused interaction with others; when standing side by side, they may stand more closely together. In the Middle East, people often stand closer to one another than is thought acceptable in the West. Westerners visiting that part of the world are likely to find themselves disconcerted by this unexpected physical proximity.

Edward T. Hall, who has worked extensively on nonverbal communication, distinguishes four zones of personal space. Intimate distance, of up to one and a half feet, is reserved for very few social contacts. Only those involved in relationships in which regular bodily touching is permitted, such as lovers or parents and children, operate within this zone of private space.

Humans, as well as several species of animals, tend to maintain a certain distance as personal space.

Personal distance (from one and a half to four feet) is the normal spacing for encounters with friends and close acquaintances. Some intimacy of contact is permitted, but this tends to be strictly limited. Social distance, from four to twelve feet, is the zone usually maintained in formal settings such as interviews. The fourth zone is that of public distance, beyond twelve feet, preserved by those who are performing to an audience.

In ordinary interaction, the most fraught zones are those of intimate and personal distance. If these zones are invaded, people try to recapture their space. We may stare at the intruder as if to say, "Move away!" or elbow him aside. When people are forced into proximity closer than they deem desirable, they might create a kind of physical boundary: a reader at a crowded library desk might physically demarcate a private space by stacking books around its edges (Hall, 1969, 1973).

INTERACTION IN TIME AND SPACE

Understanding how activities are distributed in time and space is fundamental to analyzing encounters, and also to understanding social life in general. All interaction is situated—it occurs in a particular place and has a specific duration in time. Our actions over the course of a day tend to be "zoned" in time as well as in space. Thus, for example, most people spend a zone—say, from 9:00 A.M. to 5:00 P.M.—of their daily time working. Their weekly time is also zoned: they are likely to work on weekdays and spend weekends at home, altering the pattern of their activities on the weekend days. As we move through the temporal zones of the day, we are also often moving across space as well: to get to work, we may take a bus from one area of a city to another, or perhaps commute in from the suburbs. When we analyze the contexts of social interaction, therefore, it is often useful to look at people's movements across **time-space**.

The concept of **regionalization** will help us understand how social life is zoned in time-space. Take the example of a private house. A modern house is regionalized into rooms, hallways, and floors if there is more than one story. These spaces are not just physically separate areas, but are zoned in time as well. The living rooms and kitchen are used most in the daylight hours, the bedrooms at night. The interaction that occurs in these regions is bound by both spatial and temporal divisions. Some areas of the house form back regions, with "performances" taking place in the others. At times, the whole house can become a back region. Once again, this idea is beautifully captured by Goffman:

Of a Sunday morning, a whole household can use the wall around its domestic establishment to conceal a relaxing slovenliness in dress and civil endeavor, extending to all rooms the informality that is usually restricted to kitchen and bedrooms. So, too, in American middle-class neighborhoods, on afternoons the line between children's playground and home may be defined as backstage by mothers, who pass along it wearing jeans, loafers, and a minimum of make-up.... And, of course, a region that is thoroughly established as a front region for the regular performance of a particular routine often functions as a back region before and after each performance, for at these times the permanent fixtures may undergo repairs, restoration, and rearrangement, or the performers may hold dress rehearsals. To see this we need only glance into a restaurant, or store, or home, a few minutes before these establishments are opened to us for the day. (Goffman, 1973)

Clock Time

In modern societies, the zoning of our activities is strongly influenced by clock time. Without clocks and the precise timing of activities, and thereby their coordination across space, industrialized societies could not exist (Mumford, 1973). The measuring of time by clocks is today standardized across the globe, making possible the complex international transport systems and communications we now depend on. World standard time was first introduced in 1884 at a conference of nations held in Washington. The globe was then partitioned into twenty-four time zones, each one hour apart, and an exact beginning of the universal day was fixed.

Fourteenth-century monasteries were the first organizations to try to schedule the activities of their inmates precisely across the day and week. Today, there is virtually no group or organization that does not do so—the greater the number of people and resources involved, the more precise the scheduling must be. Eviatar Zerubavel demonstrated this in his study of the temporal structure of a large modern hospital (1979, 1982). A hospital must operate on a twenty-four-hour basis, and coordinating the staff and re-

sources is a highly complex matter. For instance, the nurses work for one time period in ward A, another time period in ward B, and so on, and are also called on to alternate between day- and night-shift work. Nurses, doctors, and other staff, plus the resources they need, must be integrated together both in time and in space.

THE SOCIOLOGICAL DEBATE

THE SOCIAL CONSTRUCTION OF REALITY

Within sociology, multiple theoretical frameworks are used to explain social reality. These theories differ in their explanations of social phenomena, yet they share the assumption that social reality exists independently of people's talking about it or living in it.

Not all sociologists share this assumption. The theoretical approach called **social constructionism** believes that what individuals and society perceive and understand as reality is itself a creation of the social interaction of individuals and groups. Trying to "explain" social reality, then, would be to overlook and to reify (regard as a given truth) the processes through which such reality is constructed. Therefore, social constructionists argue that sociologists need to document and analyze these processes, and not simply the concept of social reality they give rise to.

In their 1966 classic *The Social Construction of Reality*, sociologists Peter Berger and Thomas Luckmann examine commonsense knowledge—those things that individuals take for granted as real. They emphasize that these "obvious" facts of social reality may differ among people from different cultures, and even among different people within the same culture. The task becomes an analysis of the *processes* by which individuals come to perceive what is "real" to them as real (Berger and Luckmann, 1966).

Social constructionists apply the ideas of Berger and Luckmann to the investigation of social phenomena, to illuminate the ways in which members of society come to know and simultaneously create what is real.

While social constructionists have examined such diverse topics as medicine and medical treatment, gender relations, and emotions, much of their work has focused on social problems, crime, and delinquency.

The work of Aaron Cicourel provides an example of social constructionist research in the area of juvenile delinquency. Within most of sociology, data regarding rates and cases of juvenile delinquency are taken as given (i.e., real), and theories are created to explain the patterns observed in the data. For example, arrest and court data indicate that juveniles from single-parent families are more likely to commit delinquent acts than are juveniles from two-parent homes, thus sociologists develop explanations for this observed relationship: Perhaps children from single-parent homes have less supervision, or perhaps they lack appropriate role models.

By contrast, Cicourel observed the *processes* involved in the arrest and classification of juveniles suspected of delinquency; that is, he observed the creation of the "official" delinquency data. He discovered that police procedures in the handling of juveniles rely on commonsense understandings of what juvenile delinquents are "really like."

For example, when juveniles from lower class families were arrested, police were more likely to view their offenses as results of poor supervision or a lack of proper role models, and would retain the juveniles in custody. Juveniles from upper-class homes, however, were more likely to be released to their parents' care, where police and parents believed the juvenile could receive proper discipline. Thus, the practices of police serve to formally assign the label of "juvenile delinquent" more often to juveniles from lower-class homes than to those from upper-class homes—even when the youths committed similar offenses. This assignment produces the very data which in turn confirm the relationships held by the commonsense views, e.g., that juveniles from poor families are more likely to engage in delinquency. Cicourel's study shows that through interaction, the commonsense notions of reality produce independent, "objective" proof of their own validity (Cicourel, 1968).

Social constructionism is not without its critics. Sociologists Steve Woolgar and Dorothy Pawluch argue that social constructionists aim to show the subjective creation of social reality, yet in doing so selectively view certain features as objective but others as constructed. For example, in analyses examining which juveniles become labeled as delinquent, social constructionists often argue that the initial behaviors reported for the juveniles are identical; therefore, any differences between those juveniles labeled delinquent and those avoiding such a label must be due to the construction of the label "delinquent." Critics argue that social constructionism inconsistently presents the initial behaviors as objective, while arguing that the labeling process is subjective (Woolgar and Pawluch, 1985).

Other sociologists have criticized social constructionism for its unwillingness to accept broader social forces as powerful influences on observable social outcomes. For example, some critics have argued that while reality may be a constructed perpetuation of commonsense beliefs, these beliefs themselves may be caused by existing social factors such as capitalism or patriarchy.

Ultimately, social constructionism offers a theoretical approach to understanding social reality that radically differs from most other sociological approaches. Rather than assuming that social reality objectively exists, social constructionists work to document and analyze the processes through which social reality is constructed, such that the construction then serves to confirm its own status as social reality.

Social Life and the Ordering of Space and Time

The information highway, a global electronic network, is another example of how closely forms of social life are bound up with our control of space and time. The highway will make it possible for us to interact with people we never see or meet, in any corner of the world. Such technological change "rearranges" space—we can interact with anyone without moving from our chair. It will also alter our experience of time, because communication on the electronic highway is almost immediate. Until about fifty years ago, most communication across space required a duration of time. If you sent a letter to someone abroad, there

KEY CONCEPTS IN REVIEW

Ethnomethodology, a term coined by Harold Garfinkel, is the study of the ways in which people make sense of what others do; in particular, the way people use language.

We can learn a great deal about the nature of talk by studying **response cries** (exclamations) and **slips of the tongue** (the mispronunciation or misuse of words and phrases).

Unfocused interaction refers to the mutual awareness of another's presence in a given setting, while **focused interaction** occurs when an individual pays direct attention to what another says or does. Erving Goffman termed an episode of focused interaction an **encounter.** Encounters are separated by **markers,** or what Goffman called **brackets,** which distinguish each episode of focused interaction from each other and from unfocused interaction going on in the background.

Social roles are socially defined expectations of an individual in a given status, or **social position.** Sociologists refer to an individual's group of statuses as a **status set.** Sociologists also distinguish between **ascribed status,** one based on biological factors such as as race, sex, or age, and **achieved status,** one based on an individuals' efforts. The statuses that generally determine a person's overall position in society are called **master statuses.**

Just as in theater, in the contexts of social life, there are distinctions between **front regions** (the stage itself) and **back regions,** where one prepares for one's role and relaxes afterward. Preparing for the presentation of one's social role is a form of **impression management.**

Personal space is a culturally defined boundary around which people interact with others.

---

was a time gap while the letter was carried, by ship, train, truck, or plane, to the person to whom it was written.

People still write letters today, of course, but instantaneous communication has become basic to our social world. Our lives would be almost unimaginable without it. We are so used to being able to switch on the TV and watch the news or make a phone call or send an email message to a friend in another state that it is hard for us to imagine what life would be like otherwise.

Everyday Life in Cultural and Historical Perspective

Some of the mechanisms of social interaction analyzed by Goffman, Garfinkel, and others seem to be universal. The use of markers to signal the opening and clos-

ing of encounters, for example, is characteristic of human interaction everywhere. Ways of organizing encounters, such as keeping the body turned away from others to form a conversational knot, are also found in all human gatherings. But much of Goffman's discussion of civil inattention and other kinds of interaction primarily concerns societies in which contact with strangers is commonplace. What about very small traditional societies, where there are no strangers and few settings in which more than a handful of people are together at any one time?

To see some of the contrasts between social interaction in modern and traditional societies, let's take as an example one of the least developed cultures in terms of technology remaining in the world: the !Kung (sometimes known as the Bushmen), who live in the Kalahari Desert area of Botswana and Namibia, in southern Africa (Lee, 1968, 1969; the exclamation mark refers to a click sound one makes before pronouncing the name). Although their way of life is changing because of outside influences, their traditional patterns of social life are still evident.

The !Kung live in groups of some thirty or forty people, in temporary settlements near water holes. Food is scarce in their environment, and they must walk far and wide to find it. Such roaming takes up most of the average day. Women and children often stay back in the camp, but equally often the whole group spends the day walking. Members of the community will sometimes fan out over an area of up to a hundred square miles in the course of a day, returning to the camp at night to eat and sleep. The men may be alone or in groups of two or three for much of the day. There is one period of the year, however, when the routines of their daily activities change: the winter rainy season, when water is abundant and food much easier to come by. The everyday life of the !Kung during this period is centered around ritual and ceremonial activities, the preparation for and enactment of which is very time-consuming.

The members of most !Kung groups never see anyone they don't know reasonably well. Until contacts with the outside became more common in recent years, they had no word for "stranger." While the !Kung, particularly the males, may spend long periods of the day out of contact with others, in the community itself there is little opportunity for privacy. Families sleep in flimsy, open dwellings, with virtually all activities open to public view. No one has studied the !Kung with Goffman's observations on everyday life in mind, but it is easy to see that some aspects of his

work have limited application to !Kung social life. There are few opportunities, for example, to create front and back regions. The closing off of different gatherings and encounters by the walls of rooms, separate buildings, and the various neighborhoods of cities common in modern societies are remote from the activities of the !Kung.

The Compulsion of Proximity

In modern societies, in complete contrast to the !Kung—as will be explored in the chapters that follow—we are constantly interacting with others whom we may never see or meet. Almost all of our everyday transactions, such as buying groceries or making a bank deposit, bring us into contact—but *indirect* contact—with people who may live thousands of miles away. The banking system, for example, is international. Any money you deposit is a small part of the financial investments the bank makes worldwide.

Now that it's relatively easy, why aren't more of our interactions with others indirect? Why don't we always use the phone, fax, or other means of remote communication when contacting friends or colleagues? People in business, for instance, continue to attend meetings, sometimes flying halfway around the world to do so, when it would seem much simpler and more effective to transact business through a computer or a multi-party phone line.

Deirdre Boden and Harvey Molotch have studied what they call the **compulsion of proximity**: the need

KEY CONCEPTS IN REVIEW

Social interactions are always situated in a particular time and space. **Regionalization** refers to how social life is organized in time and space. For example, our houses are divided into different regions in which different types of activity take place.

The **compulsion of proximity** refers to our need to interact with people face to face.

INTERNATIONAL TOURISM

Have you ever had a face-to-face conversation with someone from another country? Or connected to an overseas website? Have you ever traveled to another part of the world? If you answered "yes" to any of these questions, you have witnessed the effects of globalization on social interaction. Americans, of course, have always interacted with

people from foreign lands if for no other reason than America itself is an ethnically and culturally diverse nation. At the same time, globalization—a relatively recent phenomenon—has changed both the frequency and the nature of interactions between people of different nations. The historical sociologist Charles Tilly, in fact, defines globalization in terms of these changes. According to Tilly, "globalization means an increase in the geographic range of locally consequential social interactions" (1995, pp. 1–2). In other words, with globalization a greater proportion of our interactions come to involve, directly or indirectly, people from other countries.

What are the characteristics of social interactions that take place between individuals of different nations? Important contributions to the study of this problem have been made by those working in the area of the sociology of tourism. Sociologists of tourism note that globalization has greatly expanded the possibilities for international travel, both by encouraging an interest in other countries and by facilitating the movement of tourists across international borders. As a result, more than 45 million foreign tourists visited the United States in 1994—a significant increase from previous decades. These visitors pumped more than

of individuals to meet with one another in situations of **copresence,** or face-to-face interaction. People put themselves out to attend meetings, Boden and Molotch suggest, because situations of copresence, for reasons documented by Goffman in his studies of interaction, supply much richer information about how other people think and feel, and about their sincerity, than any form of electronic communication. Only by actually being in the presence of people who make de-

cisions affecting us in important ways do we feel able to learn what is going on, and confident that we can impress them with our own views and our own sincerity. "Copresence," Boden and Molotch say, "affects access to the body part that 'never lies,' the eyes—the 'windows on the soul.' Eye contact itself signals a degree of intimacy and trust; copresent interactants continuously monitor the subtle movements of this most subtle body part" (1994).

$60 billion into the U.S. economy (OECD, 1996). Americans are also traveling the world in record numbers.

High levels of international tourism, of course, translate into an increase in the number of face-to-face interactions between people of different countries. According to British sociologist John Urry (1996), many of these interactions are shaped by the "tourist gaze," the expectation on the part of the tourist that he or she will have "exotic" experiences while traveling abroad. "Exotic" experiences are those that violate our everyday expectations about how social interaction and interaction with the physical environment are "supposed" to proceed. Americans traveling in England, for example, may delight in the fact that the British drive on the left-hand side of the road. Such behavior is disconcerting to American drivers. Our rules of the road are so ingrained that we experience systematic violations of those rules as strange, weird, and exotic. Yet, as tourists, we take pleasure in this strangeness. In a sense, it is what we have paid money to see—along with Big Ben and the Tower of London. Imagine how disappointed you would be if you traveled to a different country only to find that it was almost exactly the same as the city or town in which you grew up.

Yet most tourists do not want their experiences to be *too* exotic. One of the most popular destinations for young Americans in Paris, for example, is McDonald's fast food restaurant. Some come to see if there is any truth to the line from the movie *Pulp Fiction* that because the French use the metric system, McDonald's "quarter pounder with cheese" hamburgers are called "Royales with cheese" (it is true, by the way). But many others come for the comfort of eating familiar food in a familiar setting. The contradictory demands for the exotic and the familiar are at the heart of the tourist gaze.

The tourist gaze may put strains on face-to-face interactions between tourists and "locals." Locals who are part of the tourist industry may appreciate overseas travelers for the economic benefits they bring to the places they visit. Other locals may resent tourists for their demanding attitudes or for the overdevelopment that often occurs in popular tourist destinations. Tourists may interrogate locals about aspects of their everyday lives, such as their food, work, and recreational habits; they may do this either to enhance their understanding of other cultures, or to negatively judge those who are different than themselves.

As tourism increases with the march of globalization, sociologists will have to watch carefully to see what dominant patterns of interaction emerge between tourists and locals, and to determine, among other things, whether these interactions tend to be friendly or antagonistic.

LINKING MICROSOCIOLOGY AND MACROSOCIOLOGY

As we saw in Chapter 1, **microsociology**, the study of everyday behavior in situations of face-to-face interaction, and **macrosociology**, the study of the broader features of society like class or gender hierarchies, are closely connected. We will now turn to examine social encounters on a crowded city sidewalk to illustrate this point.

Women and Men in Public

Take, for example, a situation that may seem "micro" on its face: a woman walking down the street is verbally harassed by a group of men. In her study, *Pass-*

ing By: Gender and Public Harassment, Carol Brooks Gardner found that in various settings, most famously, the edge of construction sites, these types of unwanted interaction occur as something women frequently experience as abusive.

Although the harassment of a single woman might be analyzed in microsociological terms by looking at a single interaction, it is not fruitful to view it that simply. It is typical of street talk involving men and women who are strangers (Gardner, 1995). And these kinds of interactions cannot simply be understood without also looking at the larger background of gender hierarchy in the United States. In this way we can see how micro- and macro-analysis are connected. For example, Gardner linked the harassment of women by men to the larger system of gender inequality, represented by male privilege in public spaces, women's physical vulnerability, and the omnipresent threat of rape.

Without making this link between micro- and macro-sociology, we can only have a limited understanding of these interactions. It might seem as though these types of interactions are isolated instances, or that they could be eliminated by teaching people good manners. Understanding the link between micro and macro helps us see that in order to attack the problem at its root cause, one would need to focus on eliminating the forms of gender inequality that give rise to such interactions.

Blacks and Whites in Public

Have you ever crossed to the other side of the street when you felt threatened by someone behind you or someone coming toward you? One sociologist who tried to understand simple interactions of this kind is Elijah Anderson.

Anderson began by describing social interaction on the streets of two adjacent urban neighborhoods. His book, *Streetwise: Race, Class, and Change in an Urban Community* (1990), found that studying everyday life sheds light on how social order is created by the individual building blocks of infinite micro-level interactions. He was particularly interested in understanding interactions when at least one party was viewed as threatening. Anderson showed that the ways many blacks and whites interact on the streets of a Northern city had a great deal to do with the struc-

ture of racial stereotypes, which is itself linked to the economic structure of society. In this way, he showed the link between micro interactions and the larger macro structures of society.

Anderson began by recalling Erving Goffman's description of how social roles and statuses come into existence in particular contexts or locations: "When an individual enters the presence of others, they commonly seek to acquire information about him or bring into play information already possessed. . . . Information about the individual helps to define the situation, enabling others to know in advance what he will expect of them and they may expect of him."

Following Goffman's lead, Anderson asked, what types of behavioral cues and signs make up the vocabulary of public interaction? He concluded that

> skin color, gender, age, companions, clothing, jewelry, and the objects people carry help identify them, so that assumptions are formed and communication can occur. Movements (quick or slow, false or sincere, comprehensible or incomprehensible) further refine this public communication. Factors like time of day or an activity that "explains" a person's presence can also affect in what way and how quickly the image of "stranger" is neutralized. If a stranger cannot pass inspection and be assessed as "safe," the image of predator may arise, and fellow pedestrians may try to maintain a distance consistent with that image. (Anderson, 1990, p. 167)

Anderson showed that the people most likely to pass inspection are those who do not fall into commonly accepted stereotypes of dangerous persons: "children readily pass inspection, while women and white men do so more slowly, black women, black men, and black male teenagers most slowly of all." In showing that interactional tensions derive from outside statuses such as race, class, and gender, Anderson shows that we cannot develop a full understanding of the situation by looking at the micro interactions themselves. This is how he makes the link between micro interactions and macro processes.

Anderson argues that people are "streetwise" when they develop skills such as "the art of avoidance" to deal with their felt vulnerability toward violence and crime. According to Anderson, whites who are not streetwise do not recognize the difference between different kinds of black men (e.g., middle-class youths vs. gang members). They may also not know how to alter the number of paces to walk behind a "suspicious" person or how to bypass "bad blocks" at various times of day.

SUMMARY

1. Many apparently trivial aspects of our day-to-day behavior turn out on close examination to be both complex and important aspects of *social interaction*. An example is the gaze—looking at other people. In most interactions, eye contact is fairly fleeting. To stare at another person could be taken as a sign of hostility—or on some occasions, of love. The study of social interaction is a fundamental area in sociology, illuminating many aspects of social life.

2. Many different expressions are conveyed by the human face. It is widely held that basic aspects of the facial expressions of emotion are innate. Cross-cultural studies demonstrate quite close similarities between members of different cultures both in facial expression and in the interpretation of emotions registered on the human face.

3. "Face" can also be understood in a broader sense to refer to the esteem in which an individual is held by others. Generally, in our interaction with other people, we are concerned with "saving face"—protecting our self-esteem.

4. The study of ordinary *talk* and *conversation* has come to be called *ethnomethodology*, a term first coined by Harold Garfinkel. Ethnomethodology is the analysis of the ways in which we actively—although usually in a taken-for-granted way—make sense of what others mean by what they say and do.

5. We can learn a great deal about the nature of talk by studying "*response cries*" (exclamations) and *slips of the tongue* (what happens when people mispronounce or misapply words and phrases). Slips of the tongue are often humorous and are in fact closely connected psychologically to wit and joking.

6. *Unfocused interaction* is the mutual awareness individuals have of one another in large gatherings when not directly in conversation together. *Focused interaction*, which can be divided up into distinct *encounters* or episodes of interaction, is when two or more individuals are directly attending to what the other or others are saying and doing.

7. Social interaction can often be illuminatingly studied by applying the dramaturgical model—studying social interaction as if those involved were actors on a stage, having a set and props. As in the theater, in the various contexts of social life there tend to be clear distinctions between *front regions* (the stage itself) and *back regions*, where the actors prepare themselves for the performance and relax afterward.

8. All social interaction is situated in time and space. We can analyze how our daily lives are "zoned" in time and space combined by looking at how activities occur during definite durations and at the same time involve spatial movement.

9. Some mechanisms of social interaction, such as providing *markers* in encounters, may be universal, but many are not. The !Kung of southern Africa, for example, live in small mobile bands, where there is little privacy and thus little opportunity to create front and back regions.

10. Modern societies are characterized largely by *indirect* interpersonal transactions (such as making bank deposits) which lack any *copresence*. This leads to what has been called the *compulsion of proximity*, the tendency to want to meet in person whenever possible, perhaps because this makes it easier to gather information about how others think and feel, and to accomplish impression management.

Chapter Six

Learn that what we define as deviant behavior is determined by society.

The Study of Deviant Behavior

Learn how we define deviance and how it is closely related to social power and social class. See the ways in which conformity is encouraged.

Biological and Psychological Theories of Crime and Deviance

Familiarize yourself with some traditional explanations for deviance and their limitations as theories.

Society and Crime: Sociological Theories

Know the leading sociological theories of crime and how each is useful in understanding deviance.

Crime and Crime Statistics

Recognize the helpfulness and limitations of crime statistics. Learn some important differences between men and women related to crime. Familiarize yourself with some of the varieties of crime. Think about the best solutions to reduce crime.

CONFORMITY, DEVIANCE, AND CRIME

Ishmael is a street vendor who lives and works on the corner of Eighth Street and Sixth Avenue in Greenwich Village. He earns money by taking magazines out of recycled trash and reselling them to passersby. Ishmael has lived on this corner for the past six years, ever since he was released from serving a prison sentence for committing a robbery. During the early 1990s, he was one of over 1.5 million Americans who were detained in prisons and jails, a threefold increase since 1980. This dramatic increase in incarceration had a major impact on the African-American population. In 1992, 52 percent of persons admitted to prison were black, compared to 22 percent in 1930.

The impact of the criminal justice system is shown in the lives of people like Ishmael. While they are in prison, they are not part of the labor force and thus a large amount of joblessness is not reflected in the rates of unemployment reported by the government. At the same time, incarceration also increases the long-term chances of unemployment for men like Ishmael once they are released from prison (Western and Beckett,

1999). From prison, Ishmael went directly to the streets where he now lives. He had nowhere to work and nowhere else to go. People he knew from prison were already living on this corner and he heard he could find them here.

Ishmael is a man who many people would define as a deviant. We all know who deviants are, or so we tend to think. Deviants are those individuals who refuse to live by the rules that the majority of us follow. They're violent criminals, drug addicts, or "down-and-outs," who don't fit in with what most people would define as normal standards of acceptability. Yet things are not quite as they appear—a lesson sociology often teaches us, for it encourages us to look beyond the obvious. The notion of the deviant, as we shall see, is actually not an easy one to define.

We have learned in previous chapters that human social life is governed by rules or norms. Our activities would collapse into chaos if we didn't stick to rules that define some kinds of behavior as proper in particular contexts and others as inappropriate. As we learned earlier in talking about the concept of culture, **norms** are definite principles or rules people are expected to observe; they represent the "dos" and "don'ts" of society. Orderly behavior on the highway, for example, would be impossible if drivers didn't observe the rule of driving on the right. No deviants here, you might think, except perhaps for the drunken or reckless driver. If you did think this, though, you would be wrong. When we drive, most of us are not just deviants but criminals. For most drivers regularly drive at well above the legal speed limits—assuming there isn't a police car in sight.

We are all rule breakers as well as conformists. We are all also rule creators. Most American drivers may break the law on the freeways, but in fact they've evolved informal rules that are superimposed on the legal rules. When the legal speed limit on the highway is 65 mph, most drivers don't go above 75 or so, and less when driving through urban areas.

In most European countries, the legal speed limits are higher than in the United States—between 65 and 70 mph, depending on the country. Drivers there break the law most of the time just as they do in the United States, but their informal rules about proper driving produce higher speeds than in America. People regularly drive at 80–90 mph. Conventional rules about what is and isn't reckless driving also vary. Americans who drive in the south of Italy, for example, where drivers break other traffic rules as well, are apt to find the experience a hair-raising one.

When we begin the study of deviant behavior, we must consider which rules people are observing and which they are breaking. Nobody breaks *all* rules, just as no one conforms to all rules. Even an individual who might seem wholly outside the pale of respectable society, such as Ishmael, is likely to be following many rules of the groups and societies of which he is a member.

For example, when Ishmael gets enough money for a meal, he often goes to a small Chinese restaurant around the corner from where he lives. There he sits and eats his egg rolls, chow mein, and egg drop soup with the same manners as other diners. In this restaurant, he hardly appears as a deviant. When Ishmael is out on the street, he follows the rules of the other street vendors who make a life on the street. In the world of street vendors, he appears as a conformist most of the time. Indeed, some "deviant" groups such as the homeless have strict codes of social behavior for those who live among them. Those who deviate from these informal codes of behavior may be ostracized or expelled from the group and be forced to go elsewhere (Duneier, 1999). Thus, even "deviants" are conformists at times.

THE STUDY OF DEVIANT BEHAVIOR

The study of deviant behavior is one of the most intriguing yet complex areas of sociology. It teaches us that none of us is quite as normal as we might like to think. It also helps us see that people whose behavior might appear incomprehensible or alien can be seen as rational beings when we understand why they act as they do.

The study of deviance, like other fields of sociology, directs our attention to social *power*, as well as the influence of social class—the divisions between rich and poor. When we look at deviance from or conformity to social rules or norms, we always have to bear in mind the question, *Whose* rules? As we shall see, social norms are strongly influenced by divisions of power and class.

What Is Deviance?

Deviance may be defined as nonconformity to a given set of norms that are accepted by a significant number of people in a community or society. No society, as has already been stressed, can be divided up in a simple way between those who deviate from norms and those who conform to them. Most of us on some occasions transgress generally accepted rules of behavior. We may have at some point committed minor acts of theft, like shoplifting or taking small items from work—such as office note paper and pens—for personal use. Or we may have smoked marijuana, purchased alcohol while under age, or used other illegal drugs.

The scope of the concept of deviance is very wide, as some examples will illustrate. The billionaire Howard Hughes built up his massive fortune through a mixture of hard work, inventive ideas, and shrewd decisions. In terms of his drive to succeed, his activities conformed to some of the key values in Western societies, values emphasizing the desirability of material rewards and individual achievement. On the other hand, in some areas, his behavior deviated sharply from orthodox norms. He lived the last few years of his life almost completely isolated from the outside world, hardly ever venturing out of the hotel suite he had made his home. He let his hair grow very long and cultivated a long, straggly beard, making him look more like a biblical prophet than a successful businessman.

Which of these people are deviants by your standards?

THE SOCIOLOGICAL DEBATE

DEFINING DEVIANCY

Many people take it for granted that a well-structured society is designed to prevent deviant behavior from occurring. But Émile Durkheim argued otherwise. He believed that deviance has an important part to play in a well-ordered society. Why did Durkheim think this? He said that by defining what is deviant, we become aware of what is not deviant, and thereby become aware of the standards we share as members of a society. It is not necessarily the case, then, that we should aim to completely eliminate deviance. It is more likely that society needs to keep it within acceptable limits.

Seventy years after Durkheim's work appeared, the sociologist Kai Erikson published *Wayward Puritans*, a study of deviance in seventeenth-century New England. Erikson sought "to test [Durkheim's] notion that the number of deviant offenders a community can afford to recognize is likely to remain stable over time." His research led him to conclude that

a community's capacity for handling deviance, let us say, can be roughly estimated by counting its prison cells and hospital beds, its policemen and psychiatrists, its courts and clinics. . . . The agencies of control often seem to define their job as that of keeping deviance within bounds rather than obliterating it altogether. (Erikson, 1966)

Erikson advanced the hypothesis that societies need their quotas of deviance and that they function in such a way as to keep them intact.

What does a society do when the amount of deviant behavior gets out of hand? In a controversial 1993 article, "Defining Deviancy Down," New York senator Daniel Patrick Moynihan argued that the levels of deviance in American society have increased beyond the point that it can afford to recognize. As a result, we have been "redefining deviancy so as to exempt much conduct previously stigmatized," and also quietly raising the "normal" level so that behavior seen as abnormal by an earlier standard is no longer considered to be so.

How has American society gone about this? One example that Moynihan gives is the deinstitutionalization movement within the mental health profession that began in the 1950s. Instead of being forced into institutions, the mentally ill were treated with tranquilizers and released. As a result, the number of psychiatric patients in New York dropped from 93,000 in 1955 to 11,000 by 1992.

What happened to all of those psychiatric patients? Many of them are the homeless that today are sleeping in doorways. In "defining deviancy down," people sleeping on the street are defined not as insane, but as persons lacking affordable housing. At the same time, the "normal" acceptable level of crime has risen. Moynihan points out that after the St. Valentine's Day massacre in 1929, in which seven gangsters were murdered, the nation was outraged. Today, violent gang murders are so common that there is hardly a reaction. Moynihan also sees the under-reporting of crime as another form of "normalizing" it. As he concludes, "We are getting used to a lot of behavior that is not good for us."

Hughes was both highly successful and highly deviant in his behavior. As a contrasting example, we might take the career of Ted Bundy. Bundy's way of life, on the face of things, conformed to the norms of behavior of a good citizen. He led what seemed not only a normal life, but a most worthy one. For example, he played an active role in the Samaritans, an association that organizes a twenty-four-hour phone-in service for people who are distressed or suicidal. Yet Bundy also carried out a series of horrific murders. Before sentencing him to death, the judge at his trial praised Bundy for his abilities (he had prepared his own defense) but finished by noting what a waste he had made of his life. Bundy's career shows that a person can seem entirely normal while secretly engaging in acts of extreme deviance.

Deviance does not refer only to individual behavior; it concerns the activities of groups as well. An illustration is the Heaven's Gate cult, a religious group whose beliefs and ways of life were different from those of the majority of Americans. The cult was established in the early 1970s when Marshall Herff Applewhite made his way around the West and Midwest of the United States preaching his beliefs, ultimately advertising on the Internet his belief that civilization was doomed and that the only way people could be saved was to kill themselves so their souls could be rescued by a U.F.O. On March 26, 1997, thirty-nine members of the cult followed his advice in a mass suicide at a wealthy estate in Rancho Santa Fe, California.

The Heaven's Gate cult represents an example of a **deviant subculture**. They were able to survive fairly easily within the wider society, supporting themselves by running a website business, and recruiting new members by sending e-mail messages to people they thought might be interested in their beliefs. They had plenty of money and lived together in an expensive home in a wealthy California suburb. Their position diverges from that of another deviant subculture that we just discussed: the homeless.

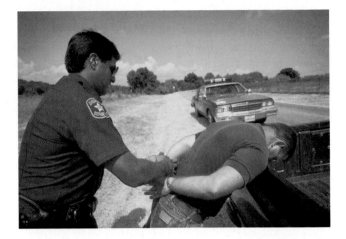

A police officer imposes sanctions on a crime suspect.

Norms and Sanctions

We most often follow social norms because, as a result of socialization, we are used to doing so. **Social control theory** holds that individuals become committed to social norms through interactions with people who obey the law. Through these interactions, we learn self-control. The more numerous these interactions, the fewer opportunities there are to deviate from conventional norms. And, over time, the longer that we interact in ways that are conventional, the more we have at stake in continuing to act in that way (Gottfredson and Hirschi, 1990).

All social norms are accompanied by sanctions that promote conformity and protect against nonconformity. A **sanction** is any reaction from others to the behavior of an individual or group that is meant to ensure that the person or group complies with a given norm. Sanctions may be positive (the offering of rewards for conformity) or negative (punishment for behavior that does not conform). They can also be formal or informal. Formal sanctions are applied by a specific body of people or an agency to ensure that a particular set of norms is followed. Informal sanctions

KEY CONCEPTS IN REVIEW

Deviance may be defined as nonconformity to a given **norm**, or set of norms, that is accepted by the majority of society. What is regarded as deviant can shift from time to time and place to place; "normal" behavior in one cultural setting may be labeled deviant in another.

A **deviant subculture** is a group that deviates from the larger society.

Social control theory asserts that individuals become committed to social norms through interactions with people who obey the law.

Sanctions, classified as formal or informal, are applied by society to reinforce social norms.

Laws are formal rules promoting conformity to government-defined norms.

are less organized and more spontaneous reactions to nonconformity, such as when a student is teasingly accused by friends of working too hard or being a "nerd" if he decides to spend an evening studying rather than going to a party.

The main types of formal sanctions in modern societies are those represented by the courts and prisons. The police, of course, are the agency charged with bringing offenders to trial and possible imprisonment. **Laws** are norms defined by governments as principles that their citizens must follow; sanctions are used against people who do not conform to them. Where there are laws, there are also **crimes,** since crime can most simply be defined as any type of behavior that breaks a law.

It is important to recognize, however, that the law is only a guide to the kind of norms that exist in a society. Oftentimes, subcultures invent their own dos and don'ts. For example, the street people that Ishmael lives among have created their own norms for determining where each of them can set up the magazines that they sell on the sidewalk. Other homeless vendors don't set up in Ishmael's spot on the sidewalk because that would show "disrespect." This example further illustrates that even members of so-called deviant groups usually live in accordance with some norms. What makes them a deviant subculture is that these norms are at odds with the norms of the mainstream of society.

At this point, we can move on to look at the main theories that have been developed to interpret and analyze deviance. Most accounts of deviance have been based particularly on studies of criminal activity, which will be our main focus as well.

BIOLOGICAL AND PSYCHOLOGICAL THEORIES OF CRIME AND DEVIANCE

The Biological View

Some of the first attempts to explain crime were essentially biological in character. The Italian criminologist Cesare Lombroso, working in the 1870s, believed that criminal types could be identified by the shape of the skull. He accepted that social learning could influence the development of criminal behavior, but he regarded most criminals as biologically degenerate or defective. Lombroso's ideas became thoroughly discredited, but similar views have repeatedly been suggested. Another popular method of trying to demonstrate the influence of heredity on criminal tendencies was to study family trees. But this demonstrates virtually nothing about the influence of heredity, because it is impossible to disentangle inherited and environmental influences.

A later theory distinguished three main types of human physique and claimed that one type was directly associated with delinquency. Muscular, active types (mesomorphs), the theory went, are more likely to become delinquent than those of thin physique (ectomorphs) or more fleshy people (endomorphs) (Sheldon, 1949; Glueck and Glueck, 1956). This research has also been widely criticized. Even if there were an overall relationship between bodily type and delinquency, this would show nothing about the influence of heredity. People of the muscular type may be drawn toward criminal activities because these offer opportunities for the physical display of athleticism. Moreover, nearly all studies in this field have been restricted to delinquents in reform schools, and it may be that the tougher, athletic-looking delinquents are more liable to be sent to such schools than fragile-looking, skinny ones. While older studies on the biological explanations of crime have been dismissed, more recent research has sought to rekindle the argument. In a study of New Zealand children, researchers sought to prove that childrens' propensity to aggression was linked to biological factors present at a child's birth (Moffitt, 1996).

However, studies such as this only show that some individuals might be inclined toward irritability and aggressiveness, and this could be reflected in crimes of physical assault on others. Yet there is no decisive evidence that any traits of personality are inherited in this way, and even if they were, their connection to criminality would at most be only a distant one. In fact, the New Zealand study did not argue that there is a biological cause to crime, but rather that biological factors, when combined with certain social factors such as one's home environment, could lead to social situations involving crime.

The Psychological View

Like biological interpretations, psychological theories of crime associate criminality with particular types of personality. Some have suggested that in a minority of individuals, an amoral, or psychopathic, personality develops. **Psychopaths** are withdrawn, emotionless characters who delight in violence for its own sake.

Individuals with psychopathic traits do sometimes commit violent crimes, but there are major problems with the concept of the psychopath. It isn't at all clear that psychopathic traits are inevitably criminal. Nearly all studies of people said to possess these characteristics have been of convicted prisoners, and their personalities inevitably tend to be presented negatively. If we describe the same traits positively, the personality type sounds quite different, and there seems no reason why people of this sort should be inherently criminal. Should we be looking for psychopathic individuals for a research study, we might place the following ad:

ARE YOU ADVENTUROUS?

Researcher wishes to contact adventurous, carefree people who've led exciting, impulsive lives. If you're the kind of person who'd do almost anything for a dare, call 337-XXXX any time. (Widom and Newman, 1985)

Such people might be explorers, spies, gamblers, or just bored with the routines of day-to-day life. They *might* be prepared to contemplate criminal adventures, but would seem just as likely to look for challenges in socially respectable ways.

Psychological theories of criminality can at best explain only some aspects of crime. While some criminals may possess personality characteristics distinct from the remainder of the population, it is highly improbable that the majority of criminals do so. There are all kinds of crimes, and it is implausible to suppose that those who commit them share some specific psychological characteristics. Even if we confine ourselves to one category of crime, such as crimes of violence, different circumstances are involved. Some such crimes are carried out by lone individuals, while oth-

Some military commandos, such as this man, might be considered psychopaths, even though they are not criminals.

ers are the work of organized groups. It is not likely that the psychological makeup of people who are loners will have much in common with the members of a close-knit gang. Even if consistent differences could be linked to forms of criminality, we still couldn't be sure which way the line of causality would run. It might be that becoming involved with criminal groups influences people's outlooks, rather than that the outlooks actually produce criminal behavior in the first place.

SOCIETY AND CRIME: SOCIOLOGICAL THEORIES

Any satisfactory account of the nature of crime must be sociological, for what crime is depends on the social institutions of a society. One of the most important emphases of sociological thinking about crime is on the interconnections between conformity and deviance in different social contexts. Modern societies contain many different subcultures, and behavior that conforms to the norms of one particular subculture may be regarded as deviant outside it; for instance, there may be strong pressure on a member of a boys' gang to prove himself by stealing a car. Moreover, there are wide divergences of wealth and power in society, which greatly influence opportunities open to different groups. Theft and burglary, not surprisingly, are carried out mainly by people from the poorer segments of the population; embezzling and tax evasion are by definition limited to persons in positions of some affluence.

Learned Deviance: Differential Association

Edwin H. Sutherland linked crime to what he called **differential association** (Sutherland, 1949). This idea is very simple. In a society that contains a variety of subcultures, some social environments tend to encourage illegal activities, whereas others do not. Individuals become delinquent through associating with people who are the carriers of criminal norms. For the most part, according to Sutherland, criminal behavior is learned within primary groups, particularly peer groups. This theory is in contrast to the view that psychological differences separate criminals from other people; it sees criminal activities as learned in much the same way as law-abiding ones, and as directed toward the same needs and values. Thieves try to make money just like people in orthodox jobs, but they choose illegal means of doing so.

Differential association can be used to assess Ishmael's life. Before Ishmael went to prison, he lived in Pennsylvania Station with a group of homeless men.

Deviant subcultures often have their own rigid norms of behavior. In the movie The Godfather, *the other mobsters treat Marlon Brando with elaborate respect.*

From this group, Ishmael learned how to target and rob restaurant delivery boys, whom he learned were unlikely to report the crime to the police because many of them were illegal immigrants from Mexico and China. Ishmael would not have known these facts unless he had learned them from associating with others who were already the carriers of criminal norms.

Structural Strain: Anomie as a Cause of Crime

Robert K. Merton's interpretation of crime, which links criminality to other types of deviant behavior, similarly emphasizes the normality of the criminal (Merton, 1957). Merton drew on the concept of **anomie** to construct a highly influential theory of deviance. The notion of anomie was first introduced by Émile Durkheim, one of the founders of sociology, who suggested that in modern societies traditional norms and standards become undermined without being replaced by new ones. Anomie exists when there are no clear standards to guide behavior in a given area of social life. In these circumstances, Durkheim believed, people feel disoriented and anxious; anomie is therefore one of the social factors influencing dispositions to suicide.

Merton modified the concept of anomie to refer to the strain put on individuals' behavior when accepted norms conflict with social reality. In American society—and to some degree in other industrial societies—generally held values emphasize material success, and the means of achieving success are supposed to be self-discipline and hard work. Accordingly, people who really work hard can succeed, no matter what their starting point in life. This idea is not in fact valid, because most of the disadvantaged are given only limited conventional opportunities for advancement, or none at all. Yet those who do not "succeed" find themselves condemned for their apparent inability to make material progress. In this situation, there is great pressure to try to get ahead by any means, legitimate or illegitimate. According to Merton, then, deviance is a by-product of economic inequalities.

Merton identifies five possible reactions to the tensions between socially endorsed values and the limited means of achieving them. *Conformists* accept both generally held values and the conventional means of realizing them, whether or not they meet with success. The majority of the population fall into this category. *Innovators* continue to accept socially approved values but use illegitimate or illegal means to follow them. Criminals who acquire wealth through illegal activities exemplify this type.

Ritualists conform to socially accepted standards although they have lost sight of the values behind these standards. The rules are followed for their own sake without a wider end in view, in a compulsive way. A ritualist would be someone who dedicates herself to a boring job, even though it has no career prospects and provides few rewards. *Retreatists* have abandoned the competitive outlook altogether, thus rejecting both the dominant values and the approved means of achieving them. An example would be the members of a self-supporting commune. Finally, *rebels* reject both the existing values and the means, but wish actively to substitute new ones and reconstruct the social system. The members of radical political groups fall into this category.

Later researchers linked Sutherland's notion of differential association (the idea that the group of people with whom individuals associate influences them for or against crime) to Merton's typology. In their study of delinquent boys' **gangs** (1960), Richard A. Cloward and Lloyd E. Ohlin argued that such gangs arise in subcultural communities where the chances of achieving success legitimately are small, such as among deprived ethnic minorities. Their work rightly emphasized connections between conformity and deviance. Lack of opportunity for success in the terms of the wider society is the main differentiating factor between those who engage in criminal behavior and those who do not.

This theory can also be used to understand Ishmael's life. When asked why he got into the street life, he says

> The reason why my style of life was like that before is that when I went through life there was no gate open for me. I am a high school graduate from Samuel Gompers High School up in the Bronx. From there I went to a school with a variety of trades. From there they sent me to apply for a job. When I went to the job there was ten other individuals who was there to apply. They

Gangs most often arise in poor communities where the chance for upward social mobility is small.

> took three from my school who were white. I did not get the job. I felt that I was denied not because of my qualifications, but pertaining to my skin color. So that drove me into other things that wrong to society. I felt that I had something to offer to society. When I completed my term in school, I felt that I would be able to get a job and live a life on my own. I had documentation from my school stating I was well enough and would be able to complete the job. But they still thought I wasn't fittable for the job situation. And they said they would call me, but as I waited for the call, the call never came through. So I chose to live the other life, which caused me to get four years in jail.

Recent research by sociologists has examined the validity of claims like Ishmael's that immediate material deprivation can lead people to commit crimes. A survey of homeless youth in Canada, for instance, shows a strong correlation between hunger, lack of shelter, and unemployment, on the one hand, and theft, prostitution, and even violent crime on the other (Hagan and McCarthy, 1992).

We should be cautious, however, about the idea that people in poorer communities, like Ishmael, aspire to the same level of success as more affluent people. Most tend to adjust their aspirations to what they see as the reality of their situation. Yet it would also be wrong to suppose that a mismatch of aspirations and opportunities is confined to the less privileged. There are pressures toward criminal activity among other groups too, as is indicated by the so-called white-collar crimes of embezzlement, fraud, and tax evasion, which we will study later.

Labeling Theory

One of the most important approaches to the understanding of criminality is called **labeling theory**—although this term itself is a label for a cluster of related ideas rather than a unified view. Labeling theory originally came to be associated with Howard S. Becker's studies of marijuana smokers (1963). In the early 1960s, marijuana use was a marginal activity carried on by subcultures rather than the lifestyle choice it is today (Hathaway, 1997). Becker found that becoming a marijuana smoker depended on one's acceptance into the subculture, close association with experienced users, and one's attitudes toward nonusers. Labeling theorists like Becker interpret deviance not as a set of characteristics of individuals or groups, but as a *process* of interaction between deviants and nondeviants. In other words, it is not the act of marijuana smoking that makes one a deviant, but the way others react to marijuana smoking that makes it deviant. In the view of labeling theorists, we must discover why some people become tagged with a "deviant" label in order to understand the nature of deviance itself.

People who represent the forces of law and order, or are able to impose definitions of conventional morality upon others, do most of the labeling. The labels that create categories of deviance thus express the power structure of society. By and large, the rules in terms of which deviance is defined are framed by the wealthy for the poor, by men for women, by older people for younger people, and by ethnic majorities for minority groups. For example, many children wander into other people's gardens, steal fruit, or play truant. In an affluent neighborhood, these might be regarded by parents, teachers, and police alike as relatively innocent pastimes of childhood. In poor areas, they might be seen as evidence of tendencies toward juvenile delinquency.

Once a child is labeled a delinquent, he is stigmatized as a criminal and is likely to be considered un-trustworthy by teachers and prospective employers. He then relapses into further criminal behavior, widening the gulf with orthodox social conventions. Edwin Lemert (1972) called the initial act of transgression **primary deviation**. **Secondary deviation** occurs when the individual comes to accept the label and sees himself as deviant. Other research has shown that how we think of ourselves and how we believe others perceive us influences our propensity for committing crime. One study examining self-appraisals of a random national sample of young men showed that such appraisals are strongly tied to levels of criminality (Matsueda, 1992).

Take, for example, Luke, who smashes a shop window while spending a Saturday night out on the town with his friends. The act may perhaps be called the accidental result of over-boisterous behavior, an excusable characteristic of young men. Luke might escape with a reprimand and a small fine. If he is from a "respectable" background, this is a likely result. And the smashing of the window stays at the level of primary deviance if the youth is seen as someone of good character who on this occasion became too rowdy. If, on the other hand, the police and courts hand out a suspended sentence and make Luke report to a social worker, the incident could become the first step on the road to secondary deviance. The process of "learning to be deviant" tends to be accentuated by the very organizations supposedly set up to correct deviant behavior—prisons and social agencies.

Labeling theory is important because it begins from the assumption that no act is intrinsically criminal. Definitions of criminality are established by the powerful, through the formulation of laws and their interpretation by police, courts, and correctional institutions. Critics of labeling theory have sometimes argued that there are certain acts that are consistently prohibited across virtually all cultures, such as murder, rape, and robbery. This view is surely incorrect; even within our own culture, killing is not always regarded as murder. In times of war, killing of the enemy is positively approved, and until recently the laws in most U.S. states did not recognize sexual intercourse forced on a woman by her husband as rape.

We can more convincingly criticize labeling theory on other grounds. First, in emphasizing the active process of labeling, labeling theorists neglect the processes that *lead* to acts defined as deviant. For labeling certain activities as deviant is not completely arbitrary; differences in socialization, attitudes, and opportunities influence how far people engage in behavior likely to be labeled deviant. For instance, children from deprived backgrounds are on average more likely to steal from shops than are richer children. It is not the labeling that leads them to steal in the first place so much as the background from which they come.

Second, it is not clear whether labeling actually does have the effect of increasing deviant conduct. Delinquent behavior tends to increase following a conviction, but is this the result of the labeling itself? Other factors, such as increased interaction with other delinquents or learning about new criminal opportunities, may be involved.

Rational Choice and "Situational" Analyses of Crime

None of the theories mentioned so far finds much place for understanding criminal behavior as a deliberate and calculated act. Each tends to see criminality as "reaction" to outside influences, rather than as conduct in which individuals actively engage in order to get definite benefits. But some writers suggest that people who engage in criminal acts, whether regularly or more sporadically, do so purposefully, and usually recognize the risks they are running. This approach to understanding criminal behavior is called **rational-choice analysis** (Cornish and Clarke, 1986).

Research indicates that many criminal actions, particularly more minor types of crime—like nonviolent theft or burglary—are "situational" decisions. An opportunity presents itself, and seems too good to pass up—as when someone sees that a house is empty, tries the back door, and finds that it is easy to get in. There are few "specialists" in crime; most people are "generalists," supplementing their other sources of income by sporadically taking part in acts of theft or burglary when opportunities to do so crop up (Walsh, 1986).

Floyd Feeney (1986) studied a sample of male robbers in California, some convicted of crimes of robbery with violence. He found that over half said they had not planned in advance for the crime or crimes

for which they were convicted. Another third reported only minor planning, such as finding a partner, thinking about where to leave a getaway car, or whether to use a weapon. Such planning usually took place the same day as the robbery, often within a few hours of it. Of the 15 percent who had used a carefully planned approach, 9 percent simply followed a pattern they had established before. Over 60 percent said that before the robbery they had not even thought of being caught. The belief was perhaps well founded: the sample included one person who had committed over 1,000 robberies by the age of twenty-six, but had only been convicted once.

The fact that many property crimes are "situational" emphasizes how similar much criminal activity is to day-to-day decisions of a nondeviant kind. Given that an individual is prepared to consider engaging in criminal activities (which some of the other theories might assist in explaining) many criminal acts involve quite ordinary decision-making processes. The decision to take something from a store when no one is looking is not so different from deciding to buy a particular product that catches the eye—in fact, a person might do both during the same shopping expedition.

Social Disorder: The Theory of "Broken Windows"

Another prominent theory of criminal behavior, which analyzes the social situation a criminal is faced with, is known as "broken windows" (Wilson and Kelling, 1982). The theory is based on a study by the social psychologist Philip Zimbardo, who abandoned cars without license plates and with their hoods up in two entirely different social settings, the wealthy community of Palo Alto, California, and a poor neighborhood in the Bronx, New York. In both places, both cars were vandalized once passersby, irregardless of class or race, sensed that the cars were abandoned and that "no one cared" (Zimbardo, 1969). Extrapolating from this study, the authors of the "broken windows" theory argued that any sign of social disorder in a community, even the appearance of a broken window, encourages more serious crime to flourish. One unrepaired broken window is a sign that no one cares, so

THE SOCIOLOGICAL DEBATE

THE RELATIONSHIP BETWEEN SOCIAL CLASS AND CRIME

The relationship between social class and crime in America is an issue that attracts attention from the media, policy makers, and sociologists. Media images of crime typically portray offenders as economically disadvantaged and poorly educated, thus perpetuating a belief that crime is primarily an activity of the poor. Early sociological research also reflected this assumption, yet more recent research acknowledges that the relationship is far more complex.

Early sociological theories designed to explain crime and delinquency assumed that, and in turn tried to explain why, members of disadvantaged social classes should be expected to commit more crime than persons from higher strata of society. As we saw earlier, Robert Merton applied Émile Durkheim's concept of anomie and argued that this feeling of normlessness arises when an individual is expected to achieve certain universal goals but does not have access to the appropriate means for achieving those goals. Merton considered material wealth a universal goal to which all Americans are taught to aspire, and the appropriate means of achieving wealth in America include receiving a good education and securing a good job. When individuals do not have access to good education and jobs, Merton predicted that they might attempt to obtain material wealth through inappropriate means, such as criminal activity. Such individuals, not surprisingly, would more likely come from the lower classes. In this way, Merton's theory explained why members of the lower classes should be more involved in crime.

In the 1970s, however, sociologists began to question whether individuals from the lower classes were more likely to engage in criminal activity than individuals from more advantaged social classes. Initial inspections of arrest data showed that poorer persons were more likely than those of upper classes to be arrested and prosecuted by the criminal justice system. However, such a finding could merely reflect biases on the part of the criminal justice system, and certainly could not account for those criminals who are not apprehended.

An analysis of crime and juvenile delinquency conducted by sociologist Charles Tittle and his colleagues (1978) revealed that when self-reported measures of crime are used, rather than official arrest statistics, the negative association between crime and class largely disappears. Other studies have since replicated this finding, and Tittle and Meier (1990) concluded that "there is no pervasive relationship between individual SES (socioeconomic status) and delinquency."

Although no relationship between class and delinquency appears to exist on the general level, sociologists have discovered strong factors linking specific economic characteristics to crime. For example, individual unemployment is frequently associated with criminal activity, particularly among the chronically unemployed. Relatedly, sociologist John Hagan argues that the reverse relationship may hold for young adults; that is, involvement in crime and delinquency as an adolescent will likely restrict an individual's future employment opportunities.

Other sociologists have examined societal-level economic factors, such as the finding that the degree of wage inequality in society (a measure of the gap between different levels of wages) is positively associated with the observed rate of violent crimes such as murder and assault (Fowles and Merva, 1996).

Sociologist Edwin Sutherland adds an additional point to consider. Sutherland (as we saw earlier, a proponent of differential association theory) argued that sociologists actually have very little idea about the causes of crime because they have incorrectly specified what should be viewed as "crime." By focusing on crimes committed predominantly by the lower classes, Sutherland argues that sociologists have ignored the crimes of society's elites—white-collar crime (committed by individuals) and corporate crime (committed by organizations). The extent of such crime and its associated damage are immense, yet sociologists generally tend to ignore such behavior in their creation of explanations of crime. Sutherland might ask: "How do we explain embezzlement by a white-collar manager using anomie theory?" Such a person would appear to have full access to the legitimate means of achieving success, after all.

Ultimately, many sociologists currently argue that

"the relationship between class and crime is class and crime specific" (Hagan, 1992). This implies that individuals from different classes engage in those crimes for which they possess the required resources. While we should not expect to see middle-class businesspeople performing armed robbery, perhaps we should also recognize that lower-class individuals are unlikely to engage in such corporate fraud as led to the insider trading crisis or the savings and loan institution debacle of the late 1980s.

breaking more windows—that is, committing more serious crimes—is a rational response by criminals to this situation of social disorder. As a result, minor acts of deviance can lead to a spiral of crime and social decay.

In the late 1980s and 1990s, the "broken windows" theory served as the basis for new policing strategies that aggressively focused on "minor" crimes such as drinking or using drugs in public or traffic violations. Studies have shown that proactive policing directed at maintaining public order can have a positive effect on reducing more serious crimes such as robbery (Sampson and Cohen, 1988). However, one flaw of the "broken windows" theory is that the police are left to identify a "social disorder" however they want. Without a systematic definition of disorder, the police are authorized to see almost anything as a sign of disorder and anyone as a threat. In fact, as crime rates fell throughout the 1990s, the number of complaints of police abuse and harassment went up, particularly by young, urban, black men who fit the "profile" of a potential criminal.

Linking Micro- and Macrosociology: The Saints and the Roughnecks

The connections between the processes by which deviant behavior occurs and the larger class structure were noted by William Chambliss in a famous study "The Saints and the Roughnecks" (Chambliss, 1973). Chambliss studied two groups of delinquents in an American high school, one from upper-middle-class families ("The Saints") and the other from poor families ("The Roughnecks"). While the Saints were constantly involved in petty crimes such as drinking, vandalism, truancy, and theft, none of their members were ever arrested. The Roughnecks were involved in similar criminal activities, yet they were constantly in trouble with the police. After Chambliss concluded that neither group was more delinquent than the other, he looked to other factors which could explain the different reaction of the police and the broader community to these two groups.

Chambliss found, for example, that the upper-class gang had automobiles and thus were able to remove themselves from the eyes of the community. The lower-class boys, through necessity, congregated in an area where everyone in the community frequently saw them. Chambliss concluded that differences of this sort were indicative of the class structure of American society, which gave certain wealthier groups advantages when it came to being labeled as deviant. For instance, the parents of the Saints saw their sons' crimes as harmless pranks while the parents of the Roughnecks acquiesced to the police's labeling of their sons' behavior as criminal. The community as a whole also seemed to agree with these different labels.

These boys went on to have lives consistent with this labeling, with the Saints living conventional middle-class lives and the Roughnecks having continual problems with the law. As we saw earlier in the chapter, this is what Lemert called "secondary deviance," because it is thought to result from the inability of a person to carry on as "normal" once he has been labeled as a "deviant."

Chambliss's study is widely cited by sociologists for showing the connection between macrosociological factors like social class and microsociological phenomena such as how people become labeled as deviant. This study provides an example of how difficult it is to isolate micro- and macro-level factors in the social construction of deviance.

Theoretical Conclusions

The contributions of the sociological theories of crime are twofold. First, these theories correctly emphasize the continuities between criminal and "respectable" behavior. The contexts in which particular types of

KEY CONCEPTS IN REVIEW

Biological and psychological theories have been developed claiming that crime and other forms of deviance are genetically determined, but these have been largely discredited. Instead, social contexts and social institutions determine whether an activity or individual is considered deviant.

The idea of **differential association**, proposed by Edwin Sutherland, states that criminals associate with others who follow criminal norms and form a subculture through their association. Criminal activities are learned in much the same way as law-abiding ones, and in general are directed toward the same needs and values.

Anomie, the lack of norms or clear standards of behavior, was modified by Robert Merton to refer to the strain put on an individual's behavior when accepted norms (such as becoming rich) conflicted with social reality (being poor).

Drawing on Merton's idea, some sociologists have argued that gangs form in subcultures when there is little chance of material success.

Labeling theory analyzes deviance as a process of interaction between deviants and nondeviants. It assumes that no act is intrinsically deviant (or normal). Instead, what is deviant is defined by people in powerful positions. Labeling someone so will only reinforce their deviant behavior.

Rational-choice analysis, unlike other sociological theories that emphasize the influence of social context on deviant behavior, analyzes deviance as a purposeful act with benefits for the deviant individual.

Sociological theories of deviance stress the continuity between deviant and nondeviant behavior and emphasize social factors and context. Thus, wealth, power, race, ethnicity, and gender all shape the definition of deviance.

---

activity are seen as criminal and punishable by law vary widely. Second, all agree that context is important in criminal activities. Whether someone engages in a criminal act or comes to be regarded as a criminal is influenced fundamentally by social learning and social surroundings.

In spite of its deficiencies, labeling theory is perhaps the most widely used approach to understanding crime and deviant behavior. This theory sensitizes us to the ways in which some activities come to be defined as punishable in law, and the power relations that form such definitions, as well as to the circumstances in which particular individuals fall foul of the law.

Now let's look directly at the nature of the criminal activities occurring in modern societies, paying particular attention to crime in the United States.

CRIME AND CRIME STATISTICS

How dangerous *are* our streets compared with yesteryear? Is American society more violent than other societies? You should be able to use the sociological skills you have developed already to answer these questions.

In Chapter 2, for example, we learned something about how to interpret statistics. The statistics of crime are a constant focus of attention on television and in the newspapers. Most TV and newspaper reporting is based on official statistics on crime, collected by the police and published by the government. But many crimes are never reported to the police at all. Some criminologists think that about half of all se-

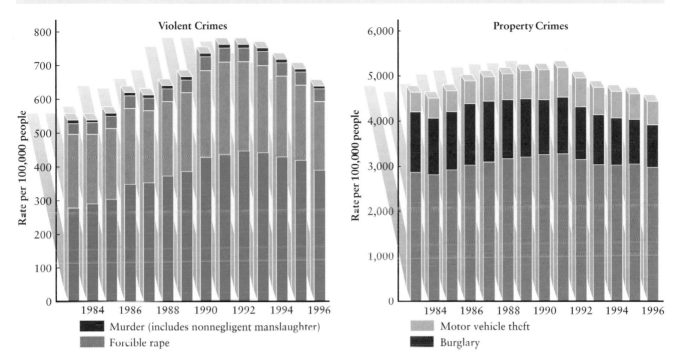

Figure 6.1
CRIME RATES IN THE UNITED STATES, 1983–1996

SOURCE: U.S. Bureau of the Census, 1998, Table No. 335, p. 210.

rious crimes, such as robbery with violence, are not reported. The proportion of less serious crimes, especially small thefts, that don't come to the attention of the police is even higher. Since 1973, the Bureau of the Census has been interviewing households across the country to find out how many members had been the victims of particular crimes over the previous six months. This procedure, which is called the National Crime Victimization Survey, has confirmed that the overall rate of crime is larger than the reported crime index. For instance, in 1991, only 59 percent of rapes were reported, 55 percent of robberies, 47 percent of assaults, and 50 percent of burglaries.

Public concern in the United States tends to focus on crimes of violence—murder, assault, and rape—even though only about 10 percent of all crimes are violent (see Figure 6.1). In the United States, the most common victims of murder and other violent crimes (with the obvious exception of rape) are young, poor,

African-American men living in the larger cities (see Figure 6.2). The rate of murder among black male teenagers is particularly high, five times the rate for their white counterparts. In general, whether indexed by police statistics or by the National Crime Victimization Survey, violent crime, burglary, and car theft are more common in cities than in the suburbs surrounding them; and they are more common in the suburbs than in smaller towns (see Table 6.1).

There can be no doubt that the United States is a dangerous place compared with other industrial countries. A comparison of murder rates, probably the most reliable of all crime statistics, shows differences between the United States and other Western societies (see Global Map 6.1). There are more reported murders each year in Detroit, for example, with a population of just over 1.5 million, than in the whole of Britain, with a population of 55 million. In recent

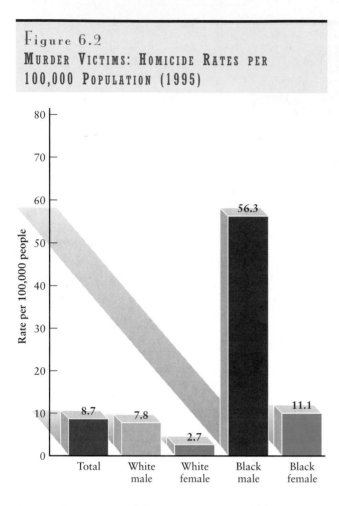

Figure 6.2

MURDER VICTIMS: HOMICIDE RATES PER 100,000 POPULATION (1995)

SOURCE: U.S. Bureau of the Census, 1998, Table No. 341, p. 213.

clining market for crack cocaine and the stigmatization of crack among young urban dwellers. Another factor has been the booming economy of the 1990s, which has provided job opportunities for those who may have been enticed to work in the drug trade (Butterfield, 1998).

One reason often given for the relatively high rates of violent crime in the United States is the widespread availability of handguns and other firearms. This is relevant, but does not provide a complete answer. Switzerland has very low rates of violent crime, yet firearms are easily accessible. All Swiss males are members of the citizen army and keep weapons in their homes, including rifles, revolvers, and sometimes other automatic weapons, plus ammunition; nor are gun licenses difficult to obtain.

Table 6.1 Crime Rates in Metropolitan vs. Rural Areas for 1996

TYPE OF CRIME	METROPOLITAN RATE (PER 100,000 POPULATION)	RURAL RATE
Violent crime	715	222
Murder	8	5
Forcible rape	38	24
Robbery	244	16
Assault	424	177
Property crime	4,798	1,828
Burglary	993	620
Larceny	3,188	1,083
Auto theft	616	126

SOURCE: U.S. Bureau of the Census, 1998, Table No. 336, p. 210.

years, there has been a drop in the overall crime rate throughout the United States to its lowest levels since 1973, when the victimization survey was started. Since 1991, rates of violent crime in particular have dropped substantially, murders by 31 percent and robberies by 32 percent. There is not any one prevailing explanation among sociologists for this decline, although many politicians would like to take credit for it. Aggressive new efforts by local police to stop the use of guns have certainly contributed to the decrease in homicides, but other social factors are also at work. Foremost among these is related to the de-

The most likely explanation for the high level of violent crime in the United States is a combination of the availability of firearms, the general influence of the "frontier tradition," and the subcultures of violence in the large cities. Violence by frontiersmen and vigilantes is an honored part of American history. Some of the first established immigrant areas in the cities developed their own informal modes of neighborhood control, backed by violence or the threat of violence. Similarly, young people in African-American and Hispanic communities today have developed subcultures of manliness and honor associated with rituals of violence, and some belong to gangs whose everyday life is one of drug dealing, territory protection, and violence.

A notable feature of most crimes of violence is their mundane character. Most assaults and homicides bear little resemblance to the murderous, random acts of gunmen or the carefully planned homicides given most prominence in the media. Murders generally happen in the context of family and other interpersonal relationships; the victim usually knows her murderer.

Gender and Crime

As in other areas of sociology, criminological studies have traditionally ignored half the population—women (Morris, 1987). Most theories of deviance similarly disregard women. An example is Robert Merton's account of social structure and anomie. Logically, one could argue that women should figure more prominently than men in the categories of deviance identified by Merton, including crime, as there are fewer opportunities open for women to get ahead than for men. Yet one of the most striking features of criminal statistics is that most crimes of all types are carried out by men (see Table 6.2). How should we interpret the extraordinary differences that seem to exist in the tendency of men and women to engage in crime? The question is an important one: the link between masculinity and crime might be relevant to trying to reduce levels of crime, particularly crimes of violence, for reasons that will be discussed later.

Table 6.2 Percentage of Crimes Committed by Men, 1996

CRIME	PERCENTAGE MALE
All serious crime	75.5
Murder	89.7
Rape	98.8
Robbery	90.3
Assault	82.1
Burglary	88.7
Theft	66.2
Auto theft	86.4
Arson	85.1

SOURCE: U.S. Bureau of the Census, 1998, Table No. 335, p. 220.

NOTE: Data represents arrests (not charges), estimated by the FBI.

MALE AND FEMALE CRIME RATES

The statistics on gender and crime are startling.[1] For example, there is an enormous imbalance in the ratio of men and women in prison, not only in the United States but in all the industrial countries: women make up only some 6 percent of the U.S. prison population. Also, as we have seen, the offenses of women rarely involve violence and are almost all small scale. Petty thefts like shoplifting and public-order offenses such as prostitution are typical female crimes.

[1] In comparing the behavior of men and women, sociologists often prefer to use the term "gender" rather than "sex." "Sex" refers to the biological/anatomical differences between women and men, "gender" to the psychological/social/cultural differences between masculinity and femininity (see Chapter 8).

GREENLAND
(DENMARK)

SWEDEN
ICELAND
NORWAY
DENMARK
GERMANY
NETHERLANDS
IRELAND
U.K.
BELGIUM
LUXEMBOURG
FRANCE
SWITZERLAND
ITALY
AZORES
PORTUGAL
SPAIN
TUNISIA

ALASKA
(U.S)

CANADA

UNITED STATES

ATLANTIC OCEAN

MOROCCO

WESTERN SAHARA
(MOROCCO)

ALGERIA

BERMUDA
BAHAMAS
HAITI
DOMINICAN REPUBLIC
Virgin Is.
PUERTO RICO
ST. CHRISTOPHER AND NEVIS
ANTIGUA AND BARBUDA
DOMINICA
BARBADOS
ST. LUCIA
ST. VINCENT AND
THE GRENADINES
GRENADA
TRINIDAD AND
TOBAGO

CUBA
MEXICO
BELIZE
JAMAICA
GUATEMALA NICARAGUA
EL SALVADOR
HONDURAS
COSTA RICA
PANAMA

Hawaiian Is.

PACIFIC OCEAN

VENEZUELA

COLOMBIA

SURINAME
GUYANA

FR. GUYANA

CAPE VERDE

MAURITANIA
SENEGAL
GAMBIA
GUINEA-BISSAU
GUINEA
SIERRA
LEONE
LIBERIA
IVORY
COAST
BOURKIN
FASO

MALI

NIGER

NIGERIA

CAMEROON

SAO TOME
AND
PRINCIPE

Galapagos Is.
ECUADOR

BRAZIL

PERU

BOLIVIA

WESTERN
SAMOA

PARAGUAY

GHANA
TOGO
BENIN

EQUATORIAL
GUINEA

GABON

CONGO
NAMIBIA

TONGA

Easter Is.

CHILE

URUGUAY

ARGENTINA

Falkland Is.

	10+
	5.0–9.9
	1.1–4.9
	1.0 or less
	No data available

SOURCE: *The Economist*, 1990.

Surprisingly, the United States does not have the highest reported murder rate in the world, although its murder rate is higher than most countries'. In general, high rates of violent crime are prevalent in societies marked by major social divisions and economic inequalities. Many of the countries not reporting any data are in the midst of internal turmoil, such as Afghanistan, Croatia, and South Africa, and it is likely that levels of violent crime there are high. Keep in mind that these statistics, like crime statistics in general, are not entirely reliable.

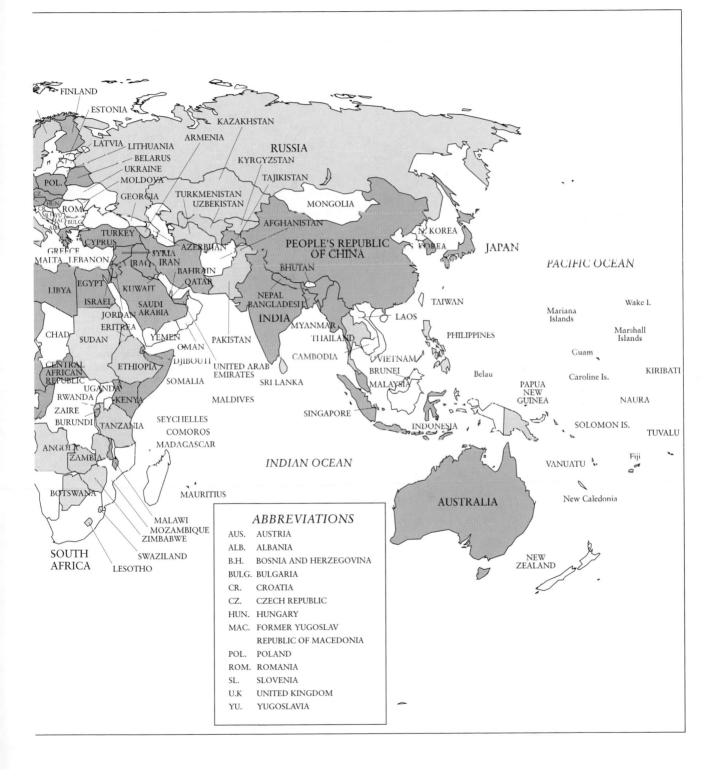

ABBREVIATIONS

AUS.   AUSTRIA
ALB.   ALBANIA
B.H.   BOSNIA AND HERZEGOVINA
BULG.   BULGARIA
CR.   CROATIA
CZ.   CZECH REPUBLIC
HUN.   HUNGARY
MAC.   FORMER YUGOSLAV
        REPUBLIC OF MACEDONIA
POL.   POLAND
ROM.   ROMANIA
SL.   SLOVENIA
U.K   UNITED KINGDOM
YU.   YUGOSLAVIA

The gender difference in crime used to be explained by the supposedly innate biological or psychological differences of women, in terms of strength, passivity, or preoccupation with reproduction (Sheldon and Glueck, 1956; Gove, 1985). Nowadays, female qualities are seen as largely socially generated, in common with the traits of masculinity. Many women are socialized to value different things from men (caring for others and the fostering of personal relationships). Even though a high proportion of women are now in the labor force, most spend much more of their lives in domestic settings than men do—not necessarily through choice, but because most men don't take equal responsibility for household chores. And in the domestic sphere, there are fewer opportunities and less motivation for most forms of criminal activity than in public settings.

The only crime where the female rate of conviction approximates that of men is shoplifting. Some have argued that this fact indicates that women will engage in criminal activities when they find themselves in a public context—out shopping—rather than in a domestic situation. In other words, when the opportunity to commit a crime is more or less equal between men and women, they are equally likely to commit offenses.

At the moment, it is difficult to say with any certainty whether female rates and patterns of crime will increasingly resemble those of men as gender divisions become more blurred. Ever since the late nineteenth century, criminologists have predicted that increasing gender equality would reduce or eliminate the differences in criminality between men and women, but as yet these differences remain pronounced.

CRIME AND THE "CRISIS OF MASCULINITY"

A recent study focused on the possible relation between gender and the high levels of crime in the poorer areas of U.S. cities. Why should so many young men in these areas turn to crime? Some answers we have already touched on. Boys are often part of gangs from an early age, a subculture in which some forms of crime are a way of life. And once gang members are labeled as criminals by the authorities, they embark on regular criminal activities. In spite of the existence today of girl gangs, such subcultures are

fundamentally masculine and infused with male values of adventure, excitement, and buddyship.

The British sociologist Beatrix Campbell, on the basis of an empirical study of the violent behavior of young men in a number of cities, has suggested that their behavior is in part a response to a "crisis of masculinity" in modern societies (Campbell, 1993). In the past, young men, even in neighborhoods where the level of criminality was high, had a clear set of goals to aim for in life: getting a legitimate job and becoming the breadwinner for a wife and family. But such a male role, Campbell argues, is now under strain, particularly for young men in more deprived areas. Where long-term unemployment is the only prospect, aiming to support a family isn't an option. Moreover, women have become more independent than they used to be, and don't need a man to achieve status in the wider society. The result is a spiral of social deterioration of the sort found in African-American ghetto areas today. Campbell's study fits closely with other recent sociological work (see Chapters 9 and 16).

Crimes of the Powerful

It is plain enough that there are connections between crime and poverty. But it would be mistaken to suppose that crime is concentrated among the poor. Crimes carried out by people in positions of power and wealth can have consequences more far-reaching than the often petty crimes of the poor.

The term **white-collar crime,** first introduced by Edwin Sutherland (1949), refers to crime carried out by people in the more affluent sectors of society. This category of criminal activity includes tax fraud, antitrust violations, illegal sales practices, securities and land fraud, embezzlement, the manufacture or sale of dangerous products, and illegal environmental pollution, as well as straightforward theft. The distribution of white-collar crimes is even harder to measure than that of other types of crime; most do not appear in the official statistics at all.

Efforts made to detect white-collar crime are ordinarily limited, and it is only on rare occasions that those who are caught go to jail. Although the authorities regard white-collar crime in a more tolerant light than crimes of the less privileged, it has been calculated that the amount of money involved in white-collar crime in the United States is forty times greater than the amount involved in crimes against property such as robberies, burglaries, larceny, forgeries, and car thefts (President's Commission on Organized Crime, 1986). Some forms of white-collar crime, moreover, affect more people than lower-class criminality. An embezzler might rob thousands—or today, via computer fraud, millions—of people.

Violent aspects of white-collar crime are less visible than cases of homicide or assault, but are just as real and just as serious. For example, the violation of regulations concerning the preparation of new drugs, safety in the workplace, or pollution may cause physical harm or death. Deaths from hazards at work far outnumber murders, although precise statistics about job accidents are difficult to obtain. We cannot assume that the majority of these deaths and injuries are the result of employer negligence about safety regulations for which they are legally liable; but some are.

"Kickbacks, embezzlement, price fixing, bribery . . . this is an extremely high-crime area."

Organized Crime

Organized crime refers to forms of activity that have some of the characteristics of orthodox business but that are illegal. Organized crime embraces illegal gambling, prostitution, large-scale theft, and protection rackets, among other activities. In America, it is a massive business, rivaling any legitimate form of economic enterprise, such as the auto industry. National and local criminal organizations provide illegal goods and services to mass consumers; some criminal networks also extend internationally.

Precise information about the nature of organized crime is difficult to obtain. In romantic portrayals of gangsters, organized crime in the United States is controlled by a secret society of national dimensions, the Mafia. The Mafia, like the cowboy, is in some degree a creation of American folklore. There is almost certainly no group of mysterious mobsters of Sicilian origin who sit at the top of a coherent nationwide organization. Yet it does seem that established criminal organizations exist in nearly all major American cities, some of which have connections with one another.

Organized crime in the United States is much more firmly established, pervasive, and tenacious than in other industrial societies. In France, for example, such crime is largely limited in its influence to two major cities, Paris and Marseilles. In southern Italy, the region of the stereotypical gangster, criminal networks are very powerful, but they are linked to traditional patterns of family organization and community control within largely poor, rural areas. Organized crime has probably become so significant in American society because of an early association with the activities of the industrial robber barons of the late nineteenth century. Many of the early industrialists made fortunes by exploiting immigrant labor, often ignoring legal regulations on working conditions and using a mixture of corruption and violence to build their industrial empires. Organized crime flourished in the deprived ethnic ghettos (where people were ignorant of their legal and political rights), using similar methods to limit competition and build networks of corruption.

DRUG TRAFFICKING

How easy would it have been for you to purchase marijuana in high school? How easy would it be to do so today? Lamentable as it may seem to some, most young people in the United States have relatively easy access to illegal drugs. According to recent Congressional testimony given by the Director of the Office of National Drug Control Policy, "nine percent of twelve to seventeen year olds are current drug users . . . 49.6 percent of high school seniors reported having tried marijuana at least once . . . [and] in every grade (eighth, tenth and twelfth) 2.1 percent of students have tried heroin" (McCaffrey, 1998).

What factors determine the availability of illegal drugs in your community? The level of police enforcement is important, of course, as is the extent of local demand. But no less important is the existence of networks of traffickers able to transport the drugs from the countries in which they are grown to your hometown. These networks have been able to flourish, in part, because of globalization.

While the cultivation of marijuana in the United States

represents a major illicit industry, almost all of the world's coca plants and opium poppies are grown in the Third World. The U.S. government spends billions of dollars each year to assist Third World nations with eradication efforts,

Illicit gambling on horse races, lotteries, and sporting events represents the greatest source of income generated by organized crime in the United States. In Western countries other than America, off-course betting is legal; the United Kingdom permits licensed public betting shops. While these do not escape all criminal influence, gambling is not controlled by illegal organizations to anything like the same extent as in the United States.

Despite numerous campaigns by the government and the police, the narcotics trade is one of the most rapidly expanding international criminal industries, with an annual growth rate of more than 10 percent in the 1980s and an extremely high level of profit. Heroin networks stretch across the Far East, particularly South Asia, North Africa, the Middle East, and Latin America. Drug trafficking is on the increase throughout the world, as is the use of illegal drugs. A report published in 1991 calculated the sales of cocaine, heroin, and cannabis at a value of $122 billion in the United States and Europe (Benn, 1991).

Are Prisons the Answer?

"What are we going to do about these kids (monsters) who kill with guns??? Line them up against the wall and get a firing squad and pull, pull, pull. I am volun-

and also devotes significant resources to stopping the flow of drugs past U.S. borders. In 1995, the federal government spent more than $8.2 billion on the "war on drugs" and since 1981 has spent a total of $65 billion (Bertram et al., 1996, p. 10). Despite this massive expenditure, there is little evidence that eradication or interdiction efforts have significantly decreased the supply of illegal drugs in the United States. Why have these efforts failed?

One answer is that the profit motive is simply too great. Farmers struggling to scratch out a living for themselves in Bolivia or Peru, members of the Colombian drug cartels, and low-level street dealers in the United States all receive substantial monetary rewards for their illegal activities. These rewards create a strong incentive to devise ways around anti-drug efforts, and to run the risk of getting caught.

Another answer—one recently discussed at a summit attended by leaders of the eight major industrial powers—is that drug traffickers have been able to take advantage of globalization. First, in their attempts to evade the authorities, traffickers make use of all the communications technologies that are available in a global age. As one commentator put it, drug traffickers "now use sophisticated technology, such as signal interceptors, to plot radar and avoid monitoring . . . [and] they can use faxes, computers and cellular phones to coordinate their activities and make their business run smoothly" (Cheepsiuk, 1998). Second, the globalization of the financial sector has helped create an

infrastructure in which large sums of money can be moved around the world electronically in a matter of seconds, making it relatively easy to "launder" drug money (that is, to make it appear to have come from a legitimate business venture). Third, recent changes in government policy designed to allow the freer flow of persons and legitimate goods across international borders have increased the opportunities for smuggling.

At the same time, globalization may create new opportunities for governments to work together to combat drug trafficking. Indeed, world leaders recently called for greater international cooperation in narcotics enforcement, stressing the need for information sharing and coordinated enforcement efforts.

teering to pull, pull, pull" (anonymous letter received by a judge in Dade County, Florida).

This letter writer isn't alone. Although as measured by police statistics (problematic, as we have seen) rates of violent crime have declined since 1990, many people in the United States have started to view crime as their most serious social concern—more so than unemployment or the state of the economy (Lacayo, 1994). Surveys show that Americans also favor tougher prison sentences for all but relatively minor crimes. The price of imprisonment, however, is enormous: it costs an average of $460,000 to keep a prisoner behind bars for twenty years. Moreover, even if the prison system were expanded, it wouldn't reduce the level of serious crime a great deal. Only about a

fifth of all cases of serious crime result in an arrest—and this is of crimes known to the police, an underestimate of the true rate of crime. And no more than half of arrests for serious crimes result in a conviction. Even so, America's prisons are so overcrowded (see Figure 6.3) that the average convict only serves a third of his sentence. The United States already locks up more people (nearly all men) per capita than any other country.

While we might suppose that imprisoning large numbers of people or stiffening sentences would deter individuals from committing crimes, there is little evidence to support this. In fact, sociological studies have demonstrated that prisons can easily become schools for crime. Instead of preventing people from commit-

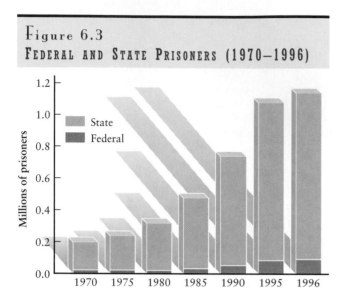

Figure 6.3
FEDERAL AND STATE PRISONERS (1970–1996)

SOURCE: U.S. Bureau of the Census, 1998, p. 206.

tiny minority of dangerous women) off the streets, evidence suggests that we need to find other means to deter crime. Robert Gangi, director of the Correctional Association of New York, says that "building more prisons to address crime is like building more graveyards to address a fatal disease" (Molowe, 1994). A sociological interpretation of crime makes clear that there are no quick fixes. The causes of crime, especially crimes of violence, are bound up with structural conditions of American society, including widespread poverty, the condition of the inner cities, and the deteriorating life circumstances of many young men. While short-term solutions like reforms that make prisons places of rehabilitation rather than simply incarceration and experiments with alternatives to prison, such as community work schemes, need to be further explored, in order to be effective solutions must address the long term (Currie, 1998).

ting crimes, prisons often actually make them more hardened criminals. The more harsh and oppressive prison conditions are, the more likely inmates are to be brutalized by the experience. Yet if prisons were made into attractive and pleasant places to live, would they have a deterrent effect?

While prisons do keep some dangerous men (and a

Crime and Community

Preventing crime, and reducing fear of crime, are both closely related to rebuilding strong communities. As we saw in our earlier discussions of the "broken windows" theory, one of the most significant innovations in criminology in recent years has been the discovery

KEY CONCEPTS IN REVIEW

The extent of crime in any society is difficult to assess, as not all crimes are reported. But some societies seem to experience much higher levels of crime than others, as is indicated by the high rates of homicide in the United States as compared with other Western countries.

Women tend to commit fewer crimes than men, probably because of general socialization differences between men and women, plus the greater involvement of men in nondomestic spheres.

White-collar crime is crime committed by the more affluent members of society. **Organized crime** refers to institutionalized forms of criminal activity, which include many of the characteristics of orthodox organizations but whose activities are illegal. Their criminal networks often extend internationally.

that the decay of day-to-day civility relates directly to criminality. For a long while attention was focused almost exclusively upon serious crime—robbery, assault, or violence. More minor crimes and forms of public disorder, however, tend to have a cumulative effect. In European and American cities, when asked to describe their problems, residents of troubled neighborhoods mention abandoned cars, graffiti, prostitution, youth gangs, and similar phenomena.

People act on their anxieties about these issues: they leave the areas in question if they can, or they buy heavy locks for their doors and bars for their windows, and abandon public places. Unchecked disorderly behavior signals to citizens that the area is unsafe. Fearful citizens stay off the streets, avoid certain neighborhoods, and curtail their normal activities and associations. As they withdraw physically, they also withdraw from roles of mutual support with fellow citizens, thereby relinquishing the social controls that formerly helped to maintain civility within the community.

COMMUNITY POLICING

What should be done to combat this development? One idea that has grown in popularity in recent years is that the police should work closely with citizens to improve local community standards and civil behavior, using education, persuasion, and counseling instead of incarceration.

"Community policing" implies not only drawing in citizens themselves, but changing the characteristic outlook of police forces. A renewed emphasis upon crime prevention rather than law enforcement can go hand in hand with the reintegration of policing with the community. The isolation of the police from those they are supposed to serve often produces a siege mentality, since the police have little regular contact with ordinary citizens.

In order to work, partnerships between government agencies, the criminal justice system, local associations, and community organizations have to be inclusive—all economic and ethnic groups must be involved (Kelling and Coles, 1997). Government and business can act together to help repair urban decay. One model is the creation of business improvement districts providing tax breaks for corporations that participate in strategic planning and offer investment

in designated areas. To be successful, such schemes demand a long-term commitment to social objectives.

Emphasizing these strategies does not mean denying the links between unemployment, poverty, and crime. Rather, the struggle against these social problems should be coordinated with community-based approaches to crime prevention. These approaches can in fact contribute directly and indirectly to furthering social justice. Where social order has decayed along with public services, other opportunities, such as new jobs, decline also. Improving the quality of life in a neighborhood can revive them.

SHAMING AS PUNISHMENT

The current emphasis on imprisonment as a means of deterring crime has a potentially crippling effect on the social ties within certain communities. In recent years, **shaming**, a form of punishing criminal and deviant behavior that attempts to maintain the ties of the offender to the community, has grown in popularity as an alternative to incarceration. According to some criminologists, the fear of being shamed within one's community is an important deterrent to crime. As a result, the public's formal disapproval could achieve the same deterring effect as incarceration, without the high costs of building and maintaining prisons.

The criminologist John Braithwaite has suggested that shaming practices can take two forms: reintegrative shaming and stigmatizing shaming. Stigmatizing shaming is related to labeling theory, which we discussed earlier in the chapter, by which a criminal is labeled as a threat to society and is treated as an outcast. As a result, the labeling process and society's efforts to marginalize the individual reinforces that person's criminal conduct, perhaps leading to future criminal behavior and higher crime rates. The much different practice of reintegrative shaming works as follows. People central to the criminal's immediate community—such as family members, employers and co-workers, and friends—are brought into court to state their condemnation of the offender's behavior. At the same time, these people must accept responsibility for reintegrating the offender back into the community. The goal is to rebuild the social bonds of the individual to the community as a means of deterring future criminal conduct.

Japan, with one of the lowest crime rates in the world, has been quite successful in implementing this approach. The process is largely based on a voluntary network of over 500,000 local crime prevention associations dedicated to facilitating reintegration into the community and a criminal justice system that is encouraged to be lenient for this purpose. As a result, in Japan only 5 percent of persons convicted for a crime serve time in prison, as compared to 30 percent in the United States. Though reintegrative shaming is not a standard practice in the American criminal justice system, it is a familiar practice in other social institutions such as the family. Think of a child who misbehaves. The parent may express disapproval of the child's behavior and try to make the child feel ashamed of her conduct, but the parent may also reassure the child that she is a loved member of the family.

Could reintegrative shaming succeed in the United States? In spite of the beliefs that these tactics are "soft" on crime, that Americans are too individualistic to participate in community-based policing, and that high-crime areas are less community-oriented, community networks have been successful in working with the police in preventing crime. These social bonds could also be fostered to increase the power of shame and reintegrate offenders into local networks of community involvement.

CRIME, DEVIANCE, AND SOCIAL ORDER

Is "harmful deviance" the price a society has to pay when that society allows considerable leeway for people to engage in nonconformist pursuits? Are high rates of criminal violence and homicide a cost that is exacted in American society in exchange for the wide range of individual liberties its citizens enjoy? Some have suggested as much. Yet in other societies in which individual freedoms are recognized and deviant activities tolerated (such as Holland), rates of violent crime are low. Conversely, countries in which the scope of individual freedom is restricted (like Guatemala) may show high levels of violence. A society that tolerates deviant behavior need not suffer social disruption. But if people find their lives largely devoid of self-fulfillment, deviant behavior is likely to be channeled toward socially destructive ends. Hence, high rates of violent crime tend to be found in societies marked by major social divisions and economic inequalities.

SUMMARY

1. Deviant behavior refers to actions that transgress commonly held *norms*. What is regarded as deviant can shift from time to time and place to place; "normal" behavior in one cultural setting may be labeled "deviant" in another.

2. *Sanctions*, formal or informal, are applied by society to reinforce social norms. *Laws* are norms defined and enforced by governments; *crimes* are acts that are not permitted by those laws.

3. Biological and psychological theories have been developed claiming that crime and other forms of deviance are genetically determined, but these have been largely discredited. Sociologists argue that conformity and deviance intertwine in different social contexts.

Divergencies of wealth and power in society strongly influence opportunities open to different groups of individuals and determine what kinds of activities are regarded as criminal. Criminal activities are learned in much the same way as are law-abiding ones, and in general are directed toward the same needs and values.

According to Edwin Sutherland, criminality is linked to *differential association*, by which behavior is learned primarily within peer groups, just as law-abiding behavior is. Criminals form a particular subculture through their association with one another.

Durkheim introduced the term *anomie*, to refer to a feeling of anxiety and disorientation that comes with the breakdown of traditional life in modern society.

Robert Merton extended the concept to include the strain felt by individuals whenever norms conflict with social reality, as when pressure to get a job conflicts with the lack of employment opportunities.

4. *Labeling theory* (which assumes that labeling someone as deviant will reinforce their deviant behavior) is important because it begins from the assumption that no act is intrinsically criminal (or normal). However, this theory needs to be supplemented with the enquiry: what caused the behavior (which has come to be labeled "deviant") in the first place?

5. The extent of crime in any society is difficult to assess, as not all crimes are reported. But some societies seem to experience much higher levels of crime than others—as is indicated by the high rates of homicide in the United States as compared to other Western countries.

6. *White-collar crime* and crimes of the powerful refer to crimes carried out by those in the more affluent sectors of society. *Organized crime* refers to institutionalized forms of criminal activity, in which many of the characteristics of orthodox organizations appear, but where the activities engaged in are systematically illegal.

7. While imprisonment has been a common solution to deter crime, other methods of deterrence that involve the community have gained in popularity. Two such methods are *community policing* and *shaming*.

structures of power

Power is an ever-present phenomenon in social life. In all human groups, some individuals have more authority or influence than others, while groups themselves have varying degrees of power. Power and inequality tend to be closely linked. The powerful are able to accumulate valued resources, such as property and wealth; possession of such resources is in turn a means of generating more power.

In this part, we look at some of the main systems of power and inequality. Chapter 7 discusses stratification and class structure—the ways in which inequalities are distributed within societies. Chapter 8 analyzes the differences and inequalities between men and women and how these inequalities are tied to other forms of inequality based on class and race. Chapter 9, on race and ethnicity, examines the tensions and hostilities often found between people who are physically or culturally different from one another. In Chapter 10, we study modern organizations and how individuals interact in such large, regimented, and impersonal settings.

Chapter 11 analyzes two types of organizations whose impact is particularly far-

reaching—the state and the military. Governments are specialists in power; they are the source of the directives that influence many of our daily activities. On the other hand, they are also the focus of resistance and rebellion. From their earliest origins, states have been associated with the development of military power. Military rivalries and wars have shaped human social development in significant ways in the past, and will continue to do so in the twenty-first century.

Chapter Seven

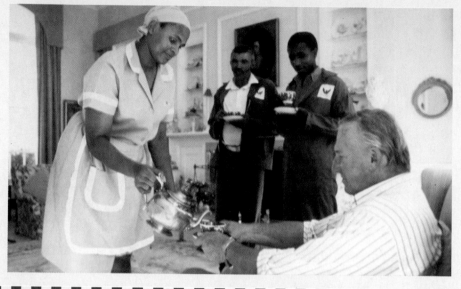

Systems of Stratification

Learn about social stratification and the importance of social background on an individual's chances for material success.

Classes in Western Societies Today

Know the class differences that exist in U.S. society and how they are defined and determined. Think about whether American society is truly a middle-class society.

Gender and Stratification

Familiarize yourself with the debate over whether class stratification determines gender inequalities.

Social Mobility

Understand the dynamics of social mobility, and think about your own mobility.

Poverty and Inequality

Learn about the conditions of poverty and homelessness in the United States today.

Theories of Stratification in Modern Societies

Become acquainted with the most influential theories of stratification—those of Marx, Weber, and Erik Olin Wright.

STRATIFICATION, CLASS, AND INEQUALITY

▰▰▰▰▰▰▰▰▰▰▰▰▰▰▰

across the street from the campus of New Mexico State University, there is a juice bar and restaurant called Island Juice. The restaurant, which specializes in fruit smoothies and tortilla-wrapped sandwiches ("wraps"), is owned by Richard Rivera, who had the idea for it while attending Chapman University in southern California, where smoothies and wraps became popular in the mid-1990s. As a college student, Rivera never thought he would own a business like Island Juice. Rivera was born in Brooklyn, New York, and grew up in a government-owned housing project. His parents did not attend college and worked most of their lives in a factory. Money was always short in Rivera's family, but his parents saved enough to send him to private Catholic schools, where he excelled in all of his classes and eventually earned a scholarship to Chapman University. He was the first in his family to ever attend college. At Chapman, he studied computer information systems and then later received a master's degree in finance. Upon receiving his master's degree, he went to work for a number of Fortune 500 companies. Meanwhile, he had the idea for Island Juice and, at the age of 27, decided to open it in Las Cruces, New Mexico. Between the success of his business and the income from his job, Rivera earns over $200,000 per year. He is living the "American dream."

Is Richard Rivera's story just an isolated incident or is it somehow representative of trends in contemporary American society? Will you, like Richard, also make more money than your parents? What about other members of your generation who, unlike you, do not go to college? How much chance does someone from a lowly background have of reaching the top of the economic ladder? For every Richard Rivera in our society, how many people struggle to make ends meet? Why do economic inequalities exist in our society? How unequal are modern societies? What are the reasons for the persistence of poverty in affluent countries like the United States? What social factors will influence your economic position in society? Are your chances any different if you are a woman? How does the globalization of the economy affect your life chances? How about the life chances of others?

These are just a few of the sorts of questions that sociologists ask and try to answer. These questions are the focus of this chapter. The study of social inequalities is one of the most important areas of sociology, because our material resources determine a great deal about our lives. To describe inequalities, sociolo-

The gap between rich and poor in the United States has concerned many sociologists.

gists speak of **social stratification,** or the existence of **structured inequalities** in a society.

We can speak of an American system of stratification because individuals' chances for material success are strongly influenced by their social background. We shall study stratification in the United States later in the chapter, but first we need to analyze the different types of stratification that exist and have existed in the past.

SYSTEMS OF STRATIFICATION

Modern stratification systems differ considerably from those of previous periods in history, and from those found in nonindustrial parts of the world today. There are four basic systems of stratification: slavery, caste, estates, and class.

Slavery

Slavery is an extreme form of inequality, in which certain people are owned as property by others. The legal conditions of slave ownership have varied considerably among different societies. Sometimes slaves were deprived of almost all rights by law—as was the case on Southern plantations in the United States—while in other societies, their position was more akin to that of servant. For example, in the ancient Greek city-state of Athens, some slaves occupied positions of great responsibility. They were excluded from political positions and from the military, but were accepted in most other types of occupation. Some were literate and worked as government administrators; many were trained in craft skills. Even so, not all slaves could count on such good fate. For the less fortunate, their days began and ended in hard labor in the mines.

Throughout history, slaves have often fought back against their subjection; the slave rebellions in the American South before the Civil War are one example. Because of such resistance, systems of slave labor have tended to be unstable. High productivity could only be achieved through constant supervision and brutal punishment. Slave-labor systems eventually broke down, partly because of the struggles they provoked, and partly because economic or other incentives motivate people to produce more effectively than direct compulsion. Slavery is simply not economically efficient. Moreover, from about the eighteenth century on, many people in Europe and America came to see slavery as morally wrong. Since the freeing of slaves in North and South America over a century ago, slavery as a formal institution has almost completely disappeared from the world.

Caste

Caste is associated above all with the cultures of the Indian subcontinent. The term "caste" itself is not an Indian one, but comes from the Portuguese *casta*, meaning "race" or "pure stock." The Indian caste system is extremely elaborate and varies in its structure from area to area—so much so that it does not really constitute one system at all, but is a loosely connected diversity of beliefs and practices. However, certain principles are widely shared. Caste membership is hereditary; no individual may move between castes. Those in the highest caste, the Brahmins, represent the most elevated condition of purity; the untouchables, the lowest. The Brahmins must avoid certain types of contact with the untouchables, and only the untouchables are allowed physical contact with animals or substances regarded as unclean.

Arhats Bestowing Alms on Beggars, *painted by Zhou Jichang in China, about 1178.*

The caste system is closely bound up with the Hindu belief in reincarnation, according to which, individuals who fail to abide by the rituals and duties of their caste will be reborn in an inferior position in their next incarnation. The Indian caste system is rigid compared with other forms of stratification, but it is not completely static. Although people are debarred from moving between castes, whole groups can change, and frequently have changed, their position within the caste hierarchy. Sociologists informally use the term "caste society" to describe a society with rigid class lines in which people have no opportunities for upward mobility.

Untouchables carrying bricks in India.

Estates

Estates were prominent in European feudalism, but they also existed in other traditional civilizations, tending to develop wherever there was a ruling group based on noble birth. The feudal estates consisted of different levels of social position, each with its own obligations and legal rights.

In Europe, the highest estate was composed of the aristocracy and gentry, whose wealth and power emanated from large-scale land holdings. The clergy formed another estate, possessing lower status but also distinctive privileges and often enormous power. The church itself owned much land and exerted considerable influence over the power of the aristocrats. Those in what came to be called the third estate were the commoners—serfs, free peasants, merchants, and artisans. A certain degree of intermarriage and individual mobility was tolerated between estates. Commoners might be knighted, for example, for having performed special services for the monarch; wealthy merchants could sometimes purchase titles and become aristocrats. A remnant of the system persists in Britain today, where hereditary titles are still recognized, though the power to rule based on these inherited titles no longer exists. Business leaders, civil servants, and others may be knighted or receive peerages in recognition of their services.

Class

The concept of **class** is most important for analyzing stratification in industrialized societies like the United States. Everyone has heard of class, but most people in everyday talk use the word in a vague way. As employed in sociology, it has some precision.

A social class is a large group of people who occupy a similar economic position in the wider society. The concept of life chances, introduced by Max Weber, is the best way to understand what class means. Your **life chances** are the opportunities you have for achieving economic prosperity. A person from a humble background, for example, has less chance of ending up wealthy than someone from a more prosperous one. And the best chance an individual has of being wealthy is to start off as wealthy in the first place.

America, it is always said, is the land of opportunity. For some, this is so. There are many examples of people who have risen from lowly circumstances to positions of wealth and power. There are many more cases, however, of people like Richard Rivera who

have done somewhat better than their parents. And yet there are more cases of people who have not, including a disproportionate share of women and members of minority groups. The idea of life chances is important because it emphasizes that while class is an important influence on what happens in our lives, it is not completely determining. Class divisions affect which neighborhoods we live in, what life-styles we follow, and even which sexual or marriage partners we choose (Mare, 1991; Massey, 1996). Yet they don't fix people for life in specific social positions, as the older systems of stratification did. A person born into a caste position has no opportunity of escaping from it; the same isn't true of class.

Class systems differ from slavery, castes, and estates in four main respects:

1. CLASS SYSTEMS ARE FLUID. Unlike the other types of strata, classes are not established by legal or religious provisions. The boundaries between classes are never clear-cut. There are no formal restrictions upon intermarriage between people from different classes.

2. CLASS POSITIONS ARE IN SOME PART ACHIEVED. An individual's class is not simply given at birth, as is the case in the other types of stratification systems. Social mobility—movement upward and downward in the class structure—is more common than in the other types.

3. CLASS IS ECONOMICALLY BASED. Classes depend on economic differences between groups of individuals—inequalities in the possession of material resources. In the other types of stratification systems, noneconomic factors (such as religion in the Indian caste system) are generally most important.

4. CLASS SYSTEMS ARE LARGE-SCALE AND IMPERSONAL. In the other types of stratification systems, inequalities are expressed primarily in personal relationships of duty or obligation—between serf and lord, slave and master, or lower- and higher-caste individuals. Class systems, by contrast, operate mainly through large-scale, impersonal associations. For instance, one major basis of class differences is in inequalities of pay and working conditions.

CLASSES IN WESTERN SOCIETIES TODAY

Let us begin our exploration of class differences in modern societies by looking at basic divisions of income, wealth, educational attainment, and occupational status within the population as a whole.

INCOME

Income refers to wages and salaries earned from paid occupations, plus unearned money from investments. One of the most significant changes occurring in Western countries over the past century has been the rising real income of the majority of the working population. (Real income is income with rises owing to inflation excluded, to provide a fixed standard of comparison from year to year.) Blue-collar workers in Western societies now earn three to four times as much in real income as their counterparts at the turn of the century, even if their real income has dropped over the past twenty years. Gains for white-collar, managerial, and professional workers have been

higher still. In terms of earnings per person (per capita) and the range of goods and services that can be purchased, the majority of the population today are vastly more affluent than any peoples have previ-

An American family with all their possessions in the front yard of their house. In the United States, real income has climbed enormously since 1900.

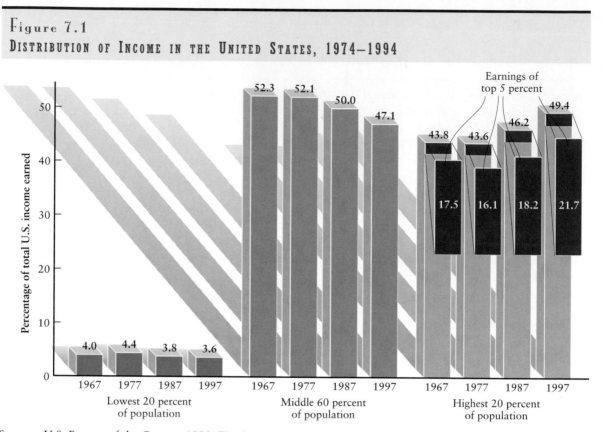

Figure 7.1
DISTRIBUTION OF INCOME IN THE UNITED STATES, 1974–1994

SOURCE: U.S. Bureau of the Census, 1998, Fig. 3, p. xii.

ously been in human history. One of the most important reasons for this growth is the increasing productivity—output per worker—that has been secured through technological development in industry. The volume of goods and services produced per worker has risen more or less continually since the 1900s.

Nevertheless, income distribution is quite unequal. The top 5 percent of earners in the United States receive 21.7 percent of total income; the highest 20 percent obtain 49.4 percent; and the bottom 20 percent receive only 3.6 percent (see Figure 7.1). Over the past two decades, income inequality has increased dramatically. The average pretax earnings of the bottom 80 percent of people in the United States declined by about 5 percent in the period from 1977 to 1992. During the same period, the richest fifth saw their incomes grow by 9 percent before taxes—and the tax burden on these people was lower in 1992 than it had

been in 1977. For the top 1 percent of earners, incomes approximately doubled during the same period. And despite the growth of the economy and the creation of millions of new jobs, these trends continued throughout the 1990s, leading some observers to deem the United States a "two-tiered society" (Freeman, 1999).

WEALTH

Wealth refers to all assets individuals own: cash, savings and checking accounts, investments in stocks, bonds, and estate properties, and so on. While most people earn their income from their work, the wealthy often derive the bulk of theirs from investments, some of them inherited. Some scholars argue that wealth—not income—is the real indicator of one's social class. Reliable information about the distribution of wealth is difficult to obtain. Some countries keep more accurate statistics than others, but there is always a considerable amount of guesswork involved. The affluent tend not to publicize the full range of their assets; we know far more about the poor. What is certain is that wealth is concentrated in the hands of a few: 1 percent of the adult population in the United States today possesses more than 20 percent of the total wealth of the country. More specifically, the wealthiest 10 percent of families own 90 percent of corporate stocks and business assets and 95 percent of bonds. The richest 0.5 percent (400,000 households) own 40 percent of corporate stocks and bonds.

Some scholars have pointed out that racial differences in wealth are even more pronounced than black-white differences in income. The sociologists Melvin Oliver and Thomas Shapiro found that, despite a generation of progress in civil rights, the average black child in America still grows up in a household with no financial assets (Oliver and Shapiro, 1995). Statistics reveal stark racial differences. The typical black family possesses on average just 11 percent of the wealth of a white family. Among those in the middle class, the figure improves slightly to 25 percent. More specifically, the average white household possesses $7,000 in net financial assets—all assets apart from home equity and the value of a person's car, minus debts. The average black family, however, has no net financial assets whatever. One-fourth of white households, 61 percent of black households, and 54 percent of Hispanic households have no net financial assets, or negative financial assets. These findings are based

In the United States, African-American families have substantially fewer monetary assets than do white families.

on data gathered from 12,000 black and white households.

What are some of the reasons for the racial disparity in wealth? Is it simply that blacks have less money with which to purchase assets? To some degree, the answer is yes. The old adage "it takes money to make money" is a fact of life for those who start with little or no wealth. Since whites historically have enjoyed higher incomes and levels of wealth than blacks, whites are able to accrue even more wealth, which they then are able to pass on to their children (Conley, 1999). In fact, economists estimate that more than half the wealth that one accumulates in a lifetime can be traced to a person's progenitors. But family advantages are not the only factors. Oliver and Shapiro argued that it is easier for whites to obtain assets, even when they have fewer resources than blacks because discrimination plays a major role in the racial gap in home ownership. Blacks are rejected for mortgages 60 percent more often than whites, even when they have the same qualifications and credit worthiness. When blacks do receive mortgages, the authors found, they pay on average a half-percent higher interest rate, or about $12,000 more over the life of a thirty-year, median fixed-rate mortgage. These issues are particularly important since homeownership is the primary means of the accumulation of wealth for most American families.

EDUCATION

Sociologists also believe that education, or the number of years of schooling a person has completed, is an important dimension of social stratification. The value of a college education has increased significantly in the past twenty years as a result of the increased demand for and wages paid to educated workers in the more computer- and information-based economy (Danziger and Gottschalk, 1995). Education is one of the strongest predictors of one's occupation, income, and wealth later in life. As we will see later in this chapter, how much education one receives is often influenced by the social class of one's parents.

Racial differences in levels of education persist, and this explains in part why racial differences in income and wealth also persist. In 1997, roughly 82 percent of whites and Asian-Americans had completed high school, while only 75 percent of African Americans had a high school degree.

INCOME INEQUALITY IN THE GLOBAL ECONOMY

Although many economists, politicians, and business people have sung the praises of globalization, there is reason to approach such claims cautiously. Globalization may well be increasing economic inequality in the world's advanced industrial societies. Although the U.S. economy has been consistently growing since the end of the recession of 1982–83, the gap between the wages of high-skilled and low-skilled workers has also been increasing. In 1979, college graduates taking entry-level positions earned on average 37 percent more than those without college degrees. By 1993, the differential had grown to 77 percent (*USA Today Magazine*, May 1998). And while this growing "wage premium" has encouraged more Americans to go to college—such that some 25 percent of the American workforce had college degrees in 1995, compared to 18 percent in 1979 (*Business Week*, December 15, 1997)—it has also helped widen the gap between the wealthiest and the poorest workers. As an analyst for the U.S. Department of Labor recently put it, "it is by now almost a platitude . . . that wage inequality has increased quite sharply since the late 1970s, for both men and women" (U.S. Dept. of Labor, 1997).

While few studies have directly implicated global-

ization as a cause of this growing inequality, there is reason to view it as an indirect causal factor. It is true that while countries like the United States, Canada, and the United Kingdom have witnessed a growth in earnings inequality since the late 1970s, countries like Germany, Japan, and France—which have, presumably, been equally affected by the forces of globalization—have seen either a decline or little change in inequality. At the same time, many of the factors that sociologists see as causes of inequality are clearly linked to globalization. First, in some cases, U.S. companies have been forced to lower wages to compete with firms that manufacture their products overseas, especially in the Third World. To the extent that globalizing tendencies have discouraged the U.S. government from raising tarriffs on foreign imports—and have also made it easier for firms to relocate their manufacturing jobs to other countries—they have arguably contributed to inequality in the United States. Second, globalization has encouraged immigration to the United States.

Immigrants—many of whom are relegated to low-wage work—increase the competition for jobs among those in the low wage labor pool, lowering wages somewhat in this segment of the labor market. Third, globalization has undermined the strength of U.S. labor unions. A number of studies have shown that when firms that used to do the bulk of their manufacturing in one region begin to spread their manufacturing base out across countries and continents, it becomes increasingly difficult for unions to organize workers and negotiate with management. But strong unions decrease earnings inequality through their commitment to raising wages.

Of course, globalization is not the only cause of inequality. Many researchers, for example, blame increasing inequality on the spectacular growth of high-tech industries, which employ mostly well-paid, white-collar workers and offer little in the way of traditional blue-collar employment. Still, it seems safe to conclude that globalization is not without its role in the growing stratification of American society.

Table 7.1 Occupational Prestige in the United States and Around the World

Occupation	United States	Average of 55 Countries	Occupation	United States	Average of 55 Countries
Supreme court judge	85	82	Professional athlete	51	48
College president	82	86	Social worker	50	56
Physician	82	78	Electrician	49	44
College professor	78	78	Secretary	46	53
Lawyer	75	73	Real estate agent	44	49
Dentist	74	70	Farmer	44	47
Architect	71	72	Carpenter	43	37
Psychologist	71	66	Plumber	41	34
Airline pilot	70	66	Mail carrier	40	33
Electrical engineer	69	65	Jazz musician	37	38
Biologist	68	69	Bricklayer	36	34
Clergy	67	60	Barber	36	30
Sociologist	65	67	Truck driver	31	33
Accountant	65	55	Factory worker	29	29
Banker	63	67	Store sales clerk	27	34
High school teacher	63	64	Bartender	25	23
Registered nurse	62	54	Lives on public aid	25	16
Pharmacist	61	64	Cab driver	22	28
Veterinarian	60	61	Gas station attendant	22	25
Classical musician	59	56	Janitor	22	21
Police officer	59	40	Waiter or waitress	20	23
Actor or actress	55	52	Garbage collector	13	13
Athletic coach	53	50	Street sweeper	11	13
Journalist	52	55	Shoe shiner	9	12

SOURCE: Treiman, 1977

OCCUPATION

Occupation is also an important indicator of one's social standing. Occupational status is highly dependent on one's level of educational attainment. In fact, in studies where persons are asked to rate jobs in terms of how "prestigious" they are, the occupations that are ranked most highly are those requiring the most education (Treiman, 1977). These studies use what is called the Standard International Occupational Prestige Scale, which ranges from 10 to 90. Research shows that physicians, college professors, lawyers, and dentists are at the top of the scale, while garbage collectors and gas station attendants are at the bottom. About at the middle are jobs such as registered nurse, computer programmer, and insurance sales representative. Interestingly, similar rankings occur regardless of who does the ranking and in what country. Comparisons of status rankings across fifty-five countries show that there is a general agreement as to how high status an occupation is (see Table 7.1).

Class Divisions

What follows is a general portrayal of the main class divisions in the United States, although there are more complexities and subcategories within the classes than can be mentioned here. Moreover, the identification of class boundaries is a debated issue among sociologists, and no detailed analysis would command universal agreement.

What are the major classes that exist in American society? The question is a very important one, because class divisions influence so many other aspects of the social order. Class division, remember, is a matter of economic differences that affect people's life chances. Possession of substantial amounts of wealth, especially when this is passed on from generation to generation, is the main characteristic distinguishing the upper class from other class groups in American society. Most Americans' livelihood does not come from any wealth they own, but from the jobs they perform. Different occupations carry different levels of income and economic reward; sociologists refer to these differences when speaking of the middle class, the working class, and the underclass in American society. Thus, for most Americans, occupation and income are important factors in categorizing class divisions.

THE UPPER CLASS

The **upper class** in American society consists of a small number of individuals and families who own considerable amounts of property—think of them as the top 1 percent of the wealthy. This class includes a core of the "super rich." There are about 250 families in the United States worth at least $100 million.

Wealth confers power. The influence of the wealthy stems in part from direct control of industrial and financial capital, and in part from their access to leading positions in the political, educational, and cultural worlds.

THE MIDDLE CLASS

The **middle class** includes people working in many different occupations. There are three distinct sectors within the middle class. The old middle class consists of the owners of small businesses, the proprietors of local shops, and small farmers. The numbers of people in this category have declined steadily over the past century, but they still compose a significant proportion of the overall working population (6 percent of the workforce in the United States). Most small enterprises fail within two years of being set up; only

some 20 percent of those established in any one year in the United States are still in business five years later. Small firms and shops are often unable to compete effectively with the large companies, supermarkets, and restaurant chains. Still, if the old middle class has not shrunk as much as some once thought would be the case, it is because there is a large reservoir of people wanting to try their hand at starting a business of their own. Most of those who go out of business are thus replaced by others.

The upper-middle class is made up mainly of people in managerial or professional occupations. About 20 percent of the U.S. population fall into this class category. Since this sector includes so many people, generalizing about their attitudes is risky. Most have experienced some form of higher education, and the proportion holding liberal views on social and political issues, especially among professional groups, is fairly high. In the United States, those from white Anglo-Saxon Protestant (WASP) and Jewish backgrounds are disproportionately represented, although there is now also a small "African-American upper middle class."

The lower-middle class, an even more heterogeneous category, includes people working as office staff, sales clerks, teachers, and nurses, among others. People in this class group tend to hold similar social and political attitudes to most blue-collar workers.

The diverse character of the middle class as a whole is a reflection of the contradictory situations in which middle-class people find themselves. Lower-middle-class people, for example, may identify with the same values of those in more profitable positions, but may find themselves living on incomes below those of the better-paid manual workers, who do not take a middle-class position.

THE WORKING CLASS

The **working class** consists of people working in blue-collar, manual occupations. As with the middle class, there tend to be marked divisions within the working class as a whole. One important source of such divisions is skill level. The upper-working class, consisting of skilled workers, has frequently made up an "aristocracy of labor"; its members have had superior incomes, better working conditions, and more job security than those in other blue-collar occupations.

Some skills, though, have been undermined by technological developments, resulting in a weakening of the position of the workers or even the extinction of certain jobs. For example, the skilled Linotype operators who used to set the type for newspapers and books have now disappeared; the Linotype machine has been supplanted by new print technology based on a computerized photoelectronic process that requires less-skilled workers.

The lower-working class is made up of those in unskilled or semiskilled jobs, like fast-food work, which need little training. Most of these jobs offer lower incomes than, and inferior job security to, skilled occupations. Sociologists have come to call this group the "working poor."

IS THE UNITED STATES A MIDDLE-CLASS SOCIETY?

At the opening of the twentieth century, about half the total workforce in the United States was made up of blue-collar workers, nearly all of them men. Only about 20 percent of the workforce were employed in white-collar jobs. Over the course of the century, these proportions have virtually become reversed—the result of a trend toward the disappearance of manufacturing jobs in particular. In 1992, about 25 percent of the workforce filled the blue-collar jobs, while over 70 percent were employed in white-collar work (the remaining small percentage held mostly farming jobs).

Do Americans live in a middle-class society since most people now fall into this class? The shrinking of the working class is undoubtedly a trend of great importance (see Figure 7.2). Think what a difference it makes, for example, to the theories of Marx (described in Chapter 1), who believed that the working class would expand in modern societies and that this would produce a situation of social revolution. The reverse has actually happened. The working class is dwindling, and thoughts of revolution are far from the minds of most blue-collar workers, who are normally more concerned with protecting their jobs and standard of living.

Yet the idea that modern America has become solidly middle class is more complicated and debatable than may at first appear. Some white-collar jobs have in fact come to resemble blue-collar ones. Is Delia, who sits in front of a computer screen all day

word processing or carrying out routine calculations, in a very different situation from Denzel, who assembles the electronic parts of TV sets on a production line? A further complicating factor is the *feminization* of the more routine forms of white-collar and service work—most of this work is now carried out by women. Many such women are married to men in blue-collar work. Should they be counted as middle class or working class? The relation between class and gender is a difficult issue in sociology, and we shall look at it in more detail in the following section.

We can draw the conclusion, however, that the United States is less of a wholly middle-class society than the bare statistics would suggest, especially if we

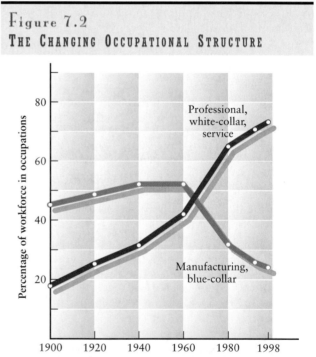

Figure 7.2
THE CHANGING OCCUPATIONAL STRUCTURE

SOURCE: *Historical Statistics of the United States*, vol. 1; U.S. Bureau of Labor Statistics, *Employment and Earnings* (January 1999).

The United States has lost a large number of manufacturing and other blue-collar jobs in the twentieth century. Many new professional/managerial or other white-collar jobs have been created. A large proportion, however, entail work in the service industries, and although these can be classified as white collar, they in fact resemble blue-collar jobs in terms of pay.

Most of the low-ranking IRS employees who process tax forms are women.

consider those at the bottom of the class structure. Large numbers of people have no permanent occupation at all, and some do not appear in the statistics of unemployment because they have never registered for work. They form one part of what is sometimes called the underclass in American society.

THE UNDERCLASS

An **underclass** can be defined as a group of people who are seen as expendable based on their value to the economy (Wright, 1978). More specifically, this refers to those who are not in stable paid work, either chronically unemployed or drifting in and out of jobs. The concept of the underclass has been most commonly used to refer to inner-city minority groups, but it applies to people of any race or location who fit the definition above.

The sociologist William Julius Wilson drew attention to the black urban underclass in his seminal book *The Declining Significance of Race.* Wilson was concerned about the persistence of some African Americans in the underclass and looked for an explanation of this pattern. Were blacks seen as expendable because of their race or was some other disadvantage a factor?

Drawing on research done in Chicago, Wilson found that a substantial black middle class—white-collar workers and professionals—had emerged over the past three or four decades in the United States. Not all African Americans still lived in city ghettos, and those who remained were kept there, Wilson maintained, not so much by active discrimination as by economic factors such as the loss of factory jobs— in other words, by class rather than by race. Wilson argued that the old racist barriers were disappearing; blacks were stuck in the ghetto as a result of economic disadvantages (Wilson, 1978).

Wilson's work ignited a controversy that still burns fiercely. The conservative political writer Charles Murray agreed about the existence of a black underclass in most big cities. According to Murray, however, African Americans find themselves at the bottom of society as a result of the very welfare policies designed to help improve their position. People become dependent upon welfare handouts and build a "culture of poverty" around such welfare dependency. They then have little incentive to find jobs, build solid communities, or make stable marriages (Murray, 1984).

In reply to Murray's claims, in the book *The Truly Disadvantaged* (1987), Wilson reiterated and extended his previous arguments, again using research carried out in Chicago. The movement of many whites from the cities to the suburbs, the decline of urban industries, and other urban economic problems, he suggested, led to high rates of joblessness among African-American men. The forms of social disintegration to which Murray pointed, including the high proportion of unmarried black mothers, Wilson explained in terms of the shrinking of the available pool of "marriageable" men, meaning men who were employed and could therefore support a family. For Wilson, the underclass lived in social isolation from the wider American society.

In his most recent study, *When Work Disappears* (1996), Wilson expanded on his previous arguments, maintaining that the existence of an underclass in urban America is a function of high levels of unemployment. He noted that the United States has witnessed a "suburbanization" of employment. That is, more and more jobs have moved out of the cities and into the suburbs. As a result, the black urban poor, who generally rely on public transportation, are often geographically excluded from obtaining these jobs, and remain isolated in neighborhoods that once featured sizable proportions of working families but now

Urban neighborhoods have suffered from the exodus of the middle-class to the suburbs.

are characterized by concentrated unemployment. Wilson observed that the consequences of neighborhood joblessness are more devastating than those of high neighborhood poverty. He argued that many of today's problems in the inner-city ghetto, such as crime, family dissolution, welfare, and low levels of social organization, are an outcome of joblessness rather than poverty. Wilson also bemoaned the lack of locally available training and education, and the dissolution of government and private support of local organizations that once supplied job information as well as job opportunities to inner-city residents.

Yet, while talking about the problems of the truly disadvantaged, Wilson is no longer willing to refer to them as "the underclass." Noting that members of a population so designated become stigmatized in popular discussions of their fate, Wilson wants to avoid the mistake of associating the term "underclass" with persons very different from conventional Americans. To avoid this, he prefers now to call this bottom rung of the American class structure "the ghetto poor" (Wilson, 1996).

GENDER AND STRATIFICATION

Studies of stratification were for many years gender-blind—they were written as though women did not exist or as though, for purposes of analyzing divisions

of power, wealth, and prestige, women were unimportant and uninteresting. Gender in fact is one of the most significant dimensions of stratification. There are no societies in which men do not possess more wealth, status, and influence than women (see also Chapter 8).

One of the main problems posed by the study of gender and stratification in modern societies sounds simple but turns out to be difficult to resolve. This is the question of whether we can understand gender inequalities in modern times mainly in terms of class divisions. Inequalities of gender are more deep-rooted historically than class systems. Men had superior standing to women even in hunting and gathering societies, where there were no classes, and where only men were allowed to take part in public and religious ceremonials. Yet there is no doubt that class divisions in modern societies overlap substantially with gender inequalities. The economic position of many women tends to reflect that of their husbands, since men are more often the main breadwinners; hence it can be argued that we have to explain gender inequalities mainly in class terms.

This view has become a matter of some debate. John Goldthorpe has defended what he calls the "conventional position" in class analysis—that the paid work of most women is relatively insignificant compared with that of most men, and that therefore women can be regarded as being in the same class as their husbands (Goldthorpe, 1983). This position is not, Goldthorpe emphasizes, based on an ideology of sexism; on the contrary, it recognizes the subordinate position in which most women find themselves in the labor force. Women hold part-time jobs more often than men, and they tend to have more intermittent experience of paid employment, since many withdraw from the workforce for lengthy periods to bear and care for children.

Goldthorpe's argument can be criticized in several ways. First, in a substantial proportion of households, the income of women is essential to maintaining the family's economic position and way of life. In these households, women's paid employment helps determine their class position. Second, a wife's employment may strongly influence that of her husband, not simply the other way around. Although women rarely earn more than their husbands, the working situation of a wife might still be the lead factor in influencing the class of her husband. This could be the case, for

KEY CONCEPTS IN REVIEW

Wealth refers to all assets individuals own: cash, savings and checking accounts, investments in stocks, bonds, and property, and other investments.

Income refers to wages and salaries from paid occupations, plus money derived from investments.

Possession of substantial amounts of wealth, especially when it is passed on from generation to generation, is the main characteristic distinguishing the **upper class** from other class groups in American society.

The **middle class** is composed broadly of those working in white-collar occupations, but it can be divided into the old middle class (such as small business owners), the upper middle class (professionals and managers), and the lower middle class (office staff, teachers, nurses, etc.).

The **working class** is composed of people working in blue-collar, or manual, occupations.

The **underclass** is composed of those who are chronically poor and without a permanent occupation. Most people in the underclass are from ethnic minority groups.

Gender is one of the most significant dimensions of stratification. There are no societies in which men do not have more wealth, status, and power than women.

---

instance, if the husband is an unskilled or semiskilled blue-collar worker and the wife the manager of a store. Her occupation would then determine the family's class position.

A study carried out in Sweden showed cross-class families to be common (Lieuffsrud and Woodward, 1987). In most such cases, the husband had the supe rior occupation; in a minority of instances, the opposite was true. The research showed that individuals tended to import views of their differing class position into the family. Decisions about who stayed at home to care for a sick child were related to the interaction of class and gender: when the husband's job was inferior to the wife's, he would usually have this responsibility.

The third criticism that can be made of Goldthorpe's position is that in an increasing proportion of families, women are the sole breadwinners. Unless a woman's income is derived from alimony, which puts her on the same economic level as her ex-husband, she is by definition the determining influence upon her own class position.

Janeen Baxter has recently made an important contribution to the debate, drawing upon material from the United States, Sweden, Norway, and Australia. On the basis of her research, she suggested that Goldthorpe's critics exaggerated the independent influence of gender on class position. In all four countries, she argued, the husband's class position is the main determinant of the wife's. However, she did find that the class position of the husband was improved when he was in a cross-class marriage in which the wife's income was superior to his (Baxter, 1994).

SOCIAL MOBILITY

In studying stratification, we must consider not only the differences between economic positions but what happens to the individuals who occupy them. **Social mobility** refers to the movement of individuals and groups between different class positions.

There are two ways of studying social mobility. First, we can look at people's own careers—how far they move up or down the socioeconomic scale in the course of their working lives. This is called **intragenerational mobility**. Alternatively, we can analyze where children are on the scale compared with their parents or grandparents. Mobility across the generations is called **intergenerational mobility**.

Another important distinction sociologists make is between structural mobility and exchange mobility. If there were such a thing as a society with complete equality of opportunity—where each person had the same chance of getting on in life as everyone else—there would be a great deal of downward as well as upward mobility. This is what is meant by **exchange mobility**: there is an exchange of positions, such that more talented people in each generation move up the economic hierarchy, while the less talented move down.

In practice, there is no society that even approaches full equality of opportunity, and most mobility, whether intra- or intergenerational, is **structural mobility**, upward mobility made possible by an expansion of better-paid occupations at the expense of more poorly paid ones. Most mobility in the United States since World War II has been dependent upon continually increasing prosperity. Levels of downward mobility, therefore, have been historically low.

Measuring Mobility

The amount of mobility in a society is a major indication of its openness. Do individuals born into the lower strata see opportunities to move up the socioeconomic ladder? How open are the industrialized countries? Is there more equality of opportunity in the United States than elsewhere? The earliest studies of comparative social mobility were done by Pitrim Sorokin (1927), who included in his analysis a vast array of societies, ranging from traditional Rome and China to the United States. Sorokin concluded that opportunities for rapid ascent in the United States were more limited than American folklore suggested. The techniques he used to gather his data, however, were relatively primitive.

A classical study of social mobility was carried out by Seymour Martin Lipset and Reinhard Bendix (1959). Their research, drawing on data from Britain, France, West Germany, Sweden, Switzerland, Japan, Denmark, Italy, and the United States, concentrated upon the mobility of men from blue-collar to white-collar work. Contrary to the researchers' expectations, they also found no evidence that the

United States was more open than the European societies. **Upward mobility** was 30 percent in the United States, with the other societies varying between 27 and 31 percent. Lipset and Bendix concluded that all the countries were experiencing a similar expansion of white-collar jobs. This led to an "upward surge of mobility" of comparable dimensions in each.

Other researchers since have questioned these findings. They have argued that there are significant differences between countries if more attention is paid to downward mobility and long-range mobility. A person with **long-range mobility** moves from a lowly social background to a high-status job. The classic case is "from log cabin to president." There seems to be more long-range mobility in the United States, for instance, than in most other Western societies. But on the whole, the similarities in patterns of mobility are more striking than the differences (Grusky and Hauser, 1984).

Robert Erikson and John Goldthorpe (1986) carried out a substantial study of cross-national similarities and variations in mobility, focusing on England, Wales, France, Sweden, Hungary, and Poland, among other countries. The results again showed a general similarity between mobility rates and patterns. However, they also indicated some significant variations: Sweden, for example, was found to be considerably more open than the other Western countries.

There are also big differences *within* societies—for example, differences in the racial or ethnic groups to which people belong (Featherman and Hauser, 1978). The obvious comparison in the United States is between African Americans and whites. The black middle class is much smaller than the white middle class, relative to the proportions of blacks and whites in the population as a whole. Someone born in a black city ghetto has only a fraction of the chance of a person from a white background of obtaining a white-collar or professional job.

Opportunities for Mobility: Who Gets Ahead?

Why is it more difficult for someone from the class of "ghetto poor" to become an upper-class professional? Many people in modern societies believe it is possible

Many studies have suggested a strong correlation between education and social status.

for anyone to reach the top through hard work and persistence. Why should it be difficult to do so? Sociologists have sought to answer these questions by trying to understand which social factors are most influential in determining an individual's status or position in society.

In a classic study of social mobility in the United States, the sociologists Peter Blau and Otis Dudley Duncan surveyed over twenty thousand men in order to assess intergenerational mobility (1967). Blau and Duncan concluded that while there has been a great deal of **vertical mobility**, nearly all of it was between occupational positions quite close to one another. Long-range mobility, that is from working class to upper-middle class, was rare. Why? Blau and Duncan sought to answer this question by assessing the impact of one's social background in determining one's ultimate social status. They concluded that the key factor behind status was educational attainment. Put simply, a child's education is influenced by the family's social status; this, in turn, affects the child's social position later in life. The sociologists William Sewell and Robert Hauser later confirmed Blau and Duncan's conclusions (1980). They added to the argument by claiming the connection between family background and educational attainment occurs because parents, teachers, and friends influence the educational and career aspirations of the child, and that these aspirations then become an important part of the status attainment process throughout the child's life. Sewell and Hauser sought to prove that social status was influ-

enced by a pattern of related social influences going back to one's birth: family background affects the child's aspirations, which in turn affect the child's educational attainment, which in turn affects the adult's later occupational prestige, and so on and so on.

The French sociologist Pierre Bourdieu has also been a major figure in examining the importance of family background to one's social status, but his emphasis is on the cultural advantages that parents can provide to their children (1984, 1988). Bourdieu argues that among the factors responsible for social status the most important is the transmission of cultural capital. Those who own economic capital often manage to pass much of it on to their children. The same is true, Bourdieu argues, of the cultural advantages that coming from a "good home" confers. These advantages are capital, which succeeding generations inherit, thus perpetuating inequalities. As we have seen, wealthier families are able to afford to send their children to better schools, an economic advantage that benefits the children's social status as adults. In addition to this material advantage, parents from the upper and middle classes are mostly highly educated themselves and tend to be more involved in their children's education—reading to them, helping with homework, purchasing books and learning materials, and encouraging their progress. Bourdieu notes that working-class parents are concerned about their children's education, but they lack the economic and cultural capital to make a difference. Bourdieu's study of French society confirmed his theory. He found that a majority of office professionals with high levels of educational attainment and income were from families of the "dominant class" in France. Likewise, office clerical workers often originated from the working classes.

The socioeconomic order in the United States is similar. Those who already hold positions of wealth and power have many chances to perpetuate their advantages and to pass them on to their offspring. They can make sure their children have the best available education, and this will often lead them into the best jobs. Most of those who reach the top had a head start; they came from professional or affluent backgrounds. Studies of people who have become wealthy show that hardly anyone begins with nothing. The large majority of people who have "made money" did so on the basis of inheriting or being given at least a modest account initially—which they then used to make more. In American society, it's better to start at the top than at the bottom (Jaher, 1973; Rubinstein, 1986).

Your Own Mobility Chances

Sometime in the next four years, you will graduate from college and be faced with the prospect of starting a new career. Do you have any idea what you will do? If you are like most of your classmates, you have no idea. Perhaps you are a person like Richard Rivera, who has a passion for something like fruit smoothies and will make a go of something that is interesting to you. Or perhaps you will go to work for someone else and become interested in something you have never heard of, working your way up the hierarchy of an organization in a formal career. What implications might be drawn from mobility studies about the career opportunities you are faced with, as someone searching for a good job? Managerial and professional jobs may continue to expand relative to lower-level positions. Those who have done well in the educational system and earned a college degree are most likely to fill these openings and make a high income. Indeed, 60 percent of Americans in the top fifth of income earners graduated from college, while in the bottom fifth, just 6 percent hold a college degree (Cox and Alm, 1999). Educational attainment seems to be

the key variable for upward mobility in the United States. Even for someone like Richard Rivera, who sells juice for a living, a college education provided him training in entrepreneurship, accounting, and computer applications (Hout, 1988).

Research indicates, however, that the impact of education on your mobility chances has decreased somewhat (Hout, 1988; Hout and Lucas, 1996). As a college student, chances are that one or both of your parents are college educated and middle class or above. Even if you earn a good income, you might not enjoy upward mobility. Additionally, as a result of global economic competition, there are not nearly enough well-paid positions open for all who wish to enter them, and some of you are bound to find that your careers do not match your expectations. Even if a higher proportion of jobs are created at managerial and professional levels than existed before, the overall number of jobs available in the future may not keep pace with the number of people with college degrees seeking work. One reason for this is the growing number of women entering the workforce. Another is the increasing use of information technology in production processes. Because computerized machinery can now handle tasks—even of a highly complicated kind—that once only humans could do, it is possible that many jobs will be eliminated in future years.

If you are a woman, although your chances of entering a good career are improving, you face certain obstacles to your progress. Male managers and employers still discriminate against female applicants, compared with males seeking the same positions. They do so at least partly because of their belief that "women are not really interested in careers" and are likely to leave the workforce to begin families. This latter factor substantially affects opportunities for women, who are often forced to choose between a career and having children. Men are rarely willing to share equal responsibility for domestic work and child care.

Downward Mobility

Although **downward mobility** is less common than upward mobility, about 20 percent of men in the United States are downwardly mobile intergenera-

KEY CONCEPTS IN REVIEW

Social mobility is the movement of individuals and groups between different class positions.

Vertical mobility is movement up or down the socioeconomic scale. People who gain in property, income, or status are **upwardly mobile**, while those who move in the opposite direction are **downwardly mobile**.

Intragenerational mobility is the study of how far up or down the socioeconomic scale an individual moves within the course of her working life.

Intergenerational mobility is upward or downward mobility between generations of a family.

Exchange mobility results from an exchange in positions on the socioeconomic scale, such that talented people move up the economic hierarchy while the less talented move down.

Structural mobility is mobility resulting from changes in the number and kinds of jobs available in a society.

tionally, although most of this movement is short-range. A person with **short-range mobility** moves from one job to another that is similar—for example, from a routine office job to semiskilled blue collar work. Downward intragenerational mobility, also a common occurrence, is often associated with psychological problems and anxieties. Some people are simply unable to sustain the life-style into which they were born. But another source of downward mobility among individuals arises through no fault of their own. During the late 1980s and early 1990s corporate America was flooded with instances in which middle-aged men lost their jobs because of company mergers or takeovers. These executives either had difficulty finding new jobs or could only find jobs that paid less than before.

Many of the intragenerational downwardly mobile are women. It is still common for women to abandon promising careers on the birth of a child. After spending some years raising children, such women often return to the paid workforce at a level lower than when they left—for instance, in poorly paid, part-time work. (This situation is changing, although not as fast as might be hoped.)

Downward mobility is particularly common today among divorced or separated women with children. As an illustration, we might take the life of Sandra Bolton, described by John Schwarz in his book *The Forgotten Americans* (1992). Sandra's fate belies the idea that people who work hard and follow the rules will be able to prosper. Sandra's husband had regularly assaulted her during the six years of their marriage, and child welfare officials considered him a threat to their two children. She divorced her husband after the Child Protective Services told her that the state would take her children if she didn't leave him.

Sandra receives no maintenance from her ex-husband, who, two weeks before the divorce was finalized, piled their furniture and valuables into a truck and drove away, not to be seen again. Whereas while married she sustained a moderately comfortable, middle-class way of life, Sandra now lives a hand-to-mouth existence. She tried to remain in college, supporting herself and her children by doing various menial jobs, but was unable to earn enough money to keep up.

A neighbor looked after her children while she took a full-time job as a secretary at a medical center. Taking courses at night and during the summers, she eventually completed a college degree. Although she applied at many places, she wasn't able to find a position paying more than her secretarial job. She took on a second job, as a checkout person in a supermarket, in the evenings just to make ends meet. "You try to do the responsible thing," she said, "and you're penalized, because the system we have right now doesn't provide you with a way to make it. I mean, I work so hard. There's only so much a person can do" (Schwarz and Volgy, 1992). As a result of her divorce, Sandra sunk from a life of some comfort to living in poverty. She is not alone.

POVERTY AND INEQUALITY

At the bottom of the class system in the United States are the millions of people who exist in conditions of poverty. Many do not maintain a proper diet and live in miserable conditions; their average life expectancy is lower than the majority of the population. In addition, the number of individuals and families who have become homeless has greatly increased over the past twenty years.

What Is Poverty?

In defining poverty, a distinction is usually made between absolute and relative poverty. **Absolute poverty** means that a person or family simply can't get enough to eat. People living in absolute poverty are undernourished and, in situations of famine, may actually starve to death. Absolute poverty is common in the poorer Third World countries.

In the industrial countries, **relative poverty** is essentially a measure of inequality. It means being poor as compared with the standards of living of the majority. It is reasonable to call a person poor in the United States if he lacks the basic resources needed to maintain a decent standard of housing and healthy living conditions.

Since the 1960s, the federal government has established a **poverty line** to designate people officially regarded as poor. The line is fixed by calculating the average cost of food that average-size families need for minimum nutrition. This figure is then tripled to cover the minimum cost of clothing, housing, medical care, and other necessities. The official poverty line for a family of four in 1996 was set at $16,036. By that measure, in that year, about 14 percent of the population—about 36.5 million people—were defined as living in poverty (U.S. Bureau of the Census, 1998).

Poverty: Myth and Reality

What do you think about poverty? Most Americans of all social classes think of the poor as people who are unemployed or on welfare. Americans also tend to display more negative attitudes toward welfare provisions and benefits than people in other Western countries. Surveys repeatedly show that the majority of Americans regard the poor as being responsible for their own poverty, and are antagonistic to those who live on "government handouts." For example, a Gallup poll found that 55 percent of the public believed that lack of effort by the poor was the principal reason for poverty. Nearly two-thirds believed that government assistance programs reduced incentives to work.

These views, however, are out of line with the realities of poverty. The poor are as diverse as other groups. About one-third of those officially living in poverty are actually working, although at low-paying jobs. Most poor people, contrary to what is believed, don't receive welfare payments, because they earn too much to qualify for welfare. Only about one-third live from welfare payments. Of the remainder, over 50 percent consist of those sixty-five and over, the ill or disabled, and children under fourteen who fall into the poverty category either because their families do or because they are in single-parent families headed by divorced women. Poverty rates are highest for single mothers and their young children (see Figure 7.3). Only a minute proportion (about 2 percent) of able-

Figure 7.3
PERCENTAGE OF AMERICANS LIVING IN POVERTY

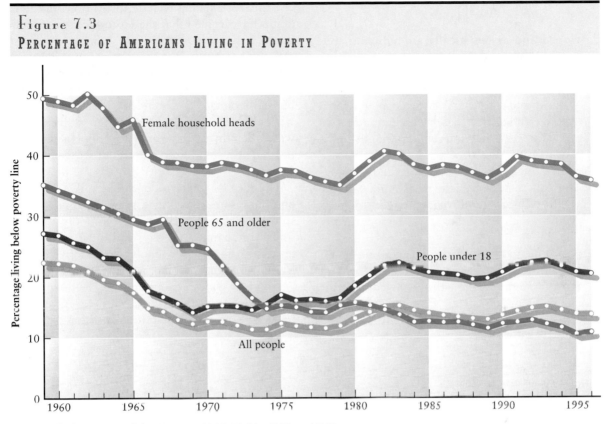

SOURCE: U.S. Bureau of the Census, 1998, Tables 759 and 762.

bodied men are on welfare. In addition, those who receive welfare payments do so for less than one year. Only one-eighth of the poor remain so for five years or more (Danziger et al., 1994).

Other myths about the poor abound. Though higher percentages of minorities fall into poverty, there are actually more numbers of whites who are poor than other groups. Families on welfare are not, as is often thought, large; the average number of children is the same for the rest of the population. And in spite of popular views about the high level of welfare cheating, fewer than 1 percent of welfare applications involve fraudulent claims—much lower than in the case of income-tax fraud, where it is estimated that more than 10 percent of tax is lost through misreporting or evasion.

Single mothers and their children constitute one of the largest groups on welfare.

Poverty and Welfare Systems

Well-developed and systematically administered welfare programs, in conjunction with government policies that actively assist in keeping down unemployment, reduce poverty levels. There exist societies such as Sweden in which poverty in effect has been eliminated (see Table 7.2). But an economic and political price has to be paid for this. Such a society requires high levels of taxation; and the government bureaucracies needed to administer the complex welfare system tend to acquire considerable power, even though they are not democratically elected.

Being poor does not necessarily mean being *mired* in poverty. A substantial proportion of people in poverty at any one time have either enjoyed superior conditions of life previously or can be expected to climb out of poverty at some time in the future.

Critics of existing welfare institutions in the United States have argued that these produce "welfare dependency," meaning that people become dependent on the very programs that are supposed to allow them to forge an independent and meaningful life for themselves. They become not just materially dependent, but psychologically dependent upon the arrival of the welfare check. Instead of taking an active attitude toward their lives, they tend to adopt a resigned and passive one, looking to the welfare system to support them.

The idea of welfare dependency is a controversial one, and some deny that such dependency is widespread. "Being on welfare" is commonly regarded as a source of shame, they say, and most people who are in such a position probably strive actively to escape from it as far as possible.

However widespread it may be, tackling welfare dependency has become a main target of attempts at reform of American welfare institutions. Among the

Table 7.2 Relative Size and Impact of Social Programs in Seven Western Nations

	PERCENTAGE OF ALL LOW-INCOME PERSONS WHOM GOVERNMENTAL BENEFITS LIFT TO HALF THE MEDIAN INCOME	PERCENTAGE OF ALL LOW-INCOME TWO-PARENT FAMILIES THAT GOVERNMENTAL BENEFITS LIFT TO HALF THE MEDIAN INCOME	PERCENTAGE OF ALL ELDERLY LOW-INCOME FAMILIES THAT GOVERNMENTAL BENEFITS LIFT TO HALF THE MEDIAN INCOME
UNITED STATES	38.1	19.4	71.5
ISRAEL	50.0	42.9	58.1
CANADA	52.7	40.5	84.4
NORWAY	80.1	56.4	94.0
(WEST) GERMANY	78.8	69.8	88.4
UNITED KINGDOM	68.5	63.1	77.0
SWEDEN	87.8	76.5	99.9

SOURCE: Adapted from Timothy M. Smeeding et al., eds., *Poverty, Inequality, and Income Distribution in Comparative Perspective* (New York: Harvester, 1990), pp. 30–31, Table 2.1, and p. 67, Table 3.5.

most significant of such reforms have been welfare-to-work programs, whose driving force is to move recipients from public assistance into paid jobs. Daniel Friedlander and Gary Burtless studied four different government-initiated programs designed to encourage welfare recipients to find paid work. The programs were roughly similar. They provided financial benefits for welfare recipients who actively searched for jobs as well as guidance in job-hunting techniques and opportunities for education and training. The target populations were mainly single-parent family heads of households who were recipients of Aid to Families with Dependent Children, at the time, the largest cash welfare program in the country. (AFDC was terminated in 1996 and replaced by state-managed block grants, called Temporary Assistance for Needy Families.) Friedlander and Burtless found that the programs did achieve results. People involved in such programs were able either to enter employment or to start working sooner than others who didn't participate. In all four programs, the earnings produced were several times greater than the net cost of the program. The programs were least effective, however, in helping those who needed them the most—those who had been out of work for a lengthy period, the long-term unemployed.

Welfare-to-work programs are designed to provide positive encouragement for welfare recipients to find paid jobs. But some welfare analysts have suggested that a more ruthless attitude should be adopted. They propose that welfare payments, under certain circumstances, should be either substantially reduced or abolished altogether. For example, benefits might be cut off if a single mother with one child has another child while still on welfare. The idea of such schemes is to dissolve the conditions that create welfare dependency and force people to look for paid work. Critics argue that such schemes are likely to lead those whose welfare benefits are reduced or taken away to turn to crime or prostitution in order to sustain a livelihood. There have been only a few experiments of this kind so far, and it is not yet possible adequately to judge what their consequences have been (Friedlander and Burtless, 1994).

The "Homeless" in America

No discussion of social stratification in America is complete without reference to the people who are traditionally seen as at the very bottom of the social hierarchy. Perhaps when you were growing up you referred to them as "bums" or "hobos" or "skids" or, most commonly, "the homeless."

"Hobo," "bum," "skid," and even "homeless" are not precise sociological concepts, but folk concepts—names we all use in our everyday lives to organize our experience of the things we see and hear about the people on the street or in shelters.

When someone refers to a "hobo," they mean a person who does seasonal work that keeps him constantly on the move (Jencks, 1994). Many of these

A homeless man sleeping in a public park.

people ride the trains between different regions of the country. In everyday language, a "bum" is a person who lives in the same community for long periods of time but has no regular work and is too poor or disorganized to rent a room on a long-term basis (Jencks, 1994).

There are also many folk explanations for how people come to be without homes. Some see the "homeless" as persons like themselves who have hit a patch of back luck. Those who see "homelessness" as a matter of bad luck often say that "we are all one step away from being homeless." Others take a harsher view. They say the "homeless" are persons who don't want to take responsibility and choose to live on the streets.

It is the role of sociology to think about these folk beliefs in a systematic manner. The first step in doing so is to ask questions about the homeless such as: How can we define an unhoused person? How many such people are there in the United States?

Like poverty, homelessness isn't as easy to define as we might imagine. Two generations ago, most Americans still thought of "home" as the family home. Homeless people were seen as individuals who lived in hotels on skid row. They were called homeless because they lived alone and rarely saw their family or kin.

Over the past two or three decades, far more people have come to live alone by choice. The **homeless** hence have become defined as people who have no place to sleep, and who either stay in free street shelters on a temporary basis or sleep in places not meant for habitation, such as doorways, subway stations, park benches, or derelict buildings.

In his study of the homeless, Christopher Jencks defined as homeless all people who slept in a public place or shelter during a given week (Jencks, 1994). His investigation didn't include those who were in rehabilitation centers, mental hospitals, welfare hotels, or jails during the week, even though many of these came from the streets and would return there as soon as they left. As he pointed out, what worries most of the population are the "visible homeless"—those who accost or can be seen by ordinary members of the public on a day-to-day basis.

Using this narrow definition, Jencks estimated that 350,000 Americans were homeless during the period of his study, March 1987. But some homeless are difficult or impossible to trace, living as they do on the margins of the wider society. The true number, he concluded, may be rather less—or quite a lot more. The numbers of people who become homeless at least for a certain time in any given year is certainly larger, perhaps amounting to 1.2 million. This is because a good deal of homelessness is temporary rather than a permanent way of life. Perhaps half the adults who became homeless in the late 1980s left the streets within two months.

Who are the homeless in America? The category is in fact a mixed one. About a quarter are people who have spent time in a mental hospital. At least some of these individuals would have been long-term inmates before the 1970s, when people with chronic mental illnesses began to be released from institutions as a result of changes in health care policy. This process of deinstitutionalization was prompted by several factors. One was the desire of states to save money—the cost of keeping people in mental hospitals, as in other types of hospitals, is high. Another, more praiseworthy motive was the belief on the part of leaders of the psychiatric profession that long-term hospitalization often did more harm than good. Anyone who could be cared for on an out-patient basis, therefore, should be. The results haven't borne out the hopes of those who saw deinstitutionalization as a positive step. Some hospitals discharged people who had nowhere to go, and who perhaps hadn't lived in the outside world for years. Often, little concrete provision for proper out-patient care was in fact made.

About a third of the homeless are people who suffer from serious problems of alcoholism. Some of these are former mental patients. From the early 1980s, alcoholism has been joined by an epidemic of crack addiction, and now it is estimated that about a quarter of the homeless are regular crack consumers (Jencks, 1994).

There isn't any clear evidence to show that alcoholism or crack addiction pushes people out onto the streets, but once they are homeless, these addictions tend to keep them there. Both types of drug consumption are expensive and swallow much of the small income individuals who live on the streets may have.

Not all of the homeless, however, are former mental patients, alcoholics, or regular consumers of illegal drugs. They are also people who find themselves on the streets because they have experienced personal

THE SOCIOLOGICAL DEBATE

STUDYING THE HOMELESS

Since the 1980s, there has been a remarkable growth in the number of homeless people in the United States. But how big is the problem? How does one know whom to count as homeless? These are questions that social scientists have sought to answer, often coming up with dramatically different results.

Until the mid-1980s, the conventional wisdom was that there were over 1 million homeless people, but the statistics were essentially undocumented. Why was it so difficult to know? The reason is that it is difficult to count people living in bus stations, subways, abandoned buildings, doorways, or dumpsters. In the absence of hard data, politicians relied on estimates provided by "homeless activists." For instance, one prominent activist, Mitch Snyder, told Ted Koppel on ABC's *Nightline* that the number was between 2 and 3 million. When asked where his numbers came from, he responded, "We got on the phone, we made a lot of calls, we talked to a lot of people, and we said, 'Okay, here are some numbers.'"

In his 1994 book *The Homeless* (discussed earlier), the sociologist Christopher Jencks stressed how important it is to look at hard data based on documented research instead of political numbers chosen to have the maximum impact on government policy. Jencks's research strategy was to carefully assess data and research collected by other social scientists or government agencies and come up with a more precise definition and count of the homeless. His definition excluded a number of people generally counted as homeless, such as those living in welfare hotels at the expense of social welfare programs, and therefore produced a number far smaller than the rough guesses of journalists and activists.

The sociologist Elliot Liebow studied homelessness entirely differently and wrote about it in his book *Tell Them Who I Am*. Liebow went out on the streets of Washington, D.C., and observed homelessness first-hand. He befriended the homeless women he was studying, volunteered to work in shelters, and helped them get along with their lives. Some would argue that in doing so, Liebow breached the rules of research discussed in Chapter 2, allowing himself to identify too closely with the group he was studying. But Liebow was able to learn something about homelessness that other research failed to illuminate: What do homeless people do all day? What are their most immediate concerns? What do they do with their limited possessions? Why do they think they are homeless?

The differences between Jencks's and Liebow's studies illustrate the differences between quantitative and qualitative research and between macrosociology and microsociology. By carefully scrutinizing the known data on the homeless, Jencks contributed a better knowledge of the extent of homelessness. By learning more about the day-to-day experiences of being homeless, Liebow contributed a better understanding of the conditions of homelessness. Both are crucial for coming to grips with the problem and forming more informed welfare policies.

disasters, often several at a time. A woman, for instance, may get divorced and at the same time lose not only her home but her job. Martha Burt's research showed that those who are most vulnerable to homelessness are people from lower-working-class backgrounds who have no specific job skills and very low incomes (Burt, 1992). Long-term joblessness is a major indicator.

With systematic data, it is possible to evaluate prevailing popular beliefs about homelessness. Jencks has shown that it is too simplistic to say that the homeless are people like you who have hit a patch of bad luck. Instead, he argues that being homeless is "the cumulative effect of many disadvantages, not just bad luck, that leads one to the street." Nor can we say that the homeless are people who don't want to take responsibility and choose to be homeless. Very few homeless people ever choose between a hit of drugs and a room. To speak about the choices people make on a day-to-day basis is to not comprehend the circumstances that led them to the street in the first place, which are often very complex.

KEY CONCEPTS IN REVIEW

Absolute poverty is defined in terms of the minimal requirements necessary to sustain a healthy existence.

Relative poverty is defined by reference to the living standards of the majority in any given society.

The **poverty line** is an official government measure to define those living in poverty in the United States.

The **homeless** are people who have no place to sleep and either stay in free shelters or sleep in public places not meant for habitation.

THEORIES OF STRATIFICATION IN MODERN SOCIETIES

So far, we have examined closely types of class division, the influence of gender, social mobility, and poverty. In this section, we step back and look at some broad theories by which thinkers have attempted to *understand* stratification. The most influential theoretical approaches are those developed by Karl Marx and Max Weber. Most subsequent theories of stratification are heavily indebted to their ideas.

Marx: Means of Production and the Analysis of Class

For Marx, a class refers to people who stand in a common relationship to the **means of production**— the means by which they gain a livelihood. In modern societies, the two main classes are those who own these new means of production—industrialists, or **capitalists**—and those who earn their living by selling their labor to them, the working class. The relationship between classes, according to Marx, is an ex-

ploitative one. In the course of the working day, Marx reasoned, workers produce more than is actually needed by employers to repay the cost of hiring them. This **surplus value** is the source of profit, which capitalists are able to put to their own use. A group of workers in a clothing factory, say, might be able to produce a hundred suits a day. Selling half the suits provides enough income for the manufacturer to pay the workers' wages. Income from the sale of the remainder of the garments is taken as profit.

Marx believed that the maturing of industrial capitalism would bring about an increasing gap between the wealth of the minority and the poverty of the mass of the population. In his view, the wages of the working class could never rise far above subsistence level, while wealth would pile up in the hands of those owning capital. In addition, laborers would daily face work that is physically wearing and mentally tedious, as is the situation in many factories. At the lowest levels of society, particularly among those frequently or permanently unemployed, there would develop an "accumulation of misery, agony of labor, slavery, ignorance, brutality, moral degradation" (1977).

Marx was right about the persistence of poverty in industrialized countries, and in anticipating that large inequalities of wealth and income would continue. He was wrong in supposing that the income of most of the population would remain extremely low, as well as in claiming that a minority would become more wealthy relative to the majority. Most people in Western countries today are much better off materially than were comparable groups in Marx's day.

Weber: Class and Status

There are two main differences between Weber's theory and that of Marx. First, according to Weber, class divisions derive not only from control or lack of control of the means of production, but from economic differences that have nothing directly to do with property. Such resources include especially people's skills and credentials, or qualifications. Those in managerial or professional occupations earn more and enjoy more favorable conditions at work, for example, than people in blue-collar jobs. The qualifications they possess, such as degrees, diplomas, and the skills they have acquired, make them more "marketable" than others without such qualifications. At a lower level, among blue-collar workers, skilled craftsmen are able to secure higher wages than the semiskilled or unskilled.

Second, Weber distinguished another aspect of stratification besides class, which he called **status**. Status refers to differences between groups in the social honor, or **prestige**, they are accorded by others. Status distinctions can vary independently of class divisions. Social honor may be either positive or negative. For instance, doctors and lawyers have high prestige in American society. **Pariah groups,** on the other hand, are negatively privileged status groups, subject to discrimination that prevents them from taking advantage of opportunities open to others. The Jews were a pariah group in medieval Europe, banned from participating in certain occupations and from holding official positions.

Possession of wealth normally tends to confer high status, but there are exceptions to this principle. In Britain, for instance, individuals from aristocratic families continue to enjoy considerable social esteem even after their fortunes have been lost. Conversely, "new money" is often looked upon with some scorn by the well-established wealthy.

Whereas class is objectively given, status depends upon people's subjective evaluations of social differences. Classes derive from the economic factors associated with property and earnings; status is governed by the varying styles of life groups follow.

Weber's writings on stratification are important because they show that other dimensions of stratification besides class strongly influence people's lives. Most sociologists hold that Weber's scheme offers a more flexible and sophisticated basis for analyzing stratification than that provided by Marx.

Davis and Moore: The Functions of Stratification

Kingsley Davis and Wilbert E. Moore (1945) provided a functionalist explanation of stratification, arguing that it has beneficial consequences to society. They claimed that certain positions or roles in society are functionally more important than others, like brain surgeons, and these positions require special skills for their performance. However, only a limited number of individuals in any society have the talents or experience appropriate to these positions. In order to attract the most qualified people, rewards need to be offered, such as money, power, and prestige. Davis and Moore concluded that since the benefits of different positions in any society must be unequal, then all societies must be stratified. They concluded that social stratification and social inequality are functional because they ensure that the most qualified people, attracted by the rewards bestowed by society, fill the roles that are most important to a smoothly functioning society.

Davis and Moore's theory suggests that a person's social position is based solely on their innate talents and efforts. Not surprisingly, their theory has been met with criticism by other sociologists. For example, Melvin Tumin critiqued the theory for several reasons (Tumin, 1953). First, he argued that the functional importance of a particular role is difficult to measure and that the rewards that a society bestows upon those in "important" roles do not reflect their actual importance. For instance, who is more important to society, a lawyer or a schoolteacher? If, on average, a lawyer earns two to three times the amount that a schoolteacher does, does that accurately reflect her relative importance to society? Second, Tumin argued that Davis and Moore overlooked the ways in which stratification limits the discovery of talent in a society.

KEY CONCEPTS IN REVIEW

Five theories of stratification:

Marx believed that class divisions are based on the **means of production,** or the means by which people earn a livelihood. In modern societies, there are two main classes: **capitalists,** who own the means of production, and the **working class,** who sell their labor. The working class produce more than they earn. This **surplus value** is the source of profits to capitalists.

Weber believed that class divisions are based not only on the means of production but on other resources as well, such as skills and credentials. He distinguished another aspect of stratification besides class—**status,** the differences between social groups in the social honor, or **prestige,** they are accorded by others. Status distinctions can vary independently of class divisions and can be either positive or negative. Negative status groups are called **pariah groups.**

Davis and Moore argued that stratification has beneficial consequences to society, by rewarding people who fill the roles that are most important to a functional society.

Wright argued that class divisions are based on exploitation and domination. Capitalists both exploit and dominate the working class. In between there are **contradictory class locations,** those who exploit and/or dominate, but are also exploited and dominated.

Parkin argued that class divisions result from the process of **social closure,** whereby groups try to maintain exclusive control over resources in a society.

As we have seen, the United States is not entirely a meritocratic society. Those at the top tend to have unequal access to economic and cultural resources, such as the highest quality education, which help the upper classes transmit their privileged status from one generation to the next. For those without access to these resources, even those with superior talents, social inequality serves as a barrier to reaching their full potential.

Erik Olin Wright: Contradictory Class Locations

The American sociologist Erik Olin Wright has developed a theoretical position that owes much to Marx, but also incorporates ideas from Weber (Wright, 1978, 1985, 1997). According to Wright, class structures are determined by two dimensions of social rela-

tions: exploitation and domination. The concept of domination is fairly straightforward: it refers to social relations within which one category of people controls the activities of another. Exploitation is a more complex idea. It refers to a particular kind of deep antagonism of economic interests between people. It exists when three basic conditions are met: first, the material well-being of exploiters depends upon the deprivations of the exploited; second, these deprivations are generated by the exclusion of the exploited from access to certain important economic resources; and third, this exclusion enables exploiters to capitalize on the labor of the exploited. If the first two of these conditions are met, but not the third, we have what might be termed "nonexploitative oppression"; if all three are present, we have exploitation. An example of nonexploitative oppression would be the relationship between European settlers in North America and Native Americans: the welfare of the settlers depended upon excluding native Americans from the land, but they generally did not rely on the labor effort of the excluded people.

The two fundamental classes in capitalist societies, capitalists and workers, are polarized on both of the underlying dimensions of class relations: capitalists, by virtue of their ownership and control of the means of production, both exploit and dominate workers. Other locations in the class structure, especially those that are generally called "middle class," are linked to exploitation and domination in more complex ways. Supervisors, for example, dominate workers but are not exploiters. High-paid professionals have a privileged relation to the dimension of exploitation, but they generally do not dominate workers. Managers, especially high-level managers, dominate workers and may indirectly exploit them, but they are in turn dominated by their own employers. As a result of these complexities, the class interests of people in the middle class are often quite confused and inconsistent. As a result Wright calls these positions in the class structure, "**contradictory class locations.**"

Wright terms the class position of such workers "contradictory," because it incorporates the characteristics of the classes both above and below them. Workers in contradictory class locations are neither capitalists nor manual workers, yet share certain common features with each.

Frank Parkin and Social Closure

Frank Parkin (1971, 1979), a British author, has proposed an approach drawing more heavily from Weber than from Marx. Parkin agrees with Marx, as Weber did, that ownership of property—the means of production—is the basic foundation of class structure. Property, however, according to Parkin, is only one form of **social closure** that can be monopolized by one group and used as a basis of power over others. We can define social closure as any process whereby groups try to maintain exclusive control over resources, limiting access to them. Besides property or wealth, most of the characteristics Weber associated with status differences, such as ethnic origin, language, or religion, may be used to create social closure.

Two types of processes are involved in social closure. The first type, *exclusion*, refers to strategies that groups adopt to separate outsiders from themselves, preventing them from having access to valued resources. Thus white unions in the United States have in the past excluded blacks from membership, as a means of maintaining power and privilege.

An emphasis on credentials is another major way by which groups exclude others in order to hold on to their power and privilege. In some U.S. school systems, for example, only those who have earned a secondary-school teaching certification in their subject, awarded by a school of education, are allowed to teach in the public schools. The second type, *usurpation*, refers to attempts by the less privileged to acquire resources previously monopolized by others—as where blacks struggle to achieve rights of union membership.

The strategies of exclusion and usurpation may be used simultaneously in some circumstances. Labor unions, for instance, might engage in usurpatory activities against employers (going on strike to obtain a greater share of the resources or a position on the board of directors of a firm) but at the same time exclude ethnic minorities from membership. Parkin calls this *dual closure*. Here there is clearly a point of similarity between Wright and Parkin. Dual closure concerns much the same processes as those discussed by Wright under contradictory class locations. Both notions indicate that those in the middle of the stratification system in some part cast their eyes toward the top, yet are also concerned with distinguishing themselves from others lower down.

CLASS, INEQUALITY, AND ECONOMIC COMPETITIVENESS

The United States, as mentioned earlier, is more unequal than most other industrial countries, and it has become yet more unequal over recent years. The chief executive of one of the hundred largest companies in the United States in 1960, on average, earned $190,000, or about forty times more than the average worker in his factory. At the end of the 1980s, the average earnings of the chief executive were $2 million, ninety-three times the average wage of the factory worker (Reich, 1991). In other industrial societies, these differentials are less.

What relation is there between inequality and economic prosperity? Some argue that high levels of economic inequality are necessary to bring about economic growth. This assumption was particularly prominent during the 1980s. The pursuit of wealth, the reasoning was, creates economic development because it is a motivating force encouraging innovation and drive. But a good deal of evidence has accumulated that runs counter to this assumption.

In his book *Capitalism vs. Capitalism* (1993), Michel Albert systematically compared two models of enterprise and economic organization. One, which he termed the "American model," is based on largely deregulated markets and low levels of state welfare systems, and evinces a high degree of economic inequality between rich and poor. The other he called the "Rhine model," because it is based on the sort of economic system found in countries that lie close to the Rhine River in Europe—Germany, Switzerland, and Holland—although it has important qualities in common with Japan and the other successful Asian economies.

In the Rhine model, collective interests tend to take precedence over individual ones. These are not aggressively individualistic societies. The communities of which the individual forms a part, whether these are business enterprises, towns, or labor unions, are regarded as crucial in providing stability. Particularly important, the Rhine model countries are egalitarian societies; the differences between rich and poor are much less than in the United States.

The Rhine model has been more successful in global economic competition, Albert argues, than the American one, largely because of its egalitarian character. Support for Albert's view can be drawn from the study of the successful Asian countries, such as Japan, Singapore, South Korea, and Taiwan, over the past thirty years. Countries where inequality is relatively low on the whole have prospered more than those where the divisions between rich and poor are greater. Including poorer people in the wider society rather than cutting them off from it gives them the means as well as the will to improve their earning power.

Economic inequality is a persistent feature of all social systems except for hunting and gathering societies—in which little wealth is produced in any case. Class divisions form the core economic inequalities in modern societies. Class exerts a great influence in our lives. But our activities are never completely determined by class divisions: many people experience some social mobility. Others, however, find themselves in situations of poverty from which it is very difficult to escape. Relative poverty is in fact a measure of inequality; American society tends to be more unequal than most other Western societies. Some have argued that such high levels of inequality, far from encouraging economic development, tend to act against it. Combatting poverty and homelessness, which is surely desirable for its own sake, might also help the United States be more competitive in the global economy.

SUMMARY

1. *Social stratification* refers to the division of people socioeconomically into layers or strata. When we talk of social stratification, we draw attention to the unequal positions occupied by individuals in society. In the larger traditional societies and in industrialized countries today there is stratification in terms of *wealth,* property, and access to material goods and cultural products.

2. Four major types of stratification systems can be distinguished: *slavery, caste, estate,* and *class.*

Whereas the first three of these depend upon legal or religiously sanctioned inequalities, class divisions are not "officially" recognized, but stem from economic factors affecting the material circumstances of people's lives.

3. Classes derive from inequalities in possession and control of material resources and access to educational and occupational opportunities. An individual's class position is at least in some part achieved, for it is not simply "given" from birth. *Social mobility*, both *upward* and *downward* in the class structure, is a fairly common feature.

4. Class is of major importance in industrialized societies, although there are many complexities in the class system within such societies. The main class divisions are between people in the *upper, middle*, and *working classes*, and the *underclass*.

5. Most people in modern societies are more affluent today than was the case several generations ago. Yet the distribution of *wealth* and *income* remains highly unequal. The wealthy have various means open to them of transmitting their property from one generation to the next.

6. Analyses of stratification have traditionally been written from a male-oriented point of view. This is partly because of the assumption that gender inequalities simply reflect class differences; but this assumption is highly questionable. Gender influences stratification in modern societies in some part independently of class.

7. In the study of social mobility, a distinction is made between *intragenerational* and *intergenerational* mobility. The first of these refers to movement up or down the social scale within an individual's working life. Intergenerational mobility is movement across the generations, as when the daughter or son from a blue-collar background becomes a professional. Social mobility is mostly of limited range. Most people remain close to the level of the family from which they came, though the expansion of white-collar jobs in the last few decades has provided the opportunity for considerable *short-range upward mobility*.

8. Poverty remains widespread in the United States. Two methods of assessing poverty exist. One involves the notion of *absolute poverty*, which is a lack of the basic resources needed to maintain a healthy existence. *Relative poverty* involves assessing the gaps between the living conditions of some groups and those enjoyed by the majority of the population.

9. The most prominent and influential theories of stratification are those developed by Marx and Weber. Marx placed the primary emphasis on *class*, which he saw as an objectively given characteristic of the economic structure of society. He saw a fundamental split between the owners of capital and the workers who do not own capital. Weber accepted a similar view, but distinguished another aspect of stratification, *status*. Status refers to the esteem or "social honor" given to individuals or groups.

Chapter Eight

Gender Differences: Nature versus Nurture

Think about whether differences between women and men are the result of biological differences or social and cultural influences.

Forms of Gender Inequality

Recognize that gender differences are a part of our social structure and create inequalities between women and men. Learn the forms these inequalities take, particularly in the workplace, family, and educational system.

Analyzing Gender Inequality

Think about various explanations for gender inequality and apply them to a real life example. Learn some feminist theories about how to achieve gender equality.

Gender
Inequality

around midnight one cold night in December, a little before the end of the second shift, Andrea Ellington is standing by the Coke machine in the workers' lounge, cleaning out her oversized pocketbook. She empties its contents, which begin with a gold plastic makeup bag, a wallet, and a bunch of monthly bills. "I gotta go wake my five-year-old daughter up at my mother's house," she says as she opens the makeup bag. "Then I go to the other babysitter and get my baby twins. Then I take them home and they've gotta go back to sleep, try to go back to sleep. By the time my daughter gets back to sleep, it's time for her to get back up again."

An African-American woman of twenty-three, Andrea Ellington has three children to support on a low-rung clerical salary of $20,000 per year. She has been working at a Chicago law firm for four years; she had taken the job believing that, with hard work, eventually she could advance enough to move her family out of public housing, her foremost goal.

Most of the five hundred or so employees in the law office where she works are not attorneys but "support staff," who work in one of many departments at the center of the floors, surrounded by plush attornies' offices on the perimeter. The Network Center where she types is solely a nighttime word processing department, with shifts from 4 P.M. to midnight and midnight to 8 A.M. The people who work as word processors are all women. They sit at computer terminals in one of four clusters separated by gray partitions. Almost all of these women who work at night are also rearing children during the day. Most live far from the law firm's gleaming downtown building.

Balancing the commitments of work and family is not only a challenge in terms of time, but also money. Raising three children on her modest income, Andrea lives from paycheck to paycheck. She seeks out extra work to help her get by with her everyday responsibilities. As she says, "[working] overtime has helped me pay bills on time, buy clothes for my children, and buy food that I normally have had to wait until each paycheck to get." As a result of Andrea's persistence, her supervisor assigned her to work an extra eight hours of overtime per week, on Sundays. Andrea came to work for the first two Sundays, and then began missing her weekend assignments when she couldn't find a babysitter for her three children. When her supervisor learned of the absences, she canceled the overtime.

Many people who encounter someone like Andrea Ellington might make certain assumptions about her life. They might assume, for example, that a disproportionate number of women become typists and word processors because it is natural for women to have certain kinds of occupations, including secretarial jobs. They might also assume that mothers should be responsible for taking care of children. Finally, they might assume that Andrea's poverty and low position in society are a result of her natural abilities. It is the job of sociology to analyze these assumptions and allow us to take a much wider view of our society and people like Andrea. Sociology allows us to understand why women are likely to work in low-paying clerical jobs, why women are likely to spend more time on child care, and why women on the whole are less powerful in society than men. Explaining the differences and inequalities between women and men in a society is now one of the most central topics in sociology.

In this chapter, we will explore a sociological approach to gender differences and gender inequality. Gender is a way for society to divide people into two categories: "men" and "women." According to this socially created division, men and women have different identities and social roles. In other words, men and women are expected to think and act in certain different ways. Since in almost all societies, men's roles are valued more than are women's roles, gender also serves as a social status. Men and women are not only different, but also unequal in terms of power, prestige, and wealth. Despite the advances that many women have made in the United States and other Western societies, this remains true today. Sociologists are interested in not only explaining how society differentiates between women and men, but also how these differences serve as the basis for social inequalities (Chafetz, 1990). Some sociologists are also concerned about the ways in which women can achieve positions of equality in society.

In this chapter, we will first look at the origins of gender differences, assessing the debate over the role of biological versus social influences on the formation of gender roles. We will also look to other cultures for evidence on this debate. We will then review the various forms of gender inequality that exist in American society. In this section, we will focus on the prominent social institutions of the workplace, family, and educational systems. We will then analyze some theories of gender inequality and apply them to the circumstances of Andrea's life. Finally, we will review the various forms of feminism and assess prospects for future change toward a gender equal society.

GENDER DIFFERENCES: NATURE VERSUS NURTURE

We begin by inquiring into the origins of the differences between boys and girls, men and women. The nature-nurture debate, noted earlier in Chapter 3, appears again with some force here. Schol-ars are divided about the degree to which inborn biological characteristics have an enduring impact upon our gender identities as "feminine" or "masculine" and the social roles based on those identities. The debate is really one about how much learning there is. No one any longer supposes that our behavior is instinctive in the sense in which the sexual activity of many lower animals—like the celebrated birds and bees—is instinctive. Some scholars, however, allow more prominence than others to social influences in analyzing gender differences.

Before we review these competing theories, we need to make an important distinction, between sex and gender. While **sex** refers to physical differences of the body, **gender** concerns the psychological, social, and cultural differences between males and females. The distinction between sex and gender is fundamental, since many differences between males and females are not biological in origin.

Some sociologists theorize that aggression is a product of culture rather than an inherent trait.

The Role of Biology

How far are differences in the behavior of women and men the result of sex rather than gender? In other words, how much are they the result of biological differences? The opinions of researchers are divided. Some hold that there are innate differences of behavior between women and men that appear in some form in all cultures, and that the findings of sociobiology point strongly in this direction. Such researchers are likely to draw attention to the fact, for example, that in almost all cultures, men rather than women

Some sociologists suggest a correlation between sex and aggression based on similarities in various cultures. In the Yanomani culture in Brazil, the tribe's men take part in a ritual to attack evil spirits.

take part in hunting and warfare. Surely, they argue, this indicates that men possess biologically based tendencies toward aggression that women lack? In the case of the word processors, they might point out that typing is a more passive occupation than being a bicycle messenger (an equivalent job category within the firm), which requires more physical strength and aggressiveness in traffic.

Other researchers are unconvinced by this argument. The level of aggressiveness of males, they say, varies widely between different cultures, and women are expected to be more passive or gentle in some cultures than in others (Elshtain, 1981). Moreover, they add, because a trait is more or less universal, it does not follow that it is biological in origin; there may be cultural factors of a general kind that produce such characteristics. For instance, in most cultures, most women spent a significant part of their lives caring for children and could not readily take part in hunting or war. According to this view, differences in the behavior of men and women develop mainly through the social learning of female and male identities.

What does the evidence show? One possible source of information is the differences in hormonal makeup between the sexes. Some have claimed that the male sex hormone, testosterone, is associated with the male propensity to violence (Rutter and Giller, 1984). Research has indicated, for instance, that if male monkeys are castrated at birth, they become less aggressive; conversely, female monkeys given testosterone will become more aggressive than normal females. However, it has also been found that providing monkeys with opportunities to dominate others actually increases the testosterone level. Aggressive behavior may thus affect the production of the hormone, rather than the hormone causing increased aggression.

Another possible source of evidence is direct observations of animal behavior. Writers who connect male aggression with biological influences often stress male aggressiveness among the higher animals. If we look at the behavior of chimpanzees, they say, male animals are invariably more aggressive than females. Yet there are in fact large differences between types of animals. Among gibbons, for instance, there are few noticeable differences in aggression between the sexes. Moreover, many female apes or monkeys are highly aggressive in some situations, such as when their young are threatened.

Another source of information comes from the experience of identical twins. Identical twins derive from a single egg and have *exactly the same* genetic makeup. In one particular case, one of a pair of identical male twins was seriously injured while being circumcised, and the decision was made to reconstruct his genitals as a female. He was thereafter raised as a girl. The twins at six years old demonstrated typical male and female traits as found in Western culture. The little girl enjoyed playing with other girls, helped with the housework, and wanted to get married when she grew up. The boy preferred the company of other boys, his favorite toys were cars and trucks, and he wanted to become a fire fighter or police officer.

For some time, this case was treated as a conclusive demonstration of the overriding influence of social learning on gender differences. However, when the girl was a teenager, she was interviewed during a television program, and the interview showed that she felt some unease about her gender identity, even perhaps that she was "really" a boy after all. She had by then learned of her unusual background, and this knowledge may very well have been responsible for this altered perception of herself (Ryan, 1985).

This case does not refute the possibility that there are biological influences on observed behavior differences between men and women. If these do exist, though, their physiological origins have not yet been identified. Many would agree that

the primary self-identification of a person as a man or a woman, with the multitude of attitudes, ideas, and desires that accompany that identification, depends on what label was attached to him or her as a child. In the normal course of events, these labels correspond to a consistent biological difference in chromosomes, hormones, and morphology. Thus biological differences become a signal for, rather than a cause of, differentiation in social roles. (Lewontin, 1982)

The Social Construction of Gender Identity

Many sociologists argue that gender differences result from socialization and interaction with others. In order to understand this argument, let's take a look at the following two scenes. Two newly born infants lie in the nursery of a hospital maternity ward. One, a male baby, is wrapped in a blue blanket, the other, a female, is in a pink blanket. Both babies are only a few hours old and are being seen by their grandparents for the first time. The conversation between one pair of grandparents runs along these lines:

Grandma A: There he is—our first grandchild, and a boy.

Grandpa A: Hey, isn't he a hefty little fellow? Look at that fist he's making. He's going to be a regular little fighter, that guy is. (Grandpa A smiles and throws out a boxing jab to his grandson.) *At-a-boy!*

Grandma A: I think he looks like you. He has your strong chin. Oh, look, he's starting to cry.

Grandpa A: Yeah—just listen to that set of lungs. He's going to be some boy.

Grandma A: Poor thing—he's still crying.

Grandpa A: It's okay. It's good for him. He's exercising and it will develop his lungs.

Grandma A: Let's go and congratulate the parents. I know they're thrilled about little Fred. They wanted a boy first.

Grandpa A: Yeah, and they were sure it would be a boy too, what with all that kicking and thumping going on even before he got here.

When they depart to congratulate the parents, the grandparents of the other child arrive. The dialogue between them goes like this:

Grandma B: There she is . . . the only one with a pink bow taped to her head. Isn't she darling.

Grandpa B: Yeah—isn't she little. Look at how tiny her fingers are. Oh, look—she's trying to make a fist.

Grandma B: Isn't she sweet . . . you know, I think she looks a little like me.

Grandpa B: Yeah, she sorta does. She has your chin.

Grandma B: Oh, look, she's starting to cry.

Grandpa B: Maybe we better call the nurse to pick her up or change her or something.

Grandma B: Yes, let's. Poor little girl. (To the baby) There, there, we'll try to help you.

Grandpa B: Let's find the nurse. I don't like to see her cry . . .

Grandma B: Hmm. I wonder when they will have their next one. I know Fred would like a son, but little Fredericka is well and healthy. After all, that's what really matters.

Grandpa B: They're young yet. They have time for more kids. I'm thankful too that she's healthy.

Grandma B: I don't think they were surprised when it was a girl anyway . . . she was carrying so low. (Walum, 1977)

The contrast between the two sets of conversations sounds so exaggerated that it is tempting to think they were made up. In fact, they are composed of transcripts of actual dialogue recorded in a maternity ward. The very first question usually asked of a parent—in Western culture at least—is, "Is it a boy or a girl?" Our images of others are fundamentally structured around gender identity. In turn, social and cul-

tural expectations for each gender create expectations about the roles and identities one should assume.

When we say that gender is "socially constructed," we mean that people create gender through social interactions with others, such as family members, friends, and colleagues. As we just saw, the **social construction of gender** begins at birth when doctors, nurses, and family members—the first to see an infant—assign the person to a gender category on the basis of physical characteristics. Babies are immediately dressed in a way that marks the sex category: "parents don't want to be constantly asked if their child is a boy or a girl" (Lorber, 1994).

Once the child is marked as male or female, everyone who interacts with the child will treat it in accordance with its gender. They do so on the basis of the society's assumptions, which lead people to treat women and men differently, even as opposites (Renzetti and Curran, 1995).

Gender Identity in Everyday Life

Our conceptions of gender identity are formed so early in life that as adults we mainly take them for granted. Yet gender is more than learning to act like a girl or boy. Gender differences are something we live with every day.

In other words, gender as a physical concept does not exist; we all, as some sociologists put it, "do gen-

Gender differentiation on a date.

der" in our daily interactions with others (West and Zimmerman, 1987). For instance, Jan Morris, the celebrated travel writer, used to be a man. As James Morris, she was a member of the British expedition, led by Sir Edmund Hillary, that successfully climbed Mount Everest. She was, in fact, a very "manly" man—a race car driver and an athlete. Yet she had always felt herself to be a woman in a male body. So she underwent a sex-change operation and since then has lived as a woman.

Jan Morris had to learn how to do gender when she discovered how differently she was expected to behave as a woman, rather than as a man. As she says, there is "no aspect of existence" that is not gendered. But she did not notice this until she changed her sex.

> It amuses me to consider, for instance, when I am taken out to lunch by one of my more urbane men friends, that not so many years ago th[e] waiter would have treated *me* as he is now treating *him*. Then he would have greeted me with respectful seriousness. Now he unfolds my napkin with a playful flourish, as if to humor me. Then he would have taken my order with grave concern, now he expects me to say something frivolous (and I do). (Morris, 1974)

The subtle ways in which we do gender are so much a part of our lives that we don't notice them until they are missing or radically altered.

This differentiation between the roles and identities that society creates for men and women occurs not only in face-to-face interaction, but is also part of society's institutions, such as the economy, political system, educational system, religions, and family forms. Because gender is so pervasive in structuring social life, gender statuses must be clearly differentiated if the society is to function in an orderly manner. However, gender differentiation can also be the basis for inequalities between men and women (Lorber, 1993; West and Fenstermaker, 1995).

The Social Construction of Masculinity

Many discussions of gender identity focus on women's roles in a society. In recent years, more scholarly attention has been paid to how men's identi-

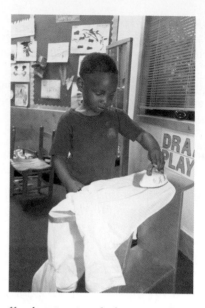

No sissy stuff: a boy ironing clothes contradicts a gender stereotype.

ties are constructed and the impact that these socially prescribed roles have on men's behavior. The traditional male role has been described by Linda Brannon as having four components (1976):

1. "No Sissy Stuff": the need to be different from women.

2. "The Big Wheel": the need to be superior to others.

3. "The Sturdy Oak": the need to be independent and self-reliant.

4. "Give 'Em Hell": the need to be more powerful than others, through violence if necessary.

These are difficult standards to measure up to. Some have argued that these stereotypical male gender roles create a strain between unattainable ideals and men's actual experiences. The stress produced by adherence to these norms may be indirectly related to men's greater risk of death due to heart disease, respiratory illness, cancer, accident, homicide, and suicide. In other words, masculinity may be dangerous to your health (Brannon, 1976; Pleck, 1981; Harrison et al., 1996).

The recognition that adherence to the stereotypical

male gender role carries with it unique pressures has led to the development of a men's movement. In the early 1970s, some men—mostly white, educated professionals—began to meet in small informal groups to discuss their experiences as men, their interpersonal relationships, their notions of masculinity, and how these influence their lives. By the mid-1970s, more than three hundred men's groups had developed, with the primary task of discussing how gender norms and stereotypes limited them (Katz, 1974).

There are two main strands to the men's movement. The first is labeled as "male-identified" and is a corollary of mainstream feminism. A main tenet is that male privilege bestows as many disadvantages as advantages. The goals of this camp are male enlightenment and personal development. Men are encouraged to explore "feminine" aspects of their personality, to develop closer relationships, and to freely express their emotions. A second strand has been labeled as "female-identified." Adherents argue that traditional masculinity is debilitating and thus the social structures that distribute power unequally must be dismantled and rebuilt (Brod, 1987).

Findings from Other Cultures

If gender differences were mostly the result of biology, then we could expect that gender roles would not vary much from culture to culture. However, one set of findings that help show gender roles are in fact socially constructed comes from anthropologists, who have studied gender in other times and cultures.

NEW GUINEA

In her classic New Guinea study, *Sex and Temperament in Three Primitive Societies*, Margaret Mead (1963) observed wide variability among gender role prescriptions—and such marked differences from those in the United States—that any claims to the universality of gender roles had to be rejected. Mead studied three separate tribes in New Guinea, which varied widely in their gender roles. The Arapesh were a society in which both males and females generally had characteristics and behaviors that would typically be associated with the Western female role. Both sexes among the Arapesh were passive, gentle, unaggressive,

and emotionally responsive to the needs of others. In contrast, Mead found that in another New Guinea group, the Mundugumor, both the males and females were characteristically aggressive, suspicious, and, from a Western observer's perspective, excessively cruel, especially toward children. In both cultures, however, men and women were expected to behave very similarly.

Mead then studied the Tchambuli tribe of New Guinea. The gender roles of the males and females were almost exactly reversed from the roles traditionally assigned to males and females in Western society. Mead reported in her autobiography that "among the Tchambuli the expected relations between men and women reversed those that are characteristic of our own culture. For it was Tchambuli women who were brisk and hearty, who managed the business affairs of life, and worked comfortably in large cooperative groups" (Mead, 1972, p. 214).

The children also exhibited these characteristics. Girls were considered the brightest and most competent and displayed "the most curiosity and the freest expression of intelligence." The Tchambuli boys "were already caught up in the rivalrous, catty, and individually competitive life of the men" (Mead, 1972, p. 214). Mead also reported that while the women managed the affairs of the family, the men were engaged differently: "Down by the lake shore in ceremonial houses the men carved and painted, gossiped and had temper tantrums, and played out their rivalries" (Mead, 1972, p. 215).

THE !KUNG

Another example can be found among the !Kung, a foraging society of bush-living people of the Kalahari Desert, where women provide from 60 to 80 percent of the society's food through their gathering activities. The !Kung division of labor conforms to the traditional "men hunt, women gather" pattern, but the game hunted by men is a much less dependable food source than the plants and small animals obtained by women. !Kung women are respected for their specialized knowledge of the bush: "Successful gathering over the years requires the ability to discriminate among hundreds of edible and inedible species of plants at various stages in their life cycle" (Draper, 1975, p. 83). In addition, women return

KEY CONCEPTS IN REVIEW

The term "sex" is ambiguous. **Sex,** which refers to biological differences between women and men, should be distinguished from sexual activity. More important, sex (in the anatomical sense) should be distinguished from **gender,** which refers to psychological, social, and cultural differences between women and men.

While biological differences contribute to our understanding of gender differences, another route is studying the **social construction of gender,** the learning of gender roles through socialization and interaction with others. Gender identities are maintained throughout life by these daily interactions with others. Gender is also a pervasive aspect of the social structure. Evidence from other cultures lends support to the view that gender differences are primarily the result of social influences.

from their gathering expeditions armed not only with food for the community but also with valuable information for hunters. Draper (1975, p. 82) noted that "women are skilled in reading the signs of the bush, and they take careful note of animal tracks, their age, and the direction of movement . . . In general, the men take advantage of women's reconnaissance and query them routinely on the evidence of game movements, the location of water and the like."

Thus, while the !Kung follow a gendered division of labor, it is not rigidly adhered to, and men and women sometimes do one another's chores. Child care is viewed as the responsibility of both parents, and "as children grow up there are few experiences which set one sex apart from the other" (Draper, 1975, p. 89). The !Kung child rearing practices are relaxed and nonauthoritarian, and aggressive behavior on the part of men and women is discouraged.

THE VANATINAI

The Vanatinai, a horticultural society on a small island southeast of Papua New Guinea, also are distin-guished by egalitarian gender relations. Both Vanatinai women and men plant, tend, and harvest garden crops. Although hunting with spears is a male activity,

women also hunt game by trapping. Members of both sexes learn and practice magic, participate in warfare, peacemaking, and community decision making; and both undertake sailing expeditions in search of ceremonial valuables. Lepkowsky (1990, p. 178) notes that the Vanatinai society "offers every adult, regardless of sex or kin group, the opportunity of excelling at prestigious activities such as participation in traditional exchange or ritual functions essential to health and prosperity."

MULTIPLE GENDERS

The understanding that only two genders (i.e., male and female) exist is not true among all societies. The *berdache* of some Asian, South Pacific, and North American societies is one such example. *Berdaches* are individuals who adopt the gender behavior ascribed to members of the opposite sex. The Mohave allow men and women to cross genders. Boys who show a preference for feminine toys and clothing undergo an initiation ceremony at puberty during which they become *alyha.* As *alyha,* they adopt feminine names, paint their faces as women do, perform female tasks, and marry men. When they marry, *alyha* pretend to menstruate by cutting their upper thighs. They also simulate pregnancy. Martin and Voorhies (1975, p. 97) wrote that "labor pains, induced by drinking a severely constipating drink, culminate in the birth of a fictitious stillborn child. Stillborn Mohave infants are customarily buried by the mother, so that an *alyha*'s failure to return to 'her' home with a living infant is explained in a culturally acceptable manner."

Likewise, Mohave women who wish to pursue a masculine lifestyle undergo an initiation ceremony to become *hwame*. *Hwame* dress and live like men; they engage in hunting, farming, and shamanism—although they are not permitted to assume leadership positions or participate in warfare. They do, though, assume paternal responsibility for children; some women, in fact, become *hwame* after they have children. Importantly, neither *hwame* or *alyha* are considered abnormal or deviant within their cultures.

Berdaches are not the counterpart of transsexuals or transvestites in the United States, however. Roscoe (1991) has studied Zuni *berdaches* and noted that although *berdaches* technically do "cross-dress," their cross-dressing is routine, public, and without erotic motives. Moreover, *berdaches* are not necessarily homosexual; rather, some are heterosexual, some homosexual, and others sexually oriented toward other *berdaches*.

In one society, Roscoe found that both males and females have characteristics typically associated with the female role in the West. In another group, both males and females are aggressive. In both cultures, men and women are expected to behave similarly. These findings demonstrate that culture—not biology—is at the root of gender differences. There was a time in the development of feminist approaches when gender roles and gender socialization were the dominant concepts in understanding why women tended to cluster in particular occupations.

In recent years, however, sociologists have noted that while society teaches people to assume certain "masculine" or "feminine" gender roles, such an approach does not tell us where these gender roles come from or how they can be changed. For this, we need to look at the way that gender is built into the institutions of society (Lorber, 1994). For example, we need to know how the schools Andrea attended and the law firm Andrea works in operate to establish "patterns of expectations" that lead people to assume certain roles (Lorber, 1994).

FORMS OF GENDER INEQUALITY

Anthropologists and historians have found that most groups, collectives, and societies throughout history differentiate between women's and men's societal roles. Although there are considerable variations in the respective roles of women and men in different cultures, there is no known instance of a society in which women are more powerful than men. Women are everywhere primarily concerned with child rearing and the maintenance of the home, while political and military activities tend to be resoundingly male. Nowhere in the world do men have primary responsibility for the rearing of children. Conversely, there are few if any cultures in which women are charged with the main responsibility for the herding of large animals, the hunting of large game, deep-sea fishing, or plow agriculture (Brown, 1977). Just because women and men perform different tasks or have different responsibilities in societies does not necessarily mean that women are unequal to men. However, if the work and activities of women and men are valued differently, then the division of labor between them can become the basis for unequal gender relations. In modern societies, the division of labor between the sexes has become less clear-cut than it was in premodern cultures, but men still outnumber women in all spheres of power and influence.

Male dominance in a society is usually referred to as **patriarchy**. Although men are favored in all of the world's societies, the degree of patriarchy varies. In the United States, women have made tremendous progress, but several forms of gender inequality still exist.

Sociologists define **gender inequality** as the difference in the status, power, and prestige women and men have in groups, collectives, and societies. In thinking about gender inequality between men and women, one can ask the following questions: Do women and men have equal access to valued societal resources—for example, food, money, power, and time? Second, do women and men have similar life options? Third, are women's and men's roles and activities valued similarly? We will turn to look at the various forms of gender inequality in the workplace, in the home, and in education systems. As you read through this section, keep the above questions in mind.

Women and the Workplace

Rates of employment of women outside the home, for all classes, were quite low until well into the twentieth century. Even as late as 1910 in the United States, more than a third of gainfully employed women were maids or house servants. The female labor force consisted mainly of young, single women and children. When they worked in factories or offices, employers often sent their wages straight home to their parents.

When they married, they withdrew from the labor force.

Since then, women's participation in the paid labor force has risen more or less continuously, especially in the past fifty years (see Figure 8.1). In 1996, 59 percent of women age sixteen and older were in the labor force. In contrast, 38 percent of working-age women were in the labor force in 1960. An even greater change in the rate of labor-force participation has occurred among married mothers of young children. In 1970, only 10 percent of married women with preschool-age children (under six years old) worked full time year round, yet this figure increased to 33 percent by 1996 (see Figure 8.2) (Spain and Bianchi, 1996).

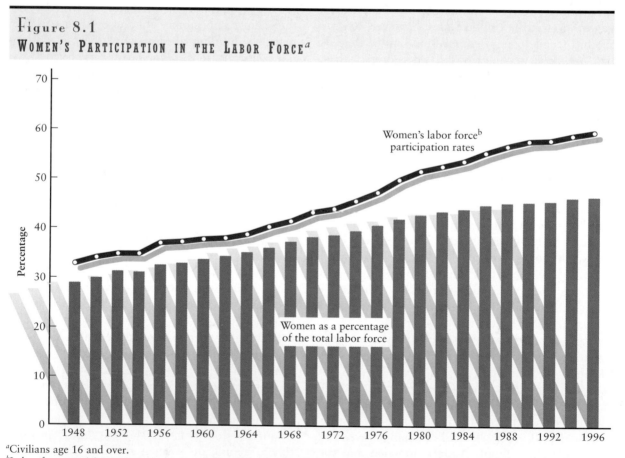

Figure 8.1
WOMEN'S PARTICIPATION IN THE LABOR FORCE[a]

Women's labor force[b] participation rates

Women as a percentage of the total labor force

[a]Civilians age 16 and over.
[b]Labor force participants as a percentage of all civilian women age 16 and over.

SOURCE: U.S. Bureau of Labor Statistics, *Handbook of Labor Statistics*, 1989, Table 2, and *Employment and Earnings*, January 1997, Table 2.

Figure 8.2
WORKING MOTHERS

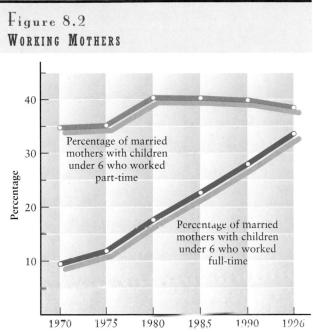

Percentage of married mothers with children under 6 who worked part-time

Percentage of married mothers with children under 6 who worked full-time

SOURCE: U.S. Bureau of Labor Statistics, *Handbook of Labor Statistics*, 1989, and unpublished data from the March Current Population Surveys of 1990 and 1996.

How can we explain this increase? One force behind women's increased entry into the labor force was the increase in demand, since 1940, for clerical and service workers like Andrea, as the U.S. economy expanded and changed (Oppenheimer, 1970). From 1940 until the mid- to late 1960s, labor-force activity increased among women who were past their prime child-rearing years. During the 1970s and 1980s, as the marriage age rose, fertility declined, and women's educational attainment increased, the growth in labor force participation spread to younger women. Many women now postpone family formation to complete their education and establish themselves in the labor force. Despite family obligations, today a majority of women of all educational levels now work outside the home during their child rearing years (Spain and Bianchi, 1996).

Inequalities at Work

Until recently, women workers were overwhelmingly concentrated in routine, poorly paid occupations. The fate of the occupation of clerk (office worker) provides a good illustration. In 1850 in the United States, clerks held responsible positions, requiring accountancy skills and carrying managerial responsibilities; less than 1 percent were women. The twentieth century saw a general mechanization of office work (starting with the introduction of the typewriter in the late nineteenth century), accompanied by a marked downgrading of the status of clerk—together with a related occupation, secretary—into a routine, low-paid occupation. Women filled these occupations as the pay and prestige of such jobs declined. Today, most secretaries and clerks are women.

Studies of particular types of occupations have shown how **gender typing** occurs in the workplace. Expanding areas of work of a lower-level kind, such as secretarial positions or retail sales, draw in a substantial proportion of women. These jobs are poorly paid and hold few career prospects. Men with good educational qualifications aspire to something higher, while others choose blue-collar work. Once an occupation has become gender typed—once it is seen as mainly a "woman's job"—inertia sets in. Job hierarchies are built around the assumption that men will occupy superior positions, while a stream of women will flow through subordinate jobs. Em-

The percentage of mothers who work outside the home has increased dramatically since 1970.

Percentage of total labor force composed of women

- 50 or higher
- 40–49.9
- 30–39.9
- 20–29.9
- Less than 20
- No data available

SOURCE: World Bank, 1998, *World Development Indicators.*

Figure 8.3
WOMEN AT WORK

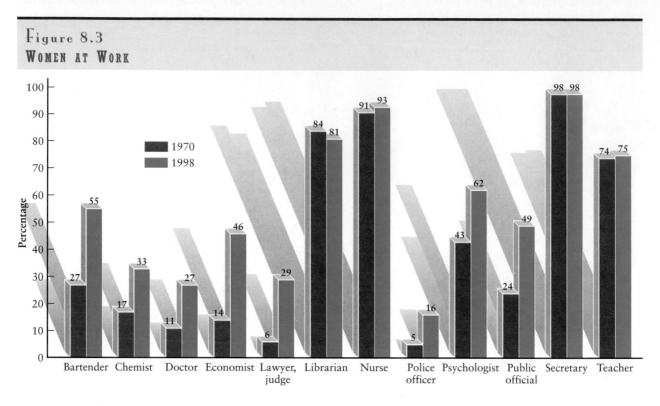

SOURCE: *New York Times,* April 27, 1995, p. B6, and U.S. Bureau of Labor Statistics, *Employment and Earnings,* January 1999, Table 11.

Of all jobs in a given occupation, the above shows the proportion held by women for each year (percentage).

ployers are guided in future hiring decisions by gender labels. And the very conditions of most female jobs lead to adaptive responses on the part of women—low job commitment, few career ambitions, high turnover, seeking alternative rewards in social relations—which fortify the image of women as suitable for only lower-level jobs. (Lowe, 1987)

These social conditions often tend to reinforce outlooks produced by early gender socialization. Women may grow up believing that they should put their husband's career before their own. (Men also are frequently brought up to believe the same thing.)

Women have recently made some inroads into occupations once defined as "men's jobs" (see Figure 8.3). By the 1990s, women constituted a majority of workers in previously male-dominated professions such as accounting, journalism, psychology, public service, and bartending. In fields such as law, medi-

cine, and engineering, their proportion has risen substantially since 1970. In 1998, a woman was more likely to be in a managerial or professional job than a clerical or service position.

Another important economic trend of the past thirty years was the narrowing of the gender gap in earnings. Between 1970 and 1998, the ratio of women's to men's earnings among full-time, year-round workers increased from 62 to 76 percent (see Table 8.1). Moreover, this ratio increased among all races and ethnic groups. During the 1980s, women's hourly wages as a percentage of men's increased from 64 to 79 percent, weekly earnings rose from 63 to 75 percent, and the ratio of annual earnings among all workers (not just those working full time) increased from 46 to 61 percent (Spain and Bianchi, 1996). Despite the lessening of the gender gap in pay, men still earn substantially more than women (see Figure 8.4). Several competing theories have been offered by economists and sociologists to explain this gap.

The medical profession is a clear example of gender typing; most doctors are men, while the majority of nurses are women.

Table.8.1 Women's Earnings as a Percentage of Men's

YEAR	EARNINGS RATIO
1970	.62
1980	.64
1990	.71
1991	.74
1992	.75
1993	.76
1994	.76
1995	.75
1996	.75
1997	.74
1998	.76

Although the earnings gap between women and men is narrowing, it remains substantial. It is also significant that since the early 1990s, the gap has remained fairly constant. Analysts wonder whether this is temporary or permanent. The table shows what women earned for each dollar earned by men.

THE SOCIOLOGICAL DEBATE

THE GENDER PAY GAP

The "gender gap" in pay is a widely recognized fact. Even as recently as 1994, women who worked full time year round (that is, more than thirty-five hours per week for fifty-two weeks per year) earned only 72 percent as much as men. What could account for this discrepancy?

Sex segregation or gender typing is viewed by many sociologists as a cause of the "gender gap" in earnings. Sex segregation refers to the fact that men and women are concentrated in different occupations. For instance, in 1989, jobs that were over 80 percent female included secretary, child care worker, hairdresser, cashier, bookkeeper, telephone operator, receptionist, typist, elementary school teacher, librarian, and nurse. Jobs that were over 80 percent male included doctor, lawyer, dentist, taxi driver, plumber, electrician, carpenter, fire fighter, auto mechanic, machinist, and truck driver (Reskin and Padavic, 1994).

In 1990, many women still worked in primarily female occupations. Of the 56 million women in the labor force in 1990, one-third worked in just ten of the 503 detailed occupations recognized in the U.S. Census. These top ten occupations included secretary, elementary school teacher, cashier, registered nurse, bookkeeper, nurse's aide, and waitress. Men were more evenly distributed across the 503 census occupational groups; only 25 percent worked in the top ten occupations (versus 33 per cent of women).

The reasons that sex segregation is problematic is because the gender composition of a job is associated with the pay received for that job. This finding has emerged in numerous studies. An analysis of 1980 census data (England, 1992) showed that both women and men are directly disadvantaged by employment in an occupation that is predominantly female. Even "after adjusting for cognitive, social, and physical skill demands, amenities, disamenities, demands for effort, and industrial and organization characteristics, jobs pay less if they contain a higher proportion of females" (England, 1992, p. 181).

Although an Equal Pay Act was established in 1963,

it has done little to eradicate pay differences attributable to gender. The Equal Pay Act requires employers to provide equal pay to workers in the *same job*. Consequently, the gender gap in pay hasn't been remedied since the 1963 Act because men and women do not work at the same jobs. As long as employers segregate men and women into separate jobs, the best hope for narrowing the pay gap is to establish a pay equity policy, meaning that pay policies remunerate workers on the basis of the worth of their work and not the sex, race, or other personal characteristics of the majority of workers in a job (Stryker, 1996). Comparable worth policies would be one such strategy.

However, economists and sociologists differ in their explanations of *how* occupational segregation leads to a gender gap in pay. Economists typically focus on the occupational choices women make, while sociologists tend to focus on the constraints women face. Specifically, many economists—as well as employers and public policy makers—endorse a **human capital theory** explanation. Human capital theory, developed by Gary Becker (1964), argues that individuals make investments in their own "human capital" in order to increase their productivity and earnings. "Human capital" includes formal schooling, on-the-job training, and work experience. Those who invest more in their own human capital are considered more productive, and consequently are paid higher wages.

This theory has been specifically applied to explain gender differences in earnings. Human capital theorists reason that women intentionally select occupations that are easy to move in and out of, while still providing moderately good incomes. Central to this argument is the assumption that women's primary allegiance is to home and family; thus they seek undemanding "dead-end" jobs that require little personal investment in training or skills acquisition so that they can better tend to their household responsibilities. When women leave the labor force to rear children, the skills they have deteriorate and they suffer a wage penalty when they re-enter. Moreover, employers may also choose to "invest" less in women workers because they believe women will work less continuously than men, and consequently employers will not realize the return on investment in women workers that they will in male workers.

Feminist sociologists critique human capital theory on several grounds. First, they dispute the claim that women freely "choose" certain occupations. The forces blocking women from freely choosing a career may be indirect or direct. For instance, childhood socialization promoting "traditional" gender roles often indirectly limits women's career choices; girls may choose occupations such as teacher or nurse, which are viewed as compatible with "feminine" traits such as warmth or nurturance. More direct obstacles to women's career choices come in the form of discriminatory bosses, coworkers, and customers. Workplace "gatekeepers" have been shown to prohibit women from entering certain occupations. For example, State Farm Insurance was successfully sued in 1992 for sex discrimination; the firm was forced to provide backpay to 814 women who were denied jobs as insurance agents because of their sex.

Sociologists further argue that human capital theory neglects power differentials between men and women in the workplace and society. Numerous studies reveal that even when men and women are in the same job, men are paid more. A study of pay practices in the British Bakers' Union showed that men were hired to bake bread for high wages, and women were hired to bake cakes and cookies for the lowest union pay rates (Beechey and Perkins, 1987, p. 64).

The implication of this study is that women's work is devalued by society and by employers, and thus women are rewarded less for performing their work. Moreover, women's relative powerlessness prevents them from redefining the work they do as "skilled." As long as jobs predominantly filled by women, such as caring for children and the elderly, are viewed as "unskilled," wages in women's jobs will remain low.

These competing explanations have very different implications for the future. According to human capital theory, the gender gap in pay could disappear if women and men receive equal amounts of education and workplace training, and if they take equal responsibility for family commitments, such as child care. If feminist sociologists are correct in arguing that women's work is devalued, a drastic change in gender ideology must occur if men and women are to become equally rewarded for their participation in the workplace.

Figure 8.4
THE GENDER PAY GAP

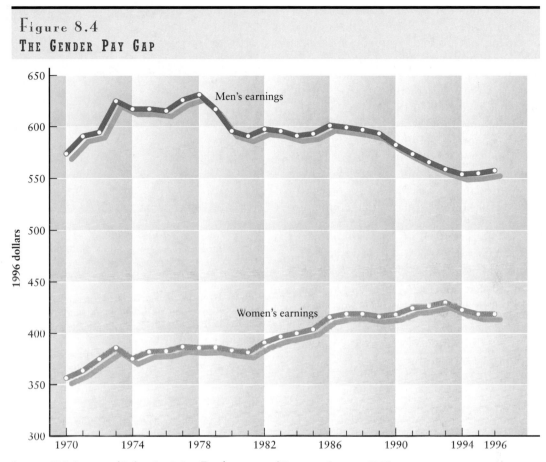

SOURCE: U.S. Bureau of Labor Statistics, *Employment and Earnings*, January 1997.

This figure, in which weekly earnings are shown in constant 1996 dollars, illustrates what has been happening to the gender pay gap over time. After narrowing gradually for years, it widened a little after 1993, when men's inflation-adjusted earnings were increasing slightly and women's were not.

COMPARABLE WORTH

Comparable worth is a policy that compares pay levels of jobs done disproportionately by women with pay levels of jobs done disproportionately by men, and tries to adjust pay so that the women and men who work in female-dominated jobs are not penalized. The policy presumes that jobs can be ranked objectively according to skill, effort, responsibility, and working conditions. After such a ranking, pay is adjusted so that equivalently ranked male- and female-dominated jobs receive equivalent pay (Hartmann et al., 1985).

Although comparable worth policies may help to reduce the gender gap in pay, only a handful of U.S. states have instituted comparable worth policies for public sector employees (Blum, 1991). One reason why comparable worth policies have not been implemented is that they raise multiple technical, political, and economic issues. Perhaps most important is the issue of job evaluation, or the technical process that reduces male- and female-dominated jobs to an underlying common denominator of skill, effort, responsibility, and working conditions so as to compare and rank them independently of the race and gender of job incumbents (Stryker, 1996). Effective implementation requires that job evaluations be free from gender bias. However, substantial research shows that gender-neutral assessments of jobs and required job skills are very difficult. Once men and women know which jobs are predominantly male and predominantly female, they tend to attribute to them the job content that best fits with gender stereotypes (Steinberg, 1990).

Opposition to comparable worth policies has been offered by both economists and feminists. Some economists worry that comparable worth is inflationary and will cause wage losses and unemployment for some (disproportionately women) because of benefits enacted for others. Feminists counter that comparable worth reinforces gender stereotyping rather than breaking down gender barriers at work (Blum, 1991).

Whether or not comparable worth policies are enacted, the surrounding debates show that what jobs society values are determined not by their market or societal worth but by power relations (Blum, 1991).

THE GLASS CEILING AND THE GLASS ESCALATOR

Although women are increasingly entering "traditionally male" jobs, their entry into such jobs may not necessarily be accompanied by increases in pay—and increases in occupational mobility—due to the "**glass ceiling.**" The glass ceiling is a promotion barrier that prevents a woman's upward mobility within an organization. The glass ceiling is particularly problematic for women who work in male-dominated occupations and the professions. Women's progress is blocked not by virtue of innate inability or lack of basic qualifications, but by not having the sponsorship of well-placed, powerful senior colleagues to articulate their value to the organization or profession (Alvarez et al., 1996). As a result, women tend to progress until mid-level management positions, but they do not, in proportionate numbers, move beyond mid-management ranks.

One explanation for women's blocked mobility is based on gender stereotypes. Research shows that college-educated white males in professional jobs tend to identify potential leaders as people who are like themselves. Women are thus assessed negatively because they deviate from this norm or standard (Cleveland, 1996).

What about men who work in female-dominated

Even in occupations dominated by women, such as elementary school teacher, the glass escalator tends to propel the few men in these jobs to executive positions.

professions? Do they also face subtle obstacles to promotion? To the contrary, the sociologist Christine Williams (1992) has observed that a "**glass escalator**" pushes these men to the top of their corporate ladders. Williams (1992) found that employers singled out male workers in traditionally female jobs, such as nurse, librarian, elementary school teacher, and social worker, and promoted them to top administrative jobs in disproportionately high numbers. "Often, despite their intentions, they face invisible pressures to move up in their professions. Like being on a moving escalator, they have to work to stay in place," writes Williams (1992). These pressures may take positive forms, such as close mentoring and encouragement from supervisors, or they may be the result of prejudicial attitudes of those outside the profession, such as clients who prefer to work with male rather than female executives. Some of the men in Williams's study faced unwelcome pressure to accept promotions, such as a male children's librarian who received negative evaluations for "not shooting high enough" in his career aspirations.

SEXUAL HARASSMENT IN THE WORKPLACE

Sexual harassment is unwanted or repeated sexual advances, remarks, or behavior that are offensive to the recipient and cause discomfort or interference with

KEY CONCEPTS IN REVIEW

Male dominance in a society is referred to as **patriarchy**.

Gender inequality—the inequality between men and women in terms of wealth, income, and status—like gender, is socially created and maintained. Gender inequalities take shape in social institutions such as the workplace, family, and educational systems.

Gender typing in the workplace occurs when women hold occupations of lower status and pay, such as secretarial and retail positions, and men hold jobs of higher status and pay, such as managerial and professional positions. The gender pay gap is a result of gender typing and sex segregation in the workplace. **Comparable worth policies** attempt to remedy the gender pay gap by adjusting pay so that those in female-dominated jobs are not paid less for equivalent work.

Women are also narrowing the gender pay gap by entering traditionally male professions, but some women are hitting the **glass ceiling**, a promotion barrier that prevents a woman's upward mobility within an organization. Men in traditionally female professions benefit from the "**glass escalator**," a rapid rise to the top of the organization. Another aspect of gender inequality in the workplace is **sexual harassment**, unwanted sexual advances, remarks, or behavior that are offensive to the recipient and interfere with job performance.

job performance. Power imbalances facilitate harassment; even though women can and do sexually harass subordinates, because men usually hold positions of authority, it is more common for men to harass women (Reskin and Padavic, 1994).

The U.S. courts have identified two types of sexual harassment. One is the *quid pro quo*, in which a supervisor demands sexual acts from a worker as a job condition, or promises work-related benefits in exchange for sexual acts. The other is the "hostile work environment," in which a pattern of sexual language, lewd posters, or sexual advances makes a worker so uncomfortable that it is difficult for her to do her job (Reskin and Padavic, 1994).

Recognition of sexual harassment, and women's willingness to report it, has increased substantially since the testimony of Anita Hill to the Senate Judiciary Committee during the confirmation hearings for Clarence Thomas's 1991 nomination to the U.S. Supreme Court. Although Thomas was ultimately confirmed as a U.S. Supreme Court Justice, Hill's recounting of his harassment raised public awareness of

Companies have become more aware of sexual harassment since Anita Hill's testimony. This demonstration was meant to encourage employee sensitivity to the issue.

the seriousness of the problem and encouraged more women to report harassment incidents (See Figure 8.5). In the first six months of 1992 alone, the number of workplace harassment complaints increased by more than 50 percent (Gross, 1992). In 1992 overall, workers filed over 10,000 complaints of sexual harassment with the Equal Employment Opportunity Commission (Equal Employment Opportunity Commission, 1993).

Despite this increased awareness, sociologists have observed that "the great majority of women who are abused by behavior that fits legal definitions of sexual harassment—and who are traumatized by the experience—do not label what has happened to them as sexual harassment" (Paludi and Barickman, 1991, p. 68).

Women's reluctance to report may be due to the following factors: (1) many still do not recognize that sexual harassment is an actionable offense; (2) victims may be reluctant to come forward with complaints, fearing that they will not be believed, that their charges will not be taken seriously, or that they will be subject to reprisals; (3) it may be difficult to differentiate between harassment and joking on the job (Giuffre and Williams, 1994).

The Family and Gender Issues

BALANCING WORK AND CHILD CARE

One of the major factors affecting women's careers is the male perception that for female employees, work comes second to having children. One study carried out in Britain investigated the views of managers interviewing female applicants for positions as technical staff in the health services. The researchers found that the interviewers always asked the women about whether or not they had, or intended to have, children (this is now illegal in the United States). They virtually never followed this practice with male applicants. When asked why, two themes ran through their answers: women with children may require extra time off for school holidays or if a child falls sick, and responsibility for child care is a mother's problem rather than a parental one.

Some managers thought their questions indicated an attitude of "caring" toward female employees. But most saw such a line of questioning as part of their task to assess how far a female applicant would prove a reliable colleague. Thus, one manager remarked:

> It's a bit of a personal question, I appreciate that, but I think it's something that has to be considered. It's something that can't happen to a man really, but I suppose in a sense it's unfair— it's not equal opportunity because the man could never find himself having a family as such. (Homans, 1987)

While men cannot biologically "have a family" in the sense of bearing children, they can be fully involved in and responsible for child care. Such a possibility was not taken into account by any of the managers studied. The same attitudes were held about the promotion of women. Women were seen as likely to interrupt their careers to care for young children, no matter how senior a position they might have reached. The few women in this study who held senior man-

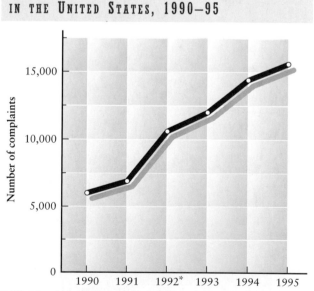

Figure 8.5

INCREASE IN SEXUAL HARASSMENT COMPLAINTS IN THE UNITED STATES, 1990–95

Number of complaints

15,000

10,000

5,000

0

1990   1991   1992*   1993   1994   1995

*Following Anita Hill's testimony before the Senate.

SOURCE: Equal Employment Opportunity Commission, Charge Data Systems National Data Base.

Women with children and careers are often assumed to have a greater role in raising children than do their husbands.

agement positions were all without children, and several of those who planned to have children in the future said they intended leaving their jobs, and would perhaps retrain for other positions subsequently.

How should we interpret these findings? Are women's job opportunities hampered mainly by male prejudices? Some managers expressed the view that women with children should *not* work, but should occupy themselves with child care and the home. Most, however, accepted the principle that women should have the same career opportunities as men. The bias in their attitudes had less to do with the workplace itself than with the domestic responsibilities of parenting. So long as most of the population take it for granted that parenting cannot be shared on an equal basis by both women and men, the problems facing women employees will persist. It will remain a fact of life, as one of the managers put it, that women are disadvantaged, compared with men, in their career opportunities.

In addition, as we saw earlier, the average wage of employed women is well below that of men, although the difference has narrowed somewhat over the past thirty years. Even within the same occupational categories, women on average earn lower salaries than men.

In her book *Working Women Don't Have Wives*, Terri Apter (1994) argues that women find themselves struggling with two contradictory forces. They want

and need economic independence, but at the same time want to be mothers to their children. Both goals are reasonable, but while men with wives who take prime responsibility for domestic work can achieve them, women cannot do likewise. Greater flexibility in working life is one partial solution. Much more difficult is getting men to alter their attitudes.

HOUSEWORK

Although there have been revolutionary changes in women's status in recent decades in the United States, including the entry of women into male-dominated professions, one area of work has lagged far behind: **housework**. Because of the increase of married women in the workforce and the resulting change in status, it was presumed that men would contribute more to housework. On the whole, this has not been the case. Although men now do more housework than they did three decades ago (about one to two hours more per week) and women do slightly less, the balance is still unequal (Shelton and John, 1993). Sociologists calculate that working women perform fifteen more hours of housework per week than their husbands, in effect a "second shift" of work (Hochschild, 1989; Shelton, 1992). These figures don't include time spent on child care, which if factored in would increase the gap. Findings like these have led Arlie Hochschild to call

The division of labor in a household.

the state of relations between women and men a "stalled revolution." Why does housework remain women's work? This question has been the focus of a good deal of research in recent years.

Some sociologists have suggested that this phenomenon is best explained as a result of economic forces: household work is exchanged for economic support. Because women earn less than men, they are more likely to remain economically dependent on their husbands and thus perform the bulk of the housework. Until the earnings gap is narrowed, women will likely remain in their dependent position. Hochschild has suggested that women are thus doubly oppressed by men: once during the "first shift" and again during the "second shift." But while this dependency model contributes to our understanding of the gendered aspects of housework, it breaks down when applied to situations where the wife earns more than her husband. For instance, of the husbands that Hochschild studied who earned less than their wives, none shared in the housework.

Some sociologists have approached the problem from a symbolic interactionist perspective, asking how the performance or nonperformance of housework is related to the gender roles created by society. For example, through interviews and participant observation, Hochschild found that the assignment of household tasks falls clearly along gendered lines. Wives do most of the daily chores, such as cooking and routine cleaning, while husbands tend to take on more occasional tasks, such as mowing the lawn or doing home repairs. The major difference between these two types of tasks is the amount of control the individual has over when they do the work. The jobs women do in the home are those that tend to bind them to a fixed schedule, whereas men's household tasks are done less regularly and are more discretionary.

The sociologist Marjorie Devault looked at how the caring activities within a household are socially constructed as women's work in her book *Feeding the Family* (1991). She argues that women perform the bulk of the housework because the family "incorporates a strong and relatively enduring association of caring activity with the woman's position in the household." Observing the division of responsibility for cooking, Devault remarks that the gendered relations of feeding and eating "convey the message that

giving service is part of being a woman, and receiving it is fundamentally part of being a man." Even in households where men contribute, an egalitarian division of household labor between spouses is greatly impeded when the couple have children—children require constant attention, and their care schedules are often unpredictable. Mothers overwhelmingly spend more time with child-rearing tasks than do their spouses (Shelton, 1992).

Sociologists argue that underlying this inequitable distribution of tasks is the implicit understanding that men and women are responsible for, and should operate in, different spheres. Men are expected to be providers, while women are expected to tend to their families—even if they are breadwinners as well as mothers. Expectations like this reinforce traditional gender roles learned during childhood socialization. By reproducing these roles in everyday life, men and women "do gender" and reinforce gender as a means for society to differentiate between men and women.

Education and Unequal Treatment in the Classroom

Sociologists have found that schools help foster gender differences in outlook and behavior. Although this has become less common today, regulations that compelled girls to wear dresses or skirts in school formed one of the most obvious ways in which gender typing occurred. The consequences went beyond mere appearance. As a result of the clothes they had to wear, girls lacked the freedom to sit casually, to join in rough-and-tumble games, or sometimes to run as fast as they were able. While the strict enforcement of styles of school dress has become quite rare, differences in informal styles of dress still persist, influencing gender behavior in school. School reading texts also help to perpetuate gender images. Although this again is changing, storybooks in elementary school often portray boys showing initiative and independence, while girls, if they appear at all, are more passive and watch their brothers. Stories written especially for girls often have an element of adventure in them, but this usually takes the form of intrigues or mysteries in a domestic or school setting. Boys' adventure stories are more wide-ranging, having heroes who travel off to distant places or who in other ways are sturdily independent (Statham, 1986).

In general, people interact differently with men and women, and boys and girls (Lorber, 1994). This is apparent even in the classrooms of elementary schools. Studies document that teachers interact differently— and often inequitably—with their male and female students. These interactions differ in at least two ways: the frequency of teacher-student interactions, and the content of those interactions. Both of the patterns are based upon—and perpetuate—traditional assumptions about male and female behavior and traits.

One study shows that regardless of the sex of the teacher, male students interact more with their teachers than female students do. Boys receive more teacher attention and instructional time than girls do. This is due in part to the fact that boys are more demanding than girls (AAUW, 1992). Another study reported that boys are eight times more likely to call out answers in class, thus grabbing their teachers' attention. This research also shows that even when boys do not voluntarily participate in class, teachers are more likely to solicit information from them than from girls. However, when girls try to bring attention to themselves by calling out in class without raising their hands, they were reprimanded by comments such as "In this class, we don't shout out answers, we raise our hands" (Sadker and Sadker, 1994).

Sociologists have also found that the content of student-teacher interactions differ, depending on the sex of the students. After observing elementary school teachers and students over many years, it was found that teachers provided boys with assistance in work-

Doonesbury BY GARRY TRUDEAU

ing out the correct answers, whereas they simply gave girls the correct answers, and did not engage them in the problem-solving process. In addition, teachers posed more academic challenges to boys, encouraging them to think through their answers in order to arrive

KEY CONCEPTS IN REVIEW

While women have been successful in overcoming gender typing, they also encounter the assumption that they put the concerns of their family before their career.

Regardless of the percentage of women in the paid workforce, women still perform the bulk of **housework,** work concentrated on maintaining the home and raising children.

Sociologists have also found that girls receive unequal treatment at school.

at the best possible response (Sadker and Sadker, 1994).

Boys were also disadvantaged in several ways, however. Because of their rowdy behavior, they were more often scolded and punished than the girl students. Moreover, boys outnumber girls in special education programs by startling percentages. Sociologists have argued that school personnel may be mislabeling boys' behavioral problems as learning disabilities.

This differential treatment of boys and girls perpetuates stereotypic gender-role behavior. Girls are trained to be quiet, well-behaved, and to turn to others for answers, while boys are encouraged to be inquisitive, outspoken, active problem solvers. Female children from ethnic minorities are in some respects doubly disadvantaged. A study of what it was like to be a black female pupil in a white school reported that unlike the boys, the black girls were initially enthusiastic about school but altered their attitudes because of the difficulties encountered there. Even when they were quite small, aged seven or eight, teachers would disperse the black girls if they were standing chatting in a group on the playground—in contrast to their treatment of the white children, whose similar behavior was tolerated. In other ways too, the black girls came to feel that they were regarded with suspicion and hostility by their teachers and by the white pupils. Once treated as "troublemakers," they rapidly became so (Bryan, Dadzie, and Scafe, 1987).

ANALYZING GENDER INEQUALITY

Sociologists have tried to explain why gender inequalities exist. One plausible explanation for gender inequality is relatively simple. Women give birth to and care for children. The helplessness of the human infant demands that such care be intensive and prolonged—hence the centrality of "mothering" to women's experience (as emphasized by Chodorow, see Chapter 4). Because of their role as mothers, women are absorbed primarily in domestic activities. Women become what the French novelist and social critic Simone de Beauvoir (1974; orig. pub. 1949) called "the second sex," because of their exclusion from the more "public" activities in which men are

free to engage. Men are not dominant over women as a result of superior physical strength, or any special intellectual powers, but because, prior to the development of birth control, women were at the mercy of their biological constitution. Constant childbirth, and continuous caring for infants, made them dependent on males for material provision (Firestone, 1971; Mitchell, 1975).

Biology versus Society

Does this explanation imply, therefore, that gender inequality is "natural" since motherhood is rooted in a woman's biological features? Some scholars would claim yes. Such essentialist explanations of gender inequalities emphasize that gender differences and gender inequalities are rooted in human biology. They explain the gender division of labor as quasi-natural, i.e., it is more efficient if women take care of children because they are often pregnant and give birth to children. Thus, the division of labor by sex is necessary for the survival of the human species. The higher the degree of development and specialization within a society the more we will see that women and men perform different roles. The devaluation of the female and the "natural" superiority of the male is, in this framework, a mere consequence of biology and therefore is inevitable and immutable.

In contrast, sociologists embracing a social constructionist approach argue that if biology determined the gender division of labor and inequalities based on gender, we would not see any variation of gender inequalities across time and across different groups and societies. Cross-cultural studies show that even though most societies distinguish between men's and women's roles, the degree to which they differentiate tasks as exclusively male or female and assign different tasks and responsibilities to women and men can vary greatly (Coltrane, 1992). The degree to which certain tasks can be shared between women and men, and even how open groups and societies are to women performing men's activities and roles, differs across cultures and across time. Finally, cultures and societies have assigned different values to women and men, and differ in the degree to which men are seen as "naturally" dominant over women. Thus, gender inequalities do not seem to be fixed or static. The division of labor based on gender and the devaluation of women relative to men have taken different forms and shapes throughout history.

Biological determinists see differences based on gender and gender inequalities as inevitable and unchangeable because they are consequences of biological necessities—not of social processes. Social constructionists disagree with biological determinists about where to find the sources of gender inequality and whether there is a potential for change: sociological approaches look at society rather than at nature to explain why gender inequalities exist and how they can change. According to many sociologists, the key to understanding gender inequality is looking at a society's gendered division of labor and the value that society assigns to men's and women's roles (Coltrane, 1992; R. Collins et al., 1993; Dunn et al., 1993; Baxter and Kane, 1995; Chafetz, 1997). It is also important to recognize that gender inequality is also tied to issues of race and class (P. Collins, 1990).

Using Sociology to Understand Andrea's Life

We have reviewed how sociologists analyze gender inequality, but let us think about how these ideas might help us illuminate the life of Andrea Ellington, the person we met at the beginning of the chapter. Andrea, a young black woman working the night shift as a word processor at an elite law firm, grew up in a poor neighborhood on the South Side of Chicago and today has three children to raise on her own.

To Andrea and women in similar life circumstances, the difficult conditions in which they find themselves may seem natural because of their sex. In other words, people may think it is natural for Andrea to be responsible for her children or to work as a word processor because she is a woman. Others might be inclined to see whether her life circumstances are all her own doing, the result of bad personal choices regarding childbearing and the decision not to be married. Part of the job of someone who thinks like a sociologist is to ask whether such explanations are convincing given what is known about gender inequality.

In conducting the exercise of thinking about An-

drea's life, we also have a chance to employ one of the key insights of contemporary feminist theory in sociology: that gender does not operate by itself, but comes together with race and class. This "coming together" is known as the intersection of gender, race, and class.

ANDREA'S JOB

The forms of gender inequality in the workplace, as discussed earlier, show that Andrea's experience as a clerical worker in the law firm is typical for women. Jobs for women have been created primarily in the service sector of the economy. Today, word processing and secretarial work are predominantly women's occupations with the characteristics of lower pay, a high degree of sex segregation, and few possibilities for promotion. Typical of jobs that have been created in the past thirty years, Andrea's job has nonstandard working hours—she works the night shift.

Although there is nothing about the biological differences between the sexes that would lead more women than men to work as word processors, societal forces tend to encourage women to aspire to such jobs. To begin with, many business colleges in Chicago advertise their secretarial programs with photographs of women, and many firms would rather hire women for their secretarial and word processing positions. Such positions have traditionally been, after all, jobs that service the clerical needs of the upper class of workers, many of whom are still men. An analysis of gender inequality would look closely at the way that people learn roles associated with gender—both the word processors and the people who do the hiring at firms. But it would also look at how those perceptions of difference become part of the structure of the organization, thereby reinforcing even more inequality.

Andrea's problems as a low-wage worker are those of many other persons similarly situated. Women are usually found at the lower end of the job ladder. One reason is that, unlike jobs in male-dominated areas, women's occupations tend to be dead-end jobs with fewer possibilities for promotion. Andrea's position on the lower end of the pay scale may be due to her age and her lower level of experience in the job, which would be equivalent to that of a poor white woman her age. However, another barrier she encounters is due to her race. Within occupations dominated by women there can also be hierarchies according to class and/or race (P. Collins 1990; Brewer, 1993). Thus, someone studying gender inequality might look at the "intersection" of race, class, and gender to ask whether white women working as support staff at many law firms tend to have better paying secretarial jobs, while black women might have word processing positions with lower pay—a plausible possibility given the circumstances at the firm where Andrea works.

Finally, we need to examine broad global economic trends. We need to look at what kinds of jobs women can get in the present economy, which is influenced by processes of globalization and economic restructuring. Thus, the mere integration of women into the labor market does not necessarily mean more gender equality in general. Differences based on class and race between women have increased because of specific economic processes (Brewer, 1993).

After her graveyard shift at the law firm, Andrea must pick up her twins from the babysitter's.

ANDREA'S FAMILY

Contemporary political debates on "welfare" in the United States have heavily focused on marriage as the solution to the financial problems Andrea faces. The idea behind these political discussions is that if black single mothers were only to get married, they would not be poor and would not need public assistance in the form of housing and health care.

It is further argued that women like Andrea must bear personal responsibility for having children out of wedlock.

A sociological analysis could begin by accepting the assumption that Andrea bears some personal responsibility for having children out of wedlock, while also trying to understand the societal conditions that lead so many poor women to make that choice. Here we can see again that there is a link between race, class, and gender. Studies of urban labor markets (Wilson, 1987) have demonstrated that the loss of jobs for poor black men in the inner city has made marriage less attractive to many black women. Why, the reasoning goes, should women get married to men who don't have jobs? This increases women's independence from men to some degree, so that women do not necessarily have to marry the fathers of their children (Huber, 1992).

In addition to the impact of this societal force on women like Andrea, there is likely also the influence of social norms. When many other women are influenced by the same structural barriers to meeting men with jobs, it comes to seem quite logical to those women to have children on their own. In these circumstances, we can begin to comprehend how women like Andrea make the choice to have children out of wedlock. The loss of jobs that might make self-support for black men possible also makes it more difficult for them to fulfill their obligations to provide child support. One reason Andrea does not have enough money to pay her bills and to attain her dream to move out of the housing project she lives in is that she has not received enough money from the father of her children.

ANDREA'S CHALLENGES IN COMBINING WORK AND FAMILY

The most prominent example of how gender inequalities in the workplace are intertwined with inequalities arising from women's roles as mothers is seen in Andrea's negotiations with her employer about overtime.

Since Andrea does not earn enough money from her low-paying job, she asks her boss if she could work extra hours. When the boss schedules these extra projects on a Sunday, Andrea is unable to find reliable child care. Because she misses work on several occasions, the boss cancels the extra projects. In the future, this boss assumed that Andrea wasn't able to work overtime and, therefore, refused to offer her extra projects. This, in turn, had an effect on how Andrea felt about her job, a process that lowers occupational aspirations (Huber, 1990).

It is quite understandable how a reasonable employer would draw such a conclusion about Andrea. Yet, a sociological approach would ask whether these incidents are due to a problem with Andrea, or with the system of child care. If the system was different, is it possible that women like Andrea would appear much more responsible?

Someone aware of gender inequality would look at the way the gender division of labor in our society places the burden of child raising on mothers. In the United States, child care is not a public responsibility, nor is it seen as the responsibility of the employer. Andrea's boss feels that it is Andrea's task to find child care, even on a Sunday. And yet, since the wages of her job are low, she needs that overtime to earn enough money to support her children and to move out of the housing project.

The ways in which societies organize the care of children, elderly, and disabled people profoundly shape gender relations. For example, if there is little public support for child care then parents have to find care givers for their children when they are working outside the home. Moreover, in societies that view child care primarily as the task of women, yet attach little value to this task, mothers in the workplace are disadvantaged. In contrast, if society valued taking care of children as an important contribution for future generations, Andrea might get financial support for taking care of her children herself; or, if taking care of children was not a low-paying job but were supported by employers and government, Andrea might find a good quality child care center open on a Sunday.

Andrea's mother usually takes care of Andrea's daughter. We can see how child care can be informally organized across generations of women. Research on African-American communities demonstrates that black women used to be tied into kinship, neighborhoods, and other networks of women who shared child raising responsibilities. But these structures of shared motherhood have been crumbling (P. Collins, 1990; Brewer, 1993; Glenn, 1994).

Feminism and the Struggle for Gender Equality

How can Andrea's life and the lives of all women change for the better? Feminist authors have been largely responsible for pointing out and analyzing forms of gender inequality, like the importance of housework. For instance, for many years, sociologists were guilty of defining "work" as "paid work outside the home." Feminists have shown how misleading such a view was, and have prompted studies of women's activities and attitudes in many areas of social life where they were previously largely ignored. Although **feminism**—the struggle to defend and expand the rights of women—has a lengthy history (which we will explore later in Chapter 18), its influence has been greatest in the past three decades. For example, feminists have pressed for economic equality, the availability of abortion, and alterations in laws concerning divorce—among other concerns. In addition to significant practical achievements, feminists today have made an intellectual impact far beyond anything previously achieved. Throughout the social sciences, and in many other fields, feminist authors have forced a rethinking of established notions and theories. A great deal of the research carried out in recent years into historical and cultural factors affecting the position of women, and into gender relations more generally, has been prompted by the influence of modern feminism.

While all feminists tend to share the same goals, they differ in the ways that they attempt to address gender inequality. In fact, at least three schools of feminist thought offer unique interpretations and explanations of gender inequality. These branches share the following assumptions: (1) a belief that women as a group are socially disadvantaged; and (2) a recognition of the extent to which social life is gendered. These strands of feminism differ substantially in their explanations of gender inequality, however, and the ways in which to redress it.

globalization and everyday life

THE INTERNATIONAL WOMEN'S MOVEMENT

Do you have any interest in joining the women's movement? Every year countless American college students are inspired by feminism and enlist in the fight for such causes as reproductive rights, equal pay, or the preservation of welfare benefits for poor women. In today's increasingly globalized world, there is a good chance that those who become active in the U.S. women's movement will come into contact with women pursuing other feminist struggles overseas.

The women's movement, of course, is not simply an American or western European phenomenon. In China, for example, women are working to secure "equal rights, employment, women's role in production, and women's partic-ipation in politics" (Zhang and Xu, 1995, p. 34). In South Africa, women played a pivotal role in the battle against apartheid, and are fighting in the post-apartheid era to improve "the material conditions of the oppressed majority; those who have been denied access to education, decent homes, health facilities, and jobs" (Kemp et al., 1995, p. 157). In Peru, activists have been working for decades to give women a greater "opportunity to participate in public life" (Blondet, 1995, p. 251), while "in Russia, women's protest was responsible for blocking the passage of legislation that the Russian Parliament considered in 1992 that encouraged women to stay home and perform 'socially necessary labor'" (Basu, 1995, p. 6).

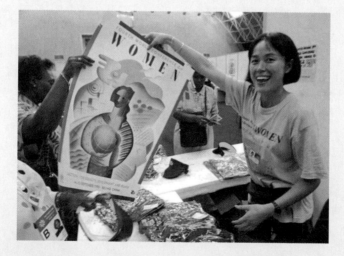

Although participants in women's movements have, for many years, cultivated ties to activists in other countries, the number and importance of such contacts has increased with globalization. A prime forum for the establishment of cross-national contacts has been the United Nation's Conference on Women, held four times since 1975. Approximately 50,000 people—of which more than two thirds were women—attended the most recent conference, held in Beijing, China, in 1995. Delegates from 181 nations were in attendance, along with representatives from thousands of nongovernmental organizations (U.N. Chronicle, 1995). Seeking ways to "ensure women's equal access to economic resources including land, credit, science and technology, vocational training, information, communication and markets," conference participants spent ten days listening to presentations on the state of women worldwide, debating ways to improve their condition, and building professional and personal ties to one another. Mallika Dutt, one of the attendees, recently wrote in the journal *Feminist Studies* that "for most women from the United States, Beijing was an eye-opening, humbling, and transformative experience. U.S. women were startled by the sophisticated analysis and well-organized and powerful voices of women from other parts of the world" (1996, p. 520). At the same time, according to Dutt, many of the conference participants left

Beijing with a "sense of global solidarity, pride, and affirmation" (1996, p. 520).

The Platform for Action finally agreed to by the conference participants called on the countries of the world to address such issues as:

"The persistant and increasing burden of poverty on women;
    Violence against women;
    The effects of armed or other kinds of conflict on women;
    Inequality between men and women in the sharing of power and decision-making;
    Stereotyping of women;
    Gender inequalities in the management of natural resources;
    Persistent discrimination against and violation of the rights of the girl child."

Must women's movements have an international orientation to be effective? Are women's interests essentially the same throughout the world? What might feminism mean to women in the Third World? These and many other questions are being hotly debated as the process of globalization continues apace.

LIBERAL FEMINISM

Liberal feminism has had the longest history of any branch of feminism and has philosophical roots in the nineteenth-century Enlightenment views of western Europe. As part of the most moderate branch of feminist theory, liberal feminists maintain that gender inequality is produced by unequal access to civil rights and certain social resources, such as education and employment, on the basis of sex. In other words, gender inequality is seen as a form of discrimination. Liberal feminists tend to seek solutions through changes in legislation that ensure that the rights of individuals are protected. This perspective underlies many mainstream programs and policies aimed at ending sex-based discrimination, including laws aimed at ending sex-based discrimination in the workplace.

MARXIST FEMINISM

Marxist feminism views gender inequality as too far reaching to be remedied with simple legislative actions. Rather, Marxist feminists view gender inequality as rooted in social class inequality. The capitalist system of production that generates social inequality also generates women's economic dependence on men. Thus, gender inequality can only be eliminated through attentiveness to the system of class relations. Marxist feminism has been criticized on the grounds that it states the importance of social class, and downplays the importance of gender as well as race, in its analysis of capitalism (Jagger, 1983).

RADICAL FEMINISM

Radical feminism disputes Marxism on the grounds that women are oppressed in societies other than capitalist ones, and therefore women's oppression by men is deeper and more harmful than any other form of oppression—including economic oppression. They argue that male domination of women permeates every aspect of life, including the family and interpersonal relationships. Because radical feminists believe that gender oppression is the most harmful of oppression, they have been criticized for ignoring the significant differences in power and privilege among various groups of women, such as those between white women and women of color. This criticism has also been leveled at liberal and Marxist feminists. In recent years, the most prominent movement within feminist sociological theory has been to consider the ways in which race and class coalesce with gender in the system of gender inequality.

SUMMARY

1. *Sex* in the sense of physical difference is distinct from *gender* (masculine and feminine), which concerns cultural and psychological differences. It is no simple matter to determine which observable differences are due to biology (sex) and which are socially constructed (gender). Arguments from animal behavior are usually ambiguous. Some researchers claim, for instance, that hormones explain such differences as greater male aggressiveness, but it may just as easily be the case that aggressive behavior causes changes in hormone levels. Studies of gender differences from a variety of human societies have shown no conclusive evidence that gender is biologically determined; rather, biological differences seem to provide a means of marking or differentiating social roles.

2. Studies of parent-infant interactions reveal that boys and girls are treated differently right from birth; the same features and behaviors are interpreted as either "masculine" or "feminine" depending on the parents' expectations.

3. Gender is continuously created and recreated by all the social actions we perform daily, and it informs our perceptions of social reality at a deep and often unconscious level. It is this circular process which maintains gender as a *social institution*.

4. *Patriarchy* refers to male dominance over women. There are no known societies that are not patriarchal, although the degree and character of inequalities between the sexes varies considerably cross-culturally.

In the United States, women have made considerable progress, yet are still unequal in many ways.

5. Women's participation in the paid labor force has risen steadily, especially married women's, and especially in expanding areas of the economy. Many women, however, are poorly paid and have dim career prospects. Even women who are successful in the corporate world face discrimination in the form of deeply held cultural expectations about the proper role of women in society.

6. The increasing number of women in the labor force has had a big impact on family responsibilities like child care and *housework*. Though men are contributing more to these responsibilities, women still shoulder the bulk of the work. For working women, these household obligations constitute a "second shift."

7. The ways schools are organized and how classes are taught have tended to sustain gender inequalities. Rules specifying distinct dress for girls and boys encourages sex typing, as do the texts containing established gender images. There is evidence that teachers treat girls and boys differently, and there is a long history of specialized subjects for separate sexes.

8. *Gender* is one of the most important dimensions of inequality, although it was neglected in the study of stratification for a long time. Although there are no societies in which women have more wealth and status than men, there are significant variations in how women's and men's roles are valued within a society. Sociologists have argued that gender inequalities are not fixed. They have also drawn attention to the links between gender inequality and race and class.

9. Recent feminist movements have called attention to forms of gender inequality and have offered solutions to address it. Indeed, this chapter would not exist (at least in the form it does) without the resurgence of feminism.

Race and Ethnicity: Key Concepts

Learn the cultural bases of race and ethnicity and how racial and ethnic differences create sharp divisions. Learn the leading psychological theories and sociological interpretations of prejudice and discrimination.

Ethnic and Racial Conflict

Recognize the importance of the historical roots, particularly in the expansion of Western colonialism, of ethnic conflict.

Ethnic Relations in the United States

Familiarize yourself with the history and social dimensions of ethnic relations in America.

Racial and Ethnic Inequality

Learn the forms of inequality experienced by different racial and ethnic groups in the United States. See that the history of prejudice and discrimination against ethnic minorities has created conditions of hardship for many but that some have succeeded despite societal barriers.

ETHNICITY AND RACE

‖▪▪▪▪ ▪▪▪ ▪▪ ▪▪▪ ▪▪ ▪▪▪ ▪▪ ▪▪▪ ▪▪‖

What are the first things you notice about a stranger when he or she passes you by on the street? It depends, of course, on where you are.

If you are in a mall or on the main street of a college campus where most of the people are alike, you might focus on items like clothing, makeup, or hairstyle, which tend to distinguish people who are otherwise alike. Is the person you pass wearing a North Face jacket? A sweatshirt from a particular high school? At many colleges such signs help distinguish people who otherwise might be alike in the sense of sharing a common college experience. They might tell us, "This person is from the East Coast," or "This person went to a particular high school," or "This person is an athlete," or "This person is in a sorority."

One thing that immediately jumps out at many people in public places is a person's skin color, which often has meanings associated with it that come from media representations and other public depictions, as well as personal experiences (Omi and Winant, 1994).

Skin color is what sociologists call a "master status" (see Chapter 5) (Hughes, 1945; Anderson, 1990), a feature that dominates our perception, often overriding in our minds a person's other characteristics. Master statuses give rise to stereotypes. Stereotypes are systematic generalizations that become vehicles for conceptions of a group of people.

For example, in the United States, the lives of black men are often accurately summarized with a number of very depressing statistics. Almost a quarter of black men in their twenties are "under the control of the criminal justice system." The life expectancy for black males is 66 years, while for white males it is 72.3 years. The homicide rate among black men is six to seven times higher than the rate among white men; they are most likely to be killed by other black men. Forty-five percent of black males are likely to become victims of violent crime three or four times in their lives.

Now, given these well-known statistics, it is not surprising that many nonviolent, law-abiding black men have trouble walking down the street without being regarded with suspicion or fear. Take, for example, the blacks who live in neighborhoods that surround urban universities—a common situation in many American cities. In such areas, interaction between poor blacks and members of the university community is common. Frequently, black men say that students respond to them as a dangerous category, a stereotype, and treat them as persons of lesser moral worth.

Ozzie, a fifty-five-year-old black man who lives near the University of Chicago, put it this way: "The University gets those students in rap sessions. They tell them not to travel alone. They get these white students when they come here from Boston and New York or wherever and they get'em in those lectures [raising his voice, imitating an imaginary professor], 'When you go out into the neighborhood, you travel in groups. Be careful who you talk to.'" Others, such as Luther, a newsstand attendant, sometimes speak with outrage about the way students respond to them: "A group of white kids is walking together and they see me, all of them, they huddle together. Well, I'm afraid of them as they are of me."

Black men will often notice pedestrians cross to the other side of the street when they approach, or they will be questioned by police or security officers for no apparent reason. This occurs because the dominant image of black men is a stereotype, a systematic generalization about an entire group that is based on limited information about part of the group.

Stereotypes are usually fixed and inflexible categories in the minds of people who hold them, but it is possible that with education and experience they can be changed. One way that sociologists have tried to move beyond stereotypes is to do systematic research in which they learn more about the people who are the subject of these generalizations.

From the standpoint of people who act on the basis of stereotypes, such behavior is sometimes necessary because they have no other information to go on. For example, where the people on the street are separated by vast economic and cultural differences, pedestrians aren't first interested in the fine distinctions between people. In many cases, they look for signals that tell them they need not feel threatened. As we walk down the sidewalk in a busy city at night, we hope to feel solidarity, or at least a sense of mutual assurance from the people who pass us by. Sometimes, we have only a split second to make a judgment about our safety, and there may be no sign to indicate to us what "kind of person" this is. One of the most prominent signs that people use is race. As a result, race is one of the most salient aspects of everyday life. Racial and ethnic identity is a primary means by which individuals differentiate themselves from others, as well as a means for a society to distinguish groups of people. Racial and ethnic distinctions are rarely neutral, but are commonly associated with inequalities of wealth and power, as well as with antagonisms between groups.

Explaining why this is so will be the main focus of this chapter. Among ethnic-group tensions, racial divisions and hostilities stand out as being particularly prevalent. We shall have to consider why this is so, and examine the concept of "race" as such—for it is a problematic one. From there we move on to discuss theoretical interpretations of ethnic prejudice and discrimination. In subsequent sections of the chapter we will analyze race relations in a comparative framework, contrasting Europe, South Africa, Brazil, and the United States. Since the ethnic composition of the United States is so complex, we shall survey American ethnic groups in some detail. We will examine the forms that racial and ethnic inequalities take and present some theories about why these inequalities have developed. But let's first begin with some basic key concepts and theories about race and ethnicity.

RACE AND ETHNICITY: KEY CONCEPTS

Race

Many people today believe, mistakenly, that humans can be readily separated into biologically different races. This is not surprising considering the numerous attempts by scholars and governments to establish racial categories of the people of the world. The United States Bureau of the Census distinguishes four races (American Indian/Alaska native, Asian and Pacific Islander, Black, and White), but too many exceptions and inconsistencies in the classifications have been found to make any of them workable without great controversy.

Black, for example, is supposed to be composed of people with dark skin, tightly curled black hair, and certain other physical characteristics. Yet the original inhabitants of Australia, the Aboriginals, possess dark skin but wavy, and sometimes blond, hair. A host of other examples can be found that defy any simple classification. There are no clear-cut "races," only a range of physical variations in human beings. Differences in physical type between groups of human beings arise from population inbreeding, which varies according to the degree of contact between different social or cultural groups. Human population groups are a continuum. The genetic diversity *within* populations that share visible physical traits is as great as the diversity *between* them. In view of these facts, many biologists, anthropologists, and sociologists believe the concept of race should be dropped because it "gives credence to the idea that there is a physical reality to which it refers" (Fredrickson, 1998, p. 78).

There are clear physical differences between human beings, and some of these differences are inherited. But the question of why some differences and not others become matters for social discrimination and prejudice has nothing to do with biology. Racial differences, therefore, should be understood as *physical variations singled out by the members of a community or society as socially significant*. Differences in skin color, for example, are treated as significant, whereas differences in color of hair are not.

Australian aborigines belong to more than one "racial" group, which illustrates the difficulty of sorting humans in this way.

Ethnicity

Ethnicity refers to cultural practices and outlooks of a given community that have emerged historically and tend to set people apart. Members of ethnic groups see themselves as culturally distinct from other groups in a society, and are seen by those other groups to be so in return. Different characteristics may serve to distinguish ethnic groups from one another, but the most common are language, history, or ancestry—real or imagined—religion, and styles of dress or adornment.

Ethnic differences are *wholly learned*, a point that seems self-evident until we remember how often some groups have been regarded as "born to rule" or "shiftless," "unintelligent," and so forth. In recent years, sociologists who study ethnicity in the United States have come to understand that larger forces that give rise to ethnic-group collective consciousness have declined. For example, people who are Jewish or Irish no longer face the kind of housing discrimination that led them to live in particular neighborhoods together. In addition, intermarriage between members of different ethnic groups has increased substantially.

In the face of such changing conditions, sociologists have noted that ethnic identity has less of an impact on the everyday lives of the members of these social groups unless they choose an ethnic label. As a result, ethnicity is now a choice of whether to be ethnic at all. More and more people must also make a choice about which ethnicity to be (Gans, 1979; Waters, 1990). Sociologists refer to *situational ethnicity* and *symbolic ethnicity*.

Situational ethnicity is a concept that illustrates one of the ways in which ethnic and racial identification is socially constructed. Some people who have Native American ancestry may choose to assert that identity when they apply for a job in which that category is favored, while downplaying that identity at other times when it might lead to discrimination. This shows that larger political forces, such as the categories devised by governments, affect the identity one chooses.

Symbolic ethnicity occurs when members of an eth-

nic group assimilate into the larger culture, perhaps moving away from the old neighborhood to the suburbs where there is a smaller percentage of people engaged in ethnic practices. Such people might only participate in ethnic customs on occasions like St. Patrick's Day or at Passover, when they attend a seder. During the rest of the year, their ethnic identity might not be very salient at all.

While ethnicity is primarily a symbolic option for white Americans, race and minority group status is not a choice for people of color. One sociologist who has studied how Americans think about their ancestry and backgrounds has written that "the social and political consequences of being Asian or Hispanic or black are not symbolic for the most part, or voluntary. They are real and often hurtful" (Waters, 1990). Minority group status can have many negative consequences for its members. One such negative consequence is segregation (see below).

In this chapter, we shall investigate the origin of divisions over ethnicity. What explains the antagonisms that so often exist between groups of different cultural or racial backgrounds? Why do these differences matter so much? Much of the discussion will center upon the experience of the United States. But, while ethnicity takes on a more benign character in areas where people can make choices about the group they will affiliate with, ethnicity is not benign in many parts of the world today.

Minority Groups

The term **minority group** as used in sociology is more than a merely numerical distinction. There are many minorities in a statistical sense, such as people having red hair or weighing more than 250 pounds, but these are not minorities according to the sociological concept. In sociology, members of a minority group are *disadvantaged* as compared with the **dominant group** (a group possessing more wealth, power, and prestige) and have some sense of *group solidarity*, of belonging together. The experience of being the subject of prejudice and discrimination usually heightens feelings of common loyalty and interests.

Members of minority groups often tend to see themselves as a people apart from the majority. Minority groups are usually physically and socially isolated from the larger community. They tend to be concentrated in certain neighborhoods, cities, or regions of a country. There is little intermarriage between those in the majority and members of the minority group, or between minority groups. People within the minority sometimes actively promote endogamy (marriage within the group) in order to keep alive their cultural distinctiveness.

Many minorities are both ethnically and physically distinct from the rest of the population. This is the case with African Americans, Native Americans, Chinese, and other groups in the United States. Physical differences such as skin color are commonly called racial. An example of an ethnic distinction in the United States is that between white Jewish groups on the one hand and the white majority population on the other. Among ethnic-group tensions, those based on race are particularly prevalent.

The Racial Divide

In *Two Nations*, a study of the divisions between blacks and whites, Queens College professor Andrew Hacker points to census counts over the last two centuries that illuminate some of the changes in the racial makeup of the United States. Each decade since 1970 shows that the two races account for a declining proportion of the population. Hispanics, Asians, Native Americans, and Hawaiians are now the nation's fastest growing groups: "By 1990, they together outnumbered blacks, and were also helping to erode white predominance."

Why, then, do so many Americans think of the nation's racial conflict in terms of a division between African Americans and whites? Part of the reason, according to Hacker, is that members of these growing racial and ethnic groups

> have been allowed to put a visible distance between themselves and black Americans. Put most simply, none of the presumptions of inferiority associated with Africa and slavery are imposed on these other ethnicities. Moreover . . . second and subsequent generations of Hispanics and Asians are merging into the "white" category, partly through intermarriage and also by personal achievement and adaptation. Indeed, the very fact that this is happening sheds light on the tensions and disparities separating two major races.

Hacker argues that while none of the presumptions of inferiority are imposed on these other races, few whites ever stop to think how they may benefit by belonging to their race. In *Two Nations*, he asks, "What is the value of being white?" He suggests that white readers suspend their belief and imagine the following.

Suppose you are visited by an official you have never met. He tells you that according to his records, you were to have been born black: to another set of parents, far from where you were raised. However, the rules being what they are, this error must be rectified. As soon as possible, you will become black. And this will mean not simply a darker skin, but the bodily and facial features associated with African ancestry.

Inside, you will be the person you always were. Your knowledge and ideas will remain intact. But outwardly, you will not be recognizable to anyone you know. Your visitor is prepared to offer you some reasonable compensation. His records show that you are scheduled to live another fifty years—as a black man or woman in America. How much financial recompense would you request?

Hacker reports that when this parable is put to white students, most seem to think that it would not be out of place to ask for $50 million, or $1 million for each coming black year. "This calculation conveys, as well as anything, the value that white people place on their own skins," writes Hacker. "And why so large a sum? The money would be used, as best it could, to buy protection from the discrimination and dangers white people know they would face once they were perceived to be black," Hacker believes.

Prejudice, Discrimination, and Racism

The concept of race is modern, but prejudice and discrimination have been widespread in human history, and we must first clearly distinguish between them. **Prejudice** refers to *opinions or attitudes* held by members of one group toward another. A prejudiced person's preconceived views are often based upon hearsay rather than on direct evidence, and are resistant to change even in the face of new information. People may harbor favorable prejudices about groups with which they identify and negative prejudices against others. Someone who is prejudiced against a particular group will refuse to give it a fair hearing.

Discrimination refers to *actual behavior* toward the other group. It can be seen in activities that disqualify members of one group from opportunities open to others, as when an African American is refused a job made available to a white person. Although prejudice is often the basis of discrimination, the two may exist separately. People may have prejudiced attitudes that they do not act upon. Equally important, discrimination does not necessarily derive directly from prejudice. For example, white house-buyers might steer away from purchasing properties in predominantly black neighborhoods not because of attitudes of hos-

tility they might feel toward African Americans, but because of worries about declining property values. Prejudiced attitudes in this case influence discrimination, but in an indirect fashion.

One widespread form of prejudice is racism. Racism is prejudice based on socially significant physical distinctions. A **racist** is someone who believes that some individuals are superior or inferior to others as a result of these racial differences. A racist would be expected to believe that if members of all groups had an equal opportunity for education, and began with the same resources, that the inferior group would have less talent represented within it at the end of a given period of time (Hacker, 1992).

Racism may take the form of distinctions made on the basis of biology or culture (Frederickson, 1998). Thus, it is possible that some people who pass a black panhandler on the street believe that the reason most of the men on this street are black is because their group is less well endowed intellectually than whites. This is biological racism. Others might argue that the panhandler is on the street because he comes from a dysfunctional culture. This is cultural racism. In both cases, such reasoning fails to take account of the historic political, social, and economic conditions that explain how and why one group disproportionately ends up on the street.

There are two other types of racism, individual and institutional. **Individual racism** occurs when an individual thinks or acts in a manner that is motivated by the conscious or unconscious belief that the people he acts toward are inferior in some way based on their race. This is the form of racism that most minorities are familiar with because it is a tangible part of everyday life. It occurs in the form of minor slights, as well as highly offensive insults and slurs (Feagin, 1991; Feagin and Sikes, 1994).

Institutional racism occurs when the norms of larger social structures conform to racist ideas. Even if people are not individual racists, by living in accordance with these larger norms, they perpetuate racism on the institutional level. For example, in many schools in the United States, minority students are referred to special education classes, even though they do not have serious mental or physical disabilities. This occurs when social structures for evaluating these students allow disciplinary problems to be the basis for referrals to special education. The result is that in

KEY CONCEPTS IN REVIEW

Ethnicity refers to cultural differences that set one group apart from another. The main distinguishing characteristics of an ethnic group are language, history or ancestry, religion, and styles of dress or adornment. Ethnic differences are wholly learned or chosen, not inherited. **Situational ethnicity** refers to ethnic identity one chooses based on the social setting or situation. **Symbolic ethnicity** refers to when people retain aspects of their ethnic identity only for symbolic purposes. In these instances, ethnicity is important only if one wants it to be.

Minority groups are disadvantaged ethnic groups compared to the **dominant group** (a group possessing more wealth, power, and prestige).

Human beings cannot be separated into biologically distinct races. Racial differences are physical variations singled out by society as significant.

Prejudice refers to the attitudes of one group toward another, while **discrimination** refers to actual behavior toward the other group. **Racism** is prejudice based on socially significant physical distinctions. **Individual racism** occurs when an individual thinks or acts in a way that is motivated by the belief that the people he acts toward are inferior based on their race. **Institutional racism** occurs when the norms of social structures reinforce racist views.

some cities, disproportionate numbers of black and Hispanic students get placed in special education classes where their learning continues to decrease, furthering their lower position in the American class structure. The teacher who makes a recommendation for a minority student to go to special education may be a person who has anti-racist views. But she is working within an institution which has norms that encourage her to send students with disciplinary problems to special education. Thus, much racism exists when anti-racists perpetuate institutional racism, often without an awareness of what they are doing.

Psychological Interpretations

Psychological theories can help us understand the nature of prejudiced and racist attitudes and also why ethnic differences matter so much to people. Two types of psychological approach are important. One employs the concept of stereotypical thinking to analyze prejudice. The other says that there is a particular type of person who is most prone to hold prejudiced attitudes against minority groups.

STEREOTYPES AND SCAPEGOATS

Prejudice operates mainly through the use of **stereotypical thinking**, which means thinking in terms of fixed and inflexible categories. Stereotyping is often closely linked to the psychological mechanism of **displacement**, in which feelings of hostility or anger are directed against objects that are not the real origin of those feelings. People vent their antagonism against **scapegoats**, people blamed for things that are not their fault. The term "scapegoat" originated with the ancient Hebrews, who each year ritually loaded all their sins onto a goat, which was then chased into the wilderness. Scapegoating is common when two deprived ethnic groups come into competition with one another for economic rewards. People who direct racial attacks against African Americans, for example, are often in a similar economic position to them. They

Children attending a meeting of the Ku Klux Klan.

blame blacks for grievances whose real causes lie elsewhere.

Scapegoating is normally directed against groups that are distinctive and relatively powerless, because they make an easy target. Protestants, Catholics, Jews, Italians, racial minorities, and others have played the unwilling role of scapegoat at various times throughout Western history.

Scapegoating frequently involves **projection,** the unconscious attribution to others of one's own desires or characteristics. Research has consistently demonstrated that when the members of a dominant group practice violence against a minority and exploit it sexually, they are likely to believe that the minority group itself displays these traits of sexual violence. For instance, the bizarre ideas held by white men in the old American South about the lustful nature of African-American men probably originated in their own frustrations, since sexual access to white women was limited by the formal nature of courtship. Similarly, in South Africa, the belief that black males are exceptionally potent sexually and that black women are promiscuous is widespread among whites. Black males are thought to be highly dangerous sexually to white women—while in fact, virtually all criminal sexual contact is initiated by white men against black women (Simpson and Yinger, 1986).

THE AUTHORITARIAN PERSONALITY

It is possible that some types of people, as a result of early socialization, are particularly prone to stereotypical thinking and projection. A famous piece of research carried out by Theodor Adorno and his associates in the 1940s diagnosed a character type they termed the **authoritarian personality** (Adorno et al., 1950). The researchers developed several measurement scales for assessing levels of prejudice. On one scale, for instance, people were asked to agree or disagree with a series of statements expressing strongly anti-Semitic views. Those who were diagnosed as prejudiced against Jews also tended to express negative attitudes toward other minorities. People with an authoritarian personality, the investigators concluded, tend to be rigidly conformist, submissive to their superiors, and dismissive toward inferiors. Such people are also highly intolerant in their religious and sexual attitudes.

The characteristics of an authoritarian personality, it was suggested by the researchers, result from a pattern of upbringing in which parents are unable to express direct love for their children and are aloof and disciplinarian. As adults, these individuals suffer from anxieties that can be controlled only by the adoption of a rigid outlook. They are unable to cope with ambiguous situations, and they ignore inconsistencies, tending to think in a stereotypical way.

Adorno's research has been subjected to a barrage of criticism. Some have doubted the value of the measurement scales used. Others have argued that authoritarianism is not a characteristic of personality, but reflects the values and norms of particular subcultures within the wider society. The investigation may be more valuable as a contribution to understanding authoritarian patterns of thought in general, rather than distinguishing a particular personality type (Wellman, 1977). Yet there are clear similarities between these findings and other research on prejudice. For example, a classic study by Eugene Hartley investigated attitudes toward thirty-five ethnic minorities and also found that those prejudiced against one ethnic group were likely to express negative feelings against others. Jews and African Americans were disliked just as much as Wallonians, Pireneans, and Danireans (Hartley, 1946). The three latter groups in fact are nonexistent; the names were coined by Hartley in order to see whether people would be prejudiced against groups they could not have even heard of.

Sociological Interpretations

The psychological mechanisms of stereotypical thinking, displacement, and projection are found among members of all societies, and help to explain why ethnic antagonism is such a common element in different cultures. However, they tell us little about the social processes involved in discrimination. To study such processes, we must call on three sociological ideas.

ETHNOCENTRISM, GROUP CLOSURE, AND ALLOCATION OF RESOURCES

Sociological concepts relevant to ethnic conflicts on a general level are those of *ethnocentrism, ethnic-group closure,* and *resource allocation.* **Ethnocentrism**—a suspicion of outsiders combined with a tendency to evaluate the culture of others in terms of one's own culture—is a concept we have encountered previously. Virtually all cultures have been ethnocentric to some degree, and it is easy to see how ethnocentrism combines with stereotypical thought. Outsiders are thought of as aliens, barbarians, or morally and mentally inferior. This was how most civilizations viewed the members of smaller cultures, for example, and the attitude has fueled innumerable ethnic clashes in history.

Ethnocentrism and **group closure** frequently go together. "Closure" refers to the process whereby groups maintain boundaries separating themselves from others. These boundaries are formed by means of exclusion devices, which sharpen the divisions between one ethnic group and another (Barth, 1969). Such devices include limiting or prohibiting intermarriage between the groups, restricting social contact or economic relationships like trading, and physically separating groups (as in the case of ethnic ghettos).

Sometimes groups of equal power mutually enforce lines of closure: their members keep separate from each other, but neither group dominates the other. More commonly, however, one ethnic group occupies a position of power over another. In these circumstances, group closure coincides with the **allocation of resources**: inequalities in the distribution of wealth and material goods.

Some of the fiercest conflicts between ethnic groups center upon the lines of closure between them precisely because these lines signal inequalities in wealth, power, or social standing. The concept of ethnic-group closure helps us understand both the dramatic and the more insidious differences that separate communities of people from one another—not just why the members of some groups get shot, lynched, beaten up, or harassed, but also why they don't get good jobs, a good education, or a desirable place to live. Wealth, power, and social status are scarce resources—some groups have more of them than others. To hold on to their distinctive positions, privileged groups sometimes undertake extreme acts of violence against others. Similarly, members of underprivileged groups may also turn to violence as a means of trying to improve their own situation.

A first-grader in New Jersey watches the arrest of a man who painted a racial slur on a school bus.

KEY CONCEPTS IN REVIEW

One psychological theory of the origins of prejudice is based on **stereotypical thinking**, or the use of fixed categories of thought. By the mechanism of **displacement** (feelings directed against objects that are not the real origins of these feelings), **scapegoating** (blaming people for things that are not their fault) may occur. Scapegoating often involves **projection**, the unconscious attribution to others of one's own desires.

A second psychological theory proposes a type called the **authoritarian personality,** the result of early socialization in stereotypical thinking and projection arising from repressed anxieties.

Three sociological concepts are helpful in understanding prejudice and ethnic-group conflict.

Ethnocentrism is the suspicion of outsiders and the evaluation of other cultures in terms of one's own.

Group closure refers to the maintenance of boundaries against others, the prohibition against intermarriage between groups, and restrictions on social contact with other groups.

Resource allocation refers to limited resources, resulting in inequalities in the distribution of wealth and goods.

Models of ethnic relations can take both positive and negative forms.

Assimilation: New immigrant groups take over the attitudes and language of the dominant community.

Melting pot: The different cultures and outlooks of the ethnic groups in a society are merged together.

Pluralism: Ethnic groups exist separately and participate in economic and political life.

Multiculturalism: Ethnic groups exist separately and share *equally* in economic and political life.

Genocide: The systematic, planned destruction of a racial, political, or cultural group.

Segregation: The practice of keeping racial and ethnic groups physically separate, thereby maintaining the superior position of the dominant group.

MODELS OF GROUP RELATIONS

Race and ethnic relations can range from positive forms such as intermarriage to negative forms such as mass genocide.

The most extreme and devastating form of group relations in human history involves the use of **genocide,** the systematic, planned destruction of a racial, political, or cultural group. The most horrific instance of brutal destructiveness against such a group was the massacre of six million Jews in the German concentration camps during World War II. Nazi ideology claimed Jews to be an inferior race to the "Aryan" people of Germany. The term "Aryan" originally referred to a group of languages spoken by people of differing physical characteristics. It was appropriated by the Nazis and their so-called "race scientists" to refer to characteristics that have little or no basis in reality. The Holocaust is not the only example of mass genocide in the twentieth century. Between 1915 and 1923 over a million Armenians were killed by the Ottoman Turkish government. In the late 1970s two million Cambodians died in the Khmer Rouge's killing fields. During the 1990s, in the African country of Rwanda, hundreds of thousands of the minority Tutsis were massacred by the dominant Hutu group. And in the former Yugoslavia, Bosnian and Kosovar Muslims were summarily executed by the Serb majority (see also Chapter 11).

In other areas of the world, exploitation of minority

groups has been an ugly part of many countries' histories. The concept of group closure, which we just reviewed, has been institutionalized in the form of **segregation,** a practice where racial and ethnic groups are kept physically separate by law, thereby maintaining the superior position of the dominant group. For instance, in South Africa (discussed further later in the chapter), laws forced blacks to live separately from whites and forbid sexual relations among races. In the United States, African Americans have also experienced legal forms of segregation. Until the 1960s, racial intermarriage was illegal in many states and economic and social segregation was enforced by law, for instance those requiring blacks and whites to use separate public bathrooms. Even today, segregated residential areas still exist in many cities, leading some

to claim that an American system of apartheid has developed (Massey and Denton, 1994).

For many years, the two most common positive models of political ethnic harmony in the United States were those of assimilation and the melting pot (see Figure 9.1). **Assimilation** meant that new immigrant groups would take over the attitudes and language of the dominant white community. The idea of the **melting pot** was different—it meant merging different cultures and outlooks by stirring them all together. A newer model of ethnic relations is **pluralism,** in which ethnic cultures are given full validity to exist separately, yet participate in the larger society's economic and political life. A recent outgrowth of pluralism is **multiculturalism,** in which ethnic groups exist separately and *equally.* It does seem at least possible

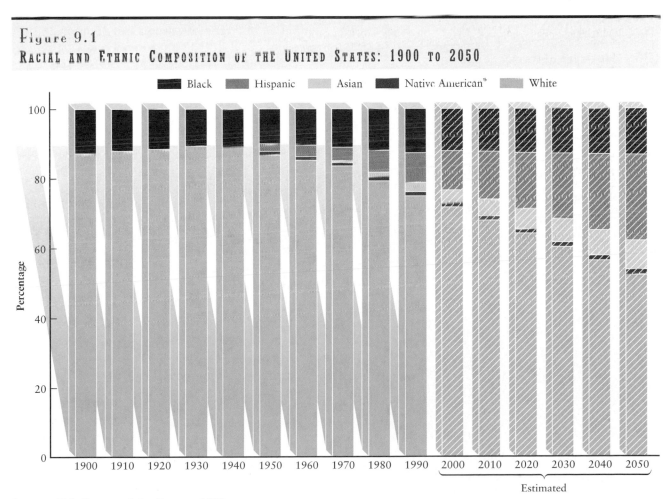

Figure 9.1

RACIAL AND ETHNIC COMPOSITION OF THE UNITED STATES: 1900 TO 2050

SOURCE: U.S. Bureau of the Census, 1998.

to create a society in which ethnic groups are separate but equal, as is demonstrated by Switzerland, where French, German, and Italian groups coexist in the same society. But this situation is unusual, and it seems unlikely that the United States could come close to mirroring this achievement in the near future.

ETHNIC AND RACIAL CONFLICT

In many parts of the world, struggles between different cultural and racial groups are being played out, some leading to intense bitterness and appalling instances of bloodshed. Bloody wars having such origins have been fought out in, among other areas, Bosnia Herzegovina and Kosovo (both are in what used to be Yugoslavia), Ethiopia (in Africa), and Georgia (part of the former Soviet Union).

At the same time, floods of refugees and emigrants move restlessly across different regions of the globe, either trying to escape from such conflicts or fleeing poverty in search of a better life. Often they reach a new country only to find they are resented by people who some generations ago were immigrants them-

Contemporary American art of the nineteenth century often stereotyped Native Americans as savage and warlike. Much of the animosity stems from a struggle between Native Americans and European Americans over North American land.

selves. Sometimes there are reversals, as has happened in Southern California and other areas of the United States along the Mexican border. Much of what is now California was once part of Mexico. Today, some Mexican Americans might say, the new waves of Mexican immigrants are reclaiming what used to be their heritage. Except that most of the existing groups in California don't quite see things this way.

In the next two sections, we shall investigate the origins of such cultural divisions. What explains the antagonisms that so often exist between groups of different cultural or racial backgrounds? Why do these differences *matter* so much? To fully analyze ethnic relations in current times, we must take a historical and comparative perspective. It is impossible to understand ethnic divisions today without giving prime place to the impact of the expansion of Western colonialism on the rest of the world (see Figure 9.2). Let's delve into this history in more detail now.

Ethnic Antagonism: A Historical Perspective

From the fifteenth century onward, Europeans began to venture into previously uncharted seas and unexplored land masses, pursuing the aims of exploration and trade but also conquering and subduing native peoples. They poured out by the millions from Europe to settle in these new areas. In the shape of the slave trade, they also occasioned a large-scale movement of people from Africa to the Americas. The following are the extraordinary shifts in population that have occurred over the past 350 years or so:

1. EUROPE TO NORTH AMERICA. From the seventeenth century to the present, some 45 million people have emigrated from Europe to what is now the United States and Canada. About 200 million in North America today can trace their ancestry to this migration.

2. EUROPE TO CENTRAL AND SOUTH AMERICA. About 20 million people from Europe, mostly from Spain, Portugal, and Italy, migrated to Central and South America. Some 50 million in these areas today are of European ancestry.

Figure 9.2
COLONIZATION AND ETHNICITY

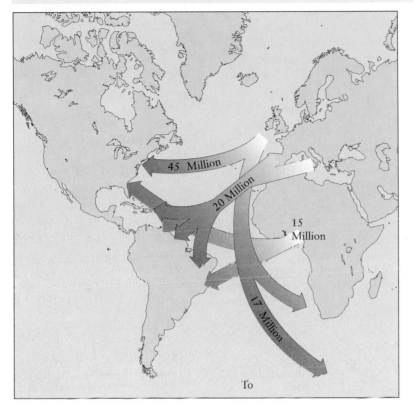

This map shows the massive movement of peoples from Europe who colonized the Americas, South Africa, Australia, and New Zealand, resulting in the ethnic composition of populations there today. People from Africa were brought to the Americas to be slaves.

3. EUROPE TO AFRICA AND AUSTRALASIA. Approximately 17 million people in these continents are of European ancestry. In Africa, the majority emigrated to the state of South Africa, which was colonized mainly by the British and Dutch.

4. AFRICA TO THE AMERICAS. Starting in the sixteenth century, about 15 million blacks were unwillingly transported to the North and South American continents. Under a million arrived in the sixteenth century; some 1.3 million in the seventeenth century; 6 million in the eighteenth century; and 2 million in the nineteenth century. Black Africans were brought to the Americas in chains to serve as slaves; families and whole communities were brutally destroyed in the process.

These population flows formed the basis of the current ethnic composition of the United States, Canada, the countries of Central and South America, South Africa, Australia, and New Zealand. In all of these societies, the indigenous populations were subjected to European rule and, in North America and Australasia, became tiny ethnic minorities. Since the Europeans were from ethnically diverse backgrounds, they implanted numerous ethnic divisions in their new homelands. At the height of the colonial era, in the nineteenth and early twentieth centuries, Europeans also ruled over native populations in many other regions: India, Burma, Malaya, and parts of the Middle East.

For most of the period of European expansion, ethnocentric attitudes were rife among the colonists, who believed that they were on a civilizing mission to the rest of the world. Even the more liberal Europeans thought themselves superior to the indigenous peoples they encountered. The fact that many of those peoples thought precisely the same about the colonists is not so relevant, since the Europeans possessed the power to make their outlook count. The early period of colonialism coincided with the rise of racism, and ever since then racial divisions and conflicts have tended to occupy a prime place in ethnic conflicts as a whole. In particular, racist views separating whites from blacks became central to European attitudes.

The Rise of Racism

Why has racism flourished? There are several reasons. One is that an opposition between white and black, as cultural symbols, was deeply rooted in European cul-

ture. White had long been associated with purity, black with evil (there is nothing natural about this symbolism; in some other cultures, it is reversed). The symbol of blackness held negative meanings *before* the West came into extensive contact with black peoples. These symbolic meanings tended to infuse the Europeans' reactions to blacks when they were first encountered on African shores. The sense that there was a radical difference between black and white peoples combined with the "heathenism" of the Africans led many Europeans to regard blacks with disdain and fear. As a seventeenth-century observer expressed it, blacks "in color as in condition are little other than Devils incarnate" (Jordan, 1968). Although the more extreme expressions of such attitudes have disappeared today, it is difficult not to believe that elements of this black-white cultural symbolism remain widespread.

A second important factor leading to modern racism was simply the invention and diffusion of the concept of race itself. Racist attitudes have been known to exist for hundreds of years. In China of 300 C.E., for example, we find recorded descriptions of barbarian peoples "who greatly resemble monkeys from whom they are descended." But the notion of race as a cluster of inherited characteristics comes from European thought of the eighteenth and nineteenth centuries. Count Joseph Arthur de Gobineau (1816–1882), who is sometimes called the father of modern racism, proposed ideas that became influential in many circles. According to de Gobineau, three races exist: the white, black, and yellow. The white race possesses superior intelligence, morality, and willpower, and these inherited qualities underlie the

spread of Western influence across the world. The blacks are the least capable, marked by an animal nature, a lack of morality, and emotional instability.

The ideas of de Gobineau and others who proposed similar views were presented as supposedly scientific theories. They later influenced Adolf Hitler, who transformed them into the ideology of the Nazi party. The notion of the superiority of the white race, although completely without value factually, remains a key element of white racism. It is an explicit element, for example, in the ideology of the Ku Klux Klan, and it was the basis of **apartheid** (separate racial development) in South Africa.

A third reason for the rise of modern racism lies in the exploitative relations that Europeans established with nonwhite peoples. The slave trade could not have been carried on had it not been widely believed by Europeans that blacks belonged to an inferior, even subhuman, race. Racism helped justify colonial rule over nonwhite peoples and denied them the rights of political participation that were being won by whites in their European homelands.

The relations between whites and nonwhites varied according to different patterns of colonial settlement—and were influenced as well by cultural differences between the Europeans themselves. To demonstrate these points, we now look at race relations in Europe, Brazil, and South Africa before analyzing racial and ethnic divisions in the United States at greater length.

Ethnic Relations in Europe

Immigration has become an explosive issue in Europe in the 1990s. Illegal immigrants from North Africa have entered European countries, particularly France and

Italy, in large numbers. The dissolution of the Soviet Union and the other changes in Eastern Europe have led governments in the western part of the Continent to fear a massive influx of immigration from the East. Hundreds of attacks on foreigners—and on Turkish workers, some of whom had been in the country for more than twenty years—took place in newly unified Germany in 1991 and 1992.

In Austria, a rightest group, the Freedom Party, has campaigned to stop foreigners from gaining access to the country. A comparable organization in Italy, called the Lombard League, has strong voting support in the North of the country. Even in the Scandanavian countries, long the bastions of liberalism in ethnic relations, hate groups with substantial support have arisen.

Over the period from the end of World War II to the opening of the Berlin Wall, over 18 million people immigrated into Germany—or what was then West Germany. Yet successive German governments clung to the idea that theirs was not a country of immigration. The Germanic notion of citizenship was one associated with blood, not place of birth. The children of "guest workers," who did not have full citizenship rights, have nonetheless quite often prospered economically. With the reunification of Germany, some erstwhile East Germans have become resentful that they are poorer than those who do not enjoy the same citizenship rights they do (Baldwin-Edwards and Schain, 1994).

Legislation pursued by the German federal parliament in 1990 included some liberalizing measures in favor of the rights of immigrants. For instance, immigrants are entitled to file for a permanent residence permit after eight years of stay. The law still talked, however, of "foreigners," rather than using the term "immigrant." The Green Party denounced the legislation as a product of "institutional racism" and called for a "minute of silence" in the parliament to "commemorate the future victims of this law."

More generally in Europe, many human rights and immigration organizations have reacted with dismay to what they see as a rising tide of racism, coupled with an attempt to construct a "fortress Europe." Yet the trends do not all go in the direction of decreasing tolerance. Anti-racist organizations have developed strongly in all the countries referred to above, and most governments have promoted measures designed to reduce discrimination.

Ethnic Relations in Brazil

Nearly 4 million Africans were transported to Brazil before the cessation of the slave trade in the middle of the nineteenth century. In the southern United States, blacks arriving from different African cultures were usually dispersed, but in Brazil, people shipped from similar culture areas were normally kept together. Hence they were able to retain more of their original culture than was possible in North America. Slaves in Brazil were allowed to marry even if their masters disapproved, as long as they continued serving them as before. A married couple could not be thereafter sold as individual slaves. Sexual contact between white men and slave women was frequent, and the children of such unions were often freed and sometimes fully accepted as part of the white family. Slavery was finally abolished in Brazil in 1888, but well before then whites had become used to the existence of free blacks (Swartz, 1985).

Following the ending of slavery, many black Brazilians moved into the towns and cities, where most of them lived (and live today) in considerable poverty. Yet they were not debarred from membership in labor unions, and a proportion have risen to positions of wealth and power. There is a much-quoted Brazilian saying, "A rich black man is a white, and a poor white man is a black." The phrase neatly catches both the relatively relaxed views of racial differences and the fact that "whiteness" is still clearly identified with superiority. Whites continue to dominate the higher positions in all sectors of the society.

Brazilians had long interpreted their own system of race relations in a charitable light, comparing it positively with the more segregated patterns of the United States. In the 1960s and 1970s, as moves to secure greater civil rights for African Americans gathered strength, such comparisons became somewhat less favorable to Brazil. In the early 1960s, the Brazilian Congress was compelled to pass a law forbidding discrimination in public places after a touring African American, dancer Katherine Dunham, complained of being refused accommodation in a São Paulo hotel. The law was largely a symbolic gesture, however, as the government made no effort to investigate the extent of possible discrimination.

Most observers agree that such discrimination has been fairly rare in Brazil, but there have been few government programs designed to improve the social and economic opportunities of nonwhites. Brazil has nonetheless avoided the recurrent lynchings and race riots that have punctuated the history of the United States, and has escaped most of the more extreme forms of antiblack prejudice (Skidmore, 1974). There are two main reasons for the different patterns of race relations in the two countries. First, as was men-

KEY CONCEPTS IN REVIEW

The history of colonialism helps to explain the prevalence of prejudice and racism in the United States and other societies.

Racism has flourished for three primary reasons: the culturally symbolic antagonism between white and black, the invention and diffusion of the concept of race, and the exploitative relations that Europeans established with nonwhite peoples.

tioned, sexual contact between whites and blacks in Brazil was from the beginning commonplace. White males also took Indian women as mates or even wives. Second, the Portuguese came from an area of Europe where the Moors—North Africans—had held considerable power; hence they did not associate dark skin with the same degree of racial inferiority as most northern Europeans. The level of racial prejudice, in other words, was from the outset lower than in North America.

Racial Division in South Africa

In South Africa, the first European settlers were Dutch. Finding the local population resistant to working in European enterprises, they began importing large numbers of slaves from elsewhere in Africa and from the Dutch East Indies. The British later established a dominant position in South Africa, putting an end to slavery in the 1830s. Divisions between whites and indigenous Africans were not at first as absolute as they later became. When slavery was abolished, new taxes were introduced for blacks, which effectively forced many of them to contract themselves to European employers, and young African men had to look for employment away from home in order to pay the tax. A system of "migrant labor" developed, which set the pattern for the subsequent evolution of

the South African economy. Many Africans went to work in gold or diamond mines, living in special camps well away from the neighborhoods where Europeans lived. Gradually a segregated system grew up which was later formalized in law.

Under the apartheid system, introduced after World War II, the population of South Africa was classified into four "registration groups"—the 4.5 million white descendants of European immigrants; the 2.5 million so-called "colored people," whose descent is traced from members of more than one "race"; the 1 million people of Asian descent; and the 23 million black Africans. Pierre van den Berghe distinguished three main levels of segregation in South African society during the years of apartheid (van den Berghe, 1970).

1. **Microsegregation**—the segregation of public places (such as used to be the case in the American South). Restrooms, waiting rooms, railroad cars, and other public areas have separate facilities for whites and nonwhites.
2. **Mezzosegregation**—the segregation of whites and nonwhites in terms of the neighborhoods where they live in urban areas. Blacks are compelled to live in specially designated zones.
3. **Macrosegregation**—the segregation of whole peoples in distinct territories set up as *native reserves*.

The South African economy was unable to function without the labor power of millions of nonwhites, living in or near the cities. Originally there were some ethnically mixed neighborhoods in the major urban areas, but more and more of the blacks were placed in "model townships," situated a number of miles away from the white areas. In addition, millions of people were herded into so-called *homelands* well away from the cities. These regions were organized into partially autonomous states subject to the overall control of the white central government. Under apartheid, non-whites had no vote, and so no representation, in the central government.

The homelands were supposed to be separate territories where the black majority could exercise the political rights denied them in white South Africa. Under the provisions of the 1970 Homelands Citizenship Act, those in a homeland were automatically deprived of their South African citizenship on the day it became "independent." So-called *frontier commuters* lived with their families in the homelands and traveled daily across the "national borders" into white South Africa.

Apartheid was universally condemned by the international community, and opposed by many from within the society. For a lengthy period South Africa was subject to economic sanctions designed to put pressure on the country to discontinue the system; in addition, South Africa was excluded from a range of international sporting events. The sanctions almost certainly had some influence, as did internal protest, but one of the major reasons why apartheid began to disintegrate in the 1980s was that many black people deliberately acted counter to it—in spite of punishments meted out by the authorities. For instance, large numbers of people migrated to urban areas in search of work in spite of laws that debarred them from doing so.

In 1990, President de Klerk lifted the ban on the African National Congress (ANC), the Communist Party, and a range of other opposition groups, which had previously been prohibited, driven underground, or forced into exile. Nelson Mandela, the ANC leader, who had been in prison since 1962, was freed. A new constitution was drawn up, which, for the first time, gave every person the vote. A referendum was held in March 1992 among white voters, and a large majority was in favor of pressing ahead with such reform.

South Africa has today become a functioning democracy, with Nelson Mandela as its elected president. Apartheid has quickly become a thing of the past. Yet there is a great deal of violent crime in the townships, as well as in some of the prosperous white neighborhoods, and it will be some while before anyone can be sure that the country will not again experience violent ethnic conflicts.

Since the ending of apartheid there has been a surge of investment in South Africa. Many large South African companies have also begun to invest in other parts of Africa. For example, in 1994–95 South African Breweries bought large holdings in the state-run brewing companies of Tanzania and Zambia. It already has outlets in Botswana, Lesotho, and Swaziland. A subsidiary of Pepkor, the biggest retailer in South Africa, opened three stores in Zambia in 1995 and plans four more for the future.

Such an expansion of South African capitalism is not without its problems. The head of a retail chain in Zimbabwe was cheered at a conference in that country when she accused South Africans of trying to "gobble up Africa." Farmers in Mozambique have staged demonstrations aimed at preventing the government from selling arable land to South African investors. Such tensions are hardly surprising, given the fact that South African governments during the period of apartheid backed military intervention in Mozambique and other surrounding countries. Racial and ethnic hostilities still simmer in these encounters, given that virtually all South African business leaders are white.

In his book about the transition from minority gov-

A picture taken in Johannesburg, South Africa, two weeks after the city integrated its previously all-white buses.

ernment in South Africa, *The Bondage of Fear* (1995), Fergal Keane notes that

> it remains a country with deep and dangerous fault lines. The years of minority rule might have created a solid infrastructure and the most developed economy in Africa, but they have also been enormously wasteful in terms of misdirected spending ... Six million people unemployed; ten million with no access to running water and twenty-three million without electricity; fewer than 50 per cent of black children under the age of fourteen attending school and nine million destitute. (p. 238)

ETHNIC RELATIONS IN THE UNITED STATES

We now concentrate for the rest of the chapter on the origins and nature of ethnic diversity in the United States (see Table 9.1)—and its consequences, which have often been tense in the extreme. More than most other societies in the world, this country is peopled almost entirely by immigrants. Only a tiny minority, less than .05 percent, of the population today are made up of Native Americans, those whom Christopher Columbus, erroneously supposing he had arrived in India, called Indians.

Before the American Revolution, British, French, and Dutch settlers established colonies in what is now the United States. Some descendants of the French colonists are still to be found in parts of Louisiana. As will be discussed in more detail later, millions of slaves were brought over from Africa to North America. Huge waves of European, Russian, Asian, and Latin-American immigrants have washed across the country at different periods since then. The United States is one of the most *ethnically diverse* countries on the face of the globe. In this section we will pay particular attention to the divisions that have separated whites and nonwhite minority groups, such as African Americans and Hispanic Americans. The emphasis is on *struggle*. Members of these groups have made repeated efforts to defend the integrity of their cultures and advance their social position in the face of persistent prejudice and discrimination from the wider social environment.

Table 9.1 Racial and Ethnic Populations in the United States, 1990

RACE OR ETHNICITY	POPULATION	PERCENTAGE OF TOTAL POPULATION
African origin	29,986,000	12.1
Hispanic origin[a]	22,354,000	9.0
Mexican	13,496,000	5.4
Puerto Rican	2,728,000	1.1
Cuban	1,044,000	0.4
Other Hispanic	5,086,000	2.0
Asian or Pacific Island origin	7,274,000	2.9
Chinese	1,645,000	0.7
Filipino	1,407,000	0.6
Japanese	848,000	0.3
Korean	799,000	0.3
Vietnamese	615,000	0.2
Hawaiian	211,000	0.1
Samoan	63,000	<[b]
Guamanian	49,000	<
Other Asian or Pacific Island	822,000	0.3
Native American	1,959,000	0.8
American Indian	1,878,000	0.8
Eskimo	57,000	<
Aleut	24,000	<
European origin	199,686,000	80.3

[a]People of Hispanic origin can be of any race.
[b]Indicates less than 1/20 of 1 percent.

SOURCE: U.S. Bureau of the Census, 1992.

Early Colonization

The first European colonists in what was to become the United States were actually of quite homogeneous background. At the time of the Declaration of Independence, the majority of the colonial population was of British descent, and almost everyone was Protestant. Settlers from outside the British Isles were at first admitted only with reluctance, but the desire for economic expansion meant having to attract immigrants from other areas. Most came from countries in northwest Europe, such as Holland, Germany, and Sweden—such migration into North America dates initially from around 1820. In the century following, about 33 million immigrants entered the United States. No migrant movement on such a scale has ever been documented before or since.

The early waves of immigrants came mostly from the same countries of origin as the groups already established in the United States. They left Europe to escape economic hardship and religious and political oppression, and because of the opportunities to acquire land as the drive westward gained momentum. As a result of successive potato famines that had produced widespread starvation, 1.5 million people migrated from Ireland, settling for the most part in the coastal areas, in contrast to most other immigrants from rural backgrounds. The Irish knew farm work as a way of life marked by hardship and despair, and most of them opted for city life and, where they could get it, industrial work.

A major new influx of immigrants arrived in the 1880s and 1890s, this time mainly from southern and eastern Europe—the Austro-Hungarian Empire, Russia, and Italy. Each successive group of immigrants was subject to considerable discrimination on the part of people previously established in the country. Negative views of the Irish, for example, emphasized their supposedly low level of intelligence and drunken behavior. Job vacancies often specifically stated, "No Irish need apply." But as they were concentrated within the cities, the Irish Americans were able to organize to protect their interests and gained a strong influence over political life. The Italians and Polish, when they reached America, were in turn discriminated against by the Irish.

Asian immigrants first arrived in the United States in large numbers in the late nineteenth century, encouraged by employers who needed cheap labor in the developing industries of the West. Some 200,000 Chinese emigrated at this period. Most were men, who came with the idea of saving money to send back to their families in China, anticipating that they would also later return there. Bitter conflicts broke out between white workers and the Chinese when employment opportunities diminished. The Chinese Exclusion Act, passed in 1882, cut down further immigration to a trickle until after World War II.

A nineteenth-century cartoon shows drunken Irish immigrants making off with a ballot box.

Japanese immigrants began to arrive not long after the ending of Chinese immigration. They were also subject to great hostility from whites. Opposition to Japanese immigration intensified in the early part of the twentieth century, leading to strict limits, or *quotas,* being placed on the numbers allowed to enter the United States.

Most immigrant groups in the early twentieth century settled in urban areas, and engaged in the developing industrial economy. They also tended to cluster in ethnic neighborhoods of their own. Chinatowns, Little Italys, and other clearly defined areas became features of most large cities. The very size of the influx provoked backlash from the Anglo-Saxon sections of the population. During the 1920s, new immigration quotas were set up, which discriminated against new arrivals from southern and eastern Europe. Many immigrants found the conditions of life in their new land little better and sometimes worse than the areas from which they originated. Eva Morawska, the author of a historical study of immigrants journeying from east central Europe to Johnstown, Pennsylvania, observes:

The ambivalence and heart-rending uncertainty that accompanied the immigrants when they made their decision to cross the ocean to try their luck in America became further sharpened in this country by feelings of bewilderment and nostalgia, and by disillusionment with the reality of the "Promised Land" as compared with the dreams they had harbored in Europe. To a number of East Central Europeans, the arrival in Johnstown was bitterly disappointing. The town was soiled and the air filled with soot and fumes from the furnace chimneys. "My disappointment was unspeakable," recalls an eighty-four-year-old Galician, "when after a twelve-day journey I saw the city of Johnstown: squalid and ugly, with those congested shabby houses, blackened with soot from the factory chimneys—this was the America I saw." (Morawska, 1986)

The immigrants may have gained greater religious and political freedom in their new home, but they met with prejudice and discrimination if their ways of life differed from those of the dominant Anglo-Saxon community. The large flow of immigration and competition for jobs allowed employers to compel workers to accept very long working days, low levels of pay, and unhealthy working conditions. Since new immigrants were commonly used as strike-breakers (people hired to replace striking workers), conflicts between them and established groups were frequent. In spite of these conditions, the economy was rapidly growing, and a substantial proportion of immigrant workers in the end managed to improve their standards of living.

African Americans in the United States

By 1780, there were nearly 4 million slaves in the American South. Since there was little incentive for them to work, physical punishment was often resorted to. Slaves who ran away were hunted with dogs and on their capture were manacled, sometimes branded with their master's mark, and occasionally even castrated. Slaves had virtually no rights in law whatsoever. But they did not passively accept the conditions their masters imposed upon them. The struggles of slaves against their oppressive conditions sometimes took the form of direct opposition or disobedience to orders, and occasionally outright rebellion (although collective slave revolts were more common in the Caribbean than in the United States). On a more subtle level, their response took the form of a cultural

creativity—a mixing of aspects of African cultures, Christian ideals, and cultural threads woven from their new environments. Some of the art forms they evolved, such as in music—for example, the invention of jazz—were genuinely new.

Feelings of hostility toward blacks on the part of the white population were in some respects more strongly developed in states where slavery had never been known than in the South itself. The celebrated French political observer Alexis de Tocqueville noted in 1835, "The prejudice of race appears to be stronger in the states that have abolished slavery than in those where it still exists; and nowhere is it so intolerant as in those states where servitude has never been known" (Tocqueville, 1969). Moral rejection of slavery seems to have been confined to a few more educated groups. The main factors underlying the Civil War were political and economic; most Northern leaders were more interested in sustaining the Union than in abolishing slavery, although this was the eventual outcome of the conflict. The formal abolition of slavery changed the real conditions of life for African Americans in the South relatively little. The "black codes"—laws limiting the rights of blacks—placed restrictions on the behavior of the former slaves and punished their transgressions in much the same way as under slavery. Acts were also passed legalizing segregation of blacks from whites in public places. One kind of slavery was thus replaced by another, based upon social, political, and economic discrimination.

INTERNAL MIGRATION FROM SOUTH TO NORTH

Industrial development in the North, combined with the mechanization of agriculture in the South, produced a progressive movement of African Americans northward from the turn of the century on. In 1900, more than 90 percent of African Americans lived in the South, mostly in rural areas. Today, less than half of the black population remains in the South; three-quarters now live in Northern urban areas. African Americans used to be farm laborers and domestic servants, but over a period of little more than two generations, they have become mainly urban, industrial, and service-economy workers. But African Americans have not become assimilated into the wider society in the way in which the successive groups of white immigrants were. They have for the most part been unable

The enslavement of millions of Africans in North and South America constituted one of the greatest population shifts in history. This is a detail of W. H. Brown's painting Hauling the Whole Week's Picking.

to break free from the conditions of neighborhood segregation and poverty that other immigrants faced on arrival. Together with those of Anglo-Saxon origin, African Americans have lived in the United States far longer than most other immigrant groups. What was a transitional experience for most of the later, white immigrants has become a seemingly permanent experience for blacks. In the majority of cities, both South and North, blacks and whites live in separate neighborhoods and are educated in different schools. It has been estimated that 80 percent of either blacks or whites would have to move in order to desegregate housing fully in the average American city.

THE CIVIL RIGHTS MOVEMENTS

Struggles by minority groups to achieve equal rights and opportunities have for a long while been a part of American history. Most minorities have been successful. African Americans, however, were largely denied opportunities for self-advancement until the early 1940s. The National Association for the Advancement of Colored People (NAACP) and the National Urban League, founded in 1909 and 1910 respectively, fought for black civil rights, but began to have some real effect only after World War II, when the NAACP instituted a campaign against segregated public education. This struggle came to a head when the organization sued five school boards, challenging the concept of separate but equal schooling that then held sway. In 1954, in *Brown v. Board of Education of Topeka, Kansas,* the U.S. Supreme Court unanimously decided that "separate educational facilities are inherently unequal."

This decision became the platform for struggles for civil rights from the 1950s to the 1970s. The strength of the resistance from many whites persuaded black leaders that mass militancy was necessary to give civil rights any real substance. In 1955, a black woman, Rosa Parks, was arrested in Montgomery, Alabama, for declining to give up her seat on a bus to a white man. As a result, almost the entire African-American population of the city, led by a Baptist minister, Martin Luther King Jr., boycotted the transportation system for 381 days. Eventually the city was forced to abolish segregation in public transportation.

Further boycotts and sit-ins followed, with the object of desegregating other public facilities. The marches and demonstrations began to achieve a mass following from blacks and white sympathizers. In 1963, a quarter of a million civil rights supporters staged a march on Washington and cheered as King announced, "We will not be satisfied until justice rolls down like the waters and righteousness like a mighty

Marchers in Washington, 1963.

IMMIGRANT AMERICA

If globalization is understood as the emergence of new patterns of interconnection among the world's peoples and cultures, then surely one of the most significant aspects of globalization is the changing racial and ethnic composition of Western societies. In the United States, shifting patterns of immigration since the end of World War II have altered the demographic structure of many regions, affecting social and cultural life in ways that can hardly be overstated. Although the United States has always been a nation of immigrants (with the obvious exception of Native Americans), most of those who arrived here prior to the early 1960s were European. Throughout the nineteenth and early twentieth centuries, vast numbers of people from Ireland, Italy, Germany, Russia, and other European and east European countries flocked to America in search of a new life, giving a distinctive European bent to American culture (of course, until the end of the Civil War, another significant group of immigrants—Africans—came not because America was a land of opportunity, but because they had been enslaved). In part because of changes in immigration policy, however, most of those admitted since 1965 have been Asian or Hispanic. In 1993, for example, of the approximately 900,000 immigrants who were legally admitted to the United States, more than 350,000 came from Asia and more than 300,000 were from Latin America. There are also an estimated 4.5 to 5 million illegal immigrants living in the United States, many of whom are Hispanic. As a result, as of 1990, 42 percent of U.S. residents who were foreign-born were from Latin America, while 25 percent were from Asia. In contrast, almost 85 percent of the foreign-born in 1900 were European (Duignan and Gann, 1998).

stream." In 1964, a Civil Rights Act was passed by Congress, comprehensively banning discrimination in public facilities, education, employment, and any agency receiving government funds. Further bills in following years were aimed at ensuring that African Americans became fully registered voters and outlawed discrimination in housing.

Attempts to implement the new civil rights legislation continued to meet with ferocious resistance from opponents. Civil rights marchers were insulted and beaten up, and some lost their lives. But in spite of barriers that hampered the full realization of its provisions, the Civil Rights Act proved to be fundamentally important. Its principles applied not just to African

Most of these new immigrants have settled in six "port-of-entry" states: California, New York, Texas, Illinois, New Jersey, and Massachusetts. These states are attractive to new immigrants not necessarily because of the job opportunities they afford, but because they house large immigrant communities into which newcomers are welcomed (Frey and Liaw, 1998). As the flow of Asian and Hispanic immigration continues, and as some non-immigrants respond by moving to regions of the country with smaller immigrant populations, the percentage of residents of port-of-entry states who are white will continue to drop. California was approximately 52 percent white in 1996; by 2010, this number is expected to fall to 40 percent (Maharidge, 1996, p. 4). "Other states will follow," Dale Maharidge (1996, p. 3) writes in the book *The Coming White Minority*, "Texas sometime around 2015, and in later years Arizona, New York, Nevada, New Jersey, and Maryland. By 2050 the nation will be almost half nonwhite."

The effect of these demographic changes on everyday social life has been profound. Take California as an example. In California's urban centers, residents fully expect street scenes to be multi-ethnic in character, and would be shocked to visit a state like Wisconsin, where the vast majority of public interactions take place between whites. In some California communities, store and street signs are printed in Spanish or Chinese or Vietnamese, as well as in English. Interracial marriages are on the rise, ethnic restaurants have proliferated, and the schools are filled with nonwhite children. In fact, nonwhites make up two thirds of the undergraduate population at the University of California at Berkeley, where Asian students are on the verge of predominating.

Unfortunately, these changes have exacerbated social tensions. Many white Californians have retreated into prosperous suburban enclaves, and have grown resentful of immigrants and nonwhites. Because rates of voter turnout are higher for whites than for other racial groups in the state, and because whites control a significant share of the state's wealth, they have managed to pass a number of laws that seek to preserve opportunities for the "coming white minority." Proposition 187, for example, passed in 1994, denied vital public services to illegal immigrants. More recently, the Regents of the University of California, in a highly controversial move, decided to abolish affirmative action for the entire nine-campus state university system. Were these decisions based on solid economic and philosophical rationales—the perception that California taxpayers were shouldering too much of the economic burden of illegal immigration, or the sense that affirmative action constitutes "reverse discrimination" against whites—or were they motivated principally by xenophobia, the fear of those different than one's self? Whatever the answer, there can be little doubt but that immigration—an important aspect of globalization—is changing the face of American society.

Americans but to anyone subject to discrimination, including other ethnic groups and women. It served as the starting point for a range of movements asserting the rights of oppressed groups.

How successful has the civil rights movement been? On one hand, a substantial black middle class has emerged over the last three to four decades. And many African Americans—such as former chairman of the Joint Chiefs of Staff Colin Powell, Chicago Bull Michael Jordan, and writer Toni Morrison—have achieved positions of power and influence in the wider society. On the other hand, a large number of African Americans, comprising an underclass, live trapped in the ghettos. Scholars have debated whether the existence of the black underclass has resulted primarily from economic disadvantage or dependency upon the welfare system. We will examine the forms of inequality that African Americans and other minority groups continue to experience later in this chapter.

Latinos in the United States

The wars of conquest that created the modern United States were not only directed against the Native American population. Much of the Southwest—along with a quarter of a million Mexicans—was taken by the United States in 1848 as a result of the American war with Mexico. The term "Chicano" includes the descendants of these people, together with subsequent immigrants from Mexico. The term "Latino" refers to anyone from Spanish-speaking areas living in the United States.

The three main groups of Latinos in the United States are Mexican Americans (around 13.5 million), Puerto Ricans (2.7 million), and Cubans (1 million). A further 5 million Spanish-speaking residents are from areas in Central and South America. The Latino population, as mentioned earlier, is increasing at an extraordinary rate—53 percent between 1980 and 1990—mainly as a result of the large-scale flow of new immigrants from across the Mexican border. If current trends continue, the Latino residents will outnumber African Americans within the next decade.

Mexican Americans continue to reside mainly in California and the Southwestern states, although there are substantial groups in some Northern cities. The majority have come, legally and illegally, to work at low-paying jobs. In the post–World War II period up to the early 1960s, Mexican workers were admitted without much restriction. This was succeeded by a phase in which numbers were limited and efforts made to deport those who had entered illegally. Illegal immigrants today continue to flood across the border. Large numbers are intercepted and sent back each year by immigration officials, but most simply try again, and it is estimated that four times as many escape officials as are stopped.

Since Mexico is a relatively poor country existing alongside the much more wealthy United States, it seems unlikely that this flow of people northward will diminish in the near future. Illegal immigrants can be

employed more cheaply than indigenous workers, and they are prepared to perform jobs that most of the rest of the population would not accept. Legislation was passed by Congress in 1986 making it possible for illegal immigrants who had lived in the United States for at least five years to claim legal residence.

Many Mexican Americans resist assimilation into the dominant English-speaking culture and, in common with other ethnic groups, have increasingly begun to display pride in their own cultural identity within the United States.

PUERTO RICANS AND CUBANS

Puerto Rico is another territory acquired by the United States through war, and Puerto Ricans have been American citizens since 1917. The island is poor, and many of its inhabitants have migrated to the mainland United States to improve their conditions of life. Puerto Ricans originally settled in New York City, but since the 1960s, they have moved elsewhere. A significant number, about 38 percent in 1990, live in considerable poverty. A reverse migration of Puerto Ricans began in the 1970s; more have left the mainland than have arrived since that date. One of the most important issues facing Puerto Rican activists is the political destiny of their homeland. Puerto Rico is at present a commonwealth, not a full state within the United States. For years, Puerto Ricans have been divided about whether the island should retain its present status, opt for independence, or attempt to become the fifty-first state of the Union.

A third Latino group in the United States, the Cubans, differs from the two others in key respects. One-half million Cubans fled Communism following the rise of Fidel Castro in 1959, and the majority settled in Florida. Unlike other Latino immigrants, they were mainly educated people from white-collar and professional backgrounds. They have managed to thrive within the United States, many finding positions comparable to those they had abandoned in Cuba. As a group, Cubans have the highest family income of all Latinos.

A further wave of Cuban immigrants, from less affluent origins, arrived in 1980. Lacking the qualifications held by the first wave, these people tend to live in circumstances closer to the rest of the Latino communities in the United States. Both sets of Cuban immigrants are mainly political refugees rather than

Many Mexican Americans in the United States, such as these mariachi students, have chosen to embrace their heritage.

economic migrants. The later immigrants to a large extent have become the "working class" for the earlier. They are paid low wages, but Cuban employers tend to take them on in preference to other ethnic groups. In Miami, nearly one-third of all businesses are owned by Cubans, and 75 percent of the labor force in construction is Cuban.

The Asian Connection

About 3 percent of the population of the United States is of Asian origin—8 million people. Chinese, Japanese, and Filipinos (immigrants from the Philippines) form the largest groups. But now there are also significant numbers of Asian Indians, Pakistanis, Koreans, and Vietnamese living in America. And as a result of the war in Vietnam, some 350,000 refugees from that country entered the United States in the 1970s.

Most of the early Chinese immigrants settled in California, where they were employed mainly in heavy industries such as mining and railroad construction. The retreat of the Chinese into distinct Chinatowns was not primarily their choice, but was made necessary by the hostility they faced. Since Chinese immigration was ended by law in 1882, the Chinese remained largely isolated from the wider society, at least until recently.

The early Japanese immigrants also settled in California and the other Pacific states. During World War II, following the attack on Pearl Harbor by Japan, all Japanese Americans in the United States were made to report to "relocation centers," which were effectively concentration camps, surrounded by barbed wire and gun turrets. In spite of the fact that most of these people were American citizens, they were compelled to live in the hastily established camps for the duration of the war. Paradoxically, this situation eventually led to their greater integration within the wider society, since, following the war, Japanese Americans did not return to the separate neighborhoods in which they had previously lived. They have become extremely successful in reaching high levels of education and income, marginally outstripping whites. The rate of intermarriage of Japanese Americans with whites is now nearly 50 percent.

Following the passing of a new Immigration Act in 1965, large-scale immigration of Asians into the United States again took place. Foreign-born Chinese Americans today outnumber those brought up in the United States. The newly arrived Chinese have avoided the Chinatowns in which the long-established Chinese have tended to remain, mostly moving into other neighborhoods.

THE SOCIOLOGICAL DEBATE

IMMIGRATION TO THE UNITED STATES

The United States is often euphemistically referred to as a "melting pot," or a nation of immigrants. The cultural and social landscape of the United States is viewed as an amalgam of diverse cultures, due largely to our nation's history as a refuge for immigrants. Today, however, policy makers and social scientists are embroiled in a dispute over the social and economic costs of immigration. Do new immigrants help or hinder the United States' economy?

Before addressing both sides of this debate, it is important to understand the current state of immigration to the United States. During the early 1990s, the United States admitted more than 800,000 legal immigrants each year, and an additional 300,000 entered and stayed in the country illegally. Unlike the major wave of immigration that occurred at the turn of the century, fewer than 10 percent of immigrants admitted into the United States in the last two decades were of European origin. In fact, between 1989 and 1993, more than half of all immigrants entering the United States came from just four countries: Mexico, the Philippines, Vietnam, and El Salvador. This change in the composition of immigrants is generally attributed to two government acts: the 1965 Immigration and Nationality Act Amendments, which abolished preference for northern and western European immigrants and gave preference to "family reunification"—rather than occupational skills—as a reason for accepting immigrants; and the 1986 Immigration Reform and Control Act, which provided amnesty for many illegal immigrants.

Consequently, many of the debates surrounding immigration focus on new immigrants' ability to secure employment and achieve economic self-sufficiency. In his 1994 essay "The Economics of Immigration," economist George Borjas argued that since the 1980s, the United States has attracted "lower quality" immigrants, who have less education and few marketable job skills. Moreover, these new immigrants are less skilled than both natives (i.e., persons born in the

United States) and earlier migrants, thus they are more reliant on government assistance for survival. Borjas's estimates show that 21 percent of immigrant households participate in some means-tested social assistance program such as Medicaid or food stamps, as compared with 14 percent of native households. Because recent immigrants are often unable to find gainful employment in the short term, economic assimilation is quite slow; Borjas estimated that recent immigrants will likely earn 20 percent less than native-born Americans for most of their working lives.

Borjas also was concerned about the effect of immigrants on natives' economic prospects. He argued that large-scale migration of less-skilled workers has done harm to the economic opportunities of less-skilled natives—particularly African Americans. This occurs because immigrants increase the number of workers in the economy; they create additional competition in the labor market and thus wages of the least-skilled workers fall.

Although Borjas described a bleak scenario, others economists and policy analysts argue that recent immigration has either a positive effect or no influence on the U.S. economy. Economist Julian Simon has written several books, including *The Ultimate Resource* (1981), and *The Economic Consequences of Immigration* (1989), which argue that immigrants provide a windfall to the U.S. economy by joining the labor force and paying into the Federal revenue system for their whole lives. By the time they retire and collect government benefits such as Social Security and Medicare, their children will be covering these costs, by working and paying into the tax system. Simon's arguments, however, are based on the assumption that immigrants earn the same wages and are as employable as natives—an assumption refuted by Borjas's research.

Simon also argues that immigrants are a cultural asset to the United States. In fact, he claims that "the notion of wanting to keep out immigrants in order to keep our institutions and our values pure is prejudice" (Brimelow, 1995, p. 110). Moreover, Simon argues that human beings have the intelligence to adapt to their surroundings, and that the more immigrants that come to the United States, the larger pool of potential innovators and problem solvers our nation will have.

Studies conducted by Simon, and the Urban Institute, a nonprofit research organization, acknowledge that while some recent immigrants may benefit from federally funded programs such as welfare, these costs are often quite short term. Immigrant children who benefit from the United States educational system go on to become productive, tax-paying workers.

Assessing the fiscal costs of immigration proves difficult, however. Although much of the public debate focuses on the costs of providing services to illegal immigrants, actual statistics documenting the number of illegal immigrants are difficult to obtain and verify. Moreover, few policy analysts can predict whether U.S. immigration policy—or the characteristics of immigrants themselves—will change drastically in the future.

RACIAL AND ETHNIC INEQUALITY

A 1996 *New York Times* headline proclaimed "Quality of Life Is Up for Many Blacks" (Holmes, 1996b). The following year, the same paper reported that "New Reports Say Minorities Benefit in Fiscal Recovery" (Holmes, 1997). Since the civil rights movement of the 1960s, has real progress been made? On the one hand, an increasing number of African Americans joined the middle class by acquiring college degrees, professional jobs, and new homes. On the other hand, blacks are far more likely than whites to live in poverty and be socially isolated from good schools and economic opportunity. Also, large numbers of immigrants came to the United States throughout the 1980s and 1990s to find new economic opportunity. Yet some of these groups, particularly immigrants from Mexico, have among the lowest levels of educational achievement and live in dire poverty. For the most part, sociologists agree on the facts about racial and ethnic inequality. There is, however, a disagreement among sociologists about how these facts should be interpreted. Are improving economic conditions for minority groups part of a long-term process or are they temporary reflections of the booming 1990s economy? Is racial and ethnic inequality primarily the result of a person's racial or ethnic background or

does it reflect a person's class position? In other words, is an African American, for example, more likely to live in poverty because of racial discrimination or because of the lower class position that many African Americans hold? In this section, we will first examine the facts: how racial and ethnic inequality is reflected in terms of educational and occupational attainment, income, health, residential segregation, and political power. We will then look at the divergent social statuses found within the largest racial and ethnic groups. We will conclude by looking at how sociologists have sought to explain racial inequality.

Educational Attainment

Differences between blacks and whites in levels of educational attainment have decreased, but these seem more the result of long-established trends rather than the direct outcome of the struggles of the 1960s. After steadily improving their levels of educational attainment for the last fifty years, young African Americans are for the first time close to whites in terms of finishing high school. The number of blacks over the age of twenty-five with high school degrees has increased from about 20 percent in 1960 to 75 percent in 1997. By contrast, just over 80 percent of whites have completed high school (see Figure 9.3). Some analysts see this development as a hopeful sign and an indicator that young blacks need not live a life of hopelessness and despair. But not all signs have been positive. While more African Americans are attending college now than in the 1960s, a much higher proportion of whites than blacks graduate from college today. In today's global economy and job market, which value college degrees, the result is a wide disparity in incomes between whites and blacks (see below). As sociologist Christopher Jencks remarked, "You have a situation where the black kids coming out of high school are better qualified, but the number of jobs that they are qualified for is actually shrinking."

Another negative trend with potentially far-reaching consequences is the large gap in educational attainment between Hispanics and both whites and blacks. Hispanics have by far the highest high-school dropout rate of any group in the United States. While rates of college attendance and success in graduation have gradually improved for other groups, the rate for

Figure 9.3
EDUCATIONAL ATTAINMENT (FOR PERSONS 25 YEARS OLD AND OVER)

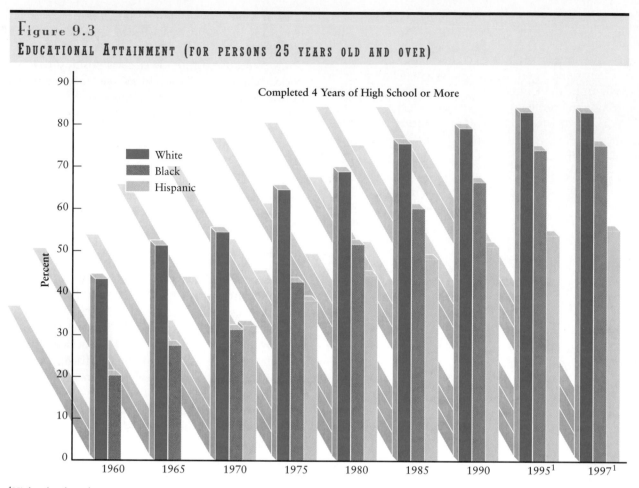

Completed 4 Years of High School or More

White
Black
Hispanic

[1]High school graduates or more.

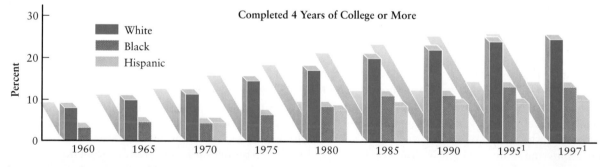

Completed 4 Years of College or More

White
Black
Hispanic

[1]B.A. degree or more.

SOURCE: Chart prepared by U.S. Bureau of the Census.

Hispanics has held relatively steady since the mid-1980s. Only about 10 percent hold a college degree. It is possible that these poor results can be attributed to the large number of poorly educated immigrants from Latin America who have come to the United States in the last two decades. Many of these immigrants have poor English language skills and their children encounter difficulties in schools. One study found, however, that even among Mexican Americans whose families have lived in the United States for three generations or more, there has been a decline in educational attainment (Bean et al., 1994). For these Hispanics with low levels of education and poor language skills, living in the United States has been "the American nightmare, not the American dream."

Employment and Income

As a result of the increase in educational attainment, African Americans now hold a slightly higher proportion of managerial and professional jobs than in 1960, though still not in proportion to their overall size. In 1998, out of the approximately 39 million managerial or professional positions in the United States, whites held about 34 million (about 87.5 percent), African Americans just under 3 million (7.5 percent), and Hispanics just under 2 million (5 percent). During that same year, black men were about twice as likely as whites to be service workers and about one and one-half times as likely to hold a blue-collar job.

The unemployment rate of black and Hispanic men outstrips that of whites by the same degree today as was the case in the early 1960s. Twice as many black and Hispanic men as white men are registered as unemployed (in 1998, 4 percent for whites versus about 8 percent for both blacks and Hispanics). There has also been some debate about whether employment opportunities for minorities have improved or worsened. Statistics on unemployment don't adequately measure economic opportunity, since it measures only those known to be looking for work. A higher proportion of blacks and Hispanics have simply opted out of the occupational system, neither working nor looking for work. They have become disillusioned by the frustration of searching for employment that is not there. Unemployment figures also do not reflect the increas-

ing numbers of young men from minority groups who have been incarcerated (see also Chapter 6). Finally, while many new jobs were created during the economic boom of the 1990s, most of them available to those without a college degree were in lower paying service occupations. As we just saw, blacks and Hispanics are underrepresented among college graduates.

Nevertheless, the disparities between the earnings of African Americans and whites are gradually diminishing. As measured in terms of weekly income, black men now earn 76 percent of the level of pay of whites. In 1959, the proportion was only 49 percent. In terms of household family income (adjusted for inflation), blacks are the only social group to have seen an improvement during the 1990s. By 1995, poverty rates for African Americans had fallen to their lowest rates since the government started tracking the figure in 1955 and continued to improve for the rest of the decade. Milton Morris, who tracks trends among African Americans, claimed "I think that this is a short period of really very substantial and significant gains. . . . [V]ery few people have been paying serious attention. And yet when you do, you see that by virtually every measure of well-being, African-Americans have been on a significant uptrend during the 90s" (quoted in Holmes, 1996). These signs of improvement appear to be felt by African Americans across the country. One Jersey City resident said "In my area, I see things getting better all the time. It used to be like hell, groups always on the corner, cussing and fighting, ripping and raiding, shooting each other. It calmed down a whole hell of a lot" (Holmes, 1996).

Some scholars have warned, however, that these gains could be reversed if the economy were to falter. They also pointed out that though there has been considerable improvement, large gaps between African Americans and whites still exist in terms of the attainment of college degrees, infant mortality, poverty rates, and household income (see Figure 9.4). Finally, though the economic status of blacks appears to have improved, prospects for Hispanics have stagnated or worsened over the same time period. Between 1980 and 1995, Hispanic household incomes (adjusted for inflation) decreased by about 10 percent. For the first time ever, the poverty rate of Hispanics surpassed that of African Americans. The large influx of immigrants, who tend to be poor, has caused some of the decline in average income, but even among Hispanics born in

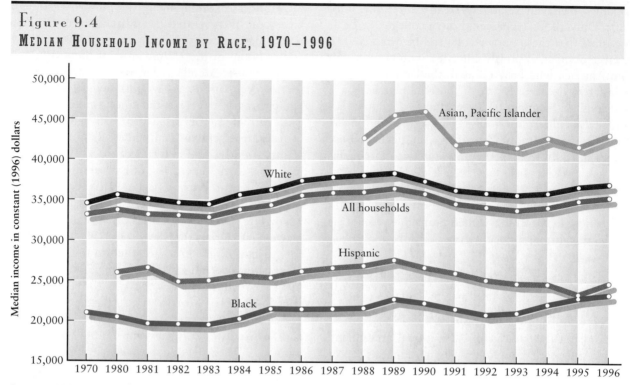

Figure 9.4
MEDIAN HOUSEHOLD INCOME BY RACE, 1970–1996

SOURCE: U.S. Bureau of the Census, 1998.

the United States, income levels declined as well. As one Latino group leader commented, "Most Hispanic residents are caught in jobs like gardener, nanny, and restaurant worker that will never pay well and from which they will never advance" (Goldberg, 1997).

Health

Jake Najman has recently surveyed the evidence linking health to racial and economic inequalities. He also considered what strategies might best be used to improve the health of the poorer groups in society. After studying data for a number of different countries, including the United States, he concluded that for people in the poorest 20 percent, as measured in terms of income, the death rates were 1.5–2.5 times those of the highest 20 percent of income earners. In the

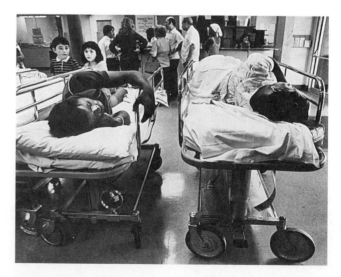

Haitian immigrants wait to be seen in a crowded emergency room in Miami. Blacks have less access to health services than do whites.

United States, the rate of infant mortality for the poorest 20 percent was four times higher than for the wealthiest 20 percent. When differences were measured between white and African American in the United States, rather than only in terms of income, the contrast in infant mortality rates was even higher—five times higher for blacks than for whites. The contrast is also becoming greater rather than less. The same is true of life expectancy—the average age to which individuals at birth can expect to live. In 1984, whites on average could expect to live 5.6 years more than African Americans. By 1996, this had increased to 6.5 years and could increase to 8.2 by 2010.

How might the influence of poverty and race on health be countered? Extensive programs of health education and disease prevention are one possibility. But such programs tend to work better among more prosperous, well-educated groups and in any case usually produce only small changes in behavior. Increased accessibility to health services would help, but probably to a limited degree. The only really effective policy option, Najman argues, would be to attack poverty itself, so as to reduce the income gap between rich and poor (Najman, 1993).

Residential Segregation

Neighborhood segregation seems to have declined little over the past quarter century. Studies show that discriminatory practices between black and white clients in the housing market continue (Lake, 1981). Black and white children now attend the same schools in most rural areas of the South, and in many of the smaller and medium-size cities throughout the country. Most black college students now also go to the same colleges and universities as whites, instead of the traditional all-black institutions (Bullock, 1984). Yet in the larger cities a high level of educational segregation persists as a result of the continuing movement of whites to suburbs or rural environs.

In *American Apartheid* (1993), Douglas Massey and Nancy A. Denton argue that the history of racial segregation and its specific urban form, the black ghetto, are responsible for the perpetuation of black poverty and the continued polarization of black and white.

The persistence of segregation, they say, is not a result of impersonal market forces. Even many middle-class blacks still find themselves segregated from the white society. For them, as for poor blacks, this becomes a self-perpetuating cycle. Affluent blacks who could afford to live in comfortable, predominantly white neighborhoods may deliberately choose not to, because of the struggle for acceptance they know they would face. The black ghetto, the authors conclude, was constructed through a series of well-defined institutional practices of racial discrimination—private behavior and public policies by which whites sought to contain growing urban black populations. Until policy makers, social scientists, and private citizens recognize the crucial role of such institutional discrimination in perpetuating urban poverty and racial injustice, the United States will remain a deeply divided and troubled society.

Political Power

Blacks have made some gains in holding local elective offices; the number of black public officials has increased from 40 in 1960 to over 8,000 today. The numbers of black mayors and judges have increased appreciably. Blacks have been voted into every major political office, except president and vice-president, including areas where white voters predominate. In 1992, after congressional districts were reshaped to give minority candidates more opportunity, a record number of African Americans and Latinos were elected to Congress. Yet these changes are still relatively small scale. Black officials still make up only about 2 percent of the elective offices in the United States. Most of these are in relatively minor local positions. The share of representation that Latinos and African Americans have in Congress is not equal to their overall size in American society. Following the defeat of Senator Carol Moseley-Braun in 1998, the U.S. Senate had no black or Latino members.

Gender and Race

The status of minority women in the United States is especially plagued by inequalities (see Figure 9.5).

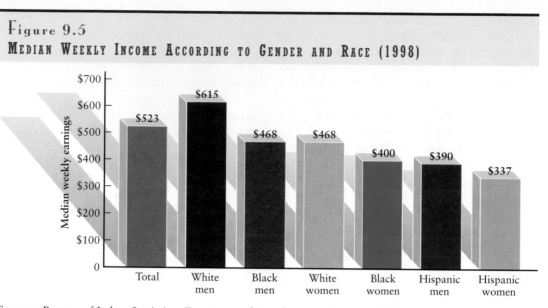

Figure 9.5
MEDIAN WEEKLY INCOME ACCORDING TO GENDER AND RACE (1998)

SOURCE: Bureau of Labor Statistics, *Earnings and Employment,* January 1999.

Gender and race discrimination combined make it particularly difficult for these women to escape conditions of poverty. They share the legacy of past discrimination against members of minority groups and women in general. Until about twenty-five years ago, most minority women worked in low-paying occupations such as household or farm work or low-wage manufacturing jobs. Changes in the law and gains in education have allowed for more minority women to enter white-collar professions, and their economic and occupational status has improved. By 1987, the average African-American female college graduate earned 90 percent of the average for white female college graduates. But in general, female college graduates earn less than men with only high school educations. And white male high school dropouts, on average, earn more than black female college graduates (Rhode, 1990; Higginbotham, 1992).

However unequal the status and pay of minority women, these women play a critical role in their communities. They are often the major or sole wage earners in their families. Yet their incomes are not always sufficient to maintain a family. About half of all households headed by African-American or Latino women live at poverty levels.

Divergent Fortunes

When we survey the development and current position of the major ethnic groups in America, one conclusion that emerges is that they have achieved varying levels of success. Whereas successive waves of European immigrants managed to overcome most of the prejudice and discrimination they originally faced and become assimilated into the wider society, other groups have not. These latter groups include two minorities that have lived in North America for centuries, Native Americans and African Americans, as well as Mexicans, Puerto Ricans, and to some extent Chinese.

THE ECONOMIC DIVIDE WITHIN THE AFRICAN-AMERICAN COMMUNITY

The situation of African Americans is the most conspicuous case of divergent fortunes. After more than two centuries of continuous presence on the North American subcontinent, longer than any other group except for Native Americans and the European settlers, blacks are in the worst situation, with the sole exception of Native Americans, of any ethnic group in the United States. The reasons for this lie in the historical backdrop of slavery and its residue in the long years of struggle that it took to free African Americans from open prejudice and discrimination.

It seems probable that a division has opened up between the minority of blacks who have obtained white-collar, managerial, or professional jobs—who form a small black middle class—and the majority whose living conditions have not improved. In 1960, most of the nonmanual-labor jobs open to blacks were those serving the black community—a small proportion of blacks could work as teachers, social workers, or less often, lawyers or doctors. No more than some 13 percent of blacks held white-collar jobs, contrasted to 44 percent of whites. Since that date, however, there have been significant changes. Between 1960 and 1970, the percentage of blacks in white-collar occupations doubled—although this level of growth slowed markedly in the 1980s. This increase was greater than that for the half century previous to 1960.

Bart Landry carried out a systematic study of the growing black middle class (1988). He surveyed white-collar blacks and whites in twenty-one metropolitan areas across the country, and also analyzed government statistics from the early 1980s. Landry found that middle-class blacks were much better off, and much more numerous, than their predecessors twenty years before. Opportunities have opened up partly through changes in legislation brought into being as a result of the civil rights movement. However, the population of blacks in middle-class jobs remains well below that of whites, and their average incomes are less.

THE ASIAN SUCCESS STORY

Unlike African Americans, other minority groups have outlasted the open prejudice and discrimination they once faced. The intense hostility once held toward the Irish, for instance, is now mostly a distant memory. Feelings of prejudice and antagonism still exist between people of Irish and Italian backgrounds in Boston and New York, and from both groups toward Jews. For the most part, however, such feelings are much less pronounced than in former times and are not widely expressed in practices of discrimination.

The changing fate of Asians in the United States is especially remarkable. Until about half a century ago, the level of prejudice and discrimination experienced by the Chinese and Japanese in North America was greater than for any other group of nonblack immigrants. Since that time, Asian Americans have achieved a steadily increasing prosperity and no longer face the same levels of antagonism from the white community. The median income of Asian Americans is now actually higher than that of whites.

This statistic conceals some big discrepancies between and within different Asian groups; there are

Asian American families have experienced a growth of real income in the last fifty years.

still many Asian Americans, including those whose families have resided in the United States for generations, who live in poverty. However, the turnaround in the fortunes of Asian Americans, on the whole, is so impressive that some have referred to the Asian-American "success story" as a prime example of what minorities can achieve in the United States.

LATINOS: A TALE OF TWO CITIES

Miami and Los Angeles both have large Latino populations. In Los Angeles, the large majority of Latinos are well down the ladder of privilege and power. But although both cities experience ethnic tensions, in Miami, Latinos have achieved a position of economic and political prominence not found elsewhere.

In *City on the Edge*, Alejandro Portes and Alex Stepik describe the ethnic transformation of Miami over recent years. In 1980, whites were already in a minority in the city, at 48 percent of the population. African Americans made up 17 percent, and those of Spanish origin, 35 percent. In that year, as Portes and Stepik put it, "the city abandoned, once and for all, the image of a sunny tourist destination and faced that of an uncertain bridge between two worlds" (1993). The reason was a large influx of Cuban immigrants. Struggles developed between the new immigrants, whites, and blacks; black leaders accused the Cubans of taking their jobs.

These struggles continue today. In Miami, those of Cuban origin have often moved into positions of considerable influence. Some Cubans have become very successful in business and have become more wealthy than the "old" white families that once ran the city. They haven't been assimilated into the white community but maintain their own customs, institutions, and language. Miami is now a place of "parallel structures" existing alongside one another, each including powerful and wealthy people, not integrated into one unified group. There is much tension, but some Anglo and Cuban politicians now speak of Miami as the capital of the Caribbean—a city not only part of the United States, but looking also to the other societies, mostly Third World countries, surrounding it.

Los Angeles points to the Pacific Rim—to what some analysts see as the future center of economic power, linking the West Coast of North America with Japan and the newly industrializing countries of Hong Kong, Taiwan, South Korea, and perhaps China. Immigrants from all of these countries have recently arrived in Los Angeles. At the same time, millions of Latinos have now settled in the city.

Los Angeles has been referred to as "the capital of the Third World" because of its large Latino and Asian populations. The city already contained the largest group of Mexicans in the United States in the 1920s. Then, as now, it was Mexicans who performed most of the menial jobs. Then, as now, most Anglos "were at once aware that this was the case," and "yet they would act as if these people, once they had finished working, went home not to the Old Plaza or, as now, to East LA, but to another planet" (Rieff, 1991).

Some optimistic observers have suggested that Los Angeles in the next century will combine Asian family loyalty, Hispanic industriousness, and Anglo-Saxon respect for individual liberty. Is such a vision possible? It would certainly take some profound social changes even to come close. Los Angeles is an ethnic mosaic that symbolizes the increasing diversity of American society as a whole. Will the Hispanic population of the city be able to achieve economic success similar to the Cubans in Miami? Will there exist separate but equal Hispanic communities in Los Angeles as well as in other U.S. cities in the future? How will such successes, if they happen, affect the black urban poor? These are all at the moment open questions, to which no one can give certain answers.

Understanding Racial Inequality

What distinguishes less fortunate groups such as African Americans and Mexican Americans is not just that they are nonwhite, but that they were originally present in America as *colonized peoples* rather than willing immigrants. In a classic analysis, Robert Blauner (1972) suggested that a sharp distinction should be drawn between groups who journeyed voluntarily to settle in the new land and those who were incorporated into the society through force or violence. Native Americans are part of American society as a result of military conquest; African Americans were transported in the slave trade; Puerto Rico was colonized as a result of war; and Mexicans were originally incorporated as a result of the conquest of the Southwest by the United States in the nineteenth century. These groups have consistently been the target of racism, which both reflects and perpetuates their separation from other ethnic communities.

But, given that this has been the case for most of American history, what explains the growth of the black middle class? William Julius Wilson (1978; see also Wilson et al., 1987) has argued that race is of diminishing importance in explaining inequalities between whites and blacks. In his view, these inequalities are now based upon class rather than skin color. The old racist barriers are crumbling. What remain are inequalities similar to those affecting all lower-class groups.

Wilson's work has proved controversial. His book was awarded a prize by the American Sociological Association, but the Association of Black Sociologists passed a resolution stating that the book "omits significant data regarding the continuing discrimination against blacks at all class levels." "It is the consensus of this organization," the resolution continues, "that this book denies the overwhelming evidence regarding the significance of race and the literature that speaks to the contrary." The resolution criticized the view that the circumstances of blacks have substantially improved, or even that racism has declined significantly. Most of the changes, it was argued, have been relatively minor, and racism has only become less vocal since the 1964 Civil Rights Act, rather than diminishing in any substantial sense (Pinkney, 1984).

Yet Wilson had made it clear in his book that the living conditions of poor blacks were deteriorating. In Wilson's view, his critics have almost completely ignored this aspect of his work. He has since extended his analysis of the most deprived sectors of the black population. Middle-class blacks today tend no longer to live in ghetto neighborhoods. Their exodus has led to an even higher concentration of the disadvantaged in these areas than previously was the case. Wilson recognizes that racism plays a part in this situation of the disadvantaged, but points out that other class-related and economic factors are at least equally important—in particular, the very high rate of unemployment and welfare dependency characteristic of the poorest neighborhoods. Wilson's argument is not so much that racism as such has declined, but that it has declined in its *significance* for blacks. Other forms of discrimination based more upon economic and class-based disadvantages are as important.

Are racial inequalities to be explained primarily in terms of class? It is true that racial divisions provide a means of social closure, whereby economic resources can be monopolized by privileged class groups. But the argument that racial inequality should be explained primarily in terms of class domination, however, has never been a satisfactory one. Ethnic discrimination, particularly of a racial kind, is partly independent of class differences: the one cannot be separated from the other. This still seems to remain true in the United States today.

For instance, opinion surveys show a general decline in hostile attitudes toward blacks over the past thirty years among white Americans (Schuman, Steel, and Bobo, 1985; Bobo and Kluegel, 1991). The overall level of prejudice seems to be diminishing fairly markedly. David Wellman has argued, however, that the concept of prejudice only captures the more open and individual forms of hostile attitudes toward ethnic minorities. Racism can also be expressed in more subtle ways—in terms of beliefs that, regardless of the intentions involved, defend the position of privileged groups. Many sociologists, according to Wellman, have underestimated the true incidence of racism, because they have looked only at its more obvious manifestations. Most studies have investigated prejudice using surveys; but these do not get at the less obvious, complex aspects of people's views about such emotive topics as ethnicity and race.

Wellman sought to illuminate these complex aspects of racism by means of in-depth interviews with 105 white Americans of varying backgrounds. Most of those he interviewed said that they believed that everyone is equal, and that they held no hostility toward blacks. Their beliefs and attitudes did not show the rigidities characteristic of prejudice and stereotypical thinking. Yet their views about contexts of social life (such as education, housing, or jobs) in which black rights threatened their own position were effectively anti-black. Their opposition to change was expressed in ways that did not directly express racial antagonism. People would say, for instance, "I'm not opposed to blacks; but if they come into the neighborhood house prices will be affected"—or, as one individual put it, "I favor anything that doesn't affect me personally" (Wellman, 1987).

These attitudes can still underlie quite rigid institutional patterns of discrimination. Ethnic inequalities are structured into existing social institutions, and patterns of behavior having no immediate connection to ethnicity can serve to reinforce them. Rights and opportunities are not the same thing. Even if it were true that every member of the population accepted that members of all ethnic groups have the same civil rights, major inequalities would persist. There are many examples that demonstrate this. A black person who wishes to obtain a bank loan in order to be able to make home improvements finds it hard to borrow money. The bank might use purely "objective" measures in reaching such decisions, based on the likeli-

hood of the loan repayments being successfully made. Nevertheless, the effect of this institutional racism is the perpetuation of ethnic discrimination (Massey and Denton, 1993).

In sum, although both individual and institutional racism seem to be declining in the United States, the differences between white and nonwhite ethnic groups are long enduring (Ringer, 1985; Conley, 1999). Moreover, the relative success of white ethnics has been to some degree purchased at the expense of nonwhites. A combination of continued white immigration and white racism, up to at least the World War II period, served to keep nonwhites out of the better-paid occupations, forcing them into the least-skilled, most marginal sectors of the economy. With the slowing down of white immigration, this situation is changing, although some newly arrived groups, like the Cubans in Miami, seem to be repeating the process.

SUMMARY

1. Ethnic groups have common cultural characteristics that separate them from others within a given population. Ethnic differences are wholly learned, although they are sometimes depicted as "natural."

2. A *minority group* is one whose members are discriminated against by the majority population in a society. Members of minority groups often have a strong sense of group solidarity, deriving in part from the collective experience of exclusion.

3. *Race* refers to physical characteristics, such as skin color, that are treated by members of a community or society as socially significant—as signaling distinct cultural characteristics. Many popular beliefs about race are mythical. There are no distinct characteristics by means of which human beings can be allocated to different races.

4. *Racism* is prejudice based on socially significant physical distinctions. A *racist* is someone who believes that some individuals are superior, or inferior, to others as a result of racial differences.

5. *Displacement* and *scapegoating* are psychological mechanisms associated with *prejudice* and *discrimination*. In displacement, feelings of hostility become directed against objects that are not the real origin of these anxieties. People project their anxieties and insecurities onto scapegoats. Prejudice involves holding preconceived views about an individual or group; discrimination refers to actual behavior that deprives members of a group of opportunities open to others. Prejudice usually involves *stereotypes*—fixed and inflexible categories of thought.

6. *Group closure* and *differential allocation of resources* are important parts of many situations of ethnic antagonism. However, some of the fundamental aspects of modern ethnic conflicts, especially racist attitudes held by whites against blacks, have to be understood in terms of the expansion of the West and of colonialism.

7. Four models of possible future developments in race and ethnic relations can be distinguished—the first stressing Anglo-conformity, or *assimilation*, the

second the *melting pot*, the third *pluralism*, and the fourth *multiculturalism*. In recent years there has been a tendency to emphasize the fourth of these avenues, whereby different ethnic identities are accepted as equal and separate within the context of the overall national culture.

8. Historical examples illustrate various ways in which societies have dealt with ethnic diversity, ranging from slavery and *apartheid* to cultural integration.

9. A remarkable diversity of ethnic minorities is found in the United States today, each group having its own distinctive cultural characteristics. Some of the most important minority communities numerically, after blacks, are Native Americans, Mexican Americans, Puerto Ricans, Cubans, Chinese, and Japanese.

10. An important distinction must be drawn between those minorities that came to America as willing immigrants, and the colonized peoples who either were here already (Native Americans, Mexican Americans) or were brought by force (African Americans, Chinese) and who were generally incorporated by violence. Racism targeted at these latter groups has been most persistent and most destructive. Gender discrimination compounds the difficulties facing women of color; about half of African American and Latino families that depend primarily on women's incomes live in poverty.

Chapter Ten

© Will Barnet. Licensed by VAGA, New York.

Learn two important theories of organization, and see how rapidly organizations are changing in the modern world.

Theories of Organizations

Know how to define an organization, and understand how they developed over the last two centuries. Learn Max Weber's theory of organization and view of bureaucracy. Understand the importance of the physical setting of organizations and Michel Foucault's theory about surveillance. Think about the potential conflicts between bureaucracy and democracy identified by these theorists.

Beyond Bureaucracy?

Familiarize yourself with some of the alternatives to bureaucracy that have developed in other societies or in recent times. Think about the influence of technology on how organizations operate.

THE RISE OF MODERN ORGANIZATIONS

Once upon a time, we were all born in our own dwellings. Women virtually always gave birth in the place where they lived, and people attached a great deal of significance to the exact spot where they were born—in the local community or village, in this house or that house, in this room or that. Usually, birth took place in the main, or communal, room of the woman's home. As soon as the first contractions started, local women would gather to assist her. Women usually gave birth in front of the hearth, especially if the weather outside was cold. Straw was brought in and scattered on the floor, in more or less the same way as it was done in the cowshed when a calf was born.

Women in childbirth had no other resources save for those the community could offer. For centuries, the idea of calling on help outside the community was alien to the ways of thinking of women of the villages. "Women helping one another" and "giving mutual assistance" are phrases that crop up constantly in the

Only for a few decades have most Americans been born in hospitals.

simply play a role in helping out in earlier phases of pregnancy. The birth process itself is controlled and monitored by the professionals within the hospital—doctors, nurses, and other medical staff.

A modern hospital is a good example of an **organization**. An organization is a large grouping of people, structured upon impersonal lines and set up to achieve specific objectives; in the case of the hospital, these objectives are the curing of illness and other forms of medical attention.

FORMAL ORGANIZATIONS

Most social systems in the traditional world developed over lengthy periods as a result of custom and habit. Organizations, on the other hand, are mostly designed—established with definite aims in view and housed in buildings or physical settings specifically constructed to help realize those aims the edifices in which hospitals, colleges, or business firms carry on their activities are mostly "custom-built."

In traditional societies, most people lived in small group settings. In a society like traditional China, it was rare for members of a local village community ever to meet a government official. Government edicts barely affected their lives.

In current times, organizations play a much more important part in our everyday lives than was ever true previously. Besides delivering us into this world, they also mark our progress through it and see us out of it when we die. Even before we are born, our mothers, and probably our fathers too, are involved in classes, pregnancy checkups, and so forth, carried out within hospitals and other medical organizations. Every child born today is registered by government organizations, which collect information on us from birth to death. Most people today die in a hospital—not at home, as was once the case—and each death must be formally registered with the government too.

Every time you use the phone, turn on the faucet or TV, or get into a car, you are in contact with, and to some extent dependent upon, organizations. And usually this will mean many organizations, all interacting in a regular way with each other besides with you. The water company, for example, makes it possible for you to take for granted that water will pour out when you turn the faucet on. But the water company is in turn dependent on other organizations, such as

writings of priests and administrators who reported on childbirth in the eighteenth and early nineteenth centuries. The key figure was the midwife, a woman experienced in assisting at births. A midwife was originally known as the "good mother": she was someone who could cope with the pains and problems of younger women at key times in their pregnancy and at the birth itself. A document written in France in the 1820s indicates the qualities the midwife was expected to have. She needed to be "strong, sturdy, nimble, graceful, with no bodily defects, with long supple hands." The spiritual side was no less important: she should be "virtuous, discreet, prudent, of good conduct and regular habits" (Gelis, 1991).

Until about the 1950s, most people in the United States were born in their own homes, and the midwife continued to play an important role. Today, however, the practice of giving birth in a hospital is almost universal, and this change has brought other important transformations in its wake. Few of us any longer feel an emotional connection with our place of birth. Why should we? That place is now a large, impersonal hospital. After having existed for many centuries, midwives have now either disappeared completely or those that construct and service reservoirs, which are themselves dependent on others . . . and so on almost indefinitely. You turn on the faucet in your own home, but the water probably comes from miles away. The water company—or, more normally, a whole group of water companies—must supply not only you but thousands or millions of others simultaneously. You can multiply what the water company does dozens of times; for counting on a regular supply of water is only one way in which we are dependent upon organizations.

It is easy to see why organizations are so important to us today. In the premodern world, families, close relatives and neighbors provided for most needs—food, the instruction of children, work and leisure-time activities. In modern times, the mass of the population is much more *interdependent* than was ever the case before. Many of our requirements are catered for by people we never meet, and who indeed might live many thousands of miles away. A tremendous amount of coordination of activities and resources—which organizations provide—is needed in such circumstances.

It should be remembered that for most of human history, before the level of organizational development became as great as it is now, people couldn't count on ways of life to which we now give barely a second thought. For example, a century ago in the United States, very few houses were equipped with a regular supply of piped water, and much

of the water people used was polluted and responsible for illnesses and epidemics. Even today, in large areas of the less developed societies (for example, Asia or Africa), there is no piped water; people gather water each day from a spring or well, and much of it contains bacteria that spread disease. In modern societies, drinking water is carefully checked for contamination; this involves yet more organizations, the health standards authorities.

One of the best ways to begin to think about the nature of organizations is to consider the university or college to which you belong. These institutions vary in size, but even the smallest are very large compared with virtually any groups in premodern societies. "Small" colleges may have two or three thousand members, while the biggest universities number seventy thousand or more. Running a college involves a permanent administrative apparatus, together with rules or procedures that students and professors are expected to follow—governing, for example, the teaching and grading of courses. Besides the student body, there are numerous different types of people involved in a college, when it is looked at as an organization. Professors, administrators, service personnel, campus officers of various sorts, police, and many others form part of the system. For the college to keep going from day to day, the activities of these groups have to be coordinated with one another, and resources have to be fed in from the outside (for example, finances to pay salaries, maintain buildings and services).

The tremendous influence organizations have come to exert over our lives cannot be seen as wholly beneficial. Organizations often have the effect of taking things out of our own hands and putting them under the control of officials or experts over whom we have little influence. For instance, we are all *required* to do certain things the government tells us—pay taxes, abide by laws, go off to fight wars—or face punishment. As sources of social power, organizations can thus subject the individual to dictates she may be powerless to resist.

In this chapter, we will look at the rise of modern organizations and the consequences this development has for our lives today. We shall first analyze the ideas of two writers who have had an especially strong impact on how sociologists think of organizations: Max Weber and Michel Foucault. We shall then look at

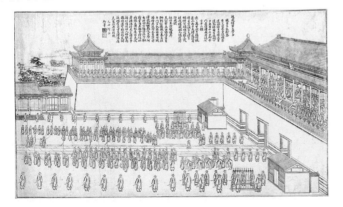

The imperial Chinese court during the Qing dynasty, a bureaucracy within a traditional civilization.

some of the ways in which organizations work. There are many different forms of organizations, from hospitals to schools, government offices, colleges, and prisons, and we will study what differences exist between these various types. In the concluding sections, we shall consider how far organizations in modern societies are becoming subject to major processes of change.

THEORIES OF ORGANIZATIONS

Max Weber developed the first systematic interpretation of the rise of modern organizations. Organizations, he argued, are ways of coordinating the activities of human beings, or the goods they produce, in a stable way across space and time. Weber emphasized that the development of organizations depends upon the control of information, and he stressed the central importance of writing in this process: an organization needs written rules for its functioning and files in which its "memory" is stored. Weber saw organizations as strongly hierarchical, with power tending to be concentrated at the top. Was Weber right? If he was, it matters a great deal to us all. For Weber detected a clash as well as a connection between modern organizations and democracy that he believed had far-reaching consequences for social life.

Weber's View of Bureaucracy

All large-scale organizations, according to Weber, tend to be bureaucratic in nature. The word "bureaucracy" was coined by a Monsieur de Gournay in 1745, who added to the word "bureau," meaning both an office and a writing table, a term derived from the Greek verb "to rule." **Bureaucracy** is thus the rule of officials. The term was first applied only to government officials, but it gradually became extended to refer to large organizations in general.

From the beginning the concept was used in a disparaging way. De Gournay spoke of the developing power of officials as "an illness called bureaumania." The French novelist Honoré de Balzac saw bureau-

cracy as "the giant power wielded by pygmies." This sort of view has persisted into current times: bureaucracy is frequently associated with red tape, inefficiency, and wastefulness. Other writers, however, have seen bureaucracy in a different light—as a model of carefulness, precision, and effective administration. Bureaucracy, they argue, is in fact the most efficient form of organization human beings have devised, because all tasks are regulated by strict rules of procedure.

Weber's account of bureaucracy steers a way between these two extremes. A limited number of bureaucratic organizations, he pointed out, existed in the traditional civilizations. For example, a bureaucratic officialdom in imperial China was responsible for the overall affairs of government. But it is only in modern times that bureaucracies have developed fully.

According to Weber, the expansion of bureaucracy is inevitable in modern societies; bureaucratic authority is the only way of coping with the administrative requirements of large-scale social systems. However, Weber also believed bureaucracy to exhibit a number of major failings, as we will see, which have important implications for the nature of modern social life.

In order to study the origins and nature of the expansion of bureaucratic organizations, Weber constructed an **ideal type of bureaucracy**. ("Ideal" here refers not to what is most desirable, but to a pure form of bureaucratic organization. An ideal type is an abstract description constructed by accentuating certain features of real cases so as to pinpoint their most essential characteristics.) Weber listed several characteristics of the ideal type of bureaucracy (1977):

1. THERE IS A CLEAR-CUT HIERARCHY OF AUTHORITY, such that tasks in the organization are distributed as "official duties." A bureaucracy looks like a pyramid, with the positions of highest authority at the top. There is a chain of command stretching from top to bottom, thus making coordinated decision-making possible. Each higher office controls and supervises the one below it in the hierarchy.

2. WRITTEN RULES GOVERN THE CONDUCT OF OFFICIALS AT ALL LEVELS OF THE ORGANIZATION. This does not mean that bureaucratic duties are just a matter of routine. The higher the office, the

more the rules tend to encompass a wide variety of cases and demand flexibility in their interpretation.

3. OFFICIALS ARE FULL-TIME AND SALARIED. Each job in the hierarchy has a definite and fixed salary attached to it. Individuals are expected to make a career within the organization. Promotion is possible on the basis of capability, seniority, or a mixture of the two.

4. THERE IS A SEPARATION BETWEEN THE TASKS OF AN OFFICIAL WITHIN THE ORGANIZATION AND HIS LIFE OUTSIDE. The home life of the official is distinct from his activities in the workplace, and is also physically separated from it.

5. NO MEMBERS OF THE ORGANIZATION OWN THE MATERIAL RESOURCES WITH WHICH THEY OPERATE. The development of bureaucracy, according to Weber, separates workers from the control of their means of production. In traditional communities, farmers and craft workers usually had control over their processes of production and owned the tools they used. In bureaucracies, officials do not own the offices they work in, the desks they sit at, or the office machinery they use.

Weber believed that the more an organization approaches the ideal type of bureaucracy, the more effective it will be in pursuing the objectives for which it was established. He often likened bureaucracies to sophisticated machines operating by the principle of **rationality** (see Chapter 1). Yet he recognized that bureaucracy could be inefficient and accepted that many bureaucratic jobs are dull, offering little opportunity for the exercise of creative capabilities. While Weber feared that the rationalization of society could have negative consequences, he concluded that bureaucratic routine and the authority of officialdom over our lives are prices we pay for the technical effectiveness of bureaucratic organizations. Since Weber's time, the rationalization of society has become more widespread. Critics of this development who share Weber's initial concerns have questioned whether the efficiency of rational organizations comes at a price greater than Weber could have imagined. The most prominent of these critiques is known as "the McDonaldization of society."

THE SOCIOLOGICAL DEBATE

THE McDONALDIZATION OF SOCIETY

In *The McDonaldization of Society* (1993), sociologist George Ritzer argues that American society and its organizations are increasingly adopting the four principles of rationalization that guide the operations of McDonald's fast-food restaurant chain: efficiency, predictability, control, and calculability. The outcome of this "McDonaldization" process? Ritzer argues that American society has become one where the human spirit is stripped of creativity, and inefficiencies and injustices are perpetuated by the mechanized, McDonaldized society. Yet several British sociologists counter that McDonaldization does not necessarily lead to a homogenized culture. To the contrary, Malcolm Waters and Shannon Peters Talbot argue that McDonaldization makes way for cultural diversity, because local cultures can influence the operations of such businesses (Waters, 1996; Talbot, 1996).

What exactly is McDonaldization? According to Ritzer, McDonaldization is "the process by which the principles of the fast-food restaurants are coming to dominate more and more sectors of American society as well as the rest of the world." The principles of rationality guide the operations of the fast-food industry. Rationality can be described as a value that emphasizes the importance of setting goals and objectives, and then achieving these goals in the most efficient way possible. Rationality has four components: efficiency, predictability, control, and calculability.

Efficiency, or an emphasis on minimizing time and cost and maximizing output and productivity, is epitomized by McDonald's, argues Ritzer. The restaurant chain offers efficiency by quickly serving its customers. Because both the customers and employees value the speed with which food can be prepared and eaten, the restaurant offers a limited, simple menu with the food prepared and served in an automated fashion. *Predictability* refers to the fact that the quality and content of food and service are uniform throughout the restaurant system, thus customers can accurately predict what their experience of eating at McDonald's will be like. This predictability is attributable to the high level of control exercised over the preparation of food, training of employees, and procedures for serving customers. *Control,* Ritzer's third principle of rationality, refers to the substitution of nonhuman technology for human judgments. For example, McDonald's has developed french-fry machines that ring or buzz when the fries are cooked. If left to an employee's judgment, the results could be undercooked or overcooked fries. Finally, *calculability* refers to the exact measurement of every aspect of the process at McDonald's. Ritzer writes that calculability is "an emphasis on the quantitative aspects of the products sold (portion, size, cost) and service offered (the time it takes to get the product)." McDonald's is not alone in their reliance on these four principles. The success of the chain has been mimicked by numerous fast-food restaurants, as well as by business and service industry firms.

Ritzer argues that the harmful effects of McDonaldization are sweeping, and he echoes Max Weber's observation that increasing rationalization has made social life more homogeneous, more rigid, and less personal. It has led to an entrapment in Weber's "iron cage," a bureaucratic culture that requires little thought and leaves virtually nothing to chance. Ritzer also questions whether McDonaldization really *does* allow society to operate most efficiently. Rather, he proposes that "the ultimate irrationality of McDonaldization is that people could lose control over the system and it would come to control us . . . Rational systems inevitably spawn a series of irrationalities that limit, eventually compromise, and perhaps even undermine their rationality."

An example is managed health care. By attempting to limit the amount of time a doctor spends with a patient, the insurance companies hope to please their customers because the doctor will be making the most efficient use of his or her time. The obvious irrationality of this is that the doctor can't know in advance how much time a patient will need. If a doctor is forced to make a diagnosis and prescription in a given amount of time, this can possibly lead to hurried diagnoses, and mistakes. Other outcomes might include longer rather than shorter wait times, more work for

the customer, the dehumanization of both the worker and customer, and dangerous anomalies that arise from these inefficiencies.

Not all sociologists concur with Ritzer's pessimistic prognosis, however. Sociologist Malcolm Waters (1995) argues that the McDonaldization process does not necessarily lead to homogenization; to the contrary, it makes way for cultural diversity, because successful corporations adapt their cultures to the local areas in which they do business. The global reach of McDonaldization leads to a far greater availability of consumer goods and services through cultural diffusion and allows individuals a wider choice of what products to purchase. A case study of the Moscow McDonald's, conducted by Shannon Peters Talbot, shows that McDonald's actually adapts to the local circumstances by offering, for example, Russian pirozhok (potato, mushroom, and cheese pies) as well as hamburgers, thus warding off the homogenization process that Ritzer fears.

Formal and Informal Relations within Bureaucracies

Weber's analysis of bureaucracy gave prime place to **formal relations** within organizations, the relations between people as stated in the rules of the organization. Weber had little to say about the informal connections and small-group relations that may exist in all organizations. But in bureaucracies, informal ways of doing things often allow for a flexibility that couldn't otherwise be achieved.

In a classic study, Peter Blau studied **informal relations** in a government agency (Blau, 1963) whose task was to investigate possible income-tax violations. Agents who came across problems they were unsure how to deal with were supposed to discuss them with their immediate supervisor; the rules of procedure stated that they should not consult colleagues working at the same level as themselves. Most officials were wary of approaching their supervisors, however, because they felt this might suggest a lack of competence on their part and reduce their promotion chances. Hence, they usually consulted each other, violating the official rules. This not only helped to provide concrete advice; it also reduced the anxieties involved in working alone. A cohesive set of loyalties of a primary group kind developed among those working at the same level. The problems these workers faced, Blau concludes, were probably coped with much more effectively as a result. The group was able to evolve informal procedures allowing for more initiative and responsibility than was provided for by the formal rules of the organization.

Informal networks tend to develop at all levels of organizations. At the very top, personal ties and connections may be more important than the formal situations in which decisions are supposed to be made. For example, meetings of boards of directors and shareholders supposedly determine the policies of business corporations. In practice, a few members of the board often really run the corporation, making their decisions informally and expecting the board to approve them. Informal networks of this sort can also stretch across different corporations. Business leaders from different firms frequently consult one another in an informal way, and may belong to the same clubs and leisure-time associations.

John Meyer and Brian Rowan (1977) argue that formal rules and procedures in organizations are usually quite distant from the practices actually adopted by the organizations' members. Formal rules, in their view, are often "myths" that people profess to follow but which have little substance in reality. They serve

Informal relations, particularly in the upper levels of power, are often as important as formal structures within bureaucracies.

to legitimate—to justify   ways in which tasks are carried out, even while these ways may diverge greatly from how things are "supposed to be done."

Formal procedures, Meyer and Rowan point out, often have a ceremonial or ritual character. People

KEY CONCEPTS IN REVIEW

An **organization** is a large association of people run on impersonal lines, set up to achieve specific objectives.

Bureaucracy literally means the rule of officials. To a large degree, all modern organizations are bureaucratic in nature.

Max Weber theorized that the **ideal type of bureaucracy** included the following characteristics: hierarchy of authority, written rules, full-time and salaried officials, separation of work and home life, ownership not in the workers' hands.

Although Weber's theory emphasizes **formal relations** within organizations, **informal relations**, such as personal connections and ties, are equally important.

will make a show of conforming to them in order to get on with their real work using other, more informal procedures. For example, rules governing ward procedure in a hospital help justify how nurses act toward patients in caring for them. Thus a nurse will faithfully fill in a patient's chart that hangs at the end of the bed, but will check the patient's progress by means of other, informal criteria—"how well the person is looking," and whether he or she seems alert and lively. Rigorously keeping up the charts impresses the patients and keeps the doctors happy, but is not always essential to the nurse's assessments.

Deciding how far informal procedures generally help or hinder the effectiveness of organizations is not a simple matter. Systems that resemble Weber's ideal type tend to give rise to a forest of unofficial ways of doing things. This is partly because the flexibility that is lacking can be achieved by unofficial tinkering with formal rules. For those in dull jobs, informal procedures often also help to create a more satisfying work environment. Informal connections between officials in higher positions may be effective in ways that aid the organization as a whole. On the other hand, these officials may be more concerned to advance or protect their own interests than to further those of the overall organization.

The Physical Setting of Organizations

Most modern organizations function in specially designed physical settings. A building that houses a particular organization possesses specific features relevant to the organization's activities, but it also shares important architectural characteristics with buildings of other organizations. The architecture of a hospital, for instance, differs in some respects from that of a business firm or a school. The hospital's separate wards, consulting rooms, operating rooms, and offices give the overall building a definite layout, while a school may consist of classrooms, laboratories, and a gymnasium. Yet there is a general resemblance: both are likely to contain hallways with doors leading off, and to use standard decoration and furnishings throughout. Apart from the differing dress of the people moving through the corridors, the buildings in

which modern organizations are usually housed have a definite sameness to them. And they often look similar from the outside as well as within their interiors. It would not be unusual to ask, on driving past a building, "Is that a school?" and receive the response "No, it's a hospital." Although major internal modifications will be required, it can happen that a school takes over buildings that once housed a hospital.

MICHEL FOUCAULT'S THEORY OF ORGANIZATIONS: THE CONTROL OF TIME AND SPACE

Michel Foucault showed that the architecture of an organization is directly involved with its social makeup and system of authority (Foucault, 1971, 1979). By studying the physical characteristics of organizations, we can shed new light on the problems Weber analyzed. The offices Weber discussed abstractly are also architectural settings—rooms, separated by corridors. The buildings of large firms are sometimes actually constructed physically as a hierarchy, in which the more elevated one's position in the hierarchy of authority, the nearer the top one's office is; the phrase "the top floor" is sometimes used to mean those who hold ultimate power in the organization.

In many other ways, the geography of an organization will affect its functioning, especially in cases where systems rely heavily on informal relationships. Physical proximity makes forming primary groups easier, while physical distance can polarize groups, resulting in a "them" and "us" attitude between departments.

SURVEILLANCE IN ORGANIZATIONS

The arrangement of rooms, hallways, and open spaces in an organization's buildings can provide basic clues to how its system of authority operates. In some organizations, groups of people work collectively in open settings. Because of the dull, repetitive nature of certain kinds of industrial work, like assembly-line production, regular supervision is needed to ensure that workers sustain the pace of labor. The same is often true of routine work carried out by typists, who sit together in the typing pool, where their activities are visible to their superiors. Foucault laid great emphasis on how visibility, or lack of it, in the architectural settings of modern organizations influences and expresses patterns of authority. Their visibility determines how easily subordinates can be subject to what Foucault calls **surveillance,** the supervision of activities in organizations. In modern organizations, everyone, even in relatively high positions of authority, is subject to surveillance; but the more lowly a person is, the more her behavior tends to be closely scrutinized.

Surveillance takes two forms. One is the direct supervision of the work of subordinates by superiors. Consider the example of a school classroom. Pupils sit at tables or desks, usually arranged in rows, all in view of the teacher. Children are supposed to look alert or otherwise be absorbed in their work. Of course, how far this actually happens in practice depends on the abilities of the teacher and the inclinations of the children to conform to what is expected of them.

The second type of surveillance is more subtle but equally important. It consists in keeping files, records, and case histories about people's lives. Weber saw the importance of written records (nowadays often computerized) in modern organizations, but did not fully explore how they can be used to regulate behavior. Employee records usually provide complete work histories, registering personal details and often giving character evaluations. Such records are used to monitor employees' behavior and assess recommendations for promotion. In many business firms, individuals at each level in the organization prepare annual reports on the performance of those in the levels just below them. School records and college transcripts are also used to monitor individuals' performance as they move through the organization. References are kept on file for academic staff, too.

Organizations cannot operate effectively if employees' work is haphazard. In business firms, as Weber pointed out, people are expected to work regular hours. Activities must be consistently coordinated in time and space, something promoted both by the physical settings and by the precise scheduling of detailed timetables. **Timetables** regularize activities across time and space—in Foucault's words, they "efficiently distribute bodies" around the organization. Timetables are the condition of organizational discipline, because they slot the activities of large numbers of people together. If a university did not strictly observe a lecture timetable, for example, it would soon collapse into complete chaos. A timetable makes possible the intensive use of time and space: each can be packed with many people and many activities.

UNDER SURVEILLANCE! THE PRISON

Foucault paid a great deal of attention to organizations, like prisons, in which individuals are physically separated for long periods from the outside world. In such organizations, people are incarcerated—kept hidden away—from the external social environment. A prison illustrates in clear detail the nature of surveillance because it seeks to maximize control over inmates' behavior. Foucault asks, "Is it surprising that

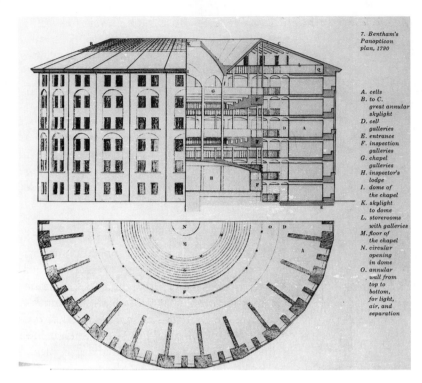

7. Bentham's
Panopticon
plan, 1790

A. cells
B. to C.
   great annular
   skylight
D. cell
   galleries
E. entrance
F. inspection
   galleries
G. chapel
   galleries
H. inspector's
   lodge
I. dome of
   the chapel
K. skylight
   to dome
L. storerooms
   with galleries
M. floor of
   the chapel
N. circular
   opening
   in dome
O. annular
   wall from
   top to
   bottom,
   for light,
   air, and
   separation

A drawing of Jeremy Bentham's proposed Panopticon, a prison designed for maximum surveillance.

prisons resemble factories, schools, barracks, hospitals, which all resemble prisons?" (1979).

According to Foucault, the modern prison has its origins in the Panopticon, an organization planned by the philosopher and social thinker Jeremy Bentham in the nineteenth century. "Panopticon" was the name Bentham gave to an ideal prison he designed, which he tried on various occasions to sell to the British government. The design was never fully implemented, but some of its main principles were incorporated in prisons built in the nineteenth century in the United States, Britain, and Europe. The Panopticon was circular in shape, with the cells built around the outside edge. In the center was an inspection tower. Two windows were placed in every cell, one facing the inspection tower and the other facing outside. The aim of the design was to make prisoners visible to guards at all times. The windows in the tower itself were equipped with venetian blinds, so that while the prison staff could keep the prisoners under constant observation, they themselves could be invisible.

THE LIMITS OF SURVEILLANCE

Foucault was right about prisons. Even today, most prisons look remarkably like the Panopticon. He was also right about the central role of surveillance in modern societies, an issue that has become even more important now, because of the growing impact of information and communications technologies. We live in what some have called the **surveillance society** (Lyon, 1994)—a society in which information about our lives is gathered by all types of organizations.

But Weber and Foucault's argument that the most effective way to run an organization is to maximize surveillance—to have clear and consistent divisions of authority—is a mistake, at least if we apply it to business firms, which don't (as prisons do) exert total control over people's lives in closed settings. Prisons are not actually a good model for organizations as a whole. Direct supervision may work tolerably well when the people involved, as in prisons, are basically hostile to those in authority over them and do not want to be where they are. But in organizations where managers desire others to cooperate with them in reaching common goals, the situation is different. Too much direct supervision alienates employees, who feel they are denied any opportunities for involvement in the work they do (Sabel, 1982; Grint, 1991).

This is one main reason why organizations founded upon the sorts of principles formulated by Weber and Foucault, such as large factories involving assembly-line production and rigid authority hierarchies, eventually ran into great difficulties. Workers weren't inclined to devote themselves to their work in such settings; continuous supervision was in fact *required* to get them to work reasonably hard at all, but it promoted resentment and antagonism (for further discussion, see Chapter 12).

People are also prone to resist high levels of surveillance in the second sense mentioned by Foucault, the collection of written information about them. That was in effect one of the main reasons why the Soviet-style Communist societies broke down. In these societies, people were spied upon in a regular way either by the secret police or by others in the pay of the secret police—even relatives and neighbors. The government also kept detailed information on its citizenry in order to clamp down on possible opposition to their rule. The result was a form of society that was politically authoritarian and, toward the end, economically inefficient. The whole society did indeed come almost to resemble a gigantic prison, with all the discontents, conflicts, and modes of opposition prisons generate—and from which, in the end, the population broke free.

Bureaucracy and Democracy

Even in democracies like the United States, government organizations hold enormous amounts of information about us, from records of our dates of birth, schools, and jobs to data on income used for tax collecting and information used to issue drivers' licenses and allocate Social Security numbers. Since we don't have access to the files of most government agencies, such surveillance activities can infringe on the principle of democracy.

The diminishing of democracy with the advance of modern forms of organization was something that worried Weber a great deal (see also Chapter 11). What especially disturbed him was the prospect of rule by faceless bureaucrats. How can democracy be

---

KEY CONCEPTS IN REVIEW

Michel Foucault's theory of organizations claimed that the architecture of organizations is directly involved with their social makeup and hierarchy of authority.

Surveillance, the supervision of activities in organizations, takes two forms: direct supervision and keeping employee records. **Surveillance society** refers to how information about our lives and activities is maintained by organizations.

Timetables are the means by which organizations regularize activities across time and space.

Oligarchy means rule by the few. The **iron law of oligarchy**, a term coined by Weber's student Robert Michels, states that large organizations tend toward centralization of power, making democracy difficult, if not impossible.

anything other than a meaningless slogan in the face of the increasing power bureaucratic organizations are wielding over us? After all, Weber reasoned, bureaucracies are necessarily specialized and hierarchical. Those near the bottom of the organization inevitably find themselves reduced to carrying out mundane tasks and have no power over what they do; power passes to those at the top. Weber's student Robert Michels (1967) invented a phrase, which has since become famous, to refer to this loss of power: in large-scale organizations, and more generally a society dominated by organizations, he argued, there is an **iron law of oligarchy. Oligarchy** means rule by the few. According to Michels, the flow of power toward the top is simply an inevitable part of an increasingly bureaucratized world—hence the term "iron law."

Was Michels right? It surely is correct to say that large-scale organizations involve the centralizing of power. Yet there is good reason to suppose that the "iron law of oligarchy" is not quite as hard and fast as Michels claimed. The connections between oligarchy and bureaucratic centralization are more ambiguous than he supposed.

We should recognize first of all that unequal power is not just a function of size. In modest-sized groups there can be very marked differences of power. In a small business, for instance, where the activities of employees are directly visible to the directors, much tighter control might be exerted than in offices in larger organizations. As organizations expand in size, power relationships often in fact become looser. Those at the middle and lower levels may have little influence over general policies forged at the top. On the other hand, because of the specialization and expertise involved in bureaucracy, people at the top also lose control of many administrative decisions, which become handled by those lower down.

As we shall see in the following section, in many modern organizations power is also quite often openly delegated downwards from superiors to subordinates. In many large companies, corporate heads are so busy coordinating different departments, coping with crises, and analyzing budget and forecast figures, that they have little time for original thinking. They hand over consideration of policy issues to others below them, whose task is to develop proposals about them. Many corporate leaders frankly admit that for the most part they simply accept the conclusions given to them.

BEYOND BUREAUCRACY?

For quite a long while in the development of Western societies, Weber's model, closely mirrored by that of Foucault, held good. In government, hospital administration, universities, and business organizations, bureaucracy seemed to be dominant. Even though, as Peter Blau showed, informal social selections always develop in bureaucratic settings and are in fact effective, it seemed as though the future might be just what Weber had anticipated: constantly increasing bureaucratization.

Bureaucracies still exist aplenty in the West, but Weber's idea that a clear hierarchy of authority, with power and knowledge concentrated at the top, is the only way to run a large organization is starting to look archaic. Numerous organizations are overhauling themselves to become less, rather than more, hierarchical. Many corporate organizations, in the face of global economic competition, have sought to be more flexible, innovative, and responsive to both customers and employees. Nowhere has this been more true than in Japan.

The Clan Model and Japanese Corporations

The economic success of Japan is frequently said to be due mainly to the distinctive characteristics of the large Japanese corporations—which differ substantially from most business firms in the West (Vogel, 1979). Japanese companies diverge from the characteristics that Weber associated with bureaucracy in several ways:

1. BOTTOM-UP DECISION MAKING. The big Japanese corporations do not form a pyramid of authority as Weber portrayed it, with each level being responsible only to the one above. Rather, workers low down in the organization are consulted about policies being considered by management, and even the top executives regularly meet with them.

2. LESS SPECIALIZATION. In Japanese organizations, employees specialize much less than their coun-

terparts in the West. Take the case of Sugao, as described by William Ouchi (1982). Sugao is a university graduate who has just joined the Mitsubeni Bank in Tokyo. He will enter the firm in a management-training position, spending his first year learning generally how the various departments of the bank operate. He will then work in a local branch for a while as a teller, and will subsequently be brought back to the bank's headquarters to learn commercial banking. Then he will move out to yet another branch dealing with loans. From there he is likely to return to headquarters to work in the personnel department. Ten years will have elapsed by this time, and Sugao will have reached the position of section chief. But the process of job rotation does not stop there. He will move on to a further branch of the bank, perhaps dealing this time with the financing of small businesses, and then return to yet a different job at headquarters.

By the time Sugao reaches the peak of his career, some thirty years after having begun as a trainee, he will have mastered all the important tasks. In contrast, a typical American bank-management trainee of the same age will almost certainly specialize in one area of banking early on, and stay in that specialty for the remainder of her working life.

3. JOB SECURITY. The large corporations in Japan are committed to the lifetime employment of those they hire; the employee is guaranteed a job. Pay and responsibility are geared to seniority—how many years a worker has been with the firm—rather than to a competitive struggle for promotion.

4. GROUP ORIENTED. At all levels of the corporation, people are involved in small cooperative "teams," or work groups. The groups, rather than individual members, are evaluated in terms of their performance. Unlike their Western counterparts, the "organization charts" of Japanese companies—maps of the authority system—show only groups, not individual positions. This is important because it contradicts the supposed iron law of oligarchy.

5. MERGING OF WORK AND PRIVATE LIVES. In Weber's depiction of bureaucracy, there is a clear division between the work of people within the organization and their activities outside. This is in fact

Japanese workers doing the company's morning exercises.

true of most Western corporations, in which the relation between firm and employee is an economic one. Japanese corporations, by contrast, provide for many of their employees' needs, expecting in return a high level of loyalty to the firm. Japanese employees, from workers on the shop floor to top executives, often wear com-

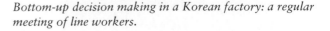

Bottom-up decision making in a Korean factory: a regular meeting of line workers.

pany uniforms. They may assemble to sing the "company song" each morning, and they regularly take part in leisure activities organized by the corporation at weekends. (A few Western corporations, like IBM and Apple, now also have company songs.) Workers receive material benefits from the company over and above their salaries. The electrical firm Hitachi, for example, studied by Ronald Dore (1980), provided housing for all unmarried workers and nearly half of its married male employees. Company loans were available for the education of children and to help with the cost of weddings and funerals.

Studies of Japanese-run plants in the United States and Britain indicate that "bottom-up" decision making does work outside Japan. Workers seem to respond positively to the greater level of involvement these plants provide (White and Trevor, 1983). It seems reasonable to conclude, therefore, that the Japanese model does carry some lessons relevant to the Weberian conception of bureaucracy. Organizations that closely resemble Weber's ideal type are probably much less effective than they appear on paper, because they do not permit lower-level employees to develop a sense of autonomy over, and involvement in, their work tasks.

Drawing upon the example of Japanese corporations, Ouchi (1979, 1982) has argued that there are clear limits to the effectiveness of bureaucratic hierarchy, as emphasized by Weber. Overly bureaucratized organizations lead to "internal failures" of functioning because of their rigid, inflexible, and uninvolving nature. Forms of authority Ouchi calls **clans**—groups having close personal connections with one another—are more efficient than bureaucratic types of organization. The work groups in Japanese firms are one example, but clan-type systems often develop informally within Western organizations as well.

Professionals and New Technology

Let us now turn back to the Western context. In pursuing the themes introduced at the beginning of the chapter—hierarchy, effectiveness, and participation in organizations—there are some further questions that need to be raised. One concerns the role of professionals—such as accountants, lawyers, doctors, or professors—in organizations. Such groups, for reasons that will be outlined, do not fit readily into hierarchical authority systems. A second question is raised by the changes occurring in organizations today, particularly as a result of the increasing use of information technology. Some have suggested that the spread of such technology might lead both to greater flexibility in organizations and to their decentralization. How valid is this idea?

PROFESSIONALS

Many positions in modern organizations depend upon detailed knowledge and expertise in the understanding and transmitting of information. Often, managers have to go outside the ranks of management personnel and hire professionals to fill such positions. **Professionals** are those who specialize in the development or application of technical knowledge (Abbott, 1988). Because a long period in higher education is presumed, and because professionals belong to national and even international bodies that define the nature of their tasks, professional expertise cannot easily be reduced to bureaucratic duties. When professionals are employed within large organizations, they do not "fit" neatly within the hierarchy of authority. Professionals usually have more autonomy in their work than others in middle and lower levels of an organization. Companies like IBM, which in so many ways epitomizes the modern corporation from organization to dress code, has under its wing research units staffed by professionals (scientists) whose work habits, hours, dress, and so on differ from those of people in other divisions.

How much control professionals within organizations enjoy over their work tasks varies according to several factors: the size and level of bureaucratization of the organization, the nature of the profession in question, and the strength of the professional association to which the individual worker belongs (Freidson, 1986). As contrasting examples, we might take nursing and law. Nurses are usually recognized as professionals, but the amount of control most have over their conditions of work is relatively limited. The larger hospitals are usually strongly bureaucratized organizations, in which nurses are subordinate to nursing supervisors as well as to other medical staff. Nursing associations set out guidelines for the employment of nurses, but do not have much power over how far these are followed within particular organizations.

For lawyers, the situation is different. Even when working in corporations rather than law firms, lawyers normally have more control over their work tasks than nurses do. The professional associations in law are very strong, and are able to define the codes of conduct which lawyers follow. Lawyers accept some administrative constraints, but their work can only be fully assessed or supervised by other members of the legal profession. Suppose a lawyer working in a given company has to prepare a legal case defending the firm against a suit that a disgruntled customer has brought against it. The company can instruct the lawyer to take charge of the case, but would not ordinarily insist on how the case would be argued in court. This is almost always assumed to be within the sphere of the lawyer's professional autonomy, and not subject to interference on the part of the employer.

Part of the power of professionals in organizations derives from their role as *gatekeepers* for the wider publics that these organizations cater to. A gatekeeper is someone who controls access to desired goods—in this case, to qualifications. For example, professional surveyors or engineers control the licenses needed before building construction can be undertaken; professors determine grades and who shall get degrees and diplomas; caseworkers assess who is eligible for various types of welfare benefits. How much autonomy professionals have in these matters is again influenced by the factors noted in the previous paragraph.

A general increase is taking place in the proportion of people working in professional occupations in modern societies (see also Chapter 12). As organizations come increasingly to rely upon their services, hierarchical bureaucratic systems are liable to come under strain. A growing tendency exists for professionals to work outside large organizations, founding smaller firms of their own, and hiring out their services as they are needed. Organizations that have a high proportion of professional workers tend to have a flexible administrative character, as compared to traditional types of organization.

INFORMATION TECHNOLOGY

The development of **information technology**—computers and electronic communication devices like the Internet—is another factor currently influencing organizational structures (Zuboff, 1988; Kanter, 1991). Anyone who draws money out of a bank, or buys an airline ticket, depends upon a computer-based communications system. Since data can be processed instantaneously in any part of the world linked to such a system, there is no need for physical proximity between those involved. As a result the introduction of new technology has allowed many companies to "reengineer" their organizational structure. The impact of these changes, while beneficial to organizational efficiency, can have both positive and negative consequences for the individuals within the organization.

For example, a particular company found the sales of some of its products falling, and was faced with the need to reduce costs. The traditional route in such circumstances would be to lay off staff. But instead, the firm set up those who might have been laid off as independent consultants, and established a computerized support network called Xanadu to provide basic office services to each of them working out of their homes. The company then "bought back" a substantial proportion of their working time for a number of years, but also left them free to use other time to work for different clients. The idea was that the new system would provide the corporation with access to the skills possessed by their former employees, but at a cheaper rate since it no longer needed to provide office space or company benefits (pension, life insurance, etc.). The former employees, in their turn, had the opportunity to build up their own businesses. Initially, at least, the scheme seems to have worked well for both parties. In such a scheme, though, the burden is placed on the former employees since they have to match the loss of company benefits with their ability to attract new business clients.

This is just one example of how large organizations have become more decentralized as the more routine tasks disappear, reinforcing the tendency toward smaller, more flexible types of enterprises (Burris, 1998). Another example of this process is the rise of "telecommuting." A good deal of office work, for instance, can be carried out at home by "telecommuters" through computer terminals linked through a telecommunications system. Several large firms in the United States and elsewhere have set up computer networks connecting employees who work from home. However, there are drawbacks to these new work arrangements. First, the employees lose the human side of work; computer terminals are not an attractive substitute for face-to-face interaction with colleagues and friends at work. In addition, female telecommuters face more stress resulting from greater housework and child-care responsibilities (Olson and Primps, 1984; Olson, 1989). Second, management cannot easily monitor the activities of employees not under direct supervision (Kling, 1996).

The experiences of telecommuters is a reminder that there can be negative consequences resulting from the implementation of information technology to reorder organizations. While computerization has resulted in a reduction in hierarchy, it has created a two-tiered occupational structure composed of technical "experts" and less-skilled production or clerical workers. In these restructured organizations, jobs are redefined based more on technical skill than rank or position. For "expert" professionals, traditional bureaucratic constraints are relaxed to allow for creativity and flexibility, but there is limited autonomy for other workers (Burris, 1993). While professionals benefit more from this expanded autonomy, computerization makes production and service workers more visible and vulnerable to supervision (Zuboff, 1988; Wellman et al., 1996). For instance, computerization allows organizations to carefully monitor employees' work patterns to the point that they can count the number of seconds per phone call or keystrokes per minute, which in turn can lead to higher levels of stress for employees.

Granted, the computerization of the workplace does have some positive effects. It has made some mundane tasks associated with clerical jobs more interesting and flexible. It can also promote social networking (Wellman et al., 1996). For example, office computers can be used for recreation, private "conversation" with other workers, friends, or family members, and work-related interaction. In some workplaces, computer-mediated communication can promote a more democratic type of workplace interaction. But in the large majority of workplaces, com-

puterization benefits the professionals who possess the knowledge and expertise to gain from it. It has not brought commensurate improvements in the career opportunities or salaries of the average worker (Kling, 1996). As Foucault thought, in the new computerized workplace, knowledge and information are important sources of power and a means of controlling people.

TIME AND SPACE IN REORDERING MODERN ORGANIZATIONS

The changes occurring in organizations today require that we rethink Weber's theory. For instance, Stanley Davis argues that organizations are increasingly coming to be **networks,** which involve bottom-up decision making, rather than hierarchies. As he puts it:

> Whether organizations shrink through downsizing, grow through alliances, or remain the same size, they will nevertheless be reorganizing their inner space. When you divide a whole into parts, it is the space between the parts that unites them together. Space is intangible and intangibility is increasingly prominent both in the new economy and in its new organizations. The industrial image of structure, for example, is the grinder-like architecture of buildings. The image of structure in the new economy, however, will be more like the architecture of atoms, built on energy and information, not steel. (1987)

Cutting down on time is the key to reorganizing activities in space. In a global marketplace, firms are under pressure from customers to deliver as quickly as possible, and the customer is as likely as not to be on the other side of the world. The system of production called "just in time," pioneered by Taiichi Ohno of Toyota, has been adopted by many business organizations outside Japan. It is called "just in time" because supplies arrive at the factory only right before they need to be used. Thus they don't need to be stored in a production plant over a long period of time. Essentially, "just in time" production means integrating all the elements of a production process—including the involvement of top management—to cut out superfluous operations where time is lost (Blackburn, 1990).

American corporations have recently tried to adopt some of these practices. Michael Hammer and James Champy give an example from the IBM Credit Corporation, a subsidiary of IBM. Until recently, requests for credit were handled in a series of steps, each carried out as a separate specialist task. In other words, the company was a bureaucracy in Weber's sense. The process of deciding about credit applications took an average of seven days, although it sometimes needed up to two weeks. Some people who were seeking credit would go elsewhere during this time.

To see whether this situation could be simplified and speeded up, a group of management consultants took a financing request themselves through all the stages of the process of authorization. The people in each office were asked to process the request as they usually would, only to do it immediately rather than adding it to the pile of work on their desks. The consultants found that the actual work took altogether only ninety minutes. The rest—most of the seven days—was taken up by passing the request from one department to the next.

It was the whole process that needed to be changed to improve efficiency, not the individual steps. The specialists in each office were replaced by generalists who could deal with the credit process from beginning to end. The result was extraordinary. The seven-*day* turnaround was slashed to four *hours*—and fewer people were required than for the older, more cumbersome way (Hammer and Champy, 1993).

Organizations in modern society are about the re-ordering of space and time. Today, information technology and electronic communication are making possible the transcendence of space and the control of time in ways that were unknown in even the relatively recent past. The fact that complex information, stored in computers, can be flashed around the world is altering many aspects of our lives. But the globalizing processes that are both produced by and the driving force behind these technologies are also serving to change the very shape and function of many organizations. This is particularly true of business corporations, which have to compete with one another in a global marketplace.

Organizations have to be somewhere, don't they? That's certainly what Foucault thought. In an important sense, his view is valid. The downtown areas of any large city, with their imposing array of buildings climbing up toward the sky, bear ample witness to this truth. These buildings, which house the executives and work staffs of large corporations, banks, and finance houses, tend to be packed into a small area.

Yet at the same time, big organizations today are "nowhere." They've become "virtual corporations." They consist of as many scattered individuals and groups as they do clusters of people working in the same physical space in office buildings. This is partly because of the ease with which people now can com-

Working at home is possible for more and more people as information becomes more vital to the business world.

THE COMPUTERIZATION OF THE WORKPLACE

For businesses competing in the global economy, investment in information technology—computer and communications equipment—is a necessity. Firms in the financial sector rely heavily on computers to engage in transactions on international financial markets; manufacturing firms depend on communications equipment to coordinate global production processes; and the customers of consumer services firms demand twenty-four-hour-a-day access to their accounts by telephone or the Internet. In short, information technology has become part of the basic infrastructure of business. In the service sector alone, businesses spent approximately $750 billion on information technology hardware between 1980 and 1990 (National Research Council, 1994, p. 4). This investment represented a doubling of the amount spent per worker on technology and has enabled firms to process vastly more transactions than they could in the past.

While some of these technologies have made workers' lives easier, there is reason to worry that the new high-tech workplace may erode workers' power and rights. First, business reliance on information technology may undermine coalitions among workers. There is great demand today for employees with high-tech skills, whereas those who finish high school or college with few such skills find themselves eligible only for a limited number of positions. Increasingly, there are coming to be two "classes" of employees in firms: a privileged class with high-tech skills, and another class relegated to lower status work. But when employees negotiate with management over such issues as wages, hours, and benefits, employee unity is essential for securing concessions. Will high-tech workers side with lower skilled employees in workplace disputes, or will they be more likely to side with management? The status of worker rights and

benefits in the next century may well hinge on the answer to this question.

Second, in part because new communications technologies allow the branch offices and production facilities of multinational firms to easily communicate with one another, a higher proportion of manufactured goods is coming to be produced on a transnational basis—a situation that may make individual workers more easily replaceable. Former U.S. Secretary of Labor Robert Reich provides the following example of a global production process: "Precision ice-hockey equipment is designed in Sweden, financed in Canada, and assembled in Cleveland and Denmark for distribution in North America and Europe, respectively, out of alloys whose molecular structure was researched and patented in Delaware and fabricated in Japan. An advertising campaign is conceived in Britain; film footage is shot in Canada, dubbed in Britain, and edited in New York" (Reich, 1991, p. 112). Although high-tech, high-skilled workers will be needed to carry out many aspects of the production process, these skills may no longer give workers the same bargaining power vis-à-vis management that skilled craftsmanship carried with it in previous eras. Because the manufacturing process has now been broken down into many small components, and because each of these components is carried out at a different production facility, the number of skills that any one worker must have is more limited than was the case in previous eras, making it easier for companies to replace contentious workers. Communications technologies thus arguably further the process that the Marxist scholar Harry Braverman called "the deskilling of labor."

Third, the nature of workplace surveillance is likely to change substantially as information technology becomes even more important for business. Employers have always watched their employees closely, monitoring performance, seeking to improve efficiency, checking to make sure they do not steal. But as a greater proportion of work comes to be done by computer, the capacity of managers to scrutinize the behavior of their employees increases. Computerized performance evaluations, scrutiny of employee email, and enhanced management access to personal employee information—such an Orwellian scenario becomes more likely as the role of information technology in the workplace expands.

Do you think these dangers are real, or is the impact of information technology on organizations essentially benign for employees? What steps, if any, do you think can be taken to counter these trends?

municate with one another in an immediate way across the world, something the Internet will further develop. It is also because of the ever-increasing importance of information, rather than physical goods, in shaping our social existence.

Physical places and goods can't occupy the same space, but physical places and information, a series of electronic blips, can. Hence, organizations themselves aren't so constrained to be somewhere as used to be the case. Where, for instance, is the stock market? Is it located at 11 Wall Street, where the traders rush around the floor exchanging slips of paper? Not today. The stock market is not, like markets once were, a physical place for the buying of stocks and shares. One might say that it is everywhere and nowhere. The stock market consists of a large number of dealers, most of whom work from computer screens in different offices and settings, and who are in continuous contact across the whole world with their counterparts in London, Paris, Tokyo, and Frankfurt.

Are networks, involving a large amount of bottom-up decision making, the path to the future, taking us completely away from Weber's more pessimistic vision? Some have suggested so, but we should be cautious about such a view. Bureaucratic systems are more internally fluid than Weber believed and are increasingly being challenged by other, less hierarchical forms of organization. But they probably won't disappear altogether, as the dinosaurs did. In the near future, there is likely to be a continuing push and pull between tendencies toward large size, impersonality, and hierarchy in organizations on the one hand and opposing influences on the other.

SUMMARY

1. All modern organizations are in some degree bureaucratic in nature. *Bureaucracy* is characterized by a clearly defined hierarchy of authority; written rules governing the conduct of officials (who work full time for a salary); and a separation between the tasks of the official within the organization and life outside it. Members of the organization do not own the material resources with which they operate. Max Weber argued that modern bureaucracy is a highly effective means of organizing large numbers of people, ensuring that decisions are made according to general criteria.

2. Informal networks tend to develop at all levels both within and between organizations. The study of these informal ties is as important as the more formal characteristics upon which Weber concentrated his attention.

3. The physical settings of organizations strongly influence their social features. The architecture of modern organizations is closely connected to surveillance as a means of securing obedience to those in authority. *Surveillance* refers to the supervision of people's activities, as well as to the keeping of files and records about them.

4. The work of Weber and Michels identifies a tension between bureaucracy and democracy. On the one hand, there are long-term processes of the centralization of decision making associated with the development of modern societies. On the other hand, one of the main features of the past two centuries has been expanding pressures toward democracy. The trends conflict, with neither one in a position of dominance.

5. Japanese corporations differ significantly from most Western companies in terms of their characteristics as organizations. There is more consultation of lower-level workers by managerial executives, pay and responsibility are linked to seniority, and groups, rather than individuals, are evaluated for their performance. Some Western firms have adopted aspects of Japanese management systems in recent years, although it is by no means proven that these explain why Japan's economic performance has outstripped that of most Western countries.

6. All modern organizations depend upon the specialization of knowledge and the transmitting of information. *Professionalization*, together with the increasing use of *information technology*, may be leading to a general increase in the flexibility of organizations. The impact of these changes—thus far, at any rate—has often been exaggerated.

7. Modern organizations are beginning to assume the form of distributed *networks* rather than hierarchies with fixed locations. Companies such as IBM are reorganizing their priorities in ways pioneered by the Japanese and empowering employees to be flexible and to make on-the-spot decisions. Ultimate success, however, depends largely on the firm's ability to manage information effectively and to communicate instantly around the world.

Chapter Eleven

Familiarize yourself with the prominent political trends around the world today: the spread of democracy and nationalism.

The Concept of the State

Learn the basic concepts underlying modern nation-states.

Democracy

Learn about different types of democracy, how this form of government has spread around the world, some theories about power in a democracy, and some of the problems associated with modern-day democracy.

The Influence of Nationalism

Know the different types of nationalism and how they are manifested today.

The Military

See the importance of military power and war in studying political sociology.

GOVERNMENT, POLITICAL POWER, AND WAR

In 1989, a drama unfolded in Tiananmen Square in Beijing, the capital of China. All over the world, television viewers watched pictures of the Chinese army clearing the square of students and others who had gathered to demonstrate in favor of freedom and democracy. Hundreds of the demonstrators lost their lives in the confrontation, and others were rounded up and imprisoned. The leaders of the demonstration had been in touch with foreign TV crews and had deliberately sought to gain a worldwide audience.

Although it is mostly a poor country by Western standards, China has in recent years been undergoing a rapid process of economic development, and many Chinese own television sets. Yet while they were beamed to much of the rest of the world, the scenes from Beijing were not transmitted on TV in China. The government simply blacked them out, and instead related the events in a light sympathetic to the army and the authorities.

Television was used in this case by the Chinese government as a blatant propaganda device (Lull, 1991). By managing the TV coverage, the government tried to reassert the place of the Communist party as the supreme political agency in the country. But it was too late for this to be more than partly successful. For television allows the Chinese access to programs—transmitted from Hong Kong, Thailand, and other nearby countries—over which the government has no control. Moreover, Chinese viewers watch a high proportion of imported programs, such as American shows and films. In these programs, viewers get a clear sense of alternative ways of life to those approved of by the government. Television is thus a force lending support to calls for political change in China—the very opposite of what the government intended.

Democratization is one of the major political forces in the world. Like so many aspects of contemporary societies, the realm of government and politics is undergoing major changes. **Government** refers to the regular enactment of policies, decisions, and matters of state on the part of the officials within a political apparatus. **Politics** concerns the means whereby power is used to affect the scope and content of governmental activities. The sphere of the *political* may range well beyond that of government itself. Television is only one influence contributing to these changes. In this chapter, we shall study the main factors affecting political life today. Many people find politics remote and uninteresting. Whether we like it or not, however, all of our lives are touched by what happens in the political sphere. Governments influence quite personal activities and, in times of war, can even order us to lay down our lives for aims they deem necessary. The sphere of government is the sphere of political *power*. All political life is about power: who holds it, how they achieve it, and what they do with it.

Power and Authority

As mentioned in Chapter 1, the study of power is of fundamental importance for sociology. **Power** is the ability of individuals or groups to make their own interests or concerns count, even when others resist. It sometimes involves the direct use of force, such as when the Chinese authorities suppressed the democracy movement in Tiananmen Square. Power is an ele-

ment in almost all social relationships, such as that between employer and employee. This chapter focuses on a narrower aspect of power, governmental power. In this form, it is almost always accompanied by ideologies, which are used to justify the actions of the powerful. For example, the Chinese government's use of force against the students demonstrating for democracy was a defense of the Communist ideology as the ultimate form of government.

Authority is a government's legitimate use of power: those subject to a government's authority consent to it. Power is thus different from authority. When pro-democracy demonstrations in China broke out and the government responded by imprisoning and killing the demonstrators, it was an exercise of power but also an indication of the government's loss of authority. Contrary to what many believe, democracy is not the only type of government people consider legitimate. Dictatorships can have legitimacy as well. But as we shall see later, democracy is presently the most widespread form of government called legitimate.

THE CONCEPT OF THE STATE

A **state** exists where there is a political apparatus of government (institutions like a parliament or congress, plus civil service officials) ruling over a given territory, whose authority is backed by a legal system and by the capacity to use military force to implement its policies. All modern societies are **nation-states.** That is, their system of government lays claim to specific territories, possesses formalized codes of law, and is backed by the control of military force. Nation-states have come into existence at various times in different parts of the world (for example, the United States in 1776 and the Czech Republic in 1993). Their main characteristics, however, contrast rather sharply with those of states in traditional civilizations.

Characteristics

Sovereignty The territories ruled by traditional states were always poorly defined, the level of control wielded by the central government being quite weak.

The notion of **sovereignty**—that a government possesses authority over an area with clear-cut borders, within which it is the supreme power—had little relevance. All nation-states, by contrast, are sovereign states.

Citizenship In traditional states, most of the population ruled by the king or emperor showed little awareness of, or interest in, those who governed them. Neither did they have any political rights or influence. Normally only the dominant classes or more affluent groups felt a sense of belonging to an overall political community. In modern societies, by contrast, most people living within the borders of the political system are **citizens**, having common rights and duties and knowing themselves to be members of a national community (Brubaker, 1992). While there are some people who are political refugees or are "stateless," almost everyone in the world today is a member of a definite national political order.

Nationalism Nation-states are associated with the rise of **nationalism,** which can be defined as a set of symbols and beliefs providing the sense of being part of a single political community. Thus, individuals feel a sense of pride and belonging in being American, Canadian, or Russian. Probably people have always felt some kind of identity with social groups of one form or another—their family, village, or religious community. Nationalism, however, made its appearance only with the development of the modern state. It is the main expression of feelings of identity with a distinct sovereign community.

Nationalistic loyalties do not always fit the physical borders marking the territories of states in the world today. Virtually all nation-states were built from communities of diverse backgrounds. As a result, **local nationalisms** have frequently arisen in opposition to those fostered by the states. Thus, in Canada, for instance, nationalist feelings among the French-speaking population in Quebec present a challenge to the feeling of "Canadianness." Yet while the relation between the nation-state and nationalism is a complicated one, the two have come into being as part of the same process. (We will return to nationalism later in the chapter as we look at its impact on international politics in the modern world.)

We can now offer a comprehensive definition of the nation-state: it is possessed of a government apparatus that is recognized to have sovereign rights within the borders of a territorial area. It is able to back its claims to sovereignty by the control of military power, and many of its citizens have positive feelings of commitment to its national identity.

Citizenship Rights

Most nation-states became centralized and effective political systems through the activities of monarchs who successfully concentrated more and more power in their own hands. Citizenship did not originally carry rights of political participation in these states. Such rights were achieved largely through struggles that limited the power of monarchs, as in Britain, or actively overthrew them—sometimes by a process of revolution, as in the cases of the United States and France, followed by a period of negotiation between the new ruling elites and their subjects (Tilly, 1996).

Three types of rights are associated with the growth of citizenship (Marshall, 1973). **Civil rights** refer to the rights of the individual in law. These include privileges many of us take for granted today, but that took a long while to achieve (and are by no means fully recognized in all countries). Examples are the freedom of individuals to live where they choose; freedom of speech and religion; the right to own property; and the right to equal justice before the law. These rights were not fully established in most European countries until the early nineteenth century (see Global Map 11.1). Even where they were generally achieved, some groups were not allowed the same privileges. Although the U.S. Constitution granted such rights to Americans well before most European states had them, African Americans were excluded. Even after the Civil War, when blacks were formally given these rights, they were not able to exercise them.

The second type of citizenship rights consists of **political rights,** especially the right to participate in elections and to run for public office. Again, these were not won easily or quickly. Except in the United States, the achievement of full voting rights even for all men is relatively recent and had to be struggled for in the face of governments reluctant to admit the principle of the universal vote. In most European countries, the vote was at first limited to male citizens owning a certain amount of property, which effectively limited voting rights to an affluent minority. Universal franchise for men was mostly won by the early years of the

GREENLAND
(DENMARK)

SWEDEN
ICELAND   NORWAY
          DENMARK
GERMANY
NETHERLANDS

ALASKA
(U.S)

CANADA

IRELAND

U.K

AUS   CZ

BELGIUM
LUXEMBOURG   FRANCE
SWITZERLAND

SL

UNITED STATES

ITALY

AZORES   PORTUGAL   SPAIN

BERMUDA   ATLANTIC OCEAN   TUNISIA

BAHAMAS
HAITI   MOROCCO
DOMINICAN REPUBLIC
Virgin Is.   WESTERN SAHARA
PUERTO RICO   (MOROCCO)   ALGERIA
CUBA   ST. CHRISTOPHER AND NEVIS
Hawaiian Is.   ANTIGUA AND BARBUDA
MEXICO   DOMINICA   MAURITANIA
BELIZE   BARBADOS   CAPE VERDE   MALI   NIGER
JAMAICA   ST. LUCIA   SENEGAL
GUATEMALA   NICARAGUA   ST. VINCENT AND   GAMBIA
EL SALVADOR   THE GRENADINES   NIGERIA
HONDURAS   GRENADA   GUINEA-BISSAU
COSTA RICA   VENEZUELA   TRINIDAD AND   GUINEA
PACIFIC OCEAN   PANAMA   TOBAGO   SIERRA   CAMEROON
COLOMBIA   FR. GUYANA   LEONE
Galapagos Is.   ECUADOR   LIBERIA   IVORY   SAO TOME
SURINAME   COAST   AND
GUYANA   PRINCIPE
BRAZIL   BOURKIN
FASO
PERU   GHANA
TOGO   GABON
BOLIVIA   BENIN
CONGO
PARAGUAY   NAMIBIA
EQUATORIAL
GUINEA
WESTERN
SAMOA

TONGA

CHILE   URUGUAY

Easter Is.   ARGENTINA

Falkland Is.

- Free
- Partly free
- Not free

SOURCE: *Freedom in the World*, 1997–1998 (New York: Freedom House, 1998).

ABBREVIATIONS

AUS.	AUSTRIA
ALB.	ALBANIA
B.H.	BOSNIA AND HERZEGOVINA
BULG.	BULGARIA
CR.	CROATIA
CZ.	CZECH REPUBLIC
HUN.	HUNGARY
MAC.	FORMER YUGOSLAV REPUBLIC OF MACEDONIA
POL.	POLAND
ROM.	ROMANIA
SL.	SLOVENIA
U.K	UNITED KINGDOM
YU.	YUGOSLAVIA

twentieth century. Women had to wait longer; in most Western countries, the vote for women was achieved partly as a result of the efforts of women's movements and partly as a consequence of the mobilization of women into the formal economy during World War I.

The third type is **social rights,** the right of every individual to enjoy a certain minimum standard of economic welfare and security. Social rights include such entitlements as sickness benefits, social security in case of unemployment, and the guarantee of minimum levels of wages. Social rights, in other words, involve welfare provisions. Although in some countries, such as nineteenth-century Germany, welfare benefits were introduced before legal and political rights were fully established, in most societies social rights have been the last to develop. This is because the establishment of civil and particularly political rights has usually been the basis on which social rights have been fought for. Social rights have been won largely as a result of the political strength poorer groups were able to develop after obtaining the vote.

The broadening of social rights is closely connected with what has come to be called the **welfare state,** which has been firmly established in Western societies only since World War II. A welfare state exists where government organizations provide material benefits for those who are unable to support themselves adequately through paid employment—the unemployed, the sick, the disabled, and the elderly. All Western countries today provide extensive welfare benefits. In many poorer countries, these benefits are virtually nonexistent.

While an extensive welfare state was seen as the culmination of the development of citizenship rights, in recent years welfare states have come under pressure from increasing global economic competition and the movement of people from poor, underdeveloped societies to richer, developed countries. As a result, the United States and some European countries have sought to reduce benefits to noncitizens and to prevent new immigrants from coming. For example, in 1994 voters in California passed Proposition 187, which denied social benefits to all illegal immigrants living there. At the national level, the welfare reform act of 1996 denied a wide range of benefits to *legal* immigrants. And for many years, the United States government has patrolled its border with Mexico and constructed walls of concrete and barbed wire in an attempt to keep illegal immigrants out of the country. Similar patterns of exclusion have occurred in Europe, particularly in Germany and Britain. In these ways, citizenship has served as a powerful instrument of social closure, whereby prosperous nation-states have attempted to exclude the migrant poor from the status and the benefits that citizenship confers (Brubaker, 1992).

Having learned some of the important characteristics of modern states, we now consider the nature of democracy in modern societies.

DEMOCRACY

The word "democracy" has its roots in the Greek term *demokratia,* the individual parts of which are *demos* ("people") and *kratos* ("rule"), and its basic meaning is therefore a political system in which the people, not monarchs (kings or queens) or aristocracies (people of noble birth like lords), rule. This sounds simple and straightforward, but it is not. What does it mean to be ruled by the people? As David Held has pointed out, questions can be raised about each part of that phrase (Held, 1987). If we start with "the people":

1. Who are the people?
2. What kind of participation are they to be allowed?
3. What conditions are assumed to be conducive to participation?

Direct democracy: A town meeting in New England.

KEY CONCEPTS IN REVIEW

Power is the capability of individuals or groups to make their own interests count, even when others resist.

Authority is a government's legitimate use of power.

A **state** exists where there is a political apparatus (government institutions) ruling a given territory. All modern states are nation-states. A **nation-state** refers to a government apparatus that is recognized to have sovereign rights within the borders of a territorial area, able to back its claims to sovereignty by military power, and many of whose citizens feel committed to its national identity. The major characteristics of a nation-state are **sovereignty** (governmental authority over a given area), **citizenship** (people having common rights and duties and conscious of their relationship with the state), and **nationalism** (symbols and beliefs that provide the sense of being part of a single political community).

Three types of rights are associated with the growth of citizenship: **civil rights** are the rights of the individual in law; **political rights** refer to the right to take part in politics (voting, for example); and **social rights** are the right of every individual to enjoy a minimum standard of living. Social rights are the basis of the **welfare state**, which helps citizens unable to support themselves through paid employment.

As regards "rule":

1. How broadly or narrowly should the scope of rule be? Should it be confined, for example, to the sphere of government, or can there be democracy in other spheres, such as industrial democracy?
2. Can rule cover the day-to-day administrative decisions governments must make, or should it refer only to major policy decisions?

In the case of "rule by":

1. Must the rule of the people be obeyed? What is the place of obligation and dissent?
2. Should some of the people act outside the law if they believe existing laws to be unjust?
3. Under what circumstances, if any, should democratic governments use coercion against those who disagree with their policies?

Answers to these questions have taken contrasting forms, at varying periods and in different societies. For example, "the people" have been variously understood as owners of property, white men, educated men, men, and adult men and women. In some societies, the officially accepted version of **democracy** is limited to the political sphere, whereas in others, it is extended to other areas of social life.

Participatory Democracy

In **participatory democracy** (or **direct democracy**), decisions are made communally by those affected by them. This was the original type of democracy practiced in ancient Greece. Those who were citizens, a small minority of the society, regularly assembled to consider policies and make major decisions. Participatory democracy is of limited importance in modern societies, where the mass of the population have polit-

THE WAVE OF DEMOCRACY

When political sociologists of the future look back on the 1980s and 1990s, one historical development in particular is likely to stand out: the democratization of many of the world's nations. Since the early 1980s, a number of countries in Latin America, such as Chile, Bolivia, and Argentina, have undergone the transition from authoritarian military rule to thriving democracy. Similarly, with the collapse of the Communist bloc in 1989, many East European states—Russia, Poland, and Czechoslovakia, for example—have become democratic, adopting written constitutions, working to ensure that disputes will be resolved according to the rule of law, and, most important, holding popular elections. The resignation of Indonesian dictator Suharto in 1998 following weeks of massive popular protest raised hopes that democratic forces will also come to prevail in that country, perhaps spurring the democratization of other Southeast Asian states. And in Africa, a number of previously undemocratic nations—including Benin, Ghana, Mozambique, and South Africa—have come to embrace democratic ideals. According to one recent estimate, 66 percent of the world's nations now rely on electoral processes to select their leaders (Schwartzman, 1998).

While a full explanation for these developments would require a detailed analysis of the social and political situations in each country that led up to the transition to democracy, there can be little doubt but that globalizing processes

played an important role in this most recent wave of democratization. First, the growing number of cross-national cultural contacts that globalization has brought with it has invigorated democratic movements in many countries. A

ical rights, and it would be impossible for everyone actively to participate in the making of all the decisions that affect them.

Yet some facets of participatory democracy do play a part in modern societies. The holding of referenda, for example, when the majority express their views on a particular issue, is one form of participatory democracy. Direct consultation of large numbers of people is

made possible by simplifying the issue down to one or two questions to be answered. Referenda are regularly used at the national level in some European countries. They are also employed frequently on a state level in the United States to decide controversial issues. Another element of participatory democracy, a meeting of the whole community, is found at the local level—for example, in some townships in New England.

globalized media, along with advances in communications technology, has exposed inhabitants of many nondemocratic nations to democratic ideals, increasing internal pressure on political elites to hold elections. Of course, such pressure does not automatically result from the diffusion of the notion of popular sovereignty. More important is that, with globalization, news of democratic revolutions, and accounts of the mobilizing processes that lead to them, are quickly spread on a regional level. News of the revolution in Poland in 1989, for example, took little time to travel to Hungary, providing pro democracy activists there with a useful, regionally appropriate model around which to orient their work.

Second, international organizations such as the United Nations and the European Union—which, in a globalized world, come to play an increasingly important role—have put external pressure on nondemocratic states to move in democratic directions. In some cases, these organizations have been able to use trade embargoes, the conditional provision of loans for economic development and stabilization, and diplomatic maneuvers of various kinds to encourage the dismantling of authoritarian regimes.

Third, democratization has been facilitated by the expansion of world capitalism. Although transnational corporations are notorious for striking deals with dictators, corporations generally prefer to do business in democratic states—not because of an inherent philosophical preference for political freedom and equality, but because democracies tend to be more stable than other kinds of states, and stability and predictability are essential for maximizing profits. Because political, economic, and military elites, particularly in the Third World and in the former Soviet Union, are often anxious to increase levels of international trade and to encourage transnationals to set up shop in their countries, they have sometimes pursued a democratic agenda of their

own, leading to what the political sociologist Barrington Moore Jr. once called "revolutions from above."

It is true that if globalization were the sole cause of the most recent wave of democratization, all countries today would be democratic. The persistence of authoritarian regimes in such countries as China, Cuba, Serbia, and Nigeria suggests that globalizing forces are not always sufficient to force a transition to democracy. But democratic moves are afoot even in several of these countries, leading some sociologists to believe that under the influence of globalization, many more nations will become democratic in the years to come.

Monarchies and Liberal Democracies

 While some modern states (such as Britain and Belgium) still have monarchs, these are few and far between. Where traditional rulers of this sort are still found, their real power is usually limited or nonexistent. In a tiny number of countries, such as Saudi Arabia and Jordan, monarchs continue to hold some degree of control over government, but in most cases they are symbols of national identity rather than personages having any direct power in political life. The queen of England, the king of Sweden, and even the emperor of Japan are all **constitutional monarchs**: their real power is severely restricted by the constitution, which vests authority in the elected representatives of the people. The vast majority of modern states are republican—there is no king or queen; almost every one, including constitutional monarchies, professes adherence to democracy.

Countries in which voters can choose between two or more parties and in which the mass of the adult population has the right to vote are usually called **liberal democracies.** The United States, the Western European countries, Japan, Australia, and New Zealand all fall into this category. Some Third World countries, such as India, also have liberal democratic systems.

The Spread of Liberal Democracy

For much of the twentieth century, the political systems of the world were divided between liberal democracy and Communism, as found in the former Soviet Union (and which still exists in China and a few other countries). **Communism** was essentially a system of one-party rule. Voters were given a choice not between different parties but between different candidates of the same party—the Communist party; there was sometimes only one candidate running.

There was thus no real choice at all. The Communist party was easily the dominant power in Soviet-style societies: it controlled not just the political system but the economy as well.

Since 1989, when the hold of the Soviet Union over Eastern Europe was broken, processes of democratization have swept across the world in a sort of chain-reaction process. The number of democratic nations almost doubled between 1989 and 1999 from 66 to 117. Countries such as Nicaragua in Central America and Zambia and South Africa in Africa have established liberal democratic governments (see Global Map 11.2). In China, which holds about a fifth of the world's population, the Communist government is facing strong pressures toward democratization. During the 1990s, thousands of people remained in prison in China for the nonviolent expression of their desire for democracy. But there are still groups, resisted by the Communist government, working actively to secure a transition to a democratic system.

Why has democracy become so popular? The reasons have to do with the social and economic changes discussed throughout this book. First, democracy tends to be associated with competitive capitalism in the economic system, and capitalism has shown itself to be superior to communism as a wealth-generating system. Second, the more social activity becomes glob-

Democracy has become the standard of government toward which most countries in the world are heading. Left, marchers carry a banner reading "Social-Democratic Association" in Moscow, 1990.

alized and people's daily lives become influenced by events happening far away, the more they start to push for information about how they are ruled—and therefore for greater democracy (Huntington, 1991).

Third is the influence of mass communications, particularly television. The chain reaction of the spread of democracy has probably been greatly affected by the visibility of events in the world today. With the coming of new television technologies, particularly satellite and cable, governments can't maintain control over what their citizens see, as happened in the Tiananmen Square incident. As in China, the Communist party in the Soviet Union and Eastern Europe used to maintain a strict control over television networks, which were all government-owned and government-run. But the spread of satellite transmission gave many people access to TV programs from the West, and thus brought them into contact with different views of their conditions of life from those churned out by orthodox government propaganda (Markoff, 1996).

Democracy in the United States

POLITICAL PARTIES

A political party is an organization of individuals, with broadly similar political aims, oriented toward achieving legitimate control of government through an electoral process. Two parties tend to dominate the political system where elections are based on the principle of winner-take-all, as in the United States. The candidate who gains the most votes wins the election, no matter what proportion of the overall vote he or she gains (Duverger, 1954). Where elections are based on different principles, such as proportional representation (in which seats in a representative assembly are allocated according to the proportions of the vote attained), five or six different parties, or even more, may be represented in the assembly. To form a government, where they lack an overall majority, some of the parties have to form a coalition—an alliance with one another.

In the United States, the system has become effectively a two-party one between the Republicans and Democrats, although no formal restriction is placed upon the number of parties. The nation's founders made no mention of parties in the Constitution because they thought that party conflict might threaten the unity of the new republic.

Two-party systems like that of the United States tend to lead to a concentration upon the "middle ground," where most votes are to be found, excluding more radical views. The parties in these countries often cultivate a moderate image, and sometimes come to resemble one another so closely that the choice they offer is relatively slight. A plurality of interests may supposedly be represented by each party, but can become blended into a bland program with few distinctive policies. Multiparty systems allow divergent interests and points of view to be expressed more directly, and provide scope for the representation of radical alternatives. Green Party representatives or representatives of Far Right parties, found in some European parliaments, are cases in point. On the other hand, no one party is likely to achieve an overall majority, and the government by coalition that results can lead to indecision and stalemate, if compromises can't be worked out, or to a rapid succession of elections and new governments, none able to stay in power for long.

Some writers have studied the connection between voting patterns and class differences: liberal and leftist parties tend to gain most of their votes from those in lower-class groups, while conservative or rightist parties are more strongly supported by affluent groups (Lipset, 1981). The party system in the United States is quite distinct from that of virtually all other Western societies, since there is no large leftist party. Class-based voting is less pronounced than in other Western democracies. While the Democratic Party has tended to appeal more to lower-class groups, and the Republicans have drawn support from the more affluent sectors of the population, the connections are far from absolute. Each party has a conservative and a liberal wing; it is relatively common for conservative and liberal members of one party to align themselves with those holding parallel opinions in the other party on particular issues such as free trade.

POLITICS AND VOTING

The founders of the American governmental system did not foresee a role for parties in the political order. George Washington recognized that interest groups would develop, but spoke out forcefully against "the

SOURCE: *Freedom in the World*, 1997–1998 (New York: Freedom House, 1998).

ABBREVIATIONS

AUS. AUSTRIA
ALB. ALBANIA
B.H. BOSNIA AND HERZEGOVINA
BULG. BULGARIA
CR. CROATIA
CZ. CZECH REPUBLIC
HUN. HUNGARY
MAC. FORMER YUGOSLAV
REPUBLIC OF MACEDONIA
POL. POLAND
ROM. ROMANIA
SL. SLOVENIA
U.K UNITED KINGDOM
YU. YUGOSLAVIA

harmful effects of the spirit of party." Thomas Jefferson echoed these sentiments, but in fact became the leader of one of the earliest party organizations, the Republicans—who were subsequently called the Democratic-Republicans, and in 1831, the Democrats. Policy disputes arose between Jefferson and Alexander Hamilton during Washington's administration. Each had a group of followers: Hamilton's faction was called the Federalists. Jefferson's Republicans were the first to endorse candidates for Congress, leading the Federalists to do likewise. The national division of parties later spread to the state legislatures, and the parties soon developed into state organizations representing specific interests and points of view. A two-party system was well established by the 1830s, and although the parties themselves underwent subsequent changes, the fundamental nature of that system has not altered greatly to this day.

Building mass support for a party in the United States is difficult, because the country is so large and includes so many different regional, cultural, and ethnic groups. The parties have each tried to develop their electoral strength by forging broad regional bases of support and by campaigning for very general political ideals.

As measured by their levels of membership, party identification, and voting support, each of the major American parties is in decline (Wattenberg, 1996). A study carried out covering the years 1952 to 1980 showed that the numbers declaring themselves to be "independent" of either party grew from 22 percent in 1952 to over 33 percent in 1994 (Wattenberg, 1996). Only some 2 percent of the adult population are active members of party organizations, nearly all of which are locally based. Most activists over the past few years have become increasingly concerned with supporting particular candidates and mobilizing support over specific issues, which has weakened party organizations even further.

Since the early 1960s the proportion of the population that turns out to vote in the United States has steadily decreased. Only about half the electorate votes in presidential elections; the turnout for congressional elections is lower still. Levels of voting are typically much lower than in the other Western societies, even with the declining patterns of voting in other countries in recent years. The average voter turnout in Britain, West Germany, and France since World War II has been over 75 percent in each country. In American presidential elections over the same period, by contrast, the average turnout was 59 percent.

The differences in voter participation between the United States and Western Europe are real, but less pronounced than they appear, for two reasons. First, voter turnout in the United States is computed rather differently from elsewhere. In most other countries, the percentage of people voting in an election is calculated on the basis of the population of *registered* voters. The American statistics are expressed as a percentage of the entire *voting-age population*. Since in the European countries some people, for one reason or another, are not on the voting register at any one time, the proportion of actual voters to those eligible to vote appears higher than in the U.S. system of calculation.

Second, there is a much more extensive range of elections in the United States than in other Western societies. There is no other country in which such a variety of offices at all levels—including sheriffs, judges, city treasurers, and many other posts—are open to election. Americans are entitled to do about three or four times as much electing as elsewhere. Low rates of voter turnout thus have to be balanced against the wider extent of voter choice.

INTEREST GROUPS

Interest groups and lobbying play a distinctive part in American politics. An interest group is any organization that attempts to influence elected officials to consider their aims when deciding on legislation. The American Medical Association, the National Organization for Women, and the National Rifle Association are but three examples. Interest groups vary in size; some are national; others, statewide. Some are permanently organized, while others are short-lived. Lobbying is the act of contacting influential officials to present arguments to convince them to vote in favor of a cause or otherwise lend support to the aims of an interest group. The word *lobby* originated in the British parliamentary system. In days past, members of Parliament did not have offices so their business was conducted in the lobby of the Parliament buildings.

The Lobbying Disclosure Act requires all organizations employing lobbyists to register with Congress and to disclose whom they represent, whom they lobby, what they are lobbying for, and how much they are paid. More than 7,000 organizations, collectively employing many thousands of lobbyists, are currently registered. Interest groups provide a great deal of money in donations to the election campaigns at all levels of political office. To run as a presidential candidate is enormously expensive. Even to run for the House or Senate costs hundreds of thousands, often millions, of dollars. About a quarter of this funding in congressional or senatorial elections comes from Political Action Committees (PACs), which are set up by interest groups to raise and distribute campaign funds. During the 1996 elections, PACs made 122,000 contributions totaling $218 million (Clawson et al., 1999).

Interest groups are not officially part of the electoral process, and this has made many people critical of them. While they ensure that a diversity of interests are represented at the higher levels of politics, it is not clear that the average voter has much influence on them; not being subject to elections, lobbyists and the more powerful interest groups are not accountable to the majority of the electorate. Also, many of their activities are carried on in secret. Thus it is possible that they contribute to the sense of powerlessness many people feel toward the state, particularly at the national level.

The Political Participation of Women

Voting has a special meaning for women against the background of their long struggle to obtain universal suffrage. The members of the early women's movements saw the vote both as the symbol of political freedom and as the means of achieving greater economic and social equality. In the United States, where the attempts by women to gain voting rights were more active, and provoked more violence, than elsewhere, women's leaders underwent considerable hardships to reach this end. Even today, in many countries, women do not have the same voting rights as men.

Women obtaining the vote has not greatly altered the nature of politics. Women's voting patterns, like those of men, are shaped by party preferences, policy options, and the choice of available candidates. The influence of women upon politics cannot be assessed solely through voting patterns, however. Feminist groups have made an impact upon political life independently of the franchise, particularly in recent decades. Since the early 1960s, the National Organization for Women (NOW) and other women's groups in the United States have played a significant role in

This enthusiastic delegate to the 1992 Democratic National Convention would not have been considered a member of "the people" less than a century ago, and would not have been able to vote.

the passing of equal opportunity acts, and have pressed for a range of issues directly affecting women to be placed on the political agenda. Such issues include equal rights at work, the availability of abortion, changes in family and divorce laws, and lesbian rights. In 1973, women achieved a legal victory when the Supreme Court ruled in *Roe v. Wade* that women had a legal right to abortion. The 1989 Court ruling in *Webster v. Reproductive Health Services*, which placed restrictions on that right, resulted in a resurgence of involvement in the women's movement.

In most of the European countries, comparable national women's organizations have been lacking, but the "second wave" of feminism, characteristic of the 1960s and since, has brought the same issues to the center of the political stage (see Chapter 8). While many of these matters—like the question of whether abortion should be freely available—have proved highly controversial among women as well as men, it seems clear that many problems and concerns that particularly affect women, which previously had seemed to be "outside politics," are now central to political debates.

Yet in general, as in so many other sectors of social life, women are poorly represented among political elites. Following the 1998 national elections in the United States, there were fifty-eight female members in the House of Representatives, making up just over 13 percent of the total membership. While this number has almost tripled since the early 1970s it is still not representative of the number of female citizens. In 1999 there were only nine women in the Senate, representing 9 percent of those sitting in the upper chamber.

What is surprising about the figures on women's involvement at the higher levels of political organizations is not this lack of representation itself, but the slowness with which things seem to be changing. In the business sector, men still monopolize the top positions, but women are now making more inroads into the strongholds of male privilege than previously. As yet at least, this does not seem to be happening in the political sphere—in spite of the fact that nearly all political parties today are nominally committed to securing equal opportunities for women and men. Since 1990, female candidates for political office have been successful *when they have run for office*. The critical factor seems to be that political parties (which are largely run by men) have not recruited as many women to run for office.

The factors that present difficulties for women's advancement in the economy also exist in the realm of politics. To rise within a political organization requires a great deal of expenditure of effort and time, which women who have major domestic burdens can rarely generate. But there may be an additional influence in political life. A high level of power is concentrated in the political area: perhaps men are especially reluctant to abandon their dominance in such a sphere.

From considering the position of women in politics, we now broaden our scope to look at some basic ideas of political power. First, we take up the issue of who actually holds the reins of power, drawing on comparative materials to help illuminate the discussion. We then consider whether democratic governments around the world are "in crisis."

Who Rules?: Theories of Democracy

DEMOCRATIC ELITISM

One of the most influential views of the nature and limits of modern democracy was set out by Max Weber and, in rather modified form, by the economist Joseph Schumpeter (1983). The ideas they developed are sometimes referred to as the theory of **democratic elitism**.

Weber began from the assumption that direct democracy is impossible as a means of regular government in large-scale societies. This is not only for the obvious logistical reason that millions of people cannot meet to make political decisions, but because running a complex society demands *expertise*. Participatory democracy can only work, Weber believed, in small organizations in which the work to be carried out is fairly simple and straightforward. Where more complicated decisions have to be made, or policies worked out, even in modest-sized groups—like a small business firm—specialized knowledge and skills are necessary. Experts have to carry out their jobs on a continuous basis; positions that require expertise cannot be subject to the regular election of people who may only have a vague knowledge of the neces-

Weber suggested that representative democracy helps guard against arbitrary decision making on the part of elected leaders, who are held accountable by voters, and of bureaucrats, who are monitored and led by elected leaders. Here, a member of Congress speaks to activists in his home district about education policy.

sary skills and information. While higher officials, responsible for overall policy decisions, are elected, there must be a large substratum of full-time bureaucratic officials who play a large part in running a country (Weber, 1979).

In Weber's view, the development of mass citizenship, which is so closely connected with the idea of general democratic participation, greatly expands the need for bureaucratic officialdom. For example, provision for welfare, health, and education demands permanent large-scale administrative systems. As Weber expresses this, "It is obvious that technically the large modern state is absolutely dependent upon a bureaucratic basis. The larger the state, and the more it is a great power, the more unconditionally this is the case . . ." (Weber, 1979).

Representative multiparty democracy, according to Weber, helps defend against both arbitrary decision making on the part of political leaders, because they are subject to popular elections, and against power being completely usurped by bureaucrats, because elected officials set overall policy. But under these circumstances the contribution of democratic institutions is less than many advocates of a more pure democracy would hope. "Rule by the people" is possi-

ble in only a very limited sense. In order to achieve power, political parties themselves must become organized in a systematic way. In short, they, too, must become bureaucratized. "Party machines" develop, which threaten the autonomy of parliaments or congresses as places in which policies are discussed and formulated. If a party with a majority representation is able to dictate policy, and if that party is itself mainly run by officials who are permanently in control, the level of democracy that has been achieved is slim indeed.

In order for democratic systems to have some degree of effectiveness, Weber argues, two conditions have to be met. First, there must be parties that represent different interests and have different outlooks. If the policies of competing parties are more or less the same, voters are denied any effective choice. Weber rejects the idea that one-party systems can be democratic in any meaningful way. Second, there must be political leaders who have the imagination and courage necessary to escape the inertia of bureaucracy. Weber places a great deal of emphasis upon the importance of *leadership* in democracy—which is why his view is referred to as "democratic elitism." He argues that rule by elites is inevitable; the best we can hope for is that those elites effectively represent our interests and that they do so in an innovative and insightful fashion. Parliaments and congresses provide a breeding ground for capable political leaders able to counter the influence of bureaucracy and to command mass support. Weber valued multiparty democracy more for the quality of leadership it generates than for the mass participation in politics it makes possible.

Joseph Schumpeter fully agreed with Weber about the limits of mass political participation. For Schumpeter, as for Weber, democracy is more important as a method of generating effective and responsible government than as a means of providing significant power for the majority. Democracy cannot offer more than the possibility of replacing a given political leader or party by another. Democracy, Schumpeter stated, is the rule of *the politician*, not *the people*. Politicians are "dealers in votes" much as brokers are dealers in shares on the stock exchange. To achieve voting support, however, politicians must be at least minimally responsive to the demands and interests of the electorate. Only if there is some degree of competition to secure votes can arbitrary rule effectively be avoided.

PLURALIST THEORIES

The ideas of Weber and Schumpeter influenced some of the **pluralist theorists** of modern democracy, although the pluralists developed their ideas somewhat differently. Pluralists accept that individual citizens can have little or no *direct* influence on political decision making. But they argue that tendencies toward the centralization of power in the hands of government officials are limited by the presence of **interest groups.** Competing interest groups or factions are vital to democracy because they divide up power, reducing the exclusive influence of any one group or class (Truman, 1981).

According to the pluralist view, government policies in a democracy are influenced by continual processes of bargaining among numerous groups representing different interests—business organizations, trade unions, ethnic groups, environmental organizations, religious groups, and so forth. A democratic political order is one in which there is a balance among competing interests, all having some impact on policy but none dominating the actual mechanisms of government. Elections are influenced by this situation also, for to achieve a broad enough base of support to lay claim to government, parties must be responsive to numerous diverse interest groups. The United States, it is held, is the most pluralistic of industrialized societies and, therefore, the most democratic. Competition between diverse interest groups occurs not only at the national level but within the states and in the politics of local communities.

THE POWER ELITE

The view suggested by C. Wright Mills in his celebrated work, *The Power Elite,* is quite different from pluralist theories (Mills, 1956). According to Mills, in earlier periods of its history, American society did show flexibility and diversity at all levels; however, this has since changed.

Mills argues that during the course of the twentieth century a process of institutional centralization occurred in the political order, the economy, and the sphere of the military. On the political side, individual state governments used to be very powerful and were only loosely coordinated by the federal government. Political power today, Mills argues, has become tightly coordinated at the federal level. Similarly, the economy was once made up of many small units, businesses, banks, and farms across the country, but has now become dominated by a cluster of very large corporations. Finally, since World War II, the military, once kept restricted in size, has grown to a giant establishment at the heart of the country's institutions.

Not only has each of these spheres become more centralized, according to Mills, but they have become increasingly merged with one another to form a unified system of power. Those who are in the highest positions in all three institutional areas come from similar social backgrounds, have parallel interests, and often know one another on a personal basis. They have become a single **power elite** that runs the country—and, given the international position of the United States, also influences a great deal of the rest of the world.

The power elite, in Mills's portrayal, is composed mainly of white Anglo-Saxon Protestants (WASPs). Many are from wealthy families, have been to the same prestigious universities, belong to the same clubs, and sit on government committees with one another. They have closely connected concerns. Business and political leaders work together, and both have close relationships with the military through weapons contracting and the supply of goods for the armed forces. There is a great deal of movement back and forth between top positions in the three spheres. Politicians have business interests; business leaders often run for public office; higher military personnel sit on the boards of the large companies.

In opposition to pluralist interpretations, Mills argues that there are three distinct levels of power in the United States. The power elite occupies the highest level, formally and informally making the most important policy decisions affecting both the domestic arena and foreign policy. Interest groups, upon which the pluralists concentrate their attention, operate at the middle levels of power, together with local government agencies. Their influence over major policy decisions is limited. At the bottom is the large mass of the population, who have virtually no influence upon the decisions at all, since these are made within the closed settings in which the members of the power elite come together. The power elite spans the top of both party organizations, each party being run by individuals with similar overall interests and outlooks. Thus the choices open to voters in presidential and congressional elections are so small as to be of little consequence.

Since Mills published his study, there have been numerous other research investigations analyzing the social background and interconnections of leading figures in the various spheres of American society (Dye, 1986). All studies agree upon the finding that the social backgrounds of those in leading positions are highly unrepresentative of the population as a whole (Domhoff, 1971, 1979, 1983, and 1998).

The main argument among sociologists about the distribution of power in the United States now focuses on the relative power of government officials and of the business leaders who run large corporations. One group of scholars argues that the government is where true power lies and that business leaders are not nearly as powerful as the experts and politicians who run the government (Skocpol, 1992; Orloff, 1993; Amenta, 1998). An alternative view holds that corporate business executives and families of great wealth form a capitalist class, which has great influence over

government officials and experts through lobbying, campaign contributions, the sponsorship of think tanks, and the appointment of top corporate leaders to important government positions (Domhoff, 1998). Both sides agree, however, that it is not inevitable that business leaders or government officials will always be dominant. Although an elite class—whether elected, expert, or corporate—rules America, the power of groups can change over time, leaving open the possibility that those who are now powerless could be dominant sometime in the future.

Democracy in Trouble?

As liberal democracy is becoming so widespread, we might expect it to be working in a highly successful way. Yet such is not the case. Democracy almost everywhere is in some difficulty. This is not only because it is proving difficult to set up a stable democratic order in Russia and other erstwhile Communist societies. Democracy is in trouble in its main countries of origin—the United States is a good example. The numbers of people voting in presidential and other elections have been in decline for some while. In surveys, many people say they don't trust politicians and regard most of them as tricksters.

In the United States, 76 percent of people in an opinion poll in 1964 answered "all" or "most of the time" when asked "How much of the time do you trust the government in Washington to do the right thing?" A repeat poll in 1994 showed the proportion had dropped to 25 percent. Of those expressing continuing trust in government, 61 percent voted in the previous presidential elections, compared with 35 percent of the less trustful. Younger people have less interest in electoral politics than older generations have, although the young have a greater interest than their elders in issues like the environment (Nye, 1997). Some have argued that trends like these indicate that people are increasingly skeptical of traditional forms of authority. Connected to this has been a shift in political values in democratic nations from "scarcity values" to "post-materialist values" (Inglehart, 1997). This means that after a certain level of economic prosperity has been reached, voters become concerned less with economic issues than with the quality of their individual (as opposed to collective) lifestyles, such as the desire for meaningful work. As a result, voters are generally less interested in national politics, except for areas involving personal liberty.

The last twenty years has also been a period in which, in several Western countries, the welfare state has come under attack. Rights and benefits, fought for over long periods, have been contested and cut back. Rightist parties have attempted to reduce levels of welfare expenditure in their countries. Even in states led by socialist governments, like France, commitment to government provision of public resources has been restricted. One reason for this governmental retrenchment is the declining revenues available to governments as a result of the general world recession beginning in the early 1970s. Yet there also seems to have developed an increasing skepticism, shared not only by some governments but by many of their citizens, about the effectiveness of relying on the state for the provision of many essential goods and services. This skepticism is based on the belief that the welfare state is bureaucratic, alienating and inefficient, and welfare benefits can create perverse consequences that undermine what they were designed to achieve (Giddens, 1998).

Why are so many people dissatisfied with the very political system that seems to be sweeping all before it across the world? The answers, curiously, are bound up with the factors that have helped spread democracy—the impact of capitalism and the globalizing of social life. For instance, while capitalist economies have proved to generate more wealth than any other type of economic system, that wealth is unevenly distributed (see Chapter 7). And economic inequalities influence who votes, joins parties, and gets elected. Wealthy individuals and corporations back interest groups that lobby for elected officials to support their aims when deciding on legislation. Not being subject to election, interest groups are not accountable to the majority of the electorate.

Economic inequalities also create an underclass of people living in poverty. About 20 percent of the population of liberal democracies live below the poverty line. Most Western liberal democracies establish poli- cies to reduce poverty levels, but they vary in how much they spend to achieve that aim. Societies that spend the most to implement a complex welfare system require a higher level of taxation and a larger

nonelected government bureaucracy. The question arises: How much of an economic and political price is a society willing to pay to reduce poverty, and what is the impact of this cost?

Two theories have been put forward by different authors to account for this changing political situation. One is the theory of **state overload** (Britain, 1975; Nordhaus, 1975). According to this view, governments in the twentieth century have acquired more responsibilities than they can capably fund and manage, from establishing public ownership of industries, utilities, and transportation, to creating extensive welfare programs. One reason for this situation is that political parties have tried to woo voters by promising to provide too many benefits and services. Governments are unable to deliver on these promises because the level of state expenditure has risen beyond the resources provided by tax revenues: state responsibilities are overloaded (Etzioni-Halvy, 1985).

Consequently, it is argued, voters have become skeptical about claims made by governments and political parties. The Democratic party in the United States and leftist parties elsewhere have lost some of their traditional support from lower-class groups, as it became apparent that states could no longer deliver the promised benefits. The rise of New Right politics is explained as an attempt to cope with this situation by trimming back the state and encouraging private enterprise.

A rival theory, developed by Jürgen Habermas, is known as the theory of **legitimation crisis** (Habermas, 1975; Offe, 1984, 1985). According to this theory, modern governments lack the legitimacy to carry out tasks they are required to undertake, such as providing highways, public housing, and health care. People who feel that they pay most for these services through higher taxes—the more affluent—are likely to believe that they gain least from them. On the one hand, governments are asked to take more and more responsibility for providing health care for those who cannot afford it; on the other, taxpayers resist any increases in taxation or even want tax payments reduced. Governments cannot cope with the contradictory demands of lower taxes and more responsibilities, leading to decreased public support and general disillusionment about government's capabilities. In sum, a legitimation crisis. According to Habermas, legitimation crises could probably be overcome if the electorate were persuaded to accept high taxation in return for a wide range of government services.

As the sociologist Daniel Bell has observed, national government is too small to respond to the big questions, such as the influence of global economic competition or the destruction of the world's environment; but it has become too big to deal with the small questions, issues that affect particular cities or regions. Governments have little power, for instance, over the activities of giant business corporations, the main actors within the global economy. A U.S. corporation may decide to shut down its production plants in America and set up a new factory in Mexico instead, in order to lower costs and compete more effectively with other corporations. The result is that thousands of American workers lose their jobs. They are likely to want the government to do something, but national governments are unable to control processes bound up with the world economy. All the government can do is try to soften the blow, like providing unemployment benefits or job retraining.

At the same time that governments have shrunk in relation to global issues, they have also become more remote from the lives of most citizens. Many Americans resent that decisions affecting their lives are made by distant "power brokers" in Washington—party officials, interest groups, lobbyists, and bureaucratic officials. They believe that the government is unable to deal with important local issues as well, such as crime and homelessness. The result is that Americans' faith in government has dropped substantially. This in turn affects people's willingness to participate in the political process.

What Is the Role of Government?: The Third Way

Many people today seem to believe that political ideas have lost their capacity to inspire and political leaders their ability to lead. This skepticism about government has led to debates about the proper role of government in democratic nations. For the past fifty years, two political ideologies have battled over the question of what governments should do. The first was the leftist belief in a strong national government and extensive welfare state. The second was the right-

ist belief that free markets are always better than government and thus the scope of government should be kept to a bare minimum. Many people tend to believe, however, that in today's world, neither of these ideologies can adequately solve the many problems that society faces, such as poverty and environmental degradation. Instead, some elected leaders are arguing that what is needed is a philosophy of government that goes beyond left and right and proposes new solutions for today's political and social problems. One such political philosophy has been called the "third way" (Giddens 1995, 1998).

The "third way" is in many respects a response to globalization and the benefits it can bring and the problems it can create. Some have argued that the advance of globalization has created a borderless world and has made politicians powerless and governments irrelevant. The "third way," however, sees a greater role for government in a globalizing world rather than a diminished one. Third way politics looks for dynamic government rather than big government. It believes that government can act in partnership with other social institutions to foster community renewal and development. It places a strong emphasis upon reviving public institutions, but no longer equates "public" with only the role of government. For example, government can act in combination with business and local community organizations to help renew economic development. Rosabeth Moss Kanter, a sociologist at the Harvard Business School, has studied the effectiveness of these endeavors in the United States. For example, in Denver, Colorado, during the late 1980s, the petroleum-based economy was in recession. A new regional coalition, the Greater Denver Cooperation, successfully led a drive to restructure the local economy. Not-for-profit and community groups, acting in conjunction with business and government, were vital to this achievement.

Third way politics also argues that government is in need of reform. Government has been mistrusted partly because it has grown bureaucratic and ineffective in some areas, such as reducing economic inequality and poverty. To regain legitimacy, governments must improve their administrative efficiency. In the United States, during the 1990s President Bill Clinton sought to "reinvent government" by changing the way government "does business" and making it more responsive to citizens. These intiatives have included

KEY CONCEPTS IN REVIEW

Democracy is a political system in which the people rule. In **participatory democracy** (or direct democracy) decisions are made by those affected by them. A **liberal democracy** is a representative multiparty democracy (such as the United States), where citizens can vote for one of at least two parties.

Several prominent theories of democracy have been developed by social theorists. The theory of **democratic elitism** as set out by Max Weber and Joseph Schumpeter argues that direct democracy is impossible because running a government requires decision making by individual experts, not the mass of citizens. As a result, the rule of elites is inevitable, but multiparty competition allows only those with political leadership to rise to the top. **Pluralist** theorists agreed that individual citizens have little or no direct influence on political decision making, but that the competition between interest groups made sure that political power was not concentrated in the hands of one group or class. While C. Wright Mills agreed that the average citizen has virtually no influence on political decisions, he disagreed with the pluralist theories, arguing instead that political power is concentrated in the hands of the **power elite.**

While democracy has become widespread, some troubles exist. In countries such as the United States, the government is unable to address many of the needs of its citizens. Dissatisfaction with government is increasing, while political participation is decreasing. Two theories attempt to account for the problems of the welfare state. The theory of **state overload** argues that states have assumed too many responsibilities. The theory of **legitimation crisis,** developed by Jürgen Habermas, argues that governments are unable to cope with the contradictory demands of lower taxes and more responsibilities. One alternative to the welfare state has been deemed "the third way." Proponents of this philosophy argue that governments need to reform by improving their administrative efficiency, adopting new social investment policies, and involving citizens more in the decision-making process.

---

cutting red tape, streamlining procurement (how the government purchases goods and services), improving the coordination of federal management, and simplifying federal rules. For example, the Food and Drug Administration (FDA) had been criticized for taking too long to approve new drugs and therapies for illnesses such as cancer and AIDS. As a result of "reinventing government," the FDA accelerated the approval process for new cancer therapies, made promising but not yet approved cancer therapies available to patients lacking other treatment possibilities, and pledged to be more responsive to the needs of cancer patients and others affected by FDA rulings.

The "third way" also emphasizes that governments must adopt new social investment strategies with the primary aim of new job creation. Rosabeth Moss Kanter has identified five main areas where government policy can assist. The first is support for entrepreneurial initiatives concerned with small business startups and technological innovation. The second is to emphasize life-long education. The third is public project partnerships, which give private enterprise a larger role in activities that governments once provided for, such as transportation to one's job. The fourth is that government policies should enhance portability of benefits. Finally, the government should encourage family-friendly workplace policies achieved through public-private collaborations.

Third way politics encourage citizens to play a greater role in the decision-making processes at the national, state, and local levels. The California Comparative Risk Project is one such example of deliberative citizen involvement. Separate committees composed of technical experts and average citizens were set up to analyze health, welfare, and environmental programs. The two committees were then brought together and required to reach joint decisions. The citizen committee raised many concerns that the experts simply ignored, leading to a rich public debate that resulted in new policy decisions.

President Bill Clinton was the world's first elected leader to talk about a "third way," and many of his administration's policies sought to adopt the type of initiatives that we have just discussed. But third way policies cannot succeed without the support and participation of the broad national community. Third way politics tries to reinstill people's trust in their government and to encourage their participation in political decision making. Although third way thinking will likely be at the core of political debates as the world enters a new century, its impact remains to be seen.

National identity, reflected in symbols like David's portrait of a heroic Napoleon on horseback, forms part of the foundation of classical nationalism.

THE INFLUENCE OF NATIONALISM

Disillusionment with politics has not made most Americans antagonistic to the wider society in which they live. Despite the United States' ethnic diversity, most think of themselves as Americans; they have a sense of national belonging. Nationalism—a feeling of belonging within a distinct national community—has been a unifying force in the United States. In other regions of the world, however, it has proved divisive. Moreover, sentiments of nationalism, especially when linked to ideas of national superiority, have often provoked wars.

For a long while, nationalism received little attention from sociologists. The classical social thinkers—Marx, Durkheim, and Weber—did not articulate a systematic account of the role of nationalist movements or symbols in the modern world. Marx believed that nationalism was essentially a sentiment through which dominant classes tried to legitimize their position. He predicted that an international workers' movement would unite the laboring classes and cause nationalism to disappear. Durkheim wrote little about nationalism; Weber proclaimed himself a "German nationalist" in his political life but never analyzed nationalism in any depth.

Why this neglect? The main reason is that all three thinkers, in common with most of their contemporaries, believed nationalism was on the decline, a worldview more of the past than the future. In this supposition, they were wrong. At the end of the twentieth century, nationalism is not only alive but—in certain parts of the world, at least—flourishing. Nationalism has played a part in all the great revolutions of this century, including those that brought down Communism in Eastern Europe in 1989.

Types of Nationalism

It is useful to draw a distinction between three types of nationalism. **Classical nationalism** refers to the nationalism associated with the rise of the nation-state in Europe from about the eighteenth century onward. This is the form of nationalism found in the creation of states such as the United States, Britain, France, Germany, and Italy. Such nationalism was partly imposed from above, as Marx argued, but was also stimulated by activist movements from below. Classical nationalism constructed an "imagined community"—a cultural interpretation of national identity, based on a specific view of the country's history (Anderson, 1991). The rise of classical nationalism was closely connected with the development of a mass education system. Through education, people learned about their national history and came to think of themselves as belonging together in the same national community. The teaching of language, such as "standard English," also played an important part (Gellner, 1983).

Postcolonial nationalism refers to nationalist movements that emerged in areas of the world once colonized by the European countries in Africa, Asia, and Latin America. Nationalism usually played a role in struggles against colonialism. Such nationalist ideas, however, were usually limited to small sectors of the society; they didn't influence the majority of the population. Once they were free from direct political colonization, many former colonial countries became what are sometimes called "state-nations." Unlike the European nation-state, where the state was

formed around the nation and the nation was the focus of nationalist sentiments, ex-colonial countries lacked a sense of the nation—of national identity. They were a state only because the colonizing country had established it, and they consisted of disparate communities and cultures that their governments fought to integrate in the face of tribalism and economic divisions. Under colonialism, some racial or ethnic groups had prospered more than others; these groups had different interests and goals and legitimately saw each other as enemies. Thus, in former colonial countries such as Nigeria and Ghana in Africa, national identity is still only weakly developed.

Subcultural nationalism refers to oppositional forms of nationalist movements that develop within mature nation-states. We find many examples today, ranging from the nationalisms that helped lead to the breakup of the Soviet Union to Scottish nationalism, Catalan nationalism (in Spain), Quebec nationalism (in Canada), and Bosnian nationalism (in the former Yugoslavia). Although such nationalism may have deep cultural roots, it shouldn't be seen as merely an extension of classical nationalism. Classical nationalism seems mostly on the decline today, while subcultural nationalism is on the rise. The latter is in some part a response to the globalization of social and economic life. Regional identities become accentuated as a response to, and defense against, the growing im-

Quebecois nationalists demonstrating, 1992.

KEY CONCEPTS IN REVIEW

It is useful to distinguish between three different types of nationalism: **classical nationalism** is associated with the rise of the nation-state in Europe from the eighteenth century onward; **postcolonial nationalism** refers to nationalist movements and ideas that emerged in areas of the world once colonized by European countries in Africa, Asia, and Latin America; **subcultural nationalism** is oppositional forms of nationalist movements that develop within mature nation-states.

pact of the wider world on people's lives; at the same time, nation-states become weakened (see Global Map 11.3).

What accounts for the importance of subcultural nationalism in the contemporary world? For one thing, nationalism is sometimes used by political elites to attempt to weld together the states over which they rule. For another, nationalism provides a sense of common identity and history that helps invigorate popular movements. More generally, nationalism makes possible a sense of belonging in a world in which many traditional bases of community have been destroyed.

Nationalist feelings often inspire antagonism, and have led to some of the most destructive conflicts of the nineteenth and twentieth centuries. On the other hand, nationalist sentiments are associated with trends toward democracy—this was true of the 1989 events in Eastern Europe. In the aftermath of the revolutions, Eastern Europe has not been entirely peaceful. One of the world's trouble spots has been the former Yugoslavia, where Communism fell in 1989 and subcultural nationalism has since risen, resulting in a bloody and devastating civil war. The nationalist aspirations of Bosnia, once an independent state until the end of World War I, led to military confrontations with Serbia, the base of the former Communist government, which sought to defend the interests of Serbians living in other regions attempting to break away. The result of conflict between the Serbian military and Bosnian nationalists was the death of 500,000 people. Subcultural nationalism was also an important influence in civil wars in Africa, where

thousands died as well. It is clear that feelings of nationalism exert a strong influence in the world today. It is to a discussion of these events, so important in their consequences, that we now turn.

Changes in Eastern Europe

The year 1989 was the two-hundredth anniversary of the French revolution. It was also a new "year of revolutions" in Europe, perhaps as far-reaching in its

implications as 1789 was. In 1989, one after the other, communist regimes in Eastern Europe relinquished their grip on power. What had seemed like a solidly and pervasively established system of rule throughout Eastern Europe was thrown off almost overnight. The communists lost power in an accelerating sequence in the countries they had dominated for half a century: Hungary (February), Poland (June), Bulgaria, East Germany, and Czechoslovakia (November), Romania (December). Every East European country, including the most underdeveloped, Albania, had freely elected governments by January 1992. Even more remarkably, by this date the Communist party had been ousted in the Soviet Union itself, and that country had broken up into myriad independent states.

With some exceptions, Eastern Europe is well advanced in the process of writing new constitutions and setting up multiparty parliamentary systems. For the most part, the spectrum of parties resembles

SOURCE: *Freedom in the World*, 1997–1998 (New York: Freedom House, 1998).

ABBREVIATIONS

AUS.	AUSTRIA
ALB.	ALBANIA
B.H.	BOSNIA AND HERZEGOVINA
BULG.	BULGARIA
CR.	CROATIA
CZ.	CZECH REPUBLIC
HUN.	HUNGARY
MAC.	FORMER YUGOSLAV REPUBLIC OF MACEDONIA
POL.	POLAND
ROM.	ROMANIA
SL.	SLOVENIA
U.K	UNITED KINGDOM
YU.	YUGOSLAVIA

that found in West European countries. Some ex-communist parties continue to exist, although quite often they have dropped the name "communist" and can no longer behave as they did in single-party systems. In the mid-nineties they have in fact done surprisingly well in elections. In the 1995 elections to the Russian Duma (parliament), for example, the re-emergent Russian Communist party secured 22 percent of the vote, making it the largest party in the parliament.

All the East European countries face major economic as well as political difficulties in the transitions they are attempting to make. Most of the population in these societies express dissatisfaction with the development of democracy in their countries, and many express disquiet about rises in crime and violence. According to the European Bank for Reconstruction and Development (EBRD) most of the East European economies have made great advances over the past several years. Yet the promises of democratic capitalism have turned out to be empty for many in Eastern Europe. Seventy-five million "newly poor" have been created as a result of unemployment and the erosion of the buying power of people on fixed incomes—and

this figure excludes the countries of the former Soviet Union. Aid to Eastern Europe from the West has been on quite a modest scale.

The changes that have occurred seem in most countries to have affected women in a particularly adverse way (Watson, 1992). The proportion of women in parliaments and other leading political bodies has in some countries fallen sharply. For instance, in the initial stages of change, in the former Czechoslovakia the percentage of female members of parliament fell from 34 percent to 4 percent; in Poland from 20 percent to 8 percent; and in Bulgaria from 21 percent to 8 percent. Women are heavily overrepresented among the growing numbers of unemployed produced by the transition to market economies in the East.

How successful will the East European societies be in instituting stable liberal democratic systems of government? Samuel Huntington (1990) has identified six influences likely to be decisive:

1. How far a country has experienced liberal democratic government at earlier periods in its history. The former Czechoslovakia has the most favorable history judged in this way, with Albania at the other extreme. In Czechoslovakia, however, there were deep tensions between the Czechs and Slovaks, and the country has now become divided into two separate states.
2. The level of economic development attained by the country—in this respect the Czech Republic and Hungary are in the lead.
3. How effectively the country was ruled under its previous communist regime. The supposition here is that a state that governed effectively under an authoritarian system would be more likely also to do so in a democratic one.
4. The strength and variety of social and political organizations that were able to stay independent of the communist rulers.
5. How capable the new governments prove to be in constructing and putting into practice radical policies of economic reform.
6. The degree of separation and hostility between subnational or ethnic groups, regions, or classes. Yugoslavia has already succumbed to disintegration as a result of such divisions, and Czechoslovakia has become divided, but how far others might follow is not yet clear.

In March 1998, thousands of ethnic Albanians in Kosovo protested the violent tactics of the Serbian military against civilians of the province.

Much the same considerations apply to the new states formed following the breakup of the Soviet Union, including Russia itself. Most start from much further back than the East European countries. The majority have no independent history of liberal democracy whatsoever, and some have not even previously existed as separate states at all. Whatever happens in the next few years, the map of Europe has changed for good and with it the global political order—since the former Soviet Union stretched right across to the far side of Asia.

Whether liberal democracy becomes firmly established is likely to depend on how far a market economy is set up. The main indicators of change are how far the privatizing of industry has proceeded; the degree of restructuring of businesses, to escape from previous styles of management; openness to competition and foreign trade; and reform of the banking system. As measured in these terms, the level of change is greatest in the Czech Republic, Hungary, and Poland; it is lowest in Azerbaijan, Georgia, Turkmenistan, and Ukraine.

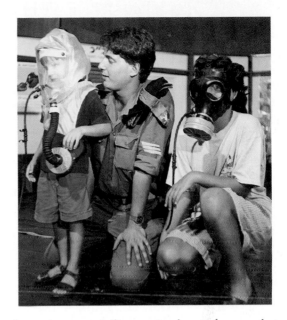

Total war threatens civilians as much as it does combatants. In Israel during the Gulf War, schoolchildren were fitted with gas masks.

THE MILITARY

The events of 1989 and after show clearly the importance of the use of military power at important social or political transitions. The sociology of military power is an important part of political sociology, as we will see at the end of the chapter. First, we look at the history of warfare and then at the Cold War and its aftermath.

From Limited to Total War

Prior to the twentieth century, even when large battles were fought, wars were limited to only small segments of the population—soldiers who did the fighting (normally a small percentage of the adult males of a society) or civilians living in the immediate regions where the wars were fought. These can be characterized as **limited wars.** But World War I (1914–18), in which enormous bodies of soldiery took part, was clearly not limited. **Total war** involves several antagonistic nations, high proportions of their male populations, the mobilization of their overall economies, and fighting throughout the world. World War I, or the "Great War," was in many ways a watershed in military development in the twentieth century. It fully justified its name; in terms of the number of countries involved—most of the European nations, together with Russia, Japan, and the United States—there were no historical parallels. The numbers of combatants and civilians killed were much higher than in any previous armed conflict. As the social historian Maurice Pearton observes, "War had changed from being the concern of the army as an elite to being the business of society as a whole, and from the limited and rational application of force to unrestricted violence" (1984).

At least two major developments promoted this transition from limited to total war: the industrialization of war and the rise of the mass-military organization. The **industrialization of war** refers to the application of modern industrial methods to the production and development of weaponry. Modern mass-military systems developed into bureaucratic organizations and significantly changed the nature of organizing and fighting wars. In addition, govern-

Table 11.1 Twentieth-Century Wars

LOCATION	DATE	IDENTIFICATION OF CONFLICT	DEATHS
LATIN AMERICA			
Mexico	1910–20	Liberals and Radicals vs. govt.	250,000
Bolivia	1932–35	Paraguay vs. Bolivia	200,000
Colombia	1949–62	"La Violencia": civil war, Liberals vs. Conservative govt.	300,000
Guatemala	1966–95	Government massacre of Indians	140,000
EUROPE			
Russia	1904–5	Japan vs. Russia	130,000
	1918–20	Civil war; Allied intervention	1,300,000
Turkey	1915	Armenians deported	1,000,000
Poland	1919–20	U.S.S.R. vs. Poland	100,000
Spain	1936–39	Civil war; Italy, Portugal, and Germany intervening	1,200,000
Greece	1945–49	Civil war; Britain intervening	160,000
Bosnia	1992–95	Civil war	263,000
FAR EAST			
China	1928	Muslim rebellion vs. govt.	200,000
	1930–35	Civil war, Communists vs. govt.	500,000
	1937–41	Japan vs. China	1,800,000
	1946–50	Civil war, Communists vs. Kuomintang govt.	1,000,000
	1950–51	Govt. executes landlords	1,000,000
	1956–59	Tibetan revolt	100,000
	1967–68	Cultural Revolution	500,000
Vietnam	1945–54	War of independence from France	600,000
	1960–65	Civil war, Vietcong vs. govt.; U.S. intervening	300,000
	1965–75	Peak of Indochina War; U.S. bombing	2,058,000
Korea	1950–53	Korean War; U.N. intervening	3,000,000
Indonesia	1965–66	Abortive coup; massacres	500,000
	1975–82	Annexation of East Timor; famine and massacres	150,000
Cambodia	1970–75	Civil war, Khmer Rouge vs. govt.; N. Vietnam, U.S. intervening	56,000
	1975–78	Pol Pot govt. vs. people; famine and massacres	1,000,000
AFRICA			
Tanzania	1905–7	Revolt against Germany; massacres	150,000
Algeria	1954–62	Civil war, Muslims vs. govt.; France intervening	100,000
Rwanda	1956–65	Tutsis vs. govt.; massacres	105,000
	1994–95	Ethnic massacres and aftermath	500,000

ments introduced **universal conscription**—the drafting of all able-bodied men within a certain age-range—as the scale of war increased.

Military Expenditure and the Cold War

The twentieth century has been unquestionably the most war-ridden and destructive in human history. Thus far, close to 100 million human beings have been killed in war, an average of 3,500 a day (see Table 11.1). Most were killed in the two world wars. Military budgets grew progressively up to 1989; military weaponry has become increasingly sophisticated and more destructive. Large-scale nuclear weapons are capable of killing millions of people.

Until the late 1980s, global military expenditure was dominated by the Cold War—the antagonistic rivalry between the United States and the former Soviet Union that lasted from the late 1940s until about

LOCATION	DATE	IDENTIFICATION OF CONFLICT	DEATHS
AFRICA *(continued)*			
Zaire	1960–65	Katanga secession; U.N., Belgium intervening	100,000
Sudan	1963–72	Christians vs. Arab govt.; massacres	500,000
	1984–95	Civil war	1,500,000
Nigeria	1967–70	Civil war, Biafrans vs. govt.; famine and massacres	2,000,000
Uganda	1971–78	Civil war, Idi Amin coup; massacres	300,000
	1981–87	Army vs. people; massacres	308,000
Burundi	1972	Hutu vs. govt., massacres	110,000
	1988–95	Tutsi massacre of Hutu civilians	170,000
Ethiopia	1974–92	Eritrean revolt and famine	575,000
Angola	1975–95	Civil war	500,000
Mozambique	1981–94	Famine worsened by civil war	1,050,000
Somalia	1988–95	Civil war	355,000
Liberia	1990–95	Rebels vs. rebels vs. govt.	150,000
MIDDLE EAST			
Iraq	1961–70	Civil war, Kurds vs. govt.; massacre of Christians	105,000
	1982–88	Iran attack following Iraqi invasion	600,000
Yemen	1962–69	Coup; civil war; Egypt intervening	101,000
Lebanon	1975–76	Civil war, Muslims vs. Christians; Syria intervening	100,000
Kuwait	1990–91	Iraqi invasion of Kuwait; U.S., U.N. intervening	200,000
SOUTH ASIA			
Bangladesh	1971	Bengalis vs. Pakistan; India invading; famine and massacres	1,000,000
India	1946–48	Muslims vs. Hindus; Britain intervening; massacres	800,000
Afghanistan	1978–91	Civil war, Muslims vs. govt.; U.S.S.R. intervening	1,500,000
WORLD WARS			
	1914–18	World War I	38,351,000
	1939–45	World War II	19,617,000
		Total	88,754,000

SOURCE: Ruth Leger Sivard, *World Military and Social Expenditures 1996*, 16th edition (Washington, D.C.: World Priorities, 1996).

1990. Each side not only spent massive sums every year on the development of armaments and on maintaining large numbers of military personnel, but constructed extensive systems of alliances with other countries, often training the armed forces of allied states. The Soviets concentrated attention on Eastern Europe but also provided weaponry and training for states in the Middle East, Asia, and Africa. The United States built a system of alliances, including the North Atlantic Treaty Organization (NATO), stretching across much of the world.

The Arms Trade

The bulk of the world trade in armaments—the **arms trade**—is weaponry sold by the industrialized nations to Third World countries. The United States and the USSR were the world's leading arms exporters. In the years before the Gulf War of 1991, the USSR and some of the Western nations provided or sold weapons and other military-related goods to Iraq,

KEY CONCEPTS IN REVIEW

Limited war is limited to only small segments of the population—soldiers directly involved with the fighting (usually a small percentage of the adult males) or civilians living in the immediate region.

Total war involves several countries, high proportions of their male populations, the mobilization of their overall economies, and fighting throughout the world. In the twentieth century, two major developments contributed to the transition from limited to total war: the **industrialization of war,** which is the application of modern industrial methods to the development and production of weapons, and the rise of the mass military organization.

which was in danger of losing its war with Iran. Certain of these weapons, particularly those furnished by the Soviet Union, proved to be old-fashioned or inadequate when faced with the very latest Western arms technology—as the outcome of the Gulf War showed. Yet the latest technology is on offer to whoever wishes and can afford to buy.

World military expenditures followed an upward trend from the 1950s until the end of the 1980s. In 1977, world expenditure on weapons exceeded $1 billion a day, representing a rate of spending of $50 million each hour. By the latter part of the 1980s, this rate had almost doubled, as measured in real terms (taking out the factor of inflation). Global military expenditure in 1993 was estimated at some 5 percent of total world income. It is greater than the economic production of the whole African continent; it is more than that of all Asia, if Japan is left out.

In light of the ending of the Cold War, one could hopefully anticipate a reduction in the developed world's military spending. Arms-related expenditure has dropped sharply in Russia and the other states that used to form the Soviet Union. The United States and other Western countries are also scaling back defense spending over the next few years. This will, however, increase the pressure to export arms to make up for lost domestic markets. It is not certain that the ending of the Cold War will reduce what Third World countries see as security requirements,

internal as well as external. As we shall see in the next sections, to what degree we can count on a global peace dividend remains far from clear.

War and Global Security

Is the world becoming a safer place as a result of the recent political developments? Certainly the prospect of an all-out nuclear holocaust is much diminished. But the possibility of nuclear war has not disappeared. There are at least 50,000 nuclear weapons still in existence. Most of these belong to the United States, Russia, and other states of the former USSR. But Britain, France, and China possess significant stockpiles; Israel has been a nuclear weapon state for some time; India and Pakistan may also now have the capability; and others have the means to follow suit.

A major problem is how to contain nuclear proliferation—the spread of nuclear weapons to states that do not currently possess them. It is hard to argue that global security would be enhanced if thirty, forty, or more states possessed nuclear weapons. Yet the Western powers, who justify their nuclear arsenals on the grounds that they deter aggression, can hardly be surprised if other countries seek to obtain them for the same reason. And if one state acquires the capability, its rival will seek to do likewise. The likelihood of proliferation thus increases.

The immediate danger resulting from the breakup of the Soviet Union would seem to have been avoided. The nuclear weapons deployed throughout what are now twelve independent republics will be concentrated on Russian territory, where adequate security and control can be provided more readily. Yet because of the expense needed to maintain weapons and materials in good condition, there are doubts about their continuing safety. Moreover, former Soviet scientists may be recruited by other countries for their expertise.

At the heart of the proliferation problem is the place that the two materials required for nuclear weapons, highly enriched uranium and plutonium, occupy in the peaceful production of nuclear power. Given the technological expertise, possession of either of these materials makes possible the building of a nuclear weapon. Japan and Germany in particular possess plutonium stocks as extensive as those in the nuclear arsenals of the United States, and could construct nuclear armaments rapidly if they so chose. The reprocessing of spent fuel from nuclear power stations also creates a large-scale proliferation threat. According to existing plans, by the turn of the new century, two thousand metric tons of plutonium will have been recovered from spent fuel in reprocessing plants in Europe and Japan. Fewer than fifteen pounds is needed to make a nuclear bomb. Since plutonium lasts for thousands of years, the problem of guaranteeing its safety and peaceful use is likely to prove formidable.

While the risk of a global nuclear war has become lessened, we will still for the indefinite future live in the shadow of a possible nuclear conflict. Even if nuclear weapons were completely scrapped, which looks unlikely, the knowledge that produced them would remain. Moreover, the application of science to the development of military technology continues. Nuclear weapons are not the only destructive armaments that people are capable of inventing. Chemical weapons, for example, are cheap to produce. Iraq used chemical weapons in its war with Iran during the 1980s and threatened to use them in its war with the United States and other Western countries in 1991. Chemical weapons mostly work by bombarding enemy troops or civilians with poisonous gases, which can be instantly fatal. One of these artificially produced poison gases was used in the attack upon commuters in the Tokyo subway system in 1995, in which several people were killed and many others had to be hospitalized.

This is a time of basic change in the world political order, however, and opportunities exist for producing a less dangerous world. The risks are easy to see: to possible nuclear proliferation and other weapons of mass destruction must be added the influence of new forms of nationalism, ethnic and religious antagonisms, and inequalities between rich and poorer nations—all potential sources of global conflicts. On the other hand, some of the main factors that promoted warfare in the past, particularly the drive to acquire new territories by conquest, have become less relevant today. Modern societies are much more interdependent globally, and for the most part their boundaries

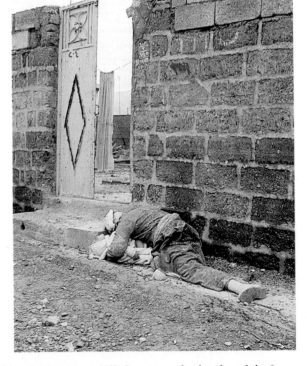

Chemical weapons killed many on both sides of the Iran-Iraq war in the 1980s.

have been fixed and agreed on by the overall community of states. Present-day warfare, especially nuclear war, has become so destructive that it cannot be used to achieve realistic political or economic objectives.

One of the most hopeful developments in recent years has been the growing recognition that the age-old adage "If you want peace, prepare for war" does not apply in the nuclear age. Even if nuclear confrontations are avoided, wars using conventional weapons would prove massively destructive.

Michael MccGwire, a well-known defense analyst, has argued that over the next twenty or thirty years the realistic possibility exists of creating a world free of nuclear weapons (McGwire, 1995). A nuclear weapons-free world (NWW) would be one where the nuclear powers agree to scrap all their nuclear armaments over an agreed period. An NWW, he says, is the only way to halt proliferation and keep nuclear weapons out of the hands of aggressive states and terrorist groups. It is a realistic option because many military and political leaders have come to see that nuclear weapons are useless for strategic purposes. The only reason for having them is that others have them or might acquire them. The risk of war will be there whatever happens; but an NWW is the only way to avoid the possibility of calamitous nuclear confrontations, which could still destroy large parts of the earth and perhaps even humanity as a whole.

SUMMARY

1. The term *government* refers to a political apparatus in which officials enact policies and make decisions. *Politics* refers to the use of power to affect government actions.

2. *Power* is the capacity to achieve one's aims even against the resistance of others, and often involves the use of force. A government is said to have *authority* when its use of power is legitimate. Such legitimacy derives from the consent of those being governed. The most common form of legitimate government is democratic, but other legitimate forms are also possible.

3. A *state* is characterized by a political apparatus (government institutions) including civil service officials, ruling over a geographically defined territory, whose authority is backed by a legal system and which has the capacity to use force to implement policies.

All modern states are *nation-states*, having certain additional features: *sovereignty*, the idea that government has authority over a given area; *citizenship*, the idea that people have common rights and duties and are aware of their part in the state; and *nationalism*, the sense of being part of a broader, unifying political community.

4. Most nation-states became centralized through the activities of monarchs who concentrated social power. Citizens initially had few rights of political participation, or none at all; such rights were achieved only through a long process of struggle which continues to this day. *Civil rights* refer to the freedoms and privileges guaranteed to individuals by law. *Political rights* ensure that citizens may participate in politics (by voting, for example). *Social rights* guarantee every individual some minimum standard of living. Social rights are the basis for the *welfare state*, which supports citizens who are unable to support themselves.

5. The term *democracy* literally means rule by the people, but this phrase can be interpreted in various ways. For instance, "the people" has often really meant "adult male property owners," while "rule" might refer to government policies, administrative decisions, or both.

Several different forms of democracy exist, including: *participatory democracy*, also called *direct democracy*, which occurs when everyone is immediately involved in all decision making, although this can be cumbersome for larger groups; *liberal democracy*, which is a system in which citizens have a choice to vote between at least two political parties for representatives who will be entrusted with decision making; and *constitutional monarchy*, which includes a royal family whose powers are severely restricted by a constitution, which puts authority in the hands of democratically elected representatives.

6. A political party is an organization oriented toward achieving legitimate control of government through an electoral process. In most Western states, the largest parties are those associated with general political interests—socialism, communism, liberalism, or conservatism. There is usually some connection between voting patterns and class differences. In many Western countries there has recently been a decline in allegiance to traditional parties and a growing disenchantment with the party system in general.

7. Women achieved the right to vote much later than men in all countries, and continue to be poorly represented among political elites. They have been influential on social and civil rights issues, and most Western countries have passed equal rights legislation over recent years.

8. According to Weber and Schumpeter, the level of democratic participation that can be achieved in a modern, large-scale society is limited. The rule of *elites* is inevitable, but multiparty systems provide the possibility of choosing *who* exercises power. The *pluralist theorists* add the claim that the competition of interest groups limits the degree to which ruling elites are able to concentrate power in few hands.

9. The number of countries with democratic governments has rapidly increased in recent years, due in large part to the effects of *globalization* and of *mass communication* and to the spread of *competitive capitalism*. But democracy is not without its problems; people everywhere have begun to lose faith in the capacity of politicians and governments to solve problems and to manage economies, and many no longer vote.

10. Sociologists assumed for some time that nationalism was in decline, but at the end of the twentieth century it seems to be flourishing, and has become the focus of renewed attention. Three types of nationalism can be distinguished: *Classical nationalism* arose in the 1700s with the emergence of mass education, which fostered a specific cultural interpretation of the past history of new nation-states. *Postcolonial nationalism* refers to movements that emerged in colonized areas of the world in resistance to domination and oppression. *Subcultural nationalism* contrasts sharply with classical nationalism; it emphasizes regional identities distinct from the larger nation-state, and so often weakens the larger state.

11. The development of states and the advance of technology and industrialization changed the nature of war. Prior to the twentieth century, most battles were fought by small segments of the population, and were thus *limited* in scope. World War I was the first of the *total wars*, and involved *universal conscription* (the drafting of all able-bodied men of a certain age) and the mobilization of entire economies.

12. The threat of global nuclear war has diminished since the end of the Cold War, but the threat of *nuclear proliferation*, the spread of nuclear capabilities to numerous smaller countries with their own private rivalries, has become a serious problem; another is the invention and stockpiling of new chemical and biological weapons. There is reason to hope, however, that the use of weapons of mass destruction is becoming less likely, as modern societies become ever more globally interdependent.

social institutions

Social institutions are the "cement" of social life. They are the basic living arrangements that human beings work out with one another, by means of which continuity is achieved across the generations.

We begin in Chapter 12 with work and economic life. Although the nature of work varies widely both within and between societies, it is one of the most pervasively important of all human pursuits.

In Chapter 13, we look at the institutions of kinship, marriage, and the family. Although the social obligations associated with kinship vary between different types of societies, the family is everywhere the context within which the young are provided with care and protection. Marriage is more or less universally connected to the family, since it is a

means of establishing new kin connections and forming a household in which children are brought up. In traditional cultures, much of the direct learning a child receives occurs within the family context. In modern societies, children spend many years of their lives in special places of instruction outside the family—schools and colleges. They also are constantly fed images and information from the mass media. Chapter 14 looks at the ways in which formal education is organized, concentrating particularly on how the educational system relates to the mass media. The subject of Chapter 15 is religion. Although religious beliefs and practices are found in all cultures, the changes affecting religion in modern societies have been particularly acute. We analyze the nature of these changes, considering in what ways traditional types of religion still maintain their influence.

Chapter Twelve

Learn the impact of global economic competition on our working lives.

The Social Significance of Work

Assess the sociological ramifications of paid and unpaid work.

The Social Organization of Work

Understand that modern economies are based on the division of labor and economic interdependence. Learn Marx's theory of alienation. Familiarize yourself with modern systems of economic production.

The Modern Economy

See the importance of the rise of large corporations; consider particularly the global impact of transnational corporations.

The Changing Nature of Work

Learn about the impact of global competition on employment. Consider how work will change over the coming years.

WORK AND ECONOMIC LIFE

For most of us, work occupies a larger part of our lives than any other single type of behavior. We live in societies where people work in a variety of occupations, but this situation has only come about with industrial development. The majority of the population in traditional cultures were engaged in one main pursuit: food gathering or food production. Crafts such as carpentry, stonemasonry, and shipbuilding were practiced in the larger traditional societies, but only a small minority engaged in them as a full-time endeavor.

Work may be defined as the carrying out of tasks requiring the expenditure of mental and physical effort, which has as its objective the production of goods and services that cater to human needs. An **occupation**, or **job**, is work that is done in exchange for a regular wage, or salary. In all cultures, work is the basis of the economic system, or economy. The **economy** consists of institutions that provide for the production and distribution of goods and services.

The study of economic institutions is of major importance in sociology, because the economy influences all segments of society and therefore social reproduction in general. Hunting and gathering, pastoralism, agriculture, industrialism—these different ways of gaining a livelihood have a fundamental influence upon the lives people lead. The distribution of goods, and variations in the economic position of those who produce them, also strongly influence social inequalities of all kinds. Wealth and power do not inevitably go together, but in general the privileged in terms of wealth are also among the more powerful groups in a society.

In this chapter, we shall analyze the nature of work in modern societies and look at the major changes affecting economic life today. We will investigate the changing nature of industrial production, the ownership structure of large business corporations, and the changing nature of work itself. Modern industry, as has been stressed in other parts of the book, differs in a fundamental way from premodern systems of production, which were based above all on agriculture. Most people worked in the fields or cared for livestock. In modern societies, by contrast, only a tiny proportion of the population works in agriculture, and farming itself has become industrialized—it is carried on largely by means of machines rather than by human hand.

Modern industry is itself always changing—technological change is one of its main features. **Technology** refers to the harnessing of science to machinery to achieve greater productive efficiency. The nature of industrial production also changes in relation to wider social and economic influences. In this chapter, we focus on both technological and economic change, showing how these are transforming industry today.

We will also see that globalization makes a great deal of difference to our working lives; the nature of the work we do is being changed by forces of global economic competition.

THE SOCIAL SIGNIFICANCE OF WORK

To tackle these problems, we need to relate work to the broad contours of our society and to industrial organization as a whole. We often associate the notion of work with drudgery—with a set of tasks that we want to minimize and, if possible, escape from altogether. You may have this very thought in mind as you set out to read this chapter! Is this most people's attitude toward their work, and if so, why? We shall try to find out in the following pages.

Work has more going for it than drudgery, or people would not feel so lost and disoriented when they become unemployed. How would you feel if you thought you would never get a job? In modern societies, having a job is important for maintaining self-

---

KEY CONCEPTS IN REVIEW

Work means performing tasks to produce goods and performing services that cater to human needs. An **occupation** or a **job** is work done in exchange for a regular wage. There is both paid work and unpaid work. The **economy** consists of institutions that provide for the production and distribution of goods and services.

In modern societies, paid work is important for several reasons: money, activity, variety, a way to structure time, social contacts, and personal identity.

The **informal economy** refers to transactions outside the sphere of regular employment and includes the exchange of cash for services provided and the direct exchange of goods or services.

Work, even when routine, can provide a person with direction and identity.

esteem. Even where work conditions are relatively unpleasant, and the tasks involved dull, work tends to be a structuring element in people's psychological makeup and the cycle of their daily activities. Several characteristics of work are relevant here.

- *Money* A wage or salary is the main resource many people depend on to meet their needs. Without such an income, anxieties about coping with day-to-day life tend to multiply.
- *Activity level* Work often provides a basis for the acquisition and exercise of skills and capacities. Even where work is routine, it offers a structured environment in which a person's energies may be absorbed. Without it, the opportunity to exercise such skills and capacities may be reduced.
- *Variety* Work provides access to contexts that contrast with domestic surroundings. In the working environment, even when the tasks are relatively dull, individuals may enjoy doing something different from home chores.
- *Temporal structure* For people in regular employment, the day is usually organized around the rhythm of work. While this may sometimes be oppressive, it provides a sense of direction in daily activities. Those who are out of work frequently find boredom a major problem and develop a sense of apathy about time. As one unemployed man remarked, "Time doesn't matter now as much as it used to. . . . There's so much of it" (Fryer and McKenna, 1987).
- *Social contacts* The work environment often provides friendships and opportunities to participate in shared activities with others. Separated from the work setting, a person's circle of possible friends and acquaintances is likely to dwindle.
- *Personal identity* Work is usually valued for the sense of stable social identity it offers. For men in particular, self-esteem is often bound up with the economic contribution they make to the maintenance of the household. In addition, job conditions, such as the opportunity to work in jobs that are challenging, not routinized, and not subject to close supervision, are known to affect a person's sense of self-worth (Kohn, 1977).

Against the backdrop of this formidable list, it is not difficult to see why being without work may undermine individuals' confidence in their social value.

Unpaid Work

We often tend to think of work, as the notion of being "out of work" implies, as equivalent to having a paid job, but in fact this is an oversimplified view. Nonpaid labor (such as repairing one's own car or housework) looms large in many people's lives. Many types of work do not conform to orthodox categories of paid employment. Much of the work done in the **informal economy**, for example, is not recorded in any direct way in the official employment statistics. The term *informal economy* refers to transactions outside the sphere of regular employment, sometimes involving the exchange of cash for services provided, but also often involving the direct exchange of goods or services.

Someone who comes to fix the television may be paid in cash, "off the books," without any receipt being given or details of the job recorded. People may exchange pilfered or stolen goods with friends or associates in return for other favors. The informal economy includes not only "hidden" cash transactions, but many forms of *self-provisioning* that people carry on inside and outside the home. Do-it-yourself activities and household appliances and tools, for instance, provide goods and services that would otherwise have to be purchased (Gershuny and Miles, 1983).

Housework, which has traditionally mostly been carried out by women, is usually unpaid. But it is work, often very hard and exhausting work, nevertheless. Volunteer work, for charities or other organizations, has an important social role. Having a paid job is important for all the reasons listed above—but the category of "work" stretches more widely.

THE SOCIAL ORGANIZATION OF WORK

One of the most distinctive characteristics of the economic system of modern societies is the existence of a highly complex **division of labor:** work has become divided into an enormous number of different occupations in which people specialize. In traditional societies, nonagricultural work entailed the mastery of a craft. Craft skills were learned through a lengthy period of apprenticeship, and the worker normally carried out all aspects of the production process from beginning to end. For example, a metalworker making a plow would forge the iron, shape it, and assemble the implement itself. With the rise of modern industrial production, most traditional crafts have dis-

appeared altogether, replaced by skills that form part of more large-scale production processes. An electrician working in an industrial setting today, for instance, may inspect and repair only a few parts of one type of machine; different people will deal with the other parts and other machines.

The contrast in the division of labor between traditional and modern societies is truly extraordinary. Even in the largest traditional societies, there usually existed no more than twenty or thirty major craft trades, together with such specialized pursuits as merchant, soldier, and priest. In a modern industrial system, there are literally thousands of distinct occupations. The U.S. Census Bureau lists some 20,000 distinct jobs in the American economy. In traditional communities, most of the population worked on farms and were economically self-sufficient. They produced their own food, clothes, and other necessities of life. One of the main features of modern societies, by contrast, is an enormous expansion of **economic interdependence**. We are all dependent on an immense number of other workers—today stretching right across the world—for the products and services that sustain our lives. With few exceptions, the vast majority of people in modern societies do not produce the food they eat, the houses in which they live, or the material goods they consume.

Taylorism and Fordism

Writing some two centuries ago, Adam Smith, one of the founders of modern economics, identified advantages that the division of labor provides in terms of increasing productivity. His most famous work, *The Wealth of Nations,* opens with a description of the division of labor in a pin factory. A person working alone could perhaps make 20 pins per day. By breaking down that worker's task into a number of simple operations, however, ten workers carrying out specialized jobs in collaboration with one another could collectively produce 48,000 pins per day. The rate of production per worker, in other words, is increased from 20 to 4,800 pins, each specialist operator producing 240 times more than when working alone.

More than a century later, these ideas reached their most developed expression in the writings of Freder-

A Ford assembly line, 1913.

ick Winslow Taylor, an American management consultant. Taylor's approach to what he called scientific management involved the detailed study of industrial processes in order to break them down into simple operations that could be precisely timed and organized. **Taylorism**, as scientific management came to be called, was not merely an academic study. It was a system of production designed to maximize industrial output, and it had a widespread impact on the organization of industrial production and technology.

Taylor was concerned with improving industrial efficiency, but he gave little consideration to the results of that efficiency. Mass production demands mass markets, and the industrialist Henry Ford was among the first to see this link. **Fordism,** an extension of Taylor's principles of scientific management, is the name used to designate the system of mass production tied to the cultivation of mass markets. Ford designed his first auto plant at Highland Park, Michigan, in 1908 to manufacture only one product—the Model T Ford—thereby allowing the introduction of specialized tools and machinery meant for speed, precision, and simplicity of operation. One of Ford's most significant innovations was the construction of a moving assembly line, said to have been inspired by Chicago slaughterhouses, in which animals were disassembled section by section on a moving line. Each worker on Ford's assembly line was assigned a specialized task, such as fitting the left-side door handles as the car

bodies moved along the line. By 1929, when production of the Model T ceased, over 15 million cars had been produced.

LIMITATIONS

At one time, it looked as though Fordism represented the likely future of industrial production as a whole. This has not proved to be the case. The system can only be applied in industries, such as the automobile, that produce standardized products for large markets. To set up mechanized production lines is enormously expensive, and once a Fordist system is established, it is quite rigid; to alter a product, for example, substantial reinvestment is needed. Fordist production is easy to copy if sufficient funding is available to set up the plant. But firms in countries in which labor power is expensive find it difficult to compete with those where wages are cheaper. This was one of the factors originally leading to the rise of the Japanese car industry (although Japanese wage levels today are no longer low) and, more recently, that of South Korea.

Work and Alienation

Karl Marx was one of the first writers to grasp that the development of modern industry would reduce many people's work to dull, uninteresting tasks. Ac-

KEY CONCEPTS IN REVIEW

For Marx, **alienation** describes industrial production within capitalist settings where workers have little or no control over their work. Fordism and Taylorism can be seen as **low-trust systems** that maximize worker alienation. A **high-trust system** allows workers control over the pace and even content of their work.

cording to Marx, the division of labor alienates human beings from their work. For Marx, **alienation** refers not only to feelings of indifference or hostility to work, but to the overall framework of industrial production within a capitalist setting.

In traditional societies, he pointed out, work was often exhausting—peasant farmers sometimes had to toil from dawn to dusk. Yet peasants held a real measure of control over their work, which required much knowledge and skill. Many industrial workers, by contrast, have little control over their jobs, only contribute a fraction to the creation of the overall product, and have no influence over how or to whom it is eventually sold. Work thus appears as something alien, a task that the worker must carry out in order to earn an income but that is intrinsically unsatisfying.

Low-Trust and High-Trust Systems

Fordism and Taylorism are what some industrial sociologists call **low-trust systems.** Jobs are set by management and are geared to machines. Those who carry out the work tasks are closely supervised and are allowed little autonomy of action. Where there are many low-trust positions, the level of worker dissatisfaction and absenteeism is high, and industrial conflict is common. A **high-trust system** is one in which workers are permitted to control the pace, and even the content, of their work, within overall guidelines. Such systems are usually concentrated at the higher levels of industrial organizations.

Industrial Conflict

There have long been conflicts between workers and those in economic and political authority over them. Riots against conscription and high taxes, and food riots at periods of harvest failure, were common in urban areas of Europe in the eighteenth century. These "premodern" forms of labor conflict continued up to not much more than a century ago in some countries. For example, there were food riots in several large Italian towns in 1868 (Geary, 1981). Such traditional forms of confrontation were not just sporadic, irrational outbursts of violence: the threat or use of violence had the effect of limiting the price of grain and other essential foodstuffs (Rudé, 1964; Thompson, 1971; Booth, 1977).

Industrial conflict between workers and employers first of all tended to follow these older patterns. In situations of confrontation, workers would quite often leave their places of employment and form crowds in the streets; they would make their grievances known through their unruly behavior or by engaging in acts of violence against the authorities. Workers in some parts of France in the late nineteenth century would threaten disliked employers with hanging (Holton, 1978). Use of the *strike* as a weapon, today commonly associated with organized bargaining between workers and management, developed only slowly and sporadically.

STRIKES

We can define a **strike** as a temporary stoppage of work by a group of employees in order to express a

The National Basketball Association's lockout of 1998 pitted the professional players' union against the owners in a battle for a percentage of league revenue. Superstars Grant Hill (foreground) and Tim Duncan poked fun at their temporary unemployment in this advertisement.

grievance or enforce a demand (Hyman, 1984). All the components of this definition are important in separating strikes from other forms of opposition and conflict. A strike is *temporary*, since workers intend to return to the same job with the same employer; where workers quit altogether, the term "strike" is not appropriate. As a *stoppage of work*, a strike is distinguishable from an overtime ban or "slow down." A *group* of workers has to be involved, because a strike is a collective action, not the response of one individual worker. That those involved are *employees* serves to separate strikes from protests such as may be conducted by tenants or students. Finally, a strike involves seeking to make known a grievance or press a demand; workers who miss work to go to a ball game could not be said to be on strike.

Strikes represent only one aspect or type of conflict in which workers and management may become involved. Other closely related expressions of organized conflict are lockouts (where the employers rather than the workers bring about a stoppage of work), output restrictions, and clashes in contract negotiations. Less-organized expressions of conflict may include high labor turnover, absenteeism, and interference with production machinery.

Workers choose to go out on strike for many specific reasons. They may be seeking to gain higher wages, forestall a proposed reduction in their earnings, protest against technological changes that make their work duller or lead to layoffs, or obtain greater security of employment. However, in all these circumstances the strike is essentially a mechanism of power: a weapon of people who are relatively powerless in the workplace, and whose working lives are affected by managerial decisions over which they have little or no control. It is usually a weapon of "last resort," to be used when other negotiations have failed, because workers on strike either receive no income, or depend upon union funds, which might be limited.

LABOR UNIONS

Although their levels of membership, and the extent of their power, vary widely, union organizations exist

The 1997 UPS strike demonstrated the power of the labor union in protecting worker interests.

in all Western countries, which also all legally recognize the right of workers to strike in pursuit of economic objectives. Why have unions become a basic feature of Western societies? Why does union-management conflict seem to be a more or less ever-present possibility in industrial settings?

Some have proposed that unions are effectively a modern version of medieval guilds—associations of people working in the same trade—reassembled in the context of modern industry. Thus, Frank Tannenbaum has suggested that unions are associations built upon the shared outlook and experience of those working in similar jobs (Tannenbaum, 1964). This interpretation might help us understand why unions often emerged first among craft workers, but does not explain why they have been so consistently associated with wage bargaining and industrial conflict. A more satisfactory explanation must look to the fact that unions developed to protect the material interests of workers in industrial settings in which they hold very little formal power.

In the early development of modern industry, workers in most countries had no political rights and little influence over the conditions of work in which they found themselves. Unions developed as a means of redressing the imbalance of power between workers and employers. Whereas workers had virtually no power as individuals, through collective organization their influence was considerably increased. An employer can do without the labor of any particular worker, but not without that of all or most of the workers in a factory or plant. Unions originally were mainly "defensive" organizations, providing the means whereby workers could counter the overwhelming power that employers wielded over their lives.

Workers today have voting rights in the political sphere, and there are established forms of negotiation with employers, by means of which economic benefits can be pressed for and grievances expressed. However, union influence, both at the level of the local plant and nationally, still remains primarily *veto power*. In other words, using the resources at their disposal, including the right to strike, unions can only *block* employers' policies or initiatives, not help formulate them in the first place. There are exceptions to this, for instance where unions and employers negotiate periodic contracts covering conditions of work.

Unions themselves, of course, have altered over the years. Some have grown very large and have become bureaucratized. These are staffed by full-time officials, who may themselves have little direct experience of the conditions under which their members work. The activities and views of union leaders can thus become quite distant from those of the members they represent. Shop-floor groups sometimes find themselves in conflict with the strategies of their own unions. Most unions have not been successful in recruiting a high level of women workers. Although some have initiated campaigns to increase their female membership, many have in the past actively discouraged women from joining.

Today, unions in Western countries are facing a threat from three related changes—the recession in world economic activity, associated with high levels of unemployment, which weakens the unions' bargaining position; the decline of the older manufacturing industries, in which the union presence has traditionally been strong; and the increasing intensity of international competition, particularly from Far Eastern countries, where wages are often lower than in the West. In the United States and several European countries, including Britain, France, Germany, and Denmark, rightist governments came to power in the 1970s or 1980s, mostly determined to limit what they saw as excessive, and negative, union influence in industry.

In the United States, unions face a crisis of even greater dimensions than their counterparts in most European countries. Union-protected working conditions and wages have been eroded in several major industries over the past twenty-five years. Workers in the trucking, steel, and car industries have all accepted lower wages than those previously negotiated. The unions came out second-best in several major strikes, perhaps the most notable example being the crushing of the air traffic controllers' union in the early 1980s.

Decline in union membership and influence is something of a general phenomenon in the industrialized countries, and is not to be explained wholly in terms of political pressure applied by rightist governments against the unions. Unions usually become weakened during periods when unemployment is high, as has been the case for a considerable while in many Western countries. Trends toward more flexible production tend to diminish the force of unionism, which flourishes more extensively where there are many people working together in large factories.

THE MODERN ECONOMY

Modern societies are, in Marx's term, capitalistic. **Capitalism** is a way of organizing economic life that is distinguished by the following important features: private ownership of the means of production; profit as incentive; free competition for markets to sell goods, acquire cheap materials, and utilize cheap labor; and restless expansion and investment to accumulate capital. Capitalism, which began to spread with the growth of the Industrial Revolution in the early nineteenth century, is a vastly more dynamic economic system than any other that preceded it in history. While the system has had many critics, like Marx, it is now the most widespread form of economic organization in the world.

So far in this chapter, we have been looking at industry mostly from the perspective of occupations and employees. We have studied how patterns of work have changed and the factors influencing the development of labor unions. But we have also to concern ourselves with the nature of the business firms in which the workforce is employed. (It should be recognized that many people today are employees of government organizations, although we shall not consider these here.) What is happening to business corporations today, and how are they run?

Corporations and Corporate Power

Since the turn of the twentieth century, modern capitalist economies have been more and more influenced by the rise of large business **corporations.** The share of total manufacturing assets held by the two hundred largest *manufacturing* firms in the United States has increased by 0.5 percent each year from 1900 to the present day; these two hundred corporations now control over half of all manufacturing assets. The two hundred largest *financial* organizations—banks, building societies, and insurance companies—account for more than half of all financial activity. There are numerous connections between large firms. For example, financial institutions hold well over 30 percent of the shares of the largest two hundred manufacturing firms.

Of course, there still exist thousands of smaller firms and enterprises within the American economy. In these companies, the image of the **entrepreneur**— the boss who owns and runs the firm—is by no means obsolete. The large corporations are a different matter. Ever since Adolf Berle and Gardiner Means published their celebrated study *The Modern Corporation and Private Property* almost seventy years ago, it has been accepted that most of the largest firms are not run by those who own them (Berle and Means, 1982). In theory, the large corporations are the property of their shareholders, who have the right to make all important decisions. But Berle and Means argued that since share ownership is so dispersed, actual control has passed into the hands of the managers who run firms on a day-to-day basis. *Ownership* of the corporations is thus separated from their *control*.

Whether run by owners or managers, the power of the major corporations is very extensive. When one or a handful of firms dominate in a given industry, they often cooperate in setting prices rather than freely competing with one another. Thus, the giant oil companies normally follow one another's lead in the price charged for gasoline. When one firm occupies a commanding position in a given industry, it is said to be in a **monopoly** position. More common is a situation of **oligopoly**, in which a small group of giant corporations predominate. In situations of oligopoly, firms are able more or less to dictate the terms on which they buy goods and services from the smaller firms that are their suppliers.

Types of Corporate Capitalism

There have been three general stages in the development of business corporations, although each overlaps with the others and all continue to coexist today. The first stage, characteristic of the nineteenth and early twentieth centuries, was dominated by **family capitalism.** Large firms were run either by individual entrepreneurs or by members of the same family and then passed on to their descendants. The famous corporate dynasties, such as the Rockefellers and Fords, belong in this category. These individuals and families did not just own a single large corporation, but held a diversity of economic interests and stood at the apex of economic empires.

KEY CONCEPTS IN REVIEW

Capitalism is a way of organizing economic life based on the following features:

- private ownership of the means of production;
- profit as an incentive;
- free competition for markets to sell goods, acquire cheap raw materials, and use cheap labor;
- restless expansion and investment to accumulate capital.

Large business **corporations** dominate in modern capitalist economies. When one corporation has a commanding position in an industry, it is a **monopoly.** More common is the **oligopoly,** in which a small group of large corporations predominate in an industry.

There have been three general stages in the development of business corporations. **Family capitalism,** enterprises run by **entrepreneurs,** was replaced by **managerial capitalism,** in which managers, not entrepreneurs or owners, made most of the decisions. The final stage was **institutional capitalism,** characterized by a consolidated network of business leaders.

With the globalizing of the economy, most large corporations have become **transnational,** or **multinational,** companies. They operate across different national boundaries in two or more countries and are of key importance to the **international division of labor**—the worldwide distribution of jobs. Transnational corporations can be divided into three types: (1) **ethnocentric transnationals,** in which management practices are standardized across all countries and are based on the cultural norms of the country where the company is based; (2) **polycentric transnationals,** in which management practices are based on broad guidelines but adapted by local managers in each country; and (3) **geocentric transnationals,** in which management is highly adaptive and mobile according to need.

Most of the big firms founded by entrepreneurial families have since become public companies—that is, shares of their stock are traded on the open market—and have passed into managerial control. But important elements of family capitalism remain, even within some of the largest corporations like the Ford Motor Company, where William Clay Ford Jr. serves as chair of the board. Among small firms, such as local shops run by their owners, small plumbing and housepainting businesses, and so forth, family capitalism continues to dominate. Some of these firms, such as shops that remain in the hands of the same family for two or more generations, are also dynasties on a minor scale. However, the small business sector is a highly unstable one, and economic failure is very common; the proportion of firms that are owned by members of the same family for extended periods of time is minuscule.

In the large corporate sector, family capitalism was increasingly succeeded by **managerial capitalism.** As managers came to have more and more influence through the growth of very large firms, the entrepreneurial families were displaced. The result has been described as the replacement of the family in the company by the company itself. The corporation emerged as a more defined economic entity. In studying the two hundred largest manufacturing corporations in the United States, Michael Allen found that in cases where profit showed a decline, family-controlled enterprises were unlikely to replace their chief executive, but manager-controlled firms did so rapidly (Allen, 1981).

Managerial capitalism has today partly ceded place to a third form of corporate system: **institutional capitalism.** This term refers to the emergence of a consolidated network of business leadership, concerned not only with decision making within single firms but also with the development of corporate power beyond them. Institutional capitalism is based on the practice of corporations holding shares in other firms. In effect, interlocking boards of directors exercise control over much of the corporate landscape. This reverses the process of increasing managerial control, since the managers' shareholdings are dwarfed by the large blocks of shares owned by other corporations. One of the main reasons for the spread of institutional capitalism is the shift in patterns of investment that has occurred over the past thirty years. Rather than investing directly by buying shares in a business, individuals now invest in money markets, trusts, insurance, and pension funds that are controlled by large financial organizations, which in turn invest these grouped savings in industrial corporations.

The Money-Changer and His Wife, *sixteenth-century Dutch ancestors of American family capitalism, by Quentin Metsys.*

The Transnational Corporations

With the intensifying of globalization, most large corporations now operate in an international economic context. When they establish branches in two or several countries, they are referred to as **transnational,** or **multinational,** companies. "Transnational" is the preferred term, indicating that these companies operate across many different national boundaries.

The largest transnationals are gigantic; their wealth outstrips that of many countries. Half of the hundred largest economic units in the world today are nations; the other half are transnational corporations. The scope of these companies' operations is staggering. The six hundred largest transnationals account for more than one-fifth of the total industrial and agricultural production in the global economy; about seventy are responsible for half of total global sales (Dicken, 1992). The revenues of the largest two hundred companies rose tenfold between the mid-1970s and the 1990s. Over the past twenty years, the transnationals' activities have become increasingly global: only three of the world's largest companies in 1950 had manufacturing subsidiaries in more than twenty countries; some fifty do so today. These are still a small minority; most of the transnationals have subsidiaries in two to five countries.

Eighty of the top two hundred transnational corporations in the world are based in the United States, contributing just over half the total sales. The share of American companies has, however, fallen significantly since 1960, during which time Japanese companies have grown dramatically; only five Japanese corporations were included in the top two hundred in 1960, as compared with twenty-eight in 1991. Contrary to common belief, three-quarters of all foreign direct investment is between the industrialized countries. Nevertheless, the involvements of transnationals in Third World countries are extensive, with Brazil, Mexico, and India showing the highest levels of foreign investment. The most rapid rate of increase in corporate investment by far has been in the Asian newly industrializing countries (NICs) of Singapore, Taiwan, Hong Kong, South Korea, and Malaysia.

The reach of the transnationals over the past thirty

years would not have been possible without advances in transport and communications. Air travel now allows people to move around the world at a speed that would have seemed inconceivable even sixty ago. The development of extremely large ocean-going vessels (superfreighters), together with containers that can be shifted directly from one type of carrier to another, makes possible the easy transport of bulk materials.

Telecommunications technologies now permit more or less instantaneous communication from one part of the world to another. Satellites have been used for commercial telecommunications since 1965, when the first satellite could carry 240 telephone conversations at once. Current satellites can carry 12,000 simultaneous conversations! The larger transnationals now have their own satellite-based communications systems. The Mitsubishi corporation, for instance, has a massive network, across which five million words are transmitted to and from its headquarters in Tokyo each day.

TYPES OF TRANSNATIONAL CORPORATIONS

The transnationals have assumed an increasingly important place in the world economy over the course of this century. They are of key importance in the **international division of labor**—the worldwide distribution of jobs. Just as national economies have become increasingly *concentrated*—dominated by a limited number of very large companies—so has the world economy. In the case of the United States and several of the other leading industrialized countries, the firms that dominate nationally also have a very wide-ranging international presence. Many sectors of world production (such as agribusiness) are *oligopolies*—production is controlled by three or four corporations, which dominate the market. Over the past two or three decades, international oligopolies have developed in automobile production, microprocessors, the electronics industry, and some other goods marketed worldwide.

H. V. Perlmutter divides transnational corporations into three types. One consists of **ethnocentric transnationals,** in which company policy is set, and as far as possible put into practice, from a headquarters in the country of origin. Companies and plants that the parent corporation owns around the world are cultural extensions of the originating company—its practices are standardized across the globe. A second category is that of **polycentric transnationals,** where overseas subsidiaries are managed by local firms in each country. The headquarters in the country or countries of origin of the main company establish broad guidelines within which local companies manage their own affairs. Finally, there are **geocentric transnationals,** which are international in their management structure. Managerial systems are integrated on a global basis, and higher managers are very mobile, moving from country to country as needs dictate (Perlmutter, 1972).

Of all transnationals, the Japanese companies tend to be most strongly ethnocentric in Perlmutter's terms. Their worldwide operations are usually controlled tightly from the parent corporation, sometimes with the close involvement of the Japanese government. The Japanese Ministry of International Trade and Industry (MITI) plays a much more direct part in the overseeing of Japanese-based foreign enterprise than Western governments do. MITI has produced a series of development plans coordinating the overseas spread of Japanese firms over the past two decades. One distinctive Japanese type of transnational consists of the giant trading companies or *sogo shosha*. These are colossal conglomerates whose main concern is with the financing and support of trade. They provide financial, organizational, and information services to other companies. About half of Japanese exports and imports are routed through the ten largest sogo

In one corner of the Global Workplace, Chinese factory workers assemble Big Bird dolls.

shosha. Some, like Mitsubishi, also have large manufacturing interests of their own.

Planning on a World Scale

The global corporations have become the first organizations able to plan on a truly world scale. Coca-Cola ads reach billions. A few companies with developed global networks are able to shape the commercial activities of diverse nations. There are four webs of interconnecting commercial activity in the new world economy. These are what Richard Barnet and John Cavanagh call the Global Cultural Bazaar, the Global Shopping Mall, the Global Workplace, and the Global Financial Network (Barnet and Cavanagh, 1994).

The Global Cultural Bazaar is the newest of the four but already the most extensive. Global images and global dreams are diffused through movies, TV programs, music, videos, games, toys, and T-shirts, sold on a worldwide basis. All over the earth, even in the poorest Third World countries, people are using the same electronic devices to see or listen to the same commercially produced songs and shows.

The Global Shopping Mall is a "planetary supermarket with a dazzling spread of things to eat, drink, wear and enjoy," according to Barnet and Cavanagh. It is more exclusive than the Cultural Bazaar because the poor haven't the resources to participate—they have the status only of window shoppers. Of the 5.5 billion people who make up the world's population, 3.5 billion lack the cash or credit to purchase any consumer goods.

The third global web, the Global Workplace, is the increasingly complex global division of labor that affects all of us. It consists of the massive array of offices, factories, restaurants, and millions of other places where goods are produced and consumed or information is exchanged. This web is closely bound up with the Global Financial Network, which it fuels and is financed by. The Global Financial Network consists of billions of bits of information stored in computers and portrayed on computer screens. It entails almost endless currency exchanges, credit-card transactions, insurance plans, and buying and selling of stocks and shares.

The Large Corporation: The Same, but Different

There are big differences between the large corporation in the late 1990s and its counterpart at mid-century. Many of the names are the same—General Motors, Ford, IBM, AT&T—but these have been joined by other giant firms, largely unknown in the 1950s, such as Texas Instruments and American Express. They all wield great power, and their top executives still inhabit the large buildings that dominate so many city centers.

The Global Financial Network includes ATMs that can do business in four languages.

But below the surface similarities between today and half a century ago, some profound transformations have taken place. The origin of these transformations lies in that process we have encountered often in this book: globalization. Over the past fifty years, the giant corporations have become more and more caught up in global competition; as a result, their internal composition, and in a way their very nature, has altered.

Robert Reich has written:

> Underneath, all is changing. America's core corporation no longer plans and implements the production of a large volume of goods and services; it no longer invests in a vast array of factories, machinery, laboratories, inventories, and other tangible assets; it no longer employs armies of production workers and middle-level managers. . . . In fact, the core corporation is no longer even American. It is, increasingly, a facade, behind which teems an array of decentralized groups and subgroups continuously contracting with similarly diffuse working units all over the world. (Reich, 1991)

The large corporation is less and less a big business than an "enterprise web"—a central organization that links smaller firms together. IBM, for example, which used to be one of the most jealously self-sufficient of all large corporations, in the 1980s and early 1990s joined with dozens of U.S.-based companies and more than eighty foreign-based firms to share strategic planning and cope with production problems.

Some corporations remain strongly bureaucratic and centered in the United States. However, most are no longer so clearly located anywhere. The old transnational corporation used to work mainly from its American headquarters, from where its overseas production plants and subsidiaries were controlled. Now, with the transformation of space and time noted earlier (Chapter 5), groups situated in any region of the world are able, via telecommunications and computer, to work with others. Nations still try to influence flows of information, resources, and money across their borders. But modern communications technologies make this more and more difficult, if not impossible. Knowledge and finances can be transferred across the world as electronic blips moving at the speed of light.

The products of the transnational companies similarly have an international character. When is something "made in America," and when not? There is no longer any clear answer. What could be more American than a Pontiac Le Mans? Yet whoever buys the Pontiac, or any other "American-made" car, is really buying a product that people of different nationalities came together to design, make, and market (see Figure 12.1). Of the $20,000 the buyer pays for the car, $6,000 goes to South Korea for basic assembly costs; $3,500 goes to Japan for advanced components; $1,500 goes to West Germany to pay for design engineering; $800 is sent to Taiwan, Singapore, and Japan for small components; Britain takes $500 to pay for advertising and marketing services; $100, for data processing, is sent to Barbados in the West Indies. The $8,000 or so that remains goes to a diversity of groups—strategists in Detroit, lawyers and bankers in New York, lobbyists in Washington, and General Motors shareholders, an increasing proportion of whom are in fact foreign nationals (Reich, 1991).

THE CHANGING NATURE OF WORK

The globalizing of economic production, together with the spread of information technology, is altering the nature of the jobs most people do. As discussed earlier in Chapter 7, the proportion of people working in blue-collar jobs in industrial countries has progressively fallen. Fewer people work in factories than before. New jobs have been created in offices and in service centers such as supermarkets and airports. Many of these new jobs are filled by women.

Changes in Industrial Production

 From the early 1970s onward, firms in Western Europe, the United States, and Japan experimented with alternatives to low-trust systems mentioned earlier. These include automated assembly lines and

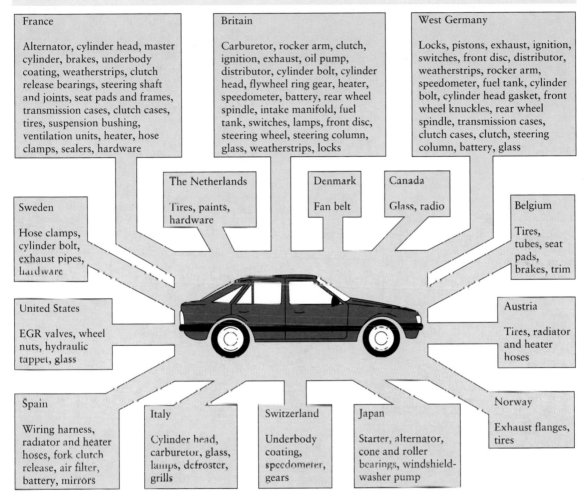

Figure 12.1
WHERE DOES YOUR CAR COME FROM?

France

Alternator, cylinder head, master cylinder, brakes, underbody coating, weatherstrips, clutch release bearings, steering shaft and joints, seat pads and frames, transmission cases, clutch cases, tires, suspension bushing, ventilation units, heater, hose clamps, sealers, hardware

Britain

Carburetor, rocker arm, clutch, ignition, exhaust, oil pump, distributor, cylinder bolt, cylinder head, flywheel ring gear, heater, speedometer, battery, rear wheel spindle, intake manifold, fuel tank, switches, lamps, front disc, steering wheel, steering column, glass, weatherstrips, locks

West Germany

Locks, pistons, exhaust, ignition, switches, front disc, distributor, weatherstrips, rocker arm, speedometer, fuel tank, cylinder bolt, cylinder head gasket, front wheel knuckles, rear wheel spindle, transmission cases, clutch cases, clutch, steering column, battery, glass

The Netherlands

Tires, paints, hardware

Denmark

Fan belt

Canada

Glass, radio

Sweden

Hose clamps, cylinder bolt, exhaust pipes, hardware

Belgium

Tires, tubes, seat pads, brakes, trim

United States

EGR valves, wheel nuts, hydraulic tappet, glass

Austria

Tires, radiator and heater hoses

Spain

Wiring harness, radiator and heater hoses, fork clutch release, air filter, battery, mirrors

Italy

Cylinder head, carburetor, glass, lamps, defroster, grills

Switzerland

Underbody coating, speedometer, gears

Japan

Starter, alternator, cone and roller bearings, windshield-washer pump

Norway

Exhaust flanges, tires

This schematic shows how automobile parts are produced in several countries and then sent to a central plant for final production of the car.

group production, in which a work group carries out a recognized role in influencing the nature of the work task. We shall now look at these strategies in turn.

AUTOMATION

The concept of **automation,** or programmable machinery, was introduced in the mid-1800s, when Christopher Spencer, an American, invented the Automat, a programmable lathe that made screws, nuts, and gears. Automation has thus far affected relatively few industries, but with advances in the design of industrial robots, its impact is certain to become greater. A robot is an automatic device that can perform functions ordinarily done by human workers. The term comes from the Czech word *robota,* or serf, popularized about fifty years ago by the playwright Karel Čapek.

Robots were first introduced into industry in some numbers in 1946, when a device was invented to automatically regulate machinery in the engineering industry. Robots of greater complexity, however, date only from the development of microprocessors—basically since the 1970s. The first robot controlled by a mini-computer was developed in 1974 by Cincinnati Milason. Robots today can execute numerous tasks like welding, spray-painting, and lifting and carrying parts. Some robots can distinguish parts by feel or touch, while others can make out a certain range of objects visually.

As Robert Ayres and Steven Miller have pointed out,

> There can be no more dedicated and untiring factory worker than a robot. Robots can repeat tasks such as spot-welding and spray-painting flawlessly on a variety of workpieces, and they can quickly be reprogrammed to perform entirely new tasks. . . . In the next few years, we can expect to see many industrial robots installed in medium-batch manufacturing plants. Robots will feed workpieces to clusters of automatic machines in workcells, which may be serialized to form a closed loop manufacturing system controlled by microprocessors. (Ayres and Miller, 1985)

The majority of the robots used in industry worldwide are to be found in automobile manufacture. The usefulness of robots in production thus far is relatively limited, because their capacity to recognize different objects and manipulate awkward shapes is still at a rudimentary level. Yet it is certain that automated production will spread rapidly in coming years; robots are becoming more sophisticated, while their costs are decreasing.

The introduction of computerized, automated technology like robots into the production process has led some sociologists to argue that labor has become deskilled and, as a result, workers have less autonomy in their jobs (Braverman, 1974; Cockburn, 1985). Other sociologists have disputed this conclusion, arguing that automation has required workers to learn more computer and other technical skills, which has resulted in an "upskilling" of labor (Blauner, 1964). More recent research confirms a general upskilling of production work, but asserts that upskilling comes at the price of limited autonomy for workers (Zuboff, 1988; Vallas and Beck, 1996).

A new study sheds some more light on this debate. The sociologist Richard Sennett studied the people who worked in a bakery that had been bought by a large food conglomerate and automated with the introduction of high-tech machinery. Computerized baking radically altered the way that bread was made. Instead of using their hands to mix the ingredients and knead the dough and their noses and eyes to judge when the bread was done baking, the bakery's workers had no physical contact with the materials or the loaves of bread. In fact, the entire process was controlled and monitored via computer screen. Computers decided the temperature and baking time of the ovens. While at times the machines produced excellent quality bread, at other times the results were burnt, blackened loaves. The workers at this bakery (it would be erroneous to call them bakers) were hired because they were skilled with computers, not because they knew how to bake bread. Ironically, these workers used very few of their computer skills. The production process involved little more than pushing buttons on a computer. In fact, one time when the computerized machinery broke down, the entire production process was halted because none of the bakery's "skilled" workers were trained or empowered to repair the problem. The workers that Sennett observed wanted to be helpful, to make things work again, but they could not, because automation had diminished their autonomy (Sennett, 1998). As we saw in Chapter 10, the introduction of computerized technology in the workplace has led to a general increase in all workers' skills, but has led to a bifurcated workforce composed of a small group of highly skilled professionals with high degrees of flexibility and autonomy in their jobs and a larger group of clerical, service, and production workers who lack autonomy in their jobs.

GROUP PRODUCTION

Group production, collaborative work groups in place of assembly lines, has sometimes been used in conjunction with automation as a way of reorganizing work. The underlying idea is to increase worker motivation by letting groups of workers collaborate in team production processes rather than requiring each worker to spend the whole day doing a single repetitive task like inserting the screws in the door handle of a car.

An example of group production is **quality circles (QCs)**, groups of between five and twenty workers who meet regularly to study and resolve production problems. Workers who belong to QCs receive extra training, enabling them to contribute technical knowledge to the discussion of production issues. QCs were initiated in the United States, taken up by a number of Japanese companies, then repopularized in the West in the 1980s. They represent a break from the assumptions of Taylorism, since they recognize that workers possess the expertise to contribute toward the definition and method of the tasks they carry out.

The positive effects of group production on workers can include the acquisition of new skills, increased autonomy, reduced managerial supervision, and growing pride in the goods and services that they produce. However, studies have identified a number of negative consequences of team production. Although direct managerial authority is less apparent in a team process, other forms of monitoring exist, such as supervision by other team workers (Smith, 1997). The sociologist Laurie Graham went to work on the assembly line at a Suburu-Isuzu factory and found that peer pressure from other workers to achieve greater productivity was relentless. One coworker told her, after initial enthusiasm for the team concept, that peer

supervision was just a new means of management trying to work people "to death." Graham also found that Suburu-Isuzu used the group-production concept as a means to resist labor unions, their argument being that if management and workers were on the same "team," then there should be no conflict between the two. In other words, the good "team player" doesn't complain. In the Suburu-Isuzu plant Graham worked in, demands for higher pay or reduced responsibilities were viewed as a lack of employee cooperativeness (Graham, 1995). Studies like Graham's have led sociologists to conclude that while team-based production processes provide workers opportunities for less monotonous forms of work, systems of power and control remain the same in the workplace.

FLEXIBLE PRODUCTION

One of the most important changes in worldwide production processes over the past few years has been the introduction of computer-aided design. While Taylorism and Fordism were successful at producing mass products (that were all the same) for mass markets, they were completely unable to produce small orders of goods, let alone goods specifically made for an individual customer. Computer-aided designs, coupled to other types of computer-based technology, have altered this situation in a radical way. Stanley Davis speaks of the emergence of "mass customizing": the new technologies allow the large-scale production of items designed for particular customers. Five thou-

KEY CONCEPTS IN REVIEW

Automation is the use of **robots** in the production process. **Group production**, sometimes used with automation, establishes collaborative work groups. An example of group production is **quality circles (QCs)**, in which workers actively participate in decision making. In **flexible production**, computers design customized products for a mass market. Industrial production has also become increasingly globalized in recent decades.

DEINDUSTRIALIZATION

In 1929, sociologists Robert and Helen Lynd published a book about the impact of industrialization on a midwestern city they called "Middletown." The Lynds observed that as an increasing number of relatively high-wage factory jobs became available over the years in the city's glass and automobile-parts industries, the habits and values of Middletown workers began to change. Thriftiness, for example, which had been an important feature of the workers' Protestant value system, was replaced by a consumer culture emphasizing car ownership. Similarly, those who engaged in the standardized labor of factory work came to prefer passive and standardized forms of leisure such as listening to the radio and reading popular magazines. Almost every aspect of social life in the community, the Lynds argued, including child-rearing practices, housing patterns, and political beliefs, was somehow affected by the industrial boom that had taken place in Middletown since 1890.

Were the Lynds to conduct their study today, they would find that an opposite process—*deindustrialization*—has been underway in many American cities since the 1970s.

Deindustrialization is defined as "a systematic decline in the industrial base" (Bluestone, 1988, p. 35), or as the process whereby the proportion of jobs in the manufacturing sector of the economy decreases over time. The consequences of deindustrialization are as significant as the changes noted by the Lynds almost seventy years ago.

sand shirts might be produced on an assembly line each day. It is now possible to customize every one of the shirts just as quickly as and at no greater expense than five thousand identical shirts (Davis, 1987).

Before computer-aided design came along, the Japanese pioneered what they called **flexible production**. By introducing production systems that differ in almost every respect from the mass production system Henry Ford pioneered at Detroit, Japanese car makers were able to notch up a remarkable increase in global sales from the mid-1970s to the early 1990s (Dertouzos, 1989). The Japanese have placed the emphasis on the creation of a skilled workforce and on ways of increasing the speed with which new product designs are introduced and new products brought to market.

Changes taking up to twenty-four hours in American car plants in the early 1980s could be made in five minutes in the Japanese factories. The goal was perfect first-time quality, with no need for subsequent improvements. Group production was brought to a high level; integrated work teams consisted of assemblers, workers, and suppliers. By means of these techniques, planners could work to a cycle (the time taken from the first conception of a new model until the last vehi-

It is estimated that factory, store, and office closings resulted in the loss of an astonishing 38 million jobs in the United States in the 1970s (Bluestone and Harrison, 1982, p. 26), with job losses continuing into the present. Hardest hit are cities in the Northeast and Upper Midwest. Manufacturing employment in Allentown, Pennsylvania, for example, decreased by almost 28 percent between 1980 and 1987, and dropped a staggering 47 percent in Gary, Indiana, during the same period (Goe, 1994, p. 981). Similar changes are occurring in cities across Europe (Lash and Urry, 1987; Byrne, 1995).

Why is deindustrialization happening? Some sociologists argue that the economies of First World nations are increasingly oriented toward the production and consumption of services such as education and recreation rather than manufactured goods; this orientation may account for the relative decline of the manufacturing sector. Others attribute deindustrialization to the globalization of the economy. As manufacturing firms develop the capacity to do business overseas, they can relocate factories to countries where labor costs are low.

Whatever its causes, the effects of deindustrialization are readily apparent. First, although many laid-off industrial workers eventually find employment elsewhere, they typically wind up in low-wage service-sector jobs. Deindustrialization may make downward mobility a common experience for blue-collar workers, with serious implications for their economic and psychological well-being as well as for the welfare of their families. Second, deindustri-

alization affects some groups of workers to a greater extent than others. The sociologist William Julius Wilson, for example, argues that the decline in manufacturing jobs has had a particularly severe impact on African Americans, many of whom live in deindustrialized cities. The consequences of job loss for inner-city life are profound and include spiraling rates of poverty, crime, and drug use (Wilson, 1996). Third, deindustrialization may undermine the strength of left-wing political parties inasmuch as the base of their working-class support narrows.

How serious has deindustrialization been in your community? If you were doing a study today like the one done by the Lynds in the 1920s, what aspects of social life would you expect to be affected by deindustrialization?

cle rolls off the production line) of seven and a half years. American planners, by contrast, until recently were working with thirteen-to-fifteen-year cycles. American car makers have now caught up a good deal, basically by trying to copy Japanese practices.

While flexible production has contributed to a stronger American economy, the effects on workers has not been wholly positive. Though workers do learn new skills and have less monotonous jobs, flexible production can create a whole new set of pressures for workers resulting from the need to carefully coordinate the complex production process and to quickly

produce the results. Laurie Graham's study of the Subaru-Isuzu factory documented instances when workers were left waiting until the last minute for critical parts in the production process. As a result, employees were forced to work longer and more intensely to keep up with the production schedule, without additional compensation. And as we saw in Chapter 7, although the American economy was booming throughout most of the 1980s and 1990s, average pay for most workers remained quite steady. The profits of these companies mostly benefitted upper management and shareholders.

GLOBAL PRODUCTION

Changes in industrial production include not only *how* products are manufactured, but, as we saw earlier with the example of an "American-made" car, *where* products are manufactured. For much of the twentieth century, the most important business organizations were large manufacturing firms that controlled both the making of goods and their final sales. Giant automobile companies such as Ford and General Motors typify this approach. Such companies employ tens of thousands of factory workers making everything from components to the final cars, which are then sold in the manufacturers' showrooms. Such manufacture-dominated production processes are organized as large bureaucracies, often controlled by a single firm.

During the past quarter century, however, another form of production has become important—one that is controlled by giant retailers. In retailer-dominated production, firms such as Walmart and Kmart buy products from manufacturers, who in turn arrange to have their products made by independently-owned factories. Sociologists Edna Bonacich and Richard Appelbaum, for example, show that in clothing manufacturing, most manufacturers actually employ no garment workers at all. Instead, they rely on thousands of factories around the world to make their apparel, which they then sell in department stores and other retail outlets. Clothing manufacturers do not own any of these factories, and therefore are not responsible for the conditions under which the clothing is made.

Two-thirds of all clothing sold in America is made in factories outside the United States, where workers are paid a fraction of U.S. wages. (In China, for example, workers are lucky to make $40 a month.) Bonacich and Appelbaum argue that such competition has resulted in a global "race to the bottom," in which retailers and manufacturers will go any place on earth where they can pay the lowest wages possible. One result is that much of the clothing we buy today was likely made in sweatshops by young workers—most likely teenage girls—who get paid pennies for clothing or athletic shoes that sell for $50, $100, or even more (Bonacich and Appelbaum, 2000).

Trends in the Occupational Structure

The occupational structure in all industrialized countries has changed very substantially since the beginning of the twentieth century (see Figure 7.2 on page 156). In 1900, about three-quarters of the employed population was in manual work, either farming or blue-collar work such as manufacturing. White-collar professional and service jobs were much fewer in number. By 1960, however, more people worked in white-collar professional and service jobs than in manual labor. By 1993, the occupational system had basically reversed its structure from 1900. Then, almost three-quarters of the employed population worked in white-collar professional and service jobs while the rest worked in blue-collar and farming jobs. By 2005, blue-collar work will decline even further, with most of the increase in new jobs occuring in the service industries. As we saw in Chapter 8, over the course of the twentieth century, numerous women joined the paid labor force. In 1998, however, 42 percent of working women had service-based or clerical positions while only 16 percent of men had these types of jobs. Likewise, 38 percent of men held blue-collar manual jobs, while only 10 percent of women were in such positions.

The reasons for the transformation of the occupational structure seem to be several. One is the continuous introduction of labor-saving machinery, culminating in the spread of information technology and computerization in industry in recent decades. Another is the rise of the manufacturing industry in other parts of the world, primarily Asia. The older industries in Western societies have experienced major job cutbacks because of their inability to compete with the more efficient Asian producers, whose labor costs are lower. As we have seen, this global economic transformation forced American companies to adopt new forms of production, which in turn forced employees to learn new skills and new occupations. A final important trend is the decline of full-time paid employment with the same employer over a long period of time. Not only has the transformation of the global economy affected the nature of day-to-day work, it has also changed the career patterns of many workers. We'll now turn to examine two such patterns that have become more prevalent today.

THE PORTFOLIO WORKER

In the light of the impact of the global economy and the demand for a "flexible" labor force, some sociologists and economists have argued that more and more people in the future will become "portfolio workers." They will have a "skill portfolio"—a number of different job skills and credentials—which they will use to move between several jobs during the course of their working lives. Only a relatively small proportion of workers will have continuous "careers" in the current sense.

Some see this move to the **portfolio worker** in a positive light: workers will not be stuck in the same job for years on end and will be able to plan their work lives in a creative way (Handy, 1994). Others hold that "flexibility" in practice means that organizations can hire and fire more or less at will, undermining any sense of security their workers might have. Employers will only have a short-term commitment to their workforces and will be able to minimize the paying of extra benefits or pension rights.

A study of Silicon Valley, California, claims that the economic success of the area is already founded on the portfolio skills of its workforce. The failure rate of firms in Silicon Valley is very high: about 300 new companies are established every year, but an equivalent number also go bust. The workforce, which has a very high proportion of professional and technical workers, has learned to adjust to this. The result, the authors say, is that talents and skills migrate rapidly from one firm to another, becoming more adaptable on the way. Technical specialists become consultants, consultants become managers, employees become venture capitalists—and back again (Bahrami and Evans, 1995).

Such a situation is as yet very definitely the exception rather than the rule. According to employment statistics, full-time workers in Britain and the United States—which have the most deregulated labor markets among industrial countries—spend as long in each job today as they did ten years ago (*The Economist*, 21 May 1995). The reasons seem to be that managers recognize that a high degree of turnover among workers is costly and bad for morale, and that they prefer to retrain their own employees rather than bring in new ones, even if this means paying above the market rate. In their book, *Built to Last* (1994), James Collins and Jerry Porras analyzed eighteen American companies that have continuously outperformed the stock-market average since 1926. They found that these companies, far from hiring and firing at will, had followed highly protective policies toward their staff. Only two of these companies over the period studied brought in a chief executive from the outside,

Portfolio workers, such as this graphic designer, often develop many different skills within their profession, making them employable in various capacities.

compared to thirteen of the less successful corporations included in the research.

These findings do not disprove the ideas of those who speak of the arrival of the portfolio worker. Organizational downsizing is a reality, throwing many thousands of workers who may have thought they had a lifetime job on to the labor market. To find work again, they may be forced to develop and diversify their skills. Many, particularly older people, might never be able to find jobs comparable to those they held before, or perhaps even paid work at all.

THE CONTINGENT WORKFORCE

Another important employment trend of the past decade has been the replacement of full-time workers by part-time workers who are hired and fired on a contingency basis. Most temporary workers are hired for the least-skilled and lowest paying jobs. But many of the "portfolio" workers that we just discussed take jobs on a part-time basis as well. As a general rule, part-time jobs do not include the benefits associated with full-time work, such as medical insurance, paid vacation time, or retirement benefits. Because employers can save on the costs of wages and benefits, the use of part-time workers has become increasingly common. Researchers estimate that contingency workers includes between 25 to 33 percent of the American workforce.

There has been some debate over the psychological effects of part-time work on the workforce. While many temporary workers fulfill their assignments in a prompt and satisfactory manner, others rebel against their tenuous positions by shirking their responsibilities or sabotaging their results. Some temporary workers have been observed trying to "look busy" or to work longer than necessary on rather simple tasks. Finally, contingency workers have tried to avoid emotionally intensive work that would require them to become psychologically committed to their employer.

However, some recent surveys of work indicate that part-time workers register higher levels of job satisfaction than those in full-time employment. This may be because most part-time workers are women, who have lower expectations of their careers than men, or who are particularly relieved to escape from domestic monotony. Yet many individuals seem to find reward precisely in the fact that they are able to balance paid work with other activities and enjoy a more varied life. Some people might choose to "peak" their lives, giving full commitment to paid work from their youth to their middle years, then perhaps changing to a second career, which would open up new interests.

THE SOCIOLOGICAL DEBATE

"GENERATION X": THE ENTREPRENEURIAL GENERATION?

Today's young adults born between 1965 and 1980 have been characterized by the mass media as "slackers." But sociologists are increasingly recognizing this group as the "entrepreneurial generation." The proportion of young adults ages eighteen to thirty-four who either own their own business, or who aspire to own their own business, is higher than any other cohort. Understanding why today's young adults are turning to entrepreneurship is a topic subject to debate among sociologists and economists.

According to Paul Reynolds, a professor of entrepreneurship at Marquette University, nearly 10 percent of Americans age twenty-five to thirty-four are actively working on starting a business—a rate nearly three times higher than in any other age group (Miniter, 1997). Even among people still in college, preferences for self-employment are widespread. In a survey of 1,000 college seniors nationwide, administered by the Graduate Management Admission Council in the mid-1990s, 49 percent of men and 31 percent of women revealed they were interested in pursuing entrepreneurship when they graduate.

Why do young adults today have such a strong proclivity toward self-employment? Economists historically have relied on two classical theories of entrepreneurship to explain such patterns: the "career" and "default" theories of self-employment. Adherents to the "career" theory view the self-employed as persons with particular abilities and skills, and self-knowledge of these abilities motivates individuals to establish their own enterprises (Knight, 1933).

The contrasting perspective regards self-employment as a "default" option (Schumpeter, 1934). The self-employed are not viewed as having unique abilities, rather, they are merely responding to environmental and structural obstacles. This theory suggests that those subject to discrimination in the workplace, such as racial and ethnic minorities, immigrants, and women, or those with few marketable job skills will form their own businesses.

Which of these explanations—if either—best explains why this generation is seeking self-employment in record numbers? Adherents to the "default" hypothesis would argue that they are turning to entrepreneurship because they face obstacles in the economy and in their own workplaces that would hinder their progress. One argument presented in defense of this theory is that the very large cohort of "baby boomers" is preventing the smaller cohort of "baby busters" from progressing in corporate careers. Dunn (1993, p. 77) notes that "as the organizational pyramid gets narrow with each higher rung, there is just not enough room at the top to handle all the boomers." Members of the younger generation might believe that their chances of advancement are hindered and may thus turn to entrepreneurship.

Other data demonstrate that the most rapidly growing entry-level jobs are relatively low-paying and do not require a college degree. Consequently, well educated young adults are not being given the opportunity to perform challenging and rewarding work for their employers. According to estimates from the Bureau of Labor Statistics, roughly 25 percent of college graduates under the age of thirty-five hold jobs that do not require college degrees. Entrepreneurship may thus be viewed as a more desirable and challenging alternative.

The evidence in defense of the "career" hypothesis is more persuasive. Today's young adults have valuable and marketable skills—particularly computer skills—that allow them to form their own businesses. As William Strauss, co-author of *Generations* (1991), has observed: this group "underprices, over-techs, and out-quicks older generations." In addition, this generation is more likely to have received specific training in business formation. The number of universities that provide degree programs for entrepreneurs has grown from just 16 in 1970, to more than 400 in 1996 (Miniter, 1997). They are also more likely than older cohorts to be computer literate—and computer and software firms represent one of the most rapidly growing industries for entrepreneurs.

An alternative explanation can also be posited: some argue that young adults are seeking self-employment because this is consistent with the socialization into "independence" they received during childhood. Strauss and Howe (1991) observe that this generation was among the first to experience parental divorce and day care during childhood. As such, they developed survival skills and a sense of independence that is compatible with self-employment. Data from attitudinal surveys support Strauss and Howe's assessment that today's young adults have greater confidence in their own skills than they do in government or business and industry. A *USA Today* poll indicated that 80 percent of Americans under age thirty-five are counting "primarily on personal savings, not government programs" to fund their retirements. Similarly, a poll by the Louis Harris organization showed that 78 percent of Americans age eighteen to twenty-four disagree with the statement: "Government can generally be trusted to look after our interests" (Miniter, 1997). Consequently, entrepreneurship may be viewed as the one sure path to financial stability among this group.

Unemployment

The idea of work is actually a complex one. All of us work in many ways besides in paid employment. Cleaning the house, planting a garden, and going shopping are plainly all work. But for two centuries or more, Western society has been built around the central importance of paid work. The experience of unemployment—being unable to find a job when one wants it—is still a largely negative one. And unemployment does bring with it unfortunate effects including, sometimes, falling into poverty. Yet as we shall see, some today are arguing that we should think about the relation between being "in work" and "out of work" in a completely different way from the recent past.

Advancements in information technology have transformed the worker base in the United States from manual to white-collar.

Rates of unemployment have fluctuated considerably over the course of this century. In Western countries, unemployment reached a peak in the early 1930s, when some 20 percent of the workforce were out of work in the United States. The economist John Maynard Keynes, who strongly influenced public policy in Europe and the United States during the postwar period, believed that unemployment results from consumers' lacking sufficient resources to buy goods. Governments can intervene to increase the level of demand in an economy, leading to the creation of new jobs; and the newly employed then have the income with which to buy more goods, thus creating yet more jobs for people who produce them. State management of economic life, most people came to believe, meant that high rates of unemployment belonged to the past. Commitment to full employment became part of government policy in virtually all Western societies. Until the 1970s, these policies seemed successful, and economic growth was more or less continuous.

Over the past twenty years or so, however, Keynesianism has largely been abandoned. In the face of economic globalization, governments have lost the

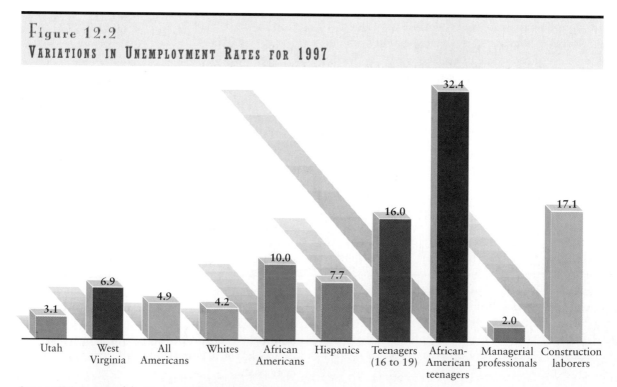

Figure 12.2
VARIATIONS IN UNEMPLOYMENT RATES FOR 1997

Utah	West Virginia	All Americans	Whites	African Americans	Hispanics	Teenagers (16 to 19)	African-American teenagers	Managerial professionals	Construction laborers
3.1	6.9	4.9	4.2	10.0	7.7	16.0	32.4	2.0	17.1

SOURCE: U.S. Bureau of the Census, 1998, pp. 423, 424, 426.

capability to control economic life as they once did. One consequence is that unemployment rates have shot up in many countries. And within countries, unemployment is not equally distributed. It varies by race or ethnic background, by age, and by industry and geographic region (see Figure 12.2). Ethnic minorities living in central cities in the United States have much higher rates of long-term unemployment than the rest of the population. A substantial proportion of young people are among the long-term unemployed, again especially among minority groups.

Several factors probably explain the increase in unemployment levels in Western countries in recent years. One is the rise of international competition in industries upon which Western prosperity used to be founded. In 1947, 60 percent of steel production in the world was carried out in the United States. Today, the figure is only about 15 percent, while steel production has risen by 300 percent in Japan and the Third World countries (principally Singapore, Taiwan, and Hong Kong, which are now undercutting Japanese prices). A second factor is the worldwide economic recession of the late 1980s, which has still not fully abated. A third reason is the increasing use of microelectronics in industry, the net effect of which has been to reduce the need for labor power. Finally, more women are seeking paid employment, meaning that more people are chasing a limited number of available jobs.

It is not certain whether the current high rates of unemployment will continue in the immediate future. Some countries seem to be better placed to combat large-scale unemployment than others. Rates of unemployment tend to be lower in the United States, for example, than in some European nations. This is perhaps because the sheer economic strength of the country gives it more power in world markets than smaller, more fragile economies. Alternatively, it may be that the exceptionally large service sector in the United States provides a greater source of new jobs than in countries where more of the population has traditionally been employed in manufacturing. It should also be noted that the United States offers weaker welfare benefits than most other industrial countries. In the latter, people don't take jobs if the salary is below what they receive from welfare. In the United States, many working people earn an income that puts them well below the poverty line. This situation—working for very low pay—by definition can't exist in countries with a high minimum wage.

The Future of Work

What counts as work, as we have seen, is a complex matter involving numerous activities in addition to orthodox employment. "Everyone has the right to work," declared the Universal Declaration of Human Rights, signed at the United Nations following World War II. At that time, this meant the right to a paid job. If, however, the trend toward large-scale unemployment proves to be long-term, the manifesto may be unrealizable. Perhaps we should rethink the nature of paid work, and in particular the dominant position it occupies in people's lives.

Unemployment tends to be considered by employers and workers alike as a negative phenomenon, but this outlook might be becoming archaic. After all, the identification of work with paid employment is peculiarly limiting. If someone spends enormous effort on an activity, such as cultivating a beautiful garden, as an avocation rather than for any material reward it might bring, why should this be regarded as clearly separate from "work"? The word "unemployment" entered the language only in the late nineteenth century. Perhaps it might disappear in the twenty-first if not having a job ceases to be regarded as equivalent to being out of work. Why not, some observers suggest, classify all the unemployed as self-employed, and give subsidies to those who need them to follow their chosen pursuits?

Over the past twenty years, in all the industrialized countries except for the United States, the average length of the working week has become reduced (U.S. Bureau of Labor Statistics, 1991). Workers still undertake long stretches of overtime, but some governments are beginning to introduce new limits on permissible working hours. In France, for example, annual overtime is restricted to a maximum of 130 hours a year. In most countries, there is a general tendency toward shortening the average working career. More people would probably quit the labor force at sixty or earlier if they could afford to do so.

If the amount of time given over to paid employment continues to shrink, and the need to have a job becomes less central, the nature of working careers might become substantially reorganized. Job sharing or flexible working hours, which arose primarily as a result of the increasing numbers of working parents trying to balance the commitments of workplace and family, for example, might become more common. Some work analysts have suggested that sabbaticals, of the university type, should be extended to workers in other spheres: people would be entitled to take a year off in order to study or pursue some form of self-improvement. Perhaps more individuals will engage in "life planning," in which they arrange to work in different ways (paid, unpaid, full or part time, etc.) at different stages in their lives. Thus, some people might choose to enter the labor force in their late thirties, having followed a period of formal education in their early twenties with time devoted to pursuits like travel. People might *opt* to work part time throughout their lives, rather than being forced to because of a lack of full-time employment opportunities.

The French sociologist André Gorz has argued that in the future paid work will play a less and less important part in people's lives. Gorz bases his views on a critical assessment of Marx's writings. Marx believed that the working class—to which more and more people would supposedly belong—would lead a revolution that would bring about a more humane type of society, in which work would be central to the satisfactions life has to offer. Although writing as a leftist, Gorz rejects this view. Rather than the working class becoming the largest grouping in society (as Marx suggested) and leading a successful revolution, it is actually shrinking. Blue-collar workers have now become a minority—and a declining minority—of the labor force.

It no longer makes much sense, in Gorz's view, to suppose that workers can take over the enterprises of which they are a part, let alone seize state power. There is no real hope of transforming the nature of paid work, because it is organized according to technical considerations that are unavoidable if an economy is to be efficient. "The point now," as Gorz puts it, "is to free oneself *from* work . . ." (Gorz, 1982, p. 67). This is particularly necessary where work is organized along Taylorist lines, or is otherwise oppressive or dull.

Rising unemployment, together with the spread of part-time work, Gorz argues, has already created what he calls a "non-class of nonworkers," alongside those in stable employment. Most people, in fact, are in this "non-class," because the proportion of the population in stable paid jobs at any one time is relatively small—if we exclude the young, the retired, the ill, and homemakers, together with people who are in part-time work or unemployed. The spread of microtechnology, Gorz believes, will further reduce the numbers of full-time jobs available. The result is likely to be a swing toward rejecting the "productivist" outlook of Western society, with its emphasis on wealth, economic growth, and material goods. A diversity of lifestyles, followed outside the sphere of permanent, paid work, will be pursued by the majority of the population in coming years.

According to Gorz, we are moving toward a "dual society." In one sector, production and political administration will be organized to maximize efficiency. The other sector will be a sphere in which individuals occupy themselves with a variety of nonwork pursuits offering enjoyment or personal fulfillment.

How likely is all this to happen? It does seem possible that more and more people will become disenchanted with "productivism"—the stress on constant economic growth and the accumulation of material possessions. It is surely valuable to see unemployment not entirely in a negative light, but as offering opportunities for individuals to pursue their interests and develop their talents.

The nature of the work most people do and the role of work in our lives, like so many other aspects of the societies in which we live, are undergoing major changes. The chief reasons are global economic competition, the widespread introduction of information technology and computerization, and the large-scale entry of women into the workforce.

How will work change in the future? It looks very likely that people will take a more active look at their lives than in the past, moving in and out of paid work at different points. These are only positive options, however, when they are deliberately chosen. The reality for most is that regular paid work remains the key to day-to-day survival and that unemployment is experienced as a hardship rather than an opportunity.

SUMMARY

1. *Work* is the carrying out of tasks, which involves the expenditure of mental and physical effort, and has as its objective the production of goods and services catering to human needs. An *occupation* is work that is done in exchange for a regular wage. In all cultures work is the basis of the *economic system*.

2. A distinctive characteristic of the economic system of modern societies is the development of a highly complex and diverse *division of labor*. The division of labor means that work is divided into different occupations requiring specialization. One result is economic interdependence: we are all dependent on each other to maintain our livelihoods.

3. One manifestation of this is *Taylorism*, or scientific management. Taylorism divides work into simple tasks that can be timed and organized. *Fordism* extended the principles of scientific management to mass production tied to mass markets. Fordism and Taylorism can be seen as *low-trust systems* that maximize worker alienation. A *high-trust system* allows workers control over the pace and even content of their work.

4. Union organizations, together with recognition of the right to *strike*, are characteristic features of economic life in all Western countries. Unions emerged as defensive organizations, concerned to provide a measure of control for workers over their conditions of labor. Today, union leaders quite often play an important role in formulating national economic policies.

5. The modern economy is dominated by the large corporations. When one firm has a commanding influence in a given industry, it is in a *monopoly* position. When a cluster of firms wields such influence, a situation of *oligopoly* exists. Through their influence upon government policy, and upon the consumption of goods, the giant corporations have a profound effect on people's lives.

6. Corporations have undergone profound transformations in recent years because of increasing world interdependence, or *globalization*. The modern corporation is increasingly an enterprise web of many smaller firms linked together, rather than a single big business.

Multinational or *transnational* companies operate across different national boundaries. The largest of them exercise tremendous economic power. Half the one hundred largest economic units are not countries, but privately owned companies.

7. In recent years computer-aided design and planning tools have provided the capability to develop *flexible production systems. Automation* involves the use of robots in the production process. *Group production*, often used with automation, establishes collaborative work groups such as the "*quality circle*" in which workers actively participate in the design and implementation of production methods.

8. Major changes have occurred in the occupational system during the course of the century. Particularly important has been the relative increase in non-manual occupations at the expense of manual ones. The interpretation of these changes, however, is disputed. Some speak of the arrival of the *portfolio worker*—the worker who has a "portfolio" of different skills, and will be able to move readily from job to job. Such workers do exist, but for many people in the workforce "flexibility" is more likely to be associated with poorly paid jobs with few career prospects.

9. Unemployment has been a recurrent problem in the industrialized countries in the twentieth century. As work is a structuring element in a person's psychological makeup, the experience of unemployment is often disorientating. The impact of new technology seems likely to further increase unemployment rates.

10. Major changes are currently occurring in the nature and organization of work. It seems certain that these will become even more important in the future. Nonetheless, work remains for many people the key basis of generating resources necessary to sustain a varied life.

Chapter Thirteen

The Family in History

Learn how the family has changed over the last five hundred years.

Changes in Family Patterns Worldwide

See that although a diversity of family forms exist in different societies today, widespread changes are occurring that relate to the spread of globalization.

Marriage and the Family in the United States

Learn about patterns of marriage, childbearing, and divorce. Analyze how different these patterns are today compared with other periods.

The Dark Side of the Family

Learn about sexual abuse and violence within families.

Alternatives to Traditional Forms of Marriage and the Family

Learn some alternatives to traditional marriage and family patterns that are becoming more widespread.

MARRIAGE AND THE FAMILY

The theme of much of this book has been change. We live in a turbulent, difficult, and unfamiliar world today. Whether we like it or not, we all must come to terms with the mixture of opportunity and risk it presents. Nowhere is this observation more true than in the domain of personal and emotional life.

In our personal lives, we now have to deal with "relationships." When someone asks you, "How is your relationship going?" she is usually asking about a sexual involvement. But we are increasingly caught up in relationships with parents, friends, and others. The term "relationship," as applied to personal life, came into general use only twenty or thirty years ago, as did the idea that there is a need for "commitment" in personal life.

The fact that most of us now think about these changes a great deal, whether we resist them or not, is indicative of the basic transformations that have affected our personal and emotional lives over the past few decades. A relationship is something *active*—you have to work at it. It depends on winning the trust of the other person if it is going to survive over time. Most kinds of sexual relations have become like this now, and so has marriage. Many troubles we see all around us in sexual and family life derive from this necessity to work at relationships, which is in some respects quite new. But opportunities of a positive kind come from it too.

For example, today the couple, married or unmarried, is at the core of what the family is. The couple came to be at the center of family life as the economic role of the family dwindled and love, or love and sexual attraction, became the basis of forming marriage ties. Most people in our society believe that a good relationship is based upon emotional communication or intimacy. The idea of intimacy, like so many other familiar notions we've discussed in this book sounds old but in fact is very new. Marriage was never in the past based upon intimacy and emotional communication. No doubt this was important to a good marriage but it was not the foundation of it. For the modern couple it is. Communication is the means of establishing a good relationship in the first place and it is the chief rationale for its continuation. A good relationship is a relationship of equals, where each party has equal rights and obligations. In such a relationship, each person has respect, and wants the best, for the other. Talk, or dialogue, is the basis of making the relationship work. Relationships function best if people don't hide too much from each other—there has to be mutual trust. And trust has to be worked at, it can't just be taken for granted. Finally, a good relationship is one free from arbitrary power, coercion, or violence.

The changes affecting the personal and emotional spheres go far beyond the borders of any particular country, even one as large as the United States. We find the same issues almost everywhere, differing only in degree and according to the cultural context in which they take place. In China, for example, the state is considering making a divorce more difficult to obtain. In the late 1960s, very liberal marriage laws were passed. Marriage is a working contract that can be dissolved "when husband and wife both desire it." Even if one partner objects, divorce can be granted when "mutual affection" has gone from the marriage. Only a two-week wait is required, after which the two pay $4 and are henceforth independent. The Chinese divorce rate is still low as com-

pared with Western countries, but it is rising rapidly—as is true in the other developing Asian societies. In Chinese cities, not only divorce, but cohabitation is becoming more frequent. In the vast Chinese countryside, by contrast, everything is different. Marriage and the family are much more traditional—in spite of the official policy of limiting childbirth through a mixture of incentives and punishment. Marriage is an arrangement between two families, fixed by the parents rather than the individuals concerned. A recent study in the province of Gansu, which has only a low level of economic development, found that 60 percent of marriages are still arranged by parents. As a Chinese saying has it: "meet once, nod your head and marry." There is a twist in the story in modernizing China. Many of those currently divorcing in the urban centers were married in the traditional manner in the country.

In China there is much talk of protecting the "traditional" family. In many Western countries the debate is even more intense and divisive. Defenders of the traditional family form argue that the emphasis on relationships comes at the expense of the family as a basic institution of society. Many of these critics now speak of the breakdown of the family. If such a breakdown is occurring, it is extremely significant. The family is the meeting point of a range of trends affecting society as a whole—increasing equality between the sexes, the widespread entry of women into the labor force, changes in sexual behavior and expectations, the changing relationship between home and work. Among all the changes going on today, none are more important than those happening in our personal lives—in sexuality, emotional life, marriage, and the family. There is a global revolution going on in how we think of ourselves and how we form ties and connections with others. It is a revolution advancing unevenly in different parts of the world, with much resistance.

How do we begin to understand the nature of these changes and their impact on our lives? It's only possible to understand what is going on in our personal lives and the family as a social institution today if we know something about how people lived in the past and how people currently live in other societies. So in this chapter, we will first look at the development of marriage and the family in earlier times, before analyzing the consequences of present-day changes both in the United States and elsewhere.

Basic Concepts

We need first of all to define some basic concepts, particularly those of family, kinship, and marriage. A **family** is a group of persons directly linked by kin connections, the adult members of which assume responsibility for caring for children. **Kinship** ties are connections between individuals, established either through marriage or through the lines of descent that connect blood relatives (mothers, fathers, offspring, grandparents, etc.). **Marriage** can be defined as a socially acknowledged and approved sexual union between two adult individuals. When two people marry, they become kin to one another; the marriage bond also, however, connects together a wider range of kinspeople. Parents, brothers, sisters, and other blood relatives become relatives of the partner through marriage.

Family relationships are always recognized within wider kinship groups. In virtually all societies, we can identify what sociologists and anthropologists call the **nuclear family**, two adults living together in a household with their own or adopted children. In most traditional societies, the nuclear family was part of a larger kinship network of some type. When close relatives other than a married couple and children live either in the same household or in a close and continuous relationship with one another, we speak of an **extended family**. An extended family may include grandparents, brothers and their wives, sisters and their husbands, aunts, and nephews.

Whether nuclear or extended, so far as the experience of each individual is concerned, families can be divided into **families of orientation** and **families of procreation**. The first is the family into which a person is born; the second is the family into which one enters as an adult and within which a new generation of children is brought up. A further important distinction concerns place of residence. In the United States, when a couple marry, they are usually expected to set up a separate household. This can be in the same area in which the bride's or groom's parents live, but may be in some different town or city altogether. In some other societies, however, everyone who marries is expected to live close to or within the same dwelling as the parents of the bride or groom. When the couple live near or with the bride's parents, the arrangement is called **matrilocal**. In a **patrilocal** pattern, the couple live near to or with the parents of the groom.

In Western societies, marriage, and therefore the family, is associated with **monogamy**. It is illegal for a man or woman to be married to more than one individual at any one time. But monogamy is not the most common type of marriage in the world as a whole. In a comparison of several hundred present-day societies, George Murdock found that **polygamy**, a marriage that allows a husband or wife to have more than one spouse, was permitted in over 80 percent (Murdock, 1949). There are two types of polygamy: **polygyny**, in which a man may be married to more than one woman at the same time, and **polyandry**, much less common, in which a woman may have two or more husbands simultaneously.

A Laotian extended family, all living in the same house.

THE FAMILY IN HISTORY

Sociologists once thought that prior to the modern period, the predominant form of family in western Europe was of the extended type. Research has shown this view to be mistaken. The nuclear family seems long to have been preeminent. Premodern household size was larger than present-day, but the difference is not especially great. In the United States, for example, throughout the seventeenth, eighteenth, and nineteenth centuries, the average household size was 4.75 persons. The current average is 3.04. Since the earlier figure includes domestic servants, the difference in family size is small. Extended family groups were more important in eastern Europe and Russia.

Children in the premodern United States and Europe were often working—helping their parents on the farm—from seven or eight years old. Those who did not remain in the family enterprise frequently left the parental household at an early age to do domestic work in the houses of others or to follow apprenticeships. Children who went away to work in other households would rarely see their parents again.

Other factors made family groups then even more impermanent than they are now, in spite of the high rates of divorce in current times. Rates of mortality (numbers of deaths per thousand of the population in any one year) for people of all ages were much higher. A quarter or more of all infants in early modern Europe did not survive beyond the first year of life (in contrast to well under 1 percent today), and women frequently died in childbirth. The death of children or of one or both spouses often dislocated or shattered family relations.

The Development of Family Life

The historical sociologist Lawrence Stone has charted some of the changes leading from premodern to modern forms of family life in Europe. Stone distinguished three phases in the development of the family from the 1500s to the 1800s. In the early part of this period, the main family form was a type of nuclear family that lived in fairly small households but main-

KEY CONCEPTS IN REVIEW

A **family** is a group of persons directly linked by kin connections, the adult members of which assume responsibility for the care of the children.

Kinship refers to family ties established through marriage or through lines of descent.

Marriage is a socially acknowledged and approved sexual union between two adults.

A **nuclear family** is a household with two adults living with their own or adopted children. An **extended family** is made up of close kin relations, other than the nuclear family, living together in the same household. Families can be divided into **families of orientation,** the family into which one is born, and **families of procreation,** the family one enters into as an adult.

When a married couple live near or with the bride's parents, this arrangement is called **matrilocal.** If the couple live near or with the groom's parents, it is called **patrilocal.**

Monogamy, or marriage to only one individual at a time, is the practice in Western societies. Some societies permit **polygamy,** or marriage to more than one spouse. The two types of polygamy are **polygyny,** when a man may be married to more than one woman at a time, and **polyandry,** when a woman may be married to more than one man at a time.

This family, painted by the sixteenth-century Dutch artist van Heemskerck, would represent the first phase in Stone's theory of the development of the family—according to which two of these children will be leaving home soon.

tained deeply embedded relationships within the community, including with other kin. This family structure was not clearly separated from the community. According to Stone (although some historians have challenged this), the family at that time was not a major focus of emotional attachment or dependence for its members. People didn't experience, or look for, the emotional intimacies we associate with family life today. Sex within marriage was not regarded as a source of pleasure but as a necessity to propagate children.

Individual freedom of choice in marriage and other matters of family life were subordinated to the interests of parents, other kin, or the community. Outside aristocratic circles, where it was sometimes actively encouraged, erotic or romantic love was regarded by moralists and theologians as a sickness. As Stone puts it, the family during this period "was an open-ended, low-keyed, unemotional, authoritarian institution. . . . It was also very short-lived, being frequently dissolved by the death of the husband or wife or the death or very early departure from the home of the children" (Stone, 1980).

This type of family was succeeded by a transitional form that lasted from the early seventeenth century to the beginning of the eighteenth. This later type was largely confined to the upper reaches of society but was nevertheless very important, because from it spread attitudes that have since become almost universal. The nuclear family became a more separate entity, distinct from ties to other kin and to the local community. There was a growing stress upon the importance of marital and parental love, although there was also an increase in the authoritarian power of fathers.

In the third phase, the type of family system we are most familiar with in the West today gradually evolved. This family is a group tied by close emotional bonds, enjoying a high degree of domestic privacy and preoccupied with the rearing of children. It is marked by the rise of **affective individualism**, the formation of marriage ties on the basis of personal selection, guided by sexual attraction or romantic love. Sexual aspects of love began to be glorified within marriage instead of in extramarital relationships. The family became geared to consumption rather than production, as a result of the increasing spread of workplaces separate from the home. Women became associated with domesticity and men with being the breadwinner. Originating among more affluent groups, this family type became more or less universal in Western countries with the spread of industrialization.

In premodern Europe marriage usually began as a property arrangement, was in its middle mostly about raising children, and ended about love. Few couples in fact married "for love," but many grew to love each other in time as they jointly managed their household, reared their offspring, and shared life's experiences. Nearly all surviving epitaphs to spouses evince profound affection. By contrast, in most of the modern West, marriage *begins* about love, in its middle is still mostly about raising children (if there are children), and ends—often—about property, by which point love is absent or a distant memory (Boswell, 1995).

The Way We Never Were: Myths of the Traditional Family

Many people in current times feel that family life is becoming undermined and contrast what they see as the decline of the family with more traditional forms of family life. What comes to mind when you hear the words "traditional family"? Most people say the following sorts of things. Marriage vows were taken seriously. The family was a supportive unit, in which people knew their place. Children respected their parents, and the authority of parents over children was firm. Mothers stayed home to care for their children, and fathers carried out a respected role as breadwinner for the family. As for sexuality—well, most people, particularly women, remained sexually inexperienced until the day of their wedding.

Not all these assumptions are false. Yet as Stephanie Coontz points out in her book *The Way We Never Were* (1992), as with other visions of a golden age of the past, the rosy light shed on the "traditional family" dissolves when we look back to previous times to see what things really were like. The notion that the traditional family was one in which a close intimacy existed between wives and husbands and where mothers devoted most of their time to their children is largely an idealized fiction. It is an expression of nostalgia for a form of family life that never really existed.

Some would like to go a long way back to retrieve the traditional family. They admire the discipline of the colonial family, which wasn't yet influenced by affective individualism and in the United States was rarely shattered by divorce. Yet were colonial families

stable? They were not. Colonial families were subject to the same disintegrative forces as their counterparts in Europe. Because of high death rates, the average length of marriages was under twelve years. More than one-half of children had lost at least one parent before they reached twenty-one. Many women died in childbirth.

Strict, indeed punitive, authority of parents over children there certainly was. But the promoters of "family values," as Coontz points out, would find attitudes toward sexuality in colonial times startlingly different from those they wish to promote now. Children were not at all protected from knowledge of sex. Spelling books for seven- and eight-year-olds in the eighteenth century, for instance, routinely offered "fornication" as an example of a four-syllable word. Sexual talk amazing in its candor was common not only between men and women but between adults and young children.

Supposing we come a bit closer to our times and stop at the Victorian family of the 1850s or so. Could

"When a grass-cutting husband lies down on the job, it's a wise wife who hurries Schlitz to the hammock." Advertising from the 1950s paints a portrait of family life that kept women in strictly defined supporting roles.

we find the ideal traditional family there? We could not. The Victorian family certainly was not a haven of security and intimacy for wives, husbands, and their children. Wives were more or less forcibly confined to the household, without means of escape. According to Victorian morality, women were supposed to be strictly virtuous. The double standard created a chasm between the sexes. Many men were sexually licentious: they visited prostitutes and paid regular visits to brothels. Wives and husbands often, in fact, had little to do with one another, communicating only through their children.

Moreover, domesticity wasn't even an option for poorer groups. African-American slaves in the South lived and worked frequently in the most appalling conditions. In the factories and workshops of the North, white families worked for fourteen hours or more per day, with little time for a home life. Some of the workers were children of nine and ten, who labored just as hard as the adults. As happened in Europe, young children in the United States often left their families even before they were in their teens to work as servants in other households.

The Later Period

To find the elusive traditional family, we should perhaps look to more recent history—the 1950s, for instance. But the 1950s, in fact, weren't a time of stable family life. Divorce rates were certainly much lower than they are now, and most women worked only in the home, while men were responsible for bringing home the family wage. Yet large numbers of women didn't actually *want* to retreat to a purely domestic role, and felt miserable and trapped in it. Women had entered paid jobs during World War II, as part of the war effort. They lost these jobs when men returned from the war. Moreover, men often observed a strong sexual double standard, seeking sexual adventures for themselves but setting strict codes for their wives.

Perhaps most important of all, the dark side of the family—which we shall look at later in more detail—was almost completely suppressed. Families were often marred by the alcoholism of one or both parents. Women and children who suffered violence at the hands of the men in their families had little means

of escape. Family violence and sexual abuse, which we know through subsequent research to have been common, were simply hidden away, as if they didn't exist. As Coontz puts it, "behind the polished facades of many *ideal* families, suburban as well as urban, was violence, terror, or simply grinding misery that only occasionally came to light" (1992).

As in other periods, for some people, family life was happy and secure. But even for these lucky ones, it was a time of transition. The idea that marriage should be a "relationship" was making its first appearance. It took the form of a demand on the part of numerous women. The majority of men were slow to respond. Betty Friedan's best-selling book *The Feminine Mystique* first appeared in 1963, but its research referred to the decade of the 1950s. Friedan struck a chord in the hearts of thousands of women when she spoke of the "problem with no name": the oppressive nature of a domestic life bound up with child care, domestic drudgery, and a husband who only occasionally put in an appearance and with whom little emotional communication was possible.

Let's now look directly at the changes affecting personal life, marriage, and the family in the world today. There is no doubt that some of these changes are profound and far-reaching. But interpreting their likely implications, particularly in the United States, means taking account of just how unrealistic it is to contrast what is happening now with a fictional or mythical view of the traditional family.

CHANGES IN FAMILY PATTERNS WORLDWIDE

There is a diversity of family forms today in different societies across the world. In some areas, such as more remote regions in Asia, Africa, and the Pacific, traditional family systems are little altered. In most Third World countries, however, widespread changes are occurring (see Global Map 13.1). The origins of these changes are complex, but several factors can be picked out as especially important. One is the spread of Western culture. Western ideals of romantic love, for example, have spread to societies in which they were previously unknown. Another factor is the de-

SOURCE: World Bank, 1994, *Human Development Report.*

FINLAND
ESTONIA
KAZAKHSTAN
ARMENIA
RUSSIA
LATVIA LITHUANIA
BELARUS
KYRGYZSTAN
UKRAINE
MOLDOVA
TAJIKISTAN
POL.
GEORGIA
TURKMENISTAN
MONGOLIA
CZ.
HUN. ROM.
UZBEKISTAN
SL. AUS. BULG.
ALB. MAC.
AFGHANISTAN
TURKEY
CYPRUS
PEOPLE'S REPUBLIC
N. KOREA
JAPA
GREECE
SYRIA
AZERBIJAN
OF CHINA
S. KOREA
PACIFIC OCEAN
LEBANON
IRAQ
IRAN
BHUTAN
EGYPT
BAHRAIN
NEPAL
LIBYA
KUWAIT
QATAR
BANGLADESH
TAIWAN
Wake I.
ISRAEL
SAUDI
INDIA
MYANMAR
LAOS
Mariana
JORDAN
ARABIA
Islands
ERITREA
PAKISTAN
THAILAND
PHILIPPINES
Marshall
CHAD
YEMEN
Islands
SUDAN
OMAN
CAMBODIA
VIETNAM
Guam
DJIBOUTI
UNITED ARAB
BRUNEI
Belau
Caroline Is.
KIRIBATI
CENTRAL
ETHIOPIA
EMIRATES
SRI LANKA
MALAYSIA
PAPUA
AFRICAN
SOMALIA
NEW
NAURA
REPUBLIC
UGANDA
MALDIVES
GUINEA
RWANDA
KENYA
SINGAPORE
SOLOMON IS.
ZAIRE
TUVALU
BURUNDI
TANZANIA
SEYCHELLES
INDONESIA
ANGOLA
Fiji
ZAMBIA
MADAGASCAR
VANUATU
INDIAN OCEAN
AUSTRALIA
New Caledonia
BOTSWANA
MAURITIUS
MALAWI
MOZAMBIQUE
ZIMBABWE
NEW
SOUTH
SWAZILAND
ZEALAND
AFRICA
LESOTHO

ABBREVIATIONS

AUS.	AUSTRIA
ALB.	ALBANIA
B.H.	BOSNIA AND HERZEGOVINA
BULG.	BULGARIA
CR.	CROATIA
CZ.	CZECH REPUBLIC
HUN.	HUNGARY
MAC.	FORMER YUGOSLAV REPUBLIC OF MACEDONIA
POL.	POLAND
ROM.	ROMANIA
SL.	SLOVENIA
U.K	UNITED KINGDOM
YU.	YUGOSLAVIA

BALANCING FAMILY AND WORK

How many hours each week did your parents spend doing paid work when you were growing up? Did their commitment to work affect the way you or your siblings were raised? One of the ways globalization has impacted family life in the United States is by increasing the amount of time that people spend each week at work. While there is some disagreement among researchers as to whether Americans, on average, are putting in more hours at work now than they did in the past, many sociologists give credence to the findings of economist Juliet Schor, author of the 1992 book *The Overworked American*. Schor argues that workers today spend on average 164 more hours each year at work than they did twenty years ago. Workers are also taking less vacation time than they did previously. Perhaps more significant, the percentage of mothers who are working full time has increased dramatically since the end of World War II. Taken together, these facts suggest that parents today have less time available to spend with their children than was the case in decades past. As a result, there has been a significant increase in the percentage of children enrolled in day-care programs—and, some would argue, a palpable increase in tension and stress within families as more of the day-to-day parental role is off-loaded onto child-care providers.

In her recent book, *The Time Bind* (1997), sociologist Arlie Hochschild suggests that these developments may be related to globalization. Globalization, of course, is not responsible for the gains women have made in securing positions in the paid labor force. Nevertheless, some corporations, according to Hochschild, have responded to the pressures of global competition by encouraging their salaried employees to put in longer hours at work, thus increasing levels of productivity. Why would employees will-

velopment of centralized government in areas previously composed of autonomous smaller societies. People's lives become influenced by their involvement in a national political system; moreover, governments make active attempts to alter traditional ways of behavior. Because of the problem of rapidly expanding population growth, states frequently introduce pro-

grams advocating smaller families, the use of contraception, and so forth.

A further influence is the large-scale migration from rural to urban areas. Often men go to work in towns or cities, leaving family members in the home village. Alternatively, a nuclear-family group will move as a unit to the city. In both cases, traditional family forms

ingly agree to spend so much time at their jobs—often considerably more than forty hours each week—when they are not paid to do so, when they know that such a commitment disrupts their family life, and in an age when computerization has greatly improved workplace efficiency? Shouldn't technological progress allow workers to spend more time with their families rather than less? Hochschild's answer to this question is that some corporations rely on the power of workplace norms to elicit a greater time commitment from their workers. New employees are socialized into a corporate culture in which working long hours is seen as a badge of dedication and professionalism. Employees, seeking status and the approval of their peers and supervisors, become motivated to put as much time into work as possible, and to make sure that those around them know precisely how much time they spend working. In some cases, such a corporate culture has arisen unintentionally, as workers respond to the threat of corporate "downsizing" by redoubling their commitment to the organization. In other cases—as with the corporation Hochschild studied—executives have consciously sought to shape the culture of the organization, reminding employees through handbooks, speeches, and newsletters that working more than forty hours a week is the mark of a "good" worker.

Although globalization has touched all the nations of the world, its effects on work-time seem to vary by country. In France and Germany, for example, workers—sometimes acting through unions, sometimes making their power known at the voting booth—have rejected corporate calls for a longer work-week, and are instead pressuring employers to reduce the work-week and to grant longer vacations. Do Europeans simply value family and leisure time more than Americans? Or would American workers be making the same demands if unions were stronger in this country?

and kinship systems may become weakened. Finally, and perhaps most important, employment opportunities away from the land and in such organizations as government bureaucracies, mines, plantations, and—where they exist—industrial firms tend to have disruptive consequences for family systems previously centered on landed production in the local community.

In general, these changes are creating a worldwide movement toward the predominance of the nuclear family, breaking down extended-family systems and other types of kinship groups. This was first documented by William J. Goode in his book *World Revolution in Family Patterns* (1963) and has been borne out by subsequent research.

Directions of Change

The most important changes occurring worldwide are the following:

1. Clans and other kin groups are declining in their influence.
2. There is a general trend toward the free choice of a spouse.
3. The rights of women are becoming more widely recognized, in respect to both the initiation of marriage and decision making within the family.
4. Kin marriages are becoming less common.
5. Higher levels of sexual freedom are developing in societies that were very restrictive.
6. There is a general trend toward the extension of children's rights.

As mentioned earlier, there are some societies in which extended families are still the norm and traditional family practices continue. Moreover, there are differences in the speed at which change is occurring, and there are reversals and countertrends. A study in the Philippines, for example, found a higher proportion of extended families in urban areas than in surrounding rural regions. These had not just developed from traditional extended-family households, but represented something new. Leaving the rural areas, cousins, nephews, and nieces went to live with their relatives in the cities to take advantage of the employment opportunities available there. Parallel examples have also been noted elsewhere in the world (Strinner, 1979), including some industrialized nations. Certain regions of Poland, for instance, show evidence of a rejuvenation of the extended family. A good number of industrial workers in Poland have farms that they tend part time. In the cities, grandparents move in with their children's family, run the household, and bring up the grandchildren, while the younger generation is engaged in outside employment (Turowski, 1977).

Given the ethnically diverse character of the United States, there are considerable variations in family and marriage within the country. Some of the most striking include differences between white and African-American family patterns, and we need to consider why this is so. We will then move on to examine divorce, remarriage, and stepparenting in relation to contemporary patterns of family life.

MARRIAGE AND THE FAMILY IN THE UNITED STATES

The United States has long been characterized by high marriage rates. Nearly every American adult eventually marries; almost 95 percent of adults in their early

KEY CONCEPTS IN REVIEW

In Europe and the United States, nuclear-family patterns were strongly implanted well before the development of industrialization, although they were profoundly influenced by it. Elsewhere in the world, there remains a diversity of family forms.

Changes in family patterns are generated by such factors as the development of a centralized government, the expansion of towns and cities, and employment within organizations outside family influence. These changes are tending to produce a worldwide movement toward nuclear-family systems, eroding extended-family forms and other types of kinship group.

fifties today are or have previously been married. The age at which first marriages are contracted has risen, however, over the past twenty years (it was also high at the turn of the century, declining in the 1922–1950 period). This is partly because of an increase in the numbers of people living together without being married (cohabitation) and partly a result of factors such as the growing proportion of the population attending college, most of whom tend to defer marriage until after completing their education. But we must be careful how we make our comparisons. While some have argued that the trend since 1970 toward later marriage is a break from tradition, it actually is close to the age of first marriage for the period 1890–1940. To say that people today are postponing marriage is true only if we compare ourselves with the 1950s generation. It might be more accurate to say that the 1950s generation married at an unusually young age.

In 1960, the average age of first marriages was 22.8 for men and 20.3 for women. The comparable ages in 1998 were 26.7 for men and 25.0 for women. Another way of measuring the relations between age and first marriage is to look at the numbers of people who remain unmarried before a certain age (see Figure 13.1). Thus, in 1960, just 28 percent of women aged less than 24 years had never married. In 1998, that proportion was 70 percent. The U.S. census now incorporates a category of "unmarried couples sharing the same household." As this practice of cohabitation is new, it is not easy to make direct comparisons with preceding years. Nonetheless, we can accurately estimate that the number of couples among younger age groups who live together without being married has risen steeply (see Figure 13.2) from 11 percent around 1970 to 44 percent in the early 1980s and probably about 50 percent today (Cherlin, 1999).

No one knows for certain how the trend toward cohabitation will develop in the future. We can get some guidance from what has happened in other industrial countries. In France, cohabiting relationships are more widespread than in the United States, and tend to be of longer duration. A survey in that country published in the late 1980s found that over half of cohabiting couples "did not think about marriage." Cohabitation, in other words, leads to marriage only for a minority; for most people, it is a phase of life in which partners want to leave their options open (Cherlin, 1992). We will return to the topic of cohabitation as an alternative to marriage at the end of the chapter.

An extraordinary increase in the proportion of people living alone in the United States has also taken place over recent years—a phenomenon that partly reflects the high levels of marital separation and divorce.

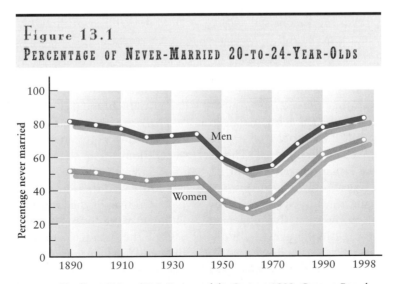

Figure 13.1
PERCENTAGE OF NEVER-MARRIED 20-TO-24-YEAR-OLDS

SOURCE: Cherlin, 1992 and U.S. Bureau of the Census, 1998, *Current Population Reports*, "Marital Status and Living Arrangements."

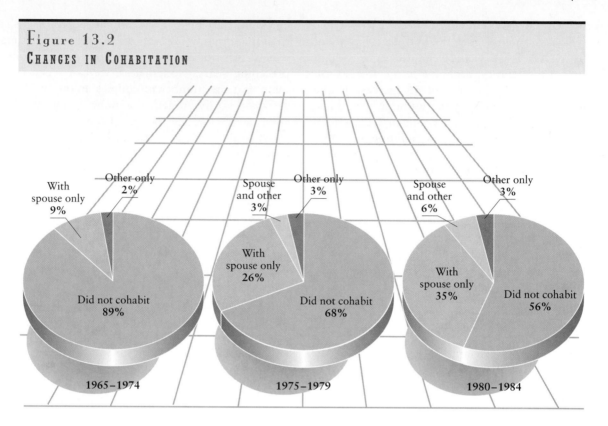

Figure 13.2
CHANGES IN COHABITATION

SOURCE: Bumpass and Sweet, 1989.

Percent cohabiting before first marriage, for persons marrying in 1965–74, 1975–79, and 1980–84.

One in every four households now consists of one person, a rise of 44 percent since 1960. There has been a particularly sharp rise in the proportion of individuals living alone in the twenty-four-to-forty-four age bracket.

Some people still suppose that the average American family is made up of a husband who works in paid employment and a wife who looks after the home, living together with their two children. This is very different from the real situation: only about 25 percent of children live in households that fit this picture. One reason is the rising rates of divorce: a substantial proportion of the population live either in single-parent households or in stepfamilies, or both. Another is the high proportion of women who work. Dual-career marriages and single-parent families are now the norm (see Figure 13.3). The majority of married women working outside the home also care for a

child or children. Although many working women are concentrated in jobs with poor or nonexistent promotion prospects, the standard of living of many American couples is dependent on the income contributed by the wife, as well as on the unpaid work she undertakes in the home (see also Chapter 12).

There are also some large differences in patterns of childbearing between parents in the 1950s and later generations. The birthrate rose sharply just after World War II and again during the 1950s. Women in the 1950s had their first child earlier in their lives than has been true of the later generations, and subsequent children were born closer together. Since the late 1960s, the average age at which women have their first child has progressively risen. And women are leaving larger gaps between children. In 1976, only 20 percent of births were to women aged over thirty. By 1995, this proportion had grown to 39 percent.

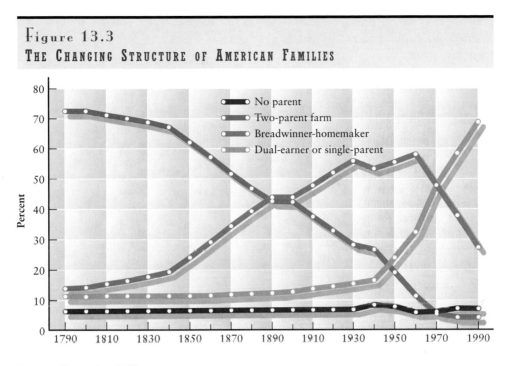

Figure 13.3
THE CHANGING STRUCTURE OF AMERICAN FAMILIES

SOURCE: Hernandez, 1993.

Percentage of American children 17 and younger living in each of four types of families, 1790–1989.

African–American Families

As mentioned earlier, there are important differences in white and black family patterns. One of the most striking is that far fewer African-American women aged twenty-five to forty-four are married and living with a husband than white women in the same age group. This fact has given rise to heated disputes about the nature of African-American families in the United States.

Thirty years ago, Senator Daniel Patrick Moynihan described black families as "disorganized" and caught up in a "tangle of pathology" (Moynihan, 1965). Moynihan, among others, looked back at the history of the black family for reasons. The early development of African-American family patterns was largely governed by the conditions imposed by slavery. The circumstances of slavery prevented blacks from maintaining the cultural customs of their societies of ori-gin. Members of similar African tribal groups were deliberately dispersed to different plantations. Some owners treated their slaves considerately, fostering the development of family life. Others, however, regarded their slaves as little better than livestock and inherently promiscuous, therefore believing marriage formalities to be unnecessary.

But slavery was not the only historical factor contributing to contemporary problems. Following emancipation, new cultural experiences and structural factors came to play upon black families. Among these were continued, yet new forms of, discrimination against African Americans, changes in the economy such as the development of sharecropping in the South after the Civil War, and the migration of black families from the South to Northern cities in the early decades of the twentieth century (Jones, 1986).

However, the divergence between black and white family patterns has become much greater since the early 1960s, when Moynihan's study was published, and it seems probable that we have to look mainly to present-day influences to explain them. In 1960, 21 percent of African-American families were headed by females; among white families, the proportion was 8 percent. By 1998, the proportion for black families had risen to more than 51 percent, while that for white families was 18 percent (see Figure 13.4). Female-headed families are more prominently represented among poorer blacks. African Americans in poor urban neighborhoods have experienced little rise in living conditions over the past two decades: many are confined to low-wage jobs or are more or less permanently unemployed. In these circumstances, there is little to foster continuity in marital relationships.

But we should not see the situation of African-American families purely in a negative light. The director of the National Urban League, a black organization, titled a research report produced in the 1970s "The Strengths of Black Families." These families, the report claimed, show characteristics that promote stability, including strong and adaptable kin ties. Extended kinship networks are important among poor blacks—much more significant, relative to marital ties, than in most white communities. A mother heading a one-parent family is likely to have a close and supportive network of relatives to depend upon.

Fathers are part of the household in only 40 percent of black families. But single-parent black families benefit more often from strong ties to other relatives than do single-parent white families.

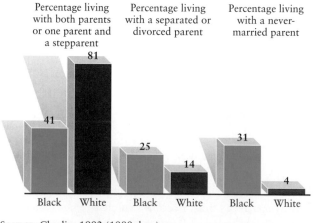

Figure 13.4
FAMILY ARRANGEMENTS FOR BLACK AND WHITE CHILDREN

Percentage living with both parents or one parent and a stepparent		Percentage living with a separated or divorced parent		Percentage living with a never-married parent	
Black	White	Black	White	Black	White
41	81	25	14	31	4

SOURCE: Cherlin, 1992 (1989 data).

This contradicts the idea that black single parents and their children form unstable families. A far higher proportion of female-headed families among African Americans have other relatives living with them than do white families headed by females.

In her book *Lifelines* (1983), Joyce Aschenbrenner provides a comprehensive portrayal of extended kin relationships in African-American families. Aschenbrenner gained a new perspective on both white and black family types in the United States as a result of fieldwork she had earlier carried out in Pakistan. From the point of view of the Pakistanis, the white family in the United States seemed weak and "disorganized." They could not understand how a mere couple, let alone a single parent, could bring up children. They viewed with abhorrence the practice of hiring a stranger to baby-sit while the parents went out. Where were the uncles and grandparents? Why weren't a woman's brothers on hand to lend assistance if she was left on her own to bring up her children? The way they thought of the family was closer to the situation of African-American families rather than to the usual family structure among whites.

Discussions of the black family, Aschenbrenner suggests, have focused too strongly on the marriage relationship. This emphasis is in line with the overriding importance of marriage in American society, but this relationship does not necessarily form the structure of the African-American family. In most societies that include extended families, relationships such as mother-daughter, father-son, or brother-sister may be more socially significant than that between husband and wife (Aschenbrenner, 1983).

Divorce and Separation

The past thirty years have seen major increases in rates of divorce, together with a relaxation of previously held attitudes of disapproval. For centuries in the West, marriage was regarded as virtually indissoluble. Divorces were granted only in limited situations, such as nonconsummation of a marriage. Yet today most countries have moved rapidly toward making divorce more easily available (see Global Map 13.2).

Divorce rates, calculated by looking at the number of divorces per thousand married men or women per year, have fluctuated in the United States in different periods (Figure 13.5). They rose, for example, following World War II, then dropped off before climbing to much higher levels. The divorce rate increased steeply from the 1960s to the late 1970s, reaching a peak in 1980 (thereafter declining somewhat). It used to be common for divorced women to move back to their parents' homes after separation; today, most set up their own households.

Divorce exerts an enormous impact upon the lives of children. Since 1970, more than 1 million American children per year have been affected by divorce. In one calculation, about one-half of children born in 1980 at some stage in their lives became members of a one-parent family. Since two-thirds of women and three-fourths of men who are divorced eventually remarry, these children nonetheless grew up in a family environment. Only just over 2 percent of children under fourteen in the United States today are not liv-

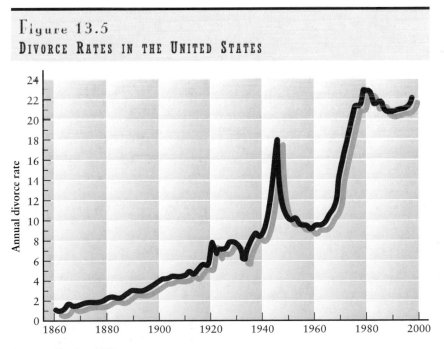

Figure 13.5
DIVORCE RATES IN THE UNITED STATES

SOURCE: Cherlin, 1999.

SWEDEN
NORWAY
ICELAND
DENMARK
GERMANY
NETHERLANDS
IRELAND
U.K.
BELGIUM
LUXEMBOURG
FRANCE
SWITZERLAND
AZORES
PORTUGAL
SPAIN
ITALY
TUNISIA

GREENLAND
(DENMARK)

ALASKA
(U.S)

CANADA

UNITED STATES

Hawaiian Is.

BERMUDA
BAHAMAS
HAITI
DOMINICAN REPUBLIC
Virgin Is.
PUERTO RICO
ST. CHRISTOPHER AND NEVIS
ANTIGUA AND BARBUDA
DOMINICA
BARBADOS
ST. LUCIA
ST. VINCENT AND
THE GRENADINES
GRENADA
TRINIDAD AND
TOBAGO
FR. GUYANA

ATLANTIC OCEAN

WESTERN SAHARA
(MOROCCO)

MOROCCO

ALGERIA

MAURITANIA
MALI
NIGER

CAPE VERDE
SENEGAL
GAMBIA
GUINEA-BISSAU
GUINEA
SIERRA
LEONE
LIBERIA
IVORY
COAST
BOURKIN
FASO
GHANA
TOGO
BENIN
EQUATORIAL
GUINEA

NIGERIA

CAMEROON
SAO TOME
AND
PRINCIPE
GABON
CONGO
NAMIBIA

CUBA
BELIZE
JAMAICA
MEXICO
GUATEMALA
EL SALVADOR
HONDURAS
COSTA RICA
PANAMA

NICARAGUA

VENEZUELA
COLOMBIA

SURINAME
GUYANA

Galapagos Is.
ECUADOR

BRAZIL

PERU

BOLIVIA

PARAGUAY

PACIFIC OCEAN

WESTERN
SAMOA

TONGA

Easter Is.

CHILE

URUGUAY

ARGENTINA

Falkland Is.

	1.0 or less
	1.0–1.99
	2.0–2.99
	3.0 or more
	No data available

SOURCE: Goode, 1993.

FINLAND
ESTONIA
KAZAKHSTAN
ARMENIA
RUSSIA
LATVIA LITHUANIA
BELARUS
KYRGYZSTAN
UKRAINE
MOLDOVA
TAJIKISTAN
POL.
CZ
HUN
CR
SL
MAC
BULG
ALB
ROM.
GEORGIA
TURKMENISTAN
UZBEKISTAN
MONGOLIA
TURKEY
CYPRUS
AFGHANISTAN
N. KOREA
JAPAN
GREECE
LEBANON
SYRIA
IRAN
AZERBIJAN
PEOPLE'S REPUBLIC
OF CHINA
S. KOREA
PACIFIC OCEAN
IRAQ
BHUTAN
BAHRAIN
EGYPT
KUWAIT
QATAR
LIBYA
ISRAEL
JORDAN
SAUDI
ARABIA
NEPAL
BANGLADESH
INDIA
TAIWAN
Wake I.
Mariana
Islands
Marshall
Islands
ERITREA
YEMEN
MYANMAR
THAILAND
LAOS
PAKISTAN
Guam
CHAD
SUDAN
OMAN
DJIBOUTI
UNITED ARAB
EMIRATES
CAMBODIA
VIETNAM
BRUNEI
PHILIPPINES
Belau
Caroline Is.
KIRIBATI
CENTRAL
AFRICAN
REPUBLIC
ETHIOPIA
UGANDA
SOMALIA
SRI LANKA
MALAYSIA
PAPUA
NEW
GUINEA
NAURU
RWANDA
KENYA
MALDIVES
ZAIRE
BURUNDI
TANZANIA
SEYCHELLES
SINGAPORE
INDONESIA
SOLOMON IS.
TUVALU
ANGOLA
ZAMBIA
MADAGASCAR
INDIAN OCEAN
VANUATU
Fiji
BOTSWANA
MAURITIUS
AUSTRALIA
New Caledonia
MALAWI
MOZAMBIQUE
ZIMBABWE
SOUTH
AFRICA
SWAZILAND
LESOTHO
NEW
ZEALAND

ABBREVIATIONS

AUS.   AUSTRIA
ALB.   ALBANIA
B.H.   BOSNIA AND HERZEGOVINA
BULG.   BULGARIA
CR.   CROATIA
CZ.   CZECH REPUBLIC
HUN.   HUNGARY
MAC.   FORMER YUGOSLAV
        REPUBLIC OF MACEDONIA
POL.   POLAND
ROM.   ROMANIA
SL.   SLOVENIA
U.K   UNITED KINGDOM
YU.   YUGOSLAVIA

ing with either parent. The remarriage figures are substantially lower for African Americans. Only 32 percent of black women and 55 percent of black men remarry within ten years. Black children are half as likely as white children to be living with both parents or one parent and a stepparent (37 percent versus 76 percent; Cherlin, 1992).

Lenore Weitzman (1985) has argued that no-fault divorce laws have helped to recast the psychological context of divorce positively (reducing some of the hostility it once generated), but they have had strong negative consequences for the economic position of women. Laws that were designed to be gender-neutral have had the unintended consequence of depriving divorced women of the financial protections that the old laws provided. Women are expected to be as capable as men of supporting themselves after divorce. Yet because most women's careers are still secondary to their work as homemakers, they may lack the qualifications and earning power of men. Weitzman's research showed that the living standards of divorced women and their children on average fell by 73 percent in the first year following the divorce settlement. The average standard of living of divorced men, by contrast, *rose* by 42 percent. Most court judgments left the former husband with a high proportion of his income intact; therefore, he had more to spend on his own needs than while he was married.

REASONS FOR DIVORCE

Divorce rates are obviously not a direct index of marital unhappiness. For one thing, they do not include people who are separated but have not been legally divorced. Moreover, people who are unhappily married may choose to stay together—because they believe in the sanctity of marriage, they are wary about the consequences they will suffer in the case of a breakup, or they wish to remain with one another for the sake of the children.

Why has divorce become much more common over recent years? There are several reasons, which involve the wider changes going on in modern societies and social institutions. As mentioned before, changes in the law have made divorce easier. Additionally, except for a small proportion of wealthy people, marriage today no longer has much connection with the desire to perpetuate property and status from generation to generation. As women become more economically independent, marriage is less of a necessary economic partnership. Greater overall prosperity means that it is easier to establish a separate household in case of marital disaffection (Lee, 1982). The fact that little stigma now attaches to divorce is in some part the result of these developments, but adds momentum to them also. A further important factor is the growing tendency to evaluate marriage in terms of the levels of personal satisfaction it offers. Rising rates of divorce do not seem to indicate a deep dissatisfaction with marriage as such, but an increased determination to make it a rewarding and satisfying relationship (Cherlin, 1990).

Other factors thought to increase the likelihood of divorce are related to an individual's life cycle. They include

- parental divorce (people whose parents divorce are more likely to divorce);
- premarital cohabitation (people who cohabitate before marriage have a higher divorce rate);
- premarital childbearing (people who marry after having children are more likely to divorce);
- marriage at an early age (people who marry as teenagers have a higher divorce rate);
- a childless marriage (couples without children are more likely to divorce); and
- low incomes (divorce is more likely among couples with low incomes) (White, 1990).

THE EXPERIENCE OF DIVORCE

It is extremely difficult to draw up a balance sheet of the social advantages and costs of high levels of divorce. More tolerant attitudes toward divorce mean that couples can terminate an unrewarding relationship without incurring social ostracism. On the other hand, marriage breakup is almost always emotionally stressful and may create financial hardship, especially for women.

In her study *Uncoupling,* Diane Vaughan (1986) carried out a series of interviews with 103 recently separated or divorced people (mainly from middle-class backgrounds) to chart the process of transition from living together to living apart. The notion of "uncoupling" refers to how people make the transition from intimate relationships to living alone. She found that in many cases, before the actual physical parting, there was a "social separation"—at least one of the partners developed a new life pattern, becoming interested in new pursuits and making new friends, in contexts in which the other was not included. This usually meant keeping secrets from the other—especially, of course, when a relationship with a lover was involved.

According to Vaughan's research, uncoupling is often unintentional in its beginnings. One individual—whom she calls the "initiator"—becomes more dissatisfied with the relationship than the other. The initiator creates a "territory" independent of the activities in which the couple engage together. For some time before this, the initiator may have been trying unsuccessfully to change the partner, to get him to behave in more acceptable ways, foster shared interests, and so forth. At some point, the initiator feels that this attempt has been a failure and that the relationship is fundamentally flawed. From then on, she becomes preoccupied with the ways in which the relationship or the partner is defective. Vaughan suggested that this is the opposite of the process of falling in love, when an individual focuses on the attractive features of the other and ignores those that may be more dubious.

Initiators seriously considering a break normally discuss their relationship extensively with others, comparing notes. In so doing, they weigh the costs and benefits as applied to their own position. Can they survive on their own? How will friends and parents react? Will the children suffer? Will they be financially solvent? Having thought about these and other problems, some decide to try again to make the marriage work. For those who go ahead with a separation, these discussions help make the break less intimidating, building confidence that they are doing the right thing. Most initiators become convinced that a responsibility for their own self-development takes priority over commitment to the other person.

But uncoupling is not always led by one individual. The other partner by this time may have also decided that the relationship cannot be changed. In some situations, an abrupt reversal of roles occurs. The person who previously wanted to save the relationship becomes determined that it should end, while the erstwhile initiator wishes to salvage it.

DIVORCE AND CHILDREN

The effects of divorce on children are difficult to gauge. How contentious the relationship is between the parents prior to separation, the ages of the children at the time, whether or not there are brothers or sisters, the availability of grandparents and other rela

A California four-year-old, sitting next to his father in divorce court, reacts as the judge awards an extra weekend of custody to his mother.

tives, the children's relationship with their individual parents, how frequently they continue to see both parents, can all affect the process of adjustment. Since children whose parents are unhappy with one another but stay together may also be affected, assessing the consequences of divorce for children is doubly problematic.

Research indicates that children often suffer a period of marked emotional anxiety following the separation of their parents. Judith Wallerstein and Joan Kelly studied 131 children of sixty families in Marin County, California, following the separation of the parents. They contacted the children at the time of the divorce, a year and a half after, and five years after. According to the authors, almost all the children experienced intense emotional disturbance at the time of the divorce. Preschool-age children were confused and frightened, tending to blame themselves for the separation. Older children were better able to understand their parents' motives for divorce, but frequently worried about its effects on their future and expressed sharp feelings of anger. At the end of the five-year period, however, the researchers found that two-thirds were coping reasonably well with their home lives and their commitments outside. A third remained dissatisfied with their lives, were subject to depression, and expressed feelings of loneliness, even in cases where the parent with whom they were living had remarried (Wallerstein and Kelly, 1980).

Wallerstein continued her study of this same group of children, following 116 of the original 131 into young adulthood with interviews at the end of ten-year and fifteen-year periods. The interviews revealed that these children brought memories and feelings of their parents' divorce into their own romantic relationships. Almost all felt that they had suffered in some way from their parents' mistakes. Not surprisingly, most of them shared a hope for something their parents had failed to achieve—a good, committed marriage based on love and faithfulness. Nearly half the group entered adulthood as "worried, underachieving, self-deprecating, and sometimes angry young men and women." Although many of them got married themselves, the legacy of their parents' divorce lived with them. Those who appeared to manage the best were often helped by supportive relationships with one or both parents (Wallerstein and Blakeslee, 1989).

We cannot say, of course, how the children might have fared if their parents had stayed together. The parents and children studied all came from an affluent white area, and might or might not be representative of the wider population. Moreover, the families were self-selected: they had approached counselors seeking help. Those who actively seek counseling might be less (or more) able to cope with separation than those who do not. One finding that does seem to emerge is that children fare better when they have a continuing relationship with both parents following separation than when they only see one parent regularly.

Remarriage and Stepparenting

Before 1900, the large majority of all marriages in the United States were first marriages. Most remarriages involved at least one widowed person. With the progressive rise in the divorce rate, the level of remarriage also began to climb, and in an increasing proportion of remarriages, at least one person was divorced.

Today, thirty-five out of every one hundred marriages involve at least one previously married person. Up to age thirty-five, the majority of remarriages are between divorced people. After that age, the proportion of remarriages with widows or widowers rises. By age fifty-five, the proportion of such remarriages is larger than those following divorce.

Odd though it might seem, the best way to maximize the chances of marriage, for both sexes, is to have been married previously. People who have been married and divorced are more likely to marry again than single people in similar age groups are to marry for the first time. At all age levels, divorced men are more likely to remarry than divorced women. Two in every three divorced women remarry, but three in every four divorced men eventually marry again. Many divorced individuals also choose to cohabitate instead of remarry. In statistical terms, at least, remarriages are less successful than first marriages: rates of divorce are higher.

This does not mean that second marriages are doomed to fail. People who have been divorced may have higher expectations of marriage than those who remain married to their first spouses. Hence, they may

KEY CONCEPTS IN REVIEW

There have been major changes in patterns of family life in the United States during the postwar period: a high percentage of women are in the paid labor force, rates of divorce have been rising, and substantial proportions of the population are either in single-parent households or living with stepfamilies. **Cohabitation** (a couple living together in a sexual relationship outside of marriage) has become increasingly common in industrial countries.

be more ready to dissolve new marriages than those only married once. The second marriages that endure are usually more satisfying, on average, than the first.

A **stepfamily** may be defined as a family in which at least one of the adults is a stepparent. Many who remarry become stepparents of children who regularly visit rather than live in the same household. By this definition, the number of stepfamilies is much greater than shown in available official statistics, since these usually refer only to families with whom stepchildren live. Stepfamilies bring into being kin ties that resemble those of some traditional societies but that are new in Western countries. Children may now have two "mothers" and two "fathers"—their natural parents and their stepparents. Some stepfamilies regard all the children and close relatives from previous marriages as part of the family. If we consider that at least some of the grandparents may be part of the family as well, the result is a situation of some complexity.

Certain particular difficulties tend to arise in stepfamilies. In the first place, there usually exists a biological parent living elsewhere whose influence over the child or children is likely to remain powerful. Cooperative relations between divorced individuals often become strained when one or both remarry. Take as an illustration the case of a woman with two children who marries a man also with two children, all six living together. If the "outside" parents demand the same times of visitation as previously, the tensions that arise from welding such a newly established family together are likely to be intense. It may prove impossible ever to have the new family all together on weekends.

Stepfamilies merge children from different backgrounds, who may have varying expectations in the family milieu. Since most stepchildren belong to two households, the possibilities of clashes of habits and outlooks are considerable. There are few established norms defining the relationship between stepparent and stepchild. Should a child call a new stepparent by name, or is "Dad" or "Mom" more appropriate? Should the stepparent play the same part in disciplining the children as the natural parent? How should a stepparent treat the new spouse of her previous partner when the children are picked up?

Members of these families are finding their own ways of adjusting to the relatively uncharted circumstances in which they find themselves. Perhaps the most appropriate conclusion to be drawn is that while marriages are broken up by divorce, families on the whole are not. Especially where children are involved, ties persist.

Single-Parent Households

Single-parent households have become increasingly common. As a result of the increase in divorce rates and births before marriage, about one-half of all children spend some time in their lives in a single-parent family (Furstenberg and Cherlin, 1991). The vast majority are headed by women, since the mother usually obtains custody of the children following a divorce (in a small proportion of single-parent households, the individual, again almost always a woman, has never

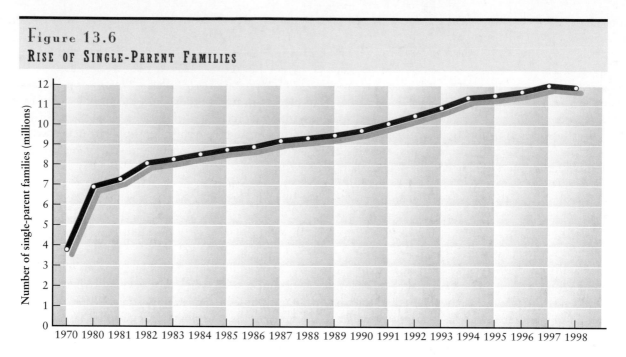

Figure 13.6
RISE OF SINGLE-PARENT FAMILIES

SOURCE: U.S. Bureau of the Census, Current Population Report, "Household and Family Characteristics," March 1998.

been married). There are about 12 million single-parent households in the United States today, and the number may continue to increase (see Figure 13.6). Such households comprise one in five of all families with dependent children. On average, they are among the poorest groups in contemporary society. Many single parents, whether they have ever been married or not, still face social disapproval as well as economic insecurity. Earlier and more judgmental terms such as "deserted wives," "fatherless families," and "broken homes" are tending to disappear, however.

The category of single-parent household is an internally diverse one. For instance, more than half of widowed mothers are homeowners, but the vast majority of never-married single mothers live in rented accommodation. Single parenthood tends to be a changing state, and its boundaries are rather blurred. In the case of a person who is widowed, the break is obviously clear-cut—although even here a person might have effectively been living on his or her own for some while if the partner was hospitalized prior to death. About 60 percent of single-parent households today, however, are brought about by separation or

divorce. In such cases, individuals may live together sporadically over a quite lengthy period. As one single mother remarks:

> I think it takes a time to come to terms with being a single mother. In my case I've only accepted what I am in the past year. I suppose before I always thought that we might get back together but when he got married I had to give up. I felt very bad at the time, but now I think it was the best thing that could have happened because it made me come to terms with my life. (Quoted in Crow and Hardey, 1992, p. 149)

Most people do not wish to be single parents, but there is a growing minority who choose to become so—who set out to have a child or children without the support of a spouse or partner. "Single mothers by choice" is an apt description of some parents, normally those who possess sufficient resources to manage satisfactorily as a single-parent household. For the majority of unmarried or never-married mothers, however, the reality is different: there is a high correlation between the rate of births outside marriage and indicators of poverty and social deprivation. As we saw earlier, these influences are very important in explaining the high proportion of single-parent households among families of African-American background in the United States.

A debate exists among sociologists about the impact on children of growing up with a single parent. The most exhaustive set of studies carried out to date, by Sara McLanahan and Gary Sandefur, rejects the claim that children raised by only one parent do just as well as children raised by both parents. A large part of the reason is economic—the sudden drop in income associated with divorce. But about half of the disadvantage comes from inadequate parental attention and lack of social ties. Separation or divorce weakens the connection between child and father, as well as the link between the child and the father's network of friends and acquaintances. On the basis of wide empirical research, the authors conclude it is a myth that there are usually strong support networks or extended family ties available to single mothers (McLanahan and Sandefur, 1994).

THE "ABSENT FATHER"

The time from the late 1930s up to the 1970s has sometimes been called the period of the "absent father." During World War II, many fathers rarely saw

Divorced women with children often find themselves struggling financially.

their children because of their war service. In the period following the war, in a high proportion of families, most women were not in the paid labor force and stayed at home to look after the children. The father was the main breadwinner and consequently was out at work all day; he would see his children only in the evenings and on weekends.

With rising divorce rates in more recent years, and the increasing number of single-parent households, the theme of the "absent father" has come to mean something different. It has come to refer to fathers who, as a result of separation or divorce, either have only infrequent contact with their children or lose touch with them altogether. In the United States, which has among the highest divorce rate in the world, this situation has provoked intense debate.

The increasing proportion of fatherless families has been said to be at the origin of a whole diversity of social problems, from rising crime to mushrooming welfare costs for child support. In his book *Fatherless America* (1995) David Blankenhorn argues that societies with high divorce rates are facing not just the loss of fathers but the very erosion of the idea of fatherhood—with lethal social consequences, because many children are growing up now without an authority figure to turn to in times of need. Marriage and fatherhood in all societies up to the present provided a means of channeling men's sexual and aggressive energies. Without them, these energies are likely to be expressed in criminality and violence. As one reviewer of Blankenhorn's book put it, "better to have a dad who comes home from a nasty job to drink beer in front of the television than no dad at all" (*The Economist*, 8 April 1995, p. 121).

Yet, is it? The issue of absent fathers overlaps with that of the more general question of the effects of divorce on children—and there, as we saw, the implications of the available evidence are far from clear. As the same reviewer put it: "Are not some fathers bad for the family?"

Evidence relevant to this controversy comes from Sweden (actually the only country in Western Europe where the birth rate has increased since 1970). About

half the babies in Sweden are born to unmarried mothers (see Table 13.1). Nineteen out of twenty of these are born in households with a father, but many will

Table 13.1 International Comparisons of Births to Single Women and Single Parenthood

	PERCENTAGE OF ALL BIRTHS TO SINGLE WOMEN		PERCENTAGE OF FAMILIES HEADED BY SINGLE PARENTS	
COUNTRY	1960	1990	1960	1988
United Kingdom	5	28	6	13
United States	5	28	9	23
Canada	4	24	9	15
Denmark	8	46	17	20
France	6	30	9	12
Germany	6	11	8	14
Italy	2	6	n.a.	n.a.
The Netherlands	1	11	9	15
Sweden	11	47	9	13

SOURCES: U.S. Bureau of the Census, *Statistical Abstract of the United States,* 1993; Constance Sorrentino, "The Changing Family in International Perspective," *Monthly Labor Review* (March 1990), pp. 41–58. From Sara McLanahan and Gary Sandefur, *Growing Up with a Single Parent: What Hurts, What Helps* (Harvard University Press, 1994).

grow up without their own fathers at home, as half of all Swedish marriages end in divorce and unmarried parents split up three times more often than married ones. Twenty percent of children in Sweden were in single-parent families in 1994.

Research in Sweden turns up little evidence of the social problems fatherlessness is supposed to bring in its wake. This might be because, in societies such as the United States, it is poverty rather than the family which is the true origin of, for example, criminality and violence. In Sweden, generous welfare benefits mean that single-parent families do not slip into poverty. In 1994 only 6.8 percent of Swedish children lived in families with less than half the average income—a much lower proportion than in the United States (*The Economist*, 9 September 1995).

THE DARK SIDE OF THE FAMILY

Since family or kin relations are part of almost everyone's experience, family life encompasses virtually the whole range of emotional experience. Family relation-

ships—between wife and husband, parents and children, brothers and sisters, or more distant relatives—can be warm and fulfilling. But they can equally be full of the most extreme tension, driving people to despair or imbuing them with a deep sense of anxiety and guilt. The dark side of family life is extensive, and belies the rosy images of family harmony frequently depicted in TV commercials and programs. It can take many forms. Among the most devastating in their consequences, however, are the incestuous abuse of children and domestic violence.

Sexual Abuse

No one knows exactly how widespread sexual abuse is, and definitions of what counts as abuse vary (Finkelhor, 1984). **Sexual abuse** can most easily be defined as the carrying out of sexual acts by adults with children below the age of consent (usually sixteen years old). Incest refers to sexual relations between close kin. Not all incest is sexual abuse. For example, sexual intercourse between brother and sister is incestuous but does not fit the definition of abuse, unless one is considerably older than the other. A sexually abusive adult essentially exploits an infant or child for sexual purposes. It is impossible to obtain precise figures on the occurrence of incest, because of its forbidden and generally secretive character. Incest and child sexual abuse more generally are phenomena that have been "discovered" only in the past ten to twenty years. It has long been known that such sexual acts occurred, but it was assumed by most researchers that the strong moral taboos that exist against such behavior meant that it was not widespread. Such, unfortunately, is not the case.

Why have incest and child sexual abuse been so hidden from public view until recently? Part of the answer seems to be that the taboos against such activity led welfare workers and social researchers to be wary of asking questions about possible abuse. The women's movement played an important role in initially drawing public attention to the issue, as one element in wider campaigns against sexual harassment and exploitation. Once researchers began to probe into suspected cases of child sexual abuse, more cases came to light. The discovery of the extent of child sexual abuse, which began in the United States, has become an international phenomenon. Studies in Britain, for example, show findings parallel to those in the United States.

We do not know exactly what proportion of child sexual abuse is incestuous, but probably most does occur in a family context. Both the nature of the incestual relation and the sexual acts committed vary widely. Most studies indicate that 70–80 percent of incest cases are father-daughter or stepfather-daughter relationships. However, uncle-niece, brother-sister, father-son, mother-daughter, and even grandparent-grandchild relationships also occur. Some incestuous contacts are short-lived and involve no more than a fondling of the child's sexual organs by the adult, or the child being encouraged to touch the adult's genitals. Others are more extensive and may be repeated over several years. The children are usually over two years old, but there are reported instances of sexual acts with infants.

Force or the threat of violence is involved in many cases of incest; children are rarely willing participants. Children are sexual beings and often engage in mild sexual play or exploration with one another. But most children subject to sexual contact from adult family members find the experience horrific, repugnant, and shameful.

UNDERSTANDING SEXUAL ABUSE

To explain why incest and, more broadly, child sexual abuse occur, we need to account for two things: why adults should be attracted to sexual activities involving children, and why men should make up the vast majority of abusers. As for the first, most child abusers do not seem to have a *preference* for sexual relationships with children over adults. Rather, it is a matter of availability coupled with power. Children within the family are dependent beings and highly vulnerable to parental demands or pressures.

Adults who commit incest mostly seem to be timid, awkward, and inadequate in their dealings with other adults. Many appear to be not just satisfying sexual impulses, but searching for affection they cannot attain elsewhere. And here is where the fact that the large majority of abusers are men comes in. Men often come to associate the expression of feeling directly with sexuality, whereas women focus more on whole relationships. Males also associate sexuality with the assertion of power and with submissiveness in their partners. Therefore, there is less of a distance for men between adult sexuality and sexual attention to children than for women.

One of the leading students of child abuse, David Finkelhor, has suggested changes that might help reduce the sexual exploitation of children:

> First, we might benefit from the opportunity to practice affection and dependency in relationships that did not involve sex, such as male-to-male friendships and nurturant interaction with children. Second, the accomplishment of heterosexual sex might be de-emphasized as the ultimate criterion of male adequacy. Third, men might learn to enjoy sexual relationships based on equality. Men who are comfortable relating to women at the same level of maturity and competence will be less likely to exploit children sexually. As men's relationships with women change, so will their relations with children. (1984)

Violence within the Family

Violence within families is also primarily a male domain, but less decisively so than in the case of child sexual abuse. We may define **domestic violence** as physical abuse directed by one member of a family against another. Studies show that the prime targets of physical abuse are again children, especially those under the age of six. In a given year, about one in twenty-two children is a victim of physical abuse (Gelles and Straus, 1989). Violence by husbands against wives is the second most common type. One in six wives reports being hit by her husband during their marriage; the average battered wife is hit three times a year. Women, however, are also perpetrators of physical violence in the household, against young children and against husbands. The home is in fact the most dangerous place in modern society. In statistical terms, a person of any age or either sex is far more likely to be subject to physical attack in the home than on the street at night. One in four murders in the United States is committed by one family member against another.

It is occasionally claimed that women are almost as violent as men in the home, and some surveys indicate that wives hit husbands nearly as often as the reverse (Straus, Gelles, and Steinmetz, 1980). However, violence by women is more restrained and less likely to cause enduring physical harm. (Violence by women is also often initiated by violence and abuse by men.) Wife battering—the regular physical brutalizing of a wife by a husband—has no real equivalent the other way around. Men who physically abuse children are also more likely to do so consistently, so as to cause long-standing injuries, than are women.

Why is domestic violence so commonplace? One factor is the emotional intensity of family life. Family ties are normally charged with strong emotions, often mixing love and hate. Quarrels that break out at home can unleash antagonisms that would not be felt in the same way in other social settings. What seems only a minor incident can precipitate full-scale hostilities between spouses or between parents and children.

A second reason is the fact that a good deal of violence within the family is culturally tolerated. Only about one-quarter of children in modern America have not at some time been slapped or spanked by a parent. Such actions can meet with general approval and are probably not even thought of as violence; but they can easily spill over into more severe forms of assault. If a stranger slapped a child in a shop because he disapproved of something the child did, it would be a different matter. Yet there is no difference in the physical assault involved.

There is also some social approval of violence between spouses. Murray Straus has even argued that parenthood provides a "license for hitting" and that "the marriage license is a hitting license" (Straus, 1978). In the workplace and other public settings, it is a general rule that no one can hit anyone else, no matter how objectionable or irritating she may be. This is not the case within the family. Research studies have shown that a substantial proportion of couples believe that in some circumstances, it is legitimate for a spouse to strike the other.

While family violence remains a problem, a recent study has concluded that it has declined since the mid-1970s as a result of changes within the broader soci-

Research suggests that many cultures approve of some forms of domestic violence.

ety. First, as we've seen, the structure of the American family has undergone changes in the last few decades. People are choosing to get married and have children later in life. There has also been a decline in the number of unwanted children, which contributes to lower rates of child abuse. In addition, there has been a big increase in paid employment for married women, which has helped equalize the balance of power in marriages and given battered women the resources necessary to leave abusive husbands. Increased protection in the way of shelters and treatment programs for battered women have contributed to the decline. Finally, changes in the law have served as a deterrence to family violence. But while these developments are a positive sign, there remain millions of victims (Gelles and Straus, 1989).

ALTERNATIVES TO TRADITIONAL FORMS OF MARRIAGE AND THE FAMILY

Communes

The family has long had its critics. In the nineteenth century, numerous thinkers proposed that family life should be replaced by more communal forms of living. Some of these ideas were acted on, one of the best-known examples being the Oneida Community of New England, which was set up in the middle of the nineteenth century. It was based on the religious beliefs of John Humphrey Noyes. Every man in the community was married to every woman, and all were supposed to be parents to the community's children. After various initial difficulties, the group expanded to include about three hundred people, and endured for about thirty years before breaking up. Many other communes have been founded since then, in Britain as well as many other Western countries. A large variety of communal groups were established in the 1960s, often involving free sexual relations within the group and collective responsibility for the raising of children. A small number of these are still in existence.

The most important current example of communal domestic life is that of the **kibbutzim** in Israel. A kibbutz is a community of families and individuals that cooperates in the raising of children. Most of the kibbutzim were originally collective farming enterprises, but today many have also moved into industrial production.

There are more than 240 kibbutzim in Israel, which have nearly 100,000 members in all. Some are small, with no more than fifty members, while others include as many as 2,000 people. Each kibbutz operates as though it were a single household, child care being treated as the responsibility of the whole community rather than the family. In some, children live in special "children's houses" rather than with their parents, although they usually spend weekends with their families.

The kibbutzim were originally established with a radical intent. Communal ownership of property, together with the group rearing of children, were to allow kibbutzim members to escape the individualistic, competitive nature of life in modern societies. These ideals have by no means been abandoned; yet over the years the majority of kibbutzim have opted for more conventional living arrangements than those favored in the early stages. It is more common for children to sleep in their parents' quarters, for instance, than used to be the case. The children's houses in the kibbutz are today perhaps better described as providing extensive child-care facilities rather than expressing communal responsibility for the raising of children.

Cohabitation

Cohabitation—in which a couple lives together in a sexual relationship without being married—has become increasingly widespread in most Western societies. Until a few decades ago, cohabitation was generally regarded as somewhat scandalous. As we saw earlier in the chapter, however, during the 1980s, the number of unmarried men and women sharing a household went up sharply. Cohabitation has become widespread among college and university students. Surveys in the United States indicate that about one in four students live with partners with whom they are involved in a sexual relationship at some point during the course of their college careers.

Cohabitation in the United States today seems to be for the most part an experimental stage before marriage. Young people come to live together usually by drifting into it, rather than through calculated planning. A couple who are already having a sexual relationship spend more and more time together, eventually giving up one of their individual homes. Young people living together almost always anticipate getting married at some date, but not necessarily to their current partners. Only a minority of such couples pool their finances.

Cohabitation has also become more popular with older adults as well. In fact, the percentage of never-married people who cohabitate is lower than the percentage of previously married people (divorced or widowed) who cohabitate.

Over the past forty years, there has been a 400 percent increase in the number of people in the United States cohabiting before marriage. Only 4 percent of women born in the 1920s cohabited and 19 percent of those born in the 1940s—but nearly half the women born in the 1960s cohabited. It has been forecast that four out of five married couples will have lived to-

gether before marriage by the year 2000 (Wilkinson and Mulgan, 1995).

The close connection between cohabitation and marriage is indicated in Figure 13.7, which shows that the most important reason for cohabiting for both women and men is so that "couples can be sure they are compatible before marriage." This is not surprising, since surveys indicate that most young people see cohabitation as "trial marriage." Sixty percent of cohabiting couples end up marrying, while a large proportion of the rest break up. Only about 10 percent of cohabiting couples remain as cohabitors (neither marrying nor breaking up) for more than five years. Thus, at least for the present time, cohabitation is less of a substitute for marriage than a possible stage in the process of becoming married.

In some European countries, particularly in rural areas, cohabitation has a long history as a legitimate practice. This is the case with the Nordic countries, which in fact have the highest rates of cohabitation today. There is not, however, a direct continuity with the past. In Sweden in 1960, for example, only 1

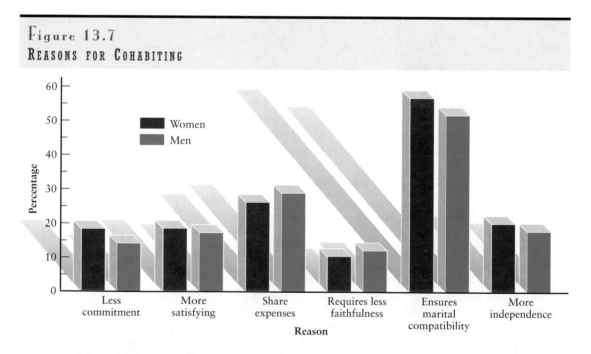

Figure 13.7
REASONS FOR COHABITING

SOURCE: Bumpass, Sweet, and Cherlin, 1991.

Percentage of cohabiting women and men under 35 who agreed that each reason was the most important for "why someone might want to live with a person of the opposite sex without being married."

percent of couples cohabited; today that figure has risen to an estimated 40 percent. As in other countries in Europe, the majority of cohabiting couples marry after a certain time, or when they have children. Cohabitation has quite often been given a legal status, such that, should a relationship break up, individuals can sue for property settlement and maintenance.

Gay-Parent Families

Many homosexual men and women now live in stable relationships as couples, and some gay couples have been formally "married" even if these ceremonies have no standing in law. Relaxation of previously intolerant attitudes toward homosexuality has been accompanied by a growing tendency for courts to allocate custody of children to mothers living in gay relationships. Techniques of artificial insemination mean that gay women may have children and become gay-parent families without any heterosexual contacts. While virtually every gay family with children in Britain involves two women, for a period in the late 1960s and early 1970s social welfare agencies in several cities in the United States placed homeless gay teenage boys in the custody of gay male couples. The practice was discontinued, largely because of adverse public reaction.

Staying Single

Several factors have combined to increase the numbers of people living alone in modern Western societies. One is a trend toward later marriages—people now marry on average about three years later than was the case in 1960; another is the rising rate of divorce. Yet another is the growing number of old people in the population whose partners have died. Being single means different things at different periods of the life-cycle. A larger proportion of people in their twenties are unmarried than used to be the case. By their mid-thirties, however, only a small minority of men and women have never been married. The majority of single people aged thirty to fifty are divorced and "in between" marriages. Most single people over fifty are widowed.

Peter Stein interviewed sixty single individuals in

Gay-parent families have had to fight in state and federal courts to obtain joint custody of children.

the age range twenty-five to forty five (Stein, 1980). Most felt ambivalent about being single. They recognized that being single often helped their career opportunities, because they could concentrate wholeheartedly on work; it made available a wider variety of sexual experiences, and promoted overall freedom and autonomy. On the other hand, they acknowledged the difficulty of being single in a world where most people their age were married, and they suffered from isolation or loneliness. On the whole, most found the pressures to marry greater than the incentives to stay single.

THE SOCIOLOGICAL DEBATE

THE FUTURE OF THE AMERICAN FAMILY

Is the American family in a state of crisis? Or are family arrangements simply changing to keep pace with rapid economic, technological, and social changes in the United States? Sociologists David Popenoe and Judith Stacey offer very different perspectives on the "future of the family." Popenoe, a Rutgers University professor, argues that the family has changed for the worse since 1960. In the last thirty-five years, divorce, non-marital births, and cohabitation rates have increased, while marriage and marital fertility rates have decreased. These trends, taken together, are at the root of countless social ills, including child poverty, adolescent pregnancy, substance abuse, and juvenile crime. Increasing rates of divorce and non-marital births have created millions of female-headed households, and have consequently removed men from the child rearing process. Popenoe argues that this is harmful for children (1993, 1996).

Stacey, a professor at the University of Southern California, counters that the traditional American family of the 1950s—praised by Popenoe and conservative politicians as the panacea for all social problems—is a dated and oppressive institution. The "breadwinner-father and child rearing–mothers" family, defined by Stacey as the "modern family," perpetuated the "segregation of the sexes by extracting men from, and consigning white married women to, an increasingly privatized domestic domain." The "modern family" has been replaced by multiple new family forms. These new forms, which Stacey has named the "postmodern family," include single mothers, blended families, cohabiting couples, lesbian and gay partners, communes, and two-worker families. The postmodern family is not inferior to the traditional two-parent family. To the contrary, it is well-suited to meet the challenges of the current economy, and is an appropriate setting for raising children: children need capable, loving caretakers—regardless of their gender, marital status, or sexual orientation, argues Stacey.

Popenoe agrees with Stacey's claim that children need capable, loving caretakers, yet maintains that "on the whole, two parents—a father and a mother—are better for a child than one parent." Why? Popenoe claims that biological fathers make "distinctive, irreplaceable contributions" to their children's welfare. Fathers offer a strong male role model to sons, they play the role of disciplinarian for trouble-prone children, they provide their daughters with a male perspective on heterosexual relationships, and, through their unique "play" styles, they teach their children about teamwork, competition, independence, self-fulfillment, self-control, and regulation of one's emotions. Mothers, alternatively, teach their children

about communion, or the feeling of being connected to others. Both needs must be met, and can be achieved only through the gender-differentiated parenting of a mother and father, argues Popenoe.

Stacey retorts that the "postmodern family" is better suited to meet the challenges of the current "postmodern economy." In the postmodern economy, employment has shifted from heavy industries to nonunionized clerical, service, and new industrial sectors. The loss of union-protected jobs means that men no longer earn enough to support a wife and children. At the same time, demand for clerical and service labor, escalating consumption standards, increases in women's educational attainment, and the persistence of high divorce rates has given more and more women reason to seek paid employment outside the home.

Stacey also takes issue with media rhetoric and claims by conservatives like Popenoe, which elevate the married, two-parent family as the ideal family form. Their condemnation of other family forms is particularly harmful to the millions of children who live with gay or lesbian parents. Rather than condemning nontraditional family forms, Stacey reasons that family sociologists and policymakers should instead develop strategies to lessen the harmful effects of divorce and single-parenthood on children. She suggests that restructuring work schedules and benefit policies to accommodate familial responsibilities, redistributing work opportunities to reduce unemployment rates, enacting comparable-worth standards of pay equity to enable women as well as men to earn a family wage, providing universal health, prenatal, and child care, sex education, and rectifying the economic inequities of divorce would be much more admirable efforts. These child-friendly efforts, she argues, are truly "profamily" (1990, 1993, 1996).

Popenoe's policy recommendations are based on the claim that "marriage must be re-established as a strong social institution." How? He argues that employers should reduce the practice of relocating married couples with children, and should provide more generous parental leave. He also supports a two-tiered system of divorce law. Marriages without minor children would be relatively easy to dissolve, but marriages with young children would be dissolvable only by mutual agreement or on grounds that clearly involve a wrong by one party against the other.

The Debate about "Family Values"

"The family is collapsing!" cry the advocates of family values, such as David Poponoe, surveying the changes of the past few decades—a more liberal and open attitude toward sexuality, steeply climbing divorce rates, and a general seeking for personal happiness at the expense of older conceptions of family duty. We must recover a moral sense of family life, they argue. We must reinstate the traditional family, which was much more stable and ordered than is the tangled web of relationships in which most of us find ourselves now.

"No!" reply their critics, such as Judith Stacey. "You think the family is collapsing. In fact, it is merely diversifying. We should actively encourage a variety of family forms and sexual life, rather than supposing that everyone has to be compressed into the same mold."

Which side is right? We should probably be critical of both views. A return to the traditional family isn't a possibility. This isn't only because, as explained earlier, the traditional family as it is usually thought of never existed, or because there were too many oppressive facets to families in the past to make them a model for today. It is also because the social changes that have transformed earlier forms of marriage and the family are mostly irreversible. Women won't return in large numbers to a domestic situation from which they have painfully managed to liberate themselves. Sexual partnerships and marriage today, for better or worse, can't be like they used to be. Emotional communication—more precisely, the active creation and sustaining of relationships—has become central to our lives in the personal and family domain.

What will be the result? The divorce rate may have leveled off from its previous steep increase, but it's not dropping. All measures of divorce are to some extent estimates, but on the basis of past trends, we can guess that some 60 percent of all marriages contracted now will end in divorce before ten years.

Divorce, as we've seen, is not always an index of unhappiness. People who may in former times have felt constrained to remain in miserable marriages can make a fresh start. But there can be no doubt that the trends affecting sexuality, marriage, and the family create deep anxieties for some people at the same time as they generate new possibilities for satisfaction and self-fulfillment for others.

Those who argue that the great diversity in family forms that exists today is to be welcomed, as freeing us from the limitations and sufferings of the past, surely have a certain amount of right on their side. Men and women can remain single if they wish, without having to face the social disapproval that once came from being a bachelor or a spinster. The number of people living alone has in fact grown rapidly over the past twenty years, although a substantial proportion are people "between" marriages or relationships. Couples in live-in relationships, which have become common, no longer face social rejection by their more "respectable" married friends. Gay couples can set up house together and bring up children without facing the same level of hostility they would have in the past.

The Future for the Democratic Family?

The family is a basic institution of society. Is there a politics of the family that reflects the social changes taking place in other social institutions? First and most fundamentally we must start from the principle of equality between the sexes, from which there can be no going back. There is only one story to tell about the family today, and that is of democracy. The family is becoming democratized, in ways that parallel processes of political democracy; and such democratization suggests how family life might combine individual choice and social solidarity.

The criteria are surprisingly close. Democracy in the public sphere involves formal equality, individual rights, public discussion of issues free from violence, and authority that is negotiated rather than given by tradition. The democratized family shares these characteristics, some of which are already protected in national and international law. Democratization in the context of the family implies equality, mutual respect, autonomy, and decision-making through communication and freedom from violence. Much the same characteristics also supply a model for parent–child relationships. Parents of course will still claim authority over children, and rightly so; but this will be more ne-gotiated and open than before. These qualities do not apply only to heterosexual families—they have exactly the same importance in homosexual relationships.

The democratized family is again an ideal. What can government do? As elsewhere, the emphasis must surely be on securing a balance of autonomy and re-sponsibility in which positive forms of encouragement go along with other sanctions. There is a widespread yearning for the family to provide stability in a chang-ing world, but realistically it is as likely to reflect other qualities of this world as it is to compensate for them. Much stress is laid upon flexibility and adaptability in the workplace: the same needs to be true of capabilities individuals bring to marriage and family relationships. The ability to sustain relationships through change, even radical changes such as divorce, becomes central not only to individuals' happiness, but to the achieve-ment of continuity in relationships with children.

The protection and care of children is the single most important thread that should guide family policy. It is not a solution to propose that divorce should be made more difficult to obtain. Such a measure might lower formal divorce rates but would not prevent sep-aration and would almost certainly mean that even fewer people would marry—the opposite effect to that desired by those who advocate stricter divorce laws.

Democratic family relationships imply shared re-sponsibility for child care, especially greater sharing among women and men, and among parents and non-parents, since in the society at large mothers bear a dis-proportionate share of the costs (and enjoy a disproportionate share of the emotional rewards) of children. Marriage and parenthood have always been thought of as tied together, but in the detraditionalized family, where having a child is an altogether different decision from in the past, the two are becoming sepa-rated. If current trends continue, the proportion of chil-dren born outside marriage probably won't decline, and lifelong sexual partnerships will become increas-ingly uncommon. Contractual commitment to a child could thus be separated from marriage, and made by each parent as a binding matter of law, with unmarried and married fathers having the same rights and the same obligations (Burgess, 1997). Both sexes would have to recognize that sexual encounters carry the chance of lifetime responsibilities, including protection from physical abuse. In combination with other cul-tural changes promoting a more positive image of fa-therhood, such a restructuring of parenthood would undermine the very idea of the "single parent."

Democracy is difficult to achieve and can be hard to live with, in the family as in other areas. As far as the care of children is concerned, it implies co-parenting, however far off this may be in current circumstances. The conservative view of the disintegration of the tra-ditional family tends to be based upon a specific idea about the limitations of men: men are intrinsically careless and morally irresponsible; unless safely locked into marriage of a traditional kind, they are a socially disruptive force.

Yet research does not support this idea (Burgess, 1998). For most men, as for women, divorce is a painful and distressing experience. The large majority of men don't feel relief at having shed their responsi-bilities for their children. Most attempt to sustain their relationships with them, even in the face of great difficulties. Many who lose contact do so because of the emotional traumas involved, or the active hostility of the ex-partner, rather than a desire to follow an ir-responsible lifestyle.

As one researcher points out, there is a very thin line between those fathers who remain closely in-volved with their children after divorce and those who do not. The most important determinant is not the at-titude of the father, but the responses of others, as well as contingent events that sway things one way rather than the other. Many fathers do lose contact with their children and do not support them economi-cally. Contrary to the "deadbeat dad" view, however, this does not seem to be a gender issue. A study by the U.S. Census Bureau found that noncustodial mothers were less likely than comparable fathers to pay child support awarded by the courts (Doherty, 1997).

Co-parenting could be encouraged by a number of innovations. Like "single mother," the term "absent parent," widely used in law, helps perpetuate a situa-tion where one parent, normally the father, is seen and treated as peripheral. Economic factors are also relevant. Why shouldn't child care be just as available for single working fathers as for working mothers? Fathers should have greater parenting rights than at present, but they should be provided, where neces-sary, with the means to fulfill their responsibilities.

These things having been said, it is difficult to resist the conclusion that we stand at a crossroads. Will the future bring about the further decay of long-term marriages or partnerships? Will we more and more inhabit an emotional and sexual landscape scarred by bitterness and violence? Such a sociological analysis of marriage and the family as we have just concluded strongly suggests that we won't resolve our problems by looking to the past. We must try to reconcile the individual freedoms most of us have come to value in our personal lives with the need to form stable and lasting relations with other people.

SUMMARY

1. *Kinship, family*, and *marriage* are closely related terms of key significance for sociology and anthropology. Kinship comprises either genetic ties or ties initiated by marriage. A family is a group of kin having responsibility for the upbringing of children. Marriage is a union of two persons living together in a socially approved sexual relationship.

2. A *nuclear family* refers to a household in which a married couple or single parent live with their own or adopted children. Where kin other than parents and children live in the same household, or are involved in close and continuous relationships, we speak of the existence of an *extended family*.

3. In Western societies, marriage, and therefore the family, is associated with *monogamy* (a culturally approved sexual relationship between one man and one woman). Many other cultures tolerate or encourage *polygamy*, in which an individual may be married to two or more spouses at the same time. *Polygyny*, in which a man may marry more than one wife, is far more common than *polyandry*, in which a woman may have more than one husband.

4. The modern Western family, which features close emotional bonds, domestic privacy, and a preoccupation with child rearing, is also characterized by *affective individualism*, meaning that marriage partners are usually selected on the basis of romantic love. This is now the norm, but it was not always so. In premodern Europe, parents, extended family members, or even landlords decided on marriage partners, basing their choices largely on social or economic considerations.

5. There are many types of families in the world, but there is a trend toward the Western norm of the nuclear family. Some reasons for this trend include: the Western ideal of romantic love, the growth of urbanization and of centralized governments, and employment in organizations outside of traditional family influence.

6. There have been major changes in patterns of family life in the United States during the postwar period: a high percentage of women are in the paid labor force, there are rising rates of divorce, and substantial proportions of the population are either in single-parent households or are living with step-families. *Co-habitation* (in which a couple lives together in a sexual relationship outside of marriage) has become increasingly common in many industrial countries.

7. Family life is by no means always a picture of harmony and happiness. The "dark side" of the family is found in the patterns of *sexual abuse* and *domestic violence* that often occur within it. Most sexual abuse of children is carried out by males and seems to connect with other types of violent behavior in which some men are involved.

8. Cohabitation and homosexuality have become more common in recent years. It seems certain that alternative forms of social and sexual relationships to those prevalent in the past will flourish still further. Yet marriage and the family remain firmly established institutions.

Chapter Fourteen

Understand that the rise of the mass media and the development of mass education are closely connected, as can be seen in the emergence of a public sphere in modern societies.

The Development of Schooling

Know how and why systems of mass education emerged in the United States.

Education and Inequality

Become familiar with the most important research on whether education reduces or perpetuates inequality. Learn the social and cultural influences on educational achievement.

Education and Literacy in the Third World

Know some basic facts about the education system and literacy rates of Third World countries.

Communication and the Mass Media

Recognize the important impact of the mass media upon society and learn some important theories about that impact.

Technological Change, Media, and Education

See the ways in which technological change is transforming both the mass media and education.

EDUCATION
AND THE MASS
MEDIA

■▄■▄■▄■▄■▄■▄■▄■▄■▄■▄■▄■

Imagine being in the shoes—or the wooden clogs—of Jean-Paul Didion, a peasant boy growing up in a French farming community two centuries ago. In 1750 Jean-Paul is fourteen years old. He cannot read or write, but this is not uncommon; only a few of the adults in his village have the ability to decipher more than the odd word or two of written texts. There are some schools in nearby districts run by monks and nuns, but these are completely removed from Jean-Paul's experience. He has never known anyone well who attended school, save for the local priest. For eight or nine years, Jean-Paul has been spending most of his days helping with domestic tasks and working in the fields. The older he gets, the longer each day he is expected to share in the backbreaking chores demanded by the intensive tilling of his father's plot of land.

Jean-Paul is likely never to leave the area in which he was born, and may spend virtually the whole of his life within the confines of the village and surrounding fields, only occasionally traveling to other local villages and towns. He may have to wait until he is in his late fifties before inheriting his father's plot of land, sharing control of it with his younger brothers. Jean-Paul is aware that he is "French," that his country is ruled over by Louis XV, and that there is a wider world beyond even France itself. But he only has a vague awareness even of "France" as a distinct political entity. There is no such thing as "news," nor any regular means by which information about events elsewhere reaches him. What he knows of the wider world comes from stories and tales he has heard told by adults and by visiting travelers. Like others in his community, he only learns about major events—like the death of the king—days, weeks, or sometimes months after they have occurred.

Although in modern terms Jean-Paul is "uneducated," he is far from "ignorant." He has a sensitive and developed understanding of the family and children, having had to care for those younger than himself since he was very young. He is already highly knowledgeable about the land, methods of crop production, and ways of preserving and storing food. His mastery of local customs and traditions is profound, and he can turn his hand to many different tasks over and above agricultural cultivation, such as weaving or basket making.

Jean-Paul is an invented figure, but the above description portrays the typical experience of a boy growing up in preindustrial Europe. Compare this with our situation today. In the industrialized countries, virtually everyone can read and write—that is, people are *literate*. We have all gone through a process of formal schooling. We are all aware of the common characteristics we share with other members of the same society, and have at least some sort of knowledge of its geographical and political position in the world, and of its past history. Our lives are influenced at all ages beyond infancy by information we pick up through books, newspapers, magazines, radio, and television, in short, the various *media*. We live in a media-saturated world. The printed word and electronic communication, combined with the formal teaching provided by schools and colleges, have become fundamental to our way of life. This being so, schooling and the media extend the process of socialization, which we took up earlier in Chapter 4 ("Socialization and the Life Cycle"). There, we focused on early influences, especially mother-infant interaction, but we only touched briefly upon schooling and the media.

In this chapter, two themes dominate: education and media as socializing processes, and education and media as sources of power. First, we shall show how present-day education developed and analyze its socializing influence, which at times complements, and at others competes with, the family. We will also look at education in relation to social inequality, and consider how far the educational system serves to encourage or to reduce such inequality. We then move to studying the nature of modern mass media.

THE DEVELOPMENT OF SCHOOLING

The term "school" has its origins in a Greek word meaning "leisure," or "recreation." In premodern societies, schooling existed for the few who had the time and resources available to pursue the cultivation of the arts and philosophy. For some, their engagement with schooling was like taking up a hobby. For others, like religious leaders or priests, schooling was a way of gaining skills and thus increasing their ability to interpret sacred texts. But for the vast majority of people, growing up meant learning by example the same social habits and work skills as their elders. Learning was a family affair—there were no schools at all for the mass of the population. Since children often started to help with domestic duties and farming work at a very young age, they rapidly became full-fledged members of the community.

Education in its modern form, the instruction of pupils within specially constructed school premises, gradually emerged in the first few years of the nineteenth century, when primary schools began to be constructed in Europe and the United States. One main reason for the rise of large educational systems was the process of industrialization, with its ensuing expansion of cities. People now worked in many different occupations, and work skills could no longer only be passed on from parents to children or even from master craftsmen to apprentices. The acquisition of knowledge based on abstract learning (of subjects like math, science, and history) became increasingly prominent. With the development of modern society, people needed the basic skills of reading, writing, and calculating; and it became important that they be able to master new, sometimes very technical, forms of information.

Sociologists have debated why formal systems of schooling developed in modern societies by studying the social functions that schools provide. For example, some have argued that mass education promotes feelings of nationalism and aided the development of national societies, constituted of citizens from different regions who would know the same history and speak a common language (Ramirez and Boli, 1987). Marxist sociologists have argued that the expansion of education was brought about by the need of employers for certain personality characteristics in their workers—self-discipline, dependability, punctuality, obedience, and the like—which are all taught in schools (Bowles and Gintis, 1976). Another influential perspective comes from the sociologist Randall Collins, who has argued that the primary social function of mass education derives from the need for diplomas and degrees to determine one's credentials for a job, even if the work involved has nothing to do with the education one has received. Over time, the practice of credentialism results in demands for higher credentials, which requires higher levels of educational attainment. Jobs, such as sales representative, that thirty years ago would have required a high school diploma now require a college degree. Since educational attainment is closely related to class position, credentialism reinforces the class structure within a society (Collins, 1971, 1979).

Schooling in the United States

Schooling in the United States has its origins in the disciplining of children. The basis of this seventeenth-century development was the Puritan belief that all children should obey their parents without question, a belief that these colonies had in fact made part of their legal statutes. A legal provision of 1642 promised severe sanctions against the "great neglect of many parents and masters in training up their children in learning and labor." Because this measure was ineffectual, however, the Puritan authorities commanded every town to provide schooling, beginning in 1647 in Massachusetts and Connecticut.

Before the Civil War, many plantation owners forbade their slaves to learn to read. Frederick Douglass, later a great abolitionist, author, and orator, held classes to educate his fellow slaves. His students risked severe beatings in order to gain the power that comes with literacy.

It was almost two centuries later before education became a common experience for the by then much-expanded American population. All states provided free elementary schooling by the 1850s, although at first attendance was not compulsory and large numbers of the population still went without any formal schooling at all. Compulsory education was introduced in most states toward the end of the nineteenth century, a period of extremely rapid expansion in the building of schools and colleges. There were only 160 public high schools in the country in 1870, but by 1900 there were in excess of 6,000.

The diverse cultural makeup of America at the turn of the century presented a particular challenge to the public school system. By that time, immigrants from Europe and elsewhere, each with a different native language and all with great hopes for the future, had settled in the United States. School then became a major transmission point in linguistically and to some extent culturally anglicizing the immigrants. In addition, the schools taught American ideals of equality of opportunity, thus encouraging the immigrants to set about making a new life. The notion that everyone is born equal led to the development of mass public education in the United States well before comparable systems were set up in other countries. Education was seen as an avenue of mobility in a society in which the aristocratic ideal—that some people are born with superior rights to others—had never held sway. And along with the idea of equality, other American values and beliefs were, and continue to be, taught more or less explicitly.

PRIMARY AND SECONDARY EDUCATION

There are wide differences between countries in ways of organizing educational systems. Some systems are highly centralized; in France, for example, all students follow nationally determined curricula and sit for exactly the same national examinations. In contrast, the American system is much more fragmentary. Individual states provide substantial funding for schools, contributing about 40 percent of the necessary finance, with the federal government providing another 40 percent. The rest comes from taxation revenue in local school districts. As a result, schools are administered by local school boards, elected by community vote, which have the power to hire teachers and other school officials and select (and occasionally ban) texts and other reading or viewing materials.

Such community control of schooling has mixed consequences. There are clear benefits in that schools are kept responsive to the needs and interests of the areas they serve. On the other hand, the system also leads to great differences in school funding, depending on how wealthy a given community is. Class size, available facilities, and the capability to attract well-qualified teachers all vary enormously between different school districts.

HIGHER EDUCATION

The system of **higher education** (education after high school, in colleges and universities) did not expand as early as the elementary and high school systems. In 1940, only 15 percent of the eighteen-to-twenty-one age group were enrolled in college. In the period after World War II, however, there was a rapid expansion that continued until the early 1970s. In 1950, the proportion of the college-age group enrolled in college

had risen to 30 percent, and a decade later had reached nearly 40 percent; 48 percent are enrolled today. The number of students carrying on through graduate school has also risen progressively over the postwar period.

In spite of the importance of public education in America, it is only since World War II that schooling has come to be considered essential to career advancement. For a long while, the Horatio Alger view of the self-made and self-educated individual held sway alongside the belief in the value of education. But this idea has moved more to the sidelines as educational qualifications have become more and more valued by employers. For this reason, the day that colleges and universities send out notices of acceptance or rejection has become a day of reckoning for many high school students.

In some countries, all universities and colleges are public agencies and receive their funding directly from government sources. Higher education in France, for instance, is organized nationally, with centralized control being almost as marked as it is in primary and secondary education. All course structures must be validated by a national regulatory body responsible to the minister of higher education. Two types of degrees can be gained, one awarded by the individual university, the other by the state. National degrees are generally regarded as more prestigious than those of specific universities, since they are supposed to conform to guaranteed uniform standards. Some occupations in government are only open to the holders of national degrees, which are also favored by most industrial employers. Virtually all teachers in schools, colleges, and universities in France are state employees. Rates of pay and teaching duties are fixed centrally.

The United States has a much higher proportion of private colleges and universities than most other industrialized countries—over half are privately funded. The difference between public and private in American higher education, however, is not as clear-cut as it is in other countries. Students at private universities are eligible for public grants and loans, and such universities receive public research funding. Public universities often receive substantial private endowments or are given donations by private firms. They also obtain research grants from private industrial sources.

Certainly one clear difference between public and private colleges in the United States is their tuition and board. The cost of studying at a private college is three to four times that of attending a public one. Private colleges generally have smaller enrollments than public ones and can therefore provide more intensive teaching. Hence, although private colleges are in the majority, only about 10 percent of all students are educated in them.

The educational sociologist Martin Trow predicted over thirty years ago that by today, almost everyone in the United States would receive some form of higher education (Trow, 1961). This hasn't happened; yet a high proportion of the American population, compared with elsewhere, has experience of higher education.

EDUCATION AND INEQUALITY

The expansion of education has always been closely linked to the ideals of democracy. Reformers value education for its own sake—for the opportunity it provides for individuals to develop their capabilities. Yet education has also consistently been seen as a means of equalization. Access to universal education, it has been argued, could help reduce disparities of wealth and power. Are educational opportunities equal for everyone? Has education in fact proved to be a great equalizer? Much research has been devoted to answering these questions.

"Savage Inequalities"

Between 1988 and 1990, the journalist Jonathan Kozol studied schools in about thirty neighborhoods around the United States. There was no special logic to the way he chose the schools, except that he went where he happened to know teachers, principals, or ministers. What startled him most was the segregation within these schools and the inequalities between them. Kozol brought these terrible conditions to the attention of the American people in his book *Savage Inequalities*, which became a best-seller (Kozol, 1991).

In his passionate opening chapter, he first took readers to East St. Louis, Illinois, a city that is 98 percent black, has no regular trash collection, and barely any jobs. Three-quarters of its residents were living on welfare at the time. City residents were forced to use their backyards as garbage dumps, which attracted a plague of flies and rats during the hot summer months. One resident told Kozol about "rats as big as puppies" that lived in his mother's yard. City residents also contended with pollution fumes from two major chemical plants in the city. Another public health problem resulted from raw sewage, which reg-

Savage inequalities: students in an affluent school district learn at a computer terminal (left) while students at a poorer school pass through metal detectors on their way to class.

THE INTERNATIONALIZATION OF EDUCATION

How many foreign students are enrolled in your sociology course? How many foreign students are there at your university? In 1943, approximately 8,000 foreign students were enrolled in American colleges and universities. By 1991, this number had skyrocketed to more than 400,000 (Lyman, 1995). Although the American university system as a whole grew considerably during this period, such that 400,000 students represented only 2.9 percent of total 1991 student enrollment, it is clear that foreign students are flocking to the United States in record numbers. Most foreign students today come from Asia—China, Japan, Taiwan, India, and South Korea all send sizeable contingents of students abroad. The United States takes in more foreign students than any other country, and there are six times as many foreign students in the United States as there are American students overseas. What do foreign students in the United States study? At the undergraduate level, more than 25 percent focus on business and management, 15 percent study engineering, and 9 percent concentrate on mathematics and computer science. More than 20 percent of foreign graduate students study engineering (Lambert, 1995).

Some scholars regard the exchange of international students as a vital component of globalization. Foreign students, in addition to serving as global "carriers" of specialized technical and scientific knowledge, have an im-

portant cultural role to play in the globalizing process. Cross-national understandings are enhanced and xenophobic and isolationist attitudes are minimized as native students in "host" countries develop social ties to their foreign classmates, and as foreign students return to their country of origin with an appreciation for the cultural mores of the nation in which they have studied.

Yet there is considerable debate in the United States about what is sometimes called the "internationalization of education." On most college campuses, it is not hard to find disgruntled students who complain that given the competitive nature of the U.S. higher education system, the influx of

ularly backed up into people's homes. East St. Louis also had some of the sickest children in the United States, with extremely high rates of infant death, asthma, and poor nutrition and extremely low rates of immunization. Only 55 percent of the children had been fully immunized for polio, diphtheria, measles,

and whooping cough. Among the city's other social problems were crime, dilapidated housing, poor health care, and lack of education.

Kozol showed how the problems of the city often spilled over into the schools, in this case literally. Over the course of two weeks, raw sewage backed up

ments unconvincing. While some Americans may lose out to foreign students in the competition for slots at prestigious universities, this is a small price to pay for the economic, political, and cultural benefits the United States receives from having educated millions of foreign business executives, policy makers, scientists, and professionals over the years—many of whom became sympathetically disposed to the United States as a result of their experiences here. And although some foreign students receive scholarships from American universities, most are supported by their parents. In fact, it is estimated that foreign students pump hundreds of millions of dollars each year into the U.S. economy. Rather than curtail the number of foreign students admitted to American universities, supporters of international education suggest that even more should be done to encourage the exchange of students. On the one hand, greater effort should be made to recruit foreign students, to help them select the university and program that will best meet their needs, and to provide them with a positive social and educational experience while they are in the United States. On the other hand, more Americans should be encouraged to study abroad. American students are notorious for having poor foreign language skills and for knowing little about global geography, much less about the cultures of other nations. This ignorance puts the United States at a disadvantage relative to other countries as the world becomes increasingly globalized; encouraging Americans to study overseas may be the best way to inculcate a global worldview.

Should there be a greater focus on international education in American colleges and universities? Should the international exchange of students be expanded? These are among the issues that educational institutions are forced to confront in the context of globalization.

foreign students deprives deserving Americans of educational opportunities. Moreover, although more than two-thirds of foreign students receive nothing in the way of scholarships, some top-notch foreign students *are* given financial inducements to attend American schools. The outcry against this practice has been loudest at public universities, which receive support from tax revenue. Critics charge that U.S. taxpayers should not shoulder the financial burden for educating foreign students whose families have not paid U.S. taxes and who are likely to return home after earning their degrees.

Supporters of international education find such argu-

into the school on three occasions, each time requiring the evacuation of students and the cancellation of classes. But the city's problems also negatively affected the school on a daily basis. Teachers often had to hold classes without chalk or paper. One teacher commented on the school's poor conditions by saying

"Our problems are severe. I don't even know where to begin. I have no materials with the exception of a single textbook given to each child. If I bring in anything else—books or tapes or magazines—I bring it in myself. The high school has no VCRs. They are such a crucial tool. So many good things run on public television. I can't make use of anything I see unless I unhook my VCR and bring it into school. The AV equipment in the school is so old that we are pressured not to use it." Comments from students reflected the same concerns. "I don't go to physics class, because my lab has no equipment," said one student. Another added, "The typewriters in my typing class don't work." A third said, "I wanted to study Latin but we don't have Latin in this school." Only 55 percent of the students in this high school ultimately graduate, about one-third of whom go on to college.

Kozol also wrote about the other end of the inequality spectrum, taking readers into a wealthy suburban school in Westchester County outside of New York City. At this school, there were 96 computers for the 546 students. Most studied a foreign language (including Latin) for four or five years. Two-thirds of the senior class were enrolled in an Advanced Placement (AP) class. Kozol visited an AP class to ask students about their perceptions of inequalities within the educational system. Students at this school were well aware of the economic advantages that they enjoyed at both home and school. With regard to their views about students less well-off than themselves, the general consensus was that equal spending between schools was a worthy goal but it would probably make little difference since poor students lack motivation and would fail because of other problems. These students also realized that equalizing spending could have adverse affects on their school. As one student said, "If you equalize the money, someone's got to be shortchanged. I don't doubt that [poor] children are getting a bad deal. But do we want everyone to get a mediocre education?"

It is impossible to read these descriptions of life in East St. Louis and Westchester County without believing that the extremes of wealth and poverty in the public schools are being exposed. Yet, many sociologists have argued that although Kozol's book is a moving portrait, it provides an inaccurate view of educational inequality. Why would Kozol's research not be compelling? There are several reasons, including the unsystematic way that he chose the schools that he studied. But the most important criticism of his work is that sociological research has shown that student achievement varies much more within schools than between schools—the proportions are about 80 percent to 20 percent. This means that differences be-

tween schools are not the main sources of inequality in achievement, even though Kozol's study may outrage us about these inequalities. This fact does not mean that Kozol was wrong—there are schools at both extremes—but these are not the kind of extremes that account for most educational inequality in America. Let's now look more closely at the work that sociologists have done to understand this complex relationship between education and inequality.

Sociological research addressing equal educational opportunities falls into two categories: research assessing "between school effects" and research assessing "within school effects." "Between school effects" refer to inequalities among children who go to different schools, asking—for example—whether students who attend schools with more resources end up ahead in the socioeconomic system. "Within school effects" are differences among students in the same school, asking—for example—if dividing students into "honors" or "remedial" classes leads to later disparities in educational attainment, occupational prestige, and wealth.

Coleman's Study of "Between School Effects" in American Education

The study of "between school effects" has been the focus of sociological research on the educational system for the past three decades. One of the classic investigations of educational inequality was undertaken in the United States in the 1960s. As a result of the Civil Rights Act of 1964, the commissioner of education was required to prepare a report on educational inequalities resulting from differences of ethnic background, religion, and national origin. James Coleman, a sociologist, was appointed director of the research program. The outcome was a study, published in 1966, based on one of the most extensive research projects ever carried out in sociology.

Information was collected on more than half a million pupils who were given a range of achievement tests assessing verbal and nonverbal abilities, reading levels, and mathematical skills. Sixty thousand teachers also completed forms providing data for about four thousand schools. The report found that a large majority of children went to schools that effectively segregated black from white. Almost 80 percent of schools attended by white students contained only 10 percent or less African-American students. White and Asian-American students scored higher on achievement tests than blacks and other ethnic minority students. Coleman had supposed his results would also show mainly African-American schools to have worse facilities, larger classes, and more inferior buildings than schools that were predominantly white. But surprisingly, the results showed far fewer differences of this type than had been anticipated.

Coleman therefore concluded that the material resources provided in schools made little difference to educational performance; the decisive influence was the children's backgrounds. In Coleman's words, "Inequalities imposed on children by their home, neighborhood, and peer environment are carried along to become the inequalities with which they confront adult life at the end of school" (Coleman et al., 1966). There was, however, some evidence that students from deprived backgrounds who formed close friendships with those from more favorable circumstances were likely to be more successful educationally.

Not long after Coleman's study, Christopher Jencks produced an equally celebrated work that reviewed empirical evidence accumulated on education and inequality up to the end of the 1960s (Jencks et al., 1972). Jencks reaffirmed two of Coleman's conclusions: (1) that educational and occupational attainment are governed mainly by family background and nonschool factors, and (2) that on their own, educational reforms can produce only minor effects on existing inequalities. Jencks' work has been criticized on methodological grounds, but his overall conclusions remain persuasive. Subsequent research has tended to confirm them.

Tracking and "Within School Effects"

The practice of **tracking**—dividing students into groups that receive different instruction on the basis of assumed similarities in ability or attainment—is common in American schools. In some schools, students are tracked only for certain subjects; in others, for all subjects. Sociologists have long believed that tracking is entirely negative in its effects. The conventional wisdom has been that tracking partly explains why schooling seems to have little effect on existing social inequalities. For being placed in a particular track labels a student as either able or otherwise. As we have seen in the case of labeling and deviance, once attached, such labels are hard to break away from. Children from more privileged backgrounds, in which academic work is encouraged, are likely to find

Though many states have attempted to equalize educational funding, situations such as this overcrowded Texas classroom still exist.

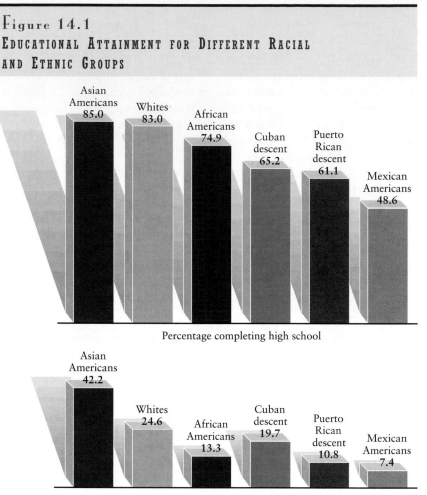

Figure 14.1
EDUCATIONAL ATTAINMENT FOR DIFFERENT RACIAL AND ETHNIC GROUPS

Asian Americans 85.0 · Whites 83.0 · African Americans 74.9 · Cuban descent 65.2 · Puerto Rican descent 61.1 · Mexican Americans 48.6

Percentage completing high school

Asian Americans 42.2 · Whites 24.6 · African Americans 13.3 · Cuban descent 19.7 · Puerto Rican descent 10.8 · Mexican Americans 7.4

Percentage completing college (or higher)

SOURCE: U.S. Bureau of the Census, 1998 (1997 data).

themselves in the higher tracks early on—and by and large stay there (see Figure 14.1).

Jeannie Oakes (1985) studied tracking in twenty-five junior and senior high schools, both large and small and in both urban and rural areas. But she concentrated on differences *within* schools rather than between them. She found that although several schools claimed they did not track students, virtually all of them had mechanisms for sorting students into groups that seemed to be alike in ability and achievement, to make teaching easier. In other words, they employed tracking but did not choose to use the term itself. Even where tracking only existed in this informal fashion, she found strong labels developing—high ability, low achieving, slow, average, and so on. Indi-

vidual students in these groups came to be defined by teachers, other students, and themselves in terms of such labels. A student in a "high-achieving" group was considered a high-achieving *person*—smart and quick. A pupil in a "low-achieving" group came to be seen as slow, below average—or, in more forthright terms, dummies, sweathogs, or yahoos. What is the impact of tracking on students in the "low" group? A subsequent study by Oakes found that these students received a poorer education in terms of the quality of courses, teachers, and textbooks made available to them (Oakes, 1990). Moreover, the negative impact of tracking affected mostly African-American, Latino, and poor students.

The usual reason given for tracking is that bright

children learn more quickly and effectively in a group of others who are equally able, and that clever students are held back if placed in mixed groups. Surveying the evidence, Oakes attempted to show that these assumptions are wrong. The results of later research investigations are not wholly consistent, but a path-breaking study by the sociologist Adam Gamoran and his colleagues concluded that Oakes was partially correct in her arguments. They agreed with Oakes's conclusions that tracking reinforces previously existing inequalities for average or poor students, but countered her argument by asserting that tracking does have positive benefits for "advanced" students (Gamoran et al., 1995). The debate about the effects of tracking is sure to continue as scholars continue to analyze more data.

The Social Reproduction of Inequality

The education system provides more than formal instruction: it socializes children to get along with each other, teaches basic skills, and transmits elements of culture such as language and values. Sociologists have looked at education as a form of social reproduction, a concept discussed in Chapter 1 and elsewhere. In the context of education, social reproduction refers to the ways in which schools help perpetuate social and economic inequalities across the generations. It also directs our attention to the means whereby schools influence the learning of values, attitudes, and habits via the hidden curriculum.

The concept of the **hidden curriculum** addresses the fact that much of what is learned in school has nothing directly to do with the formal content of lessons. Schools, by the nature of the discipline and regimentation they entail, tend to teach students "passive consumption"—an uncritical acceptance of the existing social order. These lessons are not consciously taught; they are implicit in school procedures and organization. The hidden curriculum teaches children that their role in life is "to know their place and to sit still with it" (Illich, 1983). Children spend long hours in school, and as Illich stresses, they learn a great deal more in the school context than is contained in the lessons they are actually taught. Children get an early taste of what the world of work will be like, learning

Parents with plenty of material resources are in a much better position to pass on cultural capital to their children.

that they are expected to be punctual and apply themselves diligently to the tasks that those in authority set for them.

Schools also reinforce variations in cultural values and outlooks picked up in early life. As we saw earlier in Chapter 7, the French sociologist Pierre Bourdieu calls this process the transmission of **cultural capital** (Bourdieu, 1984, 1988), whereby the cultural advantages that coming from a "good home" confers are capital, which succeeding generations inherit from one another, thus perpetuating inequalities (see Figure 14.2).

Another influential theory on the question of how schools reproduce social inequality was introduced by Samuel Bowles and Herbert Gintis. Modern education, they propose, is a response to the economic needs of industrial capitalism. Schools help to provide the technical and social skills required by industrial enterprise; and they instill discipline and respect for authority into the labor force.

Authority relations in school, which are hierarchical and place strong emphasis upon obedience, directly parallel those dominating the workplace. The rewards and punishments held out in school also replicate those found in the world of work. Schools help to motivate some individuals toward "achievement" and "success," while discouraging others, who find their way into low-paying jobs.

Bowles and Gintis accept that the development of mass education has had many beneficial consequences. Illiteracy rates are low, compared with

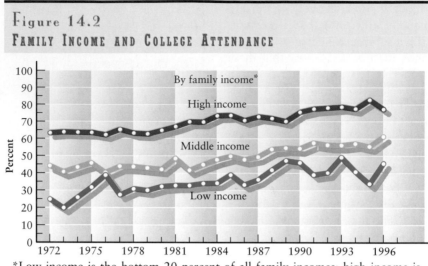

Figure 14.2
FAMILY INCOME AND COLLEGE ATTENDANCE

*Low income is the bottom 20 percent of all family incomes; high income is the top 20 percent of all family incomes; middle income is the 60 percent in between.

SOURCE: U.S. Bureau of the Census, 1991.

premodern times, and schooling provides access to learning experiences that are intrinsically self-fulfilling. Yet because education has expanded mainly as a response to economic needs, the school system falls far short of what enlightened reformers had hoped from it. That is, schooling has not become the "great equalizer," rather, schools merely produce for many the feelings of powerlessness that continue throughout their experience in industrial settings. The ideals of personal development central to education can only be achieved if people have the capability to control the conditions of their own life, and to develop their talents and abilities of self-expression. Under the current system, schools "are destined to legitimate inequality, limit personal development to forms compatible with submission to arbitrary authority, and aid in the process whereby youth are resigned to their fate" (Bowles and Gintis, 1976). If there were greater democracy in the workplace, and more equality in society at large, Bowles and Gintis argue, a system of education could be developed that would provide for greater individual fulfillment.

SOCIAL REPRODUCTION: A CASE STUDY

A classic example of social reproduction is provided in a fieldwork study that Paul Willis carried out in a school in Birmingham, England (Willis, 1981). The question Willis set out to investigate was how social reproduction occurs—or, as he put it, "how working-class kids get working-class jobs." It is often thought that, during the process of schooling, children from lower-class or minority backgrounds simply come to see that they "are not clever enough" to get well-paid or high-status jobs in their future work lives. In other words, the experience of academic failure teaches them to accept what they think are their intellectual limitations; having accepted their "inferiority," they move into occupations with limited career prospects.

As Willis points out, this interpretation does not conform at all to the reality of people's lives and experiences. The "street wisdom" of those from poor neighborhoods may be of little or no relevance to the academic setting, but it involves as subtle, skillful, and complex a set of abilities as any of the intellectual capabilities taught in school.

Few if any children leave school thinking, "I'm so stupid that it's fair and proper for me to be stacking boxes in a factory all day." If children from less-privileged backgrounds accept menial jobs, without feeling themselves throughout life to be failures, there must be other factors involved.

Willis concentrated his work upon a particular boys' group in the school he studied, spending a great deal of time with them. The members of the gang, who called themselves "the lads," were white; the school itself contained considerable numbers of black and Asian children. Willis showed how the lads had an acute and perceptive understanding of the school's authority system—but used this to fight that system rather than to pursue the academic values of the organization. The lads saw the school as an alien environment, but one that they could manipulate to their own ends. They derived positive pleasure from the running battles—confined mostly to minor skirmishes—they carried on with teachers. They were adept at seeing the weak points of the teachers' claims to authority, as well as the ways in which they were vulnerable as individuals.

In class, for instance, the children were expected to sit still, be quiet, and do their work. But the lads were all movement, except when the teacher's stare might freeze one of them momentarily; they would gossip surreptitiously or pass open remarks that were on the verge of direct insubordination, but could be explained away if challenged.

The lads referred to conformist children as "the ear-'oles" (earholes). The ear-'oles were those who actually listened to the teachers, behaving as they were instructed. The ear-'oles would go on to be more "successful," in terms of getting well-paid, comfortable jobs on leaving school, than the lads. Yet their awareness of the complexities of the school environment, according to Willis, was in many respects less profound than that of the lads. For, unlike the lads, the ear-'oles found it relatively easy to adapt to the modes of life of the school and accepted them unquestioningly. Most pupils in the school were somewhere between the lads on the one side and the ear-'oles on the other—less openly confrontational than the first group, and less consistently conformist than the second.

The lads recognized that work would be much like school, but they actively looked forward to it. They expected to gain no direct satisfaction from the work environment, but were impatient for the wages work would bring. Far from taking the jobs they did—in tire fitting, carpet laying, plumbing, painting, and decorating—from feelings of inferiority, they held an attitude of dismissive superiority toward work, as they had toward school. They enjoyed the adult status that came from working, but were uninterested in "making a career" for themselves. As Willis points out, work in blue-collar settings often involves quite simi-lar cultural features to those the lads had developed in their counter-school culture—banter, quick wit, and the skill to subvert the demands of authority figures where necessary.

Willis's work demonstrates how working-class children often tend to end up in working-class jobs by a process of the perpetuation of inequalities, but one that works in a subtle way. The lads felt uneasy in the school environment, and rebelled against it. The result of their rebellious attitudes was an orientation toward work that led them to be prepared to accept dull, poorly paid jobs—like the ones their parents had. Although they actively chose this type of work, the over-all result was still the reproduction of inequality, because they had no interest in trying to obtain well-paid jobs with better career prospects.

Intelligence and Inequality

Suppose differences in educational attainment, and in subsequent occupations and incomes, directly reflected differential intelligence? In such circumstances, it might be argued, there is in fact equality of opportunity in the school system, for people find a level equivalent to their innate potential.

WHAT IS INTELLIGENCE?

For years, psychologists, geneticists, statisticians, and others have debated whether there exists a single human capability that can be called **intelligence** and, if so, whether it rests upon innately determined differences. Intelligence is difficult to define because, as the term is usually employed, it covers qualities that may be unrelated to one another. We might suppose, for example, that the "purest" form of intelligence is the ability to solve abstract mathematical puzzles. However, people who are very good at such puzzles sometimes show low capabilities in other areas, such as history or art. Since the concept has proved so resistant to accepted definition, some psychologists have proposed (and many educators have by default accepted) that intelligence should simply be regarded as "what **IQ (intelligence quotient)** tests measure." Most IQ tests consist of a mixture of conceptual and computational problems. The tests are constructed so that the average score is 100 points: anyone scoring below is thus labeled "below-average intelligence," and anyone scoring above is "above-average intelligence." In spite of the fundamental difficulty in measuring intelligence, IQ tests are widely used in research studies, as well as in schools and businesses.

IQ AND GENETIC FACTORS

Scores on IQ tests do in fact correlate highly with academic performance (which is not surprising, since IQ tests were originally developed to predict success at school). They therefore also correlate closely with social, economic, and ethnic differences, since these are associated with variations in levels of educational attainment. White students score better, on average, than African Americans or members of other disadvantaged minorities. An article published by Arthur Jensen in 1967 caused a furor by attributing IQ differences between blacks and whites in part to genetic variations (Jensen, 1967, 1979).

More recently, psychologist Richard J. Herrnstein and sociologist Charles Murray have reopened the debate about IQ and education in a controversial way. They argue in their book *The Bell Curve: Intelligence and Class Structure in American Life* (1994) that the accumulated evidence linking IQ to genetic inheritance has now become overwhelming. The significant differences in intelligence between various racial and ethnic groups, they say, must in part be explained in terms of heredity. According to Herrnstein and Murray, the available evidence strongly indicates that some ethnic groups on average have higher IQs than other groups. Asian Americans, particularly Japanese Americans and Chinese Americans, on average possess higher IQs than whites, though the difference is not large. The average IQs of Asians and whites, however, are substantially higher than those of blacks. Summarizing the findings of 156 studies, Herrnstein and Murray find an average difference of 16 IQ points between these two racial groups. The authors argue that such differences in inherited intelligence contribute in an important way to social divisions in American society. The smarter an individual is, the greater the chance that she will rise in the social scale. Those at the top are there partly because they are smarter than the rest of the population—from which it follows that those at the bottom remain there because, on average, they are not as smart.

Critics of Herrnstein and Murray deny that IQ differences between racial and ethnic groups are genetic

KEY CONCEPTS IN REVIEW

Research by James Coleman and Christopher Jencks on the relationship between education and inequality has concluded that the decisive influence on educational performance is the student's family background. **Tracking**, or dividing students into groups according to abilities, perpetuates social inequalities because it reduces the performance of average or below students, who most often come from lower-income families.

One of the important functions of schooling is to influence the learning of values, attitudes, and habits via the **hidden curriculum**: much of what is learned in school has nothing directly to do with the formal curriculum. Schools also reinforce the transmission of **cultural capital**, the cultural advantages that well-to-do parents usually provide their children.

Because **intelligence** is difficult to define, there has been a great deal of controversy about the subject. Some argue that genetics determine one's **IQ**; others believe that social influences determine one's IQ. The weight of the evidence appears to be on the side of those arguing for social and cultural influences.

in origin. They argue that differences in IQ result from social and cultural differences (also see this chaper's "The Sociological Debate"). IQ tests, they point out, pose questions—to do with abstract reasoning, for example—more likely to be part of the experience of more affluent white students than of blacks and ethnic minorities. Scores on IQ tests may also be influenced by factors that have nothing to do with the abilities supposedly being measured, such as whether the testing is experienced as stressful. Research has demonstrated that African Americans score six points lower on IQ tests when the tester is white than when the tester is black (Kamin, 1974).

The average lower IQ score of African Americans in the United States is remarkably similar to that of deprived ethnic minorities in other countries—such as the "untouchables" in India (who are at the very bottom of the caste system), the Maori in New Zealand, and the *burakumin* of Japan. Children in these groups score an average of 10 to 15 IQ points below children belonging to the ethnic majority. The *burakumin*—descendants of people who in the eighteenth century, as a result of local wars, were dispossessed from their land and became outcasts and vagrants—are a particularly interesting example. They are not in any way physically distinct from other Japanese, although they have suffered from prejudice and discrimination for centuries. In this case, the difference in average IQ results cannot derive from genetic variations since there are no genetic differences between them and the majority population; yet the IQ difference is as thoroughly fixed as that between blacks and whites. *Burakumin* children in America, where they are treated like other Japanese, do as well on IQ tests as other Japanese.

Such observations strongly suggest that the IQ variations between African Americans and whites in the United States result from social and cultural differ- ences. This conclusion receives further support from a comparative study of fourteen nations (including the United States) showing that average IQ scores have risen substantially over the past half century for the population as a whole (Coleman, 1987). IQ tests are regularly updated. When old and new versions of the tests are given to the same group of people, they score significantly higher on the old

tests. Present-day children taking IQ tests from the 1930s outscored 1930s groups by an average of 15 points—just the kind of average difference that currently separates blacks and whites. Children today are not innately superior in intelligence to their parents or grandparents; the shift presumably derives from increasing prosperity and social advantages. The average social and economic gap between whites and African Americans is at least as great as that between the different generations, and is sufficient to explain the variation in IQ scores. While there may be genetic variations between individuals that influence scores on IQ tests, these have no overall connection to racial differences.

THE SOCIOLOGICAL DEBATE

THE BELL CURVE

Richard J. Herrnstein and Charles Murray's claim, presented in their book *The Bell Curve*, that whites are born more intelligent than blacks, created a great deal of controversy and raised the ire and indignation of countless liberals, social scientists, and members of the African-American community. Although Herrnstein and Murray's claims may be seen as racist and reprehensible, is this sufficient reason to attack their work? Or are their conclusions based on faulty social research? The answer is a resounding "both." A team of sociologists at the University of California at Berkeley have reanalyzed much of the data that Herrnstein and Murray based their conclusions on and came up with quite different findings.

In the original analysis, Herrnstein and Murray analyzed data from the National Longitudinal Study of Youth (NLSY), a survey of more than 10,000 young Americans who were interviewed multiple times over more than a decade. As part of this study, subjects were given the Armed Forces Qualifying Test (AFQT), a short test that assesses IQ. Herrnstein and Murray then conducted statistical analyses, which used the AFQT score to predict a variety of outcomes. They concluded that having a high IQ was the best predictor of later economic success, and that low IQ was the best predictor of poverty later in life.

The Berkeley sociologists, in their 1996 book *Inequality by Design: Cracking the Bell Curve Myth* (Fischer et al., 1996), countered that the AFQT does not necessarily measure intelligence, but only how much a person has learned in school. Moreover, they found that intelligence is only one factor among several that predict how well people do in life. Social factors including education, gender, community conditions, marital status, current economic conditions, and—perhaps most importantly—parents' socioeconomic status, better predict one's occupational and economic success. In the original analysis, Herrnstein and Murray measured parents' socioeconomic status by taking an average of mother's education, father's education, father's occupation, and family income.

The Berkeley sociologists recognized that each of these four factors matters differently in predicting a child's occupational outcomes, and thus weighted the four components differently. Their analysis showed that the effects of socioeconomic background on a young adult's risk of later poverty were substantially higher than Herrnstein and Murray had originally found. The Berkeley sociologists also recognized that IQ is closely associated with one's level of education. They reanalyzed the NLSY data, taking into consideration the individuals' level of education, and found that Herrnstein and Murray drastically overestimated the effects of IQ on a person's later achievements.

The relationship between race and intelligence is also best explained by social rather than biological causes, according to the Berkeley sociologists. All societies have oppressed ethnic groups. For instance, the Irish in England, the Koreans in Japan, and blacks and Latinos in the United States are afforded lower status than the majority ethnic group. This low status, often coupled with discrimination and mistreatment, leads to socioeconomic deprivation, group segregation, and a stigma of inferiority. The combination of these forces often prevents racial minorities from obtaining education, and consequently, their scores on standardized intelligence tests are lower. Citing historical and anthropological research, the Berkeley team concluded that racial inequalities in intelligence do exist, but because they are socially created, rather than biologically determined, inequities can be remedied with well-intentioned social policies.

Educational Reform in the United States

Research done by sociologists has played a big role in reforming the educational system. The object of James Coleman's research, commissioned as part of the 1964 Civil Rights Act, was not solely academic; it was undertaken to influence policy. And influence policy it certainly did. On the basis of the act, it was decided in the courts that segregated schools violated the rights of minority pupils. But rather than attacking the origins of educational inequalities directly, as Christopher Jencks' later work suggested was necessary, the courts decided that the schools in each district should achieve a similar racial balance. Thus began the practice of busing students to other schools.

Busing provoked a great deal of opposition, particularly from parents and children in white areas, and led to episodes of violence at the gates of schools where the children were bused in from other neighborhoods. White children paraded with placards reading: "We don't want them!" Busing in fact met with a good deal of success, serving to reduce levels of school segregation quite steeply, particularly in the South. But busing has also produced a number of unintended consequences. Some white parents reacted to busing by either putting their children into private schools or moving to mainly white suburbs where busing wasn't practiced. As a result, in the cities, some schools are virtually as segregated as the old schools were in the past. Busing, however, was only one factor prompting the white flight to the suburbs. Whites have also left as a reaction to urban decay: to escape city crowding, housing problems, and rising rates of crime.

While busing is less prominent today as an issue, another problem regarding the American educational system has become an important focus of research: functional illiteracy. A prominent writer on educational policy has spoken of the situation in the nation's urban public schools today as "one of the gravest social and economic crises in our history" (Littlefield, 1992). The facts are by now well established. The United States competes with other countries that lay great stress on education. As was noted in Chapter 4, Japanese students on average spend more hours a week on study than do their American

Court-ordered busing divided Boston's black and white communities. In 1976, a mob of protesters outside the Boston federal courthouse sought to impale this innocent black bystander, a lawyer on his way to his office. This Pulitzer Prize-winning photograph shows the tension and conflict resulting from the struggle for equal rights for African Americans.

counterparts. This, moreover, in the country that invented Nintendo—which doesn't seem to divert the Japanese from their schooling.

In the United States, one in every four students leaves high school without a diploma. While most of the population can read and write at a very basic level, one in every five adults is functionally illiterate—when they leave school, they can't read or write at the fourth-grade level (U.S. Department of Education, 1993). Of course, the United States is a country of immigrants, who when they arrive may not be able to read and write and who may also have trouble with English. But this doesn't explain why America lags behind most other industrial countries in terms of its level of functional illiteracy, because many people affected are not recent immigrants at all.

The situation for African Americans and Latinos is particularly serious. For example, about half of blacks leaving school are functionally illiterate. This statistic should be interpreted with some caution, because the linguistic skills that are useful in the streets of an impoverished black neighborhood aren't those taught by the school; being streetwise counts for far more. Yet street wisdom doesn't translate into job prospects. Some three-quarters of unemployed African Americans are functionally illiterate. The connection is hardly surprising. Not only do most jobs call for reading and writing ability, but the proportion of jobs demanding literacy and skills such as math is increasing as blue-collar work becomes less common.

What is to be done? Some educationists have argued that the most important change that needs to be made is to improve the quality of teaching, either by increasing teachers' pay or by introducing performance-related pay scales, with higher salaries going to the teachers who are most effective in the classroom. Others have proposed giving schools more control over their budgets (a reform that has been carried out in Britain). The idea is that more responsibility for and control over budgeting decisions will create a greater drive to improve the school. Further proposals include the refunding of federal programs such as Head Start to ensure healthy early child development and thus save millions of dollars in later costs. The problems the public school system faces, however, are so serious that probably even a combination of all these measures would only go some way toward coping with them.

The crisis in American schools won't be solved in the short term, and it won't be solved by educational reforms alone, no matter how thoroughgoing. The lesson of sociological research is that inequalities and barriers in educational opportunity reflect wider social divisions and tensions. While the United States remains wracked by racial tensions and the polarization between decaying cities and affluent suburbs persists,

the crisis in the school system is likely to prove difficult to turn around.

EDUCATION AND LITERACY IN THE THIRD WORLD

Literacy is the "baseline" of education. Without it,
schooling cannot proceed. We take it for granted in
the West that the majority of people are literate, but
as has been mentioned, this is only a recent development in Western history, and in previous times no
more than a tiny proportion of the population had
any literacy skills.

Today, some 30 percent of the population of Third
World countries are still illiterate (see Global Map
14.1). The Indian government has estimated the number of illiterate people in that country alone to be over
250 million, a number that exceeds the total population of the United States. Even if the provision of
primary education increased to match the level of
population growth, illiteracy would not become
markedly reduced for years, because a high proportion of those who cannot read or write are adults. The
absolute number of illiterate people is actually rising
(Coombs, 1985). According to UNESCO estimates,
the total grew from 569 million in 1970 to 625 million in 1980, and is likely to be 900 million by 2000.

Although countries have instituted literacy programs, these have made only a small contribution to a
problem of large-scale dimensions. Television, radio,
and the other electronic media can be used, where
they are available, to skip the stage of learning literacy
skills and convey educational programs directly to
adults. But educational programs are usually less popular than commercialized entertainment.

During the period of colonialism, the colonial governments regarded education with some trepidation.
Until the twentieth century, most believed indigenous
populations to be too primitive to be worthy of educating. Later, education was seen as a way of making
local elites responsive to European interests and ways
of life. But to some extent, the result was to foment
discontent and rebellion, since the majority of those
who led anticolonial and nationalist movements were
from educated elites who had attended schools or colleges in Europe. They were able to compare first-hand

*Third world countries have high rates of illiteracy. While
some schools exist, most do not have access to education.*

the democratic institutions of the European countries
with the absence of democracy in their lands of origin.

The education that the colonizers introduced usually pertained to Europe, not the colonial areas themselves. Educated Africans in the British colonies knew
about the kings and queens of England, read Shake-
speare, Milton, and the English poets, but knew next
to nothing about their own history or past cultural
achievements. Policies of educational reform since the
end of colonialism have not completely altered the situation even today.

Partly as a result of the legacy of colonial education, which was not directed toward the majority of
the population, the educational system in many Third
 World countries is top-heavy: higher education is disproportionately developed,
relative to primary and secondary education. The result is a correspondingly
overqualified group who, having attended
colleges and universities, cannot find white-collar or
professional jobs. Given the low level of industrial de-

velopment, most of the better-paid positions are in government, and there are not enough of those to go around.

In recent years, some Third World countries, recognizing the shortcomings of the curricula inherited from colonialism, have tried to redirect their educational programs toward the rural poor. They have had limited success, because usually there is insufficient funding to pay for the scale of the necessary innovations. As a result, countries such as India have begun programs of self-help education. Communities draw upon existing resources without creating demands for high levels of finance. Those who can read and write and who perhaps possess job skills are encouraged to take others on as apprentices, whom they coach in their spare time.

COMMUNICATION AND THE MASS MEDIA

The modern world depends upon the continuous communication or interaction between people widely separated from one another. If we were not so dependent upon "communication across distance," schooling would be less necessary. In traditional cultures—as that of Jean-Paul Didion in France, the example with which we opened the chapter—most knowledge was what the anthropologist Clifford Geertz has called **local knowledge** (Geertz, 1983). Traditions were passed on through the local community, and although general cultural ideas gradually spread across large areas, processes of cultural diffusion were long, drawn out, slow, and inconsistent. Today, we live in "the whole world" in a way that would have been quite inconceivable to Jean-Paul Didion, or anyone else living in cultures of the past.

We learn a great deal about the world from formal schooling. But we also learn much from the various communication media, which operate outside the context of schools. All of us are aware of situations and events that happen thousands of miles away—electronic communication makes such awareness almost instantaneous. Changes in the spread of information, and in information technologies, are as much a part of the development of modern societies as any aspect of industrial production (Kern, 1983).

During the twentieth century, rapid transportation and electronic communication such as the Internet greatly intensified the global diffusion of information.

The **mass media**—newspapers, magazines, movies, compact discs, TV, and the Internet—are often associated with entertainment, and therefore are seen as rather marginal to most people's lives. Such a view is quite misleading. Mass communications enter our social activities at many different points. For instance, a bank account is no longer a pile of money kept in a safe, but a series of digits printed on an account sheet and stored in a computer, and monetary transactions are now mainly performed through the exchange of information between computers. Anyone who uses a credit card is connected with a very complex system of electronically stored and transmitted information, which has now become the very basis of modern financial accounting. Today, many people use the Internet to buy CDs and books.

Even "recreational" media like newspapers or TV have a wide-ranging influence over our experience. This is not just because they affect our attitudes in specific ways, but because they are the *means of access* to the knowledge upon which many social activities depend. Voting in national elections, for example, would be quite different if information about current political events, candidates, and parties were not generally available. Even those who are largely uninterested in politics, and have little knowledge of the personalities involved, have some awareness of national and international events, such as President Bill Clinton's impeachment trial. Only a complete hermit would be entirely detached from the "news events" that impinge to some degree upon the consciousness of all of us—and we could suspect that a modern hermit might very well own a transistor radio!

The Sociological Study of the Mass Media

How do we go about studying the influence of the mass media on our lives? A basic concept needed here is that of **communication,** which means the transfer of information from one person, context, or group to another. We saw in Chapter 10 that the communication and storage of information has been fundamental to

Percentage literate

- 99.0 or higher
- 90.9–98.9
- 70.0–89.9
- 50.0–69.9
- Less than 50.0

SOURCE: World Bank, 1994, *Human Development Report*.

ABBREVIATIONS

AUS.	AUSTRIA
ALB.	ALBANIA
B.H.	BOSNIA AND HERZEGOVINA
BULG.	BULGARIA
CR.	CROATIA
CZ.	CZECH REPUBLIC
HUN.	HUNGARY
MAC.	FORMER YUGOSLAV REPUBLIC OF MACEDONIA
POL.	POLAND
ROM.	ROMANIA
SL.	SLOVENIA
U.K	UNITED KINGDOM
YU.	YUGOSLAVIA

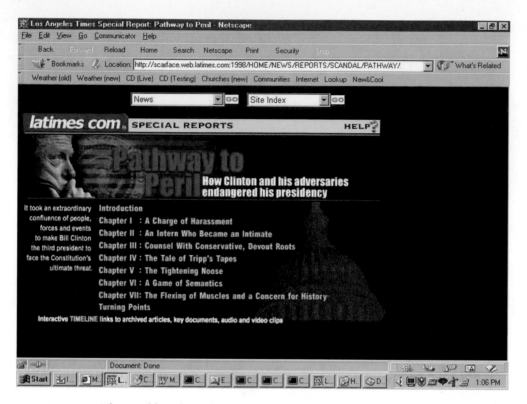

The World Wide Web has greatly expanded the public sphere.

the development of modern societies. Sociologically speaking, therefore, we need to put the rise of the mass media and popular culture in the context of the basic trends analyzed earlier.

There are close connections between the rise of the media and the development of modern systems of mass education. The two can only be properly understood sociologically in relation to one another. The German social thinker Jürgen Habermas offers a useful concept to describe this connection when he speaks of the emergence of a **public sphere** with the early development of the industrial societies. The public sphere is a sphere of communication, where public opinion is formed and attitudes shaped. In earlier forms of society, most communication was local and simply carried through speech, the ordinary daily talk of neighbors and friends in village communities. A rudimentary public sphere developed in the early civilizations, well before the emergence of the industrial societies. But it was very restricted, because only small groups were literate—could read and write. Moreover, written documents had to be laboriously pre-

pared by hand, so there weren't many in circulation. From about the sixteenth century onward in Europe, as the new technology of printing spread and levels of literacy grew, the public sphere began to expand. The first local newspapers appeared in the mid-1700s. Mass-circulation newspapers followed about a century later, to be joined in our century by the electronic media of radio, TV, and other forms.

Learning to read and write and mastering other forms of knowledge is necessary for us to play a part in this developing wider society of communication. In the industrialized countries today, most people can read and write, but in historical terms, this is a recent development, dating back no more than a hundred years. The sorts of outlooks and knowledge acquired in school allow us to participate in the public sphere—to be able to read newspapers and magazines, for example. But the mass media might often also cross-cut the goals of formal schooling. For instance, perhaps literacy and other educational skills are beginning to slump now that television and other forms of electronic media play such a large part in our

KEY CONCEPTS IN REVIEW

Communication means the transfer of information from one person, context, or group to another. The **public sphere** is the means by which people communicate in modern societies. The most prominent component of the public sphere is the **mass media**—movies, television, radio, videos, compact discs, magazines, and newspapers. The rise of the mass media and the rise of mass education are closely connected because the ability to read and write is necessary to participate in the public sphere.

lives. It isn't obvious, after all, that being able to do well at Nintendo games helps much with school achievement. The increasing influence of television is probably the single most important development in the media over the past forty years. Television is as important as books, magazines, and newspapers in the expansion of indirect forms of communication characteristic of modern societies. It frames the ways in which we interpret and respond to the social world by helping to order our experience of it. Assumptions built in to the overall character of TV production and distribution may perhaps be more significant than whatever particular programs are shown. If current trends continue, by age eighteen, the average child born today will have spent more time watching TV than any other activity save for sleeping. Virtually every household now possesses a television set (see Global Map 14.2). In the United States, the average set is switched on between five and six hours a day, and much the same is true in the European countries (Goodhardt, Ehrenberg, and Collins, 1987).

Theories of the Mass Media's Influence on Society

THE GLOBAL VILLAGE

 One influential early theorist of the mass media was the Canadian author Marshall McLuhan. According to McLuhan, "the medium is the message" (1964). That is to say, the nature of the media found in a so-ciety influences its structure much more than the content, or the messages, which the media convey. Television, for instance, is a very different medium from the printed book. It is electronic, visual, and composed of fluid images. A society in which television plays a basic role is one in which everyday life is experienced differently from one which only has print. Thus the TV news conveys global information instantaneously to millions of people. The electronic media, McLuhan thought, are creating what he called a **global village**— people throughout the world see major news items unfold and hence participate in the same events as one another. Millions of people in different countries, for example, knew about Princess Diana's life, her problems with the British royal family, and her death in an automobile accident in Paris.

Jean Baudrillard, whose ideas we will look at in this section, has been strongly influenced by the ideas of McLuhan. We turn first, however, to the theories of the German sociologist and philosopher Jürgen Habermas.

JÜRGEN HABERMAS: THE PUBLIC SPHERE

The German philosopher and sociologist Jürgen Habermas is linked to the "Frankfurt School" of social thought. The Frankfurt School was a group of authors inspired by Marx who nevertheless believed that Marx's views needed radical revision to bring them up to date. Among other things, they believed that Marx had not given enough attention to the influence of culture in modern capitalist society.

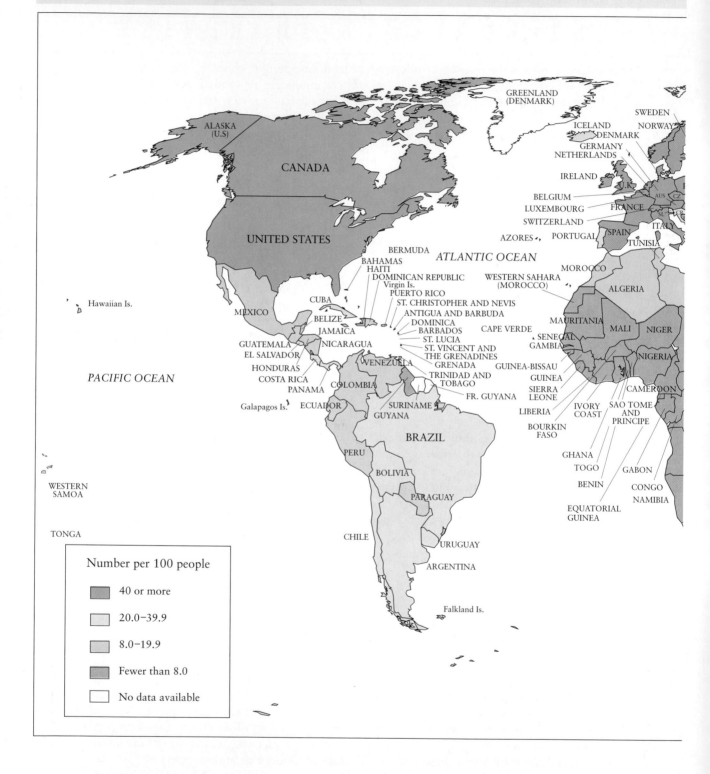

Number per 100 people

- 40 or more
- 20.0–39.9
- 8.0–19.9
- Fewer than 8.0
- No data available

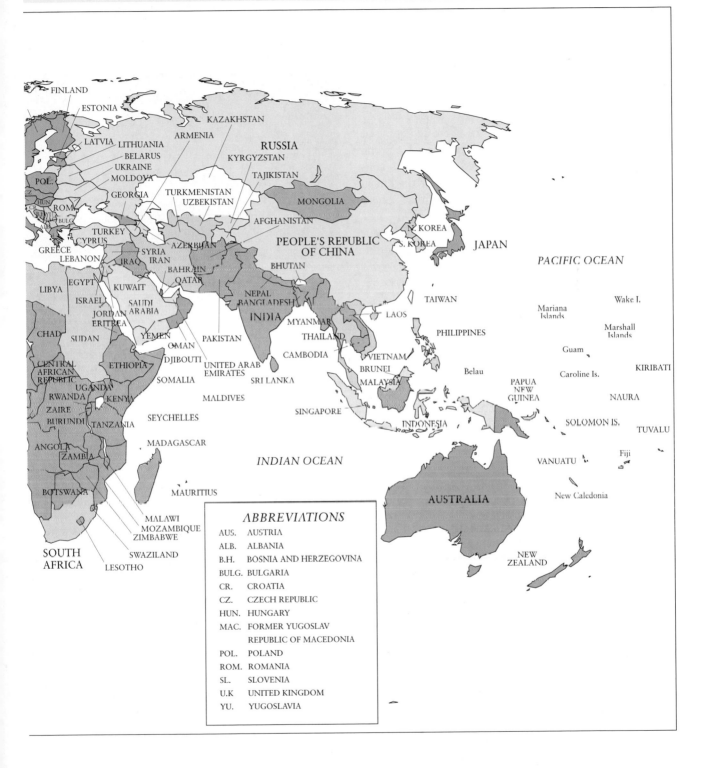

ABBREVIATIONS

AUS.	AUSTRIA
ALB.	ALBANIA
B.H.	BOSNIA AND HERZEGOVINA
BULG.	BULGARIA
CR.	CROATIA
CZ.	CZECH REPUBLIC
HUN.	HUNGARY
MAC.	FORMER YUGOSLAV REPUBLIC OF MACEDONIA
POL.	POLAND
ROM.	ROMANIA
SL.	SLOVENIA
U.K	UNITED KINGDOM
YU.	YUGOSLAVIA

The Frankfurt School made extensive study of what they called the "culture industry," meaning the entertainment industries of film, TV, popular music, radio, newspapers, and magazines. They argued that the spread of the culture industry, with its undemanding and standardized products, undermines the capacity of individuals for critical and independent thought. Art disappears, swamped by commercialization—"Mozart's Greatest Hits."

Habermas has taken up some of these themes, but developed them in a different way. He analyzes the development of media from the early eighteenth century up to the present moment, tracing out the emergence—and subsequent decay—of the public sphere (Habermas, 1989).

The public sphere, according to Habermas, developed first in the salons and coffee houses of London, Paris, and other European cities. People used to meet in such salons to discuss issues of the moment, using as a means for such debate the news sheets and newspapers that had just begun to emerge. Political debate became a matter of particular importance. Although only small numbers of the population were involved, Habermas argues that the salons were vital to the early development of democracy, for they introduced the idea of resolving political problems through public discussion. The public sphere—at least in principle—involves individuals coming together as equals in a forum for public debate.

However, the promise offered by the early development of the public sphere, Habermas concludes, has not been fully realized. Democratic debate in modern societies is stifled by the development of the culture industry. The development of the mass media and mass entertainment causes the public sphere to become largely a sham. Politics is stage-managed in government and the media, while commercial interests triumph over those of the public. "Public opinion" is not formed through open, rational discussion, but through manipulation and control—as, for example, in advertising.

BAUDRILLARD: THE WORLD OF HYPERREALITY

One of the most influential current theorists of media is the French author Jean Baudrillard. Baudrillard regards the impact of modern mass media as being quite

Reporters wait outside O.J. Simpson's estate after the not-guilty verdict in his murder trial was announced. The media covered the story exhaustively for over two years.

different from, and much more profound than, that of any other technology. The coming of the mass media, particularly electronic media such as TV, has transformed the very nature of our lives. TV does not just "represent" the world to us, it increasingly defines what the world in which we live actually *is*.

Consider as an example the O. J. Simpson trial, a celebrated court case that unfolded in Los Angeles in 1994–95. Simpson originally became famous as an American football star, but later became known around the world as a result of appearing in several popular films, including the *Naked Gun* series. He was accused of the murder of his wife, Nicole, and after a very long trial was acquitted. The trial was televised live and was watched in many countries, including Britain. In America six television channels covered the trial on a continuous basis.

The trial did not just happen in the courtroom. It was a televisual event linking millions of viewers and commentators in the media. The trial is an illustration of what Baudrillard calls **hyperreality**. There is no longer a "reality" (the events in the courtroom), which television allows us to see. The "reality" is actually the string of images on the TV screens of the world, which defined the trial as a global event.

Just before the outbreak of hostilities in the Persian Gulf in 1991, Baudrillard wrote a newspaper article entitled "The Gulf War Cannot Happen." When war was declared and a bloody conflict took place it might seem obvious that Baudrillard had been wrong. Not a bit of it. After the end of the war, Baudrillard wrote a second article, "The Gulf War Did Not Happen." What did he mean? He meant that the war was not like other wars that have happened in history. It was a war of the media age, a televisual spectacle, in which, along with other viewers throughout the world, George Bush and Saddam Hussein watched the coverage by CNN to see what was actually "happening." Baudrillard argues that, in an age where the mass media are everywhere, in effect a new reality hyper reality—is created, composed of the intermingling of people's behavior and media images.

JOHN THOMPSON: THE MEDIA AND MODERN SOCIETY

Drawing in some part on the writings of Habermas, John Thompson has analyzed the relation between the media and the development of industrial societies (Thompson, 1990, 1995). From early forms of print through to electronic communication, Thompson argues, the media have played a central role in the development of modern institutions. The main founders of sociology, including Marx, Weber, and Durkheim, Thompson believes, gave too little attention to the role of media in shaping even the early development of modern society.

Thompson's theory of the media depends on a distinction among three types of interaction. Face-to-face interaction, such as people talking at a party, is rich in clues that individuals use to make sense of what others say. **Mediated interaction** involves the use of a media technology—paper, electrical connections, electronic impulses. Characteristic of mediated interaction is that it is stretched out in time and space—it goes well beyond the contexts of ordinary face-to-face interaction. Mediated interaction takes place between individuals in a direct way—for instance, two people talking on the telephone—but there isn't the same variety of clues as when people are face to face.

A third type of interaction is **mediated quasi-interaction.** This refers to the sort of social relations created by the mass media. Such interaction is stretched across time and space, but it doesn't link individuals directly: hence the term "quasi-interaction." The two previous types are "dialogical": individuals communicate in a direct way. Mediated quasi-interaction is "monological": a TV program, for example, is a one-way form of communication. People watching the program may discuss it, and perhaps address some remarks to the TV set—but, of course, it doesn't answer back.

Thompson's point is not that the third type comes to dominate the other two—essentially the view taken by Baudrillard—rather, that all three types intermingle in our lives today. The mass media, Thompson suggests, change the balance between the public and the private in our lives. Contrary to what Habermas says, much more comes into the public domain than before, and this leads quite often to debate and controversy.

An example would be President Bill Clinton's televised testimony about his affair with Monica Lewinsky. Viewers learned a great deal about the president's private business, perhaps more details than they cared to know. At the time, Clinton's affairs were widely discussed by many Americans. The media's reporting of the affair also sparked debate about the division between the private and public, not only in newspapers and on television, but in homes, bars, offices, and Internet chat rooms across the country.

GLOBALIZATION AND MEDIA IMPERIALISM

If today we all live in "one world," it is in large part a result of the international scope of the communications media. Anyone who switches on the TV set and watches "the world news" ordinarily gets what the description suggests: a presentation of events that occurred that day or shortly before in many different parts of the world. Television programs are sold to large international markets and hundreds of millions of people watch them. The development of a **world information order**—an international system for the production, distribution, and consumption of information—like other aspects of the global society, has been uneven and reflects the divisions between the developed societies and Third World countries.

The paramount position of the industrialized countries, above all the United States, in the production and diffusion of media has led many observers to speak of *media imperialism*. A cultural empire, it is argued, has been established. Third World countries are held to be especially vulnerable, because they lack the resources to maintain their own cultural independence.

Via the electronic media, Western cultural products have certainly become widely diffused across the globe. Pico Iyer speaks of "video nights in Katmandu," of frequenting discos in Bali (Iyer, 1989). American videos are commonplace in the Islamic republic of Iran, as are audiotapes of Western popular music, brought in on the black market (Sreberny-Mohammadi, 1992). Not only more popular entertainment forms are at issue, however. Control of the world's news by the major Western agencies, it has been suggested, means the predominance of a "First World outlook" in the information conveyed. Thus it has been claimed that attention is given to the Third World in news broadcasts mainly in times of disaster, crisis, or military confrontation, and that the daily files of other types of news kept on the industrialized world are not maintained for Third World coverage.

Herbert Schiller has claimed that control of global communications by United States firms has to be seen in relation to various factors. He argues that American TV and radio networks have fallen increasingly under the influence of the federal government and particularly the Defense Department. He points out that RCA, which until 1986 owned the NBC television and radio networks, is also a leading defense subcontractor to the Pentagon. American television exports, coupled with advertising, propagate a commercialized culture that corrodes local forms of cultural expression. Even where governments prohibit commercial broadcasting within their borders, radio and television from surrounding countries can often be directly received.

Schiller argues that, although Americans were the first to be affected by the "corporate-message cocoon . . . what is now happening is the creation and global extension of a new total corporate informational-cultural environment" (Schiller, 1989, pp. 168, 128). Since U.S. corporations and culture are globally dominant, they have "overwhelmed a good part of the world," such that "American cultural domination . . . sets the boundaries for national discourse" (Schiller, 1991, p. 22).

TECHNOLOGICAL CHANGE, MEDIA, AND EDUCATION

Multimedia

Although we have concentrated so far on newspapers, television, and other parts of the "culture industry," we should not think of the media of communication only in those terms. Particularly as influenced by the computer, the media are affecting what we do in many other areas as well. New communications technologies, for example, stand behind profound changes in the world's money systems and stock markets. Money is no longer gold, or the cash in your pocket. More and more, money has become electronic, stored in computers in the world's banks. The value of whatever cash you do happen to have in your pocket is determined by the activities of traders on money markets. Such markets have been created only over the past ten to fifteen years or so: they are the product of a marriage between computers and communication satellite technology. "Technology," it has been said, "is rapidly turning the stock exchange into a seamless global market, open 24 hours a day" (Gibbons, 1990, p. 111).

Four technological trends have contributed to these developments: the constant improvement in the capabilities of computers, together with declining costs; digitization of data, making possible the integration of computer and telecommunications technologies; satellite communications development; fiber optics, which allows many different messages to travel down a single small cable. The dramatic communications explosion of recent years shows no signs of slowing down.

In his book *Being Digital* (1995), the founder of the media laboratory at the Massachusetts Institute of Technology, Nicholas Negroponte, analyzes the profound importance of digital data in current communications technologies. Any piece of information, including pictures, moving images, and sounds, can be translated into "bits." A bit is either a 1 or 0. For instance, the digital representation of 1, 2, 3, 4, 5, is 1, 10, 11, 100, 101, etc. Digitization—and speed—are at the origin of the development of **multimedia**: what used to be different media needing different technologies (such as visuals and sound) can now be *combined* on a single medium (CD-ROM/computer, etc.). The speed of computers doubles every eighteen months and the technology has now reached the stage where a videotape can be translated into a picture on a personal computer screen and back again.

Negroponte predicts that the personal computer (PC) will be the multimedia point of reference for the future. Current computers already have a range of multimedia capabilities. But these will become dramatically expanded. The PC will also be a TV set and an "electronic gateway" for cable, telephone, satellite, and the Internet. In the future there will be no separate TV industry. Digitization also permits the development of interactive media, allowing individuals actively to participate in, or structure, what they see or hear.

The **information superhighway** was much discussed in the mid-1990s. The term was repeatedly invoked by the Vice-President of the United States, Al Gore. The superhighway is more a vision of the future than a description of the present. It envisages a situation in which most or all households will be connected via fiber optic cable. The electronic gateway of which Negroponte speaks will open into every home. At the moment four separate technologies have separate electronic paths into the home: telephone, television broadcast, cable, and satellite. (Of course, not everyone has all of these.) In the future, all will travel down the same cable and have as their outlet a single computer/television.

"The information superhighway" may not be the most appropriate term to refer to the implications of the digital revolution. It suggests a road map, whereas the new interactive technologies annihilate distance and make it irrelevant. The term implies order, whereas the impact of the new technologies may very well be chaotic and disruptive.

In a world of quite stunning technological change, no one can be sure what the future holds. What is certain is that developments in media technologies are at the very heart of such change. Many see the Internet as exemplifying the new global order emerging at the close of the twentieth century. Users of the Internet live in "cyberspace." **Cyberspace** means the space of interaction formed by the global network of computers that compose the Internet. In cyberspace, much as Baudrillard might say, we are no longer "people," but messages on one another's screens. Outside of e-mail, where users identify themselves, no one on the Inter-

net knows who anyone else really is, whether they are male or female, or where they are in the world. A famous cartoon about the Internet, shows a dog sitting in front of a computer; the caption reads: "On the Internet nobody knows you're a dog."

Will we lose our identities in cyberspace? Will computerized technology dominate us rather than the reverse? Will electronic media destroy all other forms of communications media, such as the book? The answer to each of these questions, fortunately, almost certainly is "no." People don't use video conferencing if they can get together with others in an ordinary way. Business executives have far more forms of electronic communication available to them than ever before. At the same time, the number of face-to-face business conferences has shot up.

As individuals, we don't control technological change, and the sheer pace of such change threatens to swamp our lives. Yet the arrival of the wired world, thus far at any rate, hasn't led to Big Brother: rather to the contrary, it has promoted decentralization and individualism. Finally, books and other "pre-electronic" media look unlikely to disappear. Bulky as it is, this book is handier to use than a computerized version would be. Negroponte's *Being Digital* wasn't produced for the gadgets it describes, but written as a book. Even Bill Gates has found it necessary to write a book to describe the new high-tech world he anticipates.

In the meantime, the Internet spawns its own mundane problems. A recent headline announced, "Net addicts lead sad virtual lives." The article describes the lives of people who spend hours every day on the network. There is even a new support group for Internet addicts, called Caught in the Net. Cyberspace contacts can't substitute for interaction with flesh-and-blood people and aren't likely to.

EDUCATION AND NEW COMMUNICATIONS TECHNOLOGY

The spread of information technology looks set to influence education in a number of different ways, some of which may perhaps be quite fundamental. The new technologies are affecting the nature of work, replacing some types of human work by machines. The sheer pace of technological change is creating a much more rapid turnover of jobs than once was the case. Education can no longer be regarded as a stage of preparation before an individual enters work. As technology changes, necessary skills change, and even if education is seen from a purely vocational point of view—as providing skills relevant to work—most observers agree that lifelong exposure to education will be needed in the future.

TECHNOLOGIES OF EDUCATION

The rise of education in its modern sense was connected with a number of other major changes happening in the nineteenth century. One was the development of the school. One might naively think that there was a demand for education and that schools and universities were set up to meet that demand. But that was not how things happened. Schools arose, as Michel Foucault has shown, as part of the administrative apparatus of the modern state. The "hidden curriculum" was about discipline and about the control of children.

A second influence was the development of printing and the arrival of "book culture." The mass distribution of books, newspapers, and other printed media was as distinctive a feature of the development of industrial society as were machines and factories. Education developed to provide skills of literacy and computation giving access to the world of printed media. Nothing is more characteristic of the school than the schoolbook or textbook.

In the eyes of many, all this is set to change with the growing use of computers and multimedia technologies in education. It has been said that "around 70–80% of telecommunications trials conducted in the emerging multimedia technologies around the world involve education or at least have an education component" (quoted in Kenway et al., 1995). Will the computer, CD-ROM, and videotape increasingly replace the textbook? And will schools still exist in anything like the form in which they do today if children turn on their computers in order to learn, rather than sit in rows listening to a teacher?

The new technologies, it is said, will not just add to the existing curriculum, they will undermine and transform it. For young people now are already growing up in an information- and media-related society and are much more familiar with its technologies than most adults are—including their teachers. Some speak of a "classroom revolution": the arrival of "desk-top virtual reality" and the "classroom without walls."

There seems little doubt that multimedia technolo-

Schools have begun to meet the rising technological demands on today's citizen by teaching computer use as early as elementary school.

gies will find their way extensively into education. Political parties have lent their support to this in the United States as elsewhere. But one of the main driving forces is business: schools as well as homes are being targeted by the large media companies. The home computer market in the United States, for example, seemed to have reached saturation point before the marketing of new forms of educational software, which has served to give it new impetus. Companies also plan to use the Internet to market new educational programs.

As in many other areas of contemporary social life, markets and information technology are major influences on educational change. The commercializing and marketizing of education also reflect such pressures. Schools are being "re-engineered" in much the same way as business corporations.

Many of those likely to enter the education field will be organizations whose relation to schooling was previously marginal or nonexistent. They include cable companies, software houses, telecommunication groups, filmmakers, and equipment suppliers. These will not be limited in their influence to schools or universities. They are already forming part of what has been called "edutainment"—a sort of parallel education industry linked to the software industry in general, to museums, science parks, and heritage areas.

Whether the new technologies will have the radical implications for education that some claim is still an open question. Critics have pointed out that, even if they do have major effects, these may act to reinforce educational inequalities. "**Information poverty**" might become added to the material deprivations that currently have such an effect on schooling. The "classroom without walls" at the moment looks some way off. In the meantime, many schools and colleges are suffering from underfunding and long-standing neglect.

SUMMARY

1. Education in its modern form, involving the instruction of pupils within specially designated school premises, began to emerge with the spread of printed materials and higher levels of literacy. Knowledge could be retained, reproduced, and consumed by more people in more places. With industrialization, work became more specialized, and knowledge was increasingly acquired in more abstract rather than practical ways—the skills of reading, writing, and calculating.

2. The expansion of education in the twentieth century has been closely tied to perceived needs for a literate and disciplined workforce. Although reformers have seen the use of education for all as a means of reducing inequalities, its impact in this respect is fairly limited. Education tends to express and reaffirm existing inequalities more than it acts to change them.

3. The formal school curriculum is only one part of a more general process of *social reproduction* influenced by many informal aspects of learning, education, and school settings. The *hidden curriculum* plays a significant role in such reproduction.

4. Because *intelligence* is difficult to define, there has been a great deal of controversy about the subject. Some argue that genes determine one's *IQ*; others believe that social influences determine it. The weight of the evidence appears to be on the side of those arguing for social and cultural influences. A major controversy about IQ has developed as a result of the book *The Bell Curve*. The book claims that races differ in terms of their average level of inherited intelligence. Critics reject this thesis completely.

5. The *mass media* have come to play a fundamental role in modern society. The mass media are media of communication—newspapers, magazines, television, radio, movies, videos, CDs, and other forms—which reach mass audiences. The influence of the mass media on our lives is profound. The media not only provide entertainment, but provide and shape much of the information that we utilize in our daily lives.

6. A range of different theories of media and popular culture have been developed. McLuhan argued that media influence society more in terms of how they communicate than what they communicate. In McLuhan's words, "the medium is the message": TV, for example, influences people's behavior and attitudes because it is so different in nature from other media, such as newspapers or books.

7. Other important theorists include Habermas, Baudrillard, and Thompson. Habermas points to the role of the media in creating a *public sphere*—a sphere of public opinion and public debate. Baudrillard has been strongly influenced by McLuhan. He believes that new media, particularly television, actually change the "reality" we experience. Thompson argues that the mass media have created a new form of social interaction—*mediated quasi-interaction*—which is more limited, narrow, and one-way than everyday social interaction.

8. The sense today of inhabiting one world is in large part a result of the international scope of media of communication. A *world information order*—an international system of the production, distribution, and consumption of informational goods—has come into being. Given the paramount position of the industrial countries in the world information order, many believe that the Third World countries are subject to a new form of media imperialism.

9. Recent years have seen the emergence of multimedia, linked to the development of the Internet and the possible construction of an *information superhighway*. *Multimedia* refers to the combination on a single medium of what used to be different media needing different technologies, so that a CD-ROM, for example, can carry both visuals and sound and be played on a computer. Many claims have been made about the likely social effects of these developments, but it is still too early to judge how far these will be borne out.

Chapter Fifteen

What Is Religion?

Learn the elements that make up a religion. Familiarize yourself with the various forms religion takes in traditional and modern societies.

Theories of Religion

Know the sociological approaches to religion developed by Marx, Durkheim, and Weber.

Types of Religious Organizations

Learn the various ways religious communities are organized and how they have become institutionalized.

Secularization and Fundamentalism

Recognize the important influence of secularization on declining religiosity and growing revivalism around the world.

Gender and Religion

Recognize the changes taking place in the interrelationships between gender and religion.

Religion in the United States

Learn about the sociological dimensions of religion in the United States, including the rise of fundamentalism and the electronic church.

RELIGION IN MODERN SOCIETY

In his book *A Generation of Seekers,* sociologist of religion Wade Clark Roof investigated the spiritual journeys of the baby-boom generation in the United States—the generation born between 1946 and 1964, when there was a large increase in the rate of population growth. This generation includes no fewer than 76 million Americans, about a quarter of the U.S. population as a whole. The baby boomers have been tagged with many labels, including the "hippie generation" (in the 1960s), the "yuppie generation" (in the 1980s), the "Pepsi generation," the "love generation," and the "me generation."

Roof and a team of researchers interviewed hundreds of boomers over the telephone and carried out in-depth interviews in person. One thing most boomers are conscious of, Roof found, is of being "searchers." They came of age, as Roof puts it, "in a time of increased choices and optimistic dreams" in the 1960s. And even today, they continue to ask questions about the meaning of their lives, about what they want for themselves and their children. "They are still exploring, as they did in their years growing up; but they are doing so in new ways" (1993).

Spiritual and religious themes are prominent in boomers' explorations. Their involvement with religious organizations, however, is fluid and dynamic. Some have returned to orthodox religious beliefs, forms of Protestantism and Catholicism, for example, that in their twenties and thirties they rejected. Others are interested in Eastern religions, New Age teaching, twelve-step recovery programs, and spiritually inclined health regimes.

On the basis of his findings, Roof was critical of the idea of the baby boomers as the "me generation." The majority of those interviewed were not preoccupied with selfish interests. They wanted to reconcile inner and outer life, and were looking for stable frameworks and social ties. The boomers, Roof concluded, are in the vanguard of transformations affecting the religious landscape today. Many of them are seeking an all-encompassing vision of life and look to religious inspiration in order to find it. And they undertake this quest in an active way.

This phenomenon is not unique to the United States, although it is more developed there than elsewhere. New Age philosophies and diverse forms of new spiri-tual practice, for example, have become very visible in Russia with the fall of Soviet Communism. Many older Russians have returned to religious congregations to which they belonged before Communism. Religiously inclined individuals in the younger generations, however, are turning to sources similar to those of their counterparts in North America.

The spiritual quests of the baby boomers are not particularly threatening to anyone else. Other activities prompted by religious belief, however, most definitely are. Clashes between Christians and Muslims in Bosnia-Herzegovina, in the former Yugoslavia, or between Hindu fundamentalists and Muslims in India are echoed in other conflicts between different religious groups around the world. Religious convictions in these situations add fuel to struggles influenced by nationalism, ethnic divisions, and inequalities of power.

What explains the continued vitality and importance of religion in the modern world? Under what conditions does religion unite communities, and under what conditions does it divide them? To study these issues, we shall ask what religion actually is, and look at some of the different forms that religious beliefs and practices take. We will also analyze the various types of religious organizations. As in most of the other chapters in this book, the emphasis is on social change. Religious concerns today can be properly understood only in relation to social changes that have affected the position of religion in the wider world.

The study of religion is a challenging enterprise, which places special demands on the sociological imagination. In analyzing religious practices, we must be sensitive to ideals that inspire profound conviction in believers, yet at the same time take a balanced view of them. We must confront ideas that seek the eternal, while recognizing that religious groups also promote quite mundane goals, such as acquiring money or followers. We need to recognize the diversity of religious beliefs and modes of conduct, but also probe into the nature of religion as a general phenomenon.

WHAT IS RELIGION?

The variety of religious beliefs and organizations is so immense that scholars have found great difficulty in reaching a generally accepted definition of religion. In the West, most people identify religion with Christianity—a belief in Jesus Christ as the son of God, who commands them to behave in a moral fashion on this earth and promises an afterlife to come. Yet this and other beliefs that make up Christianity are *absent* from most of the world's religions. Religion is also traditionally identified with the supernatural, a world beyond this one. However, some religions, like Confucianism, are concerned with accepting the natural harmony of the world, not with finding truths that lie beyond it. Bearing these facts in mind, we can define religion in the following way: religion involves a set of **symbols**, invoking feelings of reverence or awe, which are linked to **rituals** practiced by a community of believers (Durkheim, 1965).

Each of these terms needs some elaboration. In virtually all **religions**, there are symbolic beings or objects inspiring awe or wonder. In some, people believe in a divine force, rather than personalized gods, toward which such attitudes are held. In others, figures who are not gods are nevertheless thought of with reverence; Buddha and Confucius are examples.

The rituals associated with religion may include praying, chanting, singing, eating or avoiding certain kinds of foods, fasting on certain days, and so on. Since ritual acts are oriented toward religious symbols, they are usually seen as distinct from the habits and procedures of ordinary life. Lighting a candle to honor or placate a god conveys a different significance from lighting a candle to provide illumination in the dark. Religious rituals are often carried on by individuals in isolation, but all religions also include ceremonials practiced collectively by believers. Such ceremonials normally take place within special places—churches, temples, or ceremonial grounds. Some religions also involve rituals practiced in the home, but even there, a separate place—such as a small shrine or special room—might be set aside.

Sociologists usually regard the existence of collective ceremonials as one of the main factors distinguishing religion from magic, although the boundary lines between the two are not always distinct. **Magic** is the use of potions, chantings, or ritual practices to influence natural events. It is generally practiced by individuals or small groups rather than by a community of believers. People often have resorted to magic in situations of misfortune or danger. Thus, Bronislaw Malinowski's classical study of the Trobriand Islanders of the Pacific described magical rites performed before any hazardous voyage by canoe was undertaken (Malinowski, 1982). The islanders omit-

ted these rites when they were simply going fishing on the safe and placid waters of a local lagoon.

Although magical practices have become less common in modern societies, comparable superstitions are still found. People who work in occupations that are either dangerous or depend on chance factors—such as miners, deep-sea fishermen, and athletes—sometimes indulge in small superstitious rituals or carry a charm in times of stress; a tennis player might insist on wearing a particular ring during big matches. Astrological predictions, which have been inherited from magical beliefs in medieval Europe, are still avidly attended to.

Varieties of Religion

In traditional societies, religion usually plays a comprehensive part in social life. Religious symbols and rituals are often integrated with the material and artistic culture of the society—music, painting or carving, dance, storytelling, and literature. In small hunting and gathering cultures, there is no professional priesthood, but there are always certain individuals who specialize in knowledge of religious (or magical) practices. One common specialist is the **shaman**, an individual believed to be able to direct the activities of spirits or nonnatural forces through ritual means. Shamans are sometimes essentially magicians rather than religious leaders, however, and are often consulted by people dissatisfied with what is offered in the orthodox religious rituals of the community.

TOTEMISM AND ANIMISM

Two common forms of religion in smaller cultures are **totemism** and animism. The word **totem** originated among Native American tribes, but has become widely used to refer to any species of animals or plants believed to have supernatural powers. Usually each kinship group or clan within the totemic society has its own particular totem, with its concomitant ritual activities. Totemic beliefs might at first seem quite alien to modern thinking. Yet certain symbols similar to those of totemism are not so alien: sports team mascots are totems.

Ancestor worship in China.

globalization and everyday life

THE SPREAD OF NEW AGE RELIGIONS

If you pick up a local newspaper in any U.S. city and turn to the classifieds section, you are likely to find a number of listings relating to spirituality and the New Age movement. You have no doubt seen advertisements like these before: "A course in miracles. Personal coaching by the hour." "Soul purpose, past lives, intuitive healing." "Under the guidance of a Living Spiritual Teacher, you can be guided to take the next step in your spiritual unfoldment." These ads appeal to those who feel strong spiritual yearnings, who have a sense that their lives are not going quite the way they should, and who have become disenchanted with organized religion. While some of the advertisements are clearly attempts to profit from the willingness of some to believe anything they are told, most participants in the New Age movement see themselves as being on a sincere spiritual quest for self-

enlightenment. The religious studies scholar Paul Heelas, in a recent book, describes the New Age movement that has sprung up in response to this spiritual demand as having three essential characteristics: "It explains why life—as conventionally experienced—is not what it should be; it provides an account of what it is to find perfection; and it provides the means for obtaining salvation" (1996, p. 18). By most estimates, the number of people interested in such concerns is growing. Meditation groups, psychic fairs, spirituality discussion groups, training sessions designed to help participants reach their "true" spiritual potential, Tarot card readings, books on spirituality and psychological self-help—all have proliferated since the 1960s.

From the perspective of the sociology of religion, a number of questions can be asked about these developments. To

what extent do these diverse phenomena form part of a coherent whole? What sociological factors account for the current popularity of the New Age movement? In what ways does the New Age movement differ from traditional forms of religiosity?

With respect to the last of these questions, one unique feature of the New Age movement is its eclecticism. Religions, of course, have always borrowed from one another. But most religions—no matter how much they adapt to current social and moral conditions—place a heavy emphasis on maintaining religious tradition. The faithful are often required by religious authorities to believe in the essential dogmas held by previous generations of worshippers. New Agers, however, tend to deny that there is much value in clinging to well-defined religious traditions. They see it as important, instead, that individuals pick and choose those spiritual beliefs and practices that suit them best. Heelas writes: "Much of the New Age would appear to be quite radically detraditionalized (rejecting voices of authority associated with established orders)" (1996, p. 22). Individuals, New Agers believe, should learn to listen to their intuition or "inner voice" to help them select the spiritual practices and make the life choices that are right for them.

The social organization of the New Age movement is entirely consistent with this philosophy. The movement consists of thousands of different groups, varying tremendously in size, with each group oriented around a different eclectic appropriation of the world's spiritual traditions. Many groups borrow heavily from Eastern spirituality—from Tibetan Buddhism, for example. Others incorporate certain Native American traditions. Still others combine these with elements of Christianity. There are an almost infinite number of permutations.

What does this have to do with globalization? New Agers insist that they should be free to borrow any spiritual practices that are right for them. Why, they ask, should Tibetan Buddhism be reserved for Tibetans, or Native American rituals for Native Americans? Without wishing to rob these groups of their rich cultural heritage, New Agers firmly believe that the geographic borders of nation states are entirely irrelevant to spirituality. Their eclecticism is truly global and, primarily through books and travel, they scour the world in search of meaningful forms of spirituality. If the differences between nation-states begin to fade in a globalized world, New Agers may well represent the growing penetration of globalization into the religious realm.

Animism is a belief in spirits or ghosts that have the power to influence human behavior. In some cultures, for example, spirits are believed to cause illness or madness. In medieval Europe, people believed to be possessed by evil spirits were frequently persecuted as sorcerers or witches.

Totemism and animism are mostly found in small, seemingly simple premodern societies, but some small societies practice far more complex religions. The Nuer of southern Sudan, for instance, favor an elaborate set of theological ideas centered upon the "high god," or "sky spirit" (Evans-Pritchard, 1956). Most small traditional cultures are **polytheistic**—the people believe in many gods—rather than **monotheistic,** characterized by a belief in one god.

The three most influential monotheistic religions in world history are Judaism, Christianity, and Islam. All originated in the Near East, and each has influenced the others.

JUDAISM

Judaism is the oldest of the three religions, dating from about 1000 B.C.E. The early Hebrews, a northern Semitic people, were nomads living in lands adjacent to and in ancient Egypt. The Hebrew **prophets** (inspired leaders or teachers) drew their ideas from religious beliefs existing in the region, but their commitment to a single almighty God distinguished their beliefs from those of surrounding religions, most of which were polytheistic. The prophets emphasized that obedience to God meant the following of strict moral codes. They also strongly insisted on their claim to a monopoly of truth, declaring their religion the only true one (Zeitlin, 1985, 1988).

The holy book of Judaism is the Tenakh, the Old Testament of the Christian Bible. The Tenakh is divided into three sections, the Torah, Neviím, and Ketubim. The Torah, also referred to as the Five Books of Moses, is the most important of the three and begins with the creation of the world by the word of God, who said, " 'Let there be light,' and there was light." Much of the Torah describes God's communications to Moses and through him to the Hebrew people, instructing them in how to live and how to worship. Devotion to a single God, the "jealous God" of Judaism, is expressed in the Shema, a passage in the

Scripture that contains the first religious words a Jewish child should learn and the last a Jew should utter when leaving this world:

> Hear, O Israel, the Lord God is one.
> And you shall love the Lord thy God with all thy heart.
> And with all thy soul and all thy might.

CHRISTIANITY

Christianity began as a sect of Judaism and incorporated many Judaic views. Historians are not certain that Jesus, who himself was an orthodox Jew, in-

Table 15.1 Religious Population of the World

RELIGION	NUMBER	PERCENTAGE OF TOTAL
Christians	1,869,751,000	33.5
Roman Catholics	1,042,501,000	18.7
Protestants	382,374,000	6.9
Orthodox	173,560,000	3.1
Anglicans	75,847,000	1.4
Other Christians	195,000,470	3.5
Muslims	1,014,372,000	18.2
Nonreligious	912,874,000	16.4
Hindus	751,360,000	13.5
Buddhists	334,002,000	6.0
Atheists	242,852,000	4.3
Chinese folk religions	140,956,000	2.5
New religionists	123,765,000	2.2
Tribal religionists	99,736,000	1.8
Sikhs	19,853,000	0.4
Jews	18,153,000	0.3
Other	49,280,000	1.0

SOURCE: U.S. Bureau of the Census, 1994, p. 855 (1993 data).

Adherents to Christianity live in all parts of the world. Cuban leader Fidel Castro greets Pope John Paul II, who visited Cuba in 1998.

tended to found a religion distinct from Judaism, but his disciples came to think of him as the promised "Messiah"—a Hebrew word meaning "the anointed," for which "Christ" was the Greek word. St. Paul, a Greek-speaking Roman citizen and contemporary of Jesus, was a major initiator of the spread of Christianity. He preached extensively in the Near East and Greece, though not always to receptive ears. From the crucifixion of Jesus and some of his disciples to the tearing apart of believers by lions in the Roman Colosseum, Christians were savagely persecuted. The emperor Constantine eventually adopted Christianity as the official religion of the Roman Empire, but not until the fourth century. Since then, Christianity has grown to become a dominant force in Western culture.

Christianity today commands the greatest number of adherents, and is more generally spread across the world, than any other religion. Close to 2 billion people regard themselves as Christians. Besides its main branches—Roman Catholicism, Protestantism, and Eastern Orthodoxy—there are many small subdivisions, each with its own theology and church organization.

ISLAM

The origins of Islam, presently the second largest religion in the world, overlap with those of Christianity.

Islam derives from the teachings of the seventh-century prophet Mohammed. The single God of Islam, Allah, is believed to hold sway over all human and natural life. The Pillars of Islam are the five essential religious duties of Muslims (as believers are called). The first is the compulsory recitation of the Islamic creed, "There is no God but Allah, and Mohammed is the apostle of Allah." The second pillar consists of the reciting of formal prayers five times each day, each prayer preceded by ceremonial washing. The worshipper at these prayers must always face

Muslims in Senegal praying toward Mecca.

toward the holy city of Mecca in Saudi Arabia, no matter where he is.

The third pillar is the observance of Ramadan, a month of fasting during which no food or drink may be taken during the daylight hours. The fourth is the giving of alms (money to the poor), set out in Islamic law, which often has been used as a source of taxation by the state. Finally, there is the expectation that every believer will undertake, at least once in life, a pilgrimage to Mecca. Muslims believe that Allah spoke through earlier prophets—including Moses and Jesus—but that Mohammed's teachings most directly express Allah's will.

The Islamic scriptures, known collectively as the Koran, are a collection of the messages that Muslims believe Mohammed received from God. Mohammed could not read or write, so he memorized God's words, passing them on to those who became his followers. After his death, some of the followers decided to write down his sayings in an authoritative form. "Koran" comes from an Arabic term meaning "to recite," and simply means "the recitation"—the words of God as revealed to the Prophet. Islam has come to be very widespread, with over 1 billion adherents throughout the world. The majority of Muslims are concentrated in North and East Africa, the Middle East, and Pakistan.

HINDUISM

The oldest of all the great religions still prominent in the world today is Hinduism, the core beliefs of which date back some six thousand years. Hinduism is a polytheistic religion with an array of beliefs and rituals. It is so internally diverse, in fact, that some scholars have suggested that it should be regarded as a cluster of related religions rather than a single religious orientation.

Most Hindus accept the doctrine of the cycle of reincarnation—the belief that all living beings are part of an eternal process of birth, death, and rebirth. A second key feature of Hinduism is the caste system (see Chapter 7), according to which individuals are born into their positions in the social and ritual hierarchy, their level in that hierarchy being determined by their activities in previous incarnations. There is a different set of duties and ritual prescriptions for each

caste, and a person's fate in the next life is governed mainly by how well she performs these duties.

Hindus recognize female as well as male gods, but hold that ultimately the divine force is beyond such categories, since it is found in all living beings. Hinduism accepts the possibility of numerous different religious standpoints and does not draw a clear line between believers and nonbelievers. There are almost as many Hindus as Muslims—about 750 million—however, they are virtually all situated in India. Hinduism, unlike Christianity and Islam, is not a form of religious outlook that seeks to convert others into "true believers."

BUDDHISM, CONFUCIANISM, AND TAOISM

The **ethical religions** of the East encompass Buddhism, Confucianism, and Taoism. These religions acknowledge no gods, at least not in a sense akin to the Christian God or Allah. Rather, they emphasize ethical ideals that relate the believer to the natural cohesion and unity of the universe.

Buddhism derives from the teachings of Siddhartha Gautama, the Buddha (Enlightened One), who was a Hindu prince in a small kingdom in south Nepal in the sixth century B.C.E. According to the Buddha, human beings can escape the reincarnation cycle by renouncing desire. The path of salvation lies in a life of self-discipline and meditation, separated from the tasks of the mundane world. The overall objective of Buddhism is the attainment of Nirvana, complete spiritual fulfillment. The Buddha rejected Hindu ritual and the authority of the castes. Like Hinduism, however, Buddhism tolerates local variations, including belief in local deities, and does not insist on an exclusivist view. Buddhism today is a major influence in states in the Far East such as Thailand, Myanmar, Sri Lanka, China, Japan, and Korea.

Confucianism was the basis of the culture of the ruling groups in traditional China. "Confucius" is the latinized form of Kung Futzu, who lived in the sixth century B.C.E., the same period as Buddha. Confucius was a teacher, not a religious prophet in the manner of Judaism or Islam. He is seen by his followers not as a god, but as "the wisest of wise men." Confucianism seeks to adjust human life to the inner harmony of nature and emphasizes the veneration of ancestors.

Taoism shares similar principles, stressing meditation and nonviolence as means to the higher life. Like Confucius, Lao-tzu, the founder of Taoism, was a sixth-century-B.C.E. teacher. Although some principles survive in the practices of many Chinese, Confucianism and Taoism lost much of their influence in China as a result of determined opposition from the Communist government.

THEORIES OF RELIGION

Sociological approaches to religion are still strongly influenced by the ideas of Marx, Durkheim, and Weber. None of the three was religious himself, and all believed that religion would become less and less significant in modern times. Each accepted that religion was fundamentally an illusion: the very diversity of religions and their obvious connection to different societies and regions of the world made the claims by their advocates inherently implausible. An individual born into an Australian society of hunters and gatherers would plainly hold different religious beliefs from someone born into the caste system of India or the Catholic church of medieval Europe.

Marx and Religion

In spite of the influence of his views on the subject, Karl Marx never studied religion in any detail. His thinking on religion was mostly derived from the writings of Ludwig Feuerbach, who believed that through a process he called **alienation**, human beings tend to attribute their own culturally created values and norms to alien, or separate, beings (i.e., divine forces or gods), because they do not understand their own history. Thus, the story of the Ten Commandments given to Moses by God is a mythical version of the origins of the moral precepts that govern the lives of Jewish and Christian believers.

Marx accepted the view that religion represents human self-alienation. In a famous phrase, Marx declared that religion was the "opium of the people." Religion defers happiness and rewards to the afterlife, he said, teaching the resigned acceptance of existing conditions in the earthly life. Attention is thus diverted away from inequalities and injustices in this world by the promise of what is to come in the next. Religion contains a strong ideological element: religious belief can often provide justifications for those in power. For example, "The meek shall inherit the earth" suggests attitudes of humility and nonresistance to oppression.

Durkheim: Religion and Functionalism

In contrast to Marx, Émile Durkheim spent a good part of his intellectual career studying religion, concentrating particularly on totemism as practiced by Australian aboriginal societies. *The Elementary Forms of the Religious Life*, first published in 1912, is perhaps the most influential single study in the sociology of religion (1965). Durkheim connected religion not with social inequalities or power, but with the overall nature of the institutions of a society. His argument was that totemism represented religion in its most "elementary" form—hence the title of his book.

Durkheim defined religion in terms of a distinction between the sacred and the profane. **Sacred** objects and symbols, he held, are treated as apart from the routine, utilitarian aspects of day-to-day existence—the realm of the **profane**. A totem (an animal or plant believed to have particular symbolic significance), Durkheim argued, is a sacred object, regarded with veneration and surrounded by ritual activities. These ceremonies and rituals, in Durkheim's view, are essential to binding the members of groups together.

Durkheim's theory of religion is a good example of the **functionalist** tradition of thought in sociology. To analyze the function of a social behavior or social institution like religion is to study the contribution it makes to the continuation of a group, community, or society. According to Durkheim, religion has the function of cohering a society by ensuring that people meet regularly to affirm common beliefs and values.

Weber: The World Religions and Social Change

Durkheim based his arguments on a restricted range of examples, even though he claimed his ideas applied to religion in general. Max Weber, by contrast, embarked on a massive study of religions worldwide. No

scholar before or since has undertaken a task of the scope Weber attempted.

Weber's writings on religion differ from those of Durkheim because they concentrate upon the connection between religion and social change, something to which Durkheim gave little direct attention. They also contrast with those of Marx, because Weber argued that religion was not necessarily a conservative force; on the contrary, religiously inspired movements have often produced dramatic social transformations. Thus, Protestantism, particularly Puritanism, according to Weber, was the source of the capitalistic outlook found in the modern West. The early entrepreneurs were mostly Calvinists. Their drive to succeed, which helped initiate Western economic development, was originally prompted by a desire to serve God. Material success was a sign of divine favor.

Weber conceived of his research on the world religions as a single project. His discussion of the impact of Protestantism on the development of the West was connected to a comprehensive attempt to understand the influence of religion on social and economic life in various cultures. After analyzing the Eastern religions, Weber concluded that they provided insuperable barriers to the development of industrial capitalism such as took place in the West. This was not because the non-Western civilizations were backward; they were simply oriented toward different values, such as escape from the toils of the material world, from those that came to predominate in Europe.

In traditional China and India, Weber pointed out, there was at certain periods a significant development of commerce, manufacture, and urbanism. But these did not generate the radical patterns of social change involved in the rise of industrial capitalism in the West. Religion was a major influence inhibiting such change. Consider, for example, Hinduism. Hinduism is what Weber called an "other-worldly" religion. That is to say, its highest values stress escape from the toils of the material world to a higher plane of spiritual existence. The religious feelings and motivations produced by Hinduism do not focus upon controlling or shaping the material world. On the contrary, Hinduism sees material reality as a veil hiding the true spiritual concerns to which humankind should be oriented. Confucianism also acts to direct activity away from economic "progress," as this came to be understood in the West. Confucianism emphasizes harmony with the world, rather than promoting an active mastery of it. Although China was for a long while the most powerful and culturally most developed civilization in the world, its dominant religious values acted as a brake upon a stronger commitment to economic development.

Weber regarded Christianity as a *salvation religion.* According to such religions, human beings can be "saved" if they are converted to the beliefs of the religion and follow its moral tenets. The notions of "sin," and of being rescued from sinfulness by God's grace, are important here. They generate a tension and an emotional dynamism essentially absent from the Eastern religions. Salvation religions have a "revolutionary" aspect. While the religions of the East cultivate an attitude of passivity or acceptance within the believer, Christianity demands a constant struggle against sin, and so can stimulate revolt against the existing order. Religious leaders like Luther or Calvin—have arisen, who reinterpret existing doctrines in such a way as to challenge the existing power structure.

Critical Assessment

Marx, Durkheim, and Weber each identified some important general characteristics of religion, and in some ways their views complement one another. Marx was right to claim that religion often has ideological implications, serving to justify the interests of ruling groups at the expense of others. There are innumerable instances of this in history. For example, the European missionaries who sought to convert "heathen" peoples to Christian beliefs were no doubt sincere in their efforts. Yet the effect of their teachings was in large part to reinforce the destruction of traditional cultures and the imposition of white domination. Almost all Christian denominations tolerated, or endorsed, slavery in the United States and other parts of the world up to the nineteenth century. Doctrines were developed proclaiming slavery to be based upon divine law, disobedient slaves being guilty of an offense against God as well as their masters (Stampp, 1956).

Yet Weber was certainly correct to emphasize the unsettling and often revolutionary impact of religious ideals upon the established social order. In spite of the churches' early support for slavery in the United States, church leaders later played a key role in fighting to abolish the institution. Religious beliefs have prompted social movements seeking to overthrow unjust systems of authority; for instance, religious sentiments played a prominent part in the civil rights movements of the 1960s. Religion has also generated social change through the wars fought for religious motives.

These divisive influences of religion, so prominent in history, find little mention in Durkheim's work. Durkheim emphasized above all the role of religion in promoting social cohesion. Yet it is not difficult to

KEY CONCEPTS IN REVIEW

To Marx, religion contains a strong ideological element: religion provides justification for the inequalities of wealth and power found in society.

To Durkheim, religion is important because of the cohesive functions it serves, especially in ensuring that people meet regularly to affirm common beliefs and values.

To Weber, religion is important because of the role it plays in social change, particularly the development of Western capitalism.

redirect his ideas toward explaining religious division, conflict, and change as well as solidarity. After all, much of the strength of feeling that may be generated *against* other religious groups derives from the commitment to religious values generated *within* each community of believers.

Among the most valuable points of Durkheim's writings is his stress on ritual and ceremonial. All religions comprise regular assemblies of believers, at which ritual prescriptions are observed. As Durkheim rightly points out, ritual activities also mark the major transitions of life—birth, entry to adulthood (rituals associated with puberty are found in many cultures), marriage, and death (Van Gennep, 1977).

TYPES OF RELIGIOUS ORGANIZATIONS

All religions are comprised of communities of believers. Yet such communities are organized in various ways. One of the most important ways of classifying religious organizations was first put forward by Weber and his colleague, the religious historian Ernst Troeltsch (Troeltsch, 1931), who distinguished between churches and sects. Other authors have further developed the church-sect typology. Howard Becker (1950) added two additional types: the denomination and the cult.

Churches and Sects

Churches are large, established religious bodies; one example is the Roman Catholic church. They normally have a formal, bureaucratic structure, with a hierarchy of religious officials. Churches often represent the conservative face of religion, since they are integrated within the existing institutional order. Most of their adherents are born into and grow up with the church.

Sects are smaller, less highly organized groups of committed believers, usually set up in protest against an established church, as Calvinism and Methodism were initially. Sects aim at discovering and following "the true way," and either try to change the surrounding society or withdraw from it into communities of their own, a process known as **revival**. The members of sects regard established churches as corrupt. Many sects have few or no officials, and all members are regarded as equal participants. For the most part, people are not born into sects, but actively join them in order to further commitments in which they believe.

Denominations and Cults

A **denomination** is a sect that has "cooled down" and become an institutionalized body rather than an activist protest group. Sects that survive over any period of time inevitably become denominations. Thus, Calvinism and Methodism were sects in their early period of formation, when they generated great fervor among their members; but over the years, they have become more established. (Calvinists today are called Presbyterians.) Denominations are recognized as legitimate by churches and exist alongside them, often cooperating harmoniously with them.

Cults resemble sects, but their emphases are different. Cults are the most loosely knit and transient of all religious organizations. They are composed of individuals who reject what they see as the values of the outside society, unlike sects, which try to revive an established church. They are a form of religious innovation, rather than revival. Their focus is upon individual experience, bringing like-minded people together. Like sects, cults often form around the influence of an inspirational leader. Instances of cults in modern societies include believers in spiritualism, astrology, and transcendental meditation. But cults should not necessarily be thought of as "weird." Based on the sociological definition, established religions like Buddhism and the Church of Jesus Christ of Latter-Day Saints began as cults.

Religious Movements

Religious movements represent a subtype of social movement in general. A religious movement is an association of people who join together to spread a new religion or to promote a new interpretation of an existing religion. Religious movements are larger than

KEY CONCEPTS IN REVIEW

There are four main types of religious organizations.

Churches are large and established religious bodies, normally with a formal, bureaucratic structure and a hierarchy of religious officials.

Sects are smaller, less formal groups of believers, usually set up to revive an established church.

If a sect survives over a period of time and becomes institutionalized, it is called a **denomination**.

Cults resemble sects, but rather than trying to revive an established church, cults seek to form a new religion.

Religious movement is the general term for the attempt to promote a new religion or a new interpretation of an established religion. Thus, all sects and cults can be classified as religious movements. Religious movements acquire cohesion from a powerful, charismatic leader. Max Weber defined **charisma** as the inspirational quality capable of capturing the imagination and devotion of a mass of followers. For a religious movement to survive and become a church, there must be a "routinization of charisma," the creation of formalized rules and procedures following the death of a charismatic leader.

sects and less exclusivist in their membership—although like churches and sects, movements and sects (or cults) are not always clearly distinct from one another. In fact, all sects and cults can be classified as religious movements. Examples of religious movements include the groups that originally founded and spread Christianity in the first century, the Lutheran movement that split Christianity in Europe about fifteen hundred years afterward, and the groups involved in the more recent Islamic Revolution (discussed in more detail later in the chapter).

Religious movements tend to pass through certain definite phases of development. In the first phase, the movement usually derives its life and cohesion from a powerful leader. Max Weber classified such leaders as **charismatic,** that is, having inspirational qualities capable of capturing the imagination and devotion of a mass of followers. (Charismatic leaders in Weber's formulation include political as well as religious figures—revolutionary China's Mao Tse-tung and President John F. Kennedy, as well as Jesus and Mohammed.) The leaders of religious movements are usually critical of the religious establishment and seek to proclaim a new message. In their early years, reli-

gious movements are fluid; they do not have an established authority system. Their members are normally in direct contact with the charismatic leader, and together they spread the new teachings.

The second phase of development occurs following the death of the leader. Rarely does a new charismatic

Sociologists would classify Hare Krishna followers as cultists.

leader arise from the masses, so this phase is crucial. The movement is now faced with what Weber termed the "routinization of charisma." To survive, it has to create formalized rules and procedures, since it can no longer depend on the central role of the leader in organizing the followers. Many movements fade away when their leaders die or lose their influence. A movement that survives and takes on a permanent character becomes a church. In other words, it becomes a formal organization of believers with an established authority system and established symbols and rituals. The church might itself at some later point become the origin of other movements that question its teachings and either set themselves up in opposition or break away completely.

Institutionalization versus Revivalism

These five religious classifications are useful in analyzing religious organization, but we must apply them with caution, because they partly reflect specifically Christian traditions and are not necessarily representative of non-Western religious cultures. For example, a heterogeneous religion such as Hinduism does not contain a bureaucratic hierarchy, one of the characteristics of a church; nor would it make sense to call its subdivisions denominations. Yet Hinduism is every bit as established a religion as the Christian churches.

While these concepts may be culture-bound, they do help us analyze the tension between institutionalization and revivalism present in all religions. Established religious organizations often do in fact become bureaucratic and inflexible. Yet their religious symbols retain extraordinary emotive power for believers and resist becoming reduced to the level of the routine. The more religious activities become standardized, a matter for habitual reenactment, the more the element of "sacredness" is lost, and religious ritual and belief become mundane aspects of the everyday world. Churches that are sensitive to this tension might revitalize a sense of the distinct qualities of religious experience through ceremonies. But when bureaucratic inflexibility dominates over inspirational experiences, certain sects might break away from the

main community, mobilize protest or separatist movements, or otherwise diverge from established orthodoxy. Or cults might form to attempt to establish a new religion (Stark and Bainbridge, 1985).

Millenarian Movements

The existence and number of millenarian movements show very clearly that religion frequently inspires activism and social change. A millenarian group is one that anticipates immediate, collective salvation for believers, either because of some cataclysmic change in the present, or through a recovery of a golden age supposed to have existed in the past. (The term "millenarian" actually derives from the thousand-year reign of Christ, the *millennium* prophesied in the Bible.) Millenarian movements are deeply entwined with the history of Christianity, and they have arisen in two major contexts—among the Western poor in the past and among colonized peoples in other parts of the world more recently.

THE FOLLOWERS OF JOACHIM

One European medieval millenarian movement was known as Joachimism and flourished in the thirteenth century (Cohn, 1970a, 1970b). During this period, Europe's economic prosperity was increasing rapidly and the dominant Catholic church was becoming richer. Many abbots converted their monasteries into luxurious castles, bishops built palaces where they lived as magnificently as secular feudal lords, and the popes maintained splendid courts. Joachimism developed in protest against these tendencies in the official church.

In the mid-thirteenth century, a number of Franciscan friars (whose order stressed denial of material pleasure and wealth) began to protest against the indulgent habits of church officials. They based their movement on the prophetic writings of the abbot Joachim of Fiore, who had died about fifty years earlier. Joachim's writings were interpreted to foretell that in 1260 the "Spirituals," as they called themselves, would inaugurate the Third and Last Age of Christendom. This would lead to the millennium, in which all human beings, regardless of their previous religious affiliation, would unite in a life of Christian devotion and voluntary poverty. It was prophesied that the existing church would be disbanded and that the clergy would be massacred by the German emperor.

When the year 1260 passed without the occurrence of this cataclysm, the date of the millennium was postponed—and put off again and again. The fervor of the followers of Joachim did not diminish. Condemned by the religious authorities, the Joachimite Spirituals came to see the official church as the Whore of Babylon, and the Pope as the Antichrist and the Beast of the Apocalypse. They expected a savior to emerge from their own ranks, to ascend the papal throne as the "Angelic Pope," chosen by God to convert the whole world to a life of voluntary poverty. Among the groups within the movement was one led by Fra Dolcino; with more than a thousand armed men, he waged war against the armies of the Pope in northern Italy until eventually his force was defeated and massacred. Dolcino was burned to death at the stake as a heretic, but for many years afterward other groups arose claiming to draw inspiration from him.

THE GHOST DANCE

A quite different example of a millenarian movement is the Ghost Dance cult that arose among the Plains tribes and nations of North America in the late nineteenth century. Prophets preached that a general catastrophe would occur, heralding the millennium, in which storms, earthquakes, whirlwinds, and floods would destroy all the white intruders. The Native Americans would survive to see again the prairies covered with herds of buffalo and other game. After the catastrophe all ethnic divisions would be dissolved, and any whites who came to the land would live amicably with the Native peoples. The Ghost Dance ritual spread from community to community in the area, just as religious cults have spread more recently from village to village in New Guinea. The rituals of the Ghost Dance, which included singing, chanting, and the attainment of trance-like states, were based partly on ideas derived from contact with Christianity and partly on the traditional Sun Dance, which had been performed before the arrival of the whites. The Ghost Dance died out after the massacre at Wounded Knee, in which 370 Native American men, women, and children were slaughtered by white soldiers.

THE NATURE OF MILLENARIAN MOVEMENTS

Why do millenarian movements occur? A number of common elements that most or all share can be identified. Virtually all seem to involve the activities of *prophets* ("inspired" leaders or teachers), who draw on established religious ideas and proclaim the need to revitalize them. They successfully develop a following if they manage to put into words what others only vaguely feel, and if they tap emotions that stir people to action. Prophecy has always been strongly associated with salvation religions, especially Christianity, and most of those who have led millenarian movements in colonized areas have been familiar with Christian practices and beliefs. Many have in fact been mission teachers, who have turned their adopted religion against those who schooled them in it.

Millenarian movements often arise where there is either radical cultural change or a sudden increase in poverty (Worsley, 1968). They tend to attract people who have a strong sense of deprivation as a result of such changes, which leads them to abandon their earlier acceptance of the status quo. In medieval Europe, millenarian movements were frequently the last, desperate resort of those who found themselves suddenly impoverished. Peasants in times of famine, for example, were drawn to follow prophets who offered a vision of a "world turned upside down," in which the poor would finally inherit the earth. Millenarian movements among colonized peoples tend to develop when a traditional culture is being destroyed by the impact of Western colonizers, as was the case with the Ghost Dance.

Millenarianism has sometimes been interpreted as essentially a rebellion of the poor against the privileged (Lantenari, 1963) or the oppressed against the powerful, and this is obviously a factor in many cases. But it is too simplistic: some millenarian movements, such as that of the Joachimite Spirituals, are forged through influences and sentiments that initially have little to do with material deprivation.

SECULARIZATION AND FUNDAMENTALISM

Institutionalization is not the only factor contributing to religious revival or innovation. A phenomenon associated with the spread of capitalism and other traits of modern society is **secularization,** the process by which society becomes more concerned with worldly than with spiritual matters and religious organizations lose their influence over social life. Secularization is a complex phenomenon, with a number of dimensions.

One dimension concerns the level of membership of religious organizations—how many people are active in attending services. Using this index, the United States to some degree, but particularly the Western European countries, even Catholic countries such as France, have all experienced considerable secularization over the past century.

A second dimension of secularization is how far churches and other religious organizations maintain their social influence, wealth, and prestige. Religious organizations have progressively lost much of their social and political influence, and the trend is worldwide. With some notable exceptions (such as in Iran), church leaders can no longer automatically expect to influence the powerful. Although some established churches remain wealthy by any standards and new religious movements may rapidly build up fortunes, the material circumstances of many established religious organizations are insecure.

The third dimension of secularization concerns beliefs and values, or religiosity. In some respects, religiosity has declined. Religion is not the all-pervasive force in modern societies that it was in the past. Yet many people, including nonmembers of orthodox churches, retain religious beliefs. And religion in some ways remains a dynamic force in the present world—even traditional forms of religion. We will return to secularization and its impact in the United States at the end of the chapter (see "The Sociological Debate: Is the United States a Secular or Sacred Society?").

As we learned earlier, one view that Marx, Durkheim, and Weber all shared was that traditional religion would become more and more marginal in the modern age. Of the three, probably only Weber would have suspected that a traditional religious system like Islam could undergo a major revival and become the basis of important political movements in the late twentieth century. Yet this is exactly what occurred in the 1980s in Iran. In recent years, Islamic **fundamentalism** has also had a significant impact upon other Middle Eastern countries, including Egypt, Syria, and Algeria. To understand the phenomenon, we need to look at Islam and at the secular changes affecting modern states.

Islam, like Christianity, has continually stimulated activism. The Koran is full of instructions to believers to "struggle in the way of God." This struggle is against both unbelievers and those within the Muslim community who introduce corruption. The centuries have seen successive generations of Muslim reformers, and Islam has become as internally divided as Christianity.

The Islamic Revolution was fueled initially by internal opposition to the shah (the king), Mohammed

KEY CONCEPTS IN REVIEW

Secularization is the process by which society becomes more concerned with worldly matters than with spiritual matters and religious organizations lose their influence over social life. Secularization is measured in three main ways: the level of membership in religious organizations; the social influence of religious organizations; and the level of religiosity.

Reza Pahlavi (1941–1979). The shah had tried to promote forms of modernization modeled on the West—for example, land reform, extending the vote to women, and developing secular education. He also brutally repressed those who opposed his regime, by means of the army and secret police. The movement that overthrew the shah brought together people of diverse interests, not all of whom were attached to Islamic fundamentalism. A dominant figure, however, was Ayatollah Ruhollah Khomeini, a religious leader exiled in France during the shah's reign, who provided a radical reinterpretation of Shiite ideas.

Khomeini established a government in strict accordance with traditional Islamic law, calling that government the "Representative of All." The Islamic Revolution fused religion and the state. It made Islam, as specified in the Koran, the direct basis of all politi-cal and economic life in Iran. Under the revived Islamic law, men and women are kept rigorously segregated, women are obliged to cover their heads and faces in public, homosexuals face the possibility of being shot by firing squad, and adulterers are stoned to death. The strict code is accompanied by a pronounced nationalistic outlook, strongly rejecting Western influences.

Islamic revivalism cannot be understood wholly in religious terms; it represents in part a reaction against the impact of the West, and is a movement of national and cultural assertion. It is doubtful whether Islamic revivalism, even in its most fundamentalist forms, should be seen only as a renewal of traditionally held ideas. What has occurred is something more complex. Traditional practices and modes of life have been revived, but have been combined with concerns that relate specifically to modern times.

Islamic fundamentalist movements have gained influence in many countries in North Africa, the Middle East, and South Asia over the past ten to fifteen years. Algeria is a case in point. In December 1991, the Islamic Salvation Front gained a comfortable victory in the first-round elections to the National Assembly. Its program was to turn Algeria into an Islamic state along the lines of Iran. However, the army intervened and suspended the elections (Pilkington, 1992).

In Iran, a traditional link exists between spiritual and political leadership. In recent years, however, a new liberal trend has clashed with the conservative regime, causing a backlash from the establishment.

A Clash of Civilizations?

Many worry that the Islamic world is heading for a confrontation with those parts of the world that do not share its beliefs. The Islamic countries seem resistant to the waves of democratization sweeping across much of the world. Of thirty-nine countries in which Islam is the dominant form of religion, only a handful could be thought to be liberal democracies. Turkey is one example, although it experienced several attempts at military rule in the period between 1960 and 1980.

In some other countries, which for a time were reasonably democratic, such as Algeria, democracy has been suspended or destroyed. The Algerian government permitted free elections in 1991, but refused to take them to a second round when it became clear that the Islamic party, strongly influenced by religious fundamentalism, was heading for victory. The military took control and ever since there has been something close to civil war in the country between the government and Islamic guerrillas.

If the Islamic movement comes into power in Algeria, other countries close by may also follow suit. Egypt, with 55 million people, has its own Islamic rebels, who wish to establish a religious state there. So, too, do many Muslims in Morocco and Libya.

The political scientist Samuel Huntington (1996) has argued that struggles between Western and Islamic views might become part of a worldwide "clash of civilizations" with the ending of the Cold War and with increasing globalization. The nation-state is no longer the main influence in international relations; rivalries and conflicts will therefore occur between larger cultures or civilizations. It is just such a conflict that was enacted in Bosnia, in the former Yugoslavia, where the Bosnian Muslims fought against the Serbs, who represent a Christian culture.

Islam and Christianity are each religions that lay claim to certainty, to special access to the word of God. Christianity has learned to live along with capitalism and democracy, and if Max Weber was right might even have inspired their early development. To many Islamic believers such an accommodation appears much more difficult. Capitalist enterprise and liberal democracy for them represent the impact of Western culture. Moreover, Islam refuses to draw a distinction between the private life of the believer and public issues.

Yet, as "civilizations," Christianity and Islam have more in common with one another than they have differences, originating as they do from overlapping sources. Each has inspired hundreds of bloody wars over the centuries. However, each also contains very strong traditions of tolerance and moderation. We must hope that these allow the two cultures increasingly to live peacefully alongside one another.

GENDER AND RELIGION

Churches and denominations resemble other institutions in social life in that women have been mostly excluded from power. This is clear in Christianity, but it is also characteristic of virtually all the major religions. In the following sections, we shall examine some of the interrelations of religion and gender. The issue is an important one, because this is an area in which significant changes are taking place.

Religious Images

In Christianity, while Mary, the mother of Jesus, is sometimes treated as if she had divine qualities, God is "the Father," a male figure, and Jesus took the human shape of a man. Genesis, the first book of the Bible, reveals that woman was created from a rib taken from man. These facts have not gone unnoticed by women's movements. A hundred years ago, Elizabeth Cady Stanton published a series of commentaries on the Scriptures, entitled *The Woman's Bible*. In her view, the deity had created women and men as beings of equal value, and the Bible should fully reflect this fact. Its "masculinist" character, she believed, reflected not the authentic word of God, but the fact that the Bible was written by men. In 1870, the Church of England established a Revising Committee to revise and update the biblical texts; but as Stanton pointed out, the committee contained not a single woman. She asserted that there was no reason to suppose that God is a man, since it was clear in the Scriptures that all human beings were fashioned in the image of God. When a colleague opened a women's rights conference with a prayer to "God, our Mother," there was a virulent reaction from the church authorities. Yet Stanton pressed ahead, organizing a Women's Revising Committee in America, composed of twenty-three women, to advise her in preparing *The Woman's Bible*, which was published in 1895.

In some Buddhist orders, especially Mahayana Buddhism, women are represented in a favorable light. But on the whole, Buddhism, like Christianity, is "an overwhelmingly male-created institution dominated by a patriarchal power structure," in which the feminine is mostly "associated with the secular, powerless, profane, and imperfect" (Paul, 1985). The contrasting pictures of women that appear in the Buddhist texts no doubt mirror the ambiguous attitudes of men toward women in the secular world: women are portrayed as wise, maternal, and gentle yet also as mysterious, polluting, and destructive, threatening evil.

The Role of Women in Religious Organizations

In both Buddhism and (later) Christianity, women were allowed to express strong religious convictions by choosing to become nuns. The first orders for women were probably established in the fourteenth century; their membership remained small until the 1800s. At that time, many women took religious vows in order to become teachers and nurses, since these occupations were largely controlled by the religious orders. All along, however, female religious orders remained subject to a male hierarchy, and this subjugation was reinforced by some elaborate rituals. For example, all nuns were regarded as "brides of Christ." Until changes were made in some orders in the 1950s and 1960s, "marriage" ceremonies were carried out, during the course of which the novice would cut her hair, receive her religious name, and sometimes be given a wedding ring. After several years, a novice took a vow of perpetual profession, after which she was required to receive dispensation if she chose to leave.

Women's orders today show a considerable diversity in their beliefs and modes of life. In some convents, sisters still dress in full traditional habit and live together in communities removed from the secular world. In other convents, by contrast, the nuns wear ordinary dress and may live in apartments or houses. Traditional restrictions such as not talking to others at certain periods of the day or walking with the hands folded and hidden under the habit are rarely evident.

In spite of such liberalization, women have filled only inferior positions in religious organizations. This situation is changing, in line with changes affecting women in society generally. In recent years, women's groups have pressed to achieve equal status in religious orders. Increasingly, the Catholic and Episcopalian churches are under strong pressure to allow women an equal voice in their hierarchies. Yet in 1977, the Sacred Congregation for the Doctrine of the Faith in Rome declared formally that women could not be admitted to the Catholic priesthood; the reason given was that Jesus had not called a woman

The first female Episcopal bishop, Barbara Harris.

to be one of his disciples. Ten years later, 1987 was officially designated as the "Year of the Madonna," in which women were advised to recall their traditional role as wife and mother. The barriers to Catholic women in the hierarchy of the church thus remain formidable. In a letter published in May 1994, Pope John Paul II reaffirmed the Roman Catholic church's ban on the ordination of women. The letter stated: "Wherefore, in order that all doubt may be removed regarding a matter of great importance . . . I declare that the Church has no authority to confer priestly ordination on women and that this judgment is to be definitively held by all the Church's faithful."

Since 1981, the Anglican church in Britain has permitted women to be deacons, but that role is ambiguous. They are officially part of the laity and are not allowed to conduct basic religious rituals, like pronouncing blessings or solemnizing marriages. On the other hand, at the direction of an Anglican priest, a deacon may administer certain sacraments and conduct baptisms. In 1986, the standing committee of the Anglican church's General Synod, composed of ten men and two women, examined the legislation that would be needed were women to be admitted to the priesthood. According to their report, their stated task was to consider the "safeguards necessary to meet the objections of those within the Church of England who are unable to accept, for one reason or another, the ordination of women as priests." The feelings and aspirations of women themselves found little mention.

Women were finally accepted as priests in Britain only in 1993. The change provoked much dissent and opposition (it was opposed by some women's organizations as well as by male Anglicans). Some groups left the Anglican church altogether and converted to Catholicism—in which women are still banned from becoming priests. The Anglican church in the United States (the Episcopal church) has been more open and has allowed women into its priesthood since 1976. Altogether, women have been ordained as ministers in about half of the Protestant denominations in the United States, including the Presbyterian Church (U.S.A.), the Evangelical Lutheran Church in America, the African Methodist Episcopal Church, and the United Methodist Church. And, with the exception of orthodox Judaism, women in the United States can become rabbis.

Religion in the United States has followed different paths from most other Western countries. The following sections, therefore, focus on this country.

RELIGION IN THE UNITED STATES

Freedom of religious expression was made a tenet of the American Constitution long before tolerance of varied religious beliefs and practices was widespread in any other Western society. The early settlers were refugees from religious oppression by political authorities and were suspicious of the close association between state and church that existed in their lands of origin. State and church remain more separate in the United States today than in most other industrialized countries.

The United States also contains a far greater diversity of religious groups than any other industrialized country. In most Western societies, the majority of the population are formally affiliated with a single church, such as the Italians with the Catholic church. Almost 90 percent of the American population are Christian, but they belong to a variety of churches and denominations. The largest body by far in the United States is the Catholic church, which numbers some 58 million members (see Figure 15.1). However, it makes up only about 25 percent of total membership of religious organizations. Around 63 percent of the population are Protestant, but they are divided among numerous denominations, and their relative share is declining. The Southern Baptist Convention is the largest, with over 15 million members, followed by the United Methodist church, the National Baptist Convention, and the Lutheran and Presbyterian churches. Among non-Christian groups, the largest are the Jewish congregations, numbering around 6 million members. About 10 percent of the population fall into the category of other or no religious affiliation.

Membership of religious organizations correlates quite closely with socioeconomic differences (see Table 15.2). The majority of Baptists are compara-

Table 15.2 Social and Economic Status of Religious Groups

Religious Group	% College Graduate	% Income Over $20,000
Jews	38	50
Episcopalians	34	44
Presbyterians	25	42
Catholics	12	34
Methodists	12	32
Southern Baptists	6	23
African-American Protestants	7	15

Source: Roof and McKinney, 1987.

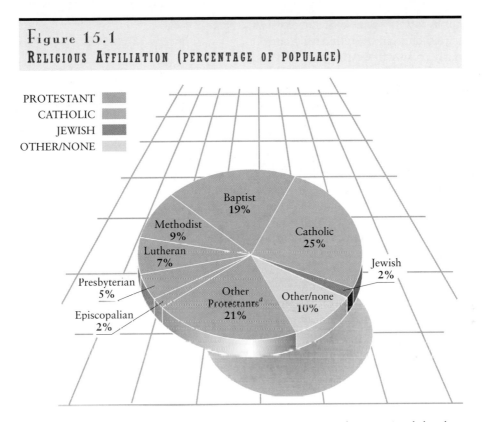

Figure 15.1
RELIGIOUS AFFILIATION (PERCENTAGE OF POPULACE)

PROTESTANT
CATHOLIC
JEWISH
OTHER/NONE

Baptist
19%

Methodist
9%

Lutheran
7%

Catholic
25%

Jewish
2%

Presbyterian
5%

Other
Protestants[a]
21%

Other/none
10%

Episcopalian
2%

[a]"Other Protestants" includes other, no denomination given, or a nondenominational church.
SOURCE: Surveys by the National Opinion Research Center, 1989, 1990, and 1991 combined.

tively poor, whereas Presbyterians and Episcopalians are disproportionately represented among those in higher income positions. Jews have a higher average income than any major Protestant denomination. These general comparisons are important, but they have to be interpreted with care. Many of the poorest groups in the United States are Catholics—including especially people of Latino background. There are large differences in income within all the major Protestant denominations.

Religion and Ethnicity

The divisions between whites and African Americans in American society are perhaps more clearly seen in religion than in any other area of social life. The saying "Eleven o'clock on a Sunday morning is the most segregated hour of the week" is as valid in 2000 as at any time in the past.

Before the Civil War, it was common for whites and blacks to attend church together as members of the same congregations. Subsequent religious segregation derived in large part from attempts on the part of whites to ensure that blacks were excluded from mixing with them culturally or socially. An additional factor, however, was the wish of leaders of some African-American denominations to secure their free and independent development. Black Baptist groups were among the first to break away, in the late 1860s. Most other denominations had followed suit by the turn of the century, at which point the independent black churches claimed nearly 3 million members in a total African-American population of just over 8 million. It has been said that black religion was the one institution over which African Americans maintained control. The price of autonomy and self-control was a separate and segregated church, one effectively cut off socially and religiously from white America (Roof and McKinney, 1987).

Numerous African-American religious organizations have been formed or have splintered off from more established groups during the course of the twentieth century. The largest black denomination today is the National Baptist Convention, with over 5 million members, followed by the National Baptist Convention of America, with just over half that number. About 85 percent of all African-American Protestant members of religious organizations belong to black denominations (compared with an estimate of 88 percent made by H. Richard Niebuhr in the 1920s [Niebuhr, 1929]).

The majority of white denominations number only 2–3 percent black members; the two groups with the largest proportions are the American Baptists and the Seventh-Day Adventists. Even in these denominations, however, African Americans mainly belong to all-black *congregations*, so it would scarcely be meaningful to speak of a significant degree of integration here. Some steps have been taken in recent years to promote wider racial inclusiveness; the United Methodists, Episcopalians, and United Church of Christ in particular have taken the lead in giving leadership positions to African Americans. Yet the general picture in the religious sphere is one of persistent and entrenched separation between whites and blacks.

Religious Behavior

Some 40 percent of the American population on average attend a church or synagogue service each week; this figure has declined somewhat since the late 1950s from 47 percent (see Table 15.3). This is much higher than comparable rates for most other industrialized countries. The upper socioeconomic groups attend church more regularly than those in the poorer sections of society, a finding that holds in the other industrialized societies also. Catholics on average attend church more regularly than Protestants, and more affluent Catholics show higher rates of attendance than their poorer counterparts.

Table 15.3 Growing Secularization?

Year	Percentage Professing No Religious Preference	Percentage Who Are Members of a Religious Body	Percentage Who Attended Religious Service
1957	3	73	47
1990	11	65	40

Year	Percentage Who Reported that Religion Is Important in Their Lives
1952	75
1965	70
1978	52.7
1990	58

SOURCE: U.S. Bureau of the Census, 1994, p. 70; *Public Opinion Quarterly* (Fall 1992), 56(3):368–69.

Religious Change in the United States

CATHOLICISM

Although Catholics continue to grow in number, church attendance especially has shown a sharp decline over the past few decades, beginning in the 1960s and leveling off in the mid-1970s. One of the main reasons was the papal encyclical of 1968, which reaffirmed the ban on the use of contraceptives among Catholics. The encyclical offered no leeway for people whose conscience allowed for the use of contraceptives. They were faced with disobeying the church, and many Catholics did just that. Over three-quarters of Catholic women of childbearing age use contraceptive devices, and more than 80 percent of all Catholics are in favor of the use of contraception (Greeley,

1977). In addition, almost half of all American Catholics reject the notion that the pope infallibly represents the voice of God. A large proportion of Catholics have therefore come to doubt or defy the church's authority over various areas of their lives.

PROTESTANTISM

Church attendance by Protestants has remained fairly stable from 1950 to the present, but other, significant changes are occurring within Protestantism today. One such change is the dividing of Protestant denominations into modernists and fundamentalists. Modernists are politically liberal, do not interpret the Bible literally, and have formed an "intellectual" commitment to their beliefs. The fundamentalists are conservative in their politics, view the Bible literally as the word of God, and are committed emotionally to their religious values and practices. Both types are found in many churches and denominations; the more established churches are primarily modernist.

The more liberal Protestant denominations include the Methodists, Episcopalians, and Lutherans. Their membership has remained stable or declined in recent years. The fundamentalist organizations, on the other hand, have been attracting a growing following. We shall return to them later, since they warrant special consideration.

JUDAISM

Jews in the United States are both a religious denomination and an ethnic minority. There are more Americans who consider themselves and are regarded by others as Jewish but who don't subscribe to any of the core religious beliefs of Judaism or participate in Jewish religious activities than there are Jews who do hold such beliefs. Attendance at temple or synagogue services has always been lower than for Christian denominations. Well under 20 percent of American Jews attend services more than once a month, although there is little indication that this proportion is declining.

Judaism is not a faith that actively seeks converts. Consequently, one change likely to affect American Jews is the rising rate of intermarriage with non-Jewish partners. Twenty-five years ago, no more than 5 percent of Jews married outside their religion;

today, more than a third do so. Given that many of the children of these marriages may be raised outside the Jewish faith, this trend seriously threatens the continuity of Judaism within the United States.

NEW CULTS

Since World War II, more religious movements have been founded in the United States than at any previous time in its history. Over this period, there has occurred an unprecedented series of mergers and divisions between denominations. Most have proved short-lived, but a few have achieved notable followings.

An example is the Unification church, founded by the Korean Sun Myung Moon. This cult was introduced into the United States at the beginning of the 1960s, and it appealed to many who at the time were rejecting traditional religion and looking for insight in Eastern religious teachings. The Unification church mixed Eastern ideas with elements of fundamentalist Christianity and showed a strong bent toward anticommunism.

The cult boasts a membership of forty thousand in the United States today. Its members are expected to fraternize only with one another, to donate their property to the cult, and to obey Moon's commands. Moon's doctrine of "heavenly deception" permits members to mislead the public when asking for money—for instance, by posing as a charity. Substantial funds were accumulated in this way, and as a result Moon was imprisoned for a year and a half in 1984 on charges of tax evasion.

The beliefs held in the new cults might seem bizarre mixtures of traditional and modern religious ideas, but in fact all long-established religions mix elements taken from diverse cultural sources. The baby boomers studied by Wade Clark Roof, referred to earlier, are experimenting with a variety of mixed religious beliefs and practices.

CHRISTIAN FUNDAMENTALISM

The growth of Christian fundamentalist religious organizations in the United States is one of the most notable features of the past thirty years. **Fundamentalism** is a loose label for a variety of viewpoints that emphasize a return to literal interpretations of the scriptural texts, which followers believe are under attack. Fundamentalists believe that "the Bible, quite bluntly, is a workable guidebook for politics, government, business, families, and all of the affairs of mankind" (Capps, 1990). Fundamentalism is a reaction against liberal theology and against attendance at church by people who do not take much active interest in religion. It is both a trend toward revivalism within existing religious organizations and an innovative force stimulating the development of new religions. The spread of fundamentalism is a worldwide phenomenon; the Islamic Revolution in Iran, for example, is a form of Islamic fundamentalism.

THE "ELECTRONIC CHURCH"

The electronic media (television and radio) have been centrally involved in changes affecting religion in the United States since the 1960s. The Reverend Billy Graham was the first to preach regularly to the nation across the airwaves, and through effective use of the media, this Baptist preacher amassed a large following. Increasingly over the last twenty years, we have seen even more sophisticated and systematic use of the media for spreading religious messages and raising money for ministries. The "electronic church"—religious organizations that operate primarily through the media rather than local congregation meetings—has come into being. Through satellite communications, religious programs can now be beamed across the world into Third World countries (for example, in Africa and Asia) as well as to other industrialized societies.

Fundamentalist and other groups seeking to convert nonbelievers have been the main pioneers of the electronic church. One reason for this is the "star system," inspirational preachers who draw followers to themselves on the basis of their personal appeal. Some such preachers are ideally suited to the electronic media, by means of which their charismatic qualities can be projected to an audience of thousands or even millions of people. Besides Billy Graham, other "electronic preachers" such as Oral Roberts, Jerry Falwell, Jimmy Swaggart, Pat Robertson, and Jim Bakker and his ex-wife Tammy Faye have made the media their main preoccupation, relying almost wholly on broadcasting to gain a following.

Some religious broadcasters, including Jim and Tammy Bakker and Jimmy Swaggart, were caught up in sexual or financial scandals that seriously damaged their reputations. Because the standing of such individuals has suffered, some have suggested that the peak of the influence of the electronic church has passed. It may be true that revivalist and fundamentalist groups are losing their dominant position, but the broader connections between religious organizations and the electronic media are unlikely to come to an end. TV, radio, and other forms of electronic communication constitute a prime influence in the modern world, and this is bound to continue to stimulate religious programming.

The electronic preaching of religion has become particularly prevalent in Latin America, where North American programs are shown. As a result, Protestant movements, most of them of the Pentecostal kind, have made a dramatic impact upon such countries as Chile and Brazil, which are predominantly Catholic (Martin, 1990).

THE SOCIOLOGICAL DEBATE

IS THE UNITED STATES A SECULAR OR SACRED SOCIETY?

Has the significance of religion in Americans' lives declined over time? Adherents of secularization theory argue that religion has declined in social significance during the last century, while opponents point to empirical and historical evidence showing that religious participation in the United States has steadily increased over time.

Sociologist Peter Berger, in his 1967 book *The Sacred Canopy*, described secularization as the process by which society becomes more concerned with worldly matters than with spiritual matters, and religious organizations lose their influence over social life. Secularization is one aspect of the massive transformation of Western society over the last two centuries, which has included industrialization, urbanization, and an emphasis on rational thought.

Berger further observed that secularization has occurred on three levels: societal, cultural, and individual. At the societal level, religious organizations no longer exercise substantial control or influence over social institutions such as the state or education. Secularization has also influenced cultural life: the arts, literature, and philosophy less frequently draw on religious sources for inspiration. Finally, at the individual level, the secularization of consciousness has occurred. Berger (1967, p. 107) explains that "the modern West has produced an increasing number of individuals who look upon the world and their own lives without benefit of religious interpretations."

The basic assumptions of secularization theory have been hotly contested, however. Critics contend that religion continues to play an important and vigorous role in modern societies—particularly in the United States. The argument against secularization theory is bolstered by an accumulation of both survey data and observation of historical trends. Observation of recent religious behavior in the United States reveals multiple new movements, including the flowering of "new religious movements" in the 1960s and 1970s; the spread of Pentecostal and charismatic movements since the 1960s; the restructuring of "American mainline religion" driven by the rapid growth of conservative Protestant churches such as the Southern Baptist Convention; and the involvement of conservative fundamentalists in politics, notably the Moral Majority and the Christian Coalition.

Surveys of nationally representative samples of Americans also reveal a remarkable persistence of religious beliefs and practices. In his 1989 book *Religious Change in America*, University of Chicago sociologist Andrew Greeley documented that in 1944, 97 percent of Americans claimed to believe in the existence of God or a universal spirit, and in 1981, 95 percent still so believed.

While Greeley's work counters secularization theory through the use of empirical sociological analyses, several sociologists have developed a new theoretical model of religion that refutes secularization theory. In their 1987 book *A Theory of Religion*, sociologists Rodney Stark and William Sims Bainbridge proposed a "religious economies" model. Drawing on rational choice theory, the authors argue that a "religious economy" consists of all religious activity occurring in a society. Religious economies are like commercial economies in that they consist of a market of current and potential customers, a set of firms serving that market, and religious "product lines" offered by various firms. Also like commercial economies, religious economies thrive when they are allowed to operate without government interference. According to this theory, deregulation (i.e., operating without government interference) leads to pluralism, pluralism to competition, competition to specialization of product (i.e., catering to a market niche) and aggressive recruitment, specialization and recruitment to higher demand, and higher demand to greater participation. Thus, as a "natural" consequence of the free market, over time the diversity of the religious market will reflect the very diversity of the population itself.

The religious economies model is supported with historical data in Roger Finke and Rodney Stark's 1992 book *The Churching of America*. The authors argue that the most striking feature of American religious history has been the "churching of America," or the growth in church membership from colonial times through the present. Finke and Stark document that between 1776 and 1990, religious "adherence" in the United States grew from 17 percent to 60 percent, and that this increase in religious adherence over time is exactly the opposite of what is predicted by secularization theory. Religious competition has stimulated, not weakened, religiosity in the United States, they conclude.

One ramification of the debate between secularization theory adherents and religious economies model proponents is that a new vision of secularization has been formulated. Sociologist Mark Chaves, in his 1994 essay "Secularization as Declining Religious Authority," concludes that secularization could be "best understood not as the decline of religion, but as the declining scope of religious authority." Specifically, secularization occurs when religious authorities have a lessened ability to influence and control societal-level institutions, and individual-level beliefs and behaviors. In a recent article, sociologist Philip Gorski adopts a similar definition of secularization ("declining religious authority") and shows that the pattern has not been one of simple decline, but of ups and downs (Gorski, 2000). Gorski argues that the only thing that can be said with any confidence is that modern people are less influenced by institutionalized and traditional forms of religion. In short, what we are witnessing is an individualization and rationalization of religiosity. Whether that is to be construed as a decline of religiosity depends on how one defines "true" religion, which is a theological question, not a sociological one.

It remains to be seen whether Chaves's and Gorski's refined secularization perspectives will be widely accepted as an alternative to the old view of secularization or the religious economies view that challenged it. Regardless of the outcome of the dispute, the debate over secularization has energized the sociological study of religion, and has reawakened sociologists to the continuing importance of religion in modern society.

Religion, Political Power, and Fundamentalism

Some fundamentalists in the United States have sought to establish direct connections between religion and politics. Those who incline toward fundamentalism tend to believe strongly in "family values," the undesirability of abortion, and the importance of patriotism, among other social issues. And they have fought to make their views on these issues count in the public domain. One expression of this political activism is the Moral Majority, founded by the Reverend Jerry Falwell in 1980. The Moral Majority is nominally a political body, but gains its membership and financial resources from its association with fundamentalist religious organizations.

Fundamentalism isn't likely to conquer America. But in some countries, such as Iran and Algeria, religious fundamentalists have either successfully or nearly come to political power. And in other countries, fundamentalist movements have made a significant impact. Fundamentalist religious beliefs hark back to the old. They are about the recovery of tradition, about rediscovering basic beliefs, values, and practices of the past that fundamentalists feel are in danger of being lost. Yet fundamentalism is actually something new. It is a *reaction*, in fact, to the changing social conditions in which we live today, both individually and globally. Fundamentalism reasserts traditional forms of morality in a world that has become increasingly **cosmopolitan**, where, as a result of globalization, many different ideas and values are brought into constant contact with one another.

But this is why fundamentalism, especially when connected to political goals, can be troubling. For fundamentalists, who proclaim the necessary truth of their beliefs, tend to be intolerant of beliefs other than their own. What is disturbing is not the existence of fundamentalist beliefs themselves, but their potential for stimulating violence. Violence is always a possibility when groups who strongly hold a particular view of the world have little concern to understand the outlooks of others. Violent clashes between religious fundamentalist groups and with government authorities, especially where those groups are trying to reach political ends, have become commonplace in the world today; examples are the conflicts between fundamentalist Hindus and Muslims in India and between Islamic fundamentalists and the government in Algeria.

CONCLUSION

In the shape of fundamentalism and in the diversity of new groups and sects found in the United States and elsewhere, religion remains a vital force in society. It might appear strange, therefore, to suggest that the influence of religion in the modern world is actually declining. However, sociologists generally agree that such a decline has taken place, considered at least as a long-term trend.

Until the modern period, the churches rivaled and frequently surpassed monarchs and governments in the political power they wielded and the wealth they managed to accumulate. The priesthood maintained control over the skills of literacy, scholarship, and learning. As in other areas of social life, much of this changed as industrialization took hold. Churches and religious organizations in Western countries lost most of their secular power. Governments took over tasks that the churches had previously controlled, including education.

Toward the end of the nineteenth century, the German philosopher Friedrich Nietzsche announced, "God is dead." Religions, he argued, used to be a point of reference for our sense of purpose and meaning. Henceforth, we would have to live without this security, and indeed without any fixed moral reference points at all. Living in a world without God means creating our own values and getting used to what Nietzsche called "the loneliness of being"—understanding that our lives are without purpose and that no superior entities watch over our fate.

There can be little doubt that the hold of religious beliefs today is less than was generally the case in the past, particularly if we include under the term "religion" the whole range of supernatural phenomena in which people once believed. Most of us do not any longer see the world as permeated by spirits and demons.

Modern rationalist thought and religious outlook exist in an uneasy state of tension. A rationalist perspective permeates a good portion of our existence, and its hold in all probability will not become weakened in the foreseeable future. Yet there are bound to be reactions against rationalism, leading to periods of religious revivalism, as is happening today. There are probably few individuals on the face of the earth who have not been touched by religious sentiments at some time in their lives. Science and rationalist thinking remain silent on questions of the meaning and purpose of life, matters that have always been at the core of religion.

SUMMARY

1. There are no known societies that do not have some form of religion, although religious beliefs and practices vary from culture to culture. All religions involve a set of *symbols*, invoking feelings of reverence, linked to *rituals* practiced by a community of believers.

2. *Totemism* and *animism* are common types of religion in smaller cultures. In totemism, a species of animal or plant is perceived as possessing supernatural powers. Animism means a belief in spirits or ghosts, populating the same world as human beings, sometimes "possessing" them.

3. The three most influential *monotheistic* religions (religions in which there is one God) in world history are Judaism, Christianity, and Islam. *Polytheism* (belief in several or many gods) is common in other religions. In some religions, like Buddhism and Confucianism, there are no gods or supernatural beings.

4. Sociological approaches to religion have been most influenced by the ideas of the three "classical" thinkers: Marx, Durkheim, and Weber. All believed that religion is fundamentally an illusion. They held that the "other" world that religion creates is *our* world, distorted through the lens of religious symbolism.

To Marx, religion contains a strong ideological element: religion provides justification for the inequalities of wealth and power found in society. To Durkheim, religion is important because of the cohesive functions it serves, especially in ensuring that people meet regularly to affirm common beliefs and values. To Weber, religion is important because of the role it plays in social change, particularly the development of Western capitalism.

5. Several different types of religious organization can be distinguished. A *church* is a large, established religious body, having a bureaucratic structure. *Sects* are small, and aim at restoring the original purity of doctrines that have become "corrupted" in the hands of official churches. A *denomination* is a sect that has become institutionalized, having a permanent form. A *cult* is a loosely knit group of people who follow the same leader or pursue similar religious ideals.

6. *Religious movements* have played a central part in the development of religion in general, as well as influencing other aspects of social life. *Millenarian movements*, which anticipate the coming of the "millennium," or "golden age," have been an important feature of the history of Christianity.

7. Secularization refers to the declining influence of religion. Measuring the level of secularization is complicated, because several dimensions of change are involved. Although the influence of religion has definitely declined, religion is certainly not on the verge of disappearing, and continues to show great diversity in the modern world. Religion can act as both a conservative and revolutionary force in society.

8. Religious organizations are generally dominated by men. In most religions, particularly Christianity, the images and symbols are mostly masculine; female imagery stresses gentleness and passivity.

social change in the modern world

All the chapters in this book emphasize the sweeping nature of the social changes that have taken place in the modern era. For virtually the whole of human history, the pace of social change was relatively slow; most people followed ways of life similar to those of their forebears. By contrast, we live today in a world subject to dramatic and continuous transformation. In the remaining chapters, we look at some of the major areas of change.

One of the most far-reaching influences of globalization is concerned with the growing field known as sociology of the body. Chapter 16 examines the many ways that global processes affect our bodies, including our diets, our health, our sexual behavior, and our aging.

The globalizing of social life also both influences and is influenced by changing patterns of urbanization, the subject of Chapter 17. This chapter also analyzes two of the most far-reaching changes occurring in modern times, the tremendous growth in world population and the increasing threat of environmental problems. Population growth has been greatly affected by the spread of Western techniques of hygiene and medicine. At the

same time, global environment threats brought on by social change require global solutions if human societies are to continue to thrive in the future.

The concluding chapter looks directly at processes of change. One of the main characteristics of the modern era is the deliberate attempt to secure social and political change through collective action. In this chapter, we study some of the major processes of social change from the eighteenth century to the present day, and also analyze general mechanisms of protest and collective violence. We also consider general interpretations of the nature of social change. What is social change actually, and why has it become so profound and constant? Finally, we consider where present-day patterns of change are likely to lead us in the twenty-first century.

Chapter Sixteen

Learn that our bodies—including our health, sexual behavior, and aging process—are strongly affected by social influences.

The Well-Functioning Body: Images of Health and Illness

Recognize that health and illness are culturally and socially determined. Learn the social and cultural differences in the distribution of disease. Learn more about AIDS as a sociological phenomenon.

Human Sexuality

Learn about the debate over the importance of biological versus social and cultural influences on human sexual behavior. Explore the cultural differences in sexual behavior and patterns of sexual behavior today.

Aging

See that aging is socially influenced and that our concept of aging is changing.

THE SOCIOLOGY OF THE BODY: HEALTH AND ILLNESS, SEXUALITY, AND AGING

Look at the two photographs on the opposite page. The images of a sunken face and an emaciated body are almost identical. The young girl on the left is Somalian, dying from a simple lack of food. The young woman on the right is an American teenager, dying because, in a society with a superabundance of food, she chose not to eat or to eat so sparingly that her life was endangered.

The social dynamics involved in each case are utterly different. Starvation from lack of food is caused by factors outside people's control and affects only the very poor. The American teenager, living in the wealthiest country in the world, is suffering from anorexia, an illness with no known physical origin; obsessed with the ideal of achieving a slim body, she has eventually given up eating altogether. Anorexia and other eating disorders are illnesses of the affluent, not of those who have little or no food. It is completely unknown in the Third World countries where food is scarce, such as Somalia.

For much of human history, a few people like saints or mystics have deliberately chosen to starve themselves for religious reasons. They were almost always men. Today, anorexia primarily affects women, and it has no specific connection to religious beliefs. It is an illness of the body, and thus we might think that we would have to look to biological or physical factors to explain it. But health and illness, like other topics we've studied, are also affected by social and cultural influences, such as the pressure to achieve a slim body.

Although it is an illness that expresses itself in physical symptoms, anorexia is closely related to the idea of being on a diet, which in turn is connected with changing views of physical attractiveness, particularly of women, in modern society. In most premodern societies, such as those described in Chapter 3, the ideal female shape was a fleshy one. Thinness wasn't regarded as desirable at all—partly because it was associated with lack of food and therefore with poverty. Even in Europe in the 1600s and 1700s, the ideal female shape was well rounded. Anyone who has seen paintings of the period, such as those by Rubens, will have noticed how curvaceous the women depicted in them are. The notion of slimness as the desirable feminine shape originated among some middle-class groups in the late nineteenth century, but it has become generalized as an ideal for most women only recently.

Anorexia thus has its origins in the changing body image of women in the recent history of modern societies. It was first identified as a disorder in France in 1874, but it remained obscure until the past thirty or forty years (Brown and Jasper, 1993). Since then, it has become increasingly common among young women. So has bulimia—bingeing on food, followed by self-induced vomiting. Anorexia and bulimia are often found together in the same individual. Someone may become extremely thin through a starvation diet, and then enter a phase of eating enormous amounts and purging in order to maintain a normal weight, followed by a period of again becoming very thin.

Anorexia and other eating disorders are no longer obscure forms of illness in modern societies. About 95 percent of U.S. college women say that they want to lose weight and up to 85 percent suffer serious problems with eating disorders at some point in their college careers. Around 25 percent experience bulimic episodes or anorexia. In American society, 60 percent of girls age thirteen have already begun to diet; this proportion rises to over 80 percent for young women of eighteen. College men also suffer similar experiences, though not in the same proportions. About 50 percent of American male college students claimed that they wanted to lose weight, while about 30 percent were on diets (Hesse-Biber, 1997).

Once again, something that may seem to be a purely personal trouble—difficulties with food and despair over one's appearance—turns out to be a public issue. If we include not just life-threatening forms of anorexia but also obsessive concern with dieting and bodily appearance, eating disorders are now part of the lives of millions of people; they are found not only in the United States today, but in all the industrial countries.

The spread of eating disorders is astonishing, and brings home clearly the influence of social factors upon our lives. The field known as **sociology of the body** investigates the ways in which our bodies are affected by these social influences. As human beings, we obviously all possess bodies. But the body isn't something we just have, and it isn't only something physical that exists outside of society. Our bodies are deeply affected by our social experiences, as well as by the norms and values of the groups to which we belong. It is only recently that sociologists have begun to recognize the profound nature of the interconnections between social life and the body. This field is therefore quite a new area, but it is one of the most exciting.

Sociology of the body draws together a number of basic themes, which we shall make use of throughout the chapter. One major theme is the effects of social change on the body—as social change itself is emphasized throughout the book. A second theme is the increasing separation of the body from "nature"—from our surrounding environment and our biological rhythms. Our bodies are being invaded by the influence of science and technology, ranging from machines to diets, and this is creating new dilemmas. The invention of a range of reproductive technologies, for example, has introduced new options but has also generated intense social controversies. We shall look at two such controversies, over genetic engineering and abortion, later in the chapter.

The term "technology" shouldn't be understood in too narrow a way here. In its most basic sense, it refers to material technologies such as those involved in modern medicine—for example, the scanning machine that allows a doctor to chart a baby's development prior to birth. But we must also take account of what Michel Foucault (1988) has called **social technologies** affecting the body. By this phrase, he means that the body is increasingly something we have to "create" rather than simply accept. A social technology is any kind of regular intervention we make into the functioning of our bodies in order to alter them in specific ways. An example is dieting, so central to anorexia.

In what follows, we will first analyze why eating disorders have become so common. From there, we will study the social dimensions of health and illness. Then we will turn to human sexuality, again by looking at the social and cultural influences on our sexual behavior. Finally, we will consider the question of the aging body. Like so many other parts of our lives in modern societies, aging is not what it once was! The aging process is not simply a physical one, and the position of older people in society today is changing in basic ways.

THE WELL-FUNCTIONING BODY: IMAGES OF HEALTH AND ILLNESS

To understand why eating disorders have become so commonplace in current times, we should think back to the social changes analyzed earlier in the book. Anorexia actually reflects certain kinds of social change, including the impact of globalization.

The rise of eating disorders in Western societies coincides directly with the globalization of food production, which has increased greatly in the last three or four decades. The invention of new modes of refrigeration plus the use of container transportation have allowed food to be stored for long periods and to be delivered from one side of the world to the other. Since the 1950s, supermarket shelves have been abundant with foods from all parts of the world (for those who can afford it—now the majority of the population in Western societies). Most of them are available all the time, not just, as was true previously, when they are in season locally.

For the past few years, almost *everyone* in the United States and the other developed countries has been on a diet. This does not mean that everyone is desperately trying to get thin. Rather, when all foods are available more or less all the time, we must *decide* what to eat—in other words construct a diet, where "diet" means the foods we habitually consume. First, we have to decide what to eat in relation to the many sorts of new medical information with which science now bombards us—for instance, that cholesterol levels are a factor in causing heart disease. Second, we can now worry about the calorie content of different foods. In a society in which food is abundant, we are able for the first time to design our bodies in relation to our lifestyle habits (jogging, yoga) and what we eat. Eating disorders have their origins in the opportunities, but also the profound strains and tensions, this situation produces.

Why do eating disorders affect women in particular and young women most acutely? To begin with, it should be pointed out that not all those suffering from eating disorders are women; about 10 percent are men. But men don't suffer from anorexia or bulimia as often as women, partly because widely held social norms stress the importance of physical attractiveness more for women than for men, and partly because desirable body images of men differ from those of women.

When men have concerned themselves with the careful cultivation of the body, the muscular body has been the ideal. For many men who have taken it up, muscle building can become as compulsive or addictive as eating disorders are for women. In his book *Muscle*, for example, Sam Fussell describes how he took up muscle building to help control his feelings of inadequacy and anxiety about himself as "weedy." From being skinny, he became very muscular indeed—but then couldn't stop. He was unable to carry on his daily activities without including hours of weight training each day. The muscle builder can never be muscular enough, just as the anorexic can never be thin enough (Fussell, 1991).

Some women have now taken up muscle building, but most don't look in this direction when trying to achieve a body that conforms to their ideals. Their anxieties concentrate on fear of fatness. The modern

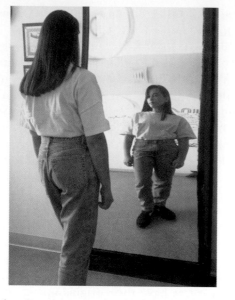

Distorted reality: Anorexia develops from deep insecurities about physical appearance.

ideal of the desirable woman is one who is thin and trim. Anorexia and bulimia are illnesses of the *active* woman. They don't just happen; they have to be actively accomplished. The anorectic individual sticks to a rigid, minimal diet and may do aerobics every day of the week.

Anorexia and other eating disorders reflect a situation in which women play a much larger part in the wider society than they used to, but are still judged as much by their appearance as their attainments. Eating disorders are rooted in feelings of shame about the body. The individual feels herself to be inadequate

and imperfect, and her anxieties about how others perceive her become focused through her feelings about her body. Ideals of slimness at that point become obsessive—shedding weight becomes the means of making everything all right in her world. Once she starts to diet and exercise compulsively, she can become locked into a pattern of refusing food altogether, or of vomiting up what she has eaten. If the pattern is not broken (and some forms of psychotherapy and medical treatment have proved effective here), the sufferer can actually starve herself to death.

The spread of eating disorders reflects the influence of science and technology upon our ways of life today: calorie counting has only been possible with the advance of technology. But the impact of technology is always conditioned by social factors. We have much more autonomy over the body than ever before, a situation that creates new possibilities of a positive kind as well as new anxieties and problems. What is happening is part of what sociologists call the **socialization of nature**. This phrase refers to the fact that phenomena that used to be "natural," or given in nature, have now become social—they depend upon our own social decisions.

Changing Conceptions of Health and Illness

Cultures differ in what they consider healthy and normal, as the discussion of eating disorders showed. All cultures have known concepts of physical health and illness, but most of what we now recognize as medicine is a consequence of developments in Western so-

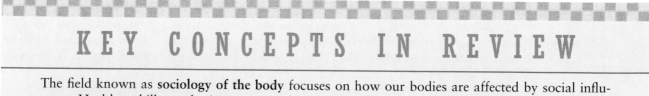

KEY CONCEPTS IN REVIEW

The field known as **sociology of the body** focuses on how our bodies are affected by social influences. Health and illness, for instance, are determined by social and cultural influences.

A **social technology** is a means by which we try to alter our bodies—for example, dieting.

The **socialization of nature** refers to the process by which we control phenomena regarded as "natural," such as reproduction.

ciety over the past three centuries. In premodern cultures, the family was the main institution coping with sickness or affliction. There have always been individuals who specialized as healers, using a mixture of physical and magical remedies, and many of these traditional systems of treatment survive today in non-Western cultures throughout the world. For instance, Ayurvedic medicine (traditional healing) has been practiced in India for nearly two thousand years. It is founded on a theory of the equilibrium of psychological and physical facets of the personality, imbalances of which are treated by nutritional and herbal remedies. Chinese folk medicine is similarly based on a conception of the overall harmony of the personality, involving the use of herbs and acupuncture, a technique in which needles are strategically inserted into a patient's skin.

Modern medicine introduced a view of disease that sees its origins and treatment as physical and explicable in scientific terms. The application of science to medical diagnosis and cure was the major feature of the development of modern health care systems. Other, closely related features were the acceptance of the hospital as the setting within which serious illnesses were to be dealt with and the development of the medical profession as a body with recognized codes of ethics and significant social power. The scientific view of disease was linked to the requirement that medical training be systematic and long-term; self-taught healers were excluded. Although professional medical practice is not limited to hospitals, the hospital provided an environment in which doctors for the first time were able to treat and study large numbers of patients, in circumstances permitting the concentration of medical technology.

In medieval times, the major illnesses were infectious diseases such as tuberculosis, cholera, malaria, and plague. The plague, or Black Death, of the four-teenth century (which was spread by fleas carried by rats) killed a quarter of the population of England and devastated large areas of Europe. Infectious diseases have now become a minor cause of death in the industrialized countries, and several have been substantially eradicated. In the industrialized countries, the most common causes of death are noninfectious diseases such as cancer and heart disease. Whereas in premodern societies the highest rates of death were among infants and young children, today

death rates (the proportion of the population who die each year) rise with increasing age.

In spite of the prestige that modern medicine has acquired, improvements in medical care accounted for only a relatively minor part of the decline in death rates prior to the twentieth century. Effective sanitation, better nutrition, control of sewage, and improved hygiene were more consequential, particularly in reducing the infant mortality rate and the number of deaths of young children. Drugs, advances in surgery, and antibiotics did not significantly decrease death rates until well into the twentieth century. Antibiotics used to treat bacterial infections first became available in the 1930s and 1940s, while immunizations (against diseases such as polio) were developed later.

Health and Illness in the Developed Countries

Within the industrial societies, there are striking differences in the distribution of the major diseases. Around 70 percent of deaths in Western countries are attributable to four major types of illness: cancer, heart disease, strokes, and lung disease. Some progress has been made in understanding their origins and in controlling their effects, but none can be effectively cured. Since the distribution of these four diseases varies among countries, regions, and classes, it seems evident that they are related to diet and lifestyle. Individuals from higher socioeconomic groups are on average healthier, taller, and stronger and live longer than those lower down the social scale. The differences are greatest when it comes to infant mortality (children dying in the first year of life) and child death, but as we saw earlier in Chapter 7, poorer people are at greater risk of dying at all ages than more affluent people. Let's now examine in more detail the uneven distribution of disease and of poor health generally among the different classes, races, and genders in American society.

SOCIAL CLASS–BASED INEQUALITIES IN HEALTH

Think about the way that we have previously defined "social class" in Chapter 7, as a concept that partakes of education, income, and occupation. In American society, people with better educations, higher incomes, and more prestigious occupations have better health. What is fascinating is that each of these dimensions of social class may be related to health and mortality for different reasons.

Income is the most obvious. In countries like the United States, where medical care is expensive and many persons are not covered by insurance, those with more financial resources have better access to physicians and medicine. But inequalities in health also persist in countries like Great Britain, which have national health insurance. One of the ways to understand this is to think beyond income about the other dimensions of social class, occupational status, and education.

Differences in occupational status may lead to inequalities in health and illness even when medical care is more or less evenly distributed. One study of health inequalities in Great Britain, *The Black Report* (Townsend and Davidson, 1982), found that manual workers had substantially higher mortality rates than professional workers, even though Britain's health service had made great strides in equalizing the distribution of health care. Indeed, different occupations are associated with different levels of on-the-job health risks.

Those who work in offices or in domestic settings are at less risk of injury or exposure to hazardous materials. The extent of industrial-based disease is difficult to calculate, because it is not always possible to determine whether an illness is acquired from working conditions or from other sources. However, some work-related diseases are well documented: lung disease is widespread in mining, as a result of dust inhalation; work with asbestos has been shown to produce certain types of cancer.

Differences in education, a third dimension of social class, also are correlated with inequalities in health and illness. Numerous studies document that education is positively related to preventative health behaviors. One set of researchers found that better educated people are significantly more likely to engage in aerobic exercise and to know their blood pressure, and are less likely to smoke or be overweight (Shea et al., 1991). Other researchers have found that poorly educated people tend to engage in more cigarette smoking; they also tend to have more problems associated with cholesterol and body weight (Winkleby et al., 1992).

RACE-BASED INEQUALITIES IN HEALTH

Life expectancy at birth in 1993 was about eighty years for white females and just seventy-four years for black females. Likewise, life expectancy at birth in 1993 was seventy-three years for white males yet just sixty-five years for black males (U.S. Bureau of the Census, 1996b).

Health differences between blacks and whites are significant. When we note such differences, we are making use of a variable—race—that, while different from social class, cannot be completely separated from it. One primary reason that there are inequalities of health between blacks and whites has to do with the fact that as a group blacks have less money than whites. Sixty-one percent of black households have no financial assets at all, twice the rate for white households (Oliver and Shapiro, 1995).

Some of the differences between black and white health go beyond economic causes to differences in cultural conditions. Take, for example, racial gaps in mortality. Young black men are more susceptible to murder than any other group. Whereas the murder rate for white males between fourteen and seventeen increased from 8 per 100,000 in 1984 to 14 in 1991, the rate for black males tripled during that time (from 32 per 100,000 to 112) (Wilson, 1996). This rise in violent crime has accompanied the rise of widespread crack-cocaine addiction, a cultural condition of poor African-American neighborhoods plagued by high levels of unemployment (Wilson, 1996).

Besides the life-expectancy and homicide rates, other race-based inequalities in health status are stark. There is a higher prevalence of hypertension among blacks—especially black men, a difference that may be biological. There are racial differences in cigarette smoking, with blacks smoking significantly more than whites. This may be due in some measure to cultural differences between blacks and whites, as well as the way in which the cigarette industry has deliberately targeted African Americans as a market.

But despite these depressing inequalities, it is important to note that some progress has been made in eradicating them. According to the National Center for Health Statistics (1996), racial differences in cigarette smoking have decreased. In 1965, half of white men and 60 percent of black men age eighteen and

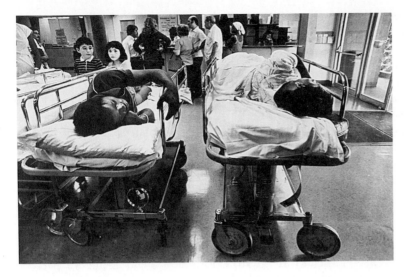

Haitian immigrants wait to be seen by doctors in a crowded emergency room in Miami. Generally, those of lower socioeconomic standing tend to suffer from a lower standard of health care.

over smoked cigarettes. By 1993, only 27 percent of white men and 33 percent of black men smoked. In 1965, roughly equal proportions of black and white women age eighteen and older smoked (33–34 percent). In 1993, a smaller proportion of black women (20 percent) smoked than did white women (23 percent).

Prevalence of hypertension among blacks has been greatly reduced. In the early 1970s, half of black adults suffered from hypertension. By 1991, however, 37 percent of black men and 31 percent of black women suffered hypertension.

Patterns of physician visitation, hospitalization, and preventative medicine have also changed. In 1987 only 30 percent of white women and 24 percent of black women age forty and older reported having a mammogram within the past two years. By 1993, the rate for white women doubled to 61 percent, and that for black women increased roughly 2.5 times to 59 percent. Between 1983 and 1993, the proportion of blacks who visited the dentist within the past year had increased from 39 percent to 47 percent, while the figures for whites increased from 57 percent to 64 percent.

How might the influence of poverty on health be countered? Extensive programs of health education and disease prevention are one possibility. But such programs tend to work better among more prosperous, well-educated groups and in any case usually produce only small changes in behavior. Increased accessibility to health services would help, but probably to a limited degree. The only really effective policy option is to attack poverty itself, so as to reduce the income gap between rich and poor (Najman, 1993).

GENDER-BASED INEQUALITIES IN HEALTH

Women in the United States are likely to live longer than men. This gender gap is, interestingly, a relatively recent phenomenon. In the United States, there was only a two-year difference in female and male life expectancies in 1900. By 1940, this gap increased to 4.4 years, and by 1970, the gap had widened to 7.7 years. The gender gap has since been stabilized at about 7 years (Cleary, 1987; National Center for Health Statistics, 1996).

How can we explain this changing gender gap? The main reason is that the leading cause of death has changed since the turn of the century. In 1900, the leading cause of death was infectious disease, which infected men, women, and children equally. Since mid-century, however, heart disease and cancer have been the leading causes of death to American adults. Heart disease and cancer are influenced by lifestyle, diet, and behavior—all of which are subject to gender differences.

Thus, social explanations for women's mortality advantage tend to focus on behavioral differences between men and women, including smoking, drinking, and preventative health behaviors. Men are more likely to smoke cigarettes than are women, and smoking is associated with heart disease and various types of cancer. Likewise, higher proportions of men than women drink alcoholic beverages, admit to "binge drinking," and smoke marijuana (see National Center for Health Statistics, 1996).

Some researchers argue that male roles lead men to adopt the Coronary Prone Behavior Pattern, or Type A personality, and that Type A personalities (i.e., persons who are competitive, impatient, ambitious, and aggressive) are twice as likely as "laid back" Type B personalities to suffer heart attacks (Spielberger et al., 1991). Indirect evidence for this hypothesis comes from examining gender differences in hypertension (i.e., elevated blood pressure or taking antihypertensive medication). In the early 1990s, 25 percent of men and 20 percent of women ages twenty to seventy-four reported having hypertension (see National Center for Health Statistics, 1996).

Sociologists tend to focus on societal factors in explaining these differences, but there are biological arguments that should also be considered. One study tested the hypothesis that higher male mortality rates are due to the greater stresses of the male role in the 1950s (competitiveness of the work force, pressure for success and high earnings) compared with the "easy life" that wives and mothers were believed to have. The study was conducted in a situation in which men and women shared equal roles and equal stresses: nuns and monks. The nuns lived longer than the monks, and both had life expectancies essentially the same as the rest of the population. Because the environment was equalized for the two groups, lifestyle factors such as diet, drinking, and stress could be ruled out as explanatory factors (Madigan, 1957). However, critics of this study note that the monks smoked more than the nuns did, so that lifestyle differences were not entirely accounted for.

Biologists have also cited the existence of genetic factors. Humans have twenty-three pairs of chromosomes, one of which determines sex. Males have XY sex chromosomes, while females have two X chromosomes. The X chromosome carries more genetic information than the Y, including some defects that can lead to physical abnormalities. Instead of making females more vulnerable to X-linked disorders, this seems to give females a genetic advantage. A female typically needs two defective X chromosomes for most genetically linked disorders to manifest them-

selves; otherwise, one healthy X chromosome can override the abnormal one. A male who has a defective X chromosome will have a genetically linked disease because there is no other X chromosome to cancel it out. This is thought to account for the higher number of miscarriages of male fetuses, and the greater ratio of male-to-female infant deaths, and deaths at all ages due to congenital abnormalities (Hayflick, 1994).

Despite the female advantage in mortality, most large surveys show women more often report poor health. Women have higher rates of illness from acute conditions and nonfatal chronic conditions, including arthritis, osteoporosis, and depressive and anxiety disorders. They are slightly more likely to report their health as fair to poor, they spend about 40 percent more days in bed each year, and their activities are restricted due to health problems about 25 percent more than men. In addition, they make more physician visits each year, and have twice the number of surgical procedures performed on them as do men (National Center for Health Statistics, 1996).

There are two main explanations for women's poorer health, yet longer lives: (1) Greater life expectancy and age brings poorer health; (2) women make greater use of medical services. In 1992, the av-

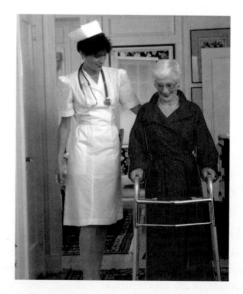

Women tend to make use of medical services more than do men.

THE WELL-FUNCTIONING BODY: IMAGES OF HEALTH AND ILLNESS

erage number of visits to physician offices, hospital emergency rooms, and hospital outpatient departments was 66 percent higher for women than for men, age fifteen to sixty-four. Men may experience as many or more health symptoms as women, but men may ignore symptoms, may underestimate the extent of their illness, or may utilize preventive services less often (Waldron, 1986).

The Third World: Colonialism and the Spread of Disease

There is good evidence that the hunting and gathering communities of the Americas, prior to the arrival of the Europeans, were not as subject to infectious disease as the European societies of the period. Many infectious organisms only thrive when human populations are living above the density characteristic of hunting and gathering life. Permanently settled communities, particularly large cities, risk contamination of water supplies by waste products. Hunters and gatherers were less vulnerable in this respect because they moved continuously across the countryside.

The expansion of the West in the colonial era transmitted certain diseases into other parts of the world where they had not existed previously. Smallpox, measles, and typhus, among other major maladies, were unknown to the indigenous populations of Central and South America prior to the Spanish conquest in the early sixteenth century. The English and French colonists brought the same diseases to North America (Dubos, 1959). Some of these illnesses produced epidemics so severe that they ravaged or completely wiped out native populations, which had little or no resistance to them.

In Africa and subtropical parts of Asia, infectious diseases have almost certainly been rife for a long period of time. Tropical and subtropical conditions are especially conducive to diseases such as malaria, carried by mosquitoes, and sleeping sickness, carried by the tsetse fly. Yet it seems probable that, prior to contact with the Europeans, levels of risk from infectious diseases were lower. There was always the threat of epidemics, drought, or natural disaster, but colonialism led to major changes in the relation between populations and their environments, producing harmful effects upon health patterns. The Europeans introduced new farming methods, upsetting the ecology of whole regions. For example, wide tracts of East Africa today are completely devoid of cattle as a result of the uncontrolled spread of the tsetse fly, which multiplied as a result of the changes the intruders introduced. Before the arrival of the Europeans, Africans successfully maintained large herds in these same areas (Kjekshus, 1977).

The most significant consequence of the colonial system was its effect upon nutrition, and therefore on levels of resistance to illness, as a result of the changed economic conditions involved in producing for world markets. In many parts of Africa in particular, the nutritional quality of native diets became substantially depressed as cash-crop production supplanted the production of native foods.

This was not simply a one-way process, however, as the early development of colonialism also radically changed Western diets, having a paradoxical impact so far as health is concerned. On the one hand, Western diets were improved by the addition of a range of new foods either previously unknown or very rare, like bananas, pineapples, and grapefruit. On the other hand, the importation of tobacco and coffee, together with raw sugar, which began increasingly to be used in all manner of foods, has had harmful consequences. Smoking tobacco, especially, has been linked to the prevalence of cancer and heart disease.

INFECTIOUS DISEASES TODAY

Although major strides have been made in reducing, and in some cases virtually eliminating, infectious diseases in the Third World (with the important exception of AIDS, which we will discuss in the next section), they remain far more common there than in the West. The most important example of a disease that has almost completely disappeared from the world is smallpox, which, even as recently as the 1960s, was a scourge of Europe as well as many other parts of the world. Campaigns against malaria have been much less successful. When the insecticide DDT was first produced, it was hoped that the mosquito, the prime carrier of malaria, could be eradicated. At first, considerable progress was made, but this has slowed down because some strains of mosquito have become resistant to DDT.

Basic medical resources are still lacking in the vast majority of Third World countries. The hospitals that do exist, together with trained doctors, tend to be heavily concentrated in urban areas, where their services are mostly monopolized by the affluent minority. Most Third World countries have introduced some form of national health service, organized by the central government, but the medical services available are usually very limited. The small section of the wealthy utilize private health care, sometimes traveling to the West when sophisticated medical treatment is needed. Conditions in many Third World cities, particularly in the shanty towns, make the control of infectious diseases very difficult: many shanty areas almost completely lack basic services such as water, sewage, and garbage disposal.

Studies carried out by the World Health Organization suggest that more than two-thirds of people living in urban areas in Third World countries draw their water from sources that fail to meet minimal safety standards (see Global Map 16.1). It has been estimated that seventeen out of the twenty-five common water-related diseases in Third World nations could either be cut by half, or eradicated altogether, simply by the provision of ready supplies of safe water (Doyal and Pennell, 1981). Only about a quarter of the city residents in Third World countries have water-borne sewage facilities; some 30 percent have no sanitation at all. These conditions provide breeding grounds for diseases such as cholera (Dwyer, 1975).

Illness as Stigma: The Impact of AIDS

Not all illnesses are found more frequently among poorer rather than more affluent groups. Anorexia, for instance, is more common among people from higher socioeconomic backgrounds. The same is true of AIDS (acquired immune deficiency syndrome), at least in the United States and other industrial countries.

AIDS is a mysterious disease, which has come from nowhere to become a major health hazard in less than twenty years. AIDS causes the body's immune system to collapse; it does not cause death itself, but the suf-ferer becomes prey to a range of fatal illnesses. Everyone who becomes infected with the virus to which most medical researchers believe it is linked, HIV (human immune-deficiency virus), seems sooner or later to develop AIDS. AIDS is believed to be transmitted either by direct blood-to-blood contact (as occurs in blood transfusions or when drug users share needles) or through sexually emitted fluids (semen or vaginal secretion).

No one knows whether AIDS had its origins in the socialization of nature, as an unintended outcome of human intervention into the world around us. Some have suggested as much, however. It has been speculated, for example, that the disease might be the result of experiments with forms of germ warfare, which unsuspectingly created a lethal virus. Others argue that AIDS and HIV have been around a long while, perhaps for centuries, in certain parts of the world. According to this theory, the symptoms now recognized as AIDS might previously have been mistaken for other diseases.

A distinctive characteristic of AIDS, compared with the majority of other illnesses, is that it can be transmitted sexually. The disease first made its appearance in North America among male homosexual groups, and initially, both among medical researchers and in the eyes of the public, AIDS was seen as a homosexual disease. AIDS came into the public consciousness at a time, the early 1980s, when it seemed that many of the preestablished prejudices against homosexuality were collapsing. But the disease seemed to those repelled by homosexuality, especially some religious groups, to provide concrete evidence of their hostile views. The idea that AIDS is a plague sent by God to punish "perversion" even found expression in some respectable medical quarters. An editorial in a medical journal asked: "Might we be witnessing, in fact, in the form of a modern communicable disorder, a fulfillment of St. Paul's pronouncement: 'The due penalty of their error'?" (Altman, 1986).

The rapid spread of AIDS was undoubtedly due in some degree to the increased opportunities for homosexual encounters provided by gay subcultures in North America and elsewhere. In fact, at first AIDS seemed to be limited almost exclusively to large American cities with significant gay populations. Headlines in the press set the early tone: "Gay plague baffling medical detectives" (*Philadelphia Daily News*, August

9, 1982); "Being gay is a health hazard" (*Saturday Evening Post*, October 1982); "Gay plague has arrived in Canada" (*Toronto Star*). The magazine *Us* reported: "Male homosexuals aren't so gay any more." At the time, it was already known that probably a third of those with AIDS in the United States were not homosexual, but in the initial publicity this was virtually ignored.

When the actor Rock Hudson died of AIDS in 1985, what shocked much of the world's press was not the nature of his illness but the fact that this symbol of male virility was homosexual. Rather than looking for the source of the disease in a particular virus, medical researchers first tried to discover its origins in specific gay practices. The discovery that AIDS can be transmitted through heterosexual contact then forced a reappraisal; most of the evidence for this came from central Africa, where AIDS was widespread but had no particular relation to male homosexuality. The "gay plague" soon became redefined by the press as a "heterosexual nightmare."

The impact of AIDS is likely to influence many forms of sexual behavior. In the homosexual community, marked changes are noticeable; the level of casual sexual encounters has been radically reduced. Some of the most widely condemned homosexual practices, paradoxically, turn out to be the safest. For example, sadomasochistic activities involving the infliction of discomfort or pain on a partner are safe because there is no direct genital contact. The dilemma facing male gay communities is how to foster procedures of "safe sex" while warding off the renewed attacks to which the gay community is subject.

AIDS AND THE HETEROSEXUAL POPULATION

In medical terms, AIDS is a moving target, new and elusive. Medical knowledge about the disease dates very quickly. And today it is becoming a global epidemic. The true number of people infected with HIV is unknown, but conservative estimates put the figure at 13 million worldwide. About 530,000 of these are in Europe, 860,000 in North America, 1.6 million in Latin America and the Caribbean, and more than 21 million in Africa (see Global Map 16.2). The main impact of the epidemic

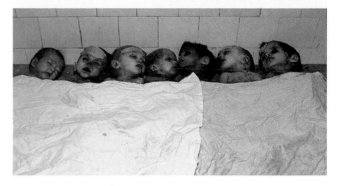

The bodies of Romanian babies who died of AIDS.

is still to come, because of the time it takes for HIV infection to develop into full-blown AIDS. The majority of people affected in the world today are heterosexuals. Worldwide, at least four HIV infections are contracted heterosexually for every instance of homosexual spread. The World Health Organization estimated that by the year 2000, more than 30 million adults and 10 million children had become infected.

The fact that at first AIDS was most prevalent among homosexuals has served to revive prejudices against homosexuality. However, new and terrifying as it is, AIDS raises fears and hostilities independent of antagonisms held toward homosexuals. Some of these were explored in the movie *Philadelphia*, in which an AIDS sufferer, played by Tom Hanks, loses his job when his employers learn about his disease. He is fired not because he is homosexual, but because of anxieties provoked by his disease. The movie traces out his struggle to sue his firm for wrongful dismissal.

AIDS is an example of illness as **stigma**. A stigma is any characteristic that sets an individual or group apart from the majority of the population, with the result that the individual or group is treated with suspicion or hostility. Most forms of illness arouse feelings of sympathy or compassion among nonsufferers. When an illness is seen as uncommonly infectious, however, or is perceived as somehow a mark of dishonor or shame, sufferers may be rejected by the "healthy" population. This was true of people afflicted with leprosy in the Middle Ages, who were popularly thought to be sinners punished by God, and were hence disowned and forced to live in separate leper colonies. In a less extreme way, AIDS often provokes such stigmatization today—in spite

Percentage

- 95 or more
- 75–94
- 50–74
- 25–49
- Less than 25

SOURCE: The World Bank, 1994.

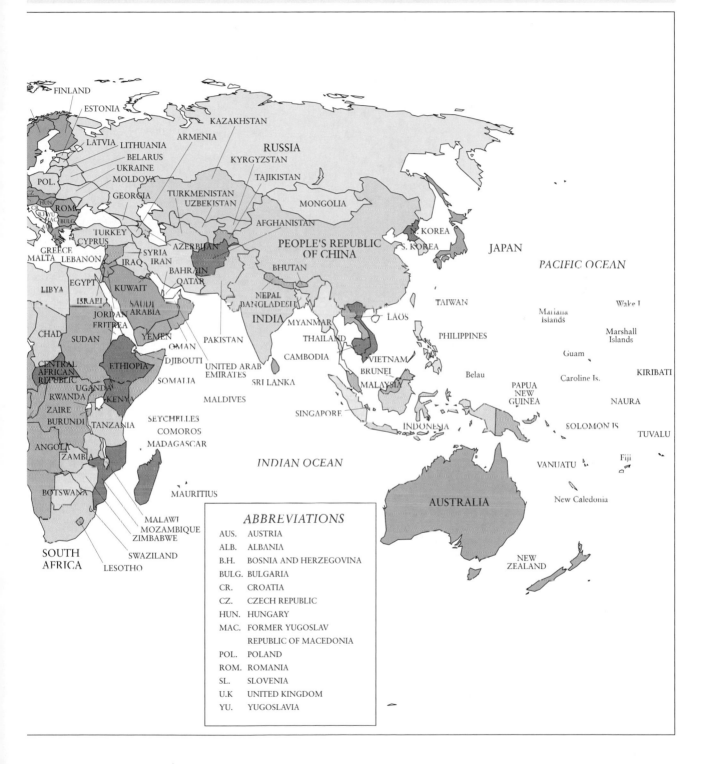

FINLAND
ESTONIA
KAZAKHSTAN
LATVIA   LITHUANIA   ARMENIA   RUSSIA
BELARUS   KYRGYZSTAN
UKRAINE
POL.   MOLDOVA   TAJIKISTAN
         GEORGIA   TURKMENISTAN   MONGOLIA
HUN.   UZBEKISTAN
CR. ROM.
YU.   AFGHANISTAN
MAC.
BULG.   TURKEY   PEOPLE'S REPUBLIC   N. KOREA   JAPAN
GREECE   CYPRUS   AZERBIJAN   OF CHINA   S. KOREA
MALTA   LEBANON SYRIA   PACIFIC OCEAN
         IRAQ   IRAN   BHUTAN
EGYPT   BAHRAIN
LIBYA   QATAR   KUWAIT   NEPAL   TAIWAN   Wake I.
ISRAEL   BANGLADESH   Mariana
JORDAN SAUDI   INDIA   MYANMAR   LAOS   Islands   Marshall
FRITREA ARABIA   Islands
CHAD   SUDAN   YEMEN   PAKISTAN THAILAND   PHILIPPINES Guam
                OMAN   CAMBODIA VIETNAM
CENTRAL   DJIBOUTI   UNITED ARAB   BRUNEI   Belau   Caroline Is.   KIRIBATI
AFRICAN ETHIOPIA EMIRATES   SRI LANKA   MALAYSIA   PAPUA
REPUBLIC UGANDA SOMALIA   NEW   NAURA
RWANDA KENYA   MALDIVES   GUINEA
ZAIRE   SINGAPORE   SOLOMON IS.
BURUNDI TANZANIA SEYCHELLES   INDONESIA   TUVALU
        COMOROS
ANGOLA   MADAGASCAR   VANUATU   Fiji
ZAMBIA   INDIAN OCEAN   AUSTRALIA
                                                                              New Caledonia
BOTSWANA   MAURITIUS
                MALAWI
                MOZAMBIQUE   ABBREVIATIONS
SOUTH   ZIMBABWE   NEW
AFRICA   SWAZILAND   ZEALAND
        LESOTHO

ABBREVIATIONS	
AUS.	AUSTRIA
ALB.	ALBANIA
B.H.	BOSNIA AND HERZEGOVINA
BULG.	BULGARIA
CR.	CROATIA
CZ.	CZECH REPUBLIC
HUN.	HUNGARY
MAC.	FORMER YUGOSLAV REPUBLIC OF MACEDONIA
POL.	POLAND
ROM.	ROMANIA
SL.	SLOVENIA
U.K	UNITED KINGDOM
YU.	YUGOSLAVIA

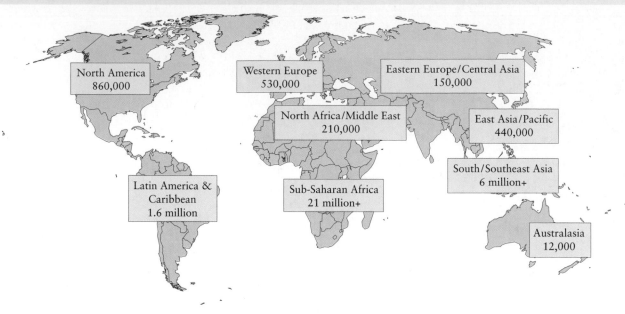

SOURCE: The World Bank, 1998.

The impact of AIDS will be greatest in sub-Saharan Africa. In countries such as Zambia, Kenya, and Zaire, more than 40 percent of the population may have AIDS by the year 2010 (World Population Profile, 1994).

of the fact that, like leprosy, the danger of contracting the disease in ordinary day-to-day situations is almost nil.

There are no effective treatments for AIDS, although some drugs seem to delay its progression. While a person who is HIV positive may live for years without developing AIDS, once the disease appears, it is effectively a death sentence. Its effects are particularly tragic, as it is most common among younger age groups. In this respect, it is unlike the other major killer illnesses in the industrial societies today, which mostly strike at older age groups.

HUMAN SEXUALITY

The global AIDS epidemic and attempts to halt its spread are further examples of the socialization of nature. As with the study of health and illness, scholars

have also differed over the importance of biological versus social and cultural influences on human sexual behavior, another important facet of the sociology of the body. We will first look at some of the biological arguments and the criticisms these arguments have created. We will then examine the social influences on sexual behavior, which will lead us into a discussion of the tremendous variations in human sexuality.

Biology and Sexual Behavior

There is clearly a biological basis to sexuality, because the female anatomy differs from that of the male, and the experience of orgasm is also different. There also exists a biological imperative to reproduce, otherwise the human species would become extinct. But human sexuality is a complex subject, and it's certain that procreation is not the only reason for sexual intercourse. While men and women may share a common end, they do exhibit different sexual behaviors, a subject scholars have sought to explain. For instance, some evolutionary biologists argue that there is an evolutionary explanation of why men tend to be more sexually promiscuous than women (see Chapter 3). The argument is that men are biologically disposed to impregnate as many women as possible in order to ensure that their seed has the greatest chance of survival. Women, who at a given time have only one egg that can be fertilized, have no such biological interests. Instead, they want a stable partner to protect the biological inheritance invested in the protection of their child. This argument was supported by studies of the sexual behavior of animals claiming to show that males are normally more promiscuous than females of the same species.

More recent studies, however, especially those carried out by women researchers, have shown that female infidelity is actually quite common in the animal kingdom, and the sexual activities of animals are more complex than was once thought. It was once believed that females mated with males who had the highest potential for a superior genetic inheritance for their offspring. But a recent study of female birds has disputed this argument, claiming that female birds take an extra mating partner not for its genes, but because it may be a better parent and offer a better home territory for raising offspring. As this study concluded, "There's more to copulation than a transfer of sperm. These females may be thinking of their futures" (Angier, 1994).

THE HOMOSEXUAL GENE?

Evolutionary biology is not the only source for explaining the biological influences upon sexual behavior. Another argument comes from the study of genetics. For example, in 1992, scientists announced that they might have isolated the "homosexual gene," a gene that would predispose someone toward homosexuality. Many homosexuals welcomed the finding. If true, it would show that some individuals possess a natural disposition toward homosexuality.

The conclusions from this research are tentative, however. Moreover, the way in which the research was reported by the media, where it received wide coverage, was misleading. The scientists did not claim that this gene would automatically make someone ho-

mosexual. It would indicate only a predisposition, not a predetermined and unchangeable sexual orientation. As we shall see later, sexuality is far too complicated to be wholly attributable to biological traits. Unlike animals, our sexual responses are not genetically given, but are largely learned.

Social Influences on Sexual Behavior

Judith Lorber distinguishes as many as ten different sexual identities: straight (heterosexual) woman, straight man, lesbian woman, gay man, bisexual woman, bisexual man, transvestite woman (a woman who regularly dresses as a man), transvestite man (a man who regularly dresses as a woman), transsexual woman (a man who becomes a woman), and transsexual man (a woman who becomes a man). Sexual practices themselves are even more diverse. Freud called human beings "polymorphously perverse." By this he meant that human beings have a wide range of sexual tastes and may follow these even when, in a given society, some are regarded as immoral or illegal. Freud first began his researches during the Victorian period, when many people were sexually prudish; yet his patients still revealed to him an amazing diversity of sexual pursuits.

Among possible sexual practices are the following: A man or woman can have sexual relations with women, men, or both. This can happen one at a time or with three or more participating. One can have sex with oneself (masturbation) or with no one (celibacy). Someone can have sexual relations with transsexuals or people who erotically cross-dress; use pornography or sexual devices; practice sadomasochism (the erotic use of bondage and the inflicting of pain); have sex with animals; and so on (Lorber, 1994). In most societies, there are sexual norms that encourage some practices and discourage or condemn others. Such norms, however, vary between different cultures. Homosexuality is a case in point. As will be discussed later, some cultures have either tolerated or actively encouraged homosexuality in certain contexts. Among the ancient Greeks, for instance, the love of men for boys was idealized as the highest form of sexual love.

THE SPREAD OF AIDS

There can be no question but that the threat of AIDS has significantly affected American sexual mores. Men and women, straight and gay, have come to realize the dangers posed by unprotected sex, and in many segments of the population, condom use has become the norm. As a result, the rate of transmission of HIV, the virus that causes AIDS, has dropped significantly in the United States. And although there remains no cure for the disease, the use of anti-retroviral drugs has greatly increased the longevity of HIV-positive Americans.

The story is very different in the Third World. According to statistics released during the 1998 World AIDS Conference, 90 percent of those with HIV live in developing nations, with the vast majority living in Africa. Because condom availability in the Third World is low, because

Accepted types of sexual behavior also vary between different cultures, which is one way we know that most sexual responses are learned rather than innate. The most extensive study was carried out five decades ago by Clellan Ford and Frank Beach (1951), who surveyed anthropological evidence from more than two hundred societies. Striking variations were found in what is regarded as "natural" sexual behavior and in norms of sexual attractiveness. For example, in some cultures, extended foreplay, perhaps lasting hours, is thought desirable and even necessary prior to intercourse; in others, foreplay is virtually nonexistent. In some societies, it is believed that overly frequent intercourse leads to physical debilitation or illness. Among the Seniang of the South Pa-

cific, advice on the desirability of spacing out lovemaking is given by the elders of the village—who also believe that a person with white hair may legitimately copulate every night!

In most cultures, norms of sexual attractiveness (held by both females and males) focus more on physical looks for women than for men, a situation that seems to be gradually changing in the West as women increasingly become active in spheres outside the home.

The traits seen as most important in female beauty, however, differ greatly. In the modern West, a slim, small body build is admired, while in other cultures a much more generous shape is regarded as most attractive. Sometimes the breasts are not seen as a source of sexual stimulus, whereas in most Third World governments offer little in the way of sex education, and because many mothers with HIV unknowingly pass the disease on to their children, in areas of Africa, one in four adults is infected with the AIDS virus. With rates of transmission showing no signs of decreasing, and with anti-retroviral therapies—which can cost thousands of dollars per patient per year—completely out of reach for all but the wealthy few, AIDS threatens to drastically reduce the average life expectancy in many developing nations.

As horrible as this situation is in itself, the spectre of AIDS in the Third World also poses a direct threat to the West—because of globalization. Westerners are travelling to the Third World in record numbers, either as tourists or on business. Although HIV cannot be transmitted through casual contact, it is certainly the case that many Americans or Europeans who travel to developing countries will have sexual contacts while they are there, some by using the services of prostitutes. Thailand, for example, has a flourishing sex-tourism business, with some major hotels and tour companies catering to foreigners who wish to take advantage of the country's semi-legal prostitution industry (Truong, 1990). Because many of these prostitutes are HIV positive, American tourists, business people, or military personnel who employ them and who fail to practice safe sex are at

risk of contracting the virus and then spreading it on their return to the United States. Diseases, no less than people or goods, cross international borders more easily in a globalized world.

some societies great erotic significance is attached to them. Some societies place great store on the shape of the face, while others emphasize the shape and color of the eyes or the size and form of the nose and lips.

Sexuality in Western Culture

Western attitudes toward sexual behavior were for nearly two thousand years molded primarily by Christianity. Although different Christian sects and denominations have held divergent views about the proper place of sexuality in life, the dominant view of the Christian church was that all sexual behavior is suspect, except that needed for reproduction. During some periods, this view produced an extreme prudishness in society at large. But at other times, many people ignored or reacted against the church's teachings, commonly engaging in practices (such as adultery) forbidden by religious authorities. As was mentioned in Chapter 1, the idea that sexual fulfillment can and should be sought through marriage was rare.

In the nineteenth century, religious presumptions about sexuality became partly replaced by medical ones. Most of the early writings by doctors about sexual behavior, however, were as stern as the views of the church. Some argued that any type of sexual activity unconnected with reproduction causes serious physical harm. Masturbation was said to bring on blindness, insanity, heart disease, and other ailments, while oral sex was claimed to cause cancer. In Victorian times, sexual hypocrisy abounded. Virtuous women were believed to be indifferent to sexuality, accepting the attentions of their husbands only as a duty. Yet in the expanding towns and cities, prostitution was rife and often openly tolerated, "loose" women being seen as in an entirely different category from their respectable sisters.

Many Victorian men, who were on the face of things sober, well-behaved citizens, devoted to their wives, regularly visited prostitutes or kept mistresses. Such behavior was treated leniently, whereas "respectable" women who took lovers were regarded as scandalous and shunned in polite society if their behavior came to light. The differing attitudes toward the sexual activities of men and women formed a double standard, which has long existed and whose residues still linger on today.

In current times, traditional attitudes exist alongside much more liberal attitudes toward sexuality, which developed particularly strongly in the 1960s. Some people, particularly those influenced by Christian teachings, believe that premarital sex is wrong and generally frown upon all forms of sexual behavior except heterosexual activity within the confines of marriage—although it is now much more commonly accepted that sexual pleasure is a desirable and important feature. Others, by contrast, condone or actively approve of premarital sex and hold tolerant attitudes toward different sexual practices. Sexual attitudes have undoubtedly become more permissive over the past thirty years in most Western countries. In movies and plays, scenes are shown that previously would have been completely unacceptable, while pornographic material is readily available to most adults who want it.

Sexual Behavior: Kinsey's Study

We can speak much more confidently about public values concerning sexuality in the past than we can about private practices, for by their nature such practices mostly go undocumented. When Alfred Kinsey began his research in the United States in the 1940s and 1950s, it was the first time a major investigation of actual sexual behavior had been undertaken. Kinsey and his co-researchers faced condemnation from

religious organizations, and his work was denounced as immoral in the newspapers and in Congress. But he persisted, and eventually obtained sexual life histories of eighteen thousand people, a reasonably representative sample of the white American population (Kinsey et al., 1948, 1953).

Kinsey's results were surprising to most and shocking to many, because they revealed a great difference between the public expectations of sexual behavior prevailing at that time and actual sexual conduct. He found that almost 70 percent of men had visited a prostitute, and 84 percent had had premarital sexual experience. Yet, following the double standard, 40 percent of men expected their wives to be virgins at the time of marriage. More than 90 percent of males had engaged in masturbation and nearly 60 percent in some form of oral sexual activity. Among women, about 50 percent had had premarital sexual experience, although mostly with their prospective husbands. Some 60 percent had masturbated, and the same percentage had engaged in oral-genital contacts.

The gap between publicly accepted attitudes and actual behavior that Kinsey's findings demonstrated was probably especially great at that particular period, just after World War II. A phase of sexual liberalization had begun rather earlier, in the 1920s, when many younger people felt freed from the strict moral codes that had governed earlier generations. Sexual behavior probably changed a good deal, but issues concerning sexuality were not openly discussed in the way that has become familiar now. People participating in sexual activities that were still strongly disapproved of on a public level concealed them, not realizing the full extent to which others were engaging in similar practices. The more permissive era of the 1960s brought openly declared attitudes more into line with the realities of behavior.

Sexual Behavior since Kinsey

In the 1960s, the social movements that challenged the existing order of things, like those associated with countercultural, or "hippy," lifestyles, also broke with existing sexual norms. These movements preached sexual freedom, and the invention of the contraceptive pill for women allowed sexual pleasure to be clearly separated from reproduction. Women's groups also started pressing for greater independence from male sexual values, the rejection of the double standard, and the need for women to achieve greater sexual satisfaction in their relationships. Until recently it was difficult to know with accuracy how much sexual behavior had changed since the time of Kinsey's research.

In the late 1980s, Lillian Rubin interviewed a thousand Americans between the ages of thirteen and forty-eight to try to discover what changes have occurred in sexual behavior and attitudes over the past thirty years or so. According to her findings, there have indeed been significant developments. Sexual activity typically begins at a younger age than was true for the previous generation; moreover, the sexual practices of teenagers tend today to be as varied and comprehensive as those of adults. There is still a double standard, but it is not as powerful as it used to be. One of the most important changes is that women now expect, and actively pursue, sexual pleasure in relationships. They expect to receive, not only to provide, sexual satisfaction—a phenomenon that Rubin argues has major consequences for both sexes.

Women are more sexually available than once was the case; but along with this development, which most men applaud, has come a new assertiveness many men find difficult to accept. The men Rubin talked to often said they "felt inadequate," were afraid they could "never do anything right," and found it "impossible to satisfy women these days" (Rubin, 1990).

Men feel inadequate? Doesn't this contradict all that we have learned in this book so far? For in modern society, men continue to dominate in most spheres, and they are in general much more violent toward women than the other way around. Such violence is substantially aimed at the control and continuing subordination of women. Yet a number of authors have begun to argue that masculinity is a burden as much as a source of reward. Much male sexuality, they add, is compulsive rather than satisfying. If men were to stop using sexuality as a means of control, not only women but they themselves would gain.

In 1994, a team of researchers, led by Edward Laumann, published *The Social Organization of Sexuality: Sexual Practices in the United States,* the most comprehensive study of sexual behavior since Kinsey. To the surprise of many, their findings reflect an es-

sential sexual conservatism among Americans. For instance, 83 percent of their subjects had had only one partner (or no partner at all) in the preceding year, and among married people the figure rises to 96 percent. Fidelity to one's spouse is also quite common: only 10 percent of women and less than 25 percent of men reported having an extramarital affair during their lifetime. According to the study, Americans average only three partners during their entire lifetime (see Table 16.1). Despite the apparent ordinariness of sexual behavior, some distinct changes emerge from this study, the most significant being a progressive increase in the level of premarital sexual experience, particularly among women. In fact, over 95 percent of Americans getting married today are sexually experienced.

THE SOCIOLOGICAL DEBATE

SEXUAL BEHAVIOR IN THE UNITED STATES

Sociologists frequently rely on responses to survey questionnaires as their main source of information on human behavior. However, obtaining detailed information on sexual behavior and attitudes is often particularly difficult. The two most comprehensive studies of sexuality in the United States—the Kinsey studies (1948, 1953) and the Laumann study (Laumann et al., 1994)—offer very different portraits of sexual preferences and behaviors. Do these conflicting results reflect historical changes in sexual mores, or are the observed differences an outcome of methodological approaches?

As we just saw, in stark contrast with Kinsey's results, which found that a high proportion of men had premarital or extramarital sex, the Laumann study revealed that 83 percent of survey respondents had only one or no sexual partners in the year prior to the study. Moreover, only 10 percent of women and fewer than 25 percent of men reported ever having had an extramarital affair during their lifetime. Certainly, it's possible that Americans have become more sexually conservative over time. Perhaps the fear of

Table 16.1 Sex in America: Social Influences on Sexual Behavior

	Sex Partners in the Past 12 Months				Sex Partners since Age 18						Median Number of Sex Partners Since Age 18
Total	None	1	2–4	5+	None	1	2–4	5–10	11–20	21+	
	12%	71%	14%	3%	3%	26%	30%	22%	11%	9%	3
Men	10%	67%	18%	5%	3%	20%	21%	23%	16%	17%	6
Women	14	75	10	2	3	32	36	20	6	3	2
Ages 18–24	11%	57%	24%	9%	8%	32%	34%	15%	8%	3%	2
25–29	6	72	17	6	2	25	31	22	10	9	4
30–34	9	73	16	2	3	21	29	25	11	10	4
35–39	10	77	11	2	2	19	30	25	14	11	4
40–44	11	75	13	1	1	22	28	24	14	12	4
45–49	15	75	9	1	2	26	24	25	10	14	4
50–54	15	79	5	0	2	34	28	18	9	9	2
55–59	32	65	4	0	1	40	28	15	8	7	2
Never married, not living with someone	25%	38%	28%	9%	12%	15%	29%	21%	12%	12%	4
Never married, living with someone	1	75	20	5	0	25	37	16	10	13	3
Married	2	94	4	1	0	37	28	19	9	7	2
Divorced, separated, or widowed, not living with someone	31	41	26	3	0	11	33	29	15	12	5
Divorced, separated, or widowed, living with someone	1	80	16	3	0	0	32	44	12	12	6

AIDS and sexually transmitted diseases have frightened men and women away from extramarital affairs and multiple sex partners.

An alternative explanation for the wildly discrepant findings is that researchers adopted different methodological approaches. Kinsey, an evolutionary biologist, originally conducted a taxonomic investigation of human sexuality. He first gave a questionnaire about sexual practices to students in his zoology classes at Indiana University. Finding this method unsatisfactory, he next conducted face-to-face interviews, and then focused his study on specific social groups. He and his colleagues eventually interviewed nearly 18,000 people.

Kinsey recognized that the ideal survey would select people at random, and thus results would represent

	SEX PARTNERS IN THE PAST 12 MONTHS				SEX PARTNERS SINCE AGE 18						MEDIAN NUMBER OF SEX PARTNERS SINCE AGE 18
TOTAL	NONE	1	2–4	5+	NONE	1	2–4	5–10	11–20	21+	
Less than high school degree	16%	67%	15%	3%	4%	27%	36%	19%	9%	6%	3
High school degree or equivalent	11	74	13	3	3	30	29	20	10	7	3
Some college or vocational school	11	71	14	4	2	24	29	23	12	9	4
College graduate	12	69	15	4	2	24	26	24	11	13	4
Advanced degree	13	74	10	3	4	25	26	23	10	13	4
No religion	11%	67%	17%	6%	3%	16%	29%	20%	16%	16%	5
Mainline Protestant	11	74	13	2	2	23	31	23	12	8	4
Conservative Protestant	13	70	14	3	3	30	30	20	10	7	3
Catholic	13	72	13	3	4	27	29	23	8	9	3
Jewish	4	78	15	4	0	24	13	30	17	17	6
Other religion	15	63	15	6	3	42	20	16	8	13	3
White	12%	73%	12%	3%	3%	26%	29%	22%	11%	9%	3
Black	13	60	21	6	2	18	34	24	11	11	4
Hispanic	11	70	17	3	3	36	27	17	8	9	2
Asian	15	77	8	0	6	46	25	14	6	3	1
Native American	12	76	10	2	5	28	35	23	5	5	3

SOURCE: Laumann et al., 1994.

the general population. However, he did not believe it was possible to persuade a randomly selected group of Americans to answer deeply personal questions about their sexual behavior. Consequently, his survey respondents were primarily college students living in sorority and fraternity houses, prisoners, psychiatric patients, and friends. To make his data more credible, Kinsey made every effort to interview 100 percent of the members of each group, such as all students living in a given fraternity house. Because Kinsey's data are based on a convenience sample, they are not representative of the American public at large. Moreover, many of his survey respondents volunteered to participate in the study. Thus, these people may be unique from nonvolunteers in that they have wider sexual experiences, or a greater interest in sexuality.

The Laumann study, in contrast, is based on data from the National Health and Social Life Survey (NHSLS). The NHSLS data were obtained from a nationally representative random sample of more than 3,000 American men and women aged eighteen to fifty-nine who spoke English. In addition, the researchers purposely oversampled among blacks and Hispanics so that they would have enough members of these minority groups to analyze their survey responses separately, with confidence that findings were statistically reliable and valid.

Recognizing that people are often hesitant to discuss sexuality, the Laumann team paid particular attention to choosing nonjudgmental language in their questionnaire. The researchers also built several "checks" into their questionnaire, to ensure the veracity of responses. Several questions were redundant, but were asked in different ways throughout the interview, to gauge whether respondents were truthful in their answers. Researchers also included eleven questions that had been asked previously on another national random sample survey of Americans. Comparisons of responses to the two sets of questions provided the NHSLS researchers with assurance that their results were consistent with other researchers' findings.

Although the Kinsey and Laumann studies are influential works on human sexuality, the studies taken together also demonstrate that the process through which sociological knowledge is obtained often is as important as the actual research findings.

Homosexuality

Homosexuality exists in all cultures. Yet the idea of a homosexual person—someone clearly marked off in terms of their sexual tastes from the majority of the population—is only a relatively recent one. In his studies of sexuality, Michel Foucault showed that before the eighteenth century, the notion seems barely to have existed (Foucault, 1978). The act of sodomy was denounced by church authorities and by the law; in England and several other European countries, it was punishable by death. However, sodomy was not de-fined specifically as a homosexual offense. It applied to relations between men and women, men and animals, as well as men among themselves. The term "homosexuality" was coined in the 1860s, and from then on, homosexuals were increasingly regarded as being a separate type of people with a particular sexual aberration (Weeks, 1986). Use of the term "lesbian" to refer to female homosexuality dates from a slightly later time.

The death penalty for "unnatural acts" was abolished in the United States following independence, and in Europe in the late eighteenth and early nineteenth centuries. Until a few decades ago, however, homosexuality remained a criminal activity in virtually all Western countries. This fact helps explain why antagonism toward homosexuals, though no longer enshrined in law, persists in many people's emotional attitudes.

HOMOSEXUALITY IN NON-WESTERN CULTURES

In some non-Western cultures, homosexual relations are accepted or even encouraged among certain groups. The Batak people of northern Sumatra, for ex- ample, permit male homosexual relationships before marriage. At puberty, a boy leaves his parents' house and sleeps in a dwelling with a dozen to fifteen males his age or older. Sexual partnerships are formed between couples in the group, and the younger boys are initiated into homosexual practices. This situation continues until young men marry women. Once married, most, but not all men, abandon homosexual activities (Money and Ehrhardt, 1972).

Among the people of East Bay, a village in Melanesia in the Pacific, homosexuality is similarly tolerated, although again only in males. Prior to marriage, while living in the men's house, young men engage in mu- tual masturbation and anal intercourse. Homosexual relationships also exist, however, between older men and younger boys, often involving boys too young to be living in the men's house. Each type of relationship is completely acceptable and discussed openly. Many married men are bisexual, having relations with younger boys while maintaining an active sexual life with their female spouses. But homosexuality without an interest in heterosexual relationships seems to be unknown in such cultures (Davenport, 1965; see also Shepherd, 1987).

HOMOSEXUALITY IN WESTERN CULTURE

Kenneth Plummer, in a classic study, distinguished four types of homosexuality within modern Western culture. Casual homosexuality is a passing homosexual encounter that does not substantially structure a person's overall sexual life. Schoolboy crushes and mutual masturbation are examples. Situated activities refer to circumstances in which homosexual acts are regularly carried out but do not become an individual's overriding preference. In settings such as prisons or military camps, where men live without women, homosexual behavior of this kind is common, and is regarded as a substitute for heterosexual behavior rather than as preferable to it.

Personalized homosexuality refers to individuals who have a preference for homosexual activities but who are isolated from groups in which this is easily accepted. Homosexuality here is a furtive activity, hidden away from friends and colleagues. Homosexuality as a way of life refers to individuals who have "come out" and have made associations with others of similar sexual tastes a key part of their lives. Such people usually belong to gay subcultures, in which homosexual activities are integrated into a distinct lifestyle (Plummer, 1975).

The proportion of the population (both male and female) who have had homosexual experiences or felt strong inclinations toward homosexuality is much larger than those who follow an openly and exclusively gay lifestyle. The probable extent of homosexuality in Western cultures first became known with the publication of Alfred Kinsey's research. According to his findings, no more than half of all American men are completely heterosexual, judged by their sexual activities and inclinations after puberty. Of Kinsey's sample, 8 percent had been involved in exclusively homosexual relationships for periods of three years or more. A further 10 percent had engaged in mixed homosexual and heterosexual activities in more or less equal quantities. Kinsey's most striking finding was that 37 percent of men had had at least one homosexual experience to the level of orgasm. An additional

A wedding ceremony in Hawaii: Same-sex marriages have been a topic of legal debate in many state courts and legislatures.

13 percent had felt homosexual desires but had not acted on them.

Rates of homosexuality among women indicated by the Kinsey researches were lower. About 2 percent of females were exclusively homosexual. Homosexual experiences were reported by 13 percent of participants, while a further 15 percent admitted they had felt homosexual desires without acting on them. Kinsey and his colleagues were startled by the level of homosexuality their studies revealed, so the results were rechecked using different methods, but the conclusions remained the same (Kinsey et al., 1948, 1953). More recent research done on a lesser scale in the United Kingdom tends to support Kinsey's figures.

However, the results from *The Social Organization of Sexuality* call into question many of the findings of Kinsey's study on the prevalence of homosexuality. In contrast to Kinsey's 37 percent, only 9 percent of men in the later study reported having a homosexual encounter to the level of orgasm, only about 8 percent of men reported having homosexual desires (compared with 13 percent), and just under 3 percent reported a sexual encounter with another man in the preceding year. Yet as the authors of this study acknowledged, the stigma that remains attached to homosexuality probably contributed to a general underreporting of homosexual behavior. And as one critic noted, the authors' random sample failed to address the geographical concentration of homosexuals

KEY CONCEPTS IN REVIEW

Although there is clearly a biological basis to sexuality, it, like gender, is largely socially constructed. Sexual practices are primarily learned behaviors, as shown by the diversity of sexual behavior among different cultures. The ways in which people make love, the norms of sexual attractiveness, and the acceptance of homosexual behavior (sexual relations between persons of the same sex) vary over time and across cultures.

In the West, Christianity has been important in shaping sexual attitudes. In societies with rigid sexual codes, double standards and hypocrisy are common. The gulf between norms and actual practice can be tremendous, as studies of sexual behavior have shown.

Homosexuality exists in all cultures, yet the category of "homosexual" is a recent phenomenon. Homosexuality is tolerated or even encouraged in many cultures.

in large cities, where homosexuals probably constitute close to 10 percent of the overall population (Robinson, 1994). Determining exact levels of homosexuality is not the central focus of studies of sexual behavior. Instead, they are an important reminder that sexual identity and behavior are constantly in flux and subject to social influences.

LESBIANISM Lesbian groups tend to be less highly organized than male gay subcultures and include a lower proportion of casual relationships. Male homosexuality tends to receive more attention than lesbianism, and lesbian activist groups are often treated as if their interests were identical with those of male organizations. But while there is sometimes close cooperation between male gays and lesbians, there are also differences, particularly where lesbians are actively involved in feminism. The specific character of lesbian women's lives is now being studied by sociologists in more detail.

Lesbian couples often have children, some through a relationship with a man, others through artificial insemination, however, it has been difficult in the past for lesbians to gain custody. In the United States, courts decide whether a mother's lesbianism makes her an "unfit" parent before allocating custody. Several cases fought through the American courts in the late 1970s and early 1980s established that lesbianism is not relevant to deciding whether or not a woman should be given custody of her child; but this has in practice been accepted only in a few states (Rights of Women Lesbian Custody Group, 1986).

Coming out (acknowledging one's sexual orientation publicly) remains a difficult process for many. Parents, other relatives and friends, and children, if there are any, must be told. However, the experience can be a rewarding one. In *There's Something I've Been Meaning to Tell You*, Loralee MacPike collected descriptions from women who had chosen to disclose their homosexuality. Of her own experience she wrote:

Like many "born-again Lesbians," I was overjoyed at my new-found self and my newly-defined life. Neither my partner nor I had ever been in a lesbian relationship before, so neither brought to our lives the social foundations and friendships that are part of gay communities; but we began making subtle approaches to others who in one way or another appeared to be coming out to us. . . . [We] have been very fortunate . . . the results have been more positive and enriching than I could have imagined. (MacPike, 1989)

ATTITUDES TOWARD HOMOSEXUALITY Attitudes of intolerance toward homosexuality have been so pronounced in the past that it is only during recent years that some of the myths surrounding the subject have been dispelled. Homosexuality is not a sickness and is not distinctively associated with any forms of psychiatric disturbance. Homosexual males are not limited to any particular sector of occupations, like hairdressing, interior decorating, or the arts.

Some kinds of male gay behavior might be seen as attempts to alter the usual connections of masculinity and power—one reason, perhaps, why homosexuals are so often thought to be threatening by the straight community. Gay men tend to reject the image of the effeminate popularly associated with them, and they deviate from this in two ways. One is through cultivating outrageous effeminacy—a "camp" femininity that parodies the stereotype. The other is by developing a "macho" image. This also is not conventionally masculine; men dressed as motorcyclists or cowboys are again parodying masculinity, by exaggerating it (Bertelson, 1986).

Sexuality and Procreative Technology

As with most of the topics in this chapter, the concept of "the socialization of nature" applies to a better sociological understanding of sexual behavior. An example is human reproduction. For hundreds of years, the lives of most women were dominated by childbirth and child rearing. In premodern times, contraception was ineffective or, in some societies, unknown. Even in Europe and the United States as late as the eighteenth century, it was common for women to experience as many as twenty pregnancies (often involving miscarriages and infant deaths). Improved methods of contraception have helped alter this situation in a fundamental way. Far from any longer being natural, it is almost unknown in the industrial countries for women to undergo so many pregnancies. Advances in contraceptive technology enable most women and men to control whether and when they choose to have children (see Global Map 16.3).

Contraception is only one example of a **procreative technology.** Some of the other areas in which natural processes have become social are described below.

CHILDBIRTH

Medical science has not always been involved with the major life transitions from birth to death. The medicalization of pregnancy and childbirth developed slowly, as local physicians and midwives were displaced by pediatric specialists. Today in the industrialized societies, most births occur in a hospital with the help of a specialized medical team.

In the past, new parents had to wait until the day of birth to learn the sex of their newborn and whether it would be healthy. Today, prenatal tests such as the sonogram (an image of the fetus produced by using ultrasonic waves) and amniocentesis (which draws off some of the amniotic fluid from around the fetus) can be used to discover structural or chromosomal abnormalities prior to birth. Such new technology presents couples and society with new ethical and legal decisions. When a disorder is detected, the couple are faced with the decision of whether or not to have the baby, knowing it may be seriously handicapped.

GENETIC ENGINEERING: DESIGNER BABIES

A great deal of scientific endeavor these days is being devoted to the expansion of genetic engineering; that is, intervening in the genetic makeup of the fetus so as to influence its subsequent development. The likely social impact of genetic engineering is starting to provoke debates almost as intense as those that surround the issue of abortion. According to its supporters, genetic engineering will bring us many benefits. It is possible, for example, to identify the genetic factors that make some people vulnerable to certain diseases. Genetic reprogramming will ensure that these illnesses are no longer passed on from generation to generation. It will be possible to "design" our bodies before birth in terms of skin color, color of hair and eyes, weight, and so forth.

There could be no better example of the mixture of opportunities and problems that the increasing socialization of nature creates for us. What choices will parents make if they can design their babies, and what

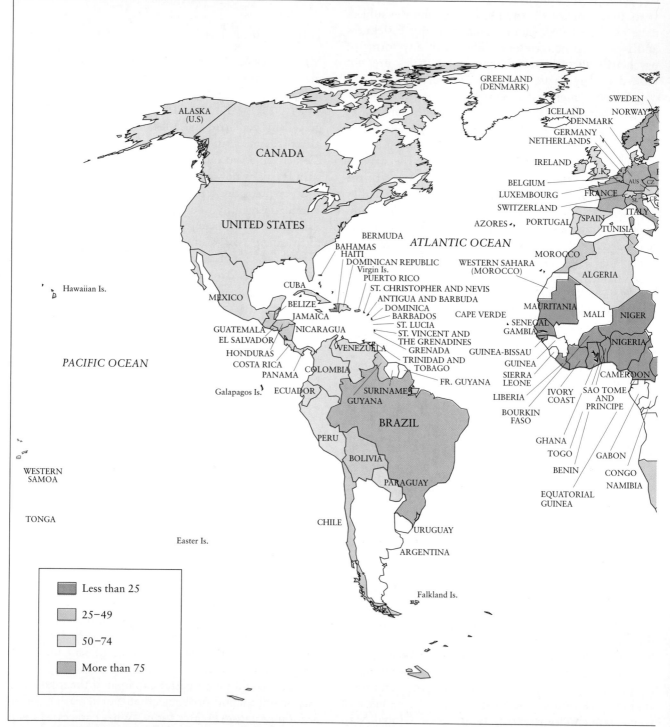

Less than 25

25–49

50–74

More than 75

SOURCE: The World Bank, 1998.

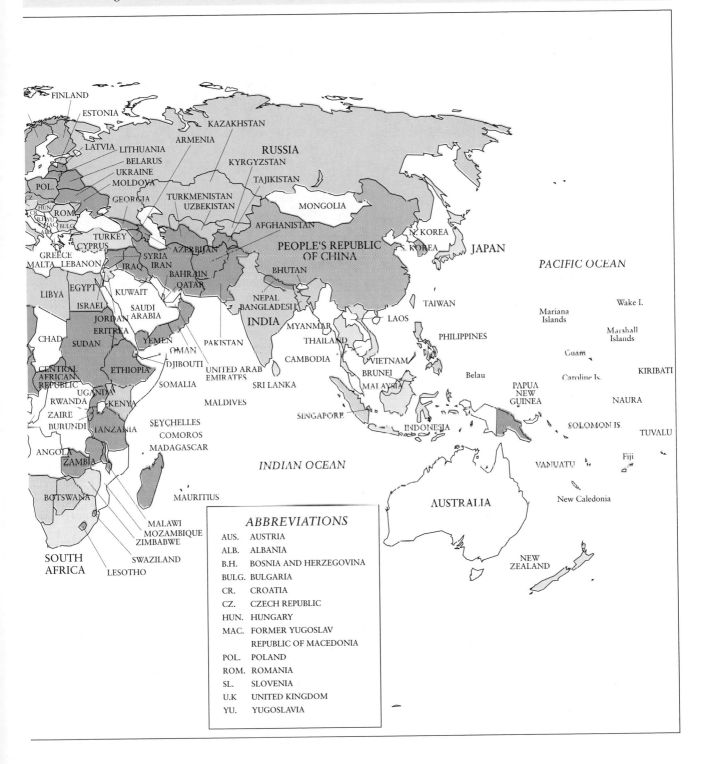

ABBREVIATIONS

AUS.	AUSTRIA
ALB.	ALBANIA
B.H.	BOSNIA AND HERZEGOVINA
BULG.	BULGARIA
CR.	CROATIA
CZ.	CZECH REPUBLIC
HUN.	HUNGARY
MAC.	FORMER YUGOSLAV REPUBLIC OF MACEDONIA
POL.	POLAND
ROM.	ROMANIA
SL.	SLOVENIA
U.K	UNITED KINGDOM
YU.	YUGOSLAVIA

limits should be placed on those choices? Genetic engineering is unlikely to be cheap. Will this mean that those who can afford to pay will be able to program out from their children any traits they see as socially undesirable? What will happen to the children of more deprived groups, who will continue to be born naturally?

Some sociologists have argued that differential access to genetic engineering might lead to the emergence of a "biological underclass." Those who don't have the physical advantages genetic engineering can bring might be subject to prejudice and discrimination by those who do enjoy these advantages. They might have difficulty finding employment and life or health insurance (Duster, 1990).

THE ABORTION DEBATE

The most controversial ethical dilemma created by modern reproductive technologies in modern societies is this: under what conditions should abortion be available to women? The abortion debate has become so intense precisely because it centers on basic ethical issues to which there are no easy solutions. Those who are "pro life" believe that abortion is always wrong except in extreme circumstances, because it is equivalent to murder. For them, ethical issues are above all subject to the value that must be placed upon human life. Those who are "pro choice" argue that the mother's control over her own body—her own right to live a rewarding life—must be the primary consideration.

The debate has led to numerous episodes of violence. Can it ever be resolved? At least one prominent social and legal theorist, Ronald Dworkin (1993), has suggested that it can. The intense divisions between those who are pro life and those who are pro choice, he argues, hide deeper sources of agreement between the two sides, and in this there is a source of hope. At previous periods of history, life was often relatively cheap. In current times, however, we have come to place a high value upon the sanctity of human life. Each side agrees with this value, but they interpret it differently, the one emphasizing the interests of the child, the other the interests of the mother. If the two sides can be persuaded that they share a common ethical value, Dworkin suggests, a more constructive dialogue may be possible.

AGING

The concept of the socialization of nature can also be used to analyze the fact that we live in an aging society, in which the proportion of people sixty-five or over is steadily increasing. For what old age actually is—the opportunities it offers and the burdens it carries—is changing dramatically.

Two rather contradictory processes are involved here. On the one hand, older people in modern societies tend to have lower status and less power than they used to have in premodern cultures. In these cultures, as in non-Western societies today (like India or China), old age was believed to bring wisdom, and the oldest people in any given community were commonly its main decision makers. Today, increasing age normally brings with it the reverse. In a society undergoing constant change, as ours is, the accumulated knowledge of older people often seems to the young no longer a valuable store of wisdom, but simply irrelevant.

On the other hand, however, older people today are much less prone to accept aging as an inevitable process. Here once more we can trace the impact of the socialization of nature. The aging process was once generally accepted as an inevitable manifestation of the ravages of time. But increasingly, aging is not something taken for granted as natural; advances in medicine and nutrition have shown that much that was once considered inevitable about aging can either be countered or slowed down. On average, people live to much older ages than was true over a century ago, as a result of improvements in nutrition, hygiene, and health care.

In the United States in 1850, the proportion of people over sixty-five was around 4 or 5 percent. The figure today is over 12 percent, and will grow over the next few decades (see Figure 16.1). The average age of Americans has been rising for more than a century and a half. In 1800, the average age was probably as low as sixteen. At the turn of the twentieth century, it had risen to twenty-three. By 1970, it was twenty-eight, and today it has reached over thirty. The average age will continue to rise for some time to come, if no major changes in current demographic trends occur. It is likely to be thirty-five by 2000 and may

Figure 16.1
THE PERCENTAGE OF U.S. SOCIETY OVER THE
AGE OF 65: PROJECTIONS FOR THE FUTURE

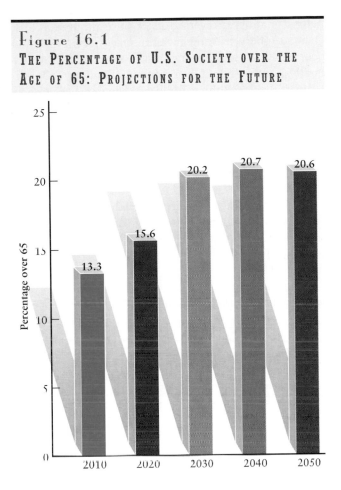

seventy-two years old, and women, to seventy-eight years old—there is debate as to whether these added years of life are happy and healthy, or whether the aged are merely experiencing a greater number of years of sickness and disability. Aging is inevitably accompanied by declines in physical health and physical strength. However, poor health is not as prevalent as many assume, especially among the "young" old (age sixty-five to seventy-four). Roughly 75 percent of non-institutionalized people (i.e., people not living in hospitals or nursing homes) age sixty-five to seventy-four in 1992 considered their health to be good, very good, or excellent compared with others their age. Among noninstitutionalized elderly people age seventy-five and older, a full 67 percent identified their health as good or better (National Center for Health Statistics, 1994).

Studies that examine health symptoms, however, show that aging is associated with disease onset and chronic conditions. Hearing loss, arthritis, heart conditions, and hypertension are among the most frequently reported symptoms among the elderly (Guralnik et al., 1989).

Because old people often experience poor health or disability in their later years, demographers occasionally differentiate between "life expectancy" and "active life expectancy." Whereas life expectancy refers to the total number of remaining years an individual can expect to live, active life expectancy refers to the total number of remaining disability-free years an in-

climb to thirty-seven by 2030. By then, there may be as many as 50 million people over sixty-five in the United States, a proportion of one in five.

There has also been an expansion in the numbers of the very old. According to some estimates, the number of Americans over eighty-five years of age will be 60 percent above present levels by the year 2000, composing over 1.5 percent of the whole population.

Biological Aspects of Aging

Gerontologists are particularly interested in the biological aspects of aging, such as the health and life quality of the aging population. Although men and women are living longer than ever before—men, to

Some people lessen the debilitating effects of aging by maintaining an active lifestyle.

dividual can expect to live. These years are defined as years of physical, emotional, and intellectual vigor, or functional well being (Katz et al., 1983).

Disability, or functional limitation, is generally measured by indicators of activities of daily living, or ADLs (Katz and Apton, 1976), and instrumental activities of daily living, or IADLs (Lawton and Brody, 1969). ADLs typically refer to a person's ability to perform basic self-care activities, such as bathing, dressing, and eating. IADLs assess independence in activities requiring adaptation to the environment, such as shopping, preparing meals, and carrying out household chores.

The need for personal assistance with everyday activities increases with age. One national sample survey showed that half of people age eighty-five and older needed assistance with everyday activities. However, for younger elderly people (age sixty-five to seventy-four) only 10 percent required such assistance. Roughly one in three people age eighty to eighty-four required help with daily activities (U.S. Bureau of the Census, 1996).

Researchers still do not agree whether more people are adding healthy years to the end of their lives, or infirm years. Some argue that mortality improvements in the 1970s and 1980s were accompanied by added years of dependent life, while others argue that this

Some senior citizens maintain an active lifestyle by continuing to work past the retirement age.

pattern may have reversed itself since the mid-1980s. Demographers reason that current cohorts of elderly people reaped benefits such as better nutrition, water quality, and hygiene when they were young and consequently are healthier in old age than earlier cohorts of elderly people (Manton, Corder, and Stallard, 1993; Crimmins, Hayward, and Saito, 1994).

Social Aspects of Aging

In addition to the biological impact of aging, the elderly can also experience dramatic changes in their social lives. In explaining the social effects of aging, sociologists have developed four different theoretical views.

Role theory assumes that people play a variety of social roles in their lifetime, and such roles identify and describe a person as a social being. These roles are the basis of one's self-concept. Age alters not only the roles expected of people, but also the manner in which they are expected to play them. How well individuals adjust to aging is assumed to depend on how well they accept the role changes typical of the later years.

Two of the primary roles held over the life course, the role of spouse and the role of worker, are often lost during old age. Some have argued that the life of retired people is "role-less" (Burgess, 1960). Because there is no social consensus about how the role of retiree should be performed, some elderly people may feel useless.

Activity theory simply assumes that older people who are active will be more satisfied and better adjusted than the less active. Since the theory presumes that a person's self-concept is validated through participation in roles characteristic of middle age, it is seen as desirable for older people to maintain as many middle-age activities as possible, and to substitute new roles for those that are lost through retirement or widowhood. Thus, advocates of activity theory believe that older people should remain active, busy, and productive in order to age optimally. This theory may be most apparent in the number of recreation events, travel tours, and classes sponsored by retirement communities and senior centers.

Disengagement theory (Cumming and Henry, 1961) challenges the assumption that older people have to be active in order to be well adjusted. Rather

Contrasting theories: The pensive satisfaction of disengagement (left) and the vigor of activity (right).

they argue that the process whereby older people decrease their activity levels, seek more passive roles, interact less frequently with others, and become increasingly preoccupied with their inner life is viewed as normal, inevitable, and personally satisfying. An underlying premise of disengagement theory is that old age is inevitably accompanied by declines in functioning, and a universal expectation of death. Advocates of this theory argue that disengagement is useful both for the aging individuals and for society at large. Older people are released from societal expectations and are allowed a sense of worth and tranquility while performing more peripheral roles. And, as old people withdraw from activities such as paid employment, younger people are ensured of a way to move into occupational roles.

Continuity theory argues that the aging person substitutes similar types of roles for lost ones, and continues to maintain typical ways of adapting to the environment in order to maintain inner psychological continuity as well as the outward continuity of social behavior and circumstances. All people are assumed to have different personalities and lifestyles, and that personality plays a major role in adjusting to aging. And the individual ages successfully if he or she maintains a mature, integrated personality while growing old (see Neugarten, Havighurst, and Toin, 1968).

THE SOCIAL EFFECTS OF AGING FOR THE INDIVIDUAL

As persons age, their relationships with others, and their ways of thinking, often change. Grandparent-grandchildren relationships are increasingly important. Increases in length of life may result in children having a greater likelihood of knowing grandparents and great-grandparents, although delayed parenthood and increased childlessness are factors that partially counter this potential. In 1990, 3.3 million grandchildren (5 percent of all children) lived in homes maintained by their grandparents, and in 30 percent of the cases the children's parents did not live with them (Moen, 1996).

Another change involves cognitive abilities, a pattern psychologists call the Classic Aging Pattern, which describes the performance of elderly people on the widely used Wechsler Adult Intelligence Scale (WAIS). People beyond the age of sixty-five perform significantly worse on performance scales, yet their scores on verbal scales remain stable over time. The performance scales assess fluid intelligence, or those skills that are biologically determined such as spatial orientation, abstract reasoning, and perceptual speed. The verbal scales, alternatively, assess crystallized intelligence, or knowledge and abilities accrued through education and experience, such as verbal comprehension and social judgment (Hooyman and Kiyak, 1993).

A third social effect of aging is emotional. Suicide rates remain high among the elderly, and older men are much more likely than older women to kill themselves. Elderly black and Hispanic males have suicide rates eight to ten times as great as their female counterparts, respectively. Elderly white males have by far the highest suicide rates among the elderly population. Lack of social networks, and lack of meaningful activity are likely associated with older white men's high rates of suicide. The percent of widowed men aged sixty-five to seventy-four and the percent of unemployed males age sixty-five and older seems to significantly contribute to the variation in the white male suicide rate among the young old (sixty-five to seventy-four) (McCall and Land, 1994). Other research suggests that lower suicide rates of older women may result from older women having more flexible and diverse coping strategies, and that relationships rather than paid employment are one important key to prevention of suicide in older men (Canetto, 1992).

Global Differences in Age Stratification

The central tenet of age stratification theory is that nearly all societies are age graded (see Riley, Johnson, and Foner, 1972). People are divided into categories such as "young," "middle-aged," and "old." That means that, as we age, we pass through a sequence of defined stages, each with its own social norms and characteristics. These groupings are defined in terms of social roles and responsibilities as well as by chronological age. Age may be linked to social roles directly (such as legally defined voting and driving ages) or indirectly (such as the socially appropriate ages for dating, marriage, and giving birth).

Thus, age is often viewed as a social construct with social meanings and social implications. The specific effects of age grading, or age stratification, vary across different cultures and historical time periods. Moreover, as the number of older people has grown and as social values have changed, the authority and power of the elderly in society has also shifted. Perhaps the greatest differences in the status of the elderly are between traditional societies and those of the modern Western world. A nonindustrial society, for instance, has very different expectations associated with stages of childhood, adolescence, and old age from our contemporary American culture. Numerous examples illustrate that age is a social construct, and elderly people are afforded different levels of respect and reverence across time, and across cultures.

In Tibet, the aged Sherpa live in a Buddhist society that idealizes old age. The elderly own their own

An elderly Sherpa man in Nepal.

homes, are in strikingly good physical condition, and have children nearby to provide care when needed. However, their younger sons move away from the community and are not available to share households and care for the old. Thus the old resist the traditional division of property and tend to keep the younger sons' share for themselves. The elderly Sherpa are also becoming proponents of birth control; since they cannot count on their sons to take care of them as they wish, they prefer to share their property among fewer children, keeping more for themselves (Beall and Goldstein, 1982).

In the subsistence society of the Chipewyan First Nation of Canada, older men are accorded low status, and old age is despised and feared. This is primarily because older men, who are no longer able to hunt, are perceived as unproductive, costing society more than they contribute. Dependent on contributions from each tribal member, the Chipewyans have sometimes been forced to abandon their old when faced with a choice between the death of older men and that of the entire tribe. Unlike older men, Chipewyan older women are still able to perform customary domestic and gathering tasks that do not require physical vigor. As a result, aging does not produce as substantial a decline in the status of older women as in that of older men (Sharp, 1981).

In seventeenth- and eighteenth-century America, old age was treated with deference and respect, in part because it was so rare. The Puritans viewed old age as a sign of God's favor and assumed that youth would inevitably defer to age. Old men occupied the highest public offices, as well as the positions of authority within the family, until they died. Fathers waited until their sixties before giving their land to their eldest sons. Church seats were given to the old. However, because the elders were exalted by law and custom, they did not develop close or loving relationships with younger relatives. Old age was not considered a time of serenity, but a time of anxiety about adequately fulfilling social obligations and keeping faith with God (Fischer, 1978).

In some societies, gerontocide or senecide—the deliberate destruction of aged community members—is viewed as functional, and is often performed with great reverence or ceremony. A team of sociologists examined sixty nonindustrialized societies and discovered that over 80 percent of these societies failed to actively maintain the existence and well-being of the aged, and for 19 percent of these societies, killing of the elderly was found. Their research also reported that in every case of killing, respect for the elderly was also present (Glascock and Feinman, 1981, 1986). The killings were viewed as regretted necessities.

Senior citizens have defended themselves against age discrimination in national and local politics.

The Future of Aging

In a society that places a high value on youth, vitality, and physical attractiveness, older people tend to become invisible. Recent years, however, have seen some changes in attitudes toward old age. Older people are unlikely to recover the full authority and prestige that used to be accorded to elders of the community in ancient societies. But as they have come to comprise a larger proportion of the population, older people have acquired more political influence than they used to have. They have already become a powerful political lobby.

Activist groups have also started to fight against **ageism**—discrimination against people on the basis of their age—seeking to encourage a positive view of old age and older people. Ageism is an ideology just as sexism and racism are. There are as many false stereotypes of older people as there are of other groups. For instance, it is often believed that most of the over sixty-five are in hospitals or homes for the elderly; that a high proportion are senile; and that older workers are less competent than younger ones. All these beliefs are erroneous. Ninety-five percent of people over sixty-five live in private dwellings; only about 7 percent of those between sixty-five and eighty show pronounced symptoms of senile decay; and the productivity and attendance records of workers over sixty are superior on average to those of younger age groups.

As the number of elderly people increases, a new crop of social and political issues will face Americans in the future.

1. Policy makers are interested in the dependency ratio or "elderly support ratio." This ratio is generally used to indicate the relationship between the proportion of the population that is employed (or "productive") and the proportion that is not in the workforce, and thus viewed as "dependent." This estimate is obtained by comparing the proportion of the population age eighteen to sixty-four years old to the proportion under age eighteen or over sixty-five. This ratio has increased steadily over time, such that there appear to be proportionately fewer employed

people to support older people today. Fear about rising costs of public pension programs are often driven by projected increases in the dependency ratio.

2. A greater number of elderly people means a greater demand for nursing homes and home-health care. The financial costs of such a trend may be overwhelming. Long-term care, such as nursing-home and home-health care, are seldom covered by private insurance or Medicare. Total expenditures for long-term care in the United States in 1993 reached $75.5 billion—$54.7 billion for nursing-home care and $20.8 billion for home care—yet only $13.7 billion was paid by Medicare. Roughly two-thirds of the total bill was paid for out of pocket by the elderly and their families (Wiener, Illston, and Hanley, 1994).

3. More demands will be placed on middle-aged people—especially women—to take care of their parents. More and more people in their fifties and sixties are likely to have surviving parents, aunts, and uncles. It has been estimated that two out of three fifty-year-old women have at least one living parent, compared to only one in three in 1950. More people will face the concern and expense of caring for their very old, frail relatives since so many people now live long enough to experience multiple, chronic illnesses. A 1992 survey of Americans found that almost one in three women and men aged fifty-five and older serve as informal caregivers of family, friends, and neighbors. Women, however, spend the most time providing care (Moen, 1996).

4. The gender gap in mortality means that many older women are living longer, and will be living without their spouses. Given that married elderly people are better off in terms of economic well-being, the number of poor women living alone may increase.

5. The population distribution in the United States could change drastically because the elderly have very distinct migration patterns. The older population is distributed very unequally in and among the fifty states. In 1994, people aged sixty-five and older accounted for 12.7 percent of the entire country's population, but more than 18 percent of Florida's (U.S. Bureau of the Census, 1996). Migration of elderly people often carries with it substantial amounts of retirement income transfers. In 1989, Florida was estimated to have received a net of $6.5 billion in transferred income due to interstate migration of the population aged sixty and older, while New York lost a net $3.3 billion to other states, with more than one-half of that loss ($1.9 billion) going to Florida (Longino, 1995).

In their book *Life After Work: The Arrival of the Ageless Society*, Michael Young and Tom Schuller (1991) argue that age has become an oppressive device used to slot people into fixed, stereotyped roles. Many older people are rebelling against such treatment and exploring new activities and modes of self-fulfillment. They are contesting what Young and Schuller call the "age-locked society."

In modern societies, both young and old are categorized by age, rather than in terms of their characteristics, pursuits, and identities. The two groups should form an alliance, according to Young and Schuller, to break out of the categories and create an ageless society. They could be pioneers in the interests not only of their own social positions, but of the majority of the population in paid work also. Young and Schuller argue that the young and the old could help shift the modern social order away from the treadmill of consumerism. More and more people, they say, quoting Virginia Woolf, could be freed from the constraints of labor, "always to be doing work that one did not wish to do, and to do it like a slave, flattering and fawning." They could develop their own unique qualities and concerns, as Woolf did in a spectacular way. Otherwise, her talent for writing, "a small one, but dear to the possessor," she thought would "perish and with it myself, my soul . . . like rust eating away the bloom of the spring."

CONCLUSION

In this chapter, we have looked at some of the diverse social influences that affect us as corporeal beings—that affect the protection and care of the body—as well as our sexual identities and reproductive strategies. As a result of both social and technological developments, we no longer experience our bodies or our sexual behavior as just a given part of our lives. There are bodily experiences into which science and technology now intrude—with mixed consequences. Many advances have been made in medicine and health care, and these have allowed people to live longer on average than once was common. At the same time, aging has changed its meaning, and older people are demanding the right to remain full members of society rather than being "pensioned off" by the young. These developments are important politically as well as socially. Making up as they do an increasing proportion of the population as a whole, older people are potentially a group with a good deal of political power.

SUMMARY

1. The field of the *sociology of the body* studies how the social world affects our bodies, and is particularly concerned with processes of social change. Modern *social technologies* have managed, for instance, to separate the body from nature; an example is the notion of dieting, which involves planned interventions in the functioning of our bodies in order to modify or regulate them in various ways.

2. Food production in the modern world has been globalized: technologies of transportation and of storage (refrigeration) have meant that now everyone is on a diet in some sense, having to *decide* what to eat everyday. Such decisions are influenced by social relations. Women especially are judged by physical appearance, but feelings of shame about the body can lead anyone to compulsive dieting, exercising, or body-building to make the body conform to social expectations.

3. Health and illness are connected to population issues as well as being strongly affected by social factors such as class, race, and gender. Modern Western medicine, which arose in the past two or three centuries, views illness as having physical origins and hence as being explicable in scientific terms. In spite of its importance, public health measures, such as better sanitation and nutrition, were more important in reducing infant mortality rates. The expansion of the West was accompanied by the spread of infectious diseases in what is now the Third World. Moreover, the colonial system, with its stress on cash crops, negatively affected the nutrition of Third World people. Susceptibility to the major illnesses is strongly influenced by socioeconomic status. For example, people in the First World tend to live longer than those in the Third World; the richer tend to be healthier, taller, and stronger than those from less-privileged backgrounds.

4. Researchers have examined both biological and cultural influences on human sexual behavior, concluding that sexuality, like gender, is mostly socially constructed. There is an extremely wide range of possible sexual practices, but in any given society only some will be approved and reflected in social norms. Because these norms also vary widely, however, we can be quite certain that most sexual responses are learned rather than innate.

5. *Reproductive technologies*—affecting fertilization, the growth of the embryo, and the nature of birth—pose difficult and controversial issues. Many debates continue to center on their use.

6. In recent years, older people, who now make up a larger proportion of the population of the industrialized countries, have started to press for more recognition of their distinctive interests and needs. The struggle against *ageism* (discrimination against people on grounds of their age) is an important aspect of this development.

Chapter Seventeen

Living in Cities

Learn how cities have changed as a result of industrialization and urbanization.

Theories of Urbanism

Learn how theories of urbanism have placed increasing emphasis on the influence of socioeconomic factors on city life.

Urbanism in the United States

Learn about the recent key developments affecting American cities in the last several decades: suburbanization, urban decay, and gentrification.

Urbanism and International Influences

See that global economic competition has a profound impact on urbanization and urban life.

World Population Growth

Learn why the world population has increased dramatically and understand the main consequences of this growth.

Urbanization, Population Growth, and the Environment

See that the environment is a sociological issue related to urbanization and population growth.

URBANIZATION, POPULATION, AND THE ENVIRONMENT

Under the leadership of Mayor Rudolph Giuliani, New York City has become what urban sociologists call a "tourist city," attracting over 30 million visitors a year from all over the globe. As in many urban areas around the world, tourism has had a great effect on both the street life and the economic well-being of the city. For example, while the neighborhood around Times Square was once full of porn shops, X-rated theaters, strip joints, drug dealers, and cheap restaurants, it is now home to the Disney Store, theme restaurants, mainstream movie theaters, and other tourist attractions. In addition, the amount of money spent by tourists on theater tickets, hotel rooms, restaurant meals, and the like has pumped billions of dollars into the local economy. Once feared and shunned because of its so-called "urban problems," New York is now one of the world's leading tourist destinations, where millions go for the "New York experience." The paradox of a "tourist city" like New York is that while the appeal of tourism is the opportunity to experience something different, cities that are remade to attract tourism seem more and more alike (Judd and Fainstein, 1999).

Nevertheless, cities like New York still offer people opportunities to escape the conformity and provincialism of life elsewhere. People who may have once flocked to Times Square now go to neighborhoods like Greenwich Village, where they hang out on St. Marks Place or Eighth Street and have access to "hip" bars, music shops, and tattoo and piercing parlors. On a weekend night, a scene like Eighth Street is a destination for high school and college students—from both New York and its surrounding suburbs—from all different social and ethnic groups. Here, they move about among older white ethnics who are long-time neighborhood residents, college professors and other urban professionals of all races who have bought apartments in the neighborhood, gays of all classes and races, drug dealers who were forced out of nearby Washington Square Park, and homeless people who make a life for themselves on the sidewalks. Every fifteen minutes or so, double-decker buses drop off tourists who spend time strolling the Village's streets.

Eighth Street is an interesting location to a sociologist because it raises two central questions about urban life: Is social life in cities distinctive from social life outside of cities? How much is urban life influenced by larger social forces? One defining characteristic of cities is the frequency of interactions between strangers. Even within the same neighborhood or apartment building, it's highly unlikely that people will know most of their neighbors. This fact alone makes life in cities today different from life elsewhere or during earlier times in history. While city life is distinctive, cities are closely tied to social processes that cut across the globe. One of the processes that we will explore in this chapter is the movement of people. So while it is easy for one to assume that "urban" problems such as crime and homelessness are unique to cities, sociologists have shown they are neither distinctive to cities nor caused by city life.

The study of cities, and the understanding that a defining feature of urban life is the interaction between strangers, has been a central concern of American sociology since the early 1920s. This was when a group of sociologists at the University of Chicago did field studies of small social worlds within that city. One such study, *The Taxi-Dance Hall* (Cress, 1932),

focused on the dance halls where immigrant men went for female companionship, buying tickets for dances with women. This early study looked at the dance hall as a place that could only exist in a city because such institutions depended on interaction between strangers. The early sociologists of the Chicago School argued that many people move from small towns to cities to get away from the suffocating atmosphere of "everyone knowing everyone else's business," and the social norms and moralistic codes that enforce conformity. But these same sociologists did not yet understand—as sociologists do today—that the conditions they observed in cities were socially constructed. They thought the patterns they observed were natural and would likely be the same in any city. In this chapter, we will see how urban sociologists ultimately came to a different understanding.

LIVING IN CITIES

An inescapable part of modern life, cities provide sociologists with a laboratory for studying the diversity of social life and conflict. Cities are the capitals of civilization: they are culturally lively, commercially dynamic, and alluring. They are efficient in providing for a large number of the population in a small amount of space. However, an entire literature has been devoted to the problems of city life, including poverty, racial and ethnic exclusion and antagonism, and crime.

In all modern societies, in contrast to the premodern era, most of the population live in urban areas, and even those who don't are affected by city life. We shall first of all study the origins of cities and the vast growth in the numbers of city dwellers that has occurred over the past century. From there, we will review the most influential theories of urban life. We then move on to consider patterns of urban development in North America, as compared with cities in the Third World. Third World cities are growing at an enormous rate. We shall consider why this is so, and at the same time look at changes now taking place in world population patterns. We will conclude by assessing the connections among urbanization, world population growth, and environmental problems.

Cities in Traditional Societies

The world's first cities appeared about 3500 B.C.E., in the river valleys of the Nile in Egypt, the Tigris and Euphrates in what is now Iraq, and the Indus in what is today Pakistan. Cities in traditional societies were very small by modern standards. Babylon, for example, one of the largest ancient Near Eastern cities, extended over an area of only 3.2 square miles and at its height, around 2000 B.C.E., probably numbered no more than 15,000–20,000 people. Rome under Emperor Augustus in the first century B.C.E. was easily the largest premodern city outside of China, with some 300,000 inhabitants—the population of Birmingham, Alabama, or Tucson, Arizona, today.

Most cities of the ancient world shared certain common features. They were usually surrounded by walls that served as a military defense and emphasized the separation of the urban community from the countryside. The central area of the city was almost always occupied by a religious temple, a royal palace, government and commercial buildings, and a public square. This ceremonial, commercial, and political center was sometimes enclosed within a second, inner wall, and was usually too small to hold more than a minority of the citizens. Although it usually contained a market, the center was different from the business districts found at the core of modern cities, because the main buildings were nearly always religious and political (Sjoberg, 1960, 1963; Fox, 1964; Wheatley, 1971).

The dwellings of the ruling class or elite tended to be concentrated in or near the center. The less privileged groups lived toward the perimeter of the city or outside the walls, moving inside if the city came under attack. Different ethnic and religious communities were often allocated to separate neighborhoods, where their members both lived and worked. Sometimes these neighborhoods were also surrounded by walls. Communication among city dwellers was erratic. Lacking any form of printing press, public officials had to shout at the tops of their voices to deliver pronouncements. "Streets" were usually strips of land on which no one had yet built. A few traditional civilizations boasted sophisticated road systems linking various cities, but these existed mainly for military purposes, and transportation for the most part was slow and limited. Merchants and soldiers were the only people who regularly traveled over long distances.

While cities were the main centers for science, the arts, and cosmopolitan culture, their influence over the rest of the country was always weak. No more than a tiny proportion of the population lived in the cities, and the division between cities and countryside

The Forum served as the political and religious center of ancient Rome.

was pronounced. By far the majority of people lived in small rural communities, and rarely came into contact with more than the occasional state official or merchant from the towns.

Industrialization and Urbanization

The contrast in size between the largest modern cities and those of premodern civilizations is extraordinary. The most populous cities in the industrialized countries number almost 20 million inhabitants. A **conurbation**—a cluster of cities and towns forming a continuous network—may include even larger numbers of people. The peak of urban life today is represented by what is called the **megalopolis**, the "city of cities." The term was originally coined in ancient Greece to refer to a city-state that was planned to be the envy of all civilizations. The current megalopolis, though, bears little relation to that utopia. The term was first applied in modern times to refer to the Northeast corridor of the United States, an area covering some 450 miles from north of Boston to below Washington, D.C. In this region, about 40 million people live at a density of over 700 persons per square mile. An urban population almost as large and dense is concentrated in the lower Great Lakes region.

Britain was the first society to undergo industrialization, beginning in the mid-eighteenth century. The process of industrialization generated increasing **ur-** **banization**—the movement of the population into towns and cities, away from the land. In 1800, fewer than 20 percent of the British population lived in towns or cities with more than 10,000 inhabitants. By 1900, this proportion had risen to 74 percent. London held about 1.1 million people in 1800; by the beginning of the twentieth century, it had increased in size to a population of over 7 million, at that date the largest city ever seen in the world. It was a vast manufacturing, commercial, and financial center at the heart of a still-expanding British Empire.

 The urbanization of most other European countries and the United States took place somewhat later. In 1800, the United States was more of a rural society than were the leading European countries.

Fewer than 10 percent lived in communities with populations of more than 2,500 people. Today, well over three-quarters of Americans are city dwellers. Between 1800 and 1900, as industrialization grew in the United States, the population of New York City leapt from 60,000 people to 4.8 million.

Urbanization in the twentieth century is a global process, into which the Third World is more and more being drawn (Kasarda and Crenshaw, 1991). From 1900 to 1950, world urbanization increased by 239 percent, compared with a global population growth of 49 percent. The past fifty years have seen a greater acceleration in the proportion of people living in cities. From 1950 to 1986, urban growth worldwide was 320 percent, while the population grew by 54 percent. Most of this growth has occurred in cities in Third World societies. In 1975, 39 percent of the world's population lived in urban areas; the figure was around 50 percent in 2000 and is predicted to be 63 percent in 2025. Eastern and southern Asia will comprise about half of the world's people in 2025. By that date, the urban populations of the Third World countries will exceed those of Europe or the United States.

Along with this worldwide urbanization come the effects of globalization. For example, the rise of urban-industrial areas in Third World countries has brought intensified economic competition to industries in U.S. cities. South Korea's shoe industry has led to the impoverishment of urban areas in Massachusetts that formerly relied on that industry for their prosperity. Similarly, Baltimore has had to adjust to losing much of the market for its steel industry to Japan. We shall examine later in the chapter how the global economy has influenced forms of city life in recent years.

Interpretations of City Life

The development of modern cities has had an enormous impact not only on people's habits and modes of behavior, but on patterns of thought and feeling. From the beginning of large urban agglomerations in the mid-eighteenth century, views about the effects of cities on social life have been polarized, and they remain so today. Some writers saw cities as representing

KEY CONCEPTS IN REVIEW

Traditional cities were mostly small by modern standards, they were surrounded by walls, and their centers were dominated by religious buildings and palaces.

In traditional societies, only a small minority of the population lived in urban areas. In the industrialized countries today, between 60 and 90 percent do so. **Urbanization** is also developing rapidly in Third World societies.

"civilized virtue," centers of dynamism and cultural creativity. For them, cities maximized opportunities for economic and cultural development and provided the means of living a comfortable and satisfying existence. James Boswell constantly praised the virtues of London, which he compared to a "museum, a garden, to endless musical combinations" (Byrd, 1978). Others branded the city a smoking inferno thronged with aggressive and mutually distrustful crowds and riddled with crime, violence, and corruption.

During the nineteenth and early twentieth centuries, as cities mushroomed in size, these contrasting views found new voices. Critics found easy targets for their attacks, as the living conditions of the poor in the most rapidly developing urban areas were frequently appalling. George Gissing, an English novelist and social analyst, personally experienced extreme poverty both in London and in Chicago in the 1870s. He portrayed the East End of London, one of the poorest sections in the city, as

a region of malodorous market streets, of factories, timber-yards, grimy warehouses, of alleys swarming with small trades and crafts, of filthy courts and passages leading into pestilential gloom; everywhere toil in its most degrading forms; the thoroughfares thundering with high-laden wagons, the pavements trodden by working folk of the coarsest type, the corners and lurking-holes showing destitution at its ugliest. (1983)

During this period, poverty in American cities received less attention than in Europe. Toward the end of the nineteenth century, however, reformers began increasingly to condemn the squalor of large parts of New York, Boston, Chicago, and other major cities. The extent of urban poverty and the vast differences

Social critics of the late nineteenth century noted the living conditions of the poorest members of industrial societies.

among city neighborhoods were some of the main factors prompting early sociological analyses of urban life. Jacob Riis, a Danish immigrant and reporter for the *New York Tribune,* traveled extensively across the United States, documenting conditions of poverty and lecturing about needed reforms. His resulting book, *How the Other Half Lives*, which appeared in 1890, reached a wide audience (Riis, 1957; Lane, 1974). Others added their voices to what became a chorus of description of grim urban life. As one anonymous poet put it, speaking of the Boston poor: "In a great, Christian city, died friendless, of hunger! Starved to death, where there's many a bright banquet hall! In a city of hospitals, died in a prison! Homeless, died in a land that boasts free homes for all! In a city of millionaires, died without money!" (Lees, 1985).

The first major sociological studies of, and theories about, modern urban conditions originated in Chicago—a city marked by a phenomenal rate of development and by very pronounced inequalities.

THEORIES OF URBANISM

The Chicago School

A number of writers associated with the University of Chicago from the 1920s to the 1940s, especially Robert Park, Ernest Burgess, and Louis Wirth, developed ideas that were for many years the chief basis of theory and research in urban sociology. Two concepts developed by the "Chicago School" are worthy of special attention. One is the so-called **ecological approach** to urban analysis; the other, the characterization of urbanism as a *way of life*, developed by Wirth (Park, 1952; Wirth, 1938). It is important to understand these ideas as they were initially conceived by the Chicago School and to see how they have been revised and even supplanted by later sociologists.

URBAN ECOLOGY

Ecology is a term taken from a physical science: the study of the adaptation of plant and animal organisms to their environment. In the natural world, organisms tend to be distributed in systematic ways over the terrain, such that a balance or equilibrium between different species is achieved. The Chicago School believed that the siting of major urban settlements and the distribution of different types of neighborhoods within them can be understood in terms of similar principles. Cities do not grow up at random, but in response to advantageous features of the environment. For example, large urban areas in modern societies tend to develop along the shores of rivers, in fertile plains, or at the intersection of trading routes or railways.

"Once set up," in Park's words, "a city is, it seems, a great sorting mechanism which . . . infallibly selects out of the population as a whole the individuals best suited to live in a particular region or a particular milieu" (Park, 1952, p. 79). Cities become ordered into "natural areas," through processes of competition, invasion, and succession—all of which occur in biological ecology. If we look at the ecology of a lake in the natural environment, we find that competition among various species of fish, insects, and other organisms operates to reach a fairly stable distribution among them. This balance is disturbed if new species invade—try to make the lake their home. Some of the organisms that used to proliferate in the central area of the lake are driven out to eke out a more precarious existence around its fringes. The invading species are their successors in the central sections.

Patterns of location, movement, and relocation in cities, according to the ecological view, have a similar form. Different neighborhoods develop through the adjustments made by inhabitants as they struggle to gain their livelihoods. A city can be pictured as a map of areas with distinct and contrasting social characteristics. In the initial stages of the growth of modern cities, industries congregate at sites suitable for the raw materials they need, close to supply lines. Population clusters around these workplaces, which come to be more and more diversified, as the number of the city's inhabitants grows. The amenities thus developed become correspondingly more attractive, and greater competition develops for their acquisition. Land values and property taxes rise, making it difficult for families to carry on living in the central neighborhood, except in cramped conditions or in decaying housing in which rents are low. The center becomes dominated by businesses and entertainment, with the more affluent private residents moving out to newly forming suburbs around the perimeter. This process follows transport routes, since these minimize the time taken in travelling to work; the areas between these routes develop more slowly.

Cities can be seen as formed in concentric rings, broken up into segments. In the center are the **inner city** areas, a mixture of big business prosperity and decaying private houses. Beyond these are older-established neighborhoods, housing workers employed in stable manual occupations. Further out still are the suburbs in which higher-income groups tend to live. Processes of invasion and succession occur within the segments of the concentric rings. Thus as property decays in a central or near-central area, ethnic minority groups might start to move into it. As they do so, more of the preexisting population start to leave, precipitating a wholesale flight to neighborhoods elsewhere in the city or out to the suburbs.

Although for a period the **urban ecology** approach fell into disrepute, it was later revived and elaborated in the writings of a number of authors, particularly Amos Hawley (Hawley, 1950, 1968). Rather than concentrating on competition for scarce resources, as his predecessors did, Hawley emphasized the *interdependence* of different city areas. *Differentiation*—the specialization of groups and occupational roles—is the main way in which human beings adapt to their environment. Groups on which many others depend will have a dominant role, often reflected in their central geographical position. Business groups, for example, like large banks or insurance companies, provide key services for many in a community, and hence are usually to be found in the central areas of settlements. But the zones that develop in urban areas, Hawley points out, arise from relationships not just of space, but of time. Business dominance, for example, is expressed not only in patterns of land use, but in the rhythm of activities in daily life—an illustration being the rush hour. The ordering in time of people's daily lives reflects the hierarchy of neighborhoods in the city.

The ecological approach has been as important for the amount of empirical research it has helped to promote as for its value as a theoretical perspective. Many studies of cities as a whole, and of particular neighborhoods, have been prompted by ecological thinking—concerned, for example, with the processes of invasion and succession just mentioned. However, various criticisms can justifiably be made. The ecological perspective tends to underemphasize the importance of conscious design and planning in city organization, regarding urban development as a natural process. The Chicago School also failed to consider how social forces such as discrimination could affect a city's development.

As we noted in the chapter's introduction, part of what it means to think like an urban sociologist today is to ask whether and how the conditions observed in cities are socially constructed or natural. We have seen that the early Chicago School leaned toward the idea that spatial patterns were natural outcomes. This all began to change when two black graduate students at the University of Chicago published the book *Black Metropolis* (1945), which posed a challenge to the human ecology framework.

Drake and Cayton's massive study, based on extensive historical and ethnographic data, showed that the black residential neighborhoods of Chicago were by no means the result of natural forces, but were constructed by unnatural, social forces. These areas were called ghettos, a term that has come to mean many things to many people, but that can be most usefully defined as a residential area where a racial or ethnic group initially comes to live as a consequence of systematic exclusion from more desirable places. Drake and Cayton showed that the ghetto was not in the poor state it was in because the people were black, but because blacks were given no choice but to live in the worst areas of the city. There was nothing natural about this placement and it would not have occurred were it not for social forces such as exclusion, violence, and restrictive covenants where neighborhood "improvement" associations passed laws making it illegal to sell land in a community to blacks. After Drake and Cayton's *Black Metropolis*, it was harder for sociologists to think of the distributions of populations in urban areas as natural.

URBANISM AS A WAY OF LIFE

Wirth's thesis of urbanism as a *way of life* is concerned less with whether cities are natural or socially constructed than with what urbanism *is* as a form of social existence. It is related to the focus, identified earlier in this chapter, with how life in cities is distinctive or different from life elsewhere. This is the other kind of question we said urban sociologists tend to ask, though we will see in the case of Wirth that the answer can be quite nuanced. Wirth observes:

> the degree to which the contemporary world may be said to be "urban" is not fully or accurately measured by the proportion of the total population living in cities. The influences which cities exert on the social life of man are greater than the ratio of the urban population would indicate; for the city is not only increasingly the dwelling-place and the workshop of modern man, but it is the initiating and controlling center of economic, political and cultural life that has drawn the most remote communities of the world into its orbit and woven diverse areas, peoples and activities into a cosmos. (Wirth, 1938, p. 342)

Here we can see that Wirth is not merely content to ask whether and how life in cities is different from life elsewhere, but he asserts that the effects of life in cities can be felt outside of cities as well. For example, have you ever noticed that many young people today dress in garments that were once thought to be distinctive to urban minority youth? It is not uncommon to find some teenagers in suburban high schools all over America dressing in baggy pants, untucked t-shirts, and hightop sneakers. If Wirth were writing today he might cite this as an example for his claim that the cultural life that begins in cities draws in the outer-lying population, so that urbanism is "a way of life" in many places outside cities as well.

Wirth's theory is important for its recognition that urbanism is not just *part* of a society, but expresses and influences the nature of the wider social system. Aspects of the urban way of life are characteristic of social life in modern societies as a whole, not just the activities of those who happen to live in big cities.

But there was another aspect to Wirth's argument that focused more on an aspect of life that he did think was distinctive to cities. In cities, Wirth points out, large numbers of people live in close proximity to one another, without knowing most others personally—a fundamental contrast to small, traditional villages. Most contacts between city-dwellers are fleeting and partial, and are means to other ends, rather than being satisfying relationships in themselves. Interactions with sales clerks in stores, cashiers in banks, pas-

sengers or ticket collectors on trains are passing encounters, entered into not for their own sake but as means to other aims.

Since those who live in urban areas tend to be highly mobile, there are relatively weak bonds between them. People are involved in many different activities and situations each day—the pace of life is faster than in rural areas. Competition prevails over cooperation. Wirth accepts that the density of social life in cities leads to the formation of neighborhoods having distinct characteristics, some of which may preserve the characteristics of small communities. In immigrant areas, for example, traditional types of connections between families are found, with most people knowing most others on a personal basis. The more such areas are absorbed into wider patterns of city life, however, the less these characteristics survive.

Wirth was among the first to address the "urban interaction problem" (Duneier and Molotoch, 1999), the necessity for city dwellers to respect social boundaries when so many people are in close physical proximity all the time. Wirth elaborates that "the reserve, the indifference, and the blasé outlook that urbanites manifest in their relationships may thus be regarded as devices for immunizing themselves against the personal claims and expectations of others." Many people walk down the street in cities acting unconcerned about the others near them. Through such appearance of apathy they can avoid unwanted transgression of social boundaries.

Wirth's ideas have deservedly enjoyed wide currency. The impersonality of many day-to-day contacts in modern cities is undeniable—but to some degree this is true of social life in general in modern societies. Although one might assume that the "immunization" urban dwellers engage in to distance themselves from others is unique to city life, urban interaction may be only a subtype of the universal social condition. While the presence of strangers is more common in cities (Lofland, 1973, 1998), all people must manage social boundaries in their face-to-face interactions with others—as has been found as far afield as Western Samoa (Duranti, 1994) or among the African Poro people (Bellman, 1984). It is always necessary to ask whether the problems one associates with cities are aspects of social life more generally. In assessing Wirth's ideas, one must also ask whether his generalizations about urban life hold true for all cities during all times.

One form of urbanism in New York: a father in the fast-paced city.

Like the ecological perspective, with which it has much in common, Wirth's theory is based mainly on observations of American cities, yet generalized to urbanism everywhere. Urbanism is not the same at all times and places. As has been mentioned, for example, ancient cities were in many respects quite different from those found in modern societies. Life for most people in the early cities was not much more anonymous or impersonal than for those living in village communities.

Wirth also exaggerates the impersonality of modern cities. Communities involving close friendship or kinship links are more persistent within modern urban communities than he supposed. Everett Hughes, a colleague of Wirth's at the University of Chicago, wrote of his associate: "Louis used to say all those things about how the city is impersonal—while living with a whole clan of kin and friends on a very personal basis" (quoted in Kasarda and Janowitz, 1974). Groups such as those Herbert Gans calls "the urban villagers" are common in modern cities (Gans, 1979). His urban villagers are Italian Americans living in an inner-city Boston neighborhood. Such "white ethnic" areas are probably becoming less significant in American cities than was once the case, but they are being replaced by inner-city communities involving newer immigrants.

More important, neighborhoods involving close kinship and personal ties seem often to be actively *created* by city life; they are not just remnants of a preexisting way of life, which survive for a period within the city. Claude Fischer has put forward an interpretation of why large-scale urbanism tends actually to promote diverse subcultures, rather than swamp everyone within an anonymous mass. Those who live in cities, he points out, are able to collaborate with others of like background or interests to develop local connections; and they can join distinctive religious, ethnic, political, and other subcultural groups. A small town or village does not allow the development of such subcultural diversity (Fischer, 1984). Those who form ethnic communities within cities, for instance, might have had little or no knowledge of one another in their land of origin. When they arrive in a new country, they gravitate to areas where others from a similar linguistic and cultural background are living, and new subcommunity structures are formed. An artist might find few others in a village or small town with whom to associate, but in a large city, on the other hand, he or she might become part of a significant artistic and intellectual subculture.

A large city is a world of strangers, yet it supports and creates personal relationships. This is not paradoxical. We have to separate urban experience into the public sphere of encounters with strangers and the more private world of family, friends, and work col-

In large cities, people can often find social and cultural groups with which to identify. Here, Asian Americans celebrate the Chinese New Year.

leagues. It may be difficult to meet people when one first moves to a large city. But anyone moving to a small, established rural community may find the friendliness of the inhabitants largely a matter of public politeness—it may take years to become accepted. This is not the case in the city. Although one finds a diversity of strangers, each is a potential friend. And once within a group or network, the possibilities for expanding one's personal connections increase considerably.

Wirth's ideas retain some validity, but in the light of subsequent contributions it is clear that they are overgeneralized. Modern cities frequently involve impersonal, anonymous social relationships, but they are also sources of diversity—and, sometimes, intimacy.

JANE JACOBS: EYES AND EARS UPON THE STREET

Like most sociologists in the twentieth century, the Chicago School researchers were professors who saw their mission as contributing to a scholarly literature and advancing the field of social science.

At certain moments in the history of sociology, however, advances have also come from thinkers working outside universities without formal training in sociology. One such person was Jane Jacobs, who

published *The Death and Life of Great American Cities* in 1961.

Jacobs is an architecture critic with a high school education, but through her own independent reading and research she transformed herself into one of the most learned figures in the emerging field of urban studies. She is known as a public intellectual, because her main goal was to speak to the educated public, rather than to contribute to a scholarly literature. Nevertheless, her work has had an impact on scholarship in sociology as well.

Like sociologists such as Louis Wirth of the Chicago School before her, Jacobs argued that "cities are, by definition, full of strangers," some of whom are dangerous. She tried to explain what makes it possible for cities to meet the challenge of "assimilating strangers" in such a way that strangers can feel comfortable together. She argued that cities are most habitable when they feature a diversity of uses, thereby ensuring that many people will be coming and going on the streets at any time. When enough people are out and about, Jacobs argued, "respectable" eyes and ears dominate the street and are fixed on strangers, who will thus not get out of hand. Underneath the seeming disorder of a busy street is the very basis for order in "the intricacy of sidewalk use, bringing with it a constant succession of eyes." The more people are out, or looking from their windows at the people who are out, the more their gazes will safeguard the street.

As sometimes happens in sociology and popular discussion, Jacobs's ideas remain influential even though the evidence for them is, at best, mixed. Only three years after her book was published, for example, a young woman named Kitty Genovese was stabbed to death in Queens, New York, while thirty-eight people watched from their windows (Rosenthal, 1999).

It is very common for people to make the mistake of believing that certain principles are natural to social life, only to discover later on that these principles only hold up under particular social conditions. The world has changed a great deal since Jacobs wrote *The Death and Life of Great American Cities*. Many of the assumptions she made about urban life may not hold up when the conditions in cities have changed. What are some of these changes? Whereas when Jacobs was writing, most of the people on the sidewalks she discussed were similar in many respects, today homeless people, drug users, panhandlers, and others representing economic inequalities, cultural differences, and extremes of behavior can make sidewalk life difficult and unpredictable (Duneier, 1999). Under these conditions, strangers do not necessarily feel the kind of solidarity and mutual assurance she described. Sociologists today must ask what happens to urban life when "the eyes and ears upon the street" represent vast inequalities and cultural differences? Do the assumptions Jacobs made still hold up? In many cases the answer is yes, but in many other cases the answer is no.

Urbanism and the Created Environment

Whereas the earlier Chicago School of sociology emphasized that the distribution of people in cities occurs naturally, we have seen that scholars like Drake and Cayton showed this was not true with regard to the black population. They demonstrated that blacks often did not get to live where their incomes would have naturally led them to live, because of violence and restrictive covenants. More recent theories of the city have stressed that urbanism is not a natural

process, but has to be analyzed in relation to major patterns of political and economic change.

According to this view, it is not the stranger on the sidewalk who is most threatening to many urban dwellers, especially the poor; instead, it is the stranger far away, working in a bank or real estate development company, who has the power to make decisions that transform whole blocks or neighborhoods (Logan and Moltoch, 1987). This focus on the political economy of cities, and on different kinds of strangers, represented a new direction for urban sociology.

HARVEY: THE RESTRUCTURING OF SPACE

Urbanism, David Harvey emphasizes, is one aspect of the **created environment** brought about by the spread of industrial capitalism. In traditional societies, city and countryside were clearly differentiated. In the modern world, industry blurs the division between city and countryside. Agriculture becomes mechanized and is run according to considerations of price and profit, just like industrial work, and this process lessens the differences in modes of social life between urban and rural people.

In modern urbanism, Harvey points out, space is continually *restructured*. The process is determined by where large firms choose to place their factories, research and development centers, and so forth; the controls that governments operate over both land and industrial production; and the activities of private investors, buying and selling houses and land. Business firms, for example, are constantly weighing up the relative advantages of new locations against existing ones. As production becomes cheaper in one area than another, or as the firm moves from one product to another, offices and factories will be closed down in one place and opened up elsewhere. Thus at one period, when there are considerable profits to be made, there may be a spate of office-block building in the center of large cities. Once the offices have been built, and the central area redeveloped, investors look for potential for further speculative building elsewhere. Often what is profitable in one period will not be so in another, when the financial climate changes.

The activities of private home buyers are strongly

influenced by how far, and where, business interests buy up land, as well as by rates of loans and taxes fixed by local and central government. After World War II, for instance, there was vast expansion of suburban development outside major cities in the United States. This was partly due to ethnic discrimination and the tendency of whites to move away from inner-city areas. However, it was only made possible, Harvey argues, because of government decisions to provide tax concessions to home buyers and construction firms, and by the setting up of special credit arrangements by financial organizations. These provided the basis for the building and buying of new homes on the peripheries of cities, and at the same time promoted demand for industrial products such as the automobile (Harvey, 1973, 1982, 1985).

CASTELLS: URBANISM AND SOCIAL MOVEMENTS

Like Harvey, Manuel Castells stresses that the spatial form of a society is closely linked to the overall mechanisms of its development. But in contrast to the Chicago sociologists, Castells sees the city not only as a distinct *location*—the urban area—but as an integral part of processes of **collective consumption**, which in turn are an inherent aspect of industrial capitalism. Homes, schools, transport services, and leisure amenities are ways in which people consume the products of modern industry. The taxation system influences who is able to buy or rent where, and who builds where. Large corporations, banks, and insurance companies, which provide capital for building projects, have a great deal of power over these processes. But government agencies also directly affect many aspects of city life, by building roads and public housing, planning parks, and so forth. The physical shape of cities is thus a product of both market forces and the power of government.

But the nature of the created environment is not just the result of the activities of wealthy and powerful people. Castells stresses the importance of the struggles of underprivileged groups to alter their living conditions. Urban problems stimulate a range of social movements, concerned with improving housing conditions, protesting against air pollution, defending parks, and combating building development that changes the nature of an area. For example, Castells has studied the gay movement in San Francisco, which succeeded in restructuring neighborhoods around its

Cities are exploring alternatives to public housing for underprivileged groups. Many are beginning to plan mixed-income neighborhoods in hopes of creating better conditions for the poor.

KEY CONCEPTS IN REVIEW

The Chicago School pioneered urban sociology. The **ecological approach** or the **urban ecology** approach sees city growth as a natural process. Cities do not grow randomly, but growth begins in the most advantageous or desirable areas. First, there is competition among different groups, the balance is upset by the invasion of new groups, and a new balance is achieved by the succession by the invaders.

Louis Wirth's idea of **urbanism** as a "way of life" stresses urbanism as a form of social existence, characterized by fleeting, impersonal interactions, the rapid pace of life, and the development of a homogeneous and anonymous mass. Many have criticized Wirth's idea for emphasizing the city as a world of strangers. Rather, urbanization often contributes to the growth of diverse subcultures and the persistence of neighborhood ties.

Unlike the Chicago School, recent theorists of urbanism draw inspiration from Marx and note political and economic influences on urban development. David Harvey argues that urbanism is an aspect of the **created environment** brought about by industrial capitalism. Manuel Castells argues that urban environments represent symbolic manifestations of broader social forces. For Castells, the city is not so much a site as a process of **collective consumption**, where people consume goods and services offered by corporations and governments. Logan and Molotch argue that the global economic forces affecting urban development are focused through local institutions.

own cultural values—allowing many gay organizations, clubs, and bars to flourish—and gained a prominent position in local politics (Castells, 1977, 1983).

Cities, Harvey and Castells both emphasize, are almost wholly artificial environments, constructed by people. Even most rural areas do not escape the influence of human intervention and modern technology, for human activity has reshaped and reordered the world of nature. Food is not produced for local inhabitants, but for national and international markets, and in mechanized farming, land is rigorously subdivided and specialized in its use, ordered into physical patterns that have little relationship to natural features of the environment. Those who live on farms and in isolated rural areas are economically, politically, and culturally tied to the larger society, however different some of their modes of behavior may be from those of city-dwellers.

In some ways, the views set out by Harvey and Castells and those of the Chicago School usefully complement each other, and can be combined to give

a comprehensive picture of urban processes. The contrasts between city areas described in urban ecology do exist, as does the overall impersonality of city life. But these are more variable than the members of the Chicago School believed, and are primarily governed by the social and economic influences analyzed by Harvey and Castells. John Logan and Harvey Molotch have suggested an approach that directly connects the perspectives of authors like Harvey and Castells with some features of the ecological standpoint (Logan and Molotch, 1987). They agree with Harvey and Castells that broad features of economic development, stretching nationally and internationally, affect urban life in a quite direct way. But these wide-ranging economic factors, they argue, are focused through local organizations, including neighborhood businesses, banks, and government agencies, together with the activities of individual house buyers.

Places—land and buildings—are bought and sold, according to Logan and Molotch, just like other goods in modern societies, but the markets that structure city environments are influenced by how different groups of people want to *use* the property they buy and sell. Many tensions and conflicts arise as a result of this process—and these are the key factors structuring city neighborhoods. For instance, an apartment house is seen as a home by its residents, but as a source of income by its landlord. Businesses are most interested in buying and selling property in an area to obtain the best production sites or to make profits in land speculation. Their interests and concerns are quite different from those of residents, for whom the neighborhood is a place to live.

In modern cities, Logan and Molotch point out, large financial and business firms continually try to intensify land use in specific areas. The more they can do so, the more there are opportunities for land speculation and for the profitable construction of new buildings. These companies have little concern with the social and physical effects of their activities on a given neighborhood—with whether or not, for example, attractive older residences are destroyed to make room for large new office buildings. The growth processes fostered by big firms involved in property development often go against the interests of local businesses or residents, who may attempt actively to resist them. People come together in neighborhood groups in order to defend their interests as residents. Such local associations may campaign for the extension of zoning restrictions, block new building on parkland, or press for more favorable rent regulations.

URBANISM IN THE UNITED STATES

What are the main trends that have affected city development in the United States over the past several decades? How can we explain the decay of central-city areas? These are questions we shall take up in the following sections. One of the major changes in urban patterns in the period since World War II is the movement of large parts of city populations to newly constructed suburbs; this movement outward has been a particularly pronounced feature of American cities and is related directly to central-city decay. We there-

fore begin with a discussion of suburbia before moving on to look at the inner city.

Suburbanization

The word "suburb" has its origins in the Latin term *sub urbe*, or "under city control," an appropriate meaning throughout most of the history of urbanism. Suburbs were originally small pockets of dwellings dependent on urban centers for their amenities and livelihood. Today, they are any residential or commercial area adjoining a city, regardless of whether or not they are subject to central-city control. Many suburbs are effectively autonomous areas, over which city administrations have little direct influence.

In the United States, **suburbanization**, the massive development and inhabiting of towns surrounding a city, rapidly increased during the 1950s and 1960s, a time of great economic growth. World War II had previously absorbed most industrial resources, and any development outside the war effort was restricted. But by the 1950s, war rationing had ended, automobiles instead of tanks were being mass produced, and people were encouraged to pursue at least one part of the "American dream"—owning a house and a piece of land. During that decade, the population in the cities increased by 10 percent, while in the suburban areas it grew by no less than 48 percent.

The prevailing economic scene also facilitated moving out of the city. The Federal Housing Administration (FHA) provided assistance in obtaining mortgage loans, making it possible in the early postwar period for families to buy housing in the suburbs for less than they would have paid for rent in the cities. The FHA did not offer financial assistance to improve older homes or to build new homes in the central areas of ethnically mixed cities; its large-scale aid went only to the builders and buyers of suburban housing. The FHA, together with the Veterans Administration, funded almost half of all suburban housing built during the 1950s and 1960s.

Early in the 1950s, lobbies promoting highway construction launched Project Adequate Roads, aimed at inducing the federal government to support the building of highways. President Eisenhower responded with a giant construction program for interstate roadways, and in 1956, the Highway Act was passed, authorizing $32 billion to be used for building such highways. This coincided with a period of expansion in the automobile industry such that families came to own more than one car; and the result was that previously out-of-the-way suburban areas, with lower property taxes, became accessible to places of work. At the same time, the highway program led to the establishment of industries and services in suburban areas themselves. Consequently, the movement of businesses from the cities to the suburbs took jobs from the manufacturing and service industries with them. Many suburban towns became essentially separate cities, connected by rapid highways to the other suburbs around them. From the 1960s on, the proportion of people commuting between suburbs increased more steadily than the proportion commuting to cities.

While suburbia in the United States is white-dominated, more and more members of racial and ethnic minorities are moving there. From 1980 to 1990, the suburban population of blacks grew by 34.4 percent, of Latinos by 69.3 percent, and of Asians by 125.9 percent. In contrast, the suburban white population grew by only 9.2 percent. Members of minority groups move to the suburbs for reasons similar to those who preceded them: better housing, schools, and amenities. Like the people who began the exodus to suburbia in the 1950s, they are mostly middle-class professionals. According to the chairman of the Chicago Housing Authority, "Suburbanization isn't about race now; it's about class. Nobody wants to be around poor people because of all the problems that go along with poor people: poor schools, unsafe streets, gangs" (DeWitt, 1994).

The suburbs nevertheless remain mostly white. Minority groups constituted only 18 percent of the total suburban population in 1990. Three out of every four African Americans continue to live in the center cities, compared with one in every four whites. Most of black suburban residents live in black-majority neighborhoods in towns bordering the city.

While the last several decades saw a movement from the cities to the suburbs, they also witnessed a shift in the regional distribution of the U.S. population from north to south and east to west. As a percentage of the nation's total population, the Northeast dropped from 25 to 20.4 percent and the Midwest from 29 to 24 percent. Meanwhile the population of the South increased from 30.7 to 34.4 percent and that of the West from 15.6 to 21.2 percent.

Urban Problems

Inner-city decay is partially a consequence of the social and economic forces involved in the movement of businesses, jobs, and middle-class residents from major cities to the outlying suburbs over the last fifty years. The manufacturing industries that provided employment for the urban blue-collar class largely vanished and were replaced by white-collar service industries. Millions of blue-collar jobs disappeared, and this affected in particular the poorly educated, drawn mostly from minority groups. While the overall educational levels of minority groups improved over this period, the improvement was not sufficient to keep up with the demands of an information-based economy (Kasarda, 1993). William Julius Wilson has argued that the problems of the urban underclass grew out of this economic transformation (1991, 1996; see Chapter 7).

These economic changes also contributed to increased residential segregation of different racial and ethnic groups and social classes, as we saw in Chapter 8. Discriminatory practices by home sellers, real estate agents, and mortgage lending institutions further added to this pattern of segregation (Massey and Denton, 1993). In the early 1990s, more than 90 percent of African Americans in the United States lived in neighborhoods, both urban and suburban, that were 60 percent or more black (Farley and Frey, 1994). The social isolation of minority groups, particularly those in the underclass or "ghetto poor," can escalate urban problems such as crime, lack of economic opportunities, poor health, and family breakdown (Massey, 1996).

Adding to these difficulties is the fact that city governments today operate against a background of almost continual financial crisis. As businesses and middle-class residents moved to the suburbs, the cities

AMERICANS ON THE MOVE

How many times did your parents move from one residence to another while you were growing up? America has a high rate of residential mobility. In 1993–94, 16.7 percent of Americans changed their place of residence at least once (Hansen, 1995, p. vii). While this number is no higher than the annual mobility rates of Canada, Australia, and New Zealand, Americans do tend to move more than residents of other industrially developed countries such as France, the United Kingdom, Japan, and Belgium. Yet except for a sharp increase in mobility in the mid-1980s, fueled by recovery from the recession of 1982–83, mobility rates in the United States are in long-term decline. In the 1950s and 1960s, approximately 20 out of every 100 Americans moved at least once every year. Mobility rates began to fall in the 1970s, and, since the late 1980s, have consistently

hovered around 17 percent. Why do people move? According to a 1991 survey, the most commonly cited reason for moving was to improve one's housing situation: to buy a better home, to make the transition from renting to owning, and so on. Many respondents also cited employment factors as a reason for moving (Gober, 1993).

Because many Americans move for job-related reasons, migration patterns tend to reflect regional patterns of economic development. For example, the Northeast and Midwest, long home to much of the nation's industrial manufacturing, has suffered what demographers call an "out-migration" as a result of the deindustrialization of the American economy. Much of the growth in service-sector work and high-tech production has occurred in the South and West, and millions of Americans have left the North-

east and Midwest in search of jobs in these areas. The Midwest has slowly been able to recover from this situation, shifting its economic base to more viable forms of production and thus attracting enough new residents from other regions to counter the out-migration to the South and West. But the Northeast continues to lose residents at a rapid pace. In 1994, the Northeast lost a total of 61,000 residents, while the West gained 379,000 and the South gained 827,000 (Hansen, 1995, p. xiii).

It is all too easy to view these demographic shifts as the result of natural and inevitable long term processes: high-tech and service-sector work comes to account for a greater share of the GNP, these industries naturally spring up in the South and West, making the regions attractive even for traditional manufacturing firms that wish to relocate, and the Northeast is depopulated.

A better explanation begins—of all places—with globalization. As globalization has proceded, a number of important transformations have taken place in the economic sector. Changes in the financial infrastructure have made it easier for investors to put their money into enterprises anywhere on the globe, and corresponding improvements in communications technology, transportation, and managerial practices have made it more practical for businesses to move their production sites to wherever their costs will be minimized. Capital, economists and sociologists say, has become increasingly mobile under the influence of globalization.

While the mobility of capital sometimes translates into American firms shifting the site of their production to the Third World, in other cases it means that firms will open in or relocate to regions of this country where their production costs will be low. All else being equal, if unions are strong in one region and weak in another, firms are more likely to do business in the region with the weak unions, because they will be able to get away with paying lower wages. Firms also prefer to operate in cities and states that are eager for new development and likely to grant substantial tax breaks. In general, state and local governments in the South and West have been more willing than governments in the Northeast to grant tax breaks to firms, and unions

tend to be weaker in these regions than in the Northeast. These factors—in addition to cheaper land and energy—have helped pull some firms out of the Northeast and into the South and West, and have encouraged many start-up firms to set up shop in the South and West. While the dynamics involved are clearly complex, globalization and the mobility of capital appear to lay behind recent trends in regional economic development, and therefore underlie key patterns in regional migration.

Should attempts be made to halt these changes? What would migration patterns look like if unions were strong in all regions, and if cities and states refused to grant generous tax breaks to corporate America? Is the depopulation of the Northeast a good or bad thing?

lost major sources of tax revenue. High rates of crime and unemployment in the city require it to spend more on welfare services, schools, police, and overall upkeep. Yet because of budget constraints, cities are forced to cut back many of these services. A cycle of deterioration develops, in which the more suburbia expands, the greater the problems faced by city dwellers become.

THE SOCIOLOGICAL DEBATE

EXPLAINING URBAN POVERTY

The plight of the American inner city has grown bleak in recent times. According to U.S. Census data, the proportion of our nation's poor who live in central cities increased from 34 percent in 1970 to 43 percent in 1990. Not only are the poor increasingly concentrated in urban areas, but the poor living in the inner city are clustered in neighborhoods overwhelmingly inhabited by other poor families. The consequences are that the urban poor—particularly the black urban poor—are living in very poor, socially isolated, racially homogeneous neighborhoods, which are increasingly plagued with troubles such as joblessness, crime, and poor quality of life.

How is it possible that the living conditions of inner city blacks have taken such a turn for the worse—especially in the three decades that follow the civil rights movements of the 1960s, and progressive public policies such as the Fair Housing Act of 1968? Two books on inner-city poverty posit distinct—yet complementary—explanations for the state of urban poverty today. In *When Work Disappears: The World of the New Urban Poor* (1996), sociologist William Julius Wilson argues, as we saw earlier in the chapter, that the loss of jobs is at the root of inner-city decline. Sociologists Douglas S. Massey and Nancy A. Denton, in their book *American Apartheid: Segregation and the Making of the Underclass* (1993), counter that the persistent poverty among urban blacks in the United States is due primarily to residential segregation.

Wilson's position can be described as the "economic restructuring" hypothesis. Wilson (1987, 1996) argues that persistent urban poverty stems primarily from the structural transformation of the inner-city economy. The decline of manufacturing industries, the "suburbanization" of employment, and the rise of a low-wage service sector have dramatically reduced the number of entry-level jobs that pay wages sufficient to support a family. The high rate of joblessness resulting from economic shifts has led to a shrinking pool of "marriageable" men (those financially able to support a family). Thus, marriage has become less attractive to poor women, unwed childbearing has increased, and female-headed families have proliferated. New generations of children are born into poverty, and the vicious cycle is perpetuated. Wilson argues that blacks suffer disproportionately due to past discrimination, and because they are concentrated in locations and occupations particularly affected by economic restructuring.

Wilson elaborated that these economic changes were accompanied by an increase in the spatial concentration of poverty within black neighborhoods. This new geography of poverty, he felt, was due in part to the civil rights movement of the 1960s, which provided middle-class blacks with new opportunities outside the ghetto. The out-migration of middle-class families from ghetto areas left behind a destitute community lacking the institutions, resources, and values necessary for success in post-industrial society. He also acknowledges that such neighborhoods lack locally available training and education, and have suffered from the dissolution of government and private support of local organizations that once supplied job information as well as employment opportunities. Thus, the urban underclass arose from a complex interplay of civil rights policy, economic restructuring, and a historical legacy of discrimination.

While Wilson emphasizes macro-level economic shifts as the cause underlying the concentration of urban poverty, Massey and Denton support the "racial residential segregation" hypothesis. This view holds that high levels of racial residential segregation may increase minority poverty by limiting access to employment opportunities. Segregation in ghettos exacerbates employment problems because it leads to weak informal employment networks and contributes to the social isolation of individuals and families, thereby reducing their chances of acquiring the skills, including adequate educational training, that facilitate mobility in a society. Since no other group in society experiences the degree of segregation, isolation, and poverty concentration that African Americans do, they are far more likely to be disadvantaged when they have to compete with other groups in society for resources and privileges.

Massey and Denton (1993) argue further that in the absence of residential segregation, the structural and economic changes observed by Wilson would not have produced the disastrous social and economic consequences observed in inner cities during the past thirty years. Although rates of black poverty were driven up by the economic dislocations Wilson identifies, it was segregation that confined the higher levels of deprivation to a small number of densely settled, tightly packed, and geographically isolated areas.

Massey and Denton (1993) also dispute Wilson's claim that concentrated poverty arose because the civil rights revolution allowed middle-class blacks to move out of the ghetto. Their principal objection to Wilson's focus on middle-class out-migration is that focusing on the flight of the black middle class deflects attention from the "real issue, which is the limitation of black residential options through segregation" (Massey and Denton, 1993, p. 9).

Wilson, in turn, argues that "to focus mainly on segregation to account for the growth of concentrated poverty is to overlook some of the dynamic aspects of the social and demographic changes occurring in cities like Chicago." Instead, Wilson calls for an approach to studying inner-city poverty that "consider[s] the way in which other changes in society have interacted with segregation to produce the dramatic and social transformation of inner-city neighborhoods, especially since the 1970s" (Wilson, 1996, p. xi).

Urban Renewal and Gentrification

Urban decay is not wholly a one-way process; it can stimulate countertrends, such as **urban renewal,** or **gentrification.** Dilapidated areas or buildings may be-come renovated as more affluent groups move back into cities. Such a renewal process is called gentrification because those areas or buildings become upgraded and return to the control of the urban "gentry"—high-income dwellers—rather than remaining in the hands of the poor.

In *Streetwise: Race, Class, and Change in an Urban Community* (1990), the sociologist Elijah Anderson analyzed the impact of gentrification on cities. While the renovation of a neighborhood generally increases its value, it rarely improves the living standards of its current low-income residents, who are usually forced to move out. In the Philadelphia neighborhood that Anderson studied, close to the ghetto, many black residences were condemned, forcing over one thousand people to leave. Although they were told that their property would be used to build low-cost housing that they would be given the first opportunity to buy, large businesses and a high school now stand there.

The poor residents who continued to live in the neighborhood received some benefits in the form of improved schools and police protection, but the resulting increase in taxes and rents forced them also to leave for a more affordable neighborhood, most often deeper into the ghetto. African-American residents Anderson interviewed expressed resentment at the influx of "yuppies," whom they held responsible for the changes that drove the poorer people away.

The white newcomers had come to the city in search of cheap "antique" housing, closer access to their city-based jobs, and a trendy urban lifestyle. They professed to be "open minded" about racial and ethnic differences; in reality, however, little fraternizing took place between the new and old residents unless they were of the same social class. Since the African-American residents were mostly poor and the white residents middle class, class differences were compounded by racial ones. While some middle-class blacks lived in the area, most chose to live far from the ghetto, fearing that otherwise they would receive the same treatment from whites reserved for the black underclass. Over time, the neighborhood became gradually transformed into a white middle-class enclave.

It is important to note that the process of gentrification parallels another trend discussed earlier: the transformation of the urban economy from a manufacturing to a service-industries base. Addressing the concerns of the victims of these economic changes is critical for the survival of the cities.

URBANISM AND INTERNATIONAL INFLUENCES

As in many areas of sociology today, urban analysis requires us to link global and local issues. The influence of global economic connections and competition has forced sociologists to reconsider how they analyze city life and urban problems. One concept that has emerged as important in the thinking of urban sociologists is the **global city**.

The Global City

Just a decade ago, many sociologists thought that cities like New York, Tokyo, and London would cease to be vibrant centers of social life. The reasoning went that as the use of computers and telecommunications became more widespread, it would become less necessary for many white-collar workers to live or work in cities. Large firms could locate outside the city without any significant cost because their connections with the expensive city could occur through faxes, email, and the Internet. A person or firm could just as easily be located in Omaha or Cedar Rapids and participate in economic transactions that it was once thought necessary to conduct in New York City.

But something unexpected occurred. The emergence of a global economy meant that the increasingly complex global production process had to be coordinated by a large number of people located in close proximity. Instead of becoming empty shells, cities like New York, London, and Tokyo emerged as vibrant places where more firms and high-income citizens located.

It is important to be very clear about what constitutes global cities. It is *not* that they produce things that are sold in many parts of the world, though they might. Nor is it a matter of them being at the center of a region like New York City is to the highly populated mid-Atlantic region. Instead, the defining feature of a

KEY CONCEPTS IN REVIEW

Suburbanization has contributed to inner-city decay. Wealthier groups and businesses tend to move out of the central city in order to take advantage of lower tax rates. This begins a cycle of deterioration: the more suburbia expands, the greater the problems faced by those living in the central cities. **Urban renewal** (also called **gentrification**)—the refurbishing of old buildings to put them to new uses—has become common in large cities.

Urban analysis today must be prepared to link global and local issues. The structure of cities and their patterns of growth and decline often reflect changes in industrial production internationally.

global city is that it is a place where the coordinating work of globalization gets done. This coordination involves connecting distant points of production and consumption. Thus, an office in a global city like New York may organize transactions between factories in Thailand and stores in Michigan. Such coordination as goes on in a global city like New York requires whole economies in financial services such as accounting, international law, and banking.

In a series of important studies, Saskia Sassen (1991, 1998) shows how important these financial services have become in coordinating globalization around the world. She shows that global cities develop a specific kind of social organization with large inequalities. On the one hand, there are highly trained "knowledge workers" who do the managerial and coordinating work of globalization. Side by side with these highly paid workers are low-wage workers who work as messengers, word processors, security guards, and the like. And beneath them is a class of immigrant workers who labor in modern sweatshop factories with no health insurance or other benefits.

In addition to large inequalities, Sassen argues that the global city also has a distinctive consumption structure. The "knowledge workers" have a set of cultural tastes in food, garments, literature, films, shows, and the like, and a whole sector of employment revolves around catering to the tastes of the knowledge workers. A subsidiary and less visible economy also emerges to cater to the needs of the labor force that services the global city.

Third World Urbanization

The Tokyo-Yokohama region in Japan is currently the world's largest urban area, with a population of about 28 million. Seven of the ten biggest urban areas in the world, however—including Mexico City, São Paolo, and Bombay—are now found in Third World countries (see Table 17.1). Between 1990 and 1995, 263 million people were added to the cities of the Third World, the equivalent of another New York or Los Angeles forming every three months. The urban population in Third World countries by 2000 was double that of the industrialized societies. Ninety percent of the world's population growth until 2030 is projected to occur in Third World cities (also see Table 17.2).

Table 17.1 The World's Ten Largest Urban Areas, 2000

CITY	POPULATION
Tokyo-Yokohama, Japan	28,000,000
Seoul, South Korea	19,065,000
Mexico City	18,100,000
Bombay, India	18,000,000
São Paulo, Brazil	17,700,000
New York	16,600,000
Shanghai, China	14,200,000
Lagos, Nigeria	13,500,000
Los Angeles	13,100,000
Beijing, China	12,400,000

SOURCE: Brown et al., 1999.

Table 17.2 Percentage of Population Living in Urban Areas, by Region, 1950–95, with Projections for 2015

REGION	1950	1975	1995	2015
Africa	14.6	25.2	34.9	46.4
Asia[1]	15.3	22.2	33.0	45.6
Latin America	41.4	61.2	73.4	79.9
Industrial Countries[2]	54.9	69.9	74.9	80.0
World	29.7	37.8	45.3	54.4

[1] Excluding Japan.
[2] Europe, Japan, Australia, New Zealand, and North America excluding Mexico.

SOURCE: United Nations, *World Urbanization Prospects: The 1996 Revision* (New York: 1998).

The urban areas now developing rapidly in Third World countries differ dramatically from cities in the industrialized countries. People are drawn to cities in the Third World either because their traditional systems of rural production have disintegrated or because the urban areas offer better job opportunities. They may intend to migrate to the city only for a short while and return to their villages once they have earned enough money. Some actually do return, but in the end, most find themselves forced to stay, having lost their positions in their former communities.

When they do arrive in Third World cities, migrants crowd into squatters' zones mushrooming around the city edges. This pattern differs from Western urban areas, where newcomers are most likely to settle in neighborhoods close to the city center. Third World city dwellers live in conditions that are almost unbelievable to someone accustomed to Western conditions of life, even in slum neighborhoods. So appalling are the conditions that these areas have come to be known as the "septic fringe" of the city.

Let's look at one major Third World city, Mexico City, in detail. Mexico City consists of an old cultural center, an international business district, an entertainment zone, and affluent housing areas, which are all most tourists see of the city; the poor and destitute live in shanty neighborhoods on the perimeter of the city. These inhabitants include recent migrants from rural areas and families who were displaced from other sections of the city because of urban renewal or highway construction. Over a third of Mexico City's population live in dwellings without running water, some also without sewerage. While there is a large amount of state-subsidized housing, only a minority of the city's population can afford it, and only about 10 percent are able to buy or rent in the private housing market. The majority, therefore, are excluded from access to available housing.

Three types of "popular housing" areas are found in Mexico City. Over half of the metropolitan residents live in *colonias proletarias*, composed of shanty dwellings mainly erected illegally by the inhabitants themselves on the edges of the city. Most of these areas were not spontaneously colonized by squatters, but were organized with the connivance of local authorities and illegal private developers. The developers form a local network of organizers, to whom regular payments are made by those living there. Most of the land occupied by the *colonias* was in fact originally public or communal, supposedly protected by the Mexican constitution from being sold or transferred.

A second type of housing is the *vecindadas*, or slums. These are mostly in the older sections of the city and are characterized by the multifamily occupation of dilapidated rental units. Two million people live in such slums, in conditions that are at least as de-

Rooftops and a market in Kampala, Uganda.

A poor family in Veracruz, Mexico, lives in typical shanty-town conditions.

prived as those in the squatters' areas. The third type is the *ciudades perdidas*, or shantytowns. These are similar to the *colonias proletarias*, but are located in the middle of the city rather than on the periphery. Some of these settlements have been demolished by city authorities in recent years, and their inhabitants have moved to the outer areas.

Ninety-four percent of the federal district of Mexico City consists of built-up areas; only 6 percent is open space. The level of green spaces—parks and open stretches of green land—is far below that found in even the most densely populated North American or European cities. Pollution is a major problem; most of it is caused by the cars, buses, and trucks that pack the inadequate roads, the rest derives from industrial pollutants. It has been estimated that living in Mexico City is equivalent to smoking forty cigarettes a day. In March 1992, pollution reached its highest level ever. Whereas an ozone level of just under 100 points is deemed satisfactory for health, in that month the level climbed to 398 points. The government ordered factories to close down for a period, schools were shut, and 40 percent of cars were banned from the streets on

any one day. One observer described the city at the time in the following way: "Seen from the air . . . its outlines barely visible beneath a dense gray-brown murk, Mexico City looked as though it was suffering a torrential rainstorm. Down on the ground, the city was bone dry and dusty—but bathed in ozone."

Cities and Overpopulation

The largest Third World cities are teeming with people, partly because of population growth and partly as a result of people seeking jobs or at least trying to avoid the extreme poverty in the regions from which they came. In the cities, they aren't necessarily any better off; but having made their move, the majority stay on anyway.

Those of us who live in industrialized countries might feel Third World population growth is not our problem, and that those societies should deal with their swelling populations as best they can. There are two reasons why such a view cannot be justified, apart from the immorality of taking a disinterested stand on the fate of three-quarters of the world's human beings.

One reason is that population growth in the Third World is largely due to factors deriving from Western influences. Some of these are intrinsically beneficial, particularly improvements in hygiene and health care. But others, such as dependence on international trade, have broken down traditional ways of life. The second reason is that if it continues at the present rate, world population growth carries the risk of global catastrophe. The pressure placed on the world's limited resources may lead to global conflict, which could end in major wars.

WORLD POPULATION GROWTH

There are currently over 6 billion people in the world. It was estimated that "baby number 6 billion" was born on October 12, 1999, although of course no one can know when and where this event happened. Paul Ehrlich calculated in the 1960s that, if the rate of population growth at that time continued, nine hundred years from now (not a long period in world history as a whole) there would be 60,000,000,000,000,000 (60 quadrillion) people on the face of the earth. There would be one hundred people for every square yard of the earth's surface, including both land and water. The physicist J. H. Fremlin worked out that housing such a population would require a continuous two-thousand-story building covering the entire planet. Even in such a stupendous structure there would only be three or four yards of floor space per person (Fremlin, 1964).

Such a picture, of course, is nothing more than nightmarish fiction designed to drive home how cataclysmic the consequences of continued population growth would be. The real issue is what will happen over the next thirty or forty years, by which time, if current trends are not reversed, the world's population will already have grown to intolerable levels. Partly because governments and other agencies heeded the warnings of Ehrlich and others twenty years ago, by introducing population control programs, there are grounds for supposing that world population growth is beginning to trail off. Estimates calculated in the 1960s of the likely world population by the year 2000 have recently been lowered. The World Bank estimated the world population was just over 6 billion in 2000, compared to some earlier estimates of over 8 billion. Nevertheless, considering that a century ago there were only 1.5 billion people in the world, this still represents growth of staggering proportions. Moreover, the factors underlying population growth are by no means completely predictable and all estimates have to be interpreted with caution.

Population Analysis: Demography

The study of population is referred to as **demography.** The term was invented about a century and a half ago, at a time when nations were beginning to keep official statistics on the nature and distribution of their populations. Demography is concerned with measuring the size of populations and explaining their rise or decline. Population patterns are governed by three factors: births, deaths, and migrations. Demography is customarily treated as a branch of sociology, because the factors that influence the level of births and deaths in a given group or society, as well as migrations of population, are largely social and cultural.

Much demographical work tends to be statistical. All the industrialized countries today gather and analyze basic statistics on their populations by carrying out censuses (systematic surveys designed to find out about the whole population of a given country). Rigorous as the modes of data collection now are, even in these nations demographic statistics are not wholly accurate. In the United States there is a comprehensive population census every ten years, and sample studies are regularly conducted. Yet for various reasons, many people are not registered in the official population statistics, including illegal immigrants, homeless people, transients, and others who for one reason or another avoided registration.

In many Third World countries, particularly those with recent high rates of population growth, demographic statistics are much more unreliable. For instance, some demographers have estimated that registered births and deaths in India may represent only about three-quarters of the actual totals (Cox, 1976). The accuracy of official statistics is even lower in parts of central Africa.

Basic Demographic Concepts

Among the basic concepts used by demographers, the most important are crude birth rates, fertility, fecundity, and crude death rates. **Crude birth rates** are expressed as the number of live births per year per thousand of the population. They are called "crude" rates because of their very general character. Crude birth rates, for example, do not tell us what proportions of a population are male or female, or what the age distribution of a population is (the relative proportions of young and old people in the population). Where statistics are collected that relate birth or death rates to such categories, demographers speak of *specific* rather than crude rates. For instance, an age-specific birth rate might specify the number of births per thousand women in different age groups.

If we wish to understand population patterns in any detail, the information provided by specific birth rates is normally necessary. Crude birth rates, however, are useful for making overall comparisons between different groups, societies, and regions. Thus the crude birth rate in the United States is 15 per thousand. Other industrialized countries have lower rates, such as 9 per thousand in Germany, Russia, and Italy. In many other parts of the world, crude birth rates are much higher. In India, for instance, the crude birth rate is 25 per thousand; in Ethiopia it is 48 per thousand (World Bank, 1998).

Birth rates are an expression of the fertility of women. **Fertility** refers to how many live-born children the average woman has. A fertility rate is usually calculated as the average number of births per thousand women of childbearing age.

Fertility is distinguished from **fecundity,** which means the potential number of children women are biologically capable of bearing. It is physically possible for a normal woman to bear a child every year during the period when she is capable of conception. There are variations in fecundity according to age at puberty and menopause, both of which differ between countries as well as among individuals. While there may be families in which a woman bears twenty or more children, fertility rates in practice are always much lower than fecundity rates, because social and cultural factors limit breeding.

Crude death rates (also called *mortality rates*) are calculated in the same way as birth rates—the number of deaths per thousand of population per year. Again there are major variations among countries, but death rates in many Third World societies are becoming reduced to levels comparable to those of the West. The death rate in the United States in 1996 was 8 per thousand. In India it was 9 per thousand; in Ethiopia it was 17 per thousand. A few countries have much higher death rates. In Sierra Leone, for example, the death rate is 27 per thousand. Like crude birth rates, crude death rates only provide a very general index of **mortality** (the number of deaths in a population). Specific death rates give more precise information. A particularly important specific death rate is the **infant mortality rate:** the number of babies per thousand births in any year who die before reaching age one. One of the key factors underlying the population explosion has been reductions in infant-mortality rates.

Declining rates of infant mortality are the most important influence on increasing **life expectancy**—that is, the number of years the average person can expect to live. In 1900, life expectancy at birth in the United States was about forty years. Today it has increased to nearly seventy-four years (see also Chapter 16 section on "Aging"). This does not mean, however, that most people at the turn of the century died when they were about forty years of age. When there is a high infant-mortality rate as there is in many Third World nations, the average life expectancy—which is a statistical average—is brought down (see Global Map 17.1). Taking the life expectancy of people surviving the first year of life, in 1900 the average person could expect to live to age fifty-eight. Illness, nutrition, and the influence of natural disasters are the other factors influencing life expectancy. Life expectancy has to be distinguished from **life span,** which is the maximum number of years that an individual could live. While life expectancy has increased in most societies in the world, life span has remained unaltered. Only a small proportion of people live to be one hundred or more.

Dynamics of Population Change

Rates of population growth or decline are measured by subtracting the number of deaths per thousand over a given period from the number of births per thousand—this is usually also calculated annually. Some European countries have negative growth rates—in other words, their populations are declining. Virtually all of the industrialized countries have growth rates of less than 0.5 percent. Rates of population growth were high in the eighteenth and nineteenth centuries in Europe and the United States, but have since leveled off. Many Third World countries today have rates of between 2–3 percent. These may not seem very different from the rates of the industrialized countries, but in fact, the difference is enormous (see Global Map 17.2).

The reason is that growth in population is **exponential.** There is an ancient Persian myth that helps to illustrate this. A courtier asked a ruler to reward him for his services by giving him twice as many grains of rice for each service than he had the time before, start-

50 and less

51 to 59

60 to 74

75 and up

SOURCE: World Bank, 1998.

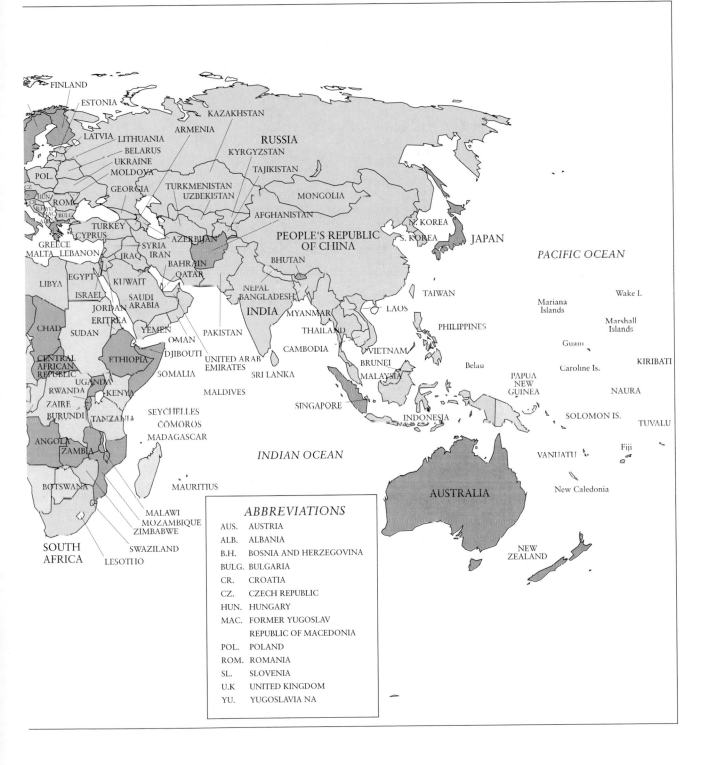

ABBREVIATIONS

AUS.   AUSTRIA

ALB.   ALBANIA

B.H.   BOSNIA AND HERZEGOVINA

BULG. BULGARIA

CR.   CROATIA

CZ.   CZECH REPUBLIC

HUN.   HUNGARY

MAC.   FORMER YUGOSLAV
       REPUBLIC OF MACEDONIA

POL.   POLAND

ROM.   ROMANIA

SL.   SLOVENIA

U.K   UNITED KINGDOM

YU.   YUGOSLAVIA NA

Annual percentage increase

- Less than 1.0
- 1.0–1.9
- 2.0–2.9
- 3.0 or more

SOURCE: World Bank, 1998.

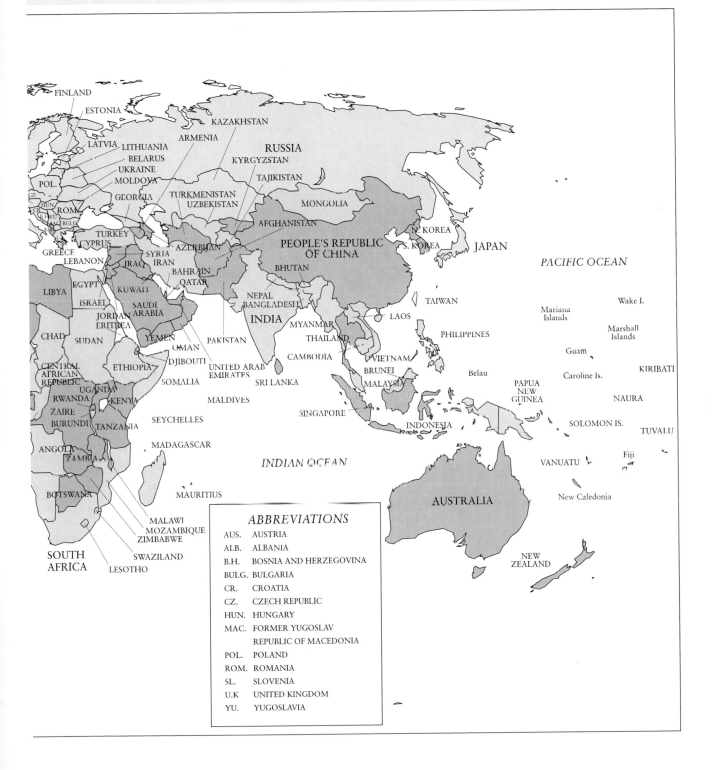

FINLAND
ESTONIA
KAZAKHSTAN
LATVIA LITHUANIA
ARMENIA
RUSSIA
BELARUS
KYRGYZSTAN
UKRAINE
MOLDOVA
TAJIKISTAN
POL.
GEORGIA
TURKMENISTAN
MONGOLIA
HUN.
UZBEKISTAN
CR. ROM.
R.HYU.
AFGHANISTAN
BULG.
TURKEY
AZERBIJAN
N. KOREA
CYPRUS
PEOPLE'S REPUBLIC
GREECE
OF CHINA
S. KOREA
JAPAN
SYRIA
LEBANON
IRAN
PACIFIC OCEAN
IRAQ
BHUTAN
LIBYA
EGYPT
BAHRAIN
QATAR
KUWAIT
NEPAL
TAIWAN
Wake I.
ISRAEL
SAUDI
BANGLADESH
JORDAN
ARABIA
INDIA
MYANMAR
Mariana
ERITREA
Islands
CHAD
YEMEN
THAILAND
PHILIPPINES
Marshall
SUDAN
LAOS
Islands
OMAN
PAKISTAN
Guam
DJIBOUTI
CAMBODIA
CENTRAL
UNITED ARAB
VIETNAM
Caroline Is.
KIRIBATI
AFRICAN
ETHIOPIA
EMIRATES
BRUNEI
Belau
REPUBLIC
SRI LANKA
PAPUA
UGANDA
SOMALIA
MALAYSIA
NEW
NAURA
RWANDA
KENYA
MALDIVES
GUINEA
ZAIRE
INDONESIA
SOLOMON IS.
BURUNDI
SINGAPORE
TUVALU
TANZANIA
SEYCHELLES
ANGOLA
Fiji
ZAMBIA
MADAGASCAR
VANUATU
INDIAN OCEAN
New Caledonia
BOTSWANA
AUSTRALIA
MAURITIUS
MALAWI
SOUTH
MOZAMBIQUE
NEW
AFRICA
ZIMBABWE
ZEALAND
SWAZILAND
LESOTHO

ABBREVIATIONS

AUS. AUSTRIA
ALB. ALBANIA
B.H. BOSNIA AND HERZEGOVINA
BULG. BULGARIA
CR.   CROATIA
CZ.   CZECH REPUBLIC
HUN. HUNGARY
MAC. FORMER YUGOSLAV
      REPUBLIC OF MACEDONIA
POL. POLAND
ROM. ROMANIA
SL.   SLOVENIA
U.K   UNITED KINGDOM
YU.   YUGOSLAVIA

ing with a single grain on the first square of a chess board. Believing himself to be on to a good thing, the king commanded grain to be brought up from his storehouse. By the twenty-first square, the storehouse was empty; the fortieth square required ten billion rice grains (Meadows et al., 1972). In other words, starting with one item and doubling it, doubling the result, and so on, rapidly leads to huge figures: 1:2:4:8:16:32:64:128, etc. In seven operations the figure has risen by 128 percent. Exactly the same principle applies to population growth. We can measure this effect by means of the **doubling time**, the period of time it takes for the population to double. A population growth of 1 percent will produce a doubling of numbers in seventy years. At 2 percent growth, a population will double in thirty-five years, while at 3 percent it will double in twenty-three years.

Malthusianism

In premodern societies, birth rates were very high by the standards of the industrialized world today. Nonetheless, population growth remained low until the eighteenth century because there was a rough overall balance between births and deaths. The general trend of numbers was upward, and there were sometimes periods of more marked population increase, but these were followed by increases in death rates. In medieval Europe, for example, when harvests were bad, marriages tended to be postponed and the number of conceptions fell, while deaths increased. These complementary trends reduced the number of mouths to be fed. No preindustrial society was able to escape from this self-regulating rhythm (Wrigley, 1968).

During the period of the rise of industrialism, many looked forward to a new age in which scarcity would be a phenomenon of the past. The development of modern industry, it was widely supposed, would create a new era of abundance. In his celebrated work *Essay on the Principle of Population* (1976; orig. pub. 1798), Thomas Malthus criticized these ideas and initiated a debate about the connection between population and food resources that continues to this day. At the time Malthus wrote, the population in Europe was growing rapidly. Malthus pointed out that, while

population increase is exponential, food supply depends on fixed resources that can be expanded only by developing new land for cultivation. Population growth therefore tends to outstrip the means of support available. The inevitable outcome is famine, which, combined with the influence of war and plagues, acts as a natural limit to population increase. Malthus predicted that human beings would always live in circumstances of misery and starvation, unless they practiced what he called "moral restraint." His cure for excessive population growth was for people to strictly limit their frequency of sexual intercourse. (The use of contraception he proclaimed to be a "vice.")

For a while, **Malthusianism** was ignored, since the population development of the Western countries followed a quite different pattern from that which he had anticipated—as we shall see below. Rates of population growth trailed off in the nineteenth and twentieth centuries. Indeed, in the 1930s there were major worries about population decline in many industrialized countries, including the United States. The upsurge in world population growth in the twentieth century has again lent some credence to Malthus's views, although few support them in their original version. Population expansion in Third World countries seems to be outstripping the resources that those countries can generate to feed their citizenry.

Population Growth in the Third World

Virtually all the industrialized countries today have low birth and death rates compared with their past history. Then why has the world population increased so dramatically? In the majority of Third World countries, because of the relatively sudden introduction of modern medicine and methods of hygiene, there has been a rapid drop in mortality. But birthrates remain high. This combination has produced a completely different age structure in Third World countries compared with the industrialized ones. In Mexico City, for example, 45 percent of the population is less than fifteen years old. In the industrialized countries, only about a quarter of the population is in

These Africans are waiting for food in a refugee camp. World population, especially in Third World countries, threatens to outgrow the earth's resources.

this age group. The imbalanced age distribution in the nonindustrialized countries adds to their social and economic difficulties. A youthful population needs support and education, during which period its members would not be economically productive. But many Third World countries lack the resources to provide universal education, and as a result, children must either work full time or scratch a living as street children, begging for whatever they can. When the street children mature, most become unemployed, homeless, or both.

A population that has disproportionate numbers of young people will continue to grow even if the birth rate should suddenly fall. If fertility declined to "replacement level"—one birth for every death in a population—it would still take seventy-five years before that population stopped increasing. In other words, until the population as a whole aged, there would be a disproportionate number of young people; the large

numbers of young women would mean a large number of babies being born, keeping the population level above zero growth (Duncan, 1971).

The Demographic Transition

Demographers often refer to the changes in the ratio of births to deaths in the industrialized countries from the nineteenth century onward as the **demographic transition.** The notion was first worked out by Warren S. Thompson, who described a three-stage process in which one type of population stability would be eventually replaced by another as a society reached an advanced level of economic development (Thompson, 1929).

Stage one refers to the conditions characteristic of most traditional societies, in which both birth and death rates are high, and the infant-mortality rate is especially large. Population grows little if at all, as the high number of births is more or less balanced by the level of deaths. Stage two, which began in Europe and the United States in the early part of the nineteenth century—with wide regional variations—occurs when death rates fall while fertility remains high. This is therefore a phase of marked population growth. It is subsequently replaced by stage three, in which, with industrial development, birth rates drop to a level such that population is again fairly stable.

Demographers do not fully agree about how this sequence of change should be interpreted, or how long lasting stage three is likely to be. Fertility in the Western countries has not been completely stable over the past century or so; there remain considerable differences in fertility between the industrialized nations, as well as between classes or regions within them. Nevertheless, it is generally accepted that this sequence accurately describes a major transformation in the demographic character of modern societies.

The theory of demographic transition directly opposes the ideas of Malthus. Whereas for Malthus, increasing prosperity would automatically bring about population increase, the thesis of demographic transition emphasizes that economic development, generated by industrialism, would actually lead to a new equilibrium of population stability.

KEY CONCEPTS IN REVIEW

Demography is the statistical study of population. **Crude birth rates** are the number of live births per year per thousand of the population. **Fertility** refers to the number of live-born children the average woman has. While fertility refers to the actual figure, **fecundity** refers to the potential number the average woman could have. **Crude death rates** are the number of deaths per thousand of population per year. **Mortality** is the number of deaths in a population. The **infant mortality rate** is the number of babies per thousand births who die before reaching the age of one. **Life expectancy** is the number of years the average person is expected to live. **Life span** refers to the potential maximum number of years an individual *could* live. Although the former has increased over the past two centuries, the latter has remained constant.

Rates of population growth are measured by subtracting the crude death rate from the crude birth rate, usually over one-year periods. Population growth tends to be **exponential** (i.e., it multiplies—hence grows quickly), rather than arithmetical. The **doubling time** refers to the period of time it takes for the population to double. **Malthusianism** is the idea that population growth tends to outstrip the means of support, leading to misery and starvation.

The changes in the ratio of births to deaths in the industrializing countries since the nineteenth century is called the **demographic transition**. Prior to industrialization, both birth and death rates were high. At the beginning of industrialization, population growth occurred as a result of a lower but steady birth rate. Currently, birth rate has also dropped to make populations stable. Thus, the demographic transition theory directly contradicts the idea of Malthusianism.

Prospects for Change

Fertility remains high in Third World societies because traditional attitudes to family size have been maintained. Having large numbers of children is often still regarded as desirable, providing a source of labor on family-run farms. Some religions are either opposed to birth control or affirm the desirability of having many children. Contraception is opposed by Islamic leaders in several countries and by the Catholic church, whose influence is especially marked in South and Central America. The motivation to reduce fertility has not always been forthcoming even from political authorities. In 1974, contraceptives were banned in Argentina as part of a program to double the population of the country as fast as possible; this was seen as a means of developing its economic and military strength.

Yet a decline in fertility levels has at last occurred in some large Third World countries. An example is China, which currently has a population of over 1.25 billion people—almost a quarter of the world's population as a whole. The Chinese government established one of the most extensive programs of population control that any country has undertaken, with the object of stabilizing the country's numbers at close to their current level. The government instituted incentives (such as better housing and free health care and education) to promote single-child families, while families who have more than one child face special hardships (wages are cut for those who have a third child). As a response to this government program, some families went to the extreme of killing their female infants. There is evidence that China's antinatal policies, however harsh they may appear, have had a substantial impact on its population (Mirsky, 1982). Yet there is also much resistance within the country. People are reluctant to regard parents with one child as a proper family.

China's program demands a degree of centralized government control that is either unacceptable or unavailable in most other developing countries. In India, for instance, many schemes for promoting family planning and the use of contraceptives have been tried, but with only relatively small success. India in 1988 had a population of 789 million. By 2000, its population just topped 1 billion. And even if its population-growth rate does diminish, by 2050, India will be the most populous country in the world with over 1.5 billion people.

A sign in Dalat, Vietnam, urges citizens to limit their child-bearing to two children per family.

Technological advances in agriculture and industry are unpredictable, so no one can be sure how large a population the world might eventually be able to support. Yet even at current population levels, global resources may already be well below those required to create living standards in the Third World comparable to those of the industrialized countries. The consumption of energy, raw materials, and other goods is vastly higher in the Western countries than in other areas of the world. Each person in the United States consumes 32 times as much energy as an individual in countries like China or India. These consumption levels partly depend, moreover, on resources transferred from Third World regions (Brown et al., 1999). Unless there are major changes in patterns of world energy consumption—such as expanding the use of solar energy and wind power—there seems little possibility of extending this Western level of energy consumption to everyone in the world. There are probably not enough known energy resources to go around (McHale et al., 1979; Gupte, 1984; Brown et al., 1999).

URBANIZATION, POPULATION GROWTH, AND THE ENVIRONMENT

Global Environmental Threats

One problem we all face concerns **environmental ecology**. Irreparable damage to the environment may already have been done by the spread of industrial production. Ecological questions concern not only how we can best cope with and contain environmental damage, but the very ways of life within industrialized societies. If the goal of continuous economic growth must be abandoned, new social institutions will probably be pioneered. Technological progress is unpredictable, and it may be that the earth will in fact yield sufficient resources for processes of industrialization. At the moment, however, this does not seem feasible, and if the Third World countries are to achieve

KEY CONCEPTS IN REVIEW

Like many areas of sociology, urbanism is subject to the influence of globalization. A new model for understanding this influence is the concept of the **global city**, the focal point of coordination of the global economy.

Massive urban development is occurring in Third World countries. The majority of the population in these cities live in illegal makeshift housing, in conditions of extreme poverty.

Population growth in the Third World, partly a result of Western influences, is one of the most significant global problems facing humanity today. Fertility rates remain high because traditional attitudes about family size have not changed. Global resources are probably inadequate to create living standards in the Third World equal to those in industrialized societies.

living standards comparable to those currently enjoyed in the West, global readjustments will be necessary.

Since the beginning of the practice of agriculture thousands of years ago, human beings have left an imprint on nature. Hunting and gathering societies mainly lived *from* nature; they existed on what the natural environment provided and made little attempt to change the world around them. With the coming of agriculture, this situation was altered. To grow crops, land must be cleared, trees cut down, and encroaching weeds and wild foliage kept at bay. Even primitive farming methods can lead to soil erosion. Once natural forests are cut down and clearings made, the wind may blow away the topsoil. The farming community then clears some fresh plots of land, and so the process goes on. Some landscapes that we today think of as natural, such as the rocky areas and scrubland in southwestern Greece, are actually the result of soil erosion created by farmers five thousand years ago.

Yet before the development of modern industry, nature dominated human life far more than the other way around. Today the human onslaught on the natural environment is so intense that there are few natural processes uninfluenced by human activity. Nearly all cultivable land is under agricultural production. What used to be almost inaccessible wildernesses are often now nature reserves, visited routinely by thou-

sands of tourists. Even the world's climate, as we shall see, has probably been affected by the global development of industry.

"Green" movements and parties (like Friends of the Earth or Greenpeace), which are themselves sometimes global organizations, have developed in response to the new environmental hazards. While there are varied green philosophies, a common thread concerns taking action to protect the world's environment, conserve rather than exhaust its resources, and protect the remaining animal species. Hundreds of animal species have become extinct even over the past fifty years, and at the moment this process is a continuing one.

Some environmental problems are particularly concentrated in specific areas. In the formerly Communist societies of Eastern Europe and the Soviet Union, rivers, forests, and the air are highly polluted by industrial wastes. The consequences of such pollution, if it goes on unchecked, are potentially worldwide. As we have learned, the societies of the earth have become much more interdependent than ever before. As travelers on "spaceship earth," no matter where we live, we are all menaced by corrosion of the environment.

Global environmental threats are of several basic sorts: pollution, the creation of waste that cannot be disposed of in the short term or recycled, and the depletion of resources that cannot be replenished. The amount of domestic waste—what goes into our garbage cans—produced each day in the industrialized societies is staggering; these countries have sometimes been called the "throw-away societies" because the volume of items discarded as a matter of course is so large. For instance, food is mostly bought in packages that are thrown away at the end of the day. Some of these can be reprocessed and reused, but most cannot. Some kinds of widely employed plastics simply become unusable waste; there is no way of recycling them, and they have to be buried in garbage dumps.

When environmental analysts speak of waste materials, however, they mean not only goods that are thrown away, but also gaseous wastes pumped into the atmosphere. Examples are the carbon dioxide released into the atmosphere by the burning of fuels like oil and coal in cars and power stations, and gases released into the air by the use of such things as aerosol cans, material for insulation, and air-conditioning units. Carbon dioxide is the main influence on the process of global warming that many scientists believe is occurring, while the other gases attack the ozone layer around the earth.

Global warming is thought to happen in the following way. The buildup of carbon dioxide in the earth's atmosphere functions like the glass of a greenhouse. It allows the sun's rays to pass through, but acts as a barrier to prevent them from passing back. The effect is to heat up the earth; global warming is sometimes termed the "greenhouse effect" for this reason. If global warming is indeed taking place, the conse-quences are likely to be devastating. Among other things, sea levels will rise as the polar ice caps melt and the oceans will warm and expand. Cities that lie near the coasts or in low-lying areas will be flooded and become uninhabitable. Large tracts of fertile land will become desert.

The ozone layer, which is high in the earth's atmosphere, forms a shield that protects against ultraviolet radiation. The gases used in aerosols and refrigerants produce particles that react with the ozone layer in such a way as to weaken it. It is thought that these chemicals have produced detectable holes in the ozone layer at both poles and thinning elsewhere. The radiation that is let into the earth's atmosphere produces a variety of potentially harmful effects, including an increase in cataracts of the eyes (which can cause blindness) and in levels of skin cancer.

Modern industry, still expanding worldwide, has led to steeply climbing demands for sources of energy and raw materials. Yet the world's supply of such energy sources and raw materials is limited. Even at current rates of use, for example, the known oil resources of the world will be completely consumed by the year 2050. New reserves of oil may be discovered, or alternative sources of cheap energy invented, but there plainly is a point at which some key resources will run out if global consumption is not limited.

The Environment: A Sociological Issue?

Why should the environment be a concern for sociologists? Aren't we talking of issues that are the province purely of scientists or technologists? Isn't the impact of human beings on nature a physical one, created by modern technologies of industrial production? Yes, but modern industry and technology have come into being in relation to distinctive social institutions. The origins of our impact on the environment are social, and so are many of its consequences.

Rescuing the global environment will thus mean social as well as technological change. Given the vast global inequalities that exist, there is little chance that the poor Third World countries will sacrifice their own economic growth because of environmental problems created largely by the rich ones. Yet the earth doesn't

The city of Lagos, Nigeria, gets its monthly cleaning. As the world's population grows, the volume of waste we create and the way we dispose of it pose serious problems.

seem to possess sufficient resources for everyone on the planet to live at the standard of living most people in the industrialized societies take for granted. Hence, if the impoverished sectors of the world are to catch up with the richer ones, the latter are likely to have to revise their expectations about constant economic growth. Some "green" authors argue that people in the rich countries must react against consumerism and return to more simple ways of life if global ecological disaster is to be avoided.

Prospects for Change

There can be no question but that global warming is a global problem. Greenhouse gases released in the atmosphere do not simply affect the climate of the country in which they were produced, but alter climatic patterns for the entire world. For this reason, many policy makers and scientists believe that any viable solution to the problem must also be global in scale. Yet the political difficulties in negotiating an international treaty to reduce greenhouse gases are enormous, and suggest that while globalization has ushered in a new era of international cooperation, the world is still far from being able to speak decisively with a unified political voice about many of the issues that it confronts.

In December 1997, delegates from 166 nations gathered in Kyoto, Japan, in an effort to hammer out an agreement to reduce global warming. The summit was the culmination of two years of informal discussion among the countries. World leaders, faced with mounting scientific evidence that global warming is indeed occurring, and under pressure from voters to adopt environmentally friendly policies, clearly recognized that international action of some kind was needed. But faced as well with intense lobbying by industry, which fears it will bear the brunt of the cost for reducing fossil fuel emissions, world leaders felt compelled to balance safeguarding the environment against the threat of economic disruption.

As a result, the pollution reductions agreed to by the countries are meager. Thirty-eight of the advanced industrial nations represented at the conference agreed to reduce total emission levels by 2010 to approximately 5 percent below what they were in 1990. But different countries agreed to different specific targets: the United States agreed to reduce emission levels

by 7 percent, the fifteen countries of the European Union pledged an 8-percent reduction, and Japan promised a 6-percent cut. The nations also tentatively agreed to establish an emissions "trading" system whereby a country that has reduced emissions levels beyond its target will be able to sell emissions "credits" to countries that have been unable to meet their goals.

While politicians hailed the accord as an important first step in dealing with global warming, there are three serious problems with the Kyoto agreement. First, several newly industrialized nations that have high levels of fossil fuel emissions—such as China and India—did not sign the accord. Unless they can be persuaded to do so, the emission reductions agreed to at Kyoto may be completely offset by increases in pollution elsewhere in the world. Second, many environmentalists warn that the reduction in greenhouse gases agreed to at Kyoto is not enough to reverse the trend toward global warming—only to slow its onset. Unless much greater emissions reductions are achieved, the world will still experience most of the disastrous consequences of global warming in the next century. Third, and most problematic, the Kyoto accord, which must be ratified by the legislative bodies of all the signatory countries, faces stiff political opposition. Industry leaders and conservative politicians in the United States, for example, claim that reaching even the 7-percent reduction agreed to by the U.S. delegation would be tremendously expensive, and that the environmental regulations required to achieve even this modest goal would hamstring U.S. business and retard economic growth. Former House Speaker Newt Gingrich said the United States "surrendered" to pressure in Kyoto and called the proposed treaty an outrage that would cripple the American economy. Unless such sentiment can be overcome, the treaty stands little chance of being ratified by the U.S. Congress. And if the United States, a world power and major polluter, does not, in the end, agree to participate, it is likely that the entire Kyoto accord will collapse.

It is clear that modern technology, science, and industry are not exclusively beneficial in their consequences. Sociologists perceive a responsibility to examine closely the social relations and institutions that brought about the current state of affairs, because rescuing the situation will require a profound consciousness of human authorship.

SUMMARY

1. Traditional cities differed in many ways from modern urban areas. They were mostly very small by modern standards, were surrounded by walls, and their centers were dominated by religious buildings and palaces.

2. In traditional societies, only a small minority of the population lived in urban areas. In the industrialized countries today, between 60 percent and 90 percent do so. Urbanism is also developing very rapidly in Third World societies.

3. Early approaches to urban sociology were dominated by the work of the Chicago School. The members of this school saw urban processes in terms of ecological models derived from biology. Louis Wirth developed the conception of urbanism as a "way of life." These approaches have more recently been challenged, without being discarded altogether.

4. Later approaches to urban theory have placed more emphasis on the influence of broader socioeconomic factors—particularly those deriving from industrial capitalism—on city life.

5. The expansion of *suburbs* has contributed to inner-city decay. Wealthier groups and businesses tend to move out of the central city in order to take advantage of lower tax rates. This begins a cycle of deterioration, in which the more suburbia expands, the greater the problems faced by those living in the central cities. *Urban renewal* (also called *gentrification*)—the refurbishing of old buildings to put them to new uses—has become common in many large cities.

6. Urban analysis today must be prepared to link global and local issues. Factors that influence urban development locally are sometimes part of much more international processes. The structure of local neighborhoods, and their patterns of growth and decline, often reflect changes in industrial production internationally.

7. Massive urban development is occurring in Third World countries. Cities in these societies differ in major respects from those characteristic of the West.

The majority of the population live in illegal makeshift housing, in conditions of extreme poverty.

8. Population growth is one of the most significant global problems currently faced by humanity. About a quarter of the world's population suffers from malnutrition, and over 10 million people die of starvation each year. This misery is concentrated in the Third World countries.

9. The study of population growth is called *demography*. Much demographic work is statistical, but demographers are also concerned with trying to explain why population patterns take the form they do. The most important concepts in population analysis are *birth rates, death rates, fertility*, and *fecundity*.

10. The changes in population patterns that have occurred in the industrialized societies are usually analyzed in terms of a process of *demographic transition*. Prior to industrialization, both birth and death rates were high. During the beginning of industrialization, there was population growth, because death rates were reduced while birth rates took longer to decline. Finally a new equilibrium was reached with low birth rates balancing low death rates.

11. World resources are finite, even if the limits of what can be produced are continually revised due to technological developments. Energy consumption and the consumption of raw materials and other goods are vastly higher in the Western countries than in other areas of the world. These consumption levels depend, moreover, upon resources transferred from Third World regions to the industrially developed nations. If resources were shared out equally, there would be a significant drop in Western living standards.

12. There are few aspects of the natural world that have not been affected by human activity. The industrialization of agriculture, the depletion of natural resources, the pollution of air and water, and the creation of vast mountains of unrecyclable waste are all sources of threat to the future survival of humanity. Addressing these issues will mean, among other things, that richer nations will have to revise their expectations of persistent economic growth.

Chapter Eighteen

Learn about patterns of social change throughout human history, and analyze why change occurs more rapidly in modern societies.

Influences on Social Change

Recognize that three main factors influence social change: the physical environment, the political organization, and cultural factors.

Change in the Modern Period

Analyze modern social change, particularly the impact of economic, political, and cultural factors.

Collective Behavior and Social Movements

Learn the different forms of collective behavior. Understand how to define and classify a social movement, learn some basic theories of social movements, and apply this understanding to the feminist movement in the United States.

Current Change and Future Prospects

Learn four different theories about current social change: postindustrialism, postmodernism, the spread of democratic capitalism, and the risk society.

Social Change: Looking into the Future

Think about where social change will lead to in the twenty-first century.

SOCIAL CHANGE AND SOCIAL MOVEMENTS

human beings have existed on earth for about half a million years. Agriculture, the necessary basis of fixed settlements, is only around twelve thousand years old. Civilizations date back no more than six thousand years or so. If we were to think of the entire span of human existence thus far as a day, agriculture would have come into existence at 11:56 P.M. and civilizations at 11:57. The development of modern societies would get under way only at 11:59 and 30 seconds! Yet perhaps as much change has taken place in the last 30 seconds of this human day as in all the time leading up to it.

 The pace of change in the modern era is easily demonstrated if we look at rates of technological development. As the economic historian David Landes has observed:

Modern technology produces not only more, faster; it turns out objects that could not have been produced under any circumstances by the craft methods of yesterday. The best Indian hand-spinner could not turn out yarn so fine and regular as that of the mule; all the forges in eighteenth century Christendom could not have produced steel sheets so large, smooth and homogeneous as those of a modern strip mill. Most important, modern technology has created things that could scarcely have been conceived in the pre-industrial era; the camera, the motor car, the airplane, the whole array of electronic devices from the radio to the high-speed computer, the nuclear power plant, and so on almost ad infinitum. . . . The result has been an enormous increase in the output and variety of goods and services and this alone has changed man's way of life more than anything since the discovery of fire: the Englishman of 1750 was closer in material things to Caesar's legionnaires than to his own great-grandchildren. (1969)

The modes of life and social institutions characteristic of the modern world are radically different from those of even the recent past. During a period of only two or three centuries—a minute sliver of time in the context of human history—human social life has been wrenched away from the types of social order in which people lived for thousands of years.

Far more than any generation before us, we face an uncertain future. To be sure, conditions of life for previous generations were always insecure: people were at the mercy of natural disasters, plagues, and famines. But though we are largely immune from plague and famine in the industrialized countries today, we must deal now with the social forces we ourselves have unleashed.

Defining Change

There is a sense in which everything changes, all of the time. Every day is a new day; every moment is a new instant in time. The Greek philosopher Heraclitus pointed out that a person cannot step into the same river twice. On the second occasion, the river is different, since the water has been flowing in the meantime, and the person has changed in subtle ways, too. While

this observation is in a sense correct, we *do* of course normally want to say that it is the same river and the same person stepping into it on two occasions. There is sufficient continuity in the shape of the river and in the physique and personality of the person with wet feet to say that each remains the same.

All accounts of change also involve showing what remains stable, as a baseline against which to measure changes. Even in the rapidly moving world of today, there are continuities with the distant past. Major religious systems, for example, like Christianity or Islam retain their ties with ideas and practices initiated some two thousand years ago. Yet most institutions in modern societies clearly change much more rapidly than did institutions of the traditional world.

How should we define social change? **Social change** is the transformation over time of the institutions and culture of a society. In this chapter, we shall look at attempts to interpret patterns of social change affecting human history as a whole; we shall then consider why the modern period should be associated with such especially profound and rapid social change. We will examine how social change is also the result of the purposeful actions of people joined in collective behavior, such as in social movements. We will then explore the types and causes of social movements and analyze the feminist movement in more depth. This will be followed by a discussion of where the major lines of social change in modern societies, and in the global order as a whole, seem to be leading.

INFLUENCES ON SOCIAL CHANGE

Social theorists have tried for the past two centuries to develop a single grand theory that explains the nature of social change. But no single-factor theory has a chance of accounting for the diversity of human social development from hunting and gathering and pastoral societies to traditional civilizations and finally to the highly complex social systems of today. In analyzing social change, we can at most accomplish two tasks. We can identify the three main factors that have consistently influenced social change: the physical environment, political organization, and cultural factors. We can also develop theories that account for particular periods of change, such as modern times.

The Physical Environment

The physical environment often has an effect on the development of human social organization (Diamond, 1997). This is clearest in more extreme environmental conditions, where people must organize their ways of life in relation to weather conditions. Peoples in polar regions necessarily develop different habits and practices from those living in subtropical areas. People who live in Alaska, where the winters are long and cold, tend to follow different patterns of social life from people who live in the much warmer American South. Alaskans spend more of their lives indoors and, except for the short period of the summer, plan outdoor activities very carefully, given the inhospitable environment in which they live.

Less extreme physical conditions can also affect society. The native population of Australia has never stopped being hunters and gatherers, since the conti-nent contained hardly any indigenous plants suitable for regular cultivation or animals that could be domesticated to develop pastoral production. The world's early civilizations mostly originated in areas that contained rich agricultural land—for instance, in river deltas. The ease of communications across land and the availability of sea routes are also important: societies cut off from others by mountain ranges, impassable jungles, or deserts often remain relatively unchanged over long periods of time.

Yet the direct influence of the environment on social change is not very great. People are often able to develop considerable productive wealth in relatively inhospitable areas. This is true, for example, of Alaskans, who have been able to develop oil and mineral resources in spite of the harsh nature of their surrounding environment. Conversely, hunting and gathering cultures have frequently lived in highly fertile regions without becoming involved in pastoral or agricultural production. For example, the Kwakiutl of Vancouver Island, whose way of life sur-

vived largely intact until about half a century ago, lived in an environment rich in fish, fruit, and edible plants. They were content with a hunting and gathering way of life in such favorable conditions, and never sought to convert to settled agriculture.

There is little direct relation between the environment and the systems of production that develop. The evolutionists' emphasis on adaptation to the environment is thus less illuminating than Marx's ideas in explaining social development. For Marx stressed that human beings rarely just adapt to their surrounding circumstances, as animals do. Humans always seek to master the world around them rather than take it as given. Moreover, there is no doubt that types of production strongly influence the level and nature of social change, although they do not have the overriding impact Marx attributed to them.

Political Organization

A second factor strongly influencing social change is the type of political organization that operates in a society. In hunting and gathering societies, this influence is at a minimum, since there are no political authorities capable of mobilizing the community. In all other types of society, however, the existence of distinct political agencies—chiefs, lords, monarchs, and governments—strongly affects the course of development a society takes. Political systems are not, as Marx argued, direct expressions of underlying economic organization; quite different types of political order may exist in societies that have similar production systems. For instance, some societies based on industrial capitalism have had authoritarian political systems (Nazi Germany and South Africa under apartheid), while others are much more democratic (the United States, Britain, and Sweden).

Military strength played a fundamental part in the establishment of most traditional states; it influenced their subsequent survival or expansion in an equally basic way. But the connections between the level of production and military strength are again indirect. A ruler may choose to channel resources into building up the military, for example, even when this impoverishes most of the rest of the population—as happened in Iraq in the 1980s under the rule of Saddam Hussein.

Cultural Factors

The third main influence on social change consists of cultural factors, which include the effects of religion, communication systems, and leadership. As we have seen, religion may be either a conservative or an innovative force in social life. Some forms of religious belief and practice have acted as a brake on change, emphasizing above all the need to adhere to traditional values and rituals. Yet, as Max Weber emphasized, religious convictions frequently play a mobilizing role in pressures for social change. For instance, American church leaders promote attempts to lessen poverty or diminish inequalities in society.

A particularly important cultural influence that affects the character and pace of change is the nature of communication systems. The invention of writing, for instance, allowed for the keeping of records, making possible increased control of material resources and the development of large-scale organizations. In addition, writing altered people's perception of the relation between past, present, and future. Societies that write keep a record of past events and know themselves to have a history. Understanding history can help in developing a sense of the overall movement or line of evolution a society is following, which people can then actively seek to promote further.

Under the general heading of cultural factors we should also place leadership. Individual leaders have had an enormous influence in world history. We have only to think of great religious figures (like Jesus), political and military leaders (like Julius Caesar), or innovators in science and philosophy (like Isaac Newton) to see that this is the case. A leader capable of pursuing dynamic policies and generating a mass following or radically altering preexisting modes of thought can overturn a previously established order.

However, individuals can only reach positions of leadership and become effective if favorable social conditions exist. Adolf Hitler was able to seize power in Germany in the 1930s, for instance, partly as a result of the tensions and crises that beset the country at that time. If those circumstances had not existed, he would likely have remained an obscure figure within a minor political faction. The same was true at a later date of Mahatma Gandhi, the famous pacifist leader in India during the period after World War II. Gandhi was able to be effective in securing his country's independence from Britain because the war and other events had unsettled the existing colonial institutions in India.

CHANGE IN THE MODERN PERIOD

What explains why the last two hundred years, the period of modernity, have seen such a tremendous acceleration in the speed of social change? This is a complex issue, but it is not difficult to pinpoint some of the factors involved. Not surprisingly, we can categorize them along lines similar to factors that have influenced social change throughout history, except that we shall subsume the impact of the physical environment within the overall importance of economic factors.

Economic Influences

Of economic influences, the most far-reaching is the impact of industrial capitalism. Capitalism differs in a fundamental way from preexisting production systems, because it involves the constant expansion of production and the ever-increasing accumulation of wealth. In traditional production systems, levels of production were fairly static as they were geared to habitual, customary needs. Capitalism promotes the constant revision of the technology of production, a process into which science is increasingly drawn. The rate of technological innovation fostered in modern industry is vastly greater than in any previous type of economic order.

Consider the current development of information technology. Over the past fifteen years, the power of computers has increased by a factor of ten thousand.

Thanks to computers, this man trades currencies from his home in California; he belongs to one of an increasing number of organizations that are "everywhere and nowhere."

A large computer in the 1960s was constructed using thousands of handmade connectors; an equivalent device today is not only much smaller, but requires only ten elements in an integrated circuit.

The impact of science and technology on how we live may be largely driven by economic factors, but it also stretches beyond the economic sphere. Science and technology both influence and are influenced by political and cultural factors. Scientific and technological development, for example, helped create modern forms of communication such as radio and television. As we have seen, such electronic forms of communication have produced changes in politics in recent years. Radio, television, and the other electronic media have also come to shape how we think and feel about the world.

Political Influences

The most important political factor that has helped to speed up patterns of change in the modern era is the

 emergence of the modern state, which has proved a vastly more efficient mechanism of government than the types that existed in pre-modern societies. Government plays a much bigger role in our lives, for better or worse, than it did before modern industrial societies came upon the scene.

Many changes in the political sphere have been spurred by economic transformations. For instance, the New Deal in the 1930s was a response to mass unemployment. But the political system affects economic life just as much as the other way around. Thus, the New Deal was a response to economic change, but the political programs it created in turn had a big impact on later economic development, serving to help reduce unemployment and introduce a period of increased prosperity before and after World War II.

Cultural Influences

Among the cultural factors affecting processes of social change in modern times, the development of science and the secularization of thought have each contributed to the *critical* and *innovative* character of the modern outlook. We no longer assume that customs or habits are acceptable merely because they have the age-old authority of tradition. On the contrary, our ways of life increasingly require a "rational" basis. For instance, a design for a hospital would

KEY CONCEPTS IN REVIEW

The modern period—from about the eighteenth century to the present day—has seen an extraordinary acceleration in **social change**, the transformation over time of the institutions and culture of a society. Probably more profound changes have occurred in this period, which is only a tiny segment of time in human history, than in the whole existence of humankind previously.

No single-factor theory can explain social change as a whole. A number of major influences on social change can be distinguished. These are the physical environment, the political organization, and cultural factors.

Among the important factors accounting for social change in the modern era are the expansion of industrial capitalism, the impact of science and technology, the development of centralized nation-states, and the emergence of "rational," or critical, ways of thought.

not be based mainly on traditional tastes, but would consider its capability for serving the purpose of a hospital—effectively caring for the sick.

In addition to *how* we think, the *content* of ideas has also changed. Ideals of self-betterment, freedom,

In 1998, Indonesian students protested and rioted against anti-democracy elements of the government. The students succeeded in ousting the nation's dictator.

equality, and democratic participation are largely creations of the past two or three centuries. Such ideals have served to mobilize processes of social and political change, including revolutions. These ideas cannot be tied to tradition, but rather suggest the constant revision of ways of life in the pursuit of human betterment. Although they initially were developed in the West, such ideals have become genuinely universal in their application, promoting change in most regions of the world.

COLLECTIVE BEHAVIOR AND SOCIAL MOVEMENTS

While we have sought to explain what factors influence social change, it bears mentioning that it is up to the people within a society to encourage or discourage social change. Sociologists identify the organized attempts of individuals to join together and either cause or prevent social change as social movements. Social movements are a form of collective behavior, which sociologists define as actions, often disorganized, taken by a large number of people gathered together usually in defiance of society's norms. Riots, for example, are a form of collective behavior.

We will now turn to look at the nature of collective

behavior and its impact on social change. We shall separate two aspects of **collective behavior:** the organizing of individuals into crowds or mobs on the one hand, and the formation of social movements on the other. While these often appear together—as for instance during the American civil rights movement in the 1950s and 1960s—they also may be quite separate. Some kinds of crowd activity, such as the action of lynch mobs in the South, are not closely related to a social movement.

Crowds and Riots

Collective behavior can occur whenever there is the chance of large numbers of people gathering together. From the first development of cities, the "urban rabble" constituted a potential danger to political authorities. In urban neighborhoods, in contrast to rural areas, many people live in close proximity to one another and can relatively easily take to the streets to demonstrate support for causes or express grievances. For example, when the "not guilty" verdict was announced in the 1992 trial of the white police officers accused of beating Rodney King, an African American, many black people in Los Angeles rioted in the streets.

The actions of urban groups are one example of **crowd activities.** A crowd is any sizable collection of people who are in direct interaction with one another in a public place. Crowds are an everyday part of urban life in one sense. We speak of a crowded shopping street or a crowded theater or amusement park, for instance, meaning that many people are jostling together in a physically confined space. These are individuals in circumstances of unfocused interaction (see Chapter 5): they are physically present in the same setting and aware of one another's presence, but they are pursuing, in small groups or as individuals, their

Part of a group of about 25,000, mostly Korean Americans, marching through the burned-out district of Los Angeles in the wake of the 1992 riots.

own aims, going their separate ways. However, when there is a **riot**, demonstration, or panic, everyone's actions become bound up with the others'. The situation suddenly becomes one of focused interaction; however temporarily, the crowd starts acting as a single unit. Crowd action in this sense has stimulated the interest of sociologists and historians for years—in fact, ever since the French Revolution of 1789.

LE BON'S THEORY OF CROWD ACTION

One of the most influential early studies of crowd action was Gustave Le Bon's book *The Crowd*, first published in 1895. Le Bon's work was stimulated by his studies of the revolutionary mobs during the French Revolution. In Le Bon's view, people act differently when caught up in the collective emotion of a crowd situation than they do in isolation. Under the influence of a **focused crowd**, individuals are capable of acts of barbarism, and of heroism, which they would not contemplate alone. The French revolutionary mobs that stormed the Bastille, for example, did so apparently regardless of the casualties they suffered. On the other hand, street crowds in 1789 also carried out numerous savageries.

What happens to produce this effect in crowd situations? According to Le Bon, when involved in the collective excitement generated by crowds, people temporarily lose some of the critical, reasoning faculties they are able to display in everyday life. They become highly suggestible and easily swayed by the exhortations of mob leaders or demagogues. Under the influence of the crowd, individuals regress to more "primitive" types of reaction than they would ordinarily produce. As Le Bon wrote, "Isolated, a person may be a cultivated individual; in a crowd, he is a barbarian—that is, a creature acting by instinct. He possesses the spontaneity, the violence, the ferocity, and also the enthusiasm and heroism of primitive beings" (Le Bon, 1960; orig. pub. 1895).

Although many subsequent authors have drawn upon Le Bon's ideas, we should treat them in historical context. Le Bon wrote as a conservative critic of democracy. He saw the French Revolution as signaling the opening of an era in which "crowds" (i.e., the mass of the ordinary population) would dominate their rightful rulers. Large groups, including parliamentary assemblies in Le Bon's eyes, cannot make rational decisions. They are liable to be as swayed by mass emotion, fashion, or whim, as street crowds are. Le Bon felt that democratic institutions would bring out the more primitive reactions of human beings, swamping the higher, more "civilized" faculties.

Some of Le Bon's ideas, however, at least regarding street crowds, do seem valid. The massing of large numbers of people together, in some circumstances, can generate an irrational, collective emotionality and produce unusual types of activity. Audiences have sometimes "gone wild" at pop concerts or rioted at sports events. When gripped by panic, people sometimes rush madly for safety, trampling others to death. Mobs have on occasion rampaged through the streets, beating up or killing those they see as their enemies—as happened, for example, in attacks upon the Jews in Nazi Germany.

RATIONAL ASPECTS OF CROWD ACTION

Yet most forms of crowd behavior are more discriminating and "rational" than in Le Bon's portrayal. Those engaging in collective action are often more clearly aware of their aims than Le Bon supposed. Nor do crowds always consist mainly of people already prone to behave irresponsibly—the criminal riffraff—as Le Bon suggested. George Rudé's studies of the French Revolution show that most of the 660 people killed in the mob that stormed the Bastille were "respectable" individuals who held orthodox occupations, not criminals or vagabonds (Rudé, 1959). Research into the urban riots of the 1960s in black neighborhoods in the United States showed that most rioters were not drawn from criminal elements, or even from people on social welfare. The average rioter was a man with a blue-collar job, more likely to be well informed about social and political issues, and to be involved in civil-rights activities, than other urban blacks. Moreover, although the rioting appeared haphazard, virtually all of the property attacked or looted was white-owned (U.S. Riot Commission, 1968).

Some authors have suggested that most crowd activities become intelligible when a quite opposite interpretation is put upon them to that given by Le Bon. Thus Richard Berk (1974) has argued that the activities of individuals in crowds are best understood as

Killings of African Americans were common after the Civil War. Mobs committed violence as a means of social control.

logical responses to specific situations. The gathering of crowds often offers opportunities to achieve aims at little personal cost. In crowd situations, individuals are relatively anonymous and can escape detection for acts that would otherwise result in their imprisonment—for instance, looting a store. When acting as a crowd, individuals temporarily have far more power than they have as isolated citizens (Turner and Killian, 1972).

Could this interpretation be applied to situations in which extreme violence toward innocent people is involved—say, to actions by lynch mobs in the South? The lynching of blacks was at one time a frequent occurrence. Following the Civil War, lynchings were regularly undertaken, in which freed slaves were sought out and put to death. Between 1889 and 1899, over 1,800 lynchings were reported—since some no doubt went unrecorded, the actual number was probably considerably higher (Cantril, 1963). The burning of blacks' homes, torture, and mutilation, were also carried out by mobs. It might seem as though only the view offered by Le Bon could make sense of such actions, and no doubt some of the features of mob violence that he identified are relevant. But there were some "rational" aspects to the lynchings. Those in-

volved were usually semi-organized vigilante groups who saw themselves as having a righteous cause. Taking action as a mob reduced their individual responsibility for the events, while publicly proclaiming their fury at the freeing of the slaves. The violence also served as a means of social control upon blacks, emphasizing to the black population as a whole that the passing of a law in the North did not change the reality of white power in the South. It could be argued that, when in focused crowds, to some extent people are able to overcome the usual forms of social control; the power and anonymity of the crowd allows them to act as they might normally wish to, but feel unable to.

Mob action and rioting, characteristically express the frustrations of people who cannot gain access to orthodox channels to express grievances or press for reforms they think necessary. Ruling authorities of all types have always feared mob activity, not just because of the direct threat it poses, but because it gives a public and tangible form to felt social injustices. But even riots that seem negative, giving rise to wanton destruction and loss of life, may stimulate change and produce at least some desired benefits. In the United States, for example, the riots in black neighborhoods in the 1960s forced the white community to pay attention to the deprivations African Americans suffered, leading to new reform programs.

Social Movements

A wide variety of social movements have existed in modern societies. Social movements are as evident a feature of the contemporary world as are the formal, bureaucratic organizations they often oppose. The study of their nature and impact forms an area of major interest in sociology.

A **social movement** may be defined as *an organized collective attempt to further a common interest or secure a common goal, through collective action outside the sphere of established institutions.* The definition has to be a broad one, precisely because of the variations among different types of movements. Some social movements are very small, numbering no more than a few dozen members; others may include thousands or even millions of people. Some movements carry on their activities within the laws of the society in which they exist, while others operate as illegal or underground groups. Often, laws are altered as a result of the action of social movements. For example, it

used to be that groups of workers that called their members out on strike were engaging in illegal activity, punished with varying degrees of severity in different countries. Eventually, however, the laws were amended, making the strike a permissible tactic of industrial conflict. Other modes of economic protest, such as sit-ins in factories or workplaces, still remain outside the law in most countries.

The dividing line between a social movement and a formal organization is sometimes blurred, because movements that become well established usually take on bureaucratic characteristics. The Salvation Army, for example, began as a social movement, but has now taken on most of the characteristics of a more permanent organization. Less frequently, an organization may devolve into a social movement, as when, for instance, a political party is banned and forced to go underground, perhaps becoming a guerrilla movement.

Classifying Social Movements

Various ways of classifying social movements have been proposed. Perhaps the neatest and most comprehensive classification is that developed by David

The environmental movement has been one of the most prevalent reformative movements internationally.

KEY CONCEPTS IN REVIEW

Collective behavior refers to the actions, often disorganized, taken by a large number of people gathered together usually in defiance of society's norms. Collective behavior can take one of several forms, including crowd activities and social movements. **Crowd activities** become focused when people act in pursuit of common objectives. **Social movements** are an organized collective attempt to further common interests through collaborative action outside the sphere of established institutions.

Social movements can be classified into four categories: **transformative movements, reformative movements, redemptive movements,** and **alterative movements.** Sociology not only studies such movements, it also responds to the issues they raise.

Aberle, who distinguishes four types of movements (Aberle, 1966). **Transformative movements** aim at far-reaching, cataclysmic, and often violent change in the society of which they are a part. Examples are revolutionary movements and some radical religious movements; many millenarian movements, as well, have foreseen a more or less complete restructuring of society when the era of salvation arrives. **Reformative movements** aspire to alter only some aspects of the existing social order. They concern themselves with specific kinds of inequality or injustice. Cases in point are the Women's Christian Temperance Union and anti-abortion groups.

Transformative and reformative movements are both concerned primarily with securing changes in society. Aberle's other two types are mainly aimed at changing the habits or outlook of individuals. **Redemptive movements** seek to rescue people from ways of life seen as corrupting. Many religious movements belong in this category, insofar as they concentrate on personal salvation. Examples are the Pentecostal sects, which believe that individuals' spiritual development is the true indication of their worth. The somewhat clumsily titled **alterative movements** aim at securing partial change in individuals. They do not seek to achieve a complete alteration in people's habits, but are concerned with changing certain specific traits. An illustration is Alcoholics Anonymous.

Why Do Social Movements Occur?

Sociology arose in the late nineteenth century as part of an effort to come to grips with the massive political and economic transformations that Europe underwent on its way from the preindustrial to the modern world (Moore, 1966). Perhaps because sociology was founded in this context, sociologists have never lost their fascination with these transformations.

Since mass social movements have been so important in world history over the past two centuries, it is not surprising that a diversity of theories exists to try to account for them. Some theories were formulated early in the history of the social sciences; the most important was that of Karl Marx. Marx, who lived well before any of the social movements undertaken in the name of his ideas took place, intended his views to be taken not just as an analysis of the conditions of revolutionary change, but as a means of furthering such change. Whatever their intrinsic validity, Marx's ideas have had an immense practical impact on twentieth-century social change.

We shall look at four frameworks for the study of social movements, many of which were developed in the context of revolution: economic deprivation, resource mobilization, structural strain, and fields of action.

ECONOMIC DEPRIVATION

Marx's view of social movements is based on his interpretation of human history in general (see Chapter 1). According to Marx, the development of societies is marked by periodic class conflicts that, when they become acute, tend to end in a process of revolutionary change. Class struggles derive from the **contradictions**—unresolvable tensions—in societies. The main sources of contradiction can be traced to economic changes, or changes in the forces of production. In any stable society, there is a balance between the economic structure, social relationships, and the political system. As the forces of production alter, contradiction is intensified, leading to open clashes between classes—and ultimately to revolution.

Marx applied this model both to the past development of feudalism and to what he saw as the probable future evolution of industrial capitalism. The traditional, feudal societies of Europe were based on peasant production; the producers were serfs ruled by a class of landed aristocrats and gentry. Economic changes within these societies gave rise to towns and cities, where trade and manufacture developed. This new economic system, created *within* feudal society, threatened its very basis. Rather than being founded on the traditional lord-serf relationship, the emerging economic order encouraged industrialists to produce goods for sale in open markets. The contradictions between the old feudal economy and the newly emerging capitalist one eventually became acute, taking the form of violent conflicts between the rising capitalist class and the feudal landowners. Revolution was the outcome of this process, the most important example being the French Revolution of 1789. Through such revolutions and revolutionary changes occurring in other European societies, Marx argued, the capitalist class managed to achieve dominance.

But the coming of industrial capitalism, according to Marx, set up new contradictions, which would eventually lead to a further series of revolutions prompted by ideals of socialism or communism. Industrial capitalism, an economic order based on the private pursuit of profit and on competition between firms to sell their products, creates a gulf between a

Relative deprivation between the peasantry and the elite in France led to the overthrow of the monarchy.

rich minority who control the industrial resources and an impoverished majority of wage workers. Workers and capitalists come into more and more intense conflict with one another. Labor movements and political parties representing the mass of the working population eventually mount a challenge to the rule of the capitalist class and overthrow the existing political system. When the position of a dominant class is particularly entrenched, Marx believed, violence is necessary to bring about the required transition. In other circumstances, this process might happen peacefully through parliamentary action; a revolution (in the sense defined above) would not be necessary.

Contrary to Marx's expectations, revolutions failed to occur in the advanced industrialized societies of the West. Why? Sociologist James Davies, a critic of Marx, pointed to periods of history when people lived in dire poverty but did not rise up in protest. Constant poverty or deprivation does not make people into revolutionaries; rather, they usually endure such conditions with resignation or mute despair. Social protest, and ultimately revolution, is more likely to occur, Davies argued, when there is an *improvement* in people's living conditions. Once standards of living have started to rise, people's levels of expectation also go up. If improvement in actual conditions subsequently slows down, propensities to revolt are created because rising expectations are frustrated (Davies, 1962).

Thus, it is not absolute deprivation that leads to protest but **relative deprivation**—the discrepancy between the lives people are forced to lead and what they think could realistically be achieved. Davies' theory is useful in understanding the connections between revolution and modern social and economic development. The influence of ideals of progress, together with expectations of economic growth, tend to induce rising hopes, which, if then frustrated, spark protest. Such protest gains further strength from the spread of ideas of equality and democratic political participation, ideas that played a basic role not only in the American Revolution of 1776 and the Russian Revolution of 1917, but also in the revolutions of 1989 in Europe.

As Charles Tilly has pointed out, however, Davies' theory does not show how and why different groups *mobilize* to seek revolutionary change. Protest might well often occur against a backdrop of rising expectations; to understand how it is transformed into a mass social movement, we need to identify how groups become collectively organized to make effective political challenges.

3. The *common interests* of those engaging in collective action, what they see as the gains and losses likely to be achieved by their policies. Some common goals always underlie mobilization to collective action. Lenin managed to weld together a broad coalition of support because many people had a common interest in removing the existing government.

4. *Opportunity*. Chance events may occur that provide opportunities to pursue revolutionary aims. Numerous forms of collective action, including revolution, are greatly influenced by such incidental events. There was no inevitability to Lenin's success, which depended on a number of contingent factors—including success in battle. If Lenin had been killed, would there have been a revolution?

Collective action itself can simply be defined as people acting together in pursuit of interests they share—for example, gathering to demonstrate in support of their cause. Some of these people may be intensely in-

RESOURCE MOBILIZATION

In *From Mobilization to Revolution*, Charles Tilly analyzed processes of revolutionary change in the context of broader forms of protest and violence (Tilly, 1978). He distinguished four main components of **collective action**, action taken to contest or overthrow an existing social order:

1. The *organization* of the group or groups involved. Protest movements are organized in many ways, varying from the spontaneous formation of crowds to tightly disciplined revolutionary groups. The Russian Revolution, for example, began as a small group of activists.

2. *Mobilization,* the ways in which a group acquires sufficient resources to make collective action possible. Such resources may include supplies of material goods, political support, and weaponry. Lenin was able to acquire material and moral support from a sympathetic peasantry, together with many townspeople.

According to Tilly, collective action, as seen in the Velvet Revolution of 1989 in Prague, requires organization, mobilization, common interests, and opportunity.

volved, others may lend more passive or irregular support. Effective collective action, such as action that culminates in revolution, usually moves through stages 1 to 4.

Social movements, in Tilly's view, tend to develop as means of mobilizing group resources either when people have no institutionalized means of making their voices heard or when their needs are directly repressed by the state authorities. Although collective action at some point involves open confrontation with the political authorities—"taking to the streets"— only when such activity is backed by groups who are systematically organized is confrontation likely to have much impact on established patterns of power.

Typical modes of collective action and protest vary with historical and cultural circumstances. In the United States today, for example, most people are familiar with forms of demonstration like mass marches, large assemblies, and street riots, whether or not they have participated in such activities. (A famous example was the historic, nonviolent march on Washington for civil rights led by Martin Luther King, Jr., in 1963.) Other types of collective protest, however, have become less common or have disappeared altogether in most modern societies (such as fights between villages, machine breaking, or lynching). Protesters can also build on examples taken from elsewhere; for instance, guerrilla movements proliferated in various parts of the world once disaffected groups learned how successful guerrilla actions can be against regular armies.

When and why does collective action become violent? After studying a large number of incidents that have occurred in Western Europe since 1800, Tilly concluded that most collective violence develops from action that is not itself initially violent. Whether violence occurs depends not so much on the nature of the activity as on other factors—in particular, how the authorities respond. A good instance is the street demonstration. The vast majority of such demonstrations take place without damage either to people or to property. A minority lead to violence, and are then labeled as riots. Sometimes the authorities step in when violence has already occurred; more often, the historical record shows, they are the originators of violence. In Tilly's words, "In the modern European experience repressive forces are themselves the most consistent initiators and performers of collective violence"

(1978). Moreover, when violent confrontations do occur, the agents of authority are responsible for the largest share of deaths and injuries. This is not surprising given their special access to arms and military discipline. The groups they are attempting to control, conversely, do greater damage to objects or property.

Revolutionary movements, according to Tilly, are a type of collective action that occurs in situations of what he calls **multiple sovereignty**—these occur when a government for some reason lacks full control over the areas it is supposed to administer. Multiple sovereignty can arise as a result of external war, internal political clashes, or the two combined. Whether a revolutionary takeover of power is accomplished depends on how far the ruling authorities maintain control over the armed forces, the extent of conflicts within ruling groups, and the level of organization of the protest movements trying to seize power.

Tilly's work represents one of the most sophisticated attempts to analyze collective violence and revolutionary struggles. The concepts he develops seem to have wide application, and his use of them is sensitive to the variabilities of historical time and place. How social movements are organized, the resources they are able to mobilize, the common interests of groups contending for power, and chance opportunities are all important facets of social transformation.

Tilly says little, however, about the circumstances that lead to multiple sovereignty. This is such a fundamental part of explaining revolution that it represents a serious omission. According to Theda Skocpol, Tilly assumes that social movements are guided by the conscious and deliberate pursuit of interests, and successful processes of revolutionary change occur when people manage to realize these interests. Skocpol, by contrast, sees social movements as more ambiguous and indecisive in their objectives. Revolutions, she emphasizes, largely emerge as unintended consequences of more partial aims:

In fact, in historical revolutions, differently situated and motivated groups have become participants in complex unfoldings of multiple conflicts. These conflicts have been powerfully shaped and limited by existing social, economic and international conditions. And they have proceeded in different ways depending upon how each revolutionary situation emerged in the first place. (1979)

KEY CONCEPTS IN REVIEW

The following are four major theories of revolution and social movements.

Economic deprivation: Marx argued that revolutions occur because of the class struggles resulting from the **contradictions** found in the economy and society. Davies contested this, arguing that revolutions result from the condition of **relative deprivation,** the discrepancy between the lives people are forced to lead and what they think could realistically be achieved.

Resource mobilization: According to Tilly, **collective action,** taken to contest or overthrow an existing social order, is a means of mobilizing a group's resources when people have no institutionalized means of making their interests known or when their interests are repressed by the government. Revolutions are a type of collective action that occurs in situations of **multiple sovereignty,** when a government lacks full control over its territory.

Structural strain: According to Smelser, social movements develop in response to situations of **structural strain.**

Fields of action: Touraine examined the historical context of social movements (an idea he called **historicity**) and the **field of action,** the arena within which social movements interact with established organizations. Touraine argued that this process of interaction was central in shaping social movements.

Skocpol's argument seems correct when we analyze the revolutionary changes that occurred in East European societies in 1989, compared with earlier revolutionary episodes (see Chapter 10: "Government, Political Power, and War").

In addition to the above theories, which sought to explain the collective behavior that led to revolutions, other theoretical perspectives on more general forms of collective action are also important. We will now look at two of those theories, structural strain and fields of action.

STRUCTURAL STRAIN

Neil Smelser (1963) distinguished six conditions underlying the origins of collective action in general, and social movements in particular. *Structural conduciveness* refers to the general social conditions promoting or inhibiting the formation of social movements of different types. For example, in Smelser's view, the sociopolitical system of the United States leaves open certain avenues of mobilization for protest because of the relative absence of state regulation in those areas. Thus there is no official state-sponsored religion. People are free to exercise their religious beliefs. This makes for a conducive environment in which religious movements might compete for individuals, so long as they do not transgress criminal or civil law.

Just because the conditions are conducive to the development of a social movement does not mean those conditions will bring them into being. There must be **structural strain**—tensions (or, in Marx's terminology, contradictions) that produce conflicting interests within societies. Uncertainties, anxieties, ambiguities, or direct clashes of goals, are expressions of such strains. Sources of strain may be quite general, or specific to particular situations. Thus sustained inequalities between ethnic groups give rise to overall tensions; these may become focused in the shape of specific conflicts when, say, blacks begin to move into a previously all-white area.

The third condition Smelser outlined is the spread of *generalized beliefs.* Social movements do not develop simply as responses to vaguely felt anxieties or

The civil rights movement met all of the criteria of Smelser's model, including having strong leadership under Dr. Martin Luther King, Jr.

hostilities. They are shaped by the influence of definite ideologies, which crystallize grievances and suggest courses of action that might be pursued to remedy them. Revolutionary movements, for instance, are based on ideas about why injustice occurs and how it can be alleviated by political struggle.

Precipitating factors are events or incidents that actually trigger direct action by those who become involved in the movement. In 1955, when a black woman named Rosa Parks refused to give up her seat to a white man on a bus in Montgomery, Alabama, her action helped spark the civil rights movement (see Chapter 9: "Ethnicity and Race").

The first four conditions combined, Smelser argued, might occasionally lead to street disturbances or outbreaks of violence. But such incidents do not lead to the development of social movements unless there is a coordinated group that becomes mobilized for action. *Leadership* and some means of *regular communication* among participants, together with funding and material resources, are necessary for a social movement to exist.

Finally, the manner in which a social movement develops is strongly influenced by the *operation of social control*. The governing authorities may respond to initial protests by intervening in the conditions of conduciveness and strain that stimulated the emergence of the movement. For instance, in a situation of ethnic tension, steps might be taken to reduce ethnic inequality that generated resentment and conflict. Other important aspects of social control concerns the responses of the police or armed forces. A harsh reaction might encourage further protest and help solidify the movement. Also, doubt and divisions within the police and military can be crucial in deciding the outcome of confrontations with revolutionary movements.

Smelser's model is useful for analyzing the sequences in the development of social movements, and collective action in general. According to Smelser, each stage in the sequence "adds value" to the overall outcome; also, each stage is a condition for the occurrence of the next one. But there are some critical comments that can be made about Smelser's theory. Some social movements become strong without any particular precipitating incidents. Conversely, a series of incidents might bring home the need to establish a movement to change the circumstances that gave rise to them. Also, a movement itself might create strains, rather than develop in response to them. For example, the women's movement has actively sought to identify and combat gender inequalities where previously these had gone unquestioned. Smelser's theory treats social movements as *responses* to situations, rather than allowing that their members might spontaneously organize to achieve desired social changes. In this respect his ideas contrast with the approach developed by Alain Touraine.

FIELDS OF ACTION

Alain Touraine (1977, 1981) developed his analysis of social movements on the basis of four main ideas. The first, which he called **historicity**, explains why there are so many more movements in the modern world than there were in earlier times. In modern societies individuals and groups know that social activism can be used to achieve social goals and reshape society.

Second, Touraine focused on the *rational objectives* of social movements. Such movements do not just come about as irrational responses to social divisions or injustices; rather, they develop from specific views and rational strategies as to how injustices can be overcome.

Third, Touraine saw a process of *interaction* in the shaping of social movements. Movements do not develop in isolation; instead, they develop in deliberate antagonism with established organizations, and sometimes with other rival social movements. All social movements have interests or aims that they are *for*; all have views and ideas they are *against*. In Touraine's view, other theories of social movements (including that of Smelser) have given insufficient consideration as to how the objectives of a social movement are shaped by encounters with others holding divergent positions, as well as by the ways in which they themselves influence the outlooks and action of their opponents. For instance, the objectives and outlook of the women's movement have been shaped in opposition to the male-dominated institutions that it seeks to alter. The goals and outlook of the movement have shifted in relation to its successes and failures, and have also influenced the perspectives of men. These changed perspectives in turn stimulated a reorientation in women's movements, and so the process of shaping and reshaping continues.

Fourth, social movements and change occur in the context of what Touraine called **fields of action**. A field of action refers to the connections between a social movement and the forces or influences against it. The process of mutual negotiation among antagonists in a field of action may lead to the social changes sought by the movement as well as to changes in the social movement itself and in its antagonists. In either circumstance the movement may evaporate—or become institutionalized as a permanent organization. For example the labor-union movements became formal organizations when they achieved the right to strike and to types of bargaining acceptable to both workers and employers. These changes in both the movement and the original worker-owner relationship were forged out of earlier processes involving widespread violent confrontation on both sides. Where there are continuing sources of conflict (as in the case of the relation between unions and employers) new movements still tend to reemerge.

Touraine's analysis can also be applied to movements concerned primarily with individual change—Aberle's redemptive and alterative categories—even though Touraine himself has said little about them.

For instance, Alcoholics Anonymous is a movement based upon medical findings about the harmful effects of alcohol upon people's health and social activities. The movement itself has been shaped by its own opposition to advertising designed to encourage alcoholic drinking, and by its attempt to confront the outside pressures faced by alcoholics in a society in which drinking is easily tolerated.

Feminist Movements

As we just saw, theories of revolution inevitably tend to overlap with those of social movements. Charles Tilly's emphasis on resource mobilization, for example, has been applied to social movements such as the feminist movement.

The first groups actively organized to promote women's rights date from the period immediately following the American and French Revolutions (Evans, 1977). In the 1790s, inspired by the ideals of freedom and equality for which the revolutions had been fought, several women's clubs were formed in Paris

In the United States, the 1910s saw great advancements in feminist issues such as women's suffrage.

and major provincial cities. The clubs provided meeting places for women, but also petitioned for equal rights in education, employment, and government. Marie Gouze, a leader of one of the clubs, drew up a statement entitled "Declaration of the Rights of Women," based on the "Declaration of the Rights of Man and Citizen," the main constitutional document of the French Revolution. How could true equality be achieved, she argued, when half the population were excluded from the privileges that men share?

The response from the male revolutionary leaders was less than sympathetic—Marie Gouze was executed in 1793, charged with "having forgotten the virtues which belong to her sex." The women's clubs were subsequently dissolved by government decree. Feminist groups and women's movements have been formed repeatedly in Western countries since that date, almost always encountering hostility, and sometimes provoking violence, from the established authorities. Marie Gouze was by no means the only feminist to give her life to the cause of achieving equal rights for her sex.

In the nineteenth century, feminism became more advanced in the United States than elsewhere, and most leaders of women's movements in other countries looked to the struggles of American women as a model. In the 1840s and 1850s, American feminists were closely involved with groups devoted to the abolition of slavery. Yet, having no formal political rights (the Constitution did not give women the right to vote), women were excluded from the political lobbying through which reformers could pursue their objectives. No women were allowed to take part in a world antislavery convention held in London in 1840. This fact led the women's groups to turn more directly to considering gender inequalities. In 1848, just as their French counterparts had done a half century before, women leaders in the United States met to approve a "Declaration of Sentiments," modeled upon the Declaration of Independence. "We hold these truths to be self-evident," it began, "that all men and women are created equal." The declaration set out a long list of the injustices to which women were subject (Hartman and Banner, 1974). However, few real gains in improving the social or political position of women were made during this period. When slavery ended, Congress ruled that only freed *male* slaves should be given the vote.

Some African-American women played a part in the early development of the women's movement in the United States, although they often had to contend with hostility and racism from their white sisters. One, Sojourner Truth, spoke out against both slavery and the disenfranchisement of women, linking the two issues closely. When she forcefully and passionately addressed an antislavery rally in Indiana in the 1850s and a white man yelled at her, "I don't believe you really are a woman," she publicly bared her breasts to prove him wrong. Although Truth played a prominent part in women's struggles of the period (Hooks, 1981), other black women who tried to participate became disillusioned with the prejudice they encountered; African-American feminists as a result were few in number.

One of the most important events in the early development of feminist movements in Europe was the presentation of a petition, signed by 1,500 women, to the British Parliament in 1866, demanding that the electoral reforms then being discussed include full voting rights for women. The petition was ignored; in response, its organizers set up the National Society for Women's Suffrage the following year. The members of the society became known as **suffragists,** and throughout the remainder of the nineteenth century they continued to petition Parliament to extend voting rights to women. By the early twentieth century, the world influence of British feminism rivaled that of feminists in the United States. Frequent marches and street demonstrations were organized in both countries. An open-air meeting held in London in June 1908 attracted a crowd of half a million people. During this period, women's movements mushroomed in all the major European countries, together with Australia and New Zealand.

Emmeline Pankhurst, a leading suffragist, participated in several speaking tours of the United States, recounting the British struggles to large audiences. Two Americans who had become involved in the campaigns in Britain, Alice Paine and Harriet Stanton Blatch, organized massive marches and parades through New York and other Eastern cities from 1910 onward.

By 1920, women had attained the right to vote in several Western countries (see Table 18.1). After achieving that right, though, most feminist movements in the United States and elsewhere fell into de-

Table 18.1 The Year in Which Women Achieved the Right to Vote on an Equal Basis with Men, by Country

1893	New Zealand	1945	France, Hungary, Italy, Japan, Vietnam, Yugoslavia, Bolivia
1902	Australia	1946	Albania, Romania, Panama
1906	Finland	1947	Argentina, Venezuela
1913	Norway	1948	Israel, Korea
1915	Denmark, Iceland	1949	China, Chile
1917	Soviet Union	1950	El Salvador, Ghana, India
1918	Canada	1951	Nepal
1919	Austria, Germany, the Netherlands, Poland, Sweden, Luxembourg, Czechoslovakia	1952	Greece
1920	United States	1953	Mexico
1922	Ireland	1954	Colombia
1928	Britain	1955	Nicaragua
1929	Ecuador	1956	Egypt, Pakistan, Senegal
1930	South Africa	1957	Lebanon
1931	Spain, Sri Lanka, Portugal	1959	Morocco
1932	Thailand	1962	Algeria
1934	Brazil, Cuba	1963	Iran, Kenya, Libya
1936	Costa Rica	1964	Sudan, Zambia
1937	Philippines	1965	Afghanistan, Guatemala
1941	Indonesia	1977	Nigeria
1942	Dominican Republic, Uruguay	1979	Peru, Zimbabwe

SOURCE: Lisa Tuttle, *Encyclopedia of Feminism* (New York: Facts on File, 1986).

cline. Radical women tended to be absorbed into other movements, such as those combating fascism, a political doctrine of the extreme right gaining ground in Germany, Italy, and elsewhere in the 1930s. Little was left of feminism as a distinct movement against male-dominated institutions. The achievement of equal political rights did little to extend equality to other spheres of women's lives.

THE RESURGENCE OF FEMINISM

In the late 1960s, women's movements again burst back to prominence (Chafe, 1974, 1977). Over the quarter century since then, feminism has become a major influence in countries throughout the world, including many in the Third World. The resurgence began in

The National Organization of Women has led the charge for women's rights.

the United States, influenced by the civil rights movement and by the student activism of the period. Women who were active in these causes often found themselves relegated by male activists to a traditionally subordinate role. Civil rights leaders were resistant to women's rights being included in their manifestos of equality. So women's groups began to establish independent organizations concerned primarily with feminist issues.

The women's movement today in fact involves a variety of interest groups and organizations. Among the most prominent in the United States is the National Organization for Women (NOW), with a membership of about 160,000 (men as well as women, although the large majority are female). Another group is the National Women's Political Caucus (NWPC), which numbers about half the membership of NOW. Some organizations are concerned with single issues such as abortion, education, or pension rights. Yet other groups consist of more long-established associations of women in various occupations, like the American Association of University Women (Palley, 1987).

FEMINIST MOVEMENTS: AN INTERPRETATION

The rise of women's movements over the past century can easily be interpreted in terms of the concepts set out by Charles Tilly. Social movements arise, Tilly argues, when people have no chance of making themselves heard or when they lack outlets for their aspirations. In the first phase of development of feminist movements, in the nineteenth and early twentieth centuries, feminist leaders sought above all to *gain a voice* for women in the political process—in other words, to obtain the right to vote. In the second phase, women's movements sought to extend the gains they had achieved, fighting for economic as well as political equality for women.

In both phases, the leaders of women's movements were able to *mobilize collective resources* to place effective pressure on the governing authorities. During the early period, women activists' chief resource was mass marches and demonstrations. Later on, organizations (like NOW) were able to fight for women's rights in a more consistent and organized way. The *common interests* to which women's group leaders have been able to appeal include the concern that women should have a role in political decision making, be able to engage in paid work if they wish, and have equal rights in divorce proceedings.

Finally, the *opportunity* of feminist activists to influence social change has been affected by a variety of factors. The outbreak of World War I, for example, helped in the aim of securing the vote: governments fighting the war needed the support and active involvement of women in the war effort. In the second phase of the development of feminism, the civil rights movement was the spark that ignited a new wave of activism.

Social movements hold a double interest for sociologists. They provide subject matter for study, but more than this, they help shift the ways in which sociologists look at certain areas of behavior. The women's movement, for instance, is not just relevant to sociology because it provides material for research. It has identified weaknesses in established frameworks of sociological thought and developed concepts (such as that of patriarchy) that help us understand issues of gender and power. There is a continuing dialogue not only between social movements and the organizations they confront, but between social movements and sociology itself.

CURRENT CHANGE AND FUTURE PROSPECTS

Where is social change leading us today? What are the main trends of development likely to affect our lives as the twenty-first century opens? Social theorists do not agree on the answers to these questions, which obviously involve a great deal of speculation. We shall look at four different perspectives: the notion that we are a postindustrial society, the idea that we have reached a postmodern period, the belief that democratic capitalism will continue to spread, and the argument that risk is the most central dynamic of society.

Toward a Postindustrial Society?

Some observers have suggested that what is occurring today is a transition to a new society no longer primarily based on industrialism. We are entering, they claim, a phase of development beyond the industrial era altogether. A variety of terms have been coined to describe this new social order, such as the **information society, service society,** and **knowledge society.** The term that has come into most common usage, however—first employed by Daniel Bell in the United States and Alain Touraine in France—is **postindustrial society** (Bell, 1976; Touraine, 1974), the "post" (meaning "after") referring to the sense that we are moving beyond the old forms of industrial development.

The diversity of names is one indication of the myriad of ideas put forward to interpret current social changes. But one theme that appears consistently is the significance of *information* or *knowledge* in the society of the future. Our way of life, based on the manufacture of material goods, centered on the power machine and the factory, is being displaced by one in which information is the basis of the productive system.

The clearest and most comprehensive portrayal of

The jobs available at this career fair represent major employment trends for the young workforce: white-collar workers specializing in systems of knowledge.

the postindustrial society is provided by Daniel Bell in *The Coming of the Post-Industrial Society* (1976). The postindustrial order, Bell argues, is distinguished by a growth of service occupations at the expense of jobs that produce material goods. The blue-collar worker, employed in a factory or workshop, is no longer the most essential type of employee. White-collar (clerical and professional) workers outnumber blue-collar, with professional and technical occupations growing fastest of all.

People working in higher level white-collar occupations specialize in the production of information and knowledge. The production and control of what Bell calls codified knowledge—systematic, coordinated information—is society's main strategic resource. Those who create and distribute this knowledge—scientists, computer specialists, economists, engineers, and professionals of all kinds—increasingly become the leading social groups, replacing the industrialists and entrepreneurs of the old system. On the level of culture, there is a shift away from the "work ethic" characteristic of industrialism; people are freer to innovate and enjoy themselves in both their work and their domestic lives.

How valid is the view that the old industrial order is being replaced by a postindustrial society? While the thesis has been widely accepted, the empirical assertions on which it depends are suspect in several ways.

1. The trend toward service occupations, accompanied by a decline in employment in other production sectors, dates back almost to the beginning of industrialism itself; it is not simply a recent phenomenon. From the early 1800s, manufacture and services both expanded at the expense of agriculture, with the service sector consistently showing a faster rate of increase than manufacture. The blue-collar worker never really was the most common type of employee; a higher proportion of paid employees has *always* worked in agriculture and services, with the service sector increasing proportionally as the numbers in agriculture dwindled. Easily the most important change has not been from industrial to service work but from farm employment to all other types of occupation.

2. The service sector is very heterogeneous. Service occupations cannot be simply treated as identical to white-collar jobs; many service jobs (such as that of gas-station attendant) are blue-collar, in the sense that they are manual. Most white-collar positions involve little specialized knowledge and have become substantially mechanized. This is true of most lower-level office work.

3. Many service jobs contribute to a process that in the end produces material goods, and therefore should really be counted as part of manufacture. Thus, a computer programmer working for an industrial firm, designing and monitoring the operation of machine tools, is directly involved in a process of making material goods.

4. No one can be sure what the long-term impact of the spreading use of microprocessing and electronic communications systems will be. At the moment, these are integrated within manufacturing production, rather than displacing it. It seems certain that such technologies will continue to show high rates of innovation and will permeate more areas of social life. But how far we yet live in a society in which codified knowledge is the main resource is unclear (Gill, 1985; Lyon, 1989).

5. The postindustrial society thesis tends to exaggerate the importance of economic factors in producing social change. Such a society is described as the outcome of developments in the economy that lead to changes in other institutions. Most of those advancing the postindustrial hypothesis have been little influenced by, or are directly critical of, Marx; but their position is a quasi-Marxist one in the sense that economic factors are held to dominate social change.

Some of the developments cited by the postindustrial theorists are important features of the current era, but it is not obvious that the concept of the postindustrial society is the best way to come to terms with them. Moreover, the forces behind the changes going on today are political and cultural as well as economic.

Postmodernity

Some authors have recently gone as far as saying that the developments now occurring are even more profound than signaling the end of the era of industrialism. What is happening is nothing short of a movement beyond modernity—the attitudes and ways of life associated with modern societies, such as our belief in progress, the benefits of science, and our capability to control the modern world. A **postmodern** era is arriving, or has already arrived.

The advocates of postmodernity claim that modern societies took their inspiration from the idea that history has a shape—it "goes somewhere" and leads to progress—and that now this notion has collapsed. There are no longer any "grand narratives"—overall conceptions of history—that make any sense (Lyotard, 1985). Not only is there no general notion of progress that can be defended, there is no such thing as history. The postmodern world is thus a highly pluralistic and diverse one. In countless films, videos, and TV programs, images circulate around the world. We come into contact with many ideas and values, but these have little connection with the history of the areas in which we live, or indeed with our own personal histories. Everything seems constantly in flux. As one group of authors expressed things:

> Our world is being remade. Mass production, the mass consumer, the big city, big-brother state, the sprawling housing estate, and the nation-state are in decline: flexibility, diversity, differentiation, and mobility, communication, decentralization and internationalization are in the ascendant. In the process our own identities, our sense of self, our own subjectivities are being transformed. We are in transition to a new era. (S. Hall et al., 1988)

History ends alongside modernity, it is said, because there is no longer any way of describing in general terms the pluralistic universe that has come into being.

The End of History

The writer whose name has come to be synonymous with the phrase "end of history" is Francis Fukuyama. But Fukuyama's conception of the end of history at first seems completely contrary to the ideas advanced by the theorists of postmodernity. His views are based not on the collapse of modernity but on its worldwide triumph, in the shape of capitalism and liberal democracy.

In the wake of the 1989 revolutions in Eastern Europe, the dissolution of the Soviet Union, and a movement toward multiparty democracy in other regions, Fukuyama argues, the ideological battles of earlier eras are over. The end of history is the end of alternatives. No one any longer defends monarchism, and fascism is a phenomenon of the past. So is communism, for so long the major rival of Western democracy. Capitalism has won in its long struggle with socialism, contrary to Marx's prediction, and liberal democracy now stands unchallenged. We have reached, Fukuyama asserts, "the end point of mankind's ideological evolution and universalization of Western democracy as the final form of human government" (1989).

The two versions of the end of history, however, are not as far apart as may appear. Liberal democracy is a framework for the expression of diverse views and interests. It does not specify how we should behave, apart from insisting that we should respect the views of others; hence it is compatible with a pluralism of attitudes and ways of life.

The Risk Society

Although it has received surprisingly little attention in the United States, *Risk Society* (1992), by German sociologist Ulrich Beck, is one of the most popular sociological books in Europe. Pointing to a series of interrelated changes in the nature of contemporary social life, including growing job insecurity, the declining role of tradition in shaping the life choices of individuals, and, most important, the increasing risk of global environmental catastrophe, Beck suggests that society is on its way to a new phase of development, a "new modernity." Whereas conflict over the distribution of wealth was the central dynamic of industrial society through the mid-twentieth century, Beck claims that this conflict is being displaced today by conflict over various forms of social risk. Individuals, of course, have always had to face risks of one sort or another. But today's risks, according to Beck, are qualitatively different than those of the past. On the one hand, risk today is *manufactured*, meaning it is the result of our own knowledge and creation. In addition, contemporary risks, such as increasing pollution levels or atmospheric temperatures, have global, as opposed to merely personal, consequences: By their nature they endanger *all* forms of life on the planet. Finally, today's risks can no longer be justified rhetorically, as they were in the past, by society's need to overcome scarcity through heightened industrial productivity.

Because contemporary risks have these characteristics, they generate important social realignments. In today's "risk society," political affiliations no longer occur primarily on the basis of class, as was true in previous eras, but on the basis of the "social risk positions" that individuals occupy. For example, although everyone is potentially affected by an accident at a nuclear power plant, some people, such as those living

The environmental risk: A farmer carries on with his daily routine in the shadow of a nuclear power plant.

near the plant, are more at risk than others. And while certain environmental hazards, like toxic waste dumps, are more likely to be located in poor communities than in wealthy ones, wealth alone may not be enough to ensure immunity from environmental disaster. New forms of affiliation therefore arise as individuals from various social strata who are nevertheless subject to the same set of risks begin to work together—for example, by joining environmental movements—to minimize the dangers that industry or government pose to them. Because environmental risks, previously the domain of experts and viewed by most people as inevitable by-products of modernization, now come to occupy center stage in social life, Beck describes society in the present period as undergoing "reflexive modernization," i.e., a form of modernization in which people begin to scrutinize aspects of the modernization process that they used to take for granted.

For environmental sociologist Ted Benton of Essex University in England, however, Beck's sweeping thesis fails to ring true. Benton does not doubt that the risk of global environmental catastrophe is real. Nor does he fail to recognize the increasing salience of environmental issues for political life. Instead, Benton objects to the assumption that, in the new "risk soci-ety," environmental dangers, rather than class relations, become the true axes around which society's core social struggles revolve. According to Benton, not only is there empirical evidence to suggest that people continue to vote along class lines, there is also reason to believe that the environmental movement is not unconnected to what Marx called the "class struggle": "Many thousands of socialist activists in their local communities and in their trade unions have been concerned with environmental health provision, with campaigning against air and water pollution, and with health and safety standards in the work-place."

Beyond this, Benton also questions the political implications of the reflexive modernization thesis. Will democratic participation alone be enough to avert environmental disaster? Benton's answer is a resounding "no." Espousing what he calls "ecological socialism," Benton maintains that environmental responsibility is virtually impossible under a capitalist system, in which pressures for "capital accumulation" are likely to create environmental problems. For Benton, environmental risks, far from signaling the end of class politics, instead provide a compelling justification for socialism (Benton, 1996).

SOCIAL CHANGE: LOOKING INTO THE FUTURE

Who can say what new forms of economic, political, or cultural order may emerge in the future? Just as the thinkers of medieval times had no inkling of the industrial society that was to emerge with the decline of feudalism, so we can't at the moment anticipate how the world will change in the coming century.

We should have reservations, therefore, about the idea of the end of history, and also about the idea of postmodernity. The postmodern theorists stress diversity and fragmentation too much, at the expense of new forms of global integration. Pluralism is important, but humanity today faces common problems, problems in our "risk society" that require for their solutions general initiatives. One-sided capitalistic expansion cannot continue indefinitely; the world has only finite resources. As collective humanity, we need to take steps to overcome the economic divisions that

KEY CONCEPTS IN REVIEW

The following are four major theories of modern social change.

A **postindustrial society** is based on knowledge and information and is distinguished by an economy made up mostly of service occupations. The person most associated with this theory is Daniel Bell.

Postmodernism is the belief that society is no longer governed by history or progress. Postmodern society is highly pluralistic and diverse, with no "grand narrative" guiding its development.

Other theorists, particularly Francis Fukuyama, believe that modernism has not collapsed, but instead has triumphed with the spread of democratic capitalism, societies based on democratic government and free enterprise.

The concept of the "risk society," as argued by Ulrich Beck, posits that the conflict over the distribution of wealth has been replaced by the conflict over various forms of social risk as the central dynamic of society today.

---

separate the rich and poor countries, as well as such divisions within societies. We need to do so while also protecting the resources on which we all depend. On the level of the political order, liberal democracy is indeed not enough. As a framework confined to the nation-state, it does not resolve the issue of how a global pluralistic order can be created.

Other common problems we face today are gender divisions and violence. Inequalities between men and women are deeply ingrained in all cultures, and the establishing of greater equality is likely to demand major changes in our social institutions. There is much debate about gender issues but no clear answer. Much the same is true of attempts to meet the threat posed by the accelerating development of weaponry and military power. The problem of how to limit—and possibly eliminate altogether—the risks of large-scale military confrontation is an urgent task facing humanity in the twenty-first century.

We cannot foresee whether the coming hundred years will be marked by peaceful social and economic development or by a multiplication of global problems perhaps beyond humanity's ability to solve. Unlike the sociologists writing two hundred years ago, we see clearly that modern industry, technology, and science are by no means wholly beneficial in their consequences. Our world is much more populous and wealthy than ever before; we see the possibility to control our destiny and shape our lives for the better, unimaginable to previous generations, yet the world hovers close to economic and ecological disaster. To say this is not in any way to encourage an attitude of resigned despair. If there is one thing sociology offers us, it is a profound consciousness of the human authorship of social institutions. Our understanding of the dark side of modern social change need not prevent us from sustaining a realistic and hopeful outlook toward the future.

1. *Social change* may be defined as the transformation, over time, of the institutions and culture of a society. The modern period, although occupying only a small fraction of human history, has shown rapid and major changes, and the pace of change is accelerating.

2. The development of social organization and institutions, from gathering and hunting to agrarian to modern industrial societies, is far too diverse to be accounted for by any single-factor theory of social change. At least three broad categories of influences can be identified: The *physical environment* includes such factors as climate or the availability of communication routes (rivers, mountain passes); these are important to consider, especially as they affect early economic development, but should not be overemphasized. *Political organization* (especially military power) affects all societies, traditional and modern, with the possible exception of gathering and hunting societies. *Cultural factors* include religion (which can act as a brake on change), communication systems (such as the invention of writing), and individual leadership.

3. The most important *economic* influence on modern social change is industrial capitalism, which depends on and promotes constant innovation and revision of productive technology. Science and technology also affect (and are affected by) *political* factors, the most important of which is the emergence of the modern state with its relatively efficient forms of government. *Cultural* influences include another effect of science and technology, the critical and innovative character of modern thinking, which constantly challenges tradition and cultural habits. These factors all interact with one another, as seen in the industrialization of military struggles, or the economic basis of many political revolutions.

4. *Crowd activities* occur not only in revolutions, but in many other circumstances of less dramatic social change—as in urban *riots*. The actions of rioting mobs might seem wholly destructive and haphazard, but often serve definite purposes for those involved.

5. Many types of *social movement* are found in modern societies. Social movements are a collective attempt to further common interests through collaborative action outside the sphere of established institutions. Sociology not only studies such movements but also responds to the issues they raise.

6. Theories of social movements and revolutions overlap. Marx argued that class struggles deriving from the *contradictions*, or unresolvable tensions within society, lead to revolutionary changes. James Davies argues that social movements occur from *relative deprivation,* a discrepancy between the lives people actually lead and what people believe to be possible. Charles Tilly analyzes revolutionary change from a broader context of *collective action*, which refers to action taken to contest or overthrow an existing social order. Collective action culminating in social movements progresses from organization, mobilization, the perception of common interests, and finally the opportunity to act. For Tilly, social movements occur in circumstances of *multiple sovereignty*, a situation in which the government lacks full control.

Neil Smelser's theory treats social movements as responses to situations, which undergo a series of stages. Alain Touraine argues that social movements rest on *historicity,* which is the idea that people know that social activism can shape history and affect society. Social movements occur in *fields of action*, which refers to the connection between a movement and the forces acting against it.

Social movements provide not only a subject matter for sociologists to study but act to challenge the establishing frameworks of thought of sociology (for instance, the impact of the women's movement on the study of gender).

7. Social theorists have speculated on where social change will lead us. One influential line of thinking about where modern society is headed holds that the industrial era is being superseded by a *postindustrial society* based on the importance of information and service, rather than on manufacturing and industrial-

ization. Some authors go further and speak not only of the end of industrialism, but of the end of modernity itself. Our beliefs in progress, in the benefits of science, and in our ability to control the modern world are diminishing, say the postmodernists; and there is such a diversity and plurality of individual concerns and points of view that it is no longer possible to have any overarching conception of history or of where we are headed.

Postmodernists seem to lay too much stress on fragmentation and diversity. Francis Fukuyama also sees the "end of history," but locates it in the triumph of Western democracy, which he regards as the "end point of mankind's ideological evolution."

APPENDIX: HOW TO USE LIBRARIES

Libraries, especially large ones, can seem like daunting places. People can feel somewhat lost when confronted with the apparently innumerable sources of information that libraries contain. They may therefore end up using only a small proportion of what a library has to offer, perhaps with damaging effects on their academic work. It is a good idea to get to know—at the beginning of your course—the range of resources libraries have. If you do this early on, the "lost" feeling won't last long!

All the information available in the library is stored and cataloged systematically, in order to make finding things easy. Most smaller libraries operate with *open stacks*—the books can be visibly inspected on the shelves, and the user can select whichever volume she wants directly. Most larger collections keep only a proportion of their books on open shelves and store others in vaults, where less space is required to keep them. In these libraries, anyone who wishes to use or borrow a book must ask for it, or fill in a request slip.

If you are looking for a particular book, you'll be able to look it up under author or title in the index or catalog. This may be a computerized list, drawers of index cards, or a microfiche—or all three. Once you find its catalog number, you can then either order it from library staff by quoting that number, or find it on the open shelves, which are always arranged by catalog number. All—or most—sociology books will be in one area. Any librarian will be able to explain how the cataloging system works. To find books on a particular topic when you don't know any names or titles, you need to use a subject index (again, this may be computerized or on cards). A subject index lists books by topics—such as "class," "bureaucracy," etc.

Many of the larger libraries today have computer-trace systems, which are very easy to operate and are normally available to all library users. You simply key in the area about which you require bibliographical information, and the computer will display a list of relevant titles.

Most libraries provide similar services, but different libraries have their own ways of doing things, and there are variations in cataloging systems. Never be afraid to ask the librarian or assistants for their help if there is any procedure that puzzles you. You should not be worried about bothering them; librarians are trained professionals, committed to making sure that the library resources are available to everyone who wants to make use of them. They are usually highly knowledgeable about the range of material the library contains, and only too willing to provide guidance.

Sources of General Information in Sociology

If you are beginning the study of a particular topic in sociology and want to find some general information about it, there are a number of useful sources. Several dictionaries of sociology are available. These provide brief discussions of major concepts and accounts of the ideas of some of the leading contributors to the discipline. The major encyclopedias—like the *World Book Encyclopedia*—contain many entries relevant to sociological topics, such as "city," "crime," "family," "middle class," "prejudice," "research," and "statistics." The entries in dictionaries and encyclopedias virtually always provide short lists of books or articles as a guide to further reading.

There are other ways in which books and articles relevant to a given issue can be traced. The *International Bibliography of the Social Sciences,* published annually by UNESCO, offers a comprehensive listing of works that have appeared in different social science subjects over the course of any year. Thus, for example, you can look up the heading "Sociology of education" and find a range of up-to-date materials in that field. An equally useful source is *Sociological Abstracts,* which not only lists books and articles in the different areas of sociology, but gives a short description of the contents of each.

Sociological Journals

It is worth familiarizing yourself with the main journals in sociology. Journals usually appear three or four times a year. The information and debates they contain are often more up-to-date than those in books, which take longer to write and publish. Journal articles are sometimes quite technical, and a person new to sociology may not find them readily understandable. But all the leading journals regularly publish articles of general interest, accessible to those with only limited knowledge of the subject.

The most important journals include the *American Sociological Review* and the *American Journal of Sociology.*

Writing Research Papers

On some occasions, you may wish to use the library to pursue a particular research project, perhaps in the course of writing a thesis. Such a task might involve carrying out a more in-depth search of relevant sources than is required for normal study.

If you need statistical information concerning the United States, a good place to start is *Statistical Abstract of the United States,* which is available from the Government Printing Office in Washington, D.C. This volume contains selected statistical information on many areas of American social life.

Newspaper articles provide a mine of valuable information for the sociological researcher. A few newspapers are what are sometimes called "journals of record." That is to say, they not only carry news stories, but also record sections from congressional speeches, government reports, and other official sources. The *New York Times, Washington Post,* and *Los Angeles Times* are the most important examples, and each produces an index of topics and names that have appeared in its pages.

Once you start using a library regularly, you are likely to find that it is more common to feel overwhelmed by the number of works available in a particular area than to experience difficulty in tracing relevant literature. One way of dealing with this problem is to base your selection of books or articles on reading lists provided by professors. Where such lists are not available, the best procedure to follow is to define the information you require as precisely as possible. This will allow you to narrow the range of choice to feasible limits. If your library is an open-stack one, it is worth looking through a number of potentially useful books or articles before selecting those you decide to work with. In making the decision, keep in mind *when* the book was written. New developments are constantly taking place in sociology and in the other social sciences, and obviously older books won't cover these.

GLOSSARY

Words in bold type within entries refer to terms found elsewhere in the glossary.

ABSOLUTE POVERTY: The minimal requirements necessary to sustain a healthy existence.

ACHIEVED STATUS: Social status based on an individual's effort.

AFFECTIVE INDIVIDUALISM: The belief in romantic attachment as a basis for contracting **marriage** ties.

AGE-GRADES: The system found in small traditional cultures according to which people belonging to a similar age-group are categorized together and hold similar rights and obligations.

AGEISM: **Discrimination** or **prejudice** against a person on the grounds of age.

AGENCIES OF SOCIALIZATION: Groups or social contexts within which processes of **socialization** take place.

AGRARIAN SOCIETIES: Societies whose means of subsistence is based on agricultural production (crop growing).

ALIENATION: The sense that our own abilities as human beings are taken over by other entities. The term was originally used by Marx to refer to the projection of human powers onto gods. Subsequently he used the term to refer to the loss of control on the part of workers over the nature and products of their labor.

ALTERATIVE MOVEMENT: A movement concerned with altering individuals' behavior or consciousness.

ANIMISM: A belief that events in the world are mobilized by the activities of spirits.

ANOMIE: A concept first brought into wide usage in sociology by Durkheim, referring to a situation in which social **norms** lose their hold over individual behavior.

APARTHEID: The system of racial segregation established in South Africa.

ARMS TRADE: The selling of armaments for profit, whether carried on by **governments** or by private contractors.

ASCRIBED STATUS: Social status based on biological factors such as race, sex, or age.

ASSIMILATION: The acceptance of a minority group by a majority population, in which the new group takes on the **values** and **norms** of the dominant **culture**.

AUTHORITARIAN PERSONALITY: A set of specific personality characteristics, including a rigid and intolerant outlook and an inability to accept ambiguity.

AUTHORITY: A **government's** legitimate use of **power**.

AUTOMATION: Production processes monitored and controlled by machines with only minimal supervision from people.

BACK REGION: An area apart from **front region** performances, as specified by Erving Goffman, in which individuals are able to relax and behave informally.

BRACKETS: See **markers**.

BUREAUCRACY: A type of **organization** marked by a clear hierarchy of authority and the existence of written rules of procedure and staffed by full-time, salaried **officials**.

CAPITALISM: An economic system based on the private ownership of wealth, which is invested and reinvested in order to produce profit.

CAPITALISTS: People who own companies, land, or stocks (shares) and use these to generate economic returns.

CASTE: A form of stratification in which a person's social position is fixed at birth and cannot be changed. There is virtually no intermarriage between the members of different castes.

CAUSAL RELATIONSHIP: A relationship in which one state of affairs (the effect) is brought about by another (the cause).

CAUSATION: The causal influence of one factor, or **variable**, upon another. A cause and effect relationship exists whenever a particular event or state of affairs (the effect) is produced by the existence of another (the cause). Causal factors in sociology include the reasons individuals give for what they do, as well as external influences on their behavior.

CHARISMA: The inspirational quality capable of capturing the imagination and devotion of a mass of followers.

CHURCH: A large body of people belonging to an established religious organization. The term is also used to refer to the place in which religious ceremonials are carried on.

CITIZEN: A member of a political community, having both rights and duties associated with that membership.

CITIZENSHIP: A people's common rights and duties and consciousness of their relationship to the **state**.

CIVIL INATTENTION: The process whereby individuals who are in the same physical setting demonstrate to one another that they are aware of each other's presence.

CIVIL RIGHTS: Legal rights held by all **citizens** in a given national community.

CLAN (business model): Work groups having close personal connections with one another, which some argue is more efficient and productive than other forms of business organization.

CLASS: Although it is one of the most frequently used concepts in sociology, there is no clear agreement about how the notion should be defined. Most sociologists use the term to refer to socioeconomic differences between groups of individuals that create differences in their material prosperity and power.

CLASSICAL NATIONALISM: Nationalism associated with the rise of the **nation-state** in Europe from the eighteenth century on.

CLOCK TIME: Time as measured by the clock, in terms of hours, minutes, and seconds. Before the invention of clocks, time-reckoning was based on events in the natural world, such as the rising and setting of the sun.

COGNITION: Human thought processes involving perception, reasoning, and remembering.

COHABITATION: Two people living together in a sexual relationship of some permanence, without being married to one another.

COLLECTIVE ACTION: Action undertaken in a relatively spontaneous way by a large number of people assembled together. One of the most important forms of collective action is crowd behavior. In crowds, individuals can seek to achieve objectives that in ordinary circumstances are denied to them.

COLLECTIVE BEHAVIOR: Actions, which are often disorganized, taken by a large number of people gathered together, usually in defiance of society's norms.

COLLECTIVE CONSUMPTION: A concept used by Manuel Castells to refer to processes of urban consumption—such as the buying and selling of property.

COLONIALISM: The process whereby Western nations established their rule in parts of the world away from their home territories.

COMMUNICATION: The transmission of information from one individual or group to another. Communication is the necessary basis of all social interaction. In face-to-face encounters, communication is carried on by the use of language, but also by bodily cues that individuals interpret. With the development of writing and electronic media such as radio, television, and computers, communication becomes in some part detached from immediate face-to-face social relationships.

COMMUNISM: A set of political ideas associated with Marx, as developed particularly by Lenin and institutionalized in the Soviet Union, Eastern Europe, and some Third World countries.

COMPARABLE WORTH: Policies that attempt to remedy the gender pay gap by adjusting pay so that those in female-dominated jobs are not paid less for equivalent work.

COMPARATIVE QUESTIONS: Questions concerned with drawing comparisons between different human societies for the purposes of sociological theory or research.

COMPARATIVE RESEARCH: Research that compares one set of findings on one society with the same type of findings on other societies.

COMPULSION OF PROXIMITY: People's need to interact with others in their presence.

CONCRETE OPERATIONAL STAGE: A stage of cognitive development, as formulated by Piaget, in which the child's thinking is based primarily on physi-

cal perception of the world. In this phase, the child is not yet capable of dealing with abstract concepts or hypothetical situations.

CONSTITUTIONAL MONARCH: A king or queen who is largely a figurehead. Real power rests in the hands of other political leaders.

CONTRADICTION: A term used by Marx to refer to mutually antagonistic tendencies in a society.

CONTRADICTORY CLASS LOCATIONS: Positions in the class structure, particularly routine white-collar and lower managerial jobs, that share characteristics of the class positions both above and below them.

CONTROL: A statistical or experimental means of holding some variables constant in order to examine the causal influence of others.

CONURBATION: An agglomeration of towns or cities into an unbroken urban environment.

CONVERSATION: Verbal communication between two or more people.

CORPORATIONS: Business firms or companies.

CORRELATION: The regular relationship between two variables, often expressed in statistical terms. Correlations may be positive or negative. A positive correlation between two variables exists when a high rank on one variable is associated with a high rank on the other. A negative correlation exists when a high rank on one variable is associated with a low rank on the other.

CORRELATION COEFFICIENT: A measure of the degree of correlation between variables.

COSMOPOLITAN: Describing people or societies that share many social qualities as a result of constant exposure to new ideas and values.

CREATED ENVIRONMENT: Constructions established by human beings to serve their needs, derived from the use of humanly created technology—including, for example, roads, railways, factories, offices, private homes, and other buildings.

CRIME: Any action that contravenes the laws established by a political authority. Although we may think of criminals as a distinct subsection of the population, there are few people who have not broken the law in one way or another during their lives. While laws are formulated by state authorities, it is not unknown for those authorities to engage in criminal behavior in certain situations.

CRIMINAL NETWORK: A network of social relations between individuals engaging in criminal activities.

CROWD ACTIVITY: Actions carried out by people when assembled together as a crowd.

CRUDE BIRTH RATE: A statistical measure representing the number of births within a given population per year, normally calculated in terms of the number of births per thousand members. Although the crude birth rate is a useful index, it is only a general measure, because it does not specify numbers of births in relation to age distribution.

CRUDE DEATH RATE: A statistical measure representing the number of deaths that occur annually in a given population per year, normally calculated as the ratio of deaths per thousand members. Crude death rates give a general indication of the mortality levels of a community or society, but are limited in their usefulness because they do not take into account the age distribution.

CULT: A fragmentary religious grouping to which individuals are loosely affiliated, but which lacks any permanent structure.

CULTURAL CAPITAL: The advantages that well-to-do parents usually provide their children.

CULTURAL RELATIVISM: The practice of judging a society by its own standards.

CULTURAL UNIVERSALS: **Values** or modes of behavior shared by all human **cultures**.

CULTURE: The **values, norms,** and material goods characteristic of a given group. Like the concept of **society**, the notion of culture is widely used in sociology as well as in the other social sciences (particularly anthropology). Culture is one of the most distinctive properties of human social association.

CYBERSPACE: Electronic networks of interaction between individuals at different computer terminals.

DEGREE OF DISPERSAL: The range or distribution of a set of figures.

DEMOCRACY: A political system that allows the citizens to participate in political decision making or to elect representatives to government bodies.

DEMOCRATIC ELITISM: A theory of the limits of democracy, which holds that in large-scale societies democratic participation is necessarily limited to the regular election of political leaders.

DEMOGRAPHIC TRANSITION: An interpretation of population change, which holds that a stable ratio of births to deaths is achieved once a certain level of economic prosperity has been reached. According to this notion, in preindustrial societies there is a rough balance between births and deaths, because population increase is kept in check by a lack of available food, and by disease or war. In modern societies, by contrast, population equilibrium is achieved because families are moved by economic incentives to limit number of children.

DEMOGRAPHY: The study of populations.

DENOMINATION: A religious **sect** that has lost its revivalist dynamism and has become an institutionalized body, commanding the adherence of significant numbers of people.

DEPENDENT VARIABLE: A **variable**, or factor, causally influenced by another (the **independent variable**).

DEVELOPMENTAL QUESTIONS: Questions that sociologists pose when looking at the origins and path of development of **social institutions** from the past to the present.

DEVIANCE: Modes of action that do not conform to the **norms** or **values** held by most members of a group or society. What is regarded as deviant is as variable as the norms and values that distinguish different cultures and subcultures from one another. Forms of behavior that are highly esteemed by one group are regarded negatively by others.

DEVIANT SUBCULTURE: A subculture whose members hold values that differ substantially from those of the majority.

DIFFERENTIAL ASSOCIATION: An interpretation of the development of criminal behavior proposed by Edwin H. Sutherland, according to whom criminal behavior is learned through association with others who regularly engage in crime.

DIRECT DEMOCRACY: A form of **participatory democracy** that allows citizens to vote directly on laws and policies.

DISCRIMINATION: Behavior that denies to the members of a particular group resources or rewards that can be obtained by others. Discrimination must be distinguished from **prejudice**: individuals who are prejudiced against others may not engage in discriminatory practices against them; conversely, people may act in a discriminatory fashion toward a group even though they are not prejudiced against that group.

DISPLACEMENT: The transferring of ideas or emotions from their true source to another object.

DIVISION OF LABOR: The specialization of work tasks, by means of which different occupations are combined within a production system. All societies have at least some rudimentary form of division of labor, especially between the tasks allocated to men and those performed by women. With the development of industrialism, the division of labor became vastly more complex than in any prior type of production system. In the modern world, the division of labor is international in scope.

DOMESTIC VIOLENCE: Violent behavior directed by one member of a household against another. Most serious domestic violence is carried out by males against females.

DOMINANT GROUP: The opposite of **minority group**; the dominant group possesses more wealth, power, and prestige in a society.

DOUBLING TIME: The time it takes for a particular level of population to double.

DOWNWARD MOBILITY: Social mobility in which individuals' wealth, income, or status is lower than what they or their parents once had.

ECOLOGICAL APPROACH: A perspective on urban analysis emphasizing the "natural" distribution of city neighborhoods into areas having contrasting characteristics.

ECONOMIC INTERDEPENDENCE: The fact that in the **division of labor**, individuals depend on others to produce many or most of the goods they need to sustain their lives.

ECONOMY: The system of production and exchange that provides for the material needs of individuals living in a given society. Economic institutions are of key importance in all social orders. What goes on in the economy usually influences other areas in social life. Modern economies differ substantially from traditional ones, because the majority of the population is no longer engaged in agricultural production.

EGOCENTRIC: According to Piaget, the characteristic quality of a child during the early years of her life. Egocentric thinking involves understanding objects and events in the environment solely in terms of the child's own position.

EMPIRICAL INVESTIGATION: Factual inquiry carried out in any area of sociological study.

ENCOUNTER: A meeting between two or more people in a situation of face-to-face interaction. Our daily lives can be seen as a series of different encounters strung out across the course of the day. In modern societies, many of these encounters are with strangers rather than people we know.

ENTREPRENEUR: The owner/founder of a business firm.

ENVIRONMENTAL ECOLOGY: A concern with preserving the integrity of the physical environment in the face of the impact of modern industry and technology.

ESTATE: A form of stratification in which inequalities between groups of individuals are established by law.

ETHICAL RELIGIONS: Religions that depend on the ethical appeal of a great teacher (like Buddha or Confucius), rather than on a belief in supernatural beings.

ETHNIC-GROUP CLOSURE: The maintenance of boundaries against others, the prohibition against intermarriage between groups, and restrictions on social contact with other groups.

ETHNICITY: Culture **values** and **norms** that distinguish the members of a given group from others. An ethnic group is one whose members share a distinct awareness of a common cultural identity, separating them from other groups. In virtually all societies, ethnic differences are associated with variations in power and material wealth. Where ethnic differences are also racial, such divisions are sometimes especially pronounced.

ETHNOCENTRIC TRANSNATIONALS: Transnational companies largely run directly from the headquarters of the parent company.

ETHNOCENTRISM: The tendency to look at other **cultures** through the eyes of one's own culture, and thereby misrepresent them.

ETHNOGRAPHY: The study of people at firsthand using **participant observation** or interviewing.

ETHNOMETHODOLOGY: The study of how people make sense of what others say and do in the course of day-to-day social interaction. Ethnomethodology is concerned with the "ethno-methods" by means of which people sustain meaningful interchanges with one another.

EXCHANGE MOBILITY: The exchange of positions on the socioeconomic scale such that talented people move up the economic hierarchy while the less talented move down.

EXPERIMENT: A research method in which **variables** can be analyzed in a controlled and systematic way, either in an artificial situation constructed by the researcher or in naturally occurring settings.

EXPONENTIAL GROWTH: A geometric, rather than linear, rate of progression, producing a fast rise in the numbers of a population experiencing such growth.

EXTENDED FAMILY: A family group consisting of more than two generations of relatives living either within the same household or very close to one another.

FACTUAL QUESTIONS: Questions that raise issues concerning matters of fact (rather than theoretical or moral issues).

FAMILY: A group of individuals related to one another by blood ties, **marriage,** or adoption, who form an economic unit, the adult members of which are responsible for the upbringing of children. All known societies involve some form of family system, although the nature of family relationships varies widely. While in modern societies the main family form is the **nuclear family, extended family** relationships are also found.

FAMILY CAPITALISM: Capitalistic enterprise owned and administered by entrepreneurial families.

FAMILY OF ORIENTATION: The family into which an individual is born.

FAMILY OF PROCREATION: The family an individual initiates through marriage or by having children.

FECUNDITY: A measure of the number of children that it is biologically possible for a woman to produce.

FEMINISM: Advocacy of the rights of women to be equal with men in all spheres of life. Feminism dates from the late eighteenth century in Europe, and feminist movements exist in most countries today.

FERTILITY: The average number of live-born children produced by women of childbearing age in a particular society.

FIELD OF ACTION: The arena within which **social movements** interact with established **organizations,** the ideas and outlook of the members of both thereby often becoming modified.

FIRST WORLD: The group of **nation-states** that possesses mature industrialized economies, based on capitalistic production.

FLEXIBLE PRODUCTION: Process in which computers design customized products for a mass market.

FOCUSED CROWD: A crowd of people acting in pursuit of common objectives.

FOCUSED INTERACTION: Interaction between individuals engaged in a common activity or in direct conversation with one another.

FORDISM: The system of production pioneered by Henry Ford, in which the assembly line was introduced.

FORMAL OPERATIONAL STAGE: According to Piaget's theory, a stage of cognitive development at which the growing child becomes capable of handling abstract concepts and hypothetical situations.

FORMAL RELATIONS: Relations that exist in groups and organizations, laid down by the **norms**, or rules, of the official system of authority.

FRONT REGION: A setting of social activity in which people seek to put on a definite "performance" for others.

FUNCTIONALISM: A theoretical perspective based on the notion that social events can best be explained in terms of the functions they perform—that is, the contributions they make to the continuity of a society.

FUNDAMENTALISM: A belief in returning to the literal meanings of scriptural texts.

GANG: An informal group of individuals meeting regularly to engage in common activities, which may be outside the framework of the law.

GENDER: Social expectations about behavior regarded as appropriate for the members of each sex. Gender refers not to the physical attributes distinguishing men and women but to socially formed traits of **masculinity** and **femininity**. The study of gender relations has become one of the most important areas of sociology in recent years.

GENDER INEQUALITY: The inequality between men and women in terms of **wealth, income,** and **status**.

GENDER ROLES: **Social roles** assigned to each sex and labeled as masculine or feminine.

GENDER SOCIALIZATION: The learning of gender roles through social factors such as schooling, the media, and family.

GENDER TYPING: Women holding occupations of lower **status** and pay, such as secretarial and retail positions, and men holding jobs of higher status and pay, such as managerial and professional positions.

GENERALIZED OTHER: A concept in the theory of George Herbert Mead, according to which the individual takes over the general **values** of a given group or society during the **socialization** process.

GENOCIDE: The systematic, planned destruction of a racial, political, or cultural group.

GENTRIFICATION: A process of urban renewal in which older, deteriorated housing is refurbished by affluent people moving into the area.

GEOCENTRIC TRANSNATIONALS: Transnational companies whose administrative structure is global, rather than organized from any particular country.

GLASS CEILING: A promotion barrier that prevents a woman's upward mobility within an organization.

GLASS ESCALATOR: The process by which men in traditionally female professions benefit from an unfair rapid rise within an organization.

GLOBAL CITY: A city, such as London, New York, or Tokyo, which has become an organizing center of the new global economy.

GLOBALIZATION: The development of social and economic relationships stretching worldwide. In current times, we are all influenced by organizations and social networks located thousands of miles away. A key part of the study of globalization is the emergency of a **world system**—for some purposes, we need to regard the world as forming a single social order.

GLOBAL VILLAGE: A notion associated with Marshall McLuhan, who believed that the world has become like a small community as a result of the spread of electronic communication. For instance, people in many different parts of the world follow the same news events through television programming.

GOVERNMENT: The enacting of policies and decisions on the part of **officials** within a political apparatus. We can speak of government as a process, or *the* government as the officialdom responsible for making binding political decisions. While in the past virtually all governments were headed by monarchs or emperors, in most modern societies governments are run by officials who do not inherit their positions of power but are elected or appointed on the basis of qualifications.

GROUP CLOSURE: The maintenance of boundaries against others, the prohibition of intermarriage between groups, and restrictions on social contact with other groups.

GROUP PRODUCTION: Production organized by means of small groups rather than individuals.

HIDDEN CURRICULUM: Traits of behavior or attitudes that are learned at school but not included within the formal curriculum—for example, gender differences.

HIGH-TRUST SYSTEMS: Organizations or work settings in which individuals are permitted a great deal of autonomy and control over the work task.

HIGHER EDUCATION: Education in colleges or universities.

HISTORICITY: The use of an understanding of history as a basis for trying to change history—that is, producing informed processes of **social change**.

HOMELESS: People who have no place to sleep and either stay in free shelters or sleep in public places not meant for habitation.

HOUSEWORK (DOMESTIC LABOR): Unpaid work carried on, usually by women, in the home; domestic chores such as cooking, cleaning, and shopping.

HUNTING AND GATHERING SOCIETIES: Societies whose mode of subsistence is gained from hunting animals, fishing, and gathering edible plants.

HYPERREALITY: An idea associated with Jean Baudrillard, who argued that, as a result of the spread of electronic communication, there is no longer a separate "reality" to which TV programs and other cultural products refer. Instead, what we take to be "reality" is structured by such communication itself. For instance, the items reported on the news are not just about a separate series of events, but actually define and construct what those events are.

HYPOTHESIS: An idea or a guess about a given state of affairs, put forward as a basis for empirical testing.

IDEAL TYPE: A "pure type," constructed by emphasizing certain traits of a social item that do not necessarily exist in reality. An example is Max Weber's ideal type of bureaucratic **organization**.

IDEOLOGY: Shared ideas or beliefs that serve to justify the interests of dominant groups. Ideologies are found in all societies in which there are systematic and ingrained inequalities between groups. The concept of ideology connects closely with that of **power**, since ideological systems serve to legitimize the power that groups hold.

IMPRESSION MANAGEMENT: Preparing for the presentation of one's **social role**.

INCOME: Payment, usually derived from wages, salaries, or investments.

INDEPENDENT VARIABLE: A **variable**, or factor, that causally affects another (the **dependent variable**).

INDIVIDUAL RACISM: Type of racism that occurs when an individual thinks or acts in a way that is motivated by the belief that the people he acts toward are inferior based on their race.

INDUSTRIALIZATION: The process of the machine production of goods. See also **industrialized societies**.

INDUSTRIALIZATION OF WAR: The application of modes of industrial production to weaponry, coupled with the organization of fighting forces as military machines. The industrialization of war is as fundamental an aspect of the development of modern societies as is industry evolved for peaceful purposes. It is closely associated with the emergence of **total war** in the twentieth century—warfare involving thousands or millions of soldiers, plus the overall mobilizing of the **economy** for war-related needs.

INDUSTRIALIZED SOCIETIES: Strongly developed **nation-states** in which the majority of the population work in factories or offices rather than in agriculture, and most people live in urban areas.

INFANT MORTALITY RATE: The number of infants who die during the first year of life, per thousand live births.

INFORMAL ECONOMY: Economic transactions carried on outside the sphere of orthodox paid employment.

INFORMAL RELATIONS: Relations that exist in groups and organizations developed on the basis of personal connections; ways of doing things that depart from formally recognized modes of procedure.

INFORMATION POVERTY: The "information poor" are those people who have little or no access to information technology, such as computers.

INFORMATION SOCIETY: A society no longer based primarily on the production of material goods but on the production of knowledge. The notion of the information society is closely bound up with the rise of information technology.

INFORMATION SUPERHIGHWAY: A network of electronic communication linking people's homes, workplaces, and schools.

INFORMATION TECHNOLOGY: Forms of technology based on information processing and requiring microelectronic circuitry.

INNER CITY: The areas composing the central neighborhoods of a city, as distinct from the **suburbs**. In many modern urban settings in the First World, inner-city areas are subject to dilapidation and decay, the more affluent residents having moved to outlying areas.

INSTINCT: A fixed pattern of behavior that has genetic origins and that appears in all normal animals within a given species.

INSTITUTIONAL CAPITALISM: Capitalistic enterprise organized on the basis of institutional shareholding.

INSTITUTIONAL RACISM: Patterns of discrimination based on ethnicity that have become structured into existing social institutions.

INTELLIGENCE: Level of intellectual ability, particularly as measured by **IQ** (intelligence quotient) tests.

INTEREST GROUP: A group organized to pursue specific interests in the political arena, operating primarily by lobbying the members of legislative bodies.

INTERGENERATIONAL MOBILITY: Movement up or down a social stratification hierarchy from one generation to another.

INTERNATIONAL DIVISION OF LABOR: The interdependence of countries or regions that trade in global markets.

INTRAGENERATIONAL MOBILITY: Movement up or down a social stratification hierarchy within the course of a personal career.

IQ (INTELLIGENCE QUOTIENT): A score attained on tests of symbolic or reasoning abilities.

IRON LAW OF OLIGARCHY: A term coined by Weber's student Robert Michels meaning that large **organizations** tend toward centralization of power, making democracy difficult.

JOB: See **occupation**.

KIBBUTZIM: Communities established in Israel in which production is carried on cooperatively, and inequalities of wealth and income are kept to a minimum.

KINSHIP: A relation that links individuals through blood ties, **marriage**, or adoption. Kinship relations are by definition part of marriage and the **family**, but extend much more broadly. While in most modern societies few social obligations are involved in kinship relations extending beyond the immediate family, in other cultures kinship is of vital importance to social life.

KNOWLEDGE SOCIETY: Another common term for **information society**—a society based on the production and consumption of knowledge and information.

LABELING THEORY: An approach to the study of **deviance** that suggests that people become "deviant" because certain labels are attached to their behavior by political authorities and others.

LANGUAGE: The primary vehicle of meaning and communication in a society, language is a system of symbols that represent objects and abstract thoughts.

LATENT FUNCTIONS: Functional consequences that are not intended or recognized by the members of a social system in which they occur.

LAW: A rule of behavior established by a political authority and backed by state power.

LEGITIMACY: The belief that a particular political order is just and valid.

LEGITIMATION CRISIS: The failure of a political order to generate a sufficient level of commitment and involvement on the part of its **citizens** to be able properly to govern.

LIBERAL DEMOCRACY: A system of **democracy** based on parliamentary institutions, coupled to the free-market system in the area of economic production.

LIBERAL FEMINISM: Form of feminist theory that believes that gender inequality is produced by unequal access to civil rights and certain social resources, such as education and employment, based on sex. Liberal feminists tend to seek solutions through changes in legislation that ensure that the rights of individuals are protected.

LIFE CHANCES: A term introduced by Max Weber to signify a person's opportunities for achieving economic prosperity.

LIFE COURSE: The various transitions people experience during their lives.

LIFE EXPECTANCY: The number of years that people at any given age can on average expect to live.

LIFE HISTORIES: Studies of the overall lives of individuals, often based on both self-reporting and documents such as letters.

LIFE SPAN: The maximum length of life that is biologically possible for a member of a given species.

LIMITED WAR: Warfare involving relatively small numbers of the population, and fought principally by soldiers.

LOCAL KNOWLEDGE: Knowledge of a local community, possessed by individuals who spend long periods of their lives in them.

LOCAL NATIONALISM: The belief that communities that share a cultural identity should have political autonomy, even within smaller units of a nation-state.

LONG-RANGE MOBILITY: Social mobility that occurs when an individual moves from the bottom to the top of the class structure.

LOW-TRUST SYSTEMS: An **organizational** or work setting in which people are allowed little responsibility for, or control over, the work task.

MACROSEGREGATION: Territorial segregation between numerous members of different racial groups.

MACROSOCIOLOGY: The study of large-scale groups, **organizations,** or social systems.

MAGIC: Rites that attempt to influence spirits or supernatural beings in order to achieve human aims. In most societies, magic exists in a relation of some tension with **religion**. In contrast to religion, magic tends to be more of an individual activity, practiced by a sorcerer, or **shaman**.

MALTHUSIANISM: A doctrine about population dynamics developed by Thomas Malthus, according to which population increase comes up against "natural limits," represented by famine and war.

MANAGERIAL CAPITALISM: Capitalistic enterprises administered by managerial executives rather than by owners.

MANIFEST FUNCTIONS: The functions of a type of social activity that are known to and intended by the individuals involved in the activity.

MARKERS: What distinguish each episode of **focused interaction** from one other and from **unfocused interaction** going on in the background; Goffman called them brackets.

MARRIAGE: A socially approved sexual relationship between two individuals. Marriage almost always involves two persons of opposite sexes, but in some cultures, types of homosexual marriage are tolerated. Marriage normally forms the basis of a **family of procreation**—that is, it is expected that the married couple will produce and bring up children. Some societies permit **polygamous** marriage, in which an individual may have several spouses at the same time.

MARXISM: A body of thought deriving its main elements from Marx's ideas.

MARXIST FEMINISM: Form of feminist theory that believes that gender inequality is rooted in social class inequality. Marxist feminists believe that the only solution to gender inequality is to address the class structure in a society.

MASS MEDIA: Forms of communication, such as newspapers, magazines, radio, and television, designed to reach mass audiences.

MASTER STATUS: The status(es) that generally determine(s) a person's overall position in society.

MATERIAL GOODS: The physical objects that a society creates, which influence the ways in which people live.

MATERIALIST CONCEPTION OF HISTORY: The view developed by Marx, according to which material, or economic, factors have a prime role in determining historical change.

MATRILOCAL FAMILY: A family system in which the husband is expected to live near the wife's parents.

MEAN: A statistical measure of central tendency, or average, based on dividing a total by the number of individual cases.

MEANS OF PRODUCTION: The means whereby the production of material goods is carried on in a society, including not just technology but the social relations between producers.

MEASURES OF CENTRAL TENDENCY: The ways of calculating averages.

MEDIAN: The number that falls halfway in a range of numbers—a way of calculating central tendency that is sometimes more useful than calculating a **mean**.

MEDIATED INTERACTION: Interaction between individuals who are not physically in one another's presence—for example, a telephone conversation.

MEDIATED QUASI-INTERACTION: Interaction that is one-sided and partial—for example, a person watching a television program.

MEGALOPOLIS: The "city of all cities" in ancient Greece—used in modern times to refer to very large **conurbations**.

MELTING POT: The idea that ethnic differences can be combined to create new patterns of behavior drawing on diverse cultural sources.

MEZZOSEGREGATION: **Segregation** between racial groups in terms of area of neighborhood residence.

MICROSEGREGATION: **Segregation** between racial groups enforced in the details of daily life—for example separate waiting rooms in bus or railway stations.

MICROSOCIOLOGY: The study of human behavior in contexts of face-to-face interaction.

MIDDLE CLASS: A social class composed broadly of those working in white-collar and lower managerial occupations.

MILLENARIAN MOVEMENT: Beliefs held by certain types of religious movements, according to which cataclysmic changes will occur in the near future, heralding the arrival of a new epoch.

MINORITY GROUP (OR ETHNIC MINORITY): A group of people in a minority in a given society who, because of their distinct physical or cultural characteristics, find themselves in situations of inequality within that society.

MOBILIZATION: The gearing up of groups for collective action.

MODE: The number that appears most often in a given set of data. This can sometimes be a helpful way of portraying central tendency.

MONOGAMY: A form of marriage in which each married partner is allowed only one spouse at any given time.

MONOPOLY: A situation in which a single firm dominates in a given industry.

MONOTHEISM: Belief in a single god.

MORTALITY: The number of deaths in a population.

MULTICULTURALISM: Ethnic groups exist separately and share *equally* in economic and political life.

MULTIMEDIA: The combination of what used to be different media requiring different technologies (for example, visuals and sound) on a single medium, such as a CD-ROM or website.

MULTINATIONALS: Business corporations located in two or more countries.

MULTIPLE SOVEREIGNTY: A situation in which there is no single sovereign power in a society.

NATIONALISM: A set of beliefs and **symbols** expressing identification with a national community.

NATION-STATE: A particular type of **state**, characteristic of the modern world, in which a government has sovereign power within a defined territorial area, and the population are **citizens** who know themselves to be part of a single nation. Nation-states are closely associated with the rise of **nationalism**, although nationalist loyalties do not always conform to the boundaries of specific states. Nation-states developed as part of an emerging nation-state system, originating in Europe; in current times, they span the whole globe.

NATURAL SELECTION: An idea associated with the founder of modern evolutionary biology, Charles Darwin. Animal species survive and prosper according to how well they have adapted to their environment; those that are less adaptive are replaced by better-adapted species.

NEO-IMPERIALISM: The dominance of some nations over others by means of unequal conditions of economic exchange. Neo-imperialism, unlike older empires, is not founded upon the direct imposition of political power by one society over another. The most important global context in which relations of neo-imperialism are established are between **industrialized societies** and the **Third World** countries.

NETWORK: A set of informal and formal social ties that links people to each other.

NEWLY INDUSTRIALIZING COUNTRIES (NICS): **Third World** countries that over the past two or three decades have begun to develop a strong industrial base, such as Singapore and Hong Kong.

NONVERBAL COMMUNICATION: Communication between individuals based on facial expression or bodily gesture rather than on language.

NORMS: Rules of conduct that specify appropriate behavior in a given range of social situations. A norm either prescribes a given type of behavior or forbids it. All human groups follow definite norms, which are always backed by sanctions of one kind or another—varying from informal disapproval to physical punishment.

NUCLEAR FAMILY: A family group consisting of wife, husband (or one of these), and dependent children.

OCCUPATION: Any form of paid employment in which an individual regularly works.

OLIGARCHY: Rule by a small minority within an **organization** or **society**.

OLIGOPOLY: The domination of a small number of firms in a given industry.

ORAL HISTORY: Interviews with people about events they witnessed or experienced at some point earlier in their lives.

ORGANIC SOLIDARITY: According to Émile Durkheim, the social cohesion that results from the various parts of a society functioning as an integrated whole.

ORGANIZATION: A large group of individuals with a definite set of authority relations. Many types of organizations exist in industrial societies, influencing most aspects of our lives. While not all organizations are bureaucratic, there are close links between the development of organizations and bureaucratic tendencies.

ORGANIZED CRIME: Criminal activities carried out by organizations established as businesses.

PARIAH GROUPS: Groups who suffer from negative **status** discrimination—they are looked down on by most other members of society. The Jews, for example, have been a pariah group throughout much of European history.

PARTICIPANT OBSERVATION (FIELDWORK): A method of research widely used in sociology and anthropology, in which the researcher takes part in the activities of the group or community being studied.

PARTICIPATORY DEMOCRACY: A system of democracy in which all members of a group or community participate collectively in making major decisions.

PASTORAL SOCIETIES: Societies whose subsistence derives from the rearing of domesticated animals.

PATRIARCHY: The dominance of men over women. All known societies are patriarchal, although there are variations in the degree and nature of the power men exercise, as compared with women. One of the prime objectives of women's movements in modern societies is to combat existing patriarchal institutions.

PATRILOCAL FAMILY: A family system in which the wife is expected to live near the husband's parents.

PEER GROUP: A friendship group composed of individuals of similar age and social status.

PERIPHERY: Countries that have a marginal role in the world economy, and are thus dependent on the core producing societies for their trading relationships.

PERSONAL SPACE: The physical space individuals maintain between themselves and others.

PILOT STUDY: A trial run in **survey research**.

PLURALISM: A model for ethnic relations in which all ethnic groups in the United States retain their independent and separate identities, yet share equally in the rights and powers of citizenship.

PLURALIST THEORIES OF DEMOCRACY: Theories that emphasize the role of diverse and competing interest groups in preventing too much power from being accumulated in the hands of political leaders.

POLITICAL RIGHTS: Rights of political participation, such as the right to vote in local and national elections, held by **citizens** of a national community.

POLITICS: The means by which power is employed to influence the nature and content of governmental activities. The sphere of the political includes the activities of those in **government**, but also the actions of others. There are many ways in which people outside the governmental apparatus seek to influence it.

POLYANDRY: A form of **marriage** in which a woman may simultaneously have two or more husbands.

POLYCENTRIC TRANSNATIONALS: Transnational companies whose administrative structure is global, but whose corporate practices are adapted according to local circumstances.

POLYGAMY: A form of **marriage** in which a person may have two or more spouses simultaneously.

POLYGYNY: A form of **marriage** in which a man may have more than one wife at the same time.

POLYTHEISM: Belief in two or more gods.

POPULATION: The people who are the focus of social research.

PORTFOLIO WORKER: A worker who possesses a diversity of skills or qualifications and is therefore able to move easily from job to job.

POSTCOLONIAL NATIONALISM: Nationalist movements and ideas that emerged in areas of the world once colonized by European countries in Africa, Asia, and Latin America.

POSTINDUSTRIAL SOCIETY: A notion advocated by those who believe that processes of social change are taking us beyond the industrialized order. A postindustrial society is based on the production of information rather than material goods. According to postindustrialists, we are currently experiencing a series of social changes as profound as those that initiated the industrial era some two hundred years ago.

POSTMODERNISM: The belief that society is no longer governed by history or progress. Postmodern society is highly pluralistic and diverse, with no "grand narrative" guiding its development.

POVERTY LINE: An official government measure to define those living in poverty in the United States.

POWER: The ability of individuals or the members of a group to achieve aims or further the interests they hold. Power is a pervasive element in all human relationships. Many **conflicts** in society are struggles over power, because how much power an individual or group is able to achieve governs how far they are able to put their wishes into practice.

POWER ELITE: Small networks of individuals who, according to C. Wright Mills, hold concentrated power in modern societies.

PREJUDICE: The holding of preconceived ideas about an individual or group, ideas that are resistant to change even in the face of new information. Prejudice may be either positive or negative.

PREOPERATIONAL STAGE: A stage of cognitive development, in Piaget's theory, in which the child has advanced sufficiently to master basic modes of logical thought.

PRESTIGE: The respect accorded to an individual or group in virtue of their **status**.

PRIMARY DEVIATION: According to Edwin Lemert, the actions that cause others to label one as a deviant.

PROFANE: That which belongs to the mundane, everyday world.

PROFESSIONALS: Occupants of jobs requiring high-level educational qualifications, whose behavior is subject to codes of conduct laid down by central bodies (or professional associations).

PROJECTION: Attributing to others feelings that a person actually has herself.

PROPHETS: Religious leaders who mobilize followers through their interpretation of sacred texts.

PSYCHOPATH: A specific personality type; such individuals lack the moral sense and concern for others held by most normal people.

PUBLIC DISTANCE: The physical space individuals maintain between themselves and others when engaged in a public performance, such as giving a lecture.

PUBLIC SPHERE: The means by which people communicate in modern societies, the most prominent component of which is the **mass media**—movies, television, radio, videos, records, magazines, and newspapers.

QUALITY CIRCLES (QCs): types of industrialized **group production**, where workers use their expertise to actively participate in decision making.

RACE: Differences in human physical characteristics used to categorize large numbers of individuals.

RACISM: The attribution of characteristics of superiority or inferiority to a population sharing certain physically inherited characteristics. Racism is one specific form of **prejudice**, focusing on physical variations between people. Racist attitudes became entrenched during the period of Western colonial expansion, but seem also to rest on mechanisms of prejudice and **discrimination** found in human societies today.

RADICAL FEMINISM: Form of feminist theory that believes that gender inequality is the result of male domination in all aspects of social and economic life.

RANDOM SAMPLING: **Sampling** method in which a sample is chosen so that every member of the population has the same probability of being included.

RATIONAL CHOICE ANALYSIS: More broadly, the theory that an individual's behavior is purposive. Within the field of criminology, rational-choice analysis argues that deviant behavior is a rational response to a specific social situation.

RATIONALITY: See also **rationalization**. The belief that rules and efficiency should guide modern societies.

RATIONALIZATION: A concept used by Max Weber to refer to the process by which modes of precise calculation and organization, involving abstract rules and procedures, increasingly come to dominate the social world.

REDEMPTIVE MOVEMENT: A **social movement** aiming to produce a return to a past state of affairs believed to be superior to the current one.

REFORMATIVE MOVEMENT: A **social movement** concerned to implement a practical but limited program of **social change**.

REGIONALIZATION: The division of social life into different regional settings or zones.

RELATIVE DEPRIVATION: Feelings of deprivation a person feels by comparing himself with a group.

RELATIVE POVERTY: Poverty defined according to the living standards of the majority in any given society.

RELIGION: A set of beliefs adhered to by the members of a community, incorporating **symbols** regarded with a sense of awe or wonder together with **ritual** practices. Religions do not universally involve a belief in supernatural entities. Although distinctions between religion and **magic** are difficult to draw, it is often held that magic is primarily practiced by individuals rather than being the focus of community ritual.

RELIGIOUS MOVEMENT: An association of people who join together to seek to spread a new religion or to promote a new interpretation of an existing religion.

REPRESENTATIVE SAMPLE: A sample from a larger population that is statistically typical of that population.

REPRODUCTIVE TECHNOLOGIES: Techniques of influencing the human reproductive process.

RESEARCH METHODS: The diverse methods of investigation used to gather empirical (factual) material. Different research methods exist in sociology, but the most commonly used are fieldwork (or **participant observation**) and **survey** methods. For many purposes, it is useful to combine two or more methods within a single research project.

RESOURCE ALLOCATION: Inequalities in the distribution of **wealth** and goods resulting from limited resources.

RESPONSE CRIES: Seemingly involuntary exclamations individuals make when, for example, being taken by surprise, dropping something inadvertently, or expressing pleasure.

REVOLUTION: A process of political change, involving the mobilizing of a mass **social movement**, which by the use of violence successfully overthrows an existing regime and forms a new government. A revolution is distinguished from a *coup d'état* by its mass movement and the occurrence of major change in the political system as a whole. Revolutions can also be distinguished from **rebellions**.

RIOT: An outbreak of illegal violence directed against persons, property, or both.

RITUAL: Formalized modes of behavior in which the members of a group or community regularly engage. **Religion** is one of the main contexts in which rituals are practiced, but the scope of ritual behavior extends further. Most groups have ritual practices of some kind or another.

ROLE: The expected behavior of a person occupying a particular **social position**. The idea of social role originally comes from the theater, referring to the parts that actors play in a stage production. In every society, individuals play a number of social roles.

SACRED: Something that inspires attitudes of awe or reverence among believers in a given set of religious ideas.

SAMPLING: Studying a proportion of individuals or cases from a larger population as representative of that population as a whole.

SANCTION: A mode of reward or punishment that reinforces socially expected forms of behavior.

SCAPEGOATING: Blaming an individual or group for wrongs that were not of their doing.

SCIENCE: In the sense of physical science, the systematic study of the physical world. Science involves the disciplined marshaling of empirical data, combined with **theoretical approaches** and **theories** that illuminate or explain those data. Scientific activity combines the creation of boldly new modes of thought with the careful testing of **hypotheses** and ideas. One major feature that helps distinguish science from other idea

systems (such as **religion**) is the assumption that *all* scientific ideas are open to criticism and revision.

SECONDARY DEVIATION: According to Edwin Lemert, following the act of **primary deviation**, secondary deviation occurs when an individual accepts the label of deviant and acts accordingly.

SECOND WORLD: Before the 1989 democracy movements, this included the industrialized Communist societies of Eastern Europe and the Soviet Union.

SECT: A religious movement that breaks away from orthodoxy.

SECULARIZATION: A process of decline in the influence of **religion**. Although modern societies have become increasingly secularized, tracing the extent of secularization is a complex matter. Secularization can refer to levels of involvement with religious organizations (such as rates of church attendance), the social and material influence wielded by religious organizations, and the degree to which people hold religious beliefs.

SEGREGATION: The practices of keeping racial and ethnic groups physically separate, thereby maintaining the superior position of the **dominant group**.

SELF-CONSCIOUSNESS: Awareness of one's distinct social identity, as a person separate from others. Human beings are not born with self-consciousness but acquire an awareness of self as a result of early **socialization**. The learning of language is of vital importance to the processes by which the child learns to become a self-conscious being.

SEMIOTICS: The study of the ways in which nonlinguistic phenomena can generate meaning—as in the example of a traffic light.

SEMIPERIPHERY: Countries that supply sources of labor and raw materials to the core industrial countries and the world economy but are not themselves fully industrialized.

SENSORIMOTOR STAGE: According to Piaget, a stage of human cognitive development in which the child's awareness of its environment is dominated by perception and touch.

SERVICE SOCIETY: A concept related to the one of **post-industrial** society, it refers to a social order distinguished by the growth of service occupations at the expense of industrial jobs that produce material goods.

SEX: The biological and anatomical differences distinguishing females from males.

SEXISM: Attitudes that falsely attribute or deny certain capacities to men or women, thereby justifying sexual inequalities.

SEXUAL ABUSE: The carrying out of sexual acts by adults with children below the age of consent (usually sixteen years old).

SEXUAL HARASSMENT: The making of unwanted sexual advances by one individual toward another, in which the first person persists even though it is clear that the other party is resistant.

SHAMAN: An individual believed to have special magical powers; a sorcerer or witch doctor.

SHAMING: A way of punishing criminal and deviant behavior based on rituals of public disapproval rather than incarceration. The goal of shaming is to maintain the ties of the offender to the community.

SHORT-RANGE MOBILITY: Social mobility that occurs when an individual moves from one position in the class structure to another of nearly equal status.

SIGNIFIER: Any vehicle of meaning and communication.

SITUATIONAL ETHNICITY: Ethnic identity that is chosen for the moment based on the social setting or situation.

SLAVERY: A form of social stratification in which some people are literally owned by others as their property.

SLIPS OF THE TONGUE: The mispronunciation or misuse of words and phrases.

SOCIAL CHANGE: Alteration in basic structures of a social group or society. Social change is an ever-present phenomenon in social life, but has become especially intense in the modern era. The origins of modern **sociology** can be traced to attempts to understand the dramatic changes shattering the traditional world and promoting new forms of social order.

SOCIAL CLOSURE: Practices by which groups separate themselves off from other groups.

SOCIAL CONSTRAINT: The conditioning influence of the groups and societies of which we are a part on our behavior. Social constraint was regarded by Emile Durkheim as one of the distinctive properties of social facts.

SOCIAL CONSTRUCTION OF GENDER: The learning of gender roles through socialization and interaction with others.

SOCIAL CONSTRUCTIONISM: Theory that social reality is a creation of the interaction of individuals and groups.

SOCIAL CONTROL THEORY: Theory that individuals become committed to social norms through interactions with people who obey the law.

SOCIAL DISTANCE: The level of spatial separation maintained when individuals interact with others whom they do not know well.

SOCIAL FACT: According to Émile Durkheim, the aspects of social life that shape our actions as individuals. Durkheim believed that social facts could be studied scientifically.

SOCIAL INSTITUTION: Basic modes of social activity followed by the majority of the members of a given society. Institutions involve **norms** and **values** to which large numbers of people conform, and all institutionalized modes of behavior are protected by strong sanctions. Institutions form the bedrock of a society, because they represent relatively fixed modes of behavior that endure over time.

SOCIAL INTERACTION: The process by which we act and react to those around us.

SOCIAL MOBILITY: Movement of individuals or groups between different social positions. **Vertical mobility** refers to movement up or down a hierarchy in a stratification system. **Lateral mobility** is movement of individuals or groups from one region to another. When analyzing vertical mobility, sociologists distinguish between how far a person is mobile in the course of his own career, and to what degree the position he reaches differs from that of his parents.

SOCIAL MOVEMENT: A large grouping of people who seek to accomplish, or to block, a process of **social change**. Social movements normally exist in relations of **conflict** with **organizations**, whose objectives and outlook they oppose. However, movements that successfully challenge power, once they become institutionalized, can develop into organizations.

SOCIAL POSITION: The social identity an individual has in a given group or society. Social positions may be general in nature (those associated with **gender** roles) or may be more specific (occupational positions).

SOCIAL REPRODUCTION: The processes that sustain or perpetuate characteristics of social structure over periods of time.

SOCIAL RIGHTS: Rights of social and welfare provision held by all **citizens** in a national community, including, for example, the right to claim unemployment benefits and sickness payments provided by the state.

SOCIAL ROLES: Socially defined expectations of an individual in a given **status,** or **social position**.

SOCIAL SELF: The basis of self-consciousness in human individuals, according to the theory of G. H. Mead. The social self is the identity conferred upon an individual by the reactions of others. A person achieves self-consciousness by becoming aware of this social identity.

SOCIAL STRATIFICATION: The existence of structured inequalities between groups in society, in terms of their access to material or symbolic rewards. While all societies involve some forms of stratification, only with the development of state-based systems did wide differences in wealth and power arise. The most distinctive form of stratification in modern societies is **class** divisions.

SOCIAL STRUCTURE: The underlying regularities or patterns in how people behave and in their relationships with one another.

SOCIAL TECHNOLOGY: A means by which we try to alter our bodies—for example, dieting.

SOCIAL TRANSFORMATION: Processes of change in societies or social systems.

SOCIALIZATION: The social processes through which children develop an awareness of social **norms** and **values** and achieve a distinct sense of self. Although socialization processes are particularly significant in infancy and childhood, they continue to some degree throughout life. No individuals are immune from the reactions of others around them, which influence and modify their behavior at all phases of the life cycle.

SOCIALIZATION OF NATURE: The process by which we control phenomena regarded as "natural," such as reproduction.

SOCIETY: A group of people who live in a particular territory, are subject to a common system of political authority, and are aware of having a distinct identity from other groups. Some societies, like those of hunters and gatherers, are small, numbering no more than a few dozen people. Others are large, numbering millions—modern Chinese society, for instance, has a population of more than a billion people.

SOCIOBIOLOGY: An approach that attempts to explain the behavior of both animals and human beings in terms of biological principles.

SOCIOLOGICAL IMAGINATION: The application of imaginative thought to the asking and answering of sociological questions. Someone using the sociological imagination "thinks himself away" from the familiar routines of daily life.

SOCIOLOGY: The study of human groups and societies, giving particular emphasis to analysis of the industrialized world. Sociology is one of a group of social sciences, which include anthropology, economics, political science, and human geography. The divisions between the various social sciences are not clear-cut, and all share a certain range of common interests, concepts, and methods.

SOCIOLOGY OF THE BODY: Field that focuses on how our bodies are affected by social influences. Health and illness, for instance, are determined by social and cultural influences.

SOVEREIGNTY: The undisputed political rule of a **state** over a given territorial area.

STANDARD DEVIATION: A way of calculating the spread of a group of figures.

STATE: A **political apparatus** (**government** institutions plus civil service **officials**) ruling over a given territorial order, whose authority is backed by **law** and the ability to use **force**. Not all societies are characterized by the existence of a state. Hunting and gathering cultures and smaller agrarian societies lack state institutions. The emergence of the state marked a distinctive transition in human history, because the centralization of political power involved in state formation introduced new dynamics into processes of **social change**.

STATE OVERLOAD: A **theory** that holds that modern states face major difficulties as a result of being overburdened with complex administrative decisions.

STATUS: The social honor or prestige that a particular group is accorded by other members of a **society**. Status groups normally display distinct styles of life—patterns of behavior that the members of a group follow. Status privilege may be positive or negative. **Pariah** status groups are regarded with disdain or treated as outcasts by the majority of the population.

STATUS SET: An individual's group of social statuses.

STEPFAMILY: A family in which at least one partner has children from a previous marriage, living either in the home or nearby.

STEREOTYPICAL THINKING: Thought processes involving rigid and inflexible categories.

STIGMA: Any physical or social characteristic that is labeled by society as undesirable.

STRIKE: A temporary stoppage of work by a group of employees in order to express a grievance or enforce a demand.

STRUCTURAL INEQUALITY: Social inequalities that result from patterns in the social structure.

STRUCTURAL MOBILITY: Mobility resulting from changes in the number and kinds of jobs available in a society.

STRUCTURAL STRAIN: Tensions that produce conflicting interests within societies.

STRUCTURATION: The two-way process by which we shape our social world through our individual actions and by which we are reshaped by society.

SUBCULTURAL NATIONALISM: Oppositional forms of nationalist movements that develop within mature **nation-states**.

SUBCULTURE: **Values** and **norms** distinct from those of the majority, held by a group within a wider society.

SUBURBANIZATION: The development of suburbia, areas of housing outside inner cities.

SUFFRAGISTS: Members of early women's movements who pressed for equal voting rights for women and men.

SURPLUS VALUE: The value of a worker's labor power, in Marxist theory, left over when an employer has repaid the cost of hiring the worker.

SURVEILLANCE: The supervising of the activities of some individuals or groups by others in order to ensure compliant behavior.

SURVEILLANCE SOCIETY: Term referring to how information about our lives and activities is maintained by **organizations**.

SURVEY: A method of sociological research in which questionnaires are administered to the population being studied.

SYMBOL: One item used to stand for or represent another—as in the case of a flag, which symbolizes a nation.

SYMBOLIC ETHNICITY: Ethnic identity that is retained only for symbolic importance.

SYMBOLIC INTERACTIONISM: A **theoretical approach** in sociology developed by George Herbert Mead, which emphasizes the role of symbols and language as core elements of all human interaction.

TAYLORISM: A set of ideas, also referred to as "scientific management," developed by Frederick Winslow Taylor, involving simple, coordinated operations in industry.

TECHNOLOGY: The application of knowledge of the material world to production; the creation of material instruments (such as machines) used in human interaction with nature.

THEORETICAL APPROACH: A perspective on social life derived from a particular theoretical tradition. Some of the major theoretical traditions in sociology include **functionalism, structuralism, symbolic interactionism,** and **Marxism**. Theoretical approaches supply overall perspectives within which sociologists work, and influence the areas of their research as well as the modes in which research problems are identified and tackled.

THEORETICAL QUESTIONS: Questions posed by sociologists when seeking to explain a particular range of observed events. The asking of theoretical questions is crucial to allowing us to generalize about the nature of social life.

THEORY: An attempt to identify general properties that explain regularly observed events. Theories form an essential element of all sociological works. While theories tend to be linked to broader theoretical approaches, they are also strongly influenced by the research results they help generate.

THIRD WORLD: The less-developed societies, in which industrial production is either virtually nonexistent or only developed to a limited degree. The majority of the world's population live in Third World countries.

TIMETABLE: The means by which organizations regularize activities across time and space.

TOTAL WAR: Warfare involving several nations, large numbers of their populations, the mobilization of their overall economies, and hundreds of thousands or millions of soldiers.

TOTEM: Any species of animal or plant believed to have supernatural powers.

TOTEMISM: A system of religious belief that attributes divine properties to a particular type of animal or plant.

TRACKING: Dividing students into groups according to abilities.

TRANSFORMATIVE MOVEMENT: A **social movement** aiming to produce major processes of **social change**.

TRANSNATIONAL COMPANIES: Business corporations located in two or more countries.

TRIANGULATION: The use of multiple research methods as a way of producing more reliable empirical data than is available from any single method.

UNDERCLASS: A class of individuals situated right at the bottom of the class system, normally composed of people from ethnic minority backgrounds.

UNFOCUSED INTERACTION: Interaction occurring among people present in a particular setting but not engaged in direct face-to-face communication.

UNINTENDED CONSEQUENCES: Consequences that result from behavior initiated for other purposes.

UNIVERSAL CONSCRIPTION: A system of national service, under which every individual of a certain age (more commonly, all males of a certain age) must undergo a period of military training.

UPPER CLASS: A social class broadly composed of the more affluent members of society, especially those who have inherited wealth, own businesses, or hold large numbers of stocks (shares).

UPWARD MOBILITY: Social mobility in which individuals' wealth, income, or prestige is higher than their parents.

URBAN ECOLOGY: An approach to the study of urban life based on an analogy with the adjustment of plants and organisms to the physical environment. According to ecological theorists, the various neighborhoods and zones within cities are formed as a result of natural processes of adjustment on the part of populations as they compete for resources.

URBAN RENEWAL: The process of renovating deteriorating neighborhoods by encouraging the renewal of old buildings and the construction of new ones.

URBANISM: A term used by Louis Wirth to denote distinctive characteristics of urban social life, such as its impersonality.

URBANIZATION: The development of towns and cities.

VALUES: Ideas held by individuals or groups about what is desirable, proper, good, and bad. What individuals value is strongly influenced by the specific **culture** in which they happen to live.

VARIABLE: A dimension along which an object, individual, or group may be categorized, such as income or height.

VERTICAL MOBILITY: Movement up or down a hierarchy of positions in a social stratification system.

WEALTH: Money and material possessions held by an individual or group.

WELFARE STATE: A political system that provides a wide range of welfare benefits for its citizens.

WHITE-COLLAR CRIME: Criminal activities carried out by those in white-collar, or professional, jobs.

WORK: The activity by which people produce from the natural world and so ensure their survival. Work should not be thought of exclusively as paid employment. In traditional cultures, there was only a rudimentary monetary system, and few people worked for money. In modern societies, there remain types of work that do not involve direct payment (such as housework).

WORKING CLASS: A social class broadly composed of people working in blue-collar, or manual, occupations.

WORLD INFORMATION ORDER: A global system of communications operating through satellite links, radio and TV transmission, and telephone and computer links.

WORLD SYSTEM: A social system of global dimensions, linking all societies within a world social order. The world system may most easily be thought of as a single global society. It has only come into being since the period of the expansion of the West from about the seventeenth century onward. Today, however, the existence of an increasingly integrated world system is one of the most important features of our lives.

WORLD-SYSTEM THEORY: Pioneered by Immanuel Wallerstein, this theory emphasizes the interconnections among countries based on the expansion of a capitalist world economy. This economy is made up of **core countries**, the **semiperiphery**, the **periphery**, and the **external arena**.

CREDITS

BIBLIOGRAPHY

ABBOTT, ANDREW. 1988. *The System of Professions: An Essay on the Division of Expert Labor.* Chicago: University of Chicago Press.

ABERLE, DAVID. 1966. *The Peyote Religion Among the Navaho.* Chicago: Aldine Press.

ADORNO, THEODORE W., ET AL. 1950. *The Authoritarian Personality.* New York: Harper and Row.

ALLEN, MICHAEL P. 1981. "Managerial power and tenure in the large corporation." *Social Forces,* vol. 60.

————. 1993. *Capitalism vs. Capitalism: How America's Obsession with Individual Achievement and Short-Term Profit Has Led It to the Brink of Collapse.* New York: Four Walls Eight Windows.

ALTMAN, DENNIS. 1986. *AIDS in the Mind of America.* Garden City, NY: Doubleday.

ALVAREZ, RODOLFO, ET AL. 1996. "Women in the professions: Assessing progress," in Paula J. Dubeck and Kathryn Borman, eds., *Women and Work: A Handbook.* New York: Garland.

AMENTA, EDWIN. 1998. *Bold Relief: Institutional Politics and the Origins of Modern American Social Policy.* Princeton: Princeton University Press.

AMERICAN ASSOCIATION OF UNIVERSITY WOMEN (AAUW). 1992. *How Schools Shortchange Girls.* Washington, DC: American Association of University Women Educational Foundation.

ANDERSON, BENEDICT. 1991. *Imagined Communities: Reflections on the Origin and Spread of Nationalism.* Revised ed. New York: Routledge.

ANDERSON, ELIJAH. 1990. *Streetwise: Race, Class, and Change in an Urban Community.* Chicago: University of Chicago Press.

ANGIER, NATALIE. 1994. "Feminists and Darwin: Scientists Try Closing the Gap." *New York Times,* June 21.

APTER, TERRI. 1994. *Working Women Don't Have Wives: Professional Success in the 1990s.* New York: St. Martin's Press.

ARIÈS, PHILIPPE. 1965. *Centuries of Childhood.* New York: Random House.

ASCHENBRENNER, JOYCE. 1983. *Lifelines: Black Families in Chicago.* Prospect Heights, IL: Waveland Press.

ASHWORTH, ANTHONY E. 1980. *Trench Warfare: 1914–1918.* London: Macmillan.

AYRES, ROBERT, and MILLER, STEVEN. 1985. "Industrial robots on the line," in Tom Forester, ed., *The Information Technology Revolution*. Cambridge, MA: MIT Press.

BAHRAMI, HOMA, and EVANS, STUART. 1995. "Flexible recycling and high-technology entrepreneurship." *California Management Review*, vol. 22.

BALDWIN-EDWARDS, MARTIN, and SCHAIN, MARTIN A., EDS. 1994. *The Politics of Immigration in Western Europe*. Portland, OR: Frank Cass.

BALSWICK, J. O. 1983. "Male inexpressiveness," in Kenneth Soloman and Norman B. Levy, eds., *Men in Transition: Theory and Therapy*. New York: Plenum Press.

BANFIELD, EDWARD. 1970. *The Unheavenly City*. Boston: Little, Brown.

BARNET, RICHARD J., and CAVANAGH, JOHN. 1994. *Global Dreams: Imperial Corporations and the New World Order*. New York: Simon and Schuster.

BARTH, FREDERICK. 1969. *Ethnic Groups and Boundaries*. London: Allen and Unwin.

BASU, AMRITA, ED. 1995. *The Challenge of Local Feminisms: Women's Movements in Global Perspective*. Boulder, CO: Westview.

BAXTER, JANEEN. 1994. "Is husband's class enough? Class location and identity in the United States, Sweden, Norway, and Australia." *American Sociological Review* (April) 59(2):220–35.

BAXTER, JEANINE, and KANE, EMILY. 1995. "Dependence and independence: A cross national analysis." *Gender & Society*, vol. 9, no. 2 (April).

BEALL, C., and GOLDSTEIN, M. C. 1982. "Work, aging, and dependency in a Sherpa population in Nepal." *Social Science and Medicine*, vol. 16, no. 2.

BEAN, FRANK D., ET AL. 1994. *Illegal Mexican Migration and the U.S./Mexico Border*. Washington, DC: U.S. Commission on Immigration Reform.

BEAUVOIR, SIMONE DE. 1974. *The Second Sex*. Originally published 1949. New York: Random House.

BECK, ULRICH. 1992. *Risk Society*. London: Sage.

BECKER, GARY. 1964. *Human Capital*. New York: National Bureau of Economic Research.

BECKER, HOWARD S. 1950. *Through Values to Social Interpretation*. Durham, NC: Duke University Press.

———. 1963. *Outsiders: Studies in the Sociology of Deviance*. New York: Macmillan.

BEECHEY, VERONICA, and PERKINS, TESSA. 1987. *A Matter of Hours: Women, Part-Time Work, and the Labour Market*. Cambridge, UK: Polity Press.

BELL, DANIEL. 1976. *The Coming of Post-Industrial Society: A Venture in Social Forecasting*. New York: Basic Books.

BELLAH, ROBERT N., ET AL. 1985. *Habits of the Heart: Individualism and Commitment in American Life*. New York: Harper and Row.

BELLMAN, BERYL. 1984. *The Language of Secrecy: Symbols and Metaphors in Poro Ritual*. New Brunswick, NJ: Rutgers University Press.

BENTON, TED, ED. 1996. *The Greening of Marxism*. New York: Guilford Books.

BERGER, PETER L. 1963. *Invitation to Sociology*. Garden City, NY: Anchor Books.

———. 1967. *The Sacred Canopy: Elements of a Sociological Theory of Religion*. Garden City, NY: Anchor Books.

———, and LUCKMANN, THOMAS. 1966. *The Social Construction of Reality: A Treatise in the Sociology of Knowledge*. Garden City, NY: Doubleday.

BERK, RICHARD A. 1974. "A gaming approach to crowd behavior." *American Sociological Review*, vol. 37.

BERLE, ADOLF, and MEANS, GARDINER C. 1982. *The Modern Corporation and Private Property*. Originally published 1932. Buffalo, NY: Heim.

BERNSTEIN, JARED, and MISTEL, LAWRENCE. 1997. "Has wage inequality stopped growing?" *Monthly Labor Review*, vol. 120.

BERTELSON, DAVID. 1986. *Snowflakes and Snowdrifts: Individualism and Sexuality in America*. Lanham, MD: University Press of America.

BERTRAM, EVA, ET AL. 1996. *Drug War Politics*. Berkeley: University of California Press.

BLACKBURN, JOSEPH C. 1990. *Time Based Competition: The Next Battleground in American Manufacturing*. Burr Ridge, IL: Irwin.

BLANKENHORN, DAVID. 1995. *Fatherless America: Confronting Our Most Urgent Social Problem.* New York: Basic Books.

BLAU, PETER. 1963. *The Dynamics of Bureaucracy,* Chicago: University of Chicago Press.

———, and DUNCAN, OTIS DUDLEY. 1967. *The American Occupational Structure.* New York: Wiley.

BLAUNER, ROBERT. 1964. *Alienation and Freedom.* Chicago: University of Chicago Press.

———. 1972. *Racial Oppression in America.* New York: Harper and Row.

BLONDET, CECILIA. 1995. "Out of the kitchen and onto the streets: Women's activism in Peru," in Amrita Basu, ed., *The Challenge of Local Feminisms.* Boulder, CO: Westview.

BLUESTONE, BARRY. 1988. "Deindustrialization and unemployment in America." *The Review of Black Political Economy,* vol. 17.

———, and HARRISON, BENNETT. 1982. *The Deindustrialization of America.* New York: Basic Books.

BLUM, LINDA M. 1991. *Between Feminism and Labor: The Significance of the Comparable Worth Movement.* Berkeley: University of California Press.

BOBO, LAWRENCE, and KLUEGEL, JAMES R. 1991. "Modern American prejudice: Stereotypes, social distance, and perceptions of discrimination toward Blacks, Hispanics, and Asians." Paper presented at the 1991 meeting of the American Sociological Association.

BODEN, DEIRDRE, and MOLOTCH, HARVEY. 1994. "The compulsion of proximity," in Deirdre Boden and Roger Friedland, eds., *Nowhere: Space, Time, and Modernity.* Berkeley: University of California Press.

BONACICH, EDNA, and APPELBAUM, RICHARD P. 2000. *Behind the Label: Inequality in the Los Angeles Garment Industry.* Berkeley: University of California Press.

BOOTH, ALAN. 1977. "Food riots in the north-west of England, 1770–1801." *Past and Present,* no. 77.

BORJAS, GEORGE J. 1994. "The economics of immigration." *Journal of Economic Literature,* vol. 32.

BOSWELL, JOHN. 1995. *The Marriage of Likeness: Same-Sex Unions in Pre-Modern Europe.* London: Fontana.

BOURDIEU, PIERRE. 1984. *Distinction: A Social Critique of Judgements of Taste.* Cambridge, MA: Harvard University Press.

———. 1988. *Language and Symbolic Power.* Cambridge, MA: Polity Press.

———. 1990. *The Logic of Practice.* Stanford, CA: Stanford University Press.

BOWLES, SAMUEL, and GINTIS, HERBERT. 1976. *Schooling in Capitalist America.* New York: Basic Books.

BRAITHWAITE, JOHN. 1996. "Crime, shame, and reintegration," in P. Cordella and L. Siegal, eds., *Readings in Contemporary Criminological Theory.* Boston: Northeastern University Press.

BRANNON, R. 1976. *The Forty-Nine Percent Majority: The Male Sex Role.* Reading, MA: Addison Wesley.

BRAVERMAN, HARRY. 1974. *Labor and Monopoly Capital.* New York: Monthly Review Press.

BRENNAN, TERESA. 1988. "Controversial discussions and feminist debate," in Naomi Segal and Edward Timms, eds., *The Origins and Evolution of Psychoanalysis.* New Haven, CT: Yale University Press.

BREWER, ROSE M. 1993. "Theorizing race, class and gender: The new scholarship of Black feminist intellectuals and Black women's labor," in Stanlie M. James and Abena P. A. Busia, eds., *Theorizing Black Feminisms: The Visionary Pragmatism of Black Women.* New York: Routledge.

BRIMELOW, PETER. 1995. *Alien Nation: Common Sense About America's Immigration Disaster.* New York: Random House.

BRITAIN, SAMUEL. 1975. "The economic contradictions of democracy." *British Journal of Political Science,* vol. 15.

BROD, HARRY, ED. 1987. *The Making of Masculinities: The New Men's Studies.* Boston: Allen & Unwin.

BROWN, CATRINA, and JASPER, KARIN, EDS. 1993. *Consuming Passions: Feminist Approaches to Eating Disorders and Weight Preoccupations.* Toronto: Second Story Press.

BROWN, JUDITH K. 1977. "A note on the division of labor by sex," in Nona Glazer and Helen Y. Waehrer, *Woman in a Man-Made World,* 2nd ed. Chicago: Rand McNally.

BROWN, LESTER R., ET AL. 1999. *State of the World 1999: A Worldwatch Institute Report on Progress Toward a Sustainable Society*. New York: Norton.

BRUBAKER, ROGERS. 1992. *The Politics of Citizenship*. Cambridge, MA: Harvard University Press.

BRYAN, BEVERLY, DADZIE, STELLA, and SCAFE, SUZANNE. 1987. "Learning to resist: Black women and education," in Gaby Weiner and Madeleine Arnot, *Gender under Scrutiny: New Inquiries in Education*. London: Hutchinson.

BULL, PETER. 1983. *Body Movement and Interpersonal Communication*. New York: Wiley.

BULLOCK, CHARLES III. 1984. "Equal education opportunity," in Charles S. Bullock III and Charles M. Lamb (eds.), *Implementation of Civil Rights Policy*. Monterey, CA: Brooks and Cole.

BUMPASS, LARRY L., and SWEET, JAMES A. 1989. "National estimates of cohabitation: Cohort levels and union stability." *Demography*, vol. 26.

———, SWEET, JAMES A., and CHERLIN, ANDREW. 1991. "The role of cohabitation in declining rates of marriage." *Journal of Marriage and the Family*, vol. 53 (November).

BURGESS, ADRIENNE. 1997. *Fatherhood Reclaimed*. London: Vermilion.

———. 1998. *A Complete Parent*. London: IPPR.

BURGESS, ERNEST WATSON. 1960. *Aging in Western Societies*. Chicago: University of Chicago Press.

BURRIS, BEVERLY H. 1993. *Technocracy at Work*. Albany: State University of New York Press.

——— 1998. "Computerization of the workplace," in *Annual Review of Sociology*, vol. 24. Palo Alto, CA: Annual Reviews.

BURT, MARTHA R. 1992. *Over the Edge: The Growth of Homelessness in the 1980s*. New York: Russell Sage.

BUTTERFIELD, FOX. 1998. "Decline of violent crimes is linked to crack market." *New York Times*, December 28, p. A18.

BYRD, MAX. 1978. *London Transformed: Images of the City in the Eighteenth Century*. New Haven, CT: Yale University Press.

BYRNE, DAVID. 1995. "Deindustrialization and dispossession." *Sociology*, vol. 29.

CAMPBELL, BEATRIX. 1993. *Goliath: Britain's Dangerous Places*. London: Methuen.

CANETTO, SILVIA SARA. 1992. "Gender and suicide in the elderly." *Suicide and Life-Threatening Behavior*, vol. 22.

CANTRIL, HADLEY. 1963. *The Psychology of Social Movements*. New York: Wiley.

CAPPS, WALTER H. 1990. *The New Religious Right: Piety, Patriotism, and Politics*. Columbia: University of South Carolina Press.

CASTELLS, MANUEL. 1977. *The Urban Question: A Marxist Approach*. Cambridge, MA: MIT Press.

———. 1983. *The City and the Grass Roots: A Cross-Cultural Theory of Urban Social Movements*. Berkeley: University of California Press.

CHAFE, WILLIAM H. 1974. *The American Woman: Her Changing Social, Economic, and Political Roles, 1920–1970*. New York: Oxford University Press.

———. 1977. *Women and Equality: Changing Patterns in American Culture*. New York: Oxford University Press.

CHAFETZ, JANET SALTZMAN. 1990. *Gender Equity: An Integrated Theory of Stability and Change*. Newbury Park, CA: Sage.

———. 1997. "Feminist theory and sociology: Underutilized contributions for mainstream theory." *Annual Review of Sociology*, vol. 23.

CHAMBLISS, WILLIAM J. 1973. "The Saints and the Roughnecks." *Society* (November).

CHAVES, MARK. 1994. "Secularization as declining religious authority." *Social Forces*, vol. 72.

CHERLIN, ANDREW. 1990. "Recent Changes in American Fertility, Marriage, and Divorce." *Annals of the American Academy of Political and Social Science*, vol. 510 (July).

———. 1992. *Marriage, Divorce, Re-Marriage*. Revised edition. Cambridge, MA: Harvard University Press.

———. 1999. *Public and Private Families: An Introduction*, 2nd ed. New York: McGraw Hill.

CHODOROW, NANCY. 1978. *The Reproduction of Mothering*. Berkeley: University of California Press.

———. 1988. *Psychoanalytic Theory and Feminism*. Cambridge: Polity Press.

CICOUREL, AARON V. 1968. *The Social Organization of Juvenile Justice*. New York: Wiley.

CISNEROS, HENRY G., ED. 1993. *Interwoven Destinies: Cities and the Nation*. New York: Norton.

CLAWSON, DAN, ET AL. 1999. *Dollars and Votes: How Business Campaign Contributions Subvert Democracy*. Philadelphia: Temple University Press.

CLEARY, PAUL D. 1987. "Gender differences in stress-related disorders," in Rosalind C. Barnett, ed., *Gender and Stress*. New York: Free Press.

CLEVELAND, JEANETTE N. 1996. "Women in high-status nontraditional occupations," in Paula J. Dubeck and Kathryn Borman, eds., *Women and Work: A Handbook*. New York: Garland.

CLOWARD, RICHARD A., and OHLIN, L. 1960. *Delinquency and Opportunity*. New York: Free Press.

COCKBURN, CYNTHIA. 1985. *Machinery of Domination*. London: Pluto.

COHN, NORMAN. 1970a. *The Pursuit of the Millenium*. London: Paladin.

———. 1970b. "Medieval millenarianism," in Slyvia L. Thrupp, ed., *Millennial Dreams in Action: Studies in Revolutionary Religious Movements*. New York: Schoeken Books.

COLEMAN, JAMES S. 1987. "Families and Schools." *Educational Researcher*, vol. 16, no. 6.

———, ET AL. 1966. *Equality of Educational Opportunity*. Washington, D.C.: Government Printing Office.

COLLIER, GEORGE ALLEN. 1994. *Basta! Land and the Zapatista Rebellion in Chiapas*. Oakland, CA: Institute for Food and Development Policy.

COLLINS, JAMES, and PORRAS, JERRY. 1994. *Built to Last*. New York: Century.

COLLINS, PATRICIA HILL. 1990. *Black Feminist Thought: Knowledge, Consciousness, and the Politics of Empowerment*. Boston: Unwin Hyman.

COLLINS, RANDALL. 1971. "Functional and conflict theories of educational stratification." *American Sociological Review*, vol. 36.

———. 1979. *The Credential Society: An Historical Sociology of Education*. New York: Academic Press.

———, ET AL. 1993. "Toward an integrated theory of gender stratification." *Sociological Perspectives*, vol. 36.

COLTRANE, SCOTT. 1992. "The micropolitics of gender in non-industrial societies." *Gender & Society*, vol. 6.

CONLEY, DALTON. 1999. *Being Black, Living in the Red: Race, Wealth, and Social Policy in America*. Berkeley and Los Angeles: University of California Press.

COOMBS, PHILIP H. 1985. *The World Crisis in Education*. New York: Oxford University Press.

COONTZ, STEPHANIE. 1992. *The Way We Never Were: American Families and the Nostalgia Trap*. New York: Basic Books.

CORNISH, DEREK B., and CLARKE, RONALD V. 1986. *The Reasoning Criminal: Rational Choice Perspectives on Offending*. New York: Springer Verlag.

CORSARO, WILLIAM. 1997. *The Sociology of Childhood*. Thousand Oaks, CA: Pine Forge Press.

COWARD, ROSALIND. 1984. *Female Desire: Women's Sexuality Today*. London: Paladin.

COX, PETER R. 1976. *Demography*, 5th ed. New York: Cambridge University Press.

COX, W. MICHAEL, and ALM, RICHARD. 1999. *Myths of Rich and Poor: Why We're Better Off Than We Think*. New York: Basic Books.

CRESSY, PAUL. 1932. *The Taxi-Dance Hall*. Chicago: University of Chicago Press.

CRIMMINS, EILEEN M., HAYWARD, MARK, and SAITO, YASUHIKO. 1994. "Changing mortality and morbidity rates and the health status and life expectancy of the older population." *Demography*, vol. 31, no. 1.

CROW, GRAHAM, and HARDEY, MICHAEL. 1992. "Diversity and ambiguity among lone-parent households in modern Britain," in Catherine Marsh and Sara Arber, eds., *Families and Households: Divisions and Change*. London: Macmillan.

CUMMING, ELAINE, and HENRY, WILLIAM E. 1961. *Growing Old: The Process of Disengagement*. New York: Basic.

CURRIE, ELLIOTT. 1998. *Crime and Punishment in America*. New York: Henry Holt.

CURTISS, SUSAN. 1977. *Genie: A Linguistic Study of a Modern Day "Wild Child."* New York: Academic Press.

DANZIGER, SHELDON H., and GOTTSCHALK, PETER. 1995. *America Unequal*. Cambridge, MA: Harvard University Press.

————, ET AL., EDS. 1994. *Confronting Poverty: Prescriptions for Change.* Cambridge, MA: Harvard University Press.

DAVENPORT, W. 1965. "Sexual patterns and their regulations in a society of the southwest Pacific," in F. Beech, ed., *Sex and Beha*vior. New York: Wiley.

DAVIES, BRONWYN. 1991. *Frogs and Snails and Feminist Tales.* Sydney: Allen and Unwin.

DAVIES, JAMES C. 1962. "Towards a theory of revolution." *American Sociological Review*, vol. 27.

DAVIS, KINGSLEY, and MOORE, WILBERT E. 1945. "Some principles of stratification." *American Sociological Review*, vol. 10 (April).

DAVIS, STANLEY M. 1987. *Future Perfect.* Reading, MA: Addison-Wesley.

DE WITT, KAREN. 1994. "Wave of suburban growth is being fed by minorities." *New York Times*, August 15, pp. A1, B6.

DERTOUZOS, MICHAEL L. 1989. *Made in America: Regaining the Productive Edge.* Cambridge, MA: MIT Press.

DEVAULT, MARJORIE L. 1991. *Feeding the Family: The Social Organization of Caring as Gendered Work.* Chicago: University of Chicago Press.

DIAMOND, JARED. 1997. *Guns, Germs, and Steel: The Fates of Human Societies.* New York: Norton.

DICKEN, PETER. 1992. *Global Shift: The Internationalization of Economic Activity*, 2nd ed. London: Chapman.

DICUM, GREGORY, and LUTTINGER, NINA. 1999. *The Coffee Book: Anatomy of an Industry from Crop to the Last Drop.* New York: New Press.

DOHERTY, W. J. 1997. "The best of times and the worst of times," in A. J. Hawkins and D. C. Dollahite, eds., *Generative Fathering.* London: Sage.

DOMHOFF, G. WILLIAM. 1998 [earlier editions 1971, 1979, 1983]. *Who Rules America?: Power and Politics in the Year 2000.* Belmont, CA: Mayfield.

DORE, RONALD. 1980. *British Factory, Japanese Factory: The Origins of National Diversity in Industrial Relations.* Berkeley: University of California Press.

DOYAL, LESLEY, and PENNELL, IMOGEN. 1981. *The Political Economy of Health.* Boston: South End Press.

DRAKE, ST. CLAIR, and CAYTON, HORACE R. 1945. *Black Metropolis: A Study of Negro Life in a Northern City.* New York: Harcourt, Brace.

DRAPER, P. 1975. "!Kung women: Contrasts in sexual egalitarianism in foraging and sedentary contexts," in R. R. Reiter, ed., *Toward an Anthropology of Women.* New York: Monthly Review Press.

DU BOIS, W. E. B. 1903. *The Souls of Black Folk.* New York: Dover.

DUBOS, RENÉ. 1959. *Mirage of Health.* New York: Doubleday/Anchor.

DUIGNAN, PETER, and GANN, L.H., EDS. 1998. *The Debate in the United States over Immigration.* Stanford: Hoover Institution Press.

DUNCAN, OTIS DUDLEY. 1971. "Observations on population." *The New Physician*, April 20.

DUNEIER, MITCHELL. 1999. *Sidewalk.* New York: Farrar, Straus, and Giroux.

DUNN, DANA, ALMQUIST, ELIZABETH M., and SALTZMAN CHAFETZ, JANET. 1993. "Macrostructural perspectives on gender inequality," in Paula England, ed., *Theory on Gender, Feminism on Theory.* New York: Aldine DeGrutyer.

DUNN, WILLIAM. 1993. *The Baby Bust: A Generation Comes of Ag*e. Ithaca, NY: American Demographics Books.

DURANTI, ALESSANDRO. 1994. *From Grammar to Politics: Linguistic Anthropology in a Western Samoan Village.* Berkeley, CA: University of California Press.

DURKHEIM, ÉMILE. 1965. *The Elementary Forms of the Religious Life.* Originally published 1912. New York: Free Press.

————. 1966. *Suicide.* Originally published 1897. New York: Free Press.

DUSTER, TROY. 1990. *Backdoor to Eugenics.* New York: Routledge.

DUTT, MALLIKA. 1996. "Some reflections on U.S. women of color and the United Nations fourth world conference on women and NGO forum in Beijing, China." *Feminist Studies*, vol. 22.

DUVERGER, MAURICE. 1954. *Political Parties.* New York: Wiley.

DWORKIN, R. M. 1993. *Life's Dominion: An Argument About Abortion, Euthanasia, and Individual Freedom.* New York: Knopf.

DWYER, D. J. 1975. *People and Housing in Third World Cities*. London: Longman.

DYE, THOMAS R. 1986. *Who's Running America?* 4th ed. Englewood Cliffs, NJ: Prentice Hall.

THE ECONOMIST. 1990. *The Economist Book of Vital World Statistics*. New York: Times Books.

EIBL-EIBESFELDT, I. 1972. "Similarities and differences between cultures in expressive movements," in Robert A. Hinde, ed., *Nonverbal Communication*. New York: Cambridge University Press.

EKMAN, PAUL, and FRIESEN, W. V. 1978. *Facial Action Coding System*. New York: Consulting Psychologists Press.

ELSHTAIN, JEAN BETHKE. 1981. *Public Man: Private Woman*. Princeton, NJ: Princeton University Press.

ENGLAND, PAULA. 1992. *Comparable Worth: Theories and Evidence*. New York: Aldine de Gruyter.

EQUAL EMPLOYMENT OPPORTUNITY COMMISSION. 1993. "National database fiscal year 1983 to fiscal year 1992." Washington, DC: Equal Employment Opportunity Commission.

ERIKSON, KAI. 1966. *Wayward Puritans: A Study in the Sociology of Deviance*. New York: Wiley.

ERIKSON, ROBERT, and GOLDTHORPE, JOHN J. 1986. "National variation in social fluidity." CAS-MIN Project Working Paper, no. 9.

ETZIONI-HALÉVY, EVA. 1985. *Bureaucracy and Democracy: A Political Dilemma*. New York: Routledge, Chapman and Hall.

EVANS-PRITCHARD, E. E. 1956. *Nuer Religion*. New York: Oxford University Press.

FABER, CAROL. 1998. "Geographical mobility." *Current Population Reports* #P20–510.

FARLEY, REYNOLDS, and FREY, WILLIAM H. 1994. "Change in the segregation of whites from blacks during the 1980s: Small steps toward a more integrated society." *American Sociological Review*, vol. 59, no. 1 (February).

FEAGIN, JOE R. 1991. "The continuing significance of race: Antiblack discrimination in public places." *American Sociological Review*, vol. 56, no. 1 (February).

———, and SIKES, MELVIN P. 1994. *Living with Racism: The Black Middle-Class Experience*. Boston: Beacon Press.

FEATHERMAN, DAVID L., and HAUSER, ROBERT M. 1978. *Opportunity and Change*. New York: Academic Press.

FEENEY, FLOYD. 1986. "Robbers as decision-makers," in Derek Cornish and Ronald Clarke, eds., *The Reasoning Criminal: Rational Choice Perspectives on Offending*. New York: Springer-Verlag.

FINKE, ROGER, and STARK, RODNEY. 1992. *The Churching of America, 1776–1990: Winners and Losers in Our Religious Economy*. New Brunswick, NJ: Rutgers University Press.

FINKELHOR, DAVID. 1984. *Child Sexual Abuse: New Theory and Research*. New York: Free Press.

FIRESTONE, SHULAMITH. 1971. *The Dialectic of Sex*. London: Paladin.

FISCHER, CLAUDE S. 1984. *The Urban Experience*, 2nd ed. New York: Harcourt Brace Jovanovich.

———, ET AL. 1996. *Inequality by Design: Cracking the Bell Curve Myth*. Princeton, NJ: Princeton University Press.

FISCHER, DAVID H. 1978. *Growing Old in America*, expanded edition. New York: Oxford University Press.

FORD, CLELLAN S., and BEACH, FRANK A. 1951. *Patterns of Sexual Behavior*. New York: Harper and Row.

FOUCAULT, MICHEL. 1971. *The Order of Things: An Archaeology of the Human Sciences*. New York: Pantheon.

———. 1978. *The History of Sexuality*. New York: Pantheon.

———. 1979. *Discipline and Punish: The Birth of the Prison*. New York: Random House.

———. 1988. "Technologies of the self," in Luther H. Martin, Huck Gutman, and Patrick H. Hutton, eds., *Technologies of the Self: A Seminar with Michel Foucault*. Amherst: University of Massachusetts Press.

FOWLES, RICHARD, and MERVA, MARY. 1996. "Wage inequality and criminal activity: An extreme bounds analysis for the United States, 1975–1990." *Criminology*, vol. 34, no. 2.

FOX, OLIVER C. 1964. "The pre-industrial city reconsidered." *Sociological Quarterly*, vol. 5.

FREDRICKSON, GEORGE M. 1998. *The Comparative Imagination: On the History of Racism, Nationalism, and Social Movements*. Berkeley and Los Angeles: University of California Press. *Freedom in the World, 1997–1998.* New York: Freedom House.

FREEMAN, RICHARD B. 1999. *The New Inequality: Creating Solutions for Poor America.* Boston: Beacon Press.

FREIDSON, ELIOT. 1986. *Professional Powers: A Study of the Institutionalization of Formal Knowledge.* Chicago: University of Chicago Press.

FREMLIN, J. H. 1964. "How many people can the world support?" *New Scientist*, October 19.

FREUD, SIGMUND. 1971. *The Psychopathology of Everyday Life.* New York: Norton.

FREY, WILLIAM, and LIAW, KAO-LEE. 1998. "The impact of recent immigration on population redistribution in the United States," in James Smith and Barry Edmonston, eds., *The Immigration Debate.* Washington, DC: National Academy Press.

FRIEDAN, BETTY. 1963. *The Feminine Mystique.* New York: Norton.

FRIEDLANDER, DANIEL, and BURTLESS, GARY. 1994. *Five Years After: The Long-Term Effects of Welfare-to-Work Programs.* New York: Russell Sage.

FRYER, DAVID, and MCKENNA, STEPHEN. 1987. "The laying off of hands—unemployment and the experience of time," in Stephen Fineman, ed., *Unemployment: Personal and Social Consequences.* London: Tavistock.

FUKUYAMA, FRANCIS. 1989. "The end of history?" *The National Interest 16* (Summer 1989).

FURSTENBERG, FRANK F., JR., and CHERLIN, ANDREW J. 1991. *Divided Families.* Cambridge, MA: Harvard University Press.

FUSSELL, SAM W. 1991. *Muscle: Confessions of an Unlikely Bodybuilder.* New York: Poseidon Press.

GAMORAN, ADAM, ET AL. 1995. "An organizational analysis of the effects of ability grouping." *American Educational Research Journal*, vol. 32, no. 4 (winter).

GANS, HERBERT J. 1979. "Symbolic ethnicity: The future of ethnic groups and cultures in America." *Ethnic and Racial Studies*, vol. 2 (January).

GARDNER, BEATRICE, and GARDNER, ALLEN. 1975. "Evidence for sentence constituents in the early utterances of child and chimpanzee." *Journal of Experimental Psychology*, vol. 104.

GARDNER, BEATRICE, and GARDNER, ALLEN. 1969. "Teaching sign language to a chimpanzee." *Science*, no. 165.

GARDNER, CAROL BROOKS. 1995. *Passing By: Gender and Public Harassment.* Berkeley and Los Angeles: University of California Press.

GARFINKEL, HAROLD. 1963. "A conception of, and experiments with, 'trust' as a condition of stable concerted actions," in O. J. Harvey, ed., *Motivation and Social Interaction.* New York: Ronald Press.

———. 1985. *Studies in Ethnomethodology.* New York: Basil Blackwell.

GEARY, DICK. 1981. *European Labor Protest, 1848–1939.* New York: St. Martin's Press.

GEERTZ, CLIFFORD. 1983. *Local Knowledge: Further Essays in Interpretative Anthropology.* New York: Basic Books.

GELB, I. J. 1952. *A Study of Writing.* Chicago: University of Chicago Press.

GELIS, JACQUES. 1991. *History of Childbirth: Fertility, Pregnancy, and Birth in Early Modern Europe.* Boston: Northeastern University Press.

GELLES, RICHARD J., and STRAUS, MURRAY A. 1989. *Intimate Violence: The Causes and Consequences of Abuse in the American Family.* New York: Simon and Schuster.

GELLNER, ERNEST. 1983. *Nations and Nationalism.* Ithaca, NY: Cornell University Press.

GERBNER, GEORGE, ET AL. 1985. "Television's mean world: violence profile no. 14–15." Annenberg School of Communication, University of Pennsylvania.

GERSHUNY, J. I., and MILES, I. D. 1983. *The New Service Economy: The Transformation of Employment in Industrial Societies.* London: Francis Pinter.

GIBBONS, JOHN H. 1990. *Trading Around the Clock: Global Securities Markets and Information Technology.* Washington, DC: Government Printing Office.

GIDDENS, ANTHONY. 1984. *The Constitution of Society.* Cambridge: Polity Press.

———. 1995. *Beyond Left and Right: The Future of Radical Politics.* Stanford, CA: Stanford University Press.

———. 1998. *The Third Way: The Renewal of Social Democracy.* Cambridge, UK: Polity Press.

GILL, COLIN. 1985. *Work, Unemployment, and the New Technolgy.* New York: Basil Blackwell.

GILLIGAN, CAROL. 1982. *In a Different Voice: Psychological Theory and Women's Development.* Cambridge, MA: Harvard University Press.

GINZBERG, ELI. 1993. "The changing urban scene: 1960–1990 and beyond," in Henry G. Cisneros, ed., *Interwoven Destinies: Cities and the Nation.* New York: Norton.

GISSING, GEORGE. 1983. *Demos: A Story of English Socialism.* Originally published 1892. New York: Routledge, Chapman and Hall.

GIUFFRE, PATTI A., and WILLIAMS, CHRISTINE L. 1994. "Boundary lines: Labeling sexual harassment in restaurants." *Gender & Society,* vol. 8.

GLASCOCK, A., and FEINMAN, S. 1981. "Social asset or social burden: An analysis of the treatment for the aged in non-industrial societies," in C. L. Fry, ed., *Dimensions: Aging, Culture, and Health.* New York: Praeger.

———. 1986. "Toward a comparative framework. Propositions concerning the treatment of the aged in non-industrial societies," in C. L. Fry and J. Keith, eds., *New Methods for Old Age Research: Strategies for Studying Diversity.* South Hadley, MA: Bergin & Garvey.

GLENN, EVELYN NAKANO. 1994. "Introduction," in Grace Change, Linda Rennie Forcey, and Evelyn Nakano Glenn, eds., *Mothering: Ideology, Experience, and Agency.* New York: Routledge.

GLUECK, SHELDON W., and GLUECK, ELEANOR. 1956. *Physique and Delinquency.* New York: Harper and Row.

GOBER, PATRICIA. 1993. *Americans on the Move.* Washington, DC: Population Reference Bureau.

GOE, W. RICHARD. 1994. "The producer services sector and development within the deindustrializing urban community." *Social Forces,* vol. 72.

GOFFMAN, ERVING. 1967. *Interaction Ritual.* New York: Doubleday/Anchor.

———. 1971. *Relations in Public: Microstudies of the Public Order.* New York: Basic Books.

———. 1973. *The Presentation of Self in Everyday Life.* New York: Overlook Press.

———. 1974. *Frame Analysis.* New York: Harper and Row.

———. 1979. *Gender Advertisements.* Cambridge, MA: Harvard University Press.

———. 1981. *Forms of Talk.* Philadelphia: University of Pennsylvania Press.

GOLDBERG, CAREY. 1997. "Hispanic households struggle amid broad decline in income." *New York Times,* January 30, pp. A1, A16.

GOLDSCHNEIDER, FRANCIS K., and WAITE, LINDA J. 1991. *New Families, No Families? The Transformation of the American Home.* Berkeley: University of California Press.

GOLDTHORPE, JOHN H. 1983. "Women and class analysis: In defense of the conventional view." *Sociology,* vol. 17.

GOODE, WILLIAM J. 1963. *World Revolution in Family Patterns.* New York: Free Press.

———. 1993. *World Changes in Divorce Patterns.* New Haven, CT: Yale University Press.

GOODHARDT, G. J., EHRENBERG, A. S. C., and COLLINS, M. A. 1987. *The Television Audience: Patterns of Voting.* 2nd ed. London: Gower.

GORSKI, PHILIP S. 2000. "Historicizing the secularization debate: Church, state, and society in late medieval and early modern Europe." *American Sociological Review,* forthcoming.

GORZ, ANDRE. 1982. *Farewell to the Working Class.* London: Pluto.

GOTTFREDSON, MICHAEL R., and HIRSCHI, TRAVIS. 1990. *A General Theory of Crime.* Stanford, CA: Stanford University Press.

GOVE, WALTER R. 1985. "The effect of age and gender on deviant behavior: A biopsychosocial perspective," in Alice S. Rossi, ed., *Gender and the Life Course.* New York: Aldine.

GRAHAM, LAURIE. 1995. *On the Line at Suburu-Isuzu.* Ithaca, NY: Cornell University Press.

GREELEY, ANDREW. 1977. *The American Catholic: A Social Portrait.* New York: Basic Books.

———. 1989. *Religious Change in America.* Cambridge, MA: Harvard University Press.

GREENFIELD, PATRICIA MARKS. 1993. "Representational competence in shared symbol systems," in R. R. Cocking and K. A. Renninger, eds., *The Development and Meaning of Psychological Distance.* Hillsdale, NJ: Erlbaum.

GRINT, KEITH. 1991. *The Sociology of Work.* Cambridge, MA: Polity Press.

GROSS, JANE. 1992. "Suffering in silence no more: Fighting sexual harassment." *New York Times*, July 13, p. A1.

GRUSKY, DAVID B., and HAUSER, ROBERT M. 1984. "Comparative social mobility revisited: Models of convergence and divergence in 16 countries." *American Sociological Review*, vol. 49.

GUPTE, PRANAY. 1984. *The Crowded Earth: People and the Politics of Population*. New York: Norton.

GURALNIK, J. M., ET AL. 1989. "Educational status and active life expectancy among older blacks and whites." *New England Journal of Medicine*, vol. 329.

HABERMAS, JÜRGEN. 1975. *Legitimation Crisis*. Trans. Thomas McCarthy. Boston: Beacon Press.

———. 1989. *The Structural Transformation of the Public Sphere: An Inquiry into a Category of Bourgeois Society*. Cambridge, UK: Polity Press.

HACKER, ANDREW. 1992. *Two Nations: Black and White, Separate, Hostile, Unequal*. New York: Scribner.

HAGAN, JOHN. 1992. "The poverty of a classless criminology." *Criminology*, vol. 30, no. 1.

———, and MCCARTHY, BILL. 1992. "Mean streets: The theoretical significance of situational delinquency among homeless youth." *American Sociological Review*, vol. 98.

HALL, EDWARD T. 1969. *The Hidden Dimension*. New York: Doubleday.

———. 1973. *The Silent Language*. New York: Doubleday.

HALL, STUART, ET AL. 1988. "New times." *Marxism Today*, October.

HAMMER, MICHAEL, and CHAMPY, JAMES. 1993. *Reengineering the Corporation: A Manifesto for Business Revolution*. New York: Harper Business.

HANSEN, KRISTIN A. 1995. "Geographical Mobility: March 1993 to March 1994," in U.S. Bureau of the Census, *Current Population Reports, P20–485*. Washington, DC: Government Printing Office.

HARRIS, JUDITH RICH. 1998. *The Nurture Assumption: Why Children Turn Out the Way They Do*. New York: Free Press.

HARRIS, MARVIN. 1978. *Cannibals and Kings: The Origins of Cultures*. New York: Random House.

HARRISON, NICK, ED. 1996. *Promises to Keep: Daily Devotions for Men of Integrity*. San Francisco: Harper San Francisco.

HARTLEY, EUGENE. 1946. *Problems in Prejudice*. New York: Kings Crown Press.

HARTMAN, MARY, and BANNER, LOIS, EDS. 1974. *Clio's Consciousness Raised: New Perspectives on the History of Women*. New York: Norton.

HARTMANN, HEIDI I., ET AL. 1985. "An agenda for basic research on comparable worth," in H. I. Hartmann et al., eds., *Comparable Worth: New Directions for Research*. Washington, DC: National Academy Press.

HARVEY, DAVID. 1973. *Social Justice and the City*. Oxford, UK: Blackwell.

———. 1982. *The Limits to Capital*. Oxford, UK: Blackwell.

———. 1985. *Consciousness and the Urban Experience: Studies in the History and Theory of Capitalist Urbanization*. Oxford, UK: Blackwell.

HATCH, S., and KICKBUSCH, R. 1983. *Self-Help and Health in Europe*. Geneva, Switzerland: World Health Organization.

HATHAWAY. 1997. "Marijuana and tolerance: Revisiting Becker's sources of control." *Deviant Behavior*, vol. 18, no. 2.

HAWKES, TERENCE. 1977. *Structuralism and Semiotics*. Berkeley, CA: University of California Press.

HAWLEY, AMOS H. 1950. *Human Ecology: A Theory of Community Structure*. New York: Ronald Press Company.

———. 1968. "Human ecology," in *International Encyclopedia of Social Science*, vol. 4. New York: Free Press.

HAYFLICK, LEONARD. 1994. *How and Why We Age*. New York: Ballantine Books.

HEBDIGE, DICK. 1997. *Cut 'n' Mix: Culture, Identity, and Caribbean Music*. London: Methuen.

HEELAS, PAUL. 1996. *The New Age Movement*. Cambridge: Blackwell.

HELD, DAVID. 1987. *Models of Democracy*. Stanford, CA: Stanford University Press.

HENSLIN, JAMES M., and BRIGGS, MAE A. 1971. "Dramaturgical desexualization: The sociology of the vaginal examination," in James M.

Henslin, ed., *Studies in the Sociology of Sex.* New York: Appleton-Century-Crofts.

———. 1997. "Behavior in public places: The sociology of the vaginal examination," in James M. Henslin, ed., *Down to Earth Sociology: Introductory Readings,* 9th ed. New York: Free Press.

HERITAGE, JOHN. 1985. *Garfinkel and Ethnomethodology.* New York: Basil Blackwell.

HERNANDEZ, D. J. 1993. *America's Children: Resources from Family, Government, and Economy.* New York: Russell Sage Foundation.

HERRNSTEIN, RICHARD J., and MURRAY, CHARLES. 1994. *The Bell Curve: Intelligence and Class Structure in American Life.* New York: Free Press.

HESSE-BIBER, SHARLENE. 1997. *Am I Thin Enough Yet?: The Cult of Thinness and the Commercialization of Identity.* New York: Oxford University Press.

HIGGINBOTHAM, ELIZABETH. 1992. "Making up with kin and community: Upward social mobility for black and white women." *Gender and Society* (September) 6(3):416–40.

HOCHSCHILD, ARLIE RUSSELL. 1983. *The Managed Heart: Commercialization of Human Feeling.* Berkeley, CA: University of California Press.

———. 1997. *The Time Bind.* New York: Metropolitan Books.

——— WITH ANNE MACHUNG. 1989. *The Second Shift: Working Parents and the Revolution at Home.* New York: Viking.

HODGE, ROBERT, and TRIPP, DAVID. 1986. *Children and Television: A Semiotic Approach.* Cambridge, MA: Polity Press.

HOLMES, STEVEN A. 1996a. "Education gap between races closes." *New York Times,* September 6, p. A18.

———. 1996b. "Quality of life is up for many blacks, data say." *New York Times,* November 18, p. A1.

———. 1997. "New reports say minorities benefit in fiscal recovery." *New York Times,* September 30, p. A1.

HOLTON, ROBERT J. 1978. "The crowds in history: Some problems of theory and method." *Social History,* vol. 3.

HOMANS, HILARY. 1987. "Man-made myth: The reality of being a woman scientist in the NHS," in Anne Spencer and David Podmore, eds., *In a Man's World: Essays on Women in Male-Dominated Professions.* London: Tavistock.

HOOKS, BELL. 1981. *Ain't I a Woman: Black Women and Feminism.* Boston: South End Press.

HOOYMAN, NANCY, and KIYAK, H. ASUMAN. 1993. *Social Gerontology: A Multidisciplinary Perspective,* 3rd ed. Needham Heights, MA: Allyn and Bacon.

HOUT, MICHAEL. 1988. "More universalism, less structural mobility: The American occupational structure in the 1980s." *American Journal of Sociology,* vol. 93.

———, and LUCAS, SAMUEL R. 1996. "Education's role in reducing income disparities." *The Education Digest,* vol. 62, no. 3 (November).

HUBER, JOAN. 1990. "Macro-micro link in gender stratification," *American Sociological Review,* vol. 55.

———, ED. 1992. *Micro-Macro Linkages in Sociology.* Newbury Park, CA: Sage.

HUGHES, EVERETT C. 1945. "Dilemmas and contradictions of status." *American Journal of Sociology,* vol. 50.

HUNTINGTON, SAMUEL P. 1990. "Democratization and security in eastern Europe," in P. Volten, ed., *Uncertain Futures: Eastern Europe and Democracy.* New York: Institute for East-West Security Studies.

———. 1991. *The Third Wave: Democratization in the Late Twentieth Century.* Norman, OK: University of Oklahoma Press.

———. 1996. *The Clash of Civilizations and the Remaking of World Order.* New York: Simon & Schuster.

HYMAN, RICHARD. 1984. *Strikes,* 2nd ed. London: Fontana.

ILLICH, IVAN D. 1983. *Deschooling Society.* New York: Harper and Row.

INGLEHART, RONALD. 1997. *Modernization and Postmodernization: Cultural, Economic and Political Change in 43 Societies.* Princeton, NJ: Princeton University Press.

IYER, PICO. 1989. *Video Nights in Katmandu.* New York: Vintage.

JACOBS, JANE. 1961. *The Death and Life of Great American Cities*. New York: Random House.

JAHER, FREDERIC COPLE, ED. 1973. *The Rich, the Well Born, and the Powerful*. Urbana, IL: University of Illinois Press.

JENCKS, CHRISTOPHER. 1994. *The Homeless*. Cambridge, MA: Harvard University Press.

———, ET AL. 1972. *Inequality: A Reassessment of the Effects of Family and School in America*. New York: Basic Books.

JENSEN, ARTHUR. 1967. "How much can we boost IQ and scholastic achievement?" *Harvard Educational Review*, vol. 29.

———. 1979. *Bias in Mental Testing*. New York: Free Press.

JONES, JACQUELINE. 1986. *Labor of Love, Labor of Sorrow: Black Women, Work, and the Family from Slavery to the Present*. New York: Random House.

JORDAN, WINTHROP. 1968. *White over Black*. Chapel Hill: University of North Carolina Press.

JUDD, DENNIS R., and FAINSTEIN, SUSAN S., EDS. 1999. *The Tourist City*. New Haven, CT: Yale University Press.

KAMIN, LEON J. 1974. *The Science and Politics of IQ*. Hillsdale, NJ: Erlbaum.

KANTER, ROSABETH MOSS. 1991. "The future of bureaucracy and hierarchy in organizational theory," in Pierre Bourdieu and James Coleman, eds., *Social Theory for a Changing Society*. Boulder, CO: Westview.

KASARDA, JOHN D., and CRENSHAW, EDWARD M. 1991. "Third world urbanization: Dimensions, theories, and determinants," in *Annual Review of Sociology 1991*, vol. 17. Palo Alto, CA: Annual Reviews.

———, and JANOWITZ, MORRIS. 1974. "Community attachment in mass society." *American Sociological Review*, vol. 39.

KASARDA, JOHN. 1993. "Urban industrial transition and the underclass," in William Julius Wilson, ed., *The Ghetto Underclass*. Newbury Park, CA: Sage.

KATZ, B. J. 1974. "A quiet march for liberation begins," in J. H. Pleck and J. Sawyers, eds., *Men and Masculinity*. Englewood Cliffs, NJ: Prentice Hall.

KATZ, S. and AKPOM, C.A. 1976. "Index of ADL." *Medical Care*, vol. 14.

KATZ. SIDNEY, ET AL. 1983. "Active life expectancy." *New England Journal of Medicine*, vol. 309.

KAUTSKY, JOHN J. 1982. *The Politics of Aristocratic Empires*. Chapel Hill: University of North Carolina Press.

KEANE, FERGAL. 1995. *The Bondage of Fear: A Journey through the Last White Empire*. London: Penguin.

KELLING, GEORGE L., and COLES, CATHERINE M. 1998. *Fixing Broken Windows: Restoring Order and Reducing Crime in Our Communities*. New York: The Free Press.

KEMP, AMANDA, ET AL. 1995. "The dawn of a new day: Redefining South African feminism," in Amrita Basu, ed., *The Challenge of Local Feminisms*. Boulder, CO: Westview.

KENWAY, JANE, ET AL. 1995. "Pulp fictions?: Education, markets, and the information superhighway." *Australian Educational Researcher*, vol. 22.

KERN, STEVEN. 1983. *The Culture of Time and Space: 1880–1918*. Cambridge, MA: Harvard University Press.

KINSEY, ALFRED C., ET AL. 1948. *Sexual Behavior in the Human Male*. Philadelphia: Saunders.

———, ET AL. 1953. *Sexual Behavior in the Human Female*. Philadelphia: Saunders.

KJEKSHUS, H. 1977. *Ecology, Control, and Economic Development in East African History*. Berkeley: University of California Press.

KLING, ROBERT. 1996. "Computerization at work," in R. Kling, ed., *Computers and Controversy*, 2nd ed. New York: Academic Press.

KLUCKHOHN, CLYDE. 1949. *Mirror for Man*. Tucson: University of Arizona Press.

KNIGHT, F. H. 1933. *Risk, Uncertainty, and Profit*. London: London School of Economics and Political Science.

KNORR-CETINA, KAREN, and CICOUREL, AARON V., EDS. 1981. *Advances in Social Theory and Methodology: Towards an Integration of Micro- and Macro-Sociologies*. Boston: Routledge and Kegan Paul.

KOHN, MELVIN. 1977. *Class and Conformity*, 2nd ed. Homewood, IL: Dorsey Press.

KOZOL, JONATHAN. 1991. *Savage Inequalities: Children in America's Schools*. New York: Crown.

LACAYO, RICHARD. 1994. "Lock 'em up!" *Time*, February 7.

LAKE, R. 1981. *The New Suburbanites: Race and Housing in the Suburbs*. New Brunswick, NJ: Center for Urban Policy Research, Rutgers University Press.

LAMBERT, RICHARD. 1995. "Foreign student flows and the internationalization of higher education," in Katharine Hanson and Joel Meyerson, eds., *International Challenges to American Colleges and Universities*. Phoenix: Orynx Press.

LANDES, DAVID S. 1969. *The Unbound Prometheus*. New York: Cambridge University Press.

LANDRY, BART. 1988. *The New Black Middle Class*. Berkeley: University of California Press.

LANE, HARLAN. 1976. *The Wild Boy of Aveyron*. Cambridge, MA: Harvard University Press.

LANE, JAMES B. 1974. *Jacob A. Riis: The American City*. New York: Kennikat Press.

LANTENARI, VITTORIO. 1963. *The Religions of the Oppressed. A Study of Modern Messianic Cults*. New York: Knopf.

LASH, SCOTT, and URRY, JOHN. 1987. *The End of Organized Capitalism*. Madison, WI: University of Wisconsin Press.

LAUMANN, EDWARD O., ET AL. 1994. *The Social Organization of Sexuality: Sexual Practices in the United States*. Chicago: University of Chicago Press.

LAWTON, M. POWELL, and BRODY, E. M. 1969. "Assessment of older people: Self-maintaining and instrumental activities of daily living." *Gerontologist*, vol. 9.

LAZARSFELD, PAUL F., BERELSON, BERNARD, and GAUDET, HAZEL. 1948. *The People's Choice*. New York: Columbia University Press.

LE BON, GUSTAVE. 1960. *The Crowd*. Originally published 1895. New York: Viking.

LEACH, EDMUND. 1976. *Culture and Communication: The Logic by Which Symbols Are Connected*. New York: Cambridge University Press.

LEE, GARY. 1982. *Family Structure and Interaction: A Comparative Analysis*. 2nd ed. Minneapolis: University of Minnesota Press.

LEE, RICHARD B. 1968. "What hunters do for a living, or how to make out on scarce resources," in Richard B. Lee and Irven DeVore, eds., *Man the Hunter*. Chicago: Aldine.

——. 1969. "!Kung Bushman subsistence: An input-output analysis," in A. P. Vayda, ed., *Environment and Cultural Behavior*. New York: Natural History Press.

LEES, ANDREW. 1985. *Cities Perceived: Urban Society in European and American Thought, 1820–1940*. New York: Columbia University Press.

LEIUFFSRUD, HAKON, and WOODWARD, ALISON. 1987. "Women at class crossroads: Repudiating conventional theories of family class." *Sociology*, vol. 21.

LEMERT, EDWIN. 1972. *Human Deviance, Social Problems, and Social Control*. Englewood Cliffs, NJ: Prentice-Hall.

LEPKOWSKY, M. 1990. "Gender in an egalitarian society: A case study from the Coral Sea," in P. R. Sandy and R. G. Goodenough, eds., *Beyond the Second Sex*. Philadelphia: University of Pennsylvania Press.

LEWIS, OSCAR. 1968. "The culture of poverty," in Daniel P. Moynihan, ed., *On Understanding Poverty: Perspectives from the Social Sciences*. New York: Basic Books.

LEWONTIN, RICHARD. 1982. *Human Diversity*. New York: Freeman.

LIEBOW, ELLIOT. 1967. *Tally's Corner: A Study of Negro Streetcorner Men*. Boston: Little, Brown.

——. 1993. *Tell Them Who I Am: The Lives of Homeless Women*. New York: Free Press.

LIPSET, SEYMOUR MARTIN, ED. 1981. *Party Coalitions in the 1980s*. San Francisco: Institute for Contemporary Affairs.

——, and BENDIX, REINHARD. 1959. *Social Mobility in Industrial Society*. Berkeley: University of California Press.

LITTLEFIELD, NICK. 1992. "Education," in Mark Green, ed., *Changing America: Blueprint for the New Administration*. New York: New Market Press.

LOFLAND, LYN H. 1973. *A World of Strangers*. New York: Basic Books.

——. 1998. *The Public Realm: Exploring the City's Quintessential Social Territory*. New York: Aldine de Gruyter.

LOGAN, JOHN R., and MOLOTCH, HARVEY L. 1987. *Urban Fortunes: The Political Economy of Place*. Berkeley: University of California Press.

LONGINO, CHARLES F. 1995. *The Old Age Challenge to the Biomedical Model: Paradigm Strain and Health Policy*. Amityville, NY.: Baywood Pub.

LORBER, JUDITH. 1994. *Paradoxes of Gender*. New Haven, CT: Yale University Press.

LOWE, GRAHAM S. 1987. *Women in the Administrative Revolution: The Feminization of Clerical Work*. Toronto: University of Toronto Press.

LULL, JAMES. 1991. *China Turned On: Television, Reform, and Resistance*. New York: Routledge.

LYMAN, RICHARD. 1995. "Overview," in Katharine Hanson and Joel Meyerson, eds., *International Challenges to American Colleges and Universities*. Phoenix: Orynx Press.

LYND, ROBERT, and LYND, HELEN. 1929. *Middletown: A Study in Contemporary American Culture*. New York: Harcourt, Brace, and Co.

LYON, DAVID. 1989. *The Information Society: Issues and Illusions*. New York: Basil Blackwell.

———. 1994. *The Electronic Eye: The Rise of Surveillance Society*. Minneapolis: University of Minnesota Press.

LYOTARD, JEAN-FRANÇOIS. 1985. *The Post-Modern Condition: A Report on Knowledge*. Minneapolis: University of Minnesota Press.

MACPIKE, LORALEE. 1989. *There's Something I've Been Meaning to Tell You*. Tallahassee: Naiad.

MAHARIDGE, DALE. 1996. *The Coming White Minority*. New York: Times Books.

MALINOWSKI, BRONISLAW. 1982. *"Magic: Science and Religion" and Other Essays*. London: Souvenir Press.

MALTHUS, THOMAS. 1976. *Essay on the Principle of Population*. Ed. Philip Appleman. Originally published 1798. New York: Norton.

MANTON, KENNETH G., CORDER, LARRY S., and STALLARD, ERIC. 1993. "Estimates of change in chronic disability and institutional evidence and prevalence rates in the U.S. elderly population from the 1982, 1984, and 1989 national long term care survey." *Gerontology*, vol. 48, no. 466.

MARE, ROBERT D. 1991. "Five decades of educational assortative mating." *American Sociological Review*, vol. 56, no. 1 (February).

MARKOFF, JOHN. 1996. *Waves of Democracy: Social Movements and Political Change*. Thousand Oaks, CA: Pine Forge Press.

MARSHALL, T. H. 1973. *Class, Citizenship, and Social Development: Essays by T. H. Marshall*. Westport, CT: Greenwood Press.

MARTIN, DAVID. 1990. *Tongues of Fire: The Explosion of Protestantism in Latin America*. Cambridge, Eng.: Blackwell.

MARTIN, KAY, and VOORHIES, BARBARA. 1975. *Female of the Species*. New York: Columbia University Press.

MARTINEAU, HARRIET. 1962 (orig. pub. 1837). *Society in America*. Garden City, NY: Doubleday.

MARX, KARL. 1977. *Capital: A Critique of Political Economy*, vol. 1. Originally published 1864. New York: Random House.

MASSEY, DOUGLAS S. 1996 "The age of extremes: Concentrated affluence and poverty in the twenty-first century." *Demography*, vol. 33, no. 4 (November).

———, and DENTON, NANCY A. 1993. *American Apartheid: Segregation and the Making of the Underclass*. Cambridge, MA: Harvard University Press.

MATSUEDA, ROSS L. 1992. "Reflected appraisals, parental labeling, and delinquency: Specifying a symbolic interactionist theory." *American Journal of Sociology*, vol. 97.

MCCAFFREY, BARRY. 1998. "Prepared statement before the senate committee on the judiciary, 6/17/98." Federal News Service, n.p.

MCCALL, PATRICIA L., and LAND, KENNETH C. 1994. "Trends in white male adolescent, young-adult, and elderly suicide: Are there common underlying structural factors?" *Social Science Research*, vol. 23 (March).

MCGWIRE, MICHAEL. 1995. "Why do we need to eliminate nuclear weapons?" Paper presented to the Canberra Commission, n.p.

MCHALE, MAGDA CORDELL, ET AL. 1979. *Children in the World*. Washington, DC: Population Reference Bureau.

MCLANAHAN, SARA, and SANDEFUR, GARY. 1994. *Growing Up With a Single Parent: What Hurts, What Helps*. Cambridge, MA: Harvard University Press.

MCLUHAN, MARSHALL. 1964. *Understanding Media.* London: Routledge and Kegan Paul.

MEAD, MARGARET. 1963 (orig. pub. 1935). *Sex and Temperament in Three Primitive Societies.* New York: William Morrow.

———. 1972. *Blackberry Winter: My Earlier Years.* New York: William Morrow.

MEADOWS, DONNELLA H., ET AL. 1972. *The Limits to Growth.* New York: Universe Books.

MERTON, ROBERT K. 1957. *Social Theory and Social Structure.* Revised ed. New York: Free Press.

MEYER, JOHN W., and ROWAN, BRIAN. 1977. "Institutionalized organizations: Formal structure as myth and ceremony." *American Journal of Sociology*, vol. 83.

MICHELS, ROBERT. 1967. *Political Parties.* Originally published 1911. New York: Free Press.

MILLS, C. WRIGHT. 1956. *The Power Elite.* New York: Oxford University Press.

———. 1959. *The Sociological Imagination.* New York: Oxford University Press.

MINER, HORACE. 1956. "Body ritual among the Nacirema." *American Anthropologist*, vol. 58.

MINITER, RICHARD. 1997. "This generation means business." *Reader's Digest*, vol. 151.

MIRSKY, JONATHAN. 1982. "China and the one child family." *New Society* (February 18), no. 59.

MITCHELL, JULIET. 1975. *Psychoanalysis and Feminism.* New York: Random House

MOEN, PHYLLIS. 1996. "Changing age trends: The pyramid upside down?" in U. Bronfenbrenner, P. McClelland, E. Wethington, P. Moen, and S. J. Ceci, eds., *The State of Americans.* New York: Free Press.

MOFFITT, TERRIE E. 1996. "The neuropsychology of conduct disorder," in P. Cordella and L. Siegel, eds., *Readings in Contemporary Criminological Theory.* Boston: Northeastern University Press.

MOLOTCH, HARVEY, and BODEN, DEIRDRE. 1985. "Talking social structure: Discourse, dominance, and the Watergate hearings." *American Sociological Review*, vol. 50.

MOLOWE, JILL. 1994. "... and throw away the key." *Time*, February 7.

MONEY, JOHN, and EHRHARDT, ANKE A. 1972. *Man and Woman, Boy and Girl.* Baltimore: Johns Hopkins University Press.

MOORE, BARRINGTON, JR. 1966. *Social Origins of Dictatorship and Democracy: Lord and Peasant in the Making of the Modern World.* Boston: Beacon Press.

MORAWSKA, EVA. 1986. *For Bread with Butter: Life Worlds of East-Central Europeans in Johnstown, Pennsylvania, 1890–1940.* New York: Cambridge University Press.

MORRIS, ALLISON. 1987. *Women, Crime, and Justice.* New York: Basil Blackwell.

MORRIS, JAN. 1974. *Conundrum.* New York: Harcourt Brace Jovanovich.

MOYNIHAN, DANIEL PATRICK. 1965. *The Negro Family: A Case for National Action.* Washington, DC: Government Printing Office.

———. 1993. "Defining deviancy down." *American Scholar* (Winter) 62(1):17–30.

MUMFORD, LEWIS. 1973. *Interpretations and Forecasts.* New York: Harcourt Brace Jovanovich.

MURDOCK, GEORGE PETER. 1949. *Social Structure.* New York: Macmillan.

MURRAY, CHARLES A. 1984. *Losing Ground: American Social Policy, 1950–1980.* New York: Basic Books.

NAJMAN, JAKE M. 1993. "Health and Poverty: Past, Present, and Prospects for the Future." *Social Science and Medicine*, vol. 36, no. 2.

NATIONAL CENTER FOR HEALTH STATISTICS. 1994. *Health—United States 1993.* Washington, DC: Government Printing Office.

———. 1996. *Health—United States 1995.* Washington, DC: Government Printing Office.

NATIONAL OPINION RESEARCH CENTER. 1989, 1990, 1991. *General Social Survey.* Chicago: National Opinion Research Center.

NATIONAL RESEARCH COUNCIL. 1994. *Information Technology in the Service Society.* Washington, DC: National Academy Press.

NEGROPONTE, NICHOLAS. 1995. *Being Digital.* London: Hodder and Stoughton.

NEUGARTEN, BERNICE, HAVINGHURST, R. J., and TOBIN, S. S. 1968. "Personality and patterns of aging," in B. Neugarten, ed., *Middle Age and Aging.* Chicago: University of Chicago Press.

NIEBUHR, H. RICHARD. 1929. *The Social Sources of Denominationalism.* New York: Holt.

NORDHAUS, W. D. 1975. "The political business cycle." *Review of Economic Studies*, vol. 42.

NYE, JOSEPH. 1997. "In government we don't trust." *Foreign Affairs* (fall).

OAKES, JEANNIE. 1985. *Keeping Track: How Schools Structure Inequality*. New Haven, CT: Yale University Press.

———. 1990. *Multiplying Inequalities: The Effects of Race, Social Class, and Tracking on Opportunities to Learn Mathematics and Science*. Santa Monica, CA: Rand.

OFFE, CLAUS. 1984. *Contradictions of the Welfare State*. Cambridge, MA: MIT Press.

———. 1985. *Disorganized Capitalism*. Cambridge, MA: MIT Press.

OLIVER, MELVIN L., and SHAPIRO, THOMAS M. 1995. *Black Wealth/White Wealth: A New Perspective on Racial Inequality*. New York: Routledge.

OLSON, M. H. 1989. "Work at home for computer professionals." *ACM Trans. Inf. Sys.*, vol. 7, no. 4.

———, and PRIMPS, S. B. 1984. "Working at home with computers." *Journal of Social Issues*, vol. 40, no. 3.

OMI, MICHAEL, and WINANT, HOWARD. 1994. *Racial Formation in the United States: From the 1960s to the 1990s*, 2nd ed. New York: Routledge.

OPPENHEIMER, VALERIE K. 1970. *The Female Labor Force in the United States*. Westport, CT: Greenwood Press.

ORGANIZATION FOR ECONOMIC COOPERATION AND DEVELOPMENT. 1996. *OECD Tourism Statistics*. Paris: OECD.

ORLOFF, ANN SHOLA. 1993. *The Politics of Pensions: A Comparative Analysis of Britain, Canada, and the United States, 1880–1940*. Madison, WI: University of Wisconsin Press.

OUCHI, WILLIAM G. 1979. "A conceptual framework for the design of organizational control mechanisms." *Management Science*, vol. 25.

———. 1982. Theory Z: *How American Business Can Meet the Japanese Challenge*. New York: Avon.

PALLEY, MARIAN LIEF. 1987. "The women's movement in recent American politics," in Sara E. Rix, *The American Woman, 1987–1988*. New York: Norton.

PALUDI, MICHELE A., and BARICKMAN, RICHARD B. 1991. *Academic and Workplace Sexual Harassment: A Resource Manual*. Albany, NY: State University of New York Press.

PARK, ROBERT E. 1952. *Human Communities: The City and Human Ecology*. New York: Free Press.

PARKIN, FRANK. 1971. *Class Inequality and Political Order: Social Stratification in Capitalist and Communist Societies*. New York: Praeger.

———. 1979. *Marxism and Class Theory: A Bourgeois Critique*. London: Tavistock.

PARSONS, TALCOTT. 1964. *The Social System*. New York: Free Press.

PATTERSON, ORLANDO. 1999. "When 'they' are 'us'." *New York Times*, April 30, p. A31.

PAUL, DIANA Y. 1985. *Women in Buddhism: Images of the Feminine in the Mahayana Tradition*. Berkeley: University of California Press.

PEARTON, MAURICE. 1984. *Diplomacy, War, and Technology since 1830*. Lawrence: University Press of Kansas.

PERLMUTTER, HOWARD V. 1972. "Towards research on and development of nations, unions, and firms as worldwide institutions," in H. Gunter, ed., *Transnational Industrial Relations*. New York: St. Martin's Press.

PILKINGTON, EDWARD. 1992. "Hapless democratic experiment." *Guardian*, 28 January.

PINKNEY, A. 1984. *The Myth of Black Progress*. New York: Cambridge University Press.

PLECK, JOSEPH H. 1981. *The Myth of Masculinity*. Cambridge, MA: MIT Press.

PLUMMER, KENNETH. 1975. *Sexual Stigma: An Interactive Account*. Boston: Routledge and Kegan Paul.

POPENOE, DAVID. 1993. "American family decline, 1960–1990: A review and appraisal." *Journal of Marriage and Family*, vol. 55.

———. 1996. *Life Without Father: Compelling New Evidence that Fatherhood and Marriage are Indispensable for the Good of Children and Society*. New York: Martin Kessler Books.

PORTES, ALEJANDRO, and STEPIK, ALEX. 1993. *City on the Edge: The Transformation of Miami*. Berkeley: University of California Press.

PRESIDENT'S COMMISSION ON ORGANIZED CRIME. 1986. *Records of Hearings, June 24–26, 1985*.

Washington, DC: Government Printing Office.

PROVENZO, EUGENE F., JR. 1991. *Video Kids: Making Sense of Nintendo*. Cambridge, MA: Harvard University Press.

RAMIREZ, FRANCISCO O., and BOLI, JOHN. 1987. "The political construction of mass schooling: European origins and worldwide institutionalism." *Sociology of Education*, vol. 60.

REICH, ROBERT. 1991. *The Work of Nations: Preparing Ourselves for 21st-Century Capitalism*. New York: Knopf.

RENZETTI, CLAIRE M., and CURRAN, DANIEL J. 1995. *Women, Men, and Society*, 3rd ed. Needham Heights, MA: Allyn & Bacon.

RESKIN, BARBARA, and PADAVIC, IRENE. 1994. *Women and Men at Work*. Thousand Oaks, CA: Pine Forge Press.

RHODE, DEBORAH L. 1990. "Gender equality and employment policy," in Sara E. Rix, ed., *The American Woman, 1990–1991: A Status Report*. New York: Norton.

RIEFF, DAVID. 1991. *Los Angeles: Capital of the Third World*. New York: Simon and Schuster.

RIGHTS OF WOMEN LESBIAN CUSTODY GROUP. 1986. *Lesbian Mothers' Legal Handbook*. London: Women's Press.

RIIS, JACOB A. 1957. *How the Other Half Lives: Studies Among the Tenements of New York*. Originally published 1890. New York: Dover.

RILEY, MATLILDA W., JOHNSON, MARILYN, and FONER, ANNE. 1972. *Aging and Society*. New York: Russell Sage Foundation.

RINGER, BENJAMIN B. 1985. *"We the People" and Others: Duality and America's Treatment of Its Racial Minorities*. New York: Tavistock.

RITZER, GEORGE. 1993. *The McDonaldization of Society*. Newbury Park, CA: Pine Forge Press.

ROBINSON, D. 1979. *Talking Out of Alcoholism: The Self-Help Process of AA*. London: Croom Helm.

———. 1980. "Self-help groups," in P. Smith, *Small Groups and Personal Change*. London: Metheun.

ROBINSON, PAUL. 1994. "The way we do the things we do." *New York Times Book Review*, October 30.

ROOF, WADE CLARK. 1993. *A Generation of Seekers: The Spiritual Journeys of the Baby Boom Generation*. San Francisco: Harper San Francisco.

———, and MCKINNEY, WILLIAM. 1987. *American Mainline Religion: Its Changing Shape and Future Prospects*. New Brunswick, NJ: Rutgers University Press.

ROSCOE, W. 1991. *The Zuni Man-Woman*. Albuquerque, NM: University of New Mexico Press.

ROSENTHAL, A. M. 1999. *Thirty-Eight Witnesses: The Kitty Genovese Case*. Berkeley: University of California Press.

ROSSI, ALICE. 1973. "The first woman sociologist: Harriett Martineau," in *The Feminist Papers: From Adams to de Beauvoir*. New York: Columbia University Press, 1973.

RUBIN, LILLIAN B. 1990. *Erotic Wars: What Happened to the Sexual Revolution?* New York: Farrar, Straus, and Giroux.

RUBINSTEIN, W. D. 1986. *Wealth and Inequality in Britain*. Winchester, MA: Faber and Faber.

RUDÉ, GEORGE. 1959. *The Crowd in the French Revolution*. Oxford: Oxford University Press.

———. 1964. *The Crowd in History: A Study of Popular Disturbances in France and England, 1730–1848*. New York: Wiley.

RUTTER, M., and GILLER, H. 1984. *Juvenile Delinquency: Trends and Perspectives*. New York: Guilford Press.

RYAN, TOM. 1985. "The roots of masculinity," in Andy Metcalf and Martin Humphries, eds., *Sexuality of Men*. London: Pluto.

SABEL, CHARLES F. 1982. *Work and Politics: The Division of Labor in Industry*. New York: Cambridge University Press.

SADKER, MYRA, and SADKER, DAVID. 1994. *Failing at Fairness*. New York: Scribner.

SAMPSON, ROBERT J., and COHEN, JACQUELINE. 1988. "Deterrent effects of the police on crime: A replication and theoretical extension." *Law and Society Review*, vol. 22, no. 1.

SASSEN, SASKIA. 1991. *The Global City: New York, London, Tokyo*. Princeton, NJ: Princeton University Press.

———. 1998. *Globalization and Its Discontents*. New York: New Press.

SAYERS, JANET. 1986. *Sexual Contradiction: Psychology, Psychoanalysis, and Feminism*. New York: Methuen.

SCHILLER, HERBERT I. 1989. *Culture Inc.: The Corporate Takeover of Public Expression*. New York: Oxford University Press.

———. 1991. "Not yet the post-imperialist era." *Critical Studies in Mass Communication*, vol. 8.

SCHOR, JULIET. 1992. *The Overworked American*. New York: Basic Books.

SCHUMAN, HOWARD, STEEL, CHARLOTTE, AND BOBO, LAWRENCE. 1985. *Racial Attitudes in America: Trends and Interpretations*. Cambridge, MA: Harvard University Press.

SCHUMPETER, JOSEPH. 1934. *The Theory of Economic Development: An Inquiry into Profits, Capital, and Credit*. Cambridge, MA: Harvard University Press.

———. 1983. *Capitalism, Socialism, and Democracy*. Originally published 1942. Magnolia, MA: Peter Smith.

SCHWARTZMAN, KATHLEEN. 1998. "Globalization and democracy." *Annual Review of Sociology*, vol. 24.

SCHWARZ, JOHN E., and VOLGY, THOMAS J. 1992. *The Forgotten Americans*. New York: Norton.

SEGURA, DENISE A., and PIERCE, JENNIFER L. 1993. "Chicana/o family structure and gender personality: Chodorow, familism, and psychoanalytic sociology revisited." *Signs*, vol. 19.

SEIBER, SAM. 1981. *Fatal Remedies: The Ironies of Social Intervention*. New York: Plenum Press.

SENNETT, RICHARD. 1998. *The Corrosion of Character: The Personal Consequences of Work in the New Capitalism*. New York: Norton.

SEWELL, WILLIAM H., and HAUSER, ROBERT M. 1980. "The Wisconsin longitudinal study of social and psychological factors in aspirations and achievements." *Research in Sociology of Education and Socialization*, vol. 1.

SHARP, H. 1981. "Old age among the Chipewyan," in Pamela T. Amoss and S. Harrells, eds., *Other Ways of Growing Old: Anthropological Perspectives*. Stanford, CA: Stanford University Press.

SHATTUCK, ROGER. 1980. *The Forbidden Experiment: The Story of the Wild Boy of Aveyron*. New York: Farrar, Straus, and Giroux.

SHEA, S., A. D., STEIN, C. E., BASCH, R., LANTIGUA, C., MAYLAHN, D., STROGATZ, and NOVICK, L. 1991. "Independent associations of educational attainment and ethnicity with behavioral risk factors for cardiovascular disease." *American Journal of Epidemiology*, vol. 134, no. 6.

SHELDON, WILLIAM A., and GLUECK, E. 1956. *Physique and Delinquency*. New York: Harper and Row.

———, ET AL. 1949. *Varieties of Delinquent Youth*. New York: Harper and Row.

SHELTON, BETH ANNE. 1992. *Women, Men, and Time: Gender Differences in Paid Work, Housework, and Leisure*. Westport, CT: Greenwood.

———, and JOHN, DAPHNE. 1993. "Does marital status make a difference?: Housework among married and cohabiting men and women." *Journal of Family Issues*, vol. 14, no. 3 (September).

SHEPHERD, GILL. 1987. "Rank, gender, and homosexuality: Mombasa as a key to understanding sexual options," in Pat Caplan, *The Social Construction of Sexuality*. New York: Tavistock.

SIMON, JULIAN. 1981. *The Ultimate Resource*. Princeton, NJ: Princeton University Press.

———. 1989. *The Economic Consequences of Immigration*. Cambridge, MA: Basil Blackwell.

SIMPSON, GEORGE EATON, and YINGER, J. MILTON. 1986. *Racial and Cultural Minorities: An Analysis of Prejudice and Discrimination*. New York: Plenum Press.

SJOBERG, GIDEON. 1960. *The Pre-Industrial City: Past and Present*. New York: Free Press.

———. 1963. "The rise and fall of cities: A theoretical perspective." *International Journal of Comparative Sociology*, vol. 4.

SKIDMORE, THOMAS E. 1974. *Black into White: Race and Nationality in Brazilian Thought*. New York: Oxford University Press.

SKOCPOL, THEDA. 1979. *States and Social Revolutions: A Comparative Analysis of France, Russia, and China*. New York: Cambridge University Press.

———. 1992. *Protecting Soldiers and Mothers: The Political Origins of Social Policy in the*

United States. Cambridge, MA: Harvard University Press.

SMELSER, NEIL J. 1963. *Theory of Collective Behavior.* New York: Free Press.

SMITH, VICKI. 1997. "New forms of work organization." *Annual Review of Sociology,* vol. 23.

SOROKIN, PITIRIM A. 1927. *Social Mobility.* New York: Harper.

SPAIN, DAPHNE, and BIANCHI, SUZANNE M. 1996. *Balancing Act: Motherhood, Marriage, and Employment among American Women.* New York: Russell Sage Foundation.

SPIELBERGER, C. D., CRANE, R. S., KEARNS, W. D., PELLEGRIN, K. L., RICKMAN, R. L., and JOHNSON, E. H. 1991. Anger and anxiety in essential hypertension. In C. D. Spielberger, I. G. Sarason, Z. Kulcs, and G. L. Van Heck, eds., *Stress and Emotion,* vol. 14. New York: Hemisphere/Taylor & Francis.

SREBERNY-MOHAMMADI, ANNABELLE. 1992. "Media integration in the third world," in B. Gronbeck et al., eds., *Media, Consciousness, and Culture.* London: Sage.

STACEY, JUDITH. 1990. *Brave New Families: Stories of Domestic Upheaval in Late Twentieth Century America.* New York: Basic Books.

———. 1993. "Good riddance to 'the family': A response to David Popenoe." *Journal of Marriage and Family,* vol. 55.

———. 1996. *In the Name of the Family: Rethinking Family Values in a Postmodern Age.* Boston: Beacon Press.

STAMPP, KENNETH. 1956. *The Peculiar Institution.* New York: Knopf.

STARK, RODNEY, and BAINBRIDGE, WILLIAM SIMS. 1985. *The Future of Religion, Secularization, Revival, and Cult Formation.* Berkeley: University of California Press.

———. 1987. *A Theory of Religion.* New Brunswick, NJ: Rutgers University Press.

STATHAM, JUNE. 1986. *Daughters and Sons: Experiences of Non-Sexist Childraising.* New York: Basil Blackwell.

STEIN, PETER J. 1981. *Single Life: Unmarried Adults in Social Context.* New York: St. Martin's Press.

STEINBERG, RONNIE J. 1990. "Social construction of skill: Gender, power, and comparable worth." *Work and Occupations,* vol. 17.

STONE, LAWRENCE. 1980. *The Family, Sex, and Marriage in England, 1500–1800.* New York: Harper and Row.

STRAUS, MURRAY A. 1978. "Wife-beating: How common and why?" *Victimology,* vol. 2.

———, GELLES, RICHARD J., and STEINMETZ, SUZANNE K. 1980. *Behind Closed Doors: Violence in the American Family.* Garden City, NY: Anchor.

STRAUSS, WILLIAM, and HOWE, NEIL. 1991. *Generations: The History of America's Future, 1584–2069.* New York: Quill.

STRINNER, WILLIAM F. 1979. "Modernization and the family extension in the Philippines: A social-demographic analysis." *Journal of Marriage and the Family,* vol. 41.

STRYKER, ROBIN. 1996. "Comparable worth and the labor market," in Paula J. Dubeck and Kathryn Borman, eds., *Women and Work: A Handbook.* New York: Garland.

SUTHERLAND, EDWIN H. 1949. *Principles of Criminology.* Chicago: Lippincott.

SUTTLES, GERALD. 1968. *The Social Order of the Slum.* Chicago: University of Chicago Press.

SWARTZ, S. 1985. *Sugar Plantations in the Formation of Brazilian Society: Bahia, 1550–1835.* Cambridge, Eng.: Cambridge University Press.

SWIDLER, ANN. 1986. "Culture in action: Symbols and strategies." *American Sociological Review,* vol. 51.

TALBOT, SHANNON PETERS. 1996. "Global localization of the world market: Case study of McDonald's in Moscow." *Sociale Wetenschappen,* December.

TANNENBAUM, FRANK. 1964. *The Fine Society: A Philosophy of Labour.* London: Cape.

THOMAS, W. I., and ZNANIECKI, FLORIAN. 1966. *The Polish Peasant in Europe and America: Monograph of Our Immigrant Group.* 5 vols. Originally published 1918–20. New York: Dover.

THOMPSON, E. P. 1971. "The moral economy of the English crowd in the eighteenth century." *Past and Present,* vol. 50.

THOMPSON, JOHN B. 1990. *Ideology and Modern Culture.* Cambridge, UK: Polity Press.

———. 1995. *The Media and Modernity: A Social Theory of the Media*. Cambridge, UK: Polity Press.

THOMPSON, WARREN S. 1929. "Population." *American Journal of Sociology*, vol. 34.

THORNE, BARRIE. 1993. *Gender Play: Girls and Boys in School*. New Brunswick, NJ: Rutgers University Press.

TILLY, CHARLES. 1978. *From Mobilization to Revolution*. Reading, MA: Addison-Wesley.

———. 1995. "Globalization threatens labor's rights." *International Labor and Working Class History*, vol. 47.

———. 1996. "The emergence of citizenship in France and elsewhere," in Charles Tilly, ed., *Citizenship, Identity, and Social History*. Cambridge, UK: Cambridge University Press.

TINBERGEN, NIKO. 1974. *The Study of Instinct*. Oxford: Oxford University Press.

TITTLE, CHARLES R., and MEIER, ROBERT F. 1990. "Specifying the SES/Delinquency relationship." *Criminology*, vol. 28, no. 2.

TOCQUEVILLE, ALEXIS DE. 1969. *Democracy in America*. Originally published 1835. New York: Doubleday.

TOURAINE, ALAIN. 1974. *The Post-Industrial Society*. London: Wildwood.

———. 1977. *The Self-Production of Society*. Chicago: University of Chicago Press.

———. 1981. *The Voice and the Eye: An Analysis of Social Movements*. New York: Cambridge University Press.

TOWNSEND, PETER, and DAVIDSON, NICK, EDS. 1982. *Inequalities in Health: The Black Report*. Harmondsworth, UK: Penguin.

TREIMAN, DONALD. 1977. *Occupational Prestige in Comparative Perspective*. New York: Academic Press.

TROELTSCH, ERNST. 1931. *The Social Teaching of the Christian Churches*. 2 vols. New York: Macmillan.

TROW, MARTIN. 1961. "The second transformation of American secondary education." *Comparative Sociology*, vol. 2.

TRUMAN, DAVID B. 1981. *The Governmental Process*. Westport, CT: Greenwood Press.

TRUONG, TRANH-DAM. 1990. *Sex, Money, and Morality*. London: Zed Books.

TUMIN, MELVIN M. 1953. "Some principles of stratification: A critical analysis." *American Sociological Review*, vol. 18 (August).

TURNBULL, COLIN. 1983. *The Human Cycle*. New York: Simon and Schuster.

TURNER, RALPH H., and KILLIAN, LEWIS M. 1972. *Collective Behavior*. Englewood Cliffs, NJ: Prentice Hall.

TUROWSKI, JAN. 1977. "Inadequacy of the theory of the nuclear family: The Polish experience," in Luis Lenero Otero, ed., *Beyond the Nuclear Family Model: Cross-Cultural Perspectives*. Beverly Hills, CA: Sage.

U.N. CHRONICLE. 1995. vol. 32 (number 4), December, p. 29.

U.S. BUREAU OF LABOR STATISTICS. 1989. *Handbook of Labor Statistics*. Washington, DC: Government Printing Office.

———. 1991. *Employment and Earnings* (January). Washington, DC: Government Printing Office.

———. 1997. "Employment and Earnings (January)." Washington, DC: Government Printing Office.

———. 1999. *Employment and Earnings* (January). Washington, DC: Government Printing Office.

U.S. BUREAU OF THE CENSUS. 1991. School Enrollment: Social and Economic Characteristics of Students, October 1991. *Current Population Reports*, series P-20, no. 469. Washington, DC: Government Printing Office.

———. 1992. *Statistical Abstract of the United States*. Washington, DC: Government Printing Office.

———. 1993. *Statistical Abstract of the United States*. Washington, DC: Government Printing Office.

———. 1994c. *World Population Profile: 1994*. Report WP/94. Washington, DC: Government Printing Office.

———. 1996. *Statistical Abstract of the United States*. Washington, DC: Government Printing Office.

———. 1998a. *Statistical Abstract of the United States*. Washington, DC: Government Printing Office.

———. 1998b. "Marital status and living arrangements," in *Current Population Reports*. Washington, DC: Government Printing Office.

————. 1998c. "Household and family characteristics (March)," in *Current Population Reports*. Washington, DC: Government Printing Office.

U.S. DEPARTMENT OF EDUCATION, NATIONAL CENTER FOR EDUCATION STATISTICS. 1993. *Adult Literacy in America: A First Look at the Results of the National Adult Literacy Survey*. Washington, DC: Government Printing Office.

U.S. RIOT COMMISSION. 1968. *Report of the National Advisory Commission on Civil Disorder*. New York: Bantam.

URRY, JOHN. 1990. *The Tourist Gaze*. London: Sage.

VALLAS, S., and BECK, J. 1996. "The transformation of work revisited: The limits of flexibility in American manufacturing." *Social Problems*, vol. 43, no. 3.

VAN DEN BERGHE, PIERRE L. 1970. *Race and Ethnicity: Essays in Comparative Sociology*. New York: Basic Books.

VAN GENNEP, ARNOLD. 1977. *The Rites of Passage*. Originally published 1908. London: Routledge and Kegan Paul.

VAUGHAN, DIANE. 1986. *Uncoupling: Turning Points in Intimate Relationships*. New York: Oxford University Press.

VIORST, JUDITH. 1986. "And the prince knelt down and tried to put the glass slipper on Cinderella's foot," in Jack Zipes, ed., *Don't Bet on the Prince: Contemporary Feminist Fairy Tales in North America and England*. New York: Methuen.

VOGEL, EZRA F. 1979. *Japan as Number One: Lessons for America*. New York: Harper Colophon.

WALDRON, INGRID. 1986. "Why do women live longer than men?" in Peter Conrad and Rachelle Kern, eds., *The Sociology of Health and Illness*. New York: St. Martin's.

WALLERSTEIN, JUDITH S., and BLAKESLEE, SANDRA. 1989. *Second Chances: Men, Women, and Children a Decade After Divorce*. New York: Ticknor and Fields.

————, and KELLY, JOAN BERLIN. 1980. *Surviving the Break-Up: How Children and Parents Cope with Divorce*. New York: Basic Books.

WALLIS, ROY. 1977. *The Road to Total Freedom*. New York: Columbia University Press.

WALSH, DERMOT. 1986. *Heavy Business: Commercial Burglary and Robbery*. New York: Routledge, Chapman and Hall.

WALUM, LAUREL RICHARDSON. 1977. *The Dynamics of Sex and Gender: A Sociological Perspective*. Chicago: Rand McNally.

WATERS, MALCOLM. 1995. *Globalization*. London: Routledge.

————. 1996. "McDonaldization and the global culture of consumption." *Sociale Wetenschappen*, December.

WATERS, MARY C. 1990. *Ethnic Options: Choosing Identities in America*. Berkeley: University of California Press.

WATSON, PEGGY. 1992. "Eastern Europe's silent revolution: Gender." Unpublished paper delivered at Cambridge University.

WATTENBERG, MARTIN P. 1996. *The Decline of American Political Parties, 1952–1994*, rev. ed. Cambridge, MA: Harvard University Press.

WEBER, MAX. 1977. *The Protestant Ethic and the Spirit of Capitalism*. New York: Macmillan.

————. 1979. *Economy and Society: An Outline of Interpretive Sociology*. 2 vols. Berkeley: University of California Press.

WEEKS, JEFFREY. 1986. *Sexuality*. New York: Routledge, Chapman and Hall.

WEITZMAN, LENORE. 1985. *Divorce Revolution: The Unexpected Social and Economic Consequences for Women and Children in America*. New York: Free Press.

————, ET AL. 1972. "Sexual socialization in picture books for preschool children." *American Journal of Sociology*, vol. 77.

WELLMAN, BARRY, ET AL. 1996. "Computer networks as social networks: Collaborative work, telework, and virtual community." *Annual Review of Sociology*, vol. 22.

WELLMAN, DAVID T., ED. 1977. *Portraits of White Racism*. New York: Cambridge University Press.

————. 1987. *Portraits of White Racism*. New York: Cambridge University Press.

WEST, CANDACE, and FENSTERMAKER, SARAH. 1995. "Doing difference." *Gender and Society*, vol. 9, no. 1 (February).

————, and ZIMMERMAN, DON. 1987. "Doing gender." *Gender and Society* 1 (June):125–51.

WESTERN, BRUCE, and BECKETT, KATHERINE. 1999. "How unregulated is the U.S. labor market?: The penal system as a labor market institution." *American Journal of Sociology*, vol. 104, no. 4 (January).

WHEATLEY, PAUL. 1971. *The Pivot of the Four Quarters*. Edinburgh: Edinburgh University Press.

WHITE, LYNN K. 1990. "Determinants of divorce: A review of research in the eighties." *Journal of Marriage and the Family* 52 (November 1990):904–12.

WHITE, MERRY I. 1993. *The Material Child: Coming of Age in Japan and America*. New York: Free Press.

WHITE, MICHAEL, and TREVOR, MALCOLM. 1983. *Under Japanese Management: The Experience of British Workers*. New York: Gower.

WIDOM, CATHY SPATZ, and NEWMAN, JOSEPH P. 1985. "Characteristics of non-institutionalized psychopaths," in David P. Farrington and John Gunn, eds., *Aggression and Dangerousness*. Chichester, Eng.: Wiley.

WIENER, J. M., ILLSTON, J., and HANLEY, F. J. 1994. *Sharing the Burden: Strategies for Public and Private Long-Term Care Insurance*. Washington, DC: Brookings Institution.

WILKSONSON, HELEN, and MULGAN, GEOFF. 1995. *Freedom's Children: Work, Relationships, and Politics for 18–34 Year Olds in Britain Today*. London: Demos.

WILL, J., P. SELF, and DATAN, N. 1976. "Maternal behavior and perceived sex of infant." *American Journal of Orthopsychiatry*, vol. 46.

WILLIAMS, CHRISTINE L. 1992. "The glass escalator: Hidden advantages for men in the 'female' professions." *Social Problems*, vol. 39.

WILLIS, PAUL. 1981. *Learning to Labor: How Working Class Kids Get Working Class Jobs*. New York: Columbia University Press.

WILSON, EDWARD O. 1975. *Sociobiology: The New Synthesis*. Cambridge, MA: Harvard University Press.

————. 1978. *On Human Nature*. Cambridge, MA: Harvard University Press.

WILSON, JAMES Q., and KELLING, GEORGE. 1982. "Broken windows," *The Atlantic*, March.

WILSON, WILLIAM JULIUS. 1978. *The Declining Significance of Race: Blacks and Changing American Institutions*. Chicago: University of Chicago Press.

————. 1987. *The Truly Disadvantaged: The Inner City, the Underclass, and Public Policy*. Chicago: University of Chicago Press.

————. 1991. "Studying inner-city social dislocations: The challenge of public agenda research." *American Sociological Review* 56 (February):1–14.

————. 1996. *When Work Disappears: The World of the New Urban Poor*. New York: Knopf.

————, ET AL. 1987. "The changing structure of urban poverty." Paper presented at the annual meeting of the American Sociological Association.

WINKLEBY, MARILYNN A., ET AL. 1992. "Socioeconomic status and health: How education, income, and occupation contribute to risk factors for cardiovascular disease." *American Journal of Public Health*, vol. 82.

WIRTH, LOUIS. 1938. "Urbanism as a way of life." *American Sociological Review*, vol. 44 (July).

WOOLGAR, STEVE, and PAWLUCH, DOROTHY. 1985. "Ontological gerrymandering: The anatomy of social problems explanations." *Social Problems*, vol. 32, no. 3.

WORLD BANK. 1994. *World Development Report, 1994*. New York: Oxford University Press.

————. 1998. *World Development Indicators*. Washington, DC: World Bank.

WORSLEY, PETER. 1968. *The Trumpet Shall Sound: A Study of Cargo Cults in Melanesia*. New York: Schocken.

————. 1984. *The Three Worlds of Culture and World Development*. Chicago: University of Chicago Press.

WRIGHT, ERIK OLIN. 1978. *Class, Crisis, and the State*. London: New Left Books.

————. 1985. *Classes*. New York: Shocken.

————. 1997. *Class Counts: Comparative Studies in Class Analysis*. New York: Cambridge University Press.

WRIGLEY, E. A. 1968. *Population and History*. New York: McGraw-Hill.

YOUNG, MICHAEL, and SCHULLER, TOM. 1991. *Life After Work: The Arrival of the Ageless Society*. London: HarperCollins London.

ZAMMUNER, VANDA LUCIA. 1986. "Children's sex-role stereotypes: A cross-cultural analysis," in Phillip Shaver and Clyde Hendrick, eds., *Sex and Gender*. Beverly Hills, CA: Sage.

ZEITLIN, IRVING. 1985. *Ancient Judaism: Biblical Criticism from Max Weber to the Present*. New York: Basil Blackwell.

——. 1988. *The Historical Jesus*. Cambridge: Polity Press.

ZERUBAVEL, EVIATAR. 1979. *Patterns of Time in Hospital Life*. Chicago: University of Chicago Press.

——. 1982. "The standardization of time: A socio-historical perspective." *American Journal of Sociology*, vol. 88.

ZHANG, NAIHU, and XU, WU. 1995. "Discovering the positive within the negative: The women's movement in a changing China," in Amrita Basu, ed., *The Challenge of Local Feminisms*. Boulder, CO: Westview.

ZIMBARDO, PHILIP G. 1969. "The human choice: Individuation, reason, and order versus deindividuation, impulse, and chaos," in W. J. Arnold and D. Levine, eds., *Nebraska Symposium on Motivation*, vol. 17. Lincoln, NE: University of Nebraska Press.

——. 1972. "Pathology of imprisonment." *Society*, vol. 9.

ZUBOFF, SHOSHANA. 1988. *In the Age of the Smart Machine: The Future of Work and Power*. New York: Basic Books.

INDEX